Student Solutions Manual

to accompany

Trigonometry

Second Edition

John W. Coburn
St. Louis Community College at Florissant Valley

J. D. Herdlick
St. Louis Community College at Meramec

Prepared by
Deana Richmond

Connect
Learn
Succeed™

The McGraw·Hill Companies

Student Solutions Manual to accompany
TRIGONOMETRY, SECOND EDITION
JOHN COBURN AND J.D. HERDLICK

Published by McGraw-Hill Higher Education, an imprint of The McGraw-Hill Companies, Inc., 1221 Avenue of the Americas, New York, NY 10020. Copyright © 2011 and 2008 by The McGraw-Hill Companies, Inc. All rights reserved.

This book is printed on recycled, acid-free paper containing 10% post consumer waste.

1 2 3 4 5 6 7 8 9 0 WDQ/WDQ 10 9 8 7 6 5 4 3 2 0

ISBN: 978–0–07–728271–4
MHID: 0–07–728271–X

www.mhhe.com

TABLE OF CONTENTS

1.1 Exercises

1. Complementary; $180°$

3. coterminal; $360°$

5. Answers will vary.

7. a. Complement $= 90° - 12.5° = 77.5°$
   b. Supplement $= 180° - 149.2° = 30.8°$

9. $\alpha = 90° - 37° = 53°$

11. $42°30' = \left[42 + 30\left(\dfrac{1}{60}\right)\right]° = 42.5°$

13. $67°33'18'' = \left[67 + 33\left(\dfrac{1}{60}\right) + 18\left(\dfrac{1}{3600}\right)\right]°$
    $= 67.555°$

15. $285°00'09'' = \left[285 + 9\left(\dfrac{1}{3600}\right)\right]°$
    $= 285.0025°$

17. $45°45'45'' = \left[45 + 45\left(\dfrac{1}{60}\right) + 45\left(\dfrac{1}{3600}\right)\right]°$
    $= 45.7625°$

19. $20.25° = 20° + 0.25(60)' = 20°15'00''$

21. $67.307° = 67° + 0.307(60)' = 67°18.42'$
    $= 67°18' + 0.42(60)'' = 67°18'25.2''$

23. $275.33° = 275° + 0.33(60)' = 275°19.8'$
    $= 275°19' + 0.8(60)'' = 275°19'48''$

25. $5.4525° = 5° + 0.4525(60)' = 5° + 27.15'$
    $= 5°27' + 0.15(60)'' = 5°27'9''$

27. $180° - 102°45' = (179° + 60') - 102°45'$
    $= (179° - 102°) + (60' - 45')$
    $= 77° + 15'$
    $= 77°15'$

29. $180° - 89°10'24''$
    $= (179° + 59' + 60'') - 89°10'24''$
    $= (179° - 89°) + (59' - 10') + (60'' - 24'')$
    $= 90° + 49' + 36''$
    $= 90°49'36''$

31. $180° - 179°03'52''$
    $= (179° + 59' + 60'') - 179°03'52''$
    $= (179° - 179°) + (59' - 3') + (60'' - 52'')$
    $= 0° + 56' + 8''$
    $= 0°56'08''$

33. $180° - 132°0'01''$
    $= (179° + 59' + 60'') - 132°0'01''$
    $= (179° - 132°) + (59' - 0') + (60'' - 1'')$
    $= 47° + 59' + 59''$
    $= 47°59'59''$

35. $\theta = 75°$; $\theta + 360k$
    $k = -2; 75 + 360(-2) = -645°$;
    $k = -1; 75 + 360(-1) = -285°$;
    $k = 1; 75 + 360(1) = 435°$;
    $k = 2; 75 + 360(2) = 795°$;
    $-645°, -285°, 435°, 795°$

37. $\theta = -45°$; $\theta + 360k$
    $k = -2; -45 + 360(-2) = -765°$;
    $k = -1; -45 + 360(-1) = -405°$;
    $k = 1; -45 + 360(1) = 315°$;
    $k = 2; -45 + 360(2) = 675°$;
    $-765°, -405°, 315°, 675°$

39. $\theta = 425°$; $\theta + 360k$
    $k = -1; 425° + 360°(-1) = 65°$

41. $\theta = 590°$; $\theta + 360k$
    $k = -2; 590° + 360°(-2) = -130°$

43. $\theta = 800°$; $\theta + 360k$
    $k = -2; 800° + 360°(-2) = 80°$

45. $c = \sqrt{2}a = \sqrt{2} \cdot 5 = 5\sqrt{2}$ cm

47. $a = b = \dfrac{c}{\sqrt{2}} = \dfrac{6\sqrt{2}}{\sqrt{2}} = 6$ ft

49. $c = \sqrt{2}a = \sqrt{2} \cdot 5\sqrt{2} = 10$ mm

51. $a = b = \dfrac{c}{\sqrt{2}} = \dfrac{8}{\sqrt{2}} = \dfrac{8}{\sqrt{2}} \cdot \dfrac{\sqrt{2}}{\sqrt{2}} = 4\sqrt{2}$ yd

53. $b = \sqrt{3}a = \sqrt{3} \cdot 3 = 3\sqrt{3}$ mm
    $c = 2a = 2 \cdot 3 = 6$ mm
    $c = 2a = 2 \cdot 9 = 18$ ft

55. $a = \dfrac{c}{2} = \dfrac{7}{2}$ in.

$b = \sqrt{3}a = \sqrt{3} \cdot \dfrac{7}{2} = \dfrac{7\sqrt{3}}{2}$ in.

57. $a = \dfrac{b}{\sqrt{3}} = \dfrac{6}{\sqrt{3}} \cdot \dfrac{\sqrt{3}}{\sqrt{3}} = 2\sqrt{3}$ cm

$c = 2a = 2 \cdot 2\sqrt{3} = 4\sqrt{3}$ cm

59. $82 = \sqrt{2} \cdot a; \quad a = \dfrac{82}{\sqrt{2}} = 41\sqrt{2} \approx 58$ ft

Height of the ladder-truck: 10 ft
Total height: 58 + 10 = 68 ft

61. $\theta = \dfrac{3600D + 60M + S}{3600}$

$= \dfrac{3600 \cdot 67 + 60 \cdot 33 + 18}{3600}$

$= \dfrac{243,198}{3600}$

$= 67.555$

$67°33'18'' = 67.555°$

63. $s = \dfrac{10}{2} = 5$ cm

$A = \dfrac{\sqrt{3}s^2}{2} = \dfrac{\sqrt{3} \cdot 5^2}{2} = \dfrac{25\sqrt{3}}{2}$ cm^2

$a = \dfrac{c}{2} = \dfrac{10}{2} = 5$ cm

$b = \sqrt{3}a = \sqrt{3} \cdot 5 = 5\sqrt{3}$ cm

$A = \dfrac{1}{2} \times \text{base} \times \text{height}$

$= \dfrac{1}{2} \times 5\sqrt{3} \times 5$

$= \dfrac{25\sqrt{3}}{2}$ cm^2

65. a. $\alpha = 90° - 34° = 56°$
The flyswatter must pass through $56°$.

b. $\dfrac{56°}{8°} = 7; \; 7 \cdot 0.1 = 0.7$ sec

It will take the swatter 0.7 seconds to strike the table.

67. $35.5575°\text{S} = 35° + 0.5575(60)' = 35° + 33.45'$
$\qquad\qquad = 35°33' + 0.45(60)'' = 35°33'27''$

$58.055°\text{W} = 58° + 0.055(60)' = 58° + 3.3'$
$\qquad\qquad = 58°3' + 0.3(60)'' = 58°3'18''\text{W}$

The coordinates are $35°33'27''\text{S}, \; 58°3'18''\text{W}$.

69. $\theta = 1080°; \; \theta + 360k$
$k = -3; 1080° + 360°(-3) = 0°$

$\theta = 1260°; \; \theta + 360k$
$k = -3; 1260° + 360°(-3) = 180°$

No, the angles of Harf's two spins were not coterminal.

$\theta = 1260°; \; \theta + 360k$
$k = -3; 1260° + 360°(-3) = 180°$
$k = -2; 1260° + 360°(-2) = 540°$

71. a. $250 \cdot 4 = 1000$ m
The change of elevation from A to B is 1000 meters.

b. $\dfrac{1 \text{ cm}}{625 \text{ m}} = \dfrac{1.6 \text{ cm}}{x}$
$\qquad 1 \cdot x = 625 \cdot 1.6$
$\qquad\quad x = 1000$ m
The horizontal distance between points A and B is 1000 meters.

c.
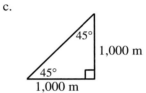

$c = \sqrt{2} \cdot 1000 = 1000\sqrt{2}$ m ≈ 1414.2 m
The length of the trail up the mountain side is approximately 1414.2 meters.

73. $a = b = 100 \cdot 0.5 = 50$ mi
In the next 0.5 hour, each plane will go 50 miles. The angle between their paths is $90°$.

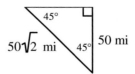

This is a 45-45-90 triangle
$c = \sqrt{2}a = \sqrt{2} \cdot 50 = 50\sqrt{2} \approx 70.7$ mi
The distance between them is $50\sqrt{2}$ or about 70.7 miles.

75. $\dfrac{\sqrt{91}}{3}$ in.

1.2 Exercises

1. sides; acute; right; obtuse

3. capital; opposite; lowercase

5. Answers will vary.

7. b

9. d

11. g

13. e

15. $\alpha = 180° - (53° + 58°) = 69°$

17. $\angle A = 180° - (90° + 65°) = 25°$

19. $\angle C = 180° - (67° + 88°) = 25°$

21. $\angle C = 180° - (23.1° + 91.4°) = 65.5°$

23. $\angle C = 180° - (98°35' + 43°15')$
$= 179°60' - 141°50'$
$= 38°10'$

25. $\angle C = 180° - (44°32'18'' + 92°5'51'')$
$= 180° - (44° + 92° + 32' + 5' + 18'' + 51'')$
$= 180° - (136° + 37' + 69'')$
$= 180° - (136° + 37' + 1' + 9'')$
$= 179°59'60'' - 136°38'09''$
$= 43°21'51''$

27. $A + B + C = 180$
$(3x - 3) + 93 + 6x = 180$
$3x - 3 + 93 + 6x = 180$
$9x + 90 = 180$
$9x = 90$
$x = 10$

$A = (3x - 3)°$ $B = 93°$ $C = 6x°$
$A = [3(10) - 3]°$ $C = 6(10)°$
$A = 27°$ $C = 60°$

29. $A + B + C = 180$
$51y + 7y + 32y = 180$
$90y = 180$
$y = 2$

$A = 51y°$ $B = 7y°$ $C = 32y°$
$A = 51(2)°$ $B = 7(2)°$ $C = 32(2)°$
$A = 102°$ $B = 14°$ $C = 64°$

31. $A = 180° - \theta$
$A = 180° - 129°$
$A = 51°$

$A + B + C = 180$
$51 + (6x - 1) + (8x + 4) = 180$
$51 + 6x - 1 + 8x + 4 = 180$
$14x + 54 = 180$
$14x = 126$
$x = 9$

$A = 51°$ $B = (6x - 1)°$ $C = (8x + 4)°$
$B = [6(9) - 1]°$ $C = [8(9) + 4]°$
$B = 53°$ $C = 76°$

33. $A + B + C = 180$
$[180 - (4x + 10)] + (2x + 10) + 72 = 180$
$(180 - 4x - 10) + (2x + 10) + 72 = 180$
$(170 - 4x) + (2x + 10) + 72 = 180$
$170 - 4x + 2x + 10 + 72 = 180$
$-2x + 252 = 180$
$-2x = -72$
$x = 36$

$A = 180° - (4x + 10)°$ $B = (2x + 10)°$
$A = 180° - [4(36) + 10]°$ $B = [2(36) + 10]°$
$A = 180° - [144 + 10]°$ $B = (72 + 10)°$
$A = 180° - 154°$ $B = 82°$
$A = 26°$

35. $\angle 1 + \angle 2 + \angle 3 = 180°$
$\angle 3 = 180° - \angle 1 - \angle 2$
$\angle 3 = 180° - 83° - 36°$
$\angle 3 = 61°$

$A = 61°$; $B = 83°$; $C = 36°$

37. $\angle 1 + \angle 2 + \angle 3 = 180°$
$\angle 3 = 180° - \angle 1 - \angle 2$
$\angle 3 = 180° - 98° - 41°$
$\angle 3 = 41°$

$A = 41°$; $B = 98°$; $C = 41°$

39. $\angle 1 + \angle 2 + \angle 3 = 180°$
$\angle 3 = 180° - \angle 1 - \angle 2$
$\angle 3 = 180° - 30° - 60°$
$\angle 3 = 90°$

$A = 60°$; $B = 90°$; $C = 30°$

41. $\angle A + \angle B + \angle C = 180°$
$\angle C = 180° - \angle A - \angle B$
$\angle C = 180° - 57° - 38°$
$\angle C = 85°$

$a = 121$ dm; $b = 89$ dm; $c = 144$ dm

43. $\angle A + \angle B + \angle C = 180°$
$$\angle C = 180° - \angle A - \angle B$$
$$\angle C = 180° - 104° - 38°$$
$$\angle C = 38°$$

$a = 7.4$ ft; $b = 4.7$ ft; $c = 4.7$ ft

45. $\angle A + \angle B + \angle C = 180°$
$$\angle C = 180° - \angle A - \angle B$$
$$\angle C = 180° - 90° - 75°$$
$$\angle C = 15°$$

$a = 2\sqrt{2}$ in.; $b = \sqrt{3}+1$ in.; $c = \sqrt{3}-1$ in.

47. No, $19 + 16 < 40$

49. Let x be the altitude of the helicopter.

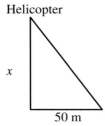

$$\frac{x}{50} = \frac{2}{1.6}$$
$$1.6x = 100$$
$$x = \frac{100}{1.6}$$
$$x = 62.5 \text{ m}$$

51. Let x be the height of the temple.
$$\frac{x}{40} = \frac{1.65}{2.2}$$
$$2.2x = 40 \cdot 1.65$$
$$2.2x = 66$$
$$x = 30 \text{ m}$$

53. $\dfrac{c}{33} = \dfrac{6}{18}$
$$\frac{c}{33} = \frac{1}{3}$$
$$3c = 33$$
$$c = 11 \text{ m}$$

55. $\dfrac{d}{3} = \dfrac{6}{10}$
$$\frac{d}{3} = \frac{3}{5}$$
$$5d = 9$$
$$d = \frac{9}{5} \text{ in.}$$

57. $\dfrac{e}{\frac{1}{5}} = \dfrac{\frac{20}{3}}{\frac{3}{5}}$
$$e \cdot \frac{5}{1} = \frac{20}{3} \cdot \frac{3}{5}$$
$$5e = 4$$
$$e = \frac{4}{5} \text{ in.}$$

59. $\dfrac{x}{18} = \dfrac{2}{x}$
$$x \cdot x = 18 \cdot 2$$
$$x^2 = 36$$
$$x = 6 \text{ m}$$

$a = x = 6$ m $g = x = 6$ m

61. $\dfrac{12}{4x} = \dfrac{x+1}{14}$
$$12 \cdot 14 = 4x(x+1)$$
$$168 = 4x^2 + 4x$$
$$0 = 4x^2 + 4x - 168$$
$$0 = 4(x^2 + x - 42)$$
$$0 = 4(x+7)(x-6)$$
$$x = -7 \quad \text{or} \quad x = 6$$

We discard $x = -7$, so $x = 6$ ft.

$a = 4x = 4(6) = 24$ ft
$e = x+1 = 6+1 = 7$ ft

63. $\dfrac{2x-1}{x-1} = \dfrac{6x}{2x}$
$$\frac{2x-1}{x-1} = 3$$
$$2x-1 = 3(x-1)$$
$$2x-1 = 3x-3$$
$$2 = x$$

$a = x-1 = 2-1 = 1$
$b = 2x = 2(2) = 4$
$e = 6x = 6(2) = 12$
$f = 2x-1 = 2(2)-1 = 4-1 = 3$

65. $a = 15$, $b = 8$, $c = 17$
$$h = \frac{ab}{c} = \frac{15(8)}{17} \approx 7.06 \text{ cm}$$
$$m = \frac{b^2}{c} = \frac{8^2}{17} \approx 3.76 \text{ cm}$$
$$n = \frac{a^2}{c} = \frac{15^2}{17} \approx 13.24 \text{ cm}$$

67. Let t be the height of the building.
$$\frac{t}{100} = \frac{12}{57}$$
$$57t = 100 \cdot 12$$
$$57t = 1200$$
$$t \approx 21 \text{ m}$$
The building is approximately 21 meters tall.

69. Let t be the height of the obelisk.
$$\frac{t}{2542} = \frac{5.9}{27}$$
$$27t = 2542 \cdot 5.9$$
$$27t = 14,997.8$$
$$t \approx 555 \text{ ft}$$
The height of the obelisk is approximately 555 feet.

71. Let h be the height of the tail light.
$$\frac{h}{16.9} = \frac{5.9}{5.3}$$
$$5.3h = 16.9 \cdot 5.9$$
$$5.3h = 99.71$$
$$h \approx 18.8 \text{ cm}$$
The height of the tail light is approximately 18.8 centimeters.

73. Let d be the distance from San Juan to Bermuda.
$$\frac{d}{1037} = \frac{19.2}{20.75}$$
$$20.75d = 1037 \cdot 19.2$$
$$20.75d = 19,910.4$$
$$d \approx 960 \text{ mi}$$
The distance from San Juan to Bermuda is approximately 960 miles.

75. Answers will vary.

77. Answers will vary.

79. $84.275° = 84° + 0.275(60)' = 84°16.5'$
$= 84°16' + 0.5(60)'' = 84°16'30''$

81. $\theta = -433°; \theta + 360k$
$k = 2; -433° + 360°(2) = 287°$

83. $a = b = \dfrac{5}{\sqrt{2}}$ cm

Mid-Chapter Check

1. $36°06'36'' = \left[36 + 6\left(\dfrac{1}{60}\right) + 36\left(\dfrac{1}{3600}\right)\right]°$
$= 36.11°\text{N}$

$115°04'48'' = \left[115 + 4\left(\dfrac{1}{60}\right) + 48\left(\dfrac{1}{3600}\right)\right]°$
$= 115.08°\text{W}$
The coordinates are $36.11°\text{N}, \ 115.08°\text{W}$.

3. a. $\theta = 18°; \theta + 360k$
$k = 1; 18° + 360°(1) = 378°$
$k = -1; 18° + 360°(-1) = -342°$

   b. $\theta = -107°; \theta + 360k$
$k = 1; -107° + 360°(1) = 253°$
$k = -1; -107° + 360°(-1) = -467°$

5. The largest angle will be opposite the largest side, the smallest angle will be opposite the smallest side, and so on.
$B = 65°; C = 55°$

7.
$$R + S + T = 180$$
$$(4x - 7) + (15x + 6) + (7x - 1) = 180$$
$$4x - 7 + 15x + 6 + 7x - 1 = 180$$
$$26x - 2 = 180$$
$$26x = 182$$
$$x = 7$$

$R = (4x - 7)°$
$R = [4(7) - 7]°$
$R = 21°$

$S = (15x + 6)°$
$S = [15(7) + 6]°$
$S = 111°$

$T = (7x - 1)°$
$T = [7(7) - 1]°$
$T = 48°$

9.
$$\frac{2x}{x+2} = \frac{15}{10}$$
$$\frac{2x}{x+2} = \frac{3}{2}$$
$$2x \cdot 2 = 3(x+2)$$
$$4x = 3x + 6$$
$$x = 6 \text{ in.}$$

Reinforcing Basic Concepts

Exercise 1:

$$a = \frac{\sqrt{6} - \sqrt{2}}{4}c$$
$$= \frac{\sqrt{6} - \sqrt{2}}{4} \cdot 8$$
$$= 2\left(\sqrt{6} - \sqrt{2}\right) \text{ cm}$$

Exercise 3:

$$c = \frac{4}{\sqrt{6} + \sqrt{2}}b$$
$$= \frac{4}{\sqrt{6} + \sqrt{2}} \cdot 5$$
$$= \frac{20}{\sqrt{6} + \sqrt{2}} \text{ ft}$$

Exercise 5:

$$b = \frac{\sqrt{6} + \sqrt{2}}{4}c$$
$$= \frac{\sqrt{6} + \sqrt{2}}{4} \cdot \left(\sqrt{6} - \sqrt{2}\right)$$
$$= \frac{6 - 2}{4} = 1 \text{ mm}$$

1.3 Exercises

1. origin; x-axis

3. $\cos\theta$; $\sin\theta$; $\tan\theta$; $\dfrac{r}{x}$; $\dfrac{r}{y}$; $\dfrac{x}{y}$

5. Answers will vary.

7. $y = \dfrac{15}{12}x$

    $y = \dfrac{5}{4}x, [0,\infty), \text{QI}$

9. $y = \dfrac{-2\sqrt{3}}{-2}x$

    $y = \sqrt{3}x, (-\infty, 0], \text{QIII}$

11. $y = \dfrac{-10.5}{6.3}x$

    $y = -\dfrac{5}{3}x, [0,\infty), \text{QIV}$

13. $y = \dfrac{\frac{3}{4}}{-\frac{5}{8}}x$

    $y = -\dfrac{3}{4} \cdot \dfrac{8}{5}x$

    $y = -\dfrac{6}{5}x, (-\infty, 0], \text{QII}$

15. At $x = -2$, $y = \dfrac{1}{2}(-2) = -1$; $(-2, -1)$

    At $x = -4$, $y = \dfrac{1}{2}(-4) = -2$; $(-4, -2)$

    At $(-2, -1)$, $\dfrac{y}{x} = \dfrac{-1}{-2} = \dfrac{1}{2}$, $\dfrac{x}{y} = \dfrac{-2}{-1} = 2$

    At $(-4, -2)$, $\dfrac{y}{x} = \dfrac{-2}{-4} = \dfrac{1}{2}$, $\dfrac{x}{y} = \dfrac{-4}{-2} = 2$

17. At $x = 1$, $y = 3(1) = 3$; $(1, 3)$

    At $x = 2$, $y = 3(2) = 6$; $(2, 6)$

    At $(1, 3)$, $\dfrac{y}{x} = \dfrac{3}{1} = 3$, $\dfrac{x}{y} = \dfrac{1}{3}$

    At $(2, 6)$, $\dfrac{y}{x} = \dfrac{6}{2} = 3$, $\dfrac{x}{y} = \dfrac{2}{6} = \dfrac{1}{3}$

19. At $x = -2$, $y = -1.5(-2) = 3$; $(-2, 3)$

    At $x = -4$, $y = -1.5(-4) = 6$; $(-4, 6)$

    At $(-2, 3)$, $\dfrac{y}{x} = \dfrac{3}{-2} = -\dfrac{3}{2}$, $\dfrac{x}{y} = \dfrac{-2}{3} = -\dfrac{2}{3}$

    At $(-4, 6)$, $\dfrac{y}{x} = \dfrac{6}{-4} = -\dfrac{3}{2}$, $\dfrac{x}{y} = \dfrac{-4}{6} = -\dfrac{2}{3}$

21. At $x = -3$, $y = \dfrac{4}{3}(-3) = -4$; $(-3, -4)$

    At $x = -6$, $y = \dfrac{4}{3}(-6) = -8$; $(-6, -8)$

    At $(-3, -4)$, $\dfrac{y}{x} = \dfrac{-4}{-3} = \dfrac{4}{3}$, $\dfrac{x}{y} = \dfrac{-3}{-4} = \dfrac{3}{4}$

    At $(-6, -8)$, $\dfrac{y}{x} = \dfrac{-8}{-6} = \dfrac{4}{3}$, $\dfrac{x}{y} = \dfrac{-6}{-8} = \dfrac{3}{4}$

23. $2x + 7y = 0$

$$7y = -2x$$

$$y = -\frac{2}{7}x$$

At $x = 7$, $y = -\frac{2}{7}(7) = -2$; $(7, -2)$

At $x = 14$, $y = -\frac{2}{7}(14) = -4$; $(14, -4)$

At $(7, -2)$, $\frac{y}{x} = \frac{-2}{7} = -\frac{2}{7}$, $\frac{x}{y} = \frac{7}{-2} = -\frac{7}{2}$

At $(14, -4)$, $\frac{y}{x} = \frac{-4}{14} = -\frac{2}{7}$, $\frac{x}{y} = \frac{14}{-4} = -\frac{7}{2}$

25. $r = \sqrt{8^2 + 15^2} = \sqrt{289} = 17$

$\sin\theta = \frac{15}{17}$; $\csc\theta = \frac{17}{15}$; $\cos\theta = \frac{8}{17}$

$\sec\theta = \frac{17}{8}$; $\tan\theta = \frac{15}{8}$; $\cot\theta = \frac{8}{15}$

27. $r = \sqrt{(-20)^2 + 21^2} = \sqrt{841} = 29$

$\sin\theta = \frac{21}{29}$; $\csc\theta = \frac{29}{21}$; $\cos\theta = -\frac{20}{29}$

$\sec\theta = -\frac{29}{20}$; $\tan\theta = -\frac{21}{20}$; $\cot\theta = -\frac{20}{21}$

29. $r = \sqrt{(7.5)^2 + (-7.5)^2} = \sqrt{2(7.5)^2} = 7.5\sqrt{2}$

$\sin\theta = -\frac{7.5}{7.5\sqrt{2}} = -\frac{\sqrt{2}}{2}$; $\csc\theta = -\frac{2}{\sqrt{2}}$

$\cos\theta = \frac{7.5}{7.5\sqrt{2}} = \frac{\sqrt{2}}{2}$; $\sec\theta = \frac{2}{\sqrt{2}}$

$\tan\theta = -1$; $\cot\theta = -1$

31. $r = \sqrt{\left(4\sqrt{3}\right)^2 + 4^2} = \sqrt{64} = 8$

$\sin\theta = \frac{4}{8} = \frac{1}{2}$; $\csc\theta = 2$

$\cos\theta = \frac{4\sqrt{3}}{8} = \frac{\sqrt{3}}{2}$; $\sec\theta = \frac{2}{\sqrt{3}}$

$\tan\theta = \frac{4}{4\sqrt{3}} = \frac{1}{\sqrt{3}}$; $\cot\theta = \sqrt{3}$

33. $r = \sqrt{2^2 + 8^2} = \sqrt{68} = 2\sqrt{17}$

$\sin\theta = \frac{8}{2\sqrt{17}} = \frac{4}{\sqrt{17}}$; $\csc\theta = \frac{\sqrt{17}}{4}$

$\cos\theta = \frac{2}{2\sqrt{17}} = \frac{1}{\sqrt{17}}$; $\sec\theta = \sqrt{17}$

$\tan\theta = \frac{8}{2} = 4$; $\cot\theta = \frac{1}{4}$

35. Based on similar triangles, we can multiply both coordinates by 4 to clear decimals.

$x = -3.75 \cdot 4 = -15$; $y = -2.5 \cdot 4 = -10$; $(-15, -10)$

$r = \sqrt{(-15)^2 + (-10)^2} = \sqrt{325} = 5\sqrt{13}$

$\sin\theta = -\frac{10}{5\sqrt{13}} = -\frac{2}{\sqrt{13}}$; $\csc\theta = -\frac{\sqrt{13}}{2}$

$\cos\theta = -\frac{15}{5\sqrt{13}} = -\frac{3}{\sqrt{13}}$; $\sec\theta = -\frac{\sqrt{13}}{3}$

$\tan\theta = \frac{-10}{-15} = \frac{2}{3}$; $\cot\theta = \frac{3}{2}$

37. Based on similar triangles, we can multiply both coordinates by 9 to clear fractions.

$x = -\frac{5}{9} \cdot 9 = -5$; $y = \frac{2}{3} \cdot 9 = 6$; $(-5, 6)$

$r = \sqrt{(-5)^2 + 6^2} = \sqrt{61}$

$\sin\theta = \frac{6}{\sqrt{61}}$; $\csc\theta = \frac{\sqrt{61}}{6}$

$\cos\theta = -\frac{5}{\sqrt{61}}$; $\sec\theta = -\frac{\sqrt{61}}{5}$

$\tan\theta = -\frac{6}{5}$; $\cot\theta = -\frac{5}{6}$

39. Based on similar triangles, we can multiply both coordinates by 4 to clear fractions.

$x = \frac{1}{4} \cdot 4 = 1$; $y = -\frac{\sqrt{5}}{2} \cdot 4 = -2\sqrt{5}$; $\left(1, -2\sqrt{5}\right)$

$r = \sqrt{1^2 + (-2\sqrt{5})^2} = \sqrt{21}$

$\sin\theta = -\frac{2\sqrt{5}}{\sqrt{21}}$; $\csc\theta = -\frac{\sqrt{21}}{2\sqrt{5}}$

$\cos\theta = \frac{1}{\sqrt{21}}$; $\sec\theta = \sqrt{21}$

$\tan\theta = -2\sqrt{5}$; $\cot\theta = -\frac{1}{2\sqrt{5}}$

41.

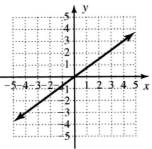

QI and QIII

For QI, we chose $(4,3)$.

$r = \sqrt{4^2 + 3^2} = \sqrt{25} = 5$

$\sin\theta = \dfrac{3}{5}$; $\cos\theta = \dfrac{4}{5}$; $\tan\theta = \dfrac{3}{4}$

For QIII, we chose $(-4,-3)$. $r = 5$

$\sin\theta = -\dfrac{3}{5}$; $\cos\theta = -\dfrac{4}{5}$; $\tan\theta = \dfrac{-3}{-4} = \dfrac{3}{4}$

43.

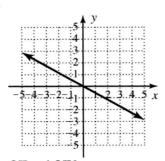

QII and QIV

For QII, we chose $\left(-3,\sqrt{3}\right)$.

$r = \sqrt{(-3)^2 + (\sqrt{3})^2} = \sqrt{12} = 2\sqrt{3}$

$\sin\theta = \dfrac{\sqrt{3}}{2\sqrt{3}} = \dfrac{1}{2}$; $\cos\theta = \dfrac{-3}{2\sqrt{3}} = -\dfrac{\sqrt{3}}{2}$

$\tan\theta = \dfrac{\sqrt{3}}{-3} = -\dfrac{1}{\sqrt{3}}$

For QIV, we chose $\left(3,-\sqrt{3}\right)$. $r = 2\sqrt{3}$.

$\sin\theta = \dfrac{-\sqrt{3}}{2\sqrt{3}} = -\dfrac{1}{2}$; $\cos\theta = \dfrac{3}{2\sqrt{3}} = \dfrac{\sqrt{3}}{2}$

$\tan\theta = \dfrac{-\sqrt{3}}{3} = -\dfrac{1}{\sqrt{3}}$

45. $\sin\theta > 0 \Rightarrow y > 0$
   $\cos\theta < 0 \Rightarrow x < 0$
   The angle θ is in quadrant II.

47. $\tan\theta < 0 \Rightarrow x$ and y differ in sign.
   $\sin\theta > 0 \Rightarrow y > 0 \Rightarrow x < 0$
   The angle θ is in quadrant II.

49. QIII; $\sin\theta\cos\theta = (-)(-)$; positive

51. QIV; $\dfrac{\cot\theta}{\cos\theta} = \dfrac{(-)}{(+)}$; negative

53. QII; $\cos\theta \cdot \dfrac{\tan\theta}{\sec\theta} = (-)\cdot\dfrac{(-)}{(-)}$; negative

55. $\cos\theta = \dfrac{4}{5} \Rightarrow x = 4,\ r = 5$
   Since $\sin\theta < 0$, y is negative.
   The angle θ is in quadrant IV.
   $y = -\sqrt{5^2 - 4^2} = -\sqrt{9} = -3$
   $\sin\theta = -\dfrac{3}{5}$; $\csc\theta = -\dfrac{5}{3}$; $\cos\theta = \dfrac{4}{5}$;
   $\sec\theta = \dfrac{5}{4}$; $\tan\theta = -\dfrac{3}{4}$; $\cot\theta = -\dfrac{4}{3}$

57. $\csc\theta = -\dfrac{37}{35} \Rightarrow y = -35,\ r = 37$
   (Since $\csc\theta < 0$ and $\tan\theta > 0$, y is negative.)
   The angle θ is in quadrant III.
   $x = -\sqrt{(37)^2 - (-35)^2} = -\sqrt{144} = -12$
   $\sin\theta = -\dfrac{35}{37}$; $\csc\theta = -\dfrac{37}{35}$; $\cos\theta = -\dfrac{12}{37}$
   $\sec\theta = -\dfrac{37}{12}$; $\tan\theta = \dfrac{35}{12}$; $\cot\theta = \dfrac{12}{35}$

59. $\csc\theta = 3 \Rightarrow y = 1,\ r = 3$
   (Since $\cos\theta > 0$, x is positive.)
   The angle θ is in quadrant I.
   $x = \sqrt{3^2 - 1^2} = \sqrt{8} = 2\sqrt{2}$
   $\sin\theta = \dfrac{1}{3}$; $\csc\theta = 3$; $\cos\theta = \dfrac{2\sqrt{2}}{3}$
   $\sec\theta = \dfrac{3}{2\sqrt{2}}$; $\tan\theta = \dfrac{1}{2\sqrt{2}}$; $\cot\theta = 2\sqrt{2}$

61. $\sin\theta = -\dfrac{7}{8} \Rightarrow y = -7,\ r = 8$

    (Since $\sec\theta < 0,\ x$ is negative.)
    The angle θ is in quadrant III.

    $x = -\sqrt{8^2 - (-7)^2} = -\sqrt{15}$

    $\sin\theta = -\dfrac{7}{8};\ \csc\theta = -\dfrac{8}{7};\ \cos\theta = -\dfrac{\sqrt{15}}{8}$

    $\sec\theta = -\dfrac{8}{\sqrt{15}};\ \tan\theta = \dfrac{7}{\sqrt{15}};\ \cot\theta = \dfrac{\sqrt{15}}{7}$

63. $\theta = 90° \Rightarrow x = 0,\ y = k;\ k > 0;\ r = |k| = k$

    $\sin 90° = \dfrac{k}{k} = 1;\ \csc 90° = 1$

    $\cos 90° = \dfrac{0}{k} = 0;\ \sec 90°$ is undefined

    $\tan 90° = \dfrac{k}{0}$ is undefined; $\cot 90° = \dfrac{0}{k} = 0$

65. $\cos\beta = \dfrac{x}{r} = 0 \Rightarrow x = 0$

    $\sin\beta = \dfrac{y}{r} = 1 \Rightarrow y = r \Rightarrow y > 0;\ \beta = 90°$

67. $\tan\beta = \dfrac{y}{x}$ is undefined $\Rightarrow x = 0$

    $\csc\beta = \dfrac{r}{y} = -1 \Rightarrow y = -r \Rightarrow y < 0;\ \beta = 270°$

69. $\tan\beta = \dfrac{y}{x} = 0 \Rightarrow y = 0$

    $\sec\beta = \dfrac{r}{x} = 1 \Rightarrow x = r \Rightarrow x > 0;\ \beta = 0°$

71. $\csc\beta = \dfrac{r}{y}$ is undefined $\Rightarrow y = 0$

    $\cos\beta = \dfrac{x}{r} = -1 \Rightarrow x = -r \Rightarrow x < 0;\ \beta = 180°$

73. $719° - 360° = 359°;\ $ QIV
    Sine is negative.

75. $-419° + 720° = 301°;\ $ QIV
    Tangent is negative.

77. $681° - 360° = 321°;\ $ QIV
    Cosecant is negative.

79. $805° - 720° = 85°;\ $ QI
    Cosine is positive.

81. $\cos\theta = \dfrac{x}{\sqrt{x^2 + y^2}}$

    a. $\cos\theta = \dfrac{3}{\sqrt{3^2 + 4^2}} = \dfrac{3}{\sqrt{25}} = \dfrac{3}{5}$

    b. $\cos\theta = \dfrac{3}{\sqrt{3^2 + 0^2}} = \dfrac{3}{\sqrt{9}} = \dfrac{3}{3} = 1$

    c. Answers will vary.

83. $\tan\theta = \dfrac{y}{x} = \dfrac{40}{-60} = -\dfrac{2}{3}$

85. $\sin\theta = \dfrac{y}{r} = \dfrac{3}{10}$

87. $\cos\theta = \dfrac{y}{r} = \dfrac{60}{70} = \dfrac{6}{7}$

89. The terminal side of α lies in QI.

    $\cos\alpha = \dfrac{a}{b} \Rightarrow x = a,\ r = b,\ y = \sqrt{b^2 - a^2}$

    $\sin\alpha = \dfrac{\sqrt{b^2 - a^2}}{b}$

    $\csc\alpha = \dfrac{b}{\sqrt{b^2 - a^2}} = \dfrac{b\sqrt{b^2 - a^2}}{b^2 - a^2}$

    $\cos\alpha = \dfrac{a}{b};\ \sec\alpha = \dfrac{b}{a}$

    $\tan\alpha = \dfrac{\sqrt{b^2 - a^2}}{a}$

    $\cot\alpha = \dfrac{a}{\sqrt{b^2 - a^2}} = \dfrac{a\sqrt{b^2 - a^2}}{b^2 - a^2}$

91. The terminal side of θ lies in QII.
    Think of $\cos\theta$ as the adjacent side divided by the hypotenuse.
    Think of $\sin\theta$ as the opposite side divided by the hypotenuse.
    Use the Pythagorean Theorem.

    $\cos\theta = \dfrac{x_1 x_2 + y_1 y_2}{r_1 r_2} \Rightarrow$

    $\sin\theta = \dfrac{\sqrt{r_1^2 r_2^2 - (x_1 x_2 + y_1 y_2)^2}}{r_1 r_2}$

93. a. $180° - 117.26° = 62.74°$

b. $180° - 85°59'37''$
$$= (179° + 59' + 60'') - 85°59'37''$$
$$= (179° - 85°) + (59' - 59') + (60'' - 37'')$$
$$= 94° + 0' + 23''$$
$$= 94°23''$$

95.
$$A + B + C = 180$$
$$(3x - 8) + 3x + (5x + 1) = 180$$
$$3x - 8 + 3x + 5x + 1 = 180$$
$$11x - 7 = 180$$
$$11x = 187$$
$$x = 17$$

$A = (3x - 8)°$ $B = 3x°$ $C = (5x + 1)°$
$A = \left[3(17) - 8\right]°$ $B = 3(17)°$ $C = \left[5(17) + 1\right]°$
$A = 43°$ $B = 51°$ $C = 86°$

97. $\theta = -93°$; $\theta + 360k$

$k = -2; -93 + 360(-2) = -813°$;

$k = -1; -93 + 360(-1) = -453°$;

$k = 1; -93 + 360(1) = 267°$;

$k = 2; -93 + 360(2) = 627°$;

$-813°, -453°, 267°, 627°$

1.4 Exercises

1. $\sin\theta$; $\sec\theta$; $\cos\theta$

3. $\cos^2\theta$; $1 + \cot^2\theta = \csc^2\theta$

5. $\dfrac{\cos\theta}{\sin\theta} - \dfrac{\sin\theta}{\sec\theta} = \dfrac{\cos\theta\sec\theta - \sin^2\theta}{\sin\theta\sec\theta}$
$$= \dfrac{1 - \sin^2\theta}{\sin\theta\sec\theta}$$
Answers will vary.

7. $\tan\theta = \dfrac{\sin\theta}{\cos\theta}$

$\tan\theta = \dfrac{\sec\theta}{\csc\theta}$

$\dfrac{\sin\theta}{\cos\theta} = \dfrac{\sec\theta}{\csc\theta}$

$\dfrac{1}{\cot\theta} = \dfrac{\sec\theta}{\csc\theta}$

$\dfrac{1}{\cot\theta} = \dfrac{\sin\theta}{\cos\theta}$

9. $1 + \tan^2\theta = \sec^2\theta$
$$1 = \sec^2\theta - \tan^2\theta$$
$$\tan^2\theta = \sec^2\theta - 1$$
$$1 = (\sec\theta + \tan\theta)(\sec\theta - \tan\theta)$$
$$\tan\theta = \pm\sqrt{\sec^2\theta - 1}$$

11. $\sin\theta\cot\theta = \cos\theta$

$\sin\theta\left(\dfrac{\cos\theta}{\sin\theta}\right) = \cos\theta$

$\cos\theta = \cos\theta$

13. $\sec^2\theta\cot^2\theta = \csc^2\theta$

$\dfrac{1}{\cos^2\theta}\left(\dfrac{\cos^2\theta}{\sin^2\theta}\right) = \csc^2\theta$

$\dfrac{1}{\sin^2\theta} = \csc^2\theta$

$\csc^2\theta = \csc^2\theta$

15. $\cos\theta(\sec\theta - \cos\theta) = \sin^2\theta$

$\cos\theta\sec\theta - \cos^2\theta = \sin^2\theta$

$\cos\theta\cdot\dfrac{1}{\cos\theta} - \cos^2\theta = \sin^2\theta$

$1 - \cos^2\theta = \sin^2\theta$

$\sin^2\theta = \sin^2\theta$

17. $\sin\theta(\csc\theta - \sin\theta) = \cos^2\theta$

$\sin\theta\csc\theta - \sin^2\theta = \cos^2\theta$

$\sin\theta\cdot\dfrac{1}{\sin\theta} - \sin^2\theta = \cos^2\theta$

$1 - \sin^2\theta = \cos^2\theta$

$\cos^2\theta = \cos^2\theta$

19. $\tan\theta(\csc\theta + \cot\theta) = \sec\theta + 1$

$\tan\theta\csc\theta + \tan\theta\cot\theta = \sec\theta + 1$

$\dfrac{\sin\theta}{\cos\theta}\cdot\dfrac{1}{\sin\theta} + \dfrac{\sin\theta}{\cos\theta}\cdot\dfrac{\cos\theta}{\sin\theta} = \sec\theta + 1$

$\dfrac{1}{\cos\theta} + 1 = \sec\theta + 1$

$\sec\theta + 1 = \sec\theta + 1$

21. $\tan^2\theta\csc^2\theta - \tan^2\theta = 1$

$\tan^2\theta(\csc^2\theta - 1) = 1$

$\tan^2\theta(\cot^2\theta) = 1$

$\dfrac{\sin^2\theta}{\cos^2\theta}\left(\dfrac{\cos^2\theta}{\sin^2\theta}\right) = 1$

$1 = 1$

23. $\dfrac{\sin\theta\cos\theta+\sin\theta}{\cos\theta+\cos^2\theta}=\tan\theta$

$\dfrac{\sin\theta(\cos\theta+1)}{\cos\theta(1+\cos\theta)}=\tan\theta$

$\dfrac{\sin\theta}{\cos\theta}=\tan\theta$

$\tan\theta=\tan\theta$

25. $\dfrac{1+\sin\theta}{\cos\theta+\cos\theta\sin\theta}=\sec\theta$

$\dfrac{1+\sin\theta}{\cos\theta(1+\sin\theta)}=\sec\theta$

$\dfrac{1}{\cos\theta}=\sec\theta$

$\sec\theta=\sec\theta$

27. $\dfrac{\sin\theta\tan\theta+\sin\theta}{\tan\theta+\tan^2\theta}=\cos\theta$

$\dfrac{\sin\theta(\tan\theta+1)}{\tan\theta(1+\tan\theta)}=\cos\theta$

$\dfrac{\sin\theta}{\tan\theta}=\cos\theta$

$\dfrac{\sin\theta}{\dfrac{\sin\theta}{\cos\theta}}=\cos\theta$

$\dfrac{\sin\theta\cos\theta}{\sin\theta}=\cos\theta$

$\cos\theta=\cos\theta$

29. $\dfrac{(\sin\theta+\cos\theta)^2}{\cos\theta}=\sec\theta+2\sin\theta$

$\dfrac{\sin^2\theta+2\sin\theta\cos\theta+\cos^2\theta}{\cos\theta}=\sec\theta+2\sin\theta$

$\dfrac{\sin^2\theta+\cos^2\theta+2\sin\theta\cos\theta}{\cos\theta}=\sec\theta+2\sin\theta$

$\dfrac{1+2\sin\theta\cos\theta}{\cos\theta}=\sec\theta+2\sin\theta$

$\dfrac{1}{\cos\theta}+\dfrac{2\sin\theta\cos\theta}{\cos\theta}=\sec\theta+2\sin\theta$

$\dfrac{1}{\cos\theta}+2\sin\theta=\sec\theta+2\sin\theta$

$\sec\theta+2\sin\theta=\sec\theta+2\sin\theta$

31. $(1+\sin\theta)(1-\sin\theta)=\cos^2\theta$

$1-\sin^2\theta=\cos^2\theta$

$\cos^2\theta=\cos^2\theta$

33. $\dfrac{(\csc\theta-\cot\theta)(\csc\theta+\cot\theta)}{\tan\theta}=\cot\theta$

$\dfrac{\csc^2\theta-\cot^2\theta}{\tan\theta}=\cot\theta$

$\dfrac{1}{\tan\theta}=\cot\theta$

$\cot\theta=\cot\theta$

35. $\dfrac{\cos^2\theta}{\sin\theta}+\dfrac{\sin\theta}{1}=\csc\theta$

$\dfrac{\cos^2\theta\cdot 1+\sin\theta\cdot\sin\theta}{\sin\theta\cdot 1}=\csc\theta$

$\dfrac{\cos^2\theta+\sin^2\theta}{\sin\theta}=\csc\theta$

$\dfrac{1}{\sin\theta}=\csc\theta$

$\csc\theta=\csc\theta$

37. $\dfrac{\tan\theta}{\csc\theta}-\dfrac{\sin\theta}{\cos\theta}=\dfrac{\sin\theta-1}{\cot\theta}$

$\dfrac{\tan\theta\cdot\cos\theta-\csc\theta\cdot\sin\theta}{\csc\theta\cdot\cos\theta}=\dfrac{\sin\theta-1}{\cot\theta}$

$\dfrac{\dfrac{\sin\theta}{\cos\theta}\cdot\cos\theta-\dfrac{1}{\sin\theta}\cdot\sin\theta}{\dfrac{1}{\sin\theta}\cdot\cos\theta}=\dfrac{\sin\theta-1}{\cot\theta}$

$\dfrac{\sin\theta-1}{\cot\theta}=\dfrac{\sin\theta-1}{\cot\theta}$

39. $\dfrac{\sec\theta}{\sin\theta}-\dfrac{\csc\theta}{\sec\theta}=\tan\theta$

$\dfrac{\sec\theta\cdot\sec\theta-\sin\theta\cdot\csc\theta}{\sin\theta\cdot\sec\theta}=\tan\theta$

$\dfrac{\sec^2\theta-\sin\theta\csc\theta}{\sin\theta\sec\theta}=\tan\theta$

$\dfrac{\sec^2\theta-\sin\theta\cdot\dfrac{1}{\sin\theta}}{\sin\theta\cdot\dfrac{1}{\cos\theta}}=\tan\theta$

$\dfrac{\sec^2\theta-1}{\tan\theta}=\tan\theta$

$\dfrac{\tan^2\theta}{\tan\theta}=\tan\theta$

$\tan\theta=\tan\theta$

41. $\tan\theta$ in terms of $\sin\theta$

$$\tan\theta = \frac{\sin\theta}{\cos\theta}$$

$$\cos^2\theta = 1 - \sin^2\theta \Rightarrow \cos\theta = \pm\sqrt{1-\sin^2\theta}$$

$$\Rightarrow \tan\theta = \frac{\sin\theta}{\pm\sqrt{1-\sin^2\theta}}$$

43. $\sec\theta$ in terms of $\cot\theta$

$$\sec^2\theta = \tan^2\theta + 1 \Rightarrow \sec^2\theta = \frac{1}{\cot^2\theta} + 1$$

$$\Rightarrow \sec\theta = \pm\sqrt{\frac{1}{\cot^2\theta} + 1}$$

45. $\cot\theta$ in terms of $\sin\theta$

Note that $\csc\theta = \dfrac{1}{\sin\theta}$.

$$\cot^2\theta = \csc^2\theta - 1 \Rightarrow$$

$$\cot\theta = \pm\sqrt{\csc^2\theta - 1}$$

$$\cot\theta = \pm\sqrt{\frac{1}{\sin^2\theta} - 1}$$

$$\cot\theta = \pm\sqrt{\frac{1-\sin^2\theta}{\sin^2\theta}}$$

$$\cot\theta = \frac{\pm\sqrt{1-\sin^2\theta}}{\sin\theta}$$

47. $\cos\theta = -\dfrac{20}{29}$ with θ in QII

$$\sec\theta = -\frac{29}{20} \text{ (reciprocal identities)}$$

$$\sin^2\theta = 1 - \cos^2\theta \Rightarrow \sin\theta = \pm\sqrt{1-\cos^2\theta}$$

$$\sin\theta = \pm\sqrt{1 - \left(-\frac{20}{29}\right)^2}$$

$$= \pm\sqrt{\frac{841}{841} - \frac{400}{841}} = \pm\sqrt{\frac{441}{841}} = \pm\frac{21}{29}$$

$\sin\theta$ is positive in QII, so $\sin\theta = \dfrac{21}{29}$, and

$$\csc\theta = \frac{29}{21}. \text{ (reciprocal identities)}$$

$$\tan\theta = \frac{\sin\theta}{\cos\theta} = \frac{\frac{21}{29}}{-\frac{20}{29}} = \frac{21}{29}\cdot\left(-\frac{29}{20}\right) = -\frac{21}{20}$$

$$\cot\theta = -\frac{20}{21} \text{ (reciprocal identities)}$$

49. $\tan\theta = \dfrac{15}{8}$ with θ in QIII

$$\cot\theta = \frac{8}{15} \text{ (reciprocal identities)}$$

$$\sec^2\theta = \tan^2\theta + 1 \Rightarrow \sec\theta = \pm\sqrt{\tan^2\theta + 1}$$

$$\sec\theta = \pm\sqrt{\left(\frac{15}{8}\right)^2 + 1} = \pm\sqrt{\frac{225}{64} + \frac{64}{64}}$$

$$= \pm\sqrt{\frac{289}{64}} = \pm\frac{17}{8}$$

$\sec\theta$ is negative in QIII, so $\sec\theta = -\dfrac{17}{8}$, and

$$\cos\theta = -\frac{8}{17}. \text{ (reciprocal identities)}$$

$$\sin^2\theta = 1 - \cos^2\theta \Rightarrow \sin\theta = \pm\sqrt{1-\cos^2\theta}$$

$$\sin\theta = \pm\sqrt{1^2 - \left(-\frac{8}{17}\right)^2} = \pm\sqrt{\frac{289}{289} - \frac{64}{289}}$$

$$= \pm\sqrt{\frac{225}{289}} = \pm\frac{15}{17}$$

$\sin\theta$ is negative in QIII, so $\sin\theta = -\dfrac{15}{17}$, and

$$\csc\theta = -\frac{17}{15}. \text{ (reciprocal identities)}$$

51. $\cot\theta = \dfrac{x}{5}$ with θ in QI (Note $x > 0$.)

$$\tan\theta = \frac{5}{x} \text{ (reciprocal identities)}$$

$$\sec^2\theta = \tan^2\theta + 1 \Rightarrow \sec\theta = \pm\sqrt{\tan^2\theta + 1}$$

$$\sec\theta = \pm\sqrt{\left(\frac{5}{x}\right)^2 + 1} = \pm\sqrt{\frac{25}{x^2} + \frac{x^2}{x^2}} = \pm\frac{\sqrt{25+x^2}}{x}$$

$\sec\theta$ is positive in QI, so $\sec\theta = \dfrac{\sqrt{25+x^2}}{x}$,

and $\cos\theta = \dfrac{x}{\sqrt{25+x^2}}$. (reciprocal identities)

$$\csc^2\theta = 1 + \cot^2\theta \Rightarrow \csc\theta = \pm\sqrt{1+\cot^2\theta}$$

$$\csc\theta = \pm\sqrt{1 + \left(\frac{x}{5}\right)^2} = \pm\sqrt{\frac{25}{25} + \frac{x^2}{25}} = \pm\frac{\sqrt{25+x^2}}{5}$$

$\csc\theta$ is positive in QI, so $\csc\theta = \dfrac{\sqrt{25+x^2}}{5}$,

and $\sin\theta = \dfrac{5}{\sqrt{25+x^2}}$. (reciprocal identities)

53. $\sin\theta = -\dfrac{7}{13}$ with θ in QIII

$\csc\theta = -\dfrac{13}{7}$ (reciprocal identities)

$\cos^2\theta = 1 - \sin^2\theta \Rightarrow \cos\theta = \pm\sqrt{1-\sin^2\theta}$

$\cos\theta = \pm\sqrt{1-\left(-\dfrac{7}{13}\right)^2} = \pm\sqrt{\dfrac{169}{169} - \dfrac{49}{169}}$

$\qquad = \pm\sqrt{\dfrac{120}{169}} = \pm\dfrac{2\sqrt{30}}{13}$

$\cos\theta$ is negative in QIII, so $\cos\theta = -\dfrac{2\sqrt{30}}{13}$,

and $\sec\theta = -\dfrac{13}{2\sqrt{30}}$. (reciprocal identities)

$\tan\theta = \dfrac{\sin\theta}{\cos\theta} = \dfrac{-\dfrac{7}{13}}{-\dfrac{2\sqrt{30}}{13}} = -\dfrac{7}{13}\cdot\left(-\dfrac{13}{2\sqrt{30}}\right) = \dfrac{7}{2\sqrt{30}}$

$\cot\theta = \dfrac{2\sqrt{30}}{7}$ (reciprocal identities)

55. $\sec\theta = -\dfrac{9}{7}$ with θ in QII

$\cos\theta = -\dfrac{7}{9}$ (reciprocal identities)

$\sin^2\theta = 1 - \cos^2\theta \Rightarrow \sin\theta = \pm\sqrt{1-\cos^2\theta}$

$\sin\theta = \pm\sqrt{1-\left(-\dfrac{7}{9}\right)^2} = \pm\sqrt{\dfrac{81}{81} - \dfrac{49}{81}}$

$\qquad = \pm\sqrt{\dfrac{32}{81}} = \pm\dfrac{4\sqrt{2}}{9}$

$\sin\theta$ is positive in QII, so $\sin\theta = \dfrac{4\sqrt{2}}{9}$, and

$\csc\theta = \dfrac{9}{4\sqrt{2}}$. (reciprocal identities)

$\tan\theta = \dfrac{\sin\theta}{\cos\theta} = \dfrac{\dfrac{4\sqrt{2}}{9}}{-\dfrac{7}{9}} = \dfrac{4\sqrt{2}}{9}\cdot\left(-\dfrac{9}{7}\right) = -\dfrac{4\sqrt{2}}{7}$

$\cot\theta = -\dfrac{7}{4\sqrt{2}}$ (reciprocal identities)

57. $V = 2\sin^2\theta = 2\left(1-\cos^2\theta\right)$

59. $\cos^3\theta = \left(\cos\theta\right)\left(\cos^2\theta\right)$

$\qquad = \cos\theta\left(1-\sin^2\theta\right)$

61. $\tan\theta + \tan^3\theta = \tan\theta\left(1+\tan^2\theta\right) = \tan\theta\left(\sec^2\theta\right)$

63. $\tan^2\theta\sec\theta - 4\tan^2\theta$

$\qquad = \left(\tan^2\theta\right)\left(\sec\theta - 4\right)$

$\qquad = \left(\sec\theta - 4\right)\left(\tan^2\theta\right)$

$\qquad = \left(\sec\theta - 4\right)\left(\sec^2\theta - 1\right)$

$\qquad = \left(\sec\theta - 4\right)\left(\sec\theta - 1\right)\left(\sec\theta + 1\right)$

65. $\cos^2\theta\sin\theta - \cos^2\theta$

$\qquad = \cos^2\theta\left(\sin\theta - 1\right)$

$\qquad = \left(1-\sin^2\theta\right)\left(\sin\theta - 1\right)$

$\qquad = \left(1+\sin\theta\right)\left(1-\sin\theta\right)\left(\sin\theta - 1\right)$

$\qquad = \left(1+\sin\theta\right)\left(-1\right)\left(1-\sin\theta\right)\left(1-\sin\theta\right)$

$\qquad = -1\left(1+\sin\theta\right)\left(1-\sin\theta\right)^2$

67. $\left(m_2 - m_1\right)\cos\theta = \sin\theta + m_1 m_2\sin\theta$

$\qquad \left(m_2 - m_1\right)\cos\theta = \sin\theta\left(1 + m_1 m_2\right)$

$\qquad \dfrac{m_2 - m_1}{1 + m_1 m_2} = \dfrac{\sin\theta}{\cos\theta}$

$\qquad \tan\theta = \dfrac{m_2 - m_1}{1 + m_1 m_2}$

69. $\tan\theta = \dfrac{m_2 - m_1}{1 + m_1 m_2}$

$\tan\theta = \dfrac{-2-3}{1+3(-2)} = \dfrac{-5}{1-6} = \dfrac{-5}{-5} = 1$,

so $\theta = 45°$.

71. $-2\sin^4\theta + \sqrt{3}\sin^3\theta + 2\sin^2\theta - \sqrt{3}\sin\theta$

$\qquad = \sin\theta\left(-2\sin^3\theta + \sqrt{3}\sin^2\theta + 2\sin\theta - \sqrt{3}\right)$

$\qquad = \sin\theta\left[\left(-2\sin^3\theta + \sqrt{3}\sin^2\theta\right) + \left(2\sin\theta - \sqrt{3}\right)\right]$

$\qquad = \sin\theta\left[-\sin^2\theta\left(2\sin\theta - \sqrt{3}\right) + 1\left(2\sin\theta - \sqrt{3}\right)\right]$

$\qquad = \sin\theta\left[\left(1-\sin^2\theta\right)\left(2\sin\theta - \sqrt{3}\right)\right]$

$\qquad = \sin\theta\left(\cos^2\theta\right)\left(2\sin\theta - \sqrt{3}\right)$

73. $a = b = \dfrac{c}{\sqrt{2}} = \dfrac{7}{\sqrt{2}} = \dfrac{7}{\sqrt{2}}\cdot\dfrac{\sqrt{2}}{\sqrt{2}} = \dfrac{7\sqrt{2}}{2}$ in.

75. No, because $17 + 22 < 40$.

77. The figure shown is a right isosceles triangle.

Summary and Concept Review 1.1

1. $90° - 47°03'49''$
    $= (89° + 59' + 60'') - 47°03'49''$
    $= (89° - 47°) + (59' - 03') + (60'' - 49'')$
    $= 42° + 56' + 11''$
    $= 42°56'11''$

3. $147°36'48'' = \left[147 + 36\left(\dfrac{1}{60}\right) + 48\left(\dfrac{1}{3600}\right)\right]°$
    $= 147.61\overline{3}°$

5. $\theta = 207°$; $\theta + 360k$
    $k = -2; 207 + 360(-2) = -513°$;
    $k = -1; 207 + 360(-1) = -153°$;
    $k = 1; 207 + 360(1) = 567°$;
    $k = 2; 207 + 360(2) = 927°$;
    $-513°, -153°, 567°, 927°$

7. $d = \sqrt{3} \cdot 400 = 400\sqrt{3} \approx 692.82$ yd

Summary and Concept Review 1.2

9. The figure shown is an obtuse isosceles triangle.

11. $\angle A = 180° - (32° + 87°) = 61°$

13. Let x be the length of the hypotenuse of the smallest triangle.
     $x = \sqrt{3^2 + 4^2} = \sqrt{25} = 5$

     Let a be the height of the largest triangle.
     $\dfrac{a}{3} = \dfrac{16.875}{5}$
     $5a = 3 \cdot 16.875$
     $5a = 50.625$
     $a = 10.125$

     Let b be the base of the largest triangle.
     $b = \sqrt{16.875^2 - 10.125^2}$
     $= \sqrt{182.25}$
     $= \sqrt{13.5}$
     The dimensions of the largest triangle are
     $10.125 \times 13.5 \times 16.875$.

15.
$$\dfrac{x-1}{9} = \dfrac{7}{5x+1}$$
$$(x-1)(5x+1) = 9 \cdot 7$$
$$5x^2 - 4x - 1 = 63$$
$$5x^2 - 4x - 64 = 0$$
$$(5x+16)(x-4) = 0$$
$$x = -\dfrac{16}{5} \quad \text{or} \quad x = 4$$

We discard $x = -\dfrac{16}{5}$, so $x = 4$ in.

$x - 1 = 4 - 1 = 3$ in.
$5x + 1 = 5(4) + 1 = 21$ in.

Summary and Concept Review 1.3

17. For QIII, choose $x = -1$.
     $y = 3(-1) = -3 \Rightarrow (-1, -3)$
     $r = \sqrt{(-1)^2 + (-3)^2} = \sqrt{10}$

     $\sin\theta = \dfrac{-3}{\sqrt{10}} = -\dfrac{3\sqrt{10}}{10}$; $\csc\theta = -\dfrac{\sqrt{10}}{3}$

     $\cos\theta = \dfrac{-1}{\sqrt{10}} = -\dfrac{\sqrt{10}}{10}$; $\sec\theta = -\sqrt{10}$

     $\tan\theta = \dfrac{-3}{-1} = 3$; $\cot\theta = \dfrac{1}{3}$

19. a. $\cos\theta = \dfrac{4}{5} \Rightarrow x = 4, r = 5$

     Since $\sin\theta < 0$, y is negative.
     The angle θ is in quadrant IV.
     $y = -\sqrt{5^2 - 4^2} = -\sqrt{9} = -3$

     $\sin\theta = -\dfrac{3}{5}$; $\csc\theta = -\dfrac{5}{3}$; $\cos\theta = \dfrac{4}{5}$;

     $\sec\theta = \dfrac{5}{4}$; $\tan\theta = -\dfrac{3}{4}$; $\cot\theta = -\dfrac{4}{3}$

     b. $\tan\theta = -\dfrac{12}{5} \Rightarrow x = 5, y = -12$

     (Since $\cos\theta > 0$ and $\tan\theta < 0$,
     y is negative.)
     The angle θ is in quadrant IV.
     $r = \sqrt{5^2 + (-12)^2} = \sqrt{169} = 13$

     $\sin\theta = -\dfrac{12}{13}$; $\csc\theta = -\dfrac{13}{12}$; $\cos\theta = \dfrac{5}{13}$

     $\sec\theta = \dfrac{13}{5}$; $\tan\theta = -\dfrac{12}{5}$; $\cot\theta = -\dfrac{5}{12}$

21. a. $\sec 90° = \dfrac{1}{\cos 90°} = \dfrac{1}{0}$ is undefined

    b. $\tan 180° = \dfrac{\sin 180°}{\cos 180°} = \dfrac{0}{-1} = 0$

    c. $\cot 270° = \dfrac{\cos 270°}{\sin 270°} = \dfrac{0}{-1} = 0$

    d. $\csc 360° = \dfrac{1}{\sin 360°} = \dfrac{1}{0}$ is undefined

Summary and Concept Review 1.4

23. $\dfrac{\tan^2\theta \csc\theta + \csc\theta}{\sec^2} = \csc\theta$

$$\dfrac{\csc\theta\left(\tan^2\theta + 1\right)}{\sec^2} = \csc\theta$$

$$\dfrac{\csc\theta\left(\sec^2\theta\right)}{\sec^2} = \csc\theta$$

$$\csc\theta = \csc\theta$$

25. $\dfrac{\sec^2\theta}{\csc\theta} - \sin\theta = \dfrac{\tan^2\theta}{\csc\theta}$

$$\dfrac{\sec^2\theta}{\csc\theta} - \dfrac{\sin\theta}{1} = \dfrac{\tan^2\theta}{\csc\theta}$$

$$\dfrac{\sec^2\theta \cdot 1 - \csc\theta\sin\theta}{\csc\theta} = \dfrac{\tan^2\theta}{\csc\theta}$$

$$\dfrac{\sec^2\theta - 1}{\csc\theta} = \dfrac{\tan^2\theta}{\csc\theta}$$

$$\dfrac{\tan^2\theta}{\csc\theta} = \dfrac{\tan^2\theta}{\csc\theta}$$

27. $\sec\theta = \dfrac{25}{23}$ with θ in QIV

$\cos\theta = \dfrac{23}{25}$ (reciprocal identities)

$\sin^2\theta = 1 - \cos^2\theta \Rightarrow \sin\theta = \pm\sqrt{1 - \cos^2\theta}$

$\sin\theta = \pm\sqrt{1 - \left(\dfrac{23}{25}\right)^2} = \pm\sqrt{\dfrac{625}{625} - \dfrac{529}{625}}$

$= \pm\sqrt{\dfrac{96}{625}} = \pm\dfrac{4\sqrt{6}}{25}$

$\sin\theta$ is negative in QIV, so $\sin\theta = -\dfrac{4\sqrt{6}}{25}$,

and $\csc\theta = -\dfrac{25}{4\sqrt{6}}$ (reciprocal identities)

---

27. (continued)

$\tan\theta = \dfrac{\sin\theta}{\cos\theta} = \dfrac{-\dfrac{4\sqrt{6}}{25}}{\dfrac{23}{25}}$

$= -\dfrac{4\sqrt{6}}{25}\cdot\dfrac{25}{23} = -\dfrac{4\sqrt{6}}{23}$

$\cot\theta = -\dfrac{23}{4\sqrt{6}}$ (reciprocal identities)

Mixed Review

1. a. $b = \sqrt{3}a = \sqrt{3}\cdot 5\sqrt{3} = 5\cdot 3 = 15$ cm
    b. $c = 2a = 2\cdot 5\sqrt{3} = 10\sqrt{3}$ cm

3. At $x = -16$, $y = -\dfrac{7}{8}(-16) = 14$; $(-16, 14)$

    At $x = -8$, $y = -\dfrac{7}{8}(-8) = 7$; $(-8, 7)$

5. $220.8138\overline{3}°$

$= 220° + 0.8138\overline{3}(60)' = 220° + 48.8\overline{3}'$

$= 220°48' + 0.8\overline{3}(60)'' = 220°48'50''$

7. Let x be the length of the diagonal cut.
$x = \sqrt{12^2 + 12^2} = \sqrt{288} = 12\sqrt{2}$ in.
The length of each cut is $12\sqrt{2}$ inches.

$5\cdot 12\sqrt{2} = 60\sqrt{2} \approx 84.9$ in.
The width of the wall covered by tiles is 84.9 inches.

9. a. $\sin\theta > 0 \Rightarrow y > 0$
      $\cos\theta > 0 \Rightarrow x > 0$
      The angle θ is in quadrant I.

    b. $\tan\theta < 0 \Rightarrow x$ and y differ in sign.
      $\sec\theta > 0 \Rightarrow x > 0 \Rightarrow y < 0$
      The angle θ is in quadrant IV.

    c. $\cot\theta > 0 \Rightarrow x$ and y have the same sign.
      $\csc\theta < 0 \Rightarrow y < 0 \Rightarrow x < 0$
      The angle θ is in quadrant III.

    d. $\sec\theta < 0 \Rightarrow x < 0$
      $\csc\theta > 0 \Rightarrow y > 0$
      The angle θ is in quadrant II.

11. $86°54'54'' = \left[86 + 54\left(\dfrac{1}{60}\right) + 54\left(\dfrac{1}{3600}\right)\right]°$

$\qquad = 86.915°$

13. $r = \sqrt{15^2 + (-8)^2} = \sqrt{289} = 17$

$\sin\theta = -\dfrac{8}{17}; \ \csc\theta = -\dfrac{17}{8}; \ \cos\theta = \dfrac{15}{17}$

$\sec\theta = \dfrac{17}{15}; \ \tan\theta = -\dfrac{8}{15}; \ \cot\theta = -\dfrac{15}{8}$

15. $\csc\theta\tan\theta - \cos\theta = \dfrac{\sin^2\theta}{\cos\theta}$

$\dfrac{1}{\sin\theta}\cdot\dfrac{\sin\theta}{\cos\theta} - \cos\theta = \dfrac{\sin^2\theta}{\cos\theta}$

$\dfrac{1}{\cos\theta} - \cos\theta = \dfrac{\sin^2\theta}{\cos\theta}$

$\dfrac{1}{\cos\theta} - \dfrac{\cos^2\theta}{\cos\theta} = \dfrac{\sin^2\theta}{\cos\theta}$

$\dfrac{1 - \cos^2\theta}{\cos\theta} = \dfrac{\sin^2\theta}{\cos\theta}$

$\dfrac{\sin^2\theta}{\cos\theta} = \dfrac{\sin^2\theta}{\cos\theta}$

17. $\csc\theta = \dfrac{\sqrt{117}}{6} = \dfrac{3\sqrt{13}}{6} = \dfrac{\sqrt{13}}{2}$ with θ in QII

$\sin\theta = \dfrac{2}{\sqrt{13}} = \dfrac{2\sqrt{13}}{13}$ (reciprocal identities)

$\cos^2\theta = 1 - \sin^2\theta \Rightarrow \cos\theta = \pm\sqrt{1 - \sin^2\theta}$

$\cos\theta = \pm\sqrt{1 - \left(\dfrac{2}{\sqrt{13}}\right)^2} = \pm\sqrt{\dfrac{13}{13} - \dfrac{4}{13}}$

$\qquad = \pm\sqrt{\dfrac{9}{13}} = \pm\dfrac{3}{\sqrt{13}} = \pm\dfrac{3\sqrt{13}}{13}$

$\cos\theta$ is negative in QII, so $\cos\theta = -\dfrac{3\sqrt{13}}{13}$,

and $\sec\theta = -\dfrac{\sqrt{13}}{3}$ (reciprocal identities)

$\tan\theta = \dfrac{\sin\theta}{\cos\theta} = \dfrac{\dfrac{2\sqrt{13}}{13}}{-\dfrac{3\sqrt{13}}{13}} = \dfrac{2\sqrt{13}}{13}\cdot\left(-\dfrac{13}{3\sqrt{13}}\right) = -\dfrac{2}{3}$

$\cot\theta = -\dfrac{3}{2}$ (reciprocal identities)

19. $\tan\theta = \dfrac{\sin\theta}{\cos\theta} = \dfrac{\pm\sqrt{1 - \cos^2\theta}}{\cos\theta}$

Practice Test

1. Complement = $90° - 55° = 55°$
Supplement = $180° - 35° = 145°$

3. $\theta = 30°; \ \theta + 360k$
$k = -2; \ 30° + 360°(-2) = -690°$
$k = -1; \ 30° + 360°(-1) = -330°$
$k = 1; \ 30° + 360°(1) = 390°$
$k = 2; \ 30° + 360°(2) = 750°$

5. a. $c = 2a = 2\cdot215 = 430$ mi
The distance from Four Corners USA to point P is 430 miles.

   b. $b = \sqrt{3}a = \sqrt{3}\cdot215 = 215\sqrt{3}$ mi
Colorado's southern border is $215\sqrt{3}$ miles long.

7. $2A = 180° - \dfrac{3}{2}(30°) = 135°$
$A = 135° \div 2 = 67.5°$
The measure of the upper angles will be 67.5°.

9. $\dfrac{3x}{2x} = \dfrac{2x+2}{8}$
$3x\cdot8 = 2x\cdot(2x+2)$
$24x = 4x^2 + 4x$
$0 = 4x^2 - 20x$
$0 = 4x(x-5)$

$\begin{array}{ll} 4x = 0 & x - 5 = 0 \\ x = 0 & x = 5 \end{array}$

Discard $x = 0$. It doesn't make sense.

$a = 3x = 3(5) = 15$ yd
$c = 2x + 2 = 2(5) + 2 = 12$ yd
$d = 2x = 2(5) = 10$ yd

11. a. $y = \dfrac{9}{-7}x = -\dfrac{9}{7}x$

   b. At $x = -14$, $y = -\dfrac{9}{7}(-14) = 18; \ (-14, 18)$

13. $\cos\theta = \dfrac{2}{5} \Rightarrow x = 2,\, r = 5$

    Since $\tan\theta < 0$, and x is positive,
    y is negative.
    The angle θ is in quadrant IV.

    $y = -\sqrt{5^2 - 2^2} = -\sqrt{21}$

    $\sin\theta = -\dfrac{\sqrt{21}}{5}$; $\csc\theta = -\dfrac{5}{\sqrt{21}}$; $\cos\theta = \dfrac{2}{5}$;

    $\sec\theta = \dfrac{5}{2}$; $\tan\theta = -\dfrac{\sqrt{21}}{2}$; $\cot\theta = -\dfrac{2}{\sqrt{21}}$

15. a. QIV; $\sin\theta\cos\theta\tan\theta = (-)(+)(-) = $ positive

    b. QII; $\csc\theta\cot^3\theta = (+)(-)^3$; negative

    c. QI; $\dfrac{\sin\theta\sec\theta}{\csc\theta} = \dfrac{(+)(+)}{(+)}$; positive

    d. QIII; $\dfrac{1}{\cot\theta\cos\theta} = \dfrac{1}{(+)(-)}$; negative

17. $\dfrac{(\csc\theta - \cot\theta)(\csc\theta + \cot\theta)}{\sec\theta} = \cos\theta$

    $\dfrac{\csc^2\theta - \cot^2\theta}{\sec\theta} = \cos\theta$

    $\dfrac{1}{\sec\theta} = \cos\theta$

    $\cos\theta = \cos\theta$

19. $\cos\theta = \dfrac{48}{73}$ with θ in QIV

    $\sec\theta = \dfrac{73}{48}$ (reciprocal identities)

    $\sin^2\theta = 1 - \cos^2\theta \Rightarrow \sin\theta = \pm\sqrt{1 - \cos^2\theta}$

    $\sin\theta = \pm\sqrt{1 - \left(\dfrac{48}{73}\right)^2} = \pm\sqrt{\dfrac{5329}{5329} - \dfrac{2304}{5329}}$

    $= \pm\sqrt{\dfrac{3025}{5329}} = \pm\dfrac{55}{73}$

    $\sin\theta$ is negative in QIV, so $\sin\theta = -\dfrac{55}{73}$, and

    $\csc\theta = -\dfrac{73}{55}$ (reciprocal identities)

    $\tan\theta = \dfrac{\sin\theta}{\cos\theta} = \dfrac{-\dfrac{55}{73}}{\dfrac{48}{73}} = -\dfrac{55}{73} \cdot \left(\dfrac{73}{48}\right) = -\dfrac{55}{48}$

    $\cot\theta = -\dfrac{48}{55}$ (reciprocal identities)

Calculator Exploration and Discovery

Exercise 1:

$\sin \to -1$

The range of $y = \sin\theta$ appears to be $[-1, 1]$.

Exercise 3:

$\cos \to -1$

The range of $y = \cos\theta$ appears to be $[-1, 1]$.

Strengthening Core Skills

Exercise 1:

$\sec\theta + \tan\theta = \dfrac{1}{\cos\theta} + \dfrac{\sin\theta}{\cos\theta}$

$= \dfrac{1 + \sin\theta}{\cos\theta}$

Exercise 3:

$(1 - \sin^2\theta)\sec\theta = \cos^2\theta\left(\dfrac{1}{\cos\theta}\right)$

$= \cos\theta$

Exercise 5:

$\dfrac{\sin\theta - \sin\theta\cos\theta}{\sin^2\theta} = \dfrac{\sin\theta(1 - \cos\theta)}{\sin^2\theta}$

$= \dfrac{\sin\theta(1 - \cos\theta)}{\sin^2\theta}$

$= \dfrac{1 - \cos\theta}{\sin\theta}$

2.1 Exercises

1. complementary; cotangent

3. opposite; hypotenuse

5. Answers will vary.

7. a. $\sec 30° = \dfrac{\text{hyp}}{\text{adj}} = \dfrac{2}{\sqrt{3}} = \dfrac{2\sqrt{3}}{3}$

    b. $\csc 30° = \dfrac{\text{hyp}}{\text{opp}} = \dfrac{2}{1} = 2$

    c. $\cot 30° = \dfrac{\text{adj}}{\text{opp}} = \dfrac{\sqrt{3}}{1} = \sqrt{3}$

9. a. $\cos 45° = \dfrac{\text{adj}}{\text{hyp}} = \dfrac{1}{\sqrt{2}} = \dfrac{\sqrt{2}}{2}$

    b. $\sin 45° = \dfrac{\text{opp}}{\text{hyp}} = \dfrac{1}{\sqrt{2}} = \dfrac{\sqrt{2}}{2}$

    c. $\tan 45° = \dfrac{\text{opp}}{\text{adj}} = \dfrac{1}{1} = 1$

11. a. $\cos A = \dfrac{\text{adj}}{\text{hyp}} = \dfrac{4}{5}$

    b. $\sin A = \dfrac{\text{opp}}{\text{hyp}} = \dfrac{3}{5}$

    c. $\tan A = \dfrac{\text{opp}}{\text{adj}} = \dfrac{3}{4}$

13. a. $\sec B = \dfrac{\text{hyp}}{\text{adj}} = \dfrac{5}{3}$

    b. $\csc B = \dfrac{\text{hyp}}{\text{opp}} = \dfrac{5}{4}$

    c. $\cot B = \dfrac{\text{adj}}{\text{opp}} = \dfrac{3}{4}$

Use the following diagram in 15 – 24. Note that it is not drawn to scale.

15. $\cos \theta = \dfrac{5}{13} = \dfrac{\text{adj}}{\text{hyp}}$

    $\text{opp} = \sqrt{13^2 - 5^2} = \sqrt{144} = 12$

    $\sin \theta = \dfrac{12}{13}; \ \csc \theta = \dfrac{13}{12}; \ \sec \theta = \dfrac{13}{5};$

    $\tan \theta = \dfrac{12}{5}; \ \cot \theta = \dfrac{5}{12}$

17. $\tan \theta = \dfrac{84}{13} = \dfrac{\text{opp}}{\text{adj}}$

    $\text{hyp} = \sqrt{13^2 + 84^2} = \sqrt{7225} = 85$

    $\cos \theta = \dfrac{13}{85}; \ \sec \theta = \dfrac{85}{13}; \ \cot \theta = \dfrac{13}{84};$

    $\sin \theta = \dfrac{84}{85}; \ \csc \theta = \dfrac{85}{84}$

19. $\cot \theta = \dfrac{2}{11} = \dfrac{\text{adj}}{\text{opp}}$

    $\text{hyp} = \sqrt{2^2 + 11^2} = \sqrt{125} = 5\sqrt{5}$

    $\sin \theta = \dfrac{11}{5\sqrt{5}}; \ \tan \theta = \dfrac{11}{2}; \ \csc \theta = \dfrac{5\sqrt{5}}{11}$

    $\cos \theta = \dfrac{2}{5\sqrt{5}}; \ \sec \theta = \dfrac{5\sqrt{5}}{2}$

21. $\tan \theta = 2 = \dfrac{2}{1} = \dfrac{\text{opp}}{\text{adj}}$

    $\text{hyp} = \sqrt{1^2 + 2^2} = \sqrt{5}$

    $\cos \theta = \dfrac{1}{\sqrt{5}} = \dfrac{\sqrt{5}}{5}; \ \sin \theta = \dfrac{2}{\sqrt{5}} = \dfrac{2\sqrt{5}}{5}$

    $\sec \theta = \sqrt{5}; \ \csc \theta = \dfrac{\sqrt{5}}{2}; \ \cot \theta = \dfrac{1}{2}$

23. $\cot \theta = t = \dfrac{t}{1} = \dfrac{\text{adj}}{\text{opp}}$

    $\text{hyp} = \sqrt{t^2 + 1^2} = \sqrt{t^2 + 1}$

    $\cos \theta = \dfrac{t}{\sqrt{t^2 + 1}} = \dfrac{t\sqrt{t^2 + 1}}{t^2 + 1};$

    $\sin \theta = \dfrac{1}{\sqrt{t^2 + 1}} = \dfrac{\sqrt{t^2 + 1}}{t^2 + 1};$

    $\tan \theta = \dfrac{1}{t}; \ \sec \theta = \dfrac{\sqrt{t^2 + 1}}{t}; \ \csc \theta = \sqrt{t^2 + 1}$

25. For $\angle A$, $(\text{adj, opp}) = (21, 20)$.

27. For $\angle A$, $(\text{adj, opp}) = \left(\sqrt{5}, 2\right)$.

29. For $\angle B$, $(\text{adj, opp}) = (6.5, 7.2)$.

31. For $\angle B$, $(\text{adj, opp}) = (a, b)$.

33. For $\angle A$, $\text{adj} = \sqrt{73^2 - 48^2} = \sqrt{3025} = 55$
     $(\text{adj, opp}) = (55, 48)$

35. $\sin 47° = \cos(90° - 47°) = \cos 43°$

37. $\cot 69° = \tan(90° - 69°) = \tan 21°$

39. $\sin(4x)° = \cos(5x)°$
     $\sin(4x)° = \cos(90 - 4x)°$
     $5x = 90 - 4x$
     $9x = 90$
     $x = 10$

41. $\cot(6x - 1)° = \tan(5x + 3)°$
     $\cot(6x - 1)° = \tan[90 - (6x - 1)]°$
     $5x + 3 = 90 - (6x - 1)$
     $5x + 3 = 90 - 6x + 1$
     $5x + 3 = 91 - 6x$
     $11x = 88$
     $x = 8$

43.

θ	30°	θ	30°
$\sin \theta$	$\frac{1}{2}$	$\tan(90 - \theta)$	$\sqrt{3}$
$\cos \theta$	$\frac{\sqrt{3}}{2}$	$\csc \theta$	2
$\tan \theta$	$\frac{\sqrt{3}}{3}$	$\sec \theta$	$\frac{2\sqrt{3}}{3}$
$\sin(90 - \theta)$	$\frac{\sqrt{3}}{2}$	$\cot \theta$	$\sqrt{3}$
$\cos(90 - \theta)$	$\frac{1}{2}$		

45. $\sqrt{6} \csc 15° = \sqrt{6} \sec 75° = \sqrt{6}(\sqrt{6} + \sqrt{2})$
     $= 6 + \sqrt{12} = 6 + 2\sqrt{3}$

47. $\cot^2 15° = \tan^2 75° = (2 + \sqrt{3})^2$
     $= 4 + 4\sqrt{3} + 3 = 7 + 4\sqrt{3}$

49. $\dfrac{\sin \alpha}{\sin \beta} = \dfrac{\sin \alpha}{\cos \alpha} = \tan \alpha$

51. $\sec^2 \alpha = \tan^2 \alpha + 1 = \cot^2 \beta + 1$

53. $\tan^2 \alpha \sec^2 \beta - \cot^2 \beta$
     $= \tan^2 \alpha \csc^2 \alpha - \tan^2 \alpha$
     $= \tan^2 \alpha(\csc^2 \alpha - 1)$
     $= \tan^2 \alpha \cot^2 \alpha$
     $= 1$

55. $v = \dfrac{32kt}{\cos \theta}$
     $= \dfrac{32(0.2)(0.8)}{\cos 45°}$
     $= \dfrac{5.12}{\frac{\sqrt{2}}{2}}$
     ≈ 7.2 ft/sec

57. $\tan \theta = \dfrac{\text{opp}}{\text{adj}} = \dfrac{30}{8} = 3.75$

59. $\sec \theta = \dfrac{\text{hyp}}{\text{adj}} = \dfrac{12}{8} = 1.5$

61. $\text{hyp} = \sqrt{12^2 + 9^2} = \sqrt{225} = 15$
     $\cos \theta = \dfrac{\text{adj}}{\text{hyp}} = \dfrac{12}{15} = 0.8$

63. a. Let x be the length of the diagonal of one side of the box.
         $x = \sqrt{10^2 + 10^2} = \sqrt{200} = 10\sqrt{2}$ cm
         Now, let d be the length of the diagonal that passes through the center of the box.
         $x = \sqrt{10^2 + (10\sqrt{2})^2} = \sqrt{300} = 10\sqrt{3}$ cm

     b. $\sin \theta = \dfrac{\text{opp}}{\text{hyp}} = \dfrac{10}{10\sqrt{3}} = \dfrac{\sqrt{3}}{3}$

65. $\cot u = \dfrac{x}{h} \to x = h \cot u$
     $\cot v = \dfrac{x - d}{h} \to \cot v = \dfrac{h \cot u - d}{h}$
     $h \cot v = h \cot u - d$
     $d = h \cot u - h \cot v = h(\cot u - \cot v)$
     $h = \dfrac{d}{\cot u - \cot v}$

67. $\dfrac{\sin \theta}{\tan^2 \theta} = \cot \theta \cos \theta$
     $\sin \theta \cdot \cot^2 \theta = \cot \theta \cos \theta$
     $\sin \theta \cdot \dfrac{\cos^2 \theta}{\sin^2 \theta} = \cot \theta \cos \theta$
     $\dfrac{\cos^2 \theta}{\sin \theta} = \cot \theta \cos \theta$
     $\cot \theta \cos \theta = \cot \theta \cos \theta$

69. $c = \sqrt{a^2 + b^2}$

$\quad = \sqrt{7^2 + 9^2}$

$\quad = \sqrt{130}$

$e = \sqrt{c^2 + d^2}$ $\qquad \cos \beta = \dfrac{\sqrt{d^2 - a^2}}{d} = \dfrac{d}{e}$

$\quad = \sqrt{\left(\sqrt{130}\right)^2 + (8.75)^2}$

$\quad = \sqrt{130 + 76.5625}$

$\quad \approx 14.4$ m

71. $\text{hyp} = \sqrt{(-2)^2 + (-5)^2} = \sqrt{29}$

$\cos^2 \theta \tan^2 \theta = \left(\cos \theta \tan \theta\right)^2$

$\qquad = \left[\left(-\dfrac{2}{\sqrt{29}}\right)\left(\dfrac{5}{2}\right)\right]^2 = \dfrac{25}{29}$

2.2 Exercises

1. $\theta = \tan^{-1} x$

3. Pythagorean; hypotenuse; $\tan^{-1}$; angle

5. To find the measure of all three angles and all three sides.

7. $B = 90° - 30° = 60°$

$\sin 30° = \dfrac{a}{196}; \ a = 196 \sin 30° = 98$ cm

$\cos 30° = \dfrac{b}{196}; \ b = 196 \cos 30° = 98\sqrt{3}$ cm

Angle	Side
$A = 30°$	$a = 98$ cm
$B = 60°$	$b = 98\sqrt{3}$ cm
$C = 90°$	$c = 196$ cm

9. $B = 90° - 45° = 45°$

$\sin 45° = \dfrac{9.9}{c}; \ c \sin 45° = 9.9$

$c = \dfrac{9.9}{\sin 45°} = \dfrac{9.9}{\sqrt{2}/2} = \dfrac{19.8}{\sqrt{2}} = 9.9\sqrt{2}$ mm

$\cos 45° = \dfrac{a}{9.9\sqrt{2}}$

$a = 9.9\sqrt{2} \cos 45° = 9.9\sqrt{2} \cdot \dfrac{\sqrt{2}}{2} = 9.9$

9. (continued)

Angle	Side
$A = 45°$	$a = 9.9$ mm
$B = 45°$	$b = 9.9$ mm
$C = 90°$	$c = 9.9\sqrt{2}$ mm

11. $B = 90° - 22° = 68°$

$\sin 22° = \dfrac{14}{c}; \ c \sin 22° = 14$

$c = \dfrac{14}{\sin 22°} \approx 37.37$ m

$\tan 22° = \dfrac{14}{b}; \ b \tan 22° = 14$

$b = \dfrac{14}{\tan 22°} \approx 34.65$ m

Angle	Side
$A = 22°$	$a = 14$ m
$B = 68°$	$b \approx 34.65$ m
$C = 90°$	$c \approx 37.37$ m

13. $A = 90° - 58° = 32°$

$\cos 58° = \dfrac{5.6}{c}; \ c \cos 58° = 5.6$

$c = \dfrac{5.6}{\cos 58°} \approx 10.57$ mi

$\tan 58° = \dfrac{b}{5.6}$

$b = 5.6 \tan 58° \approx 8.96$ mi

Angle	Side
$A = 32°$	$a = 5.6$ mi
$B = 58°$	$b \approx 8.96$ mi
$C = 90°$	$c \approx 10.57$ mi

15. $B = 90° - 65° = 25°$

$\sin 65° = \dfrac{625}{c}; \ c \sin 65° = 625;$

$c = \dfrac{625}{\sin 65°} \approx 689.61$ mm

$\tan 65° = \dfrac{625}{b}; \ b \tan 65° = 625;$

$b = \dfrac{625}{\tan 65°} \approx 291.44$ mm

Angle	Side
$A = 65°$	$a = 625$ mm
$B = 25°$	$b \approx 291.44$ mm
$C = 90°$	$c \approx 689.61$ mm

17. $\sin 27° = 0.4540$

19. $\tan 40° = 0.8391$

21. $\sec 40.9° = 1.3230$

23. $\sin 65° = 0.9063$

25. $A = \sin^{-1}(0.4540) \approx 27°$

27. $\theta = \tan^{-1}(0.8390) \approx 40°$

29. $B = \cos^{-1}\left(\dfrac{1}{1.3230}\right) \approx 40.9°$

31. $A = \sin^{-1}(0.9063) \approx 65°$

33. $\alpha = \tan^{-1}(0.9896) \approx 44.7°$

35. $\alpha = \sin^{-1}(0.3453) \approx 20.2°$

37. $\tan\theta = \dfrac{6}{18}$; $\theta = \tan^{-1}\left(\dfrac{1}{3}\right) \approx 18.4°$

39. $\tan\gamma = \dfrac{19.5}{18.7}$; $\gamma = \tan^{-1}\left(\dfrac{19.5}{18.7}\right) \approx 46.2°$

41. $\cos B = \dfrac{20}{42}$; $B = \cos^{-1}\left(\dfrac{20}{42}\right) \approx 61.6°$

43.

$\sin 25° = \dfrac{a}{52}$; $a = 52\sin 25° \approx 21.98$ mm

45.

$\tan 32° = \dfrac{1.9}{b}$; $b\tan 32° = 1.9$

$b = \dfrac{1.9}{\tan 32°} \approx 3.04$ mi

47. $\cos 62.3° = \dfrac{82.5}{c}$; $c\cos 62.3° = 82.5$

$c = \dfrac{82.5}{\cos 62.3°} \approx 177.48$ furlongs

57. b.   Now we can find the angle using cosine.

49. $\sin\theta = \dfrac{2A}{ab} = \dfrac{2(38.9)}{(17)(24)}$

$\theta = \sin^{-1}\left(\dfrac{2(38.9)}{(17)(24)}\right) \approx 11.0°$

Repeat for β using 24 and 8 for a and b.

$\sin\beta = \dfrac{2(38.9)}{8(24)}$; $\beta = \sin^{-1}\dfrac{2(38.9)}{8(24)} \approx 23.9°$

$\gamma = 180° - (11.0° + 23.9°) = 145.1°$

51. $\cos 34° = \dfrac{320}{Z}$; $Z\cos 34° = 320$

$Z = \dfrac{320}{\cos 34°} \approx 386.0\,\Omega$

53. a.   Five contour lines, so change in elevation is $5(175) = 875$ m.

   b. $\dfrac{2.4\,\text{cm}}{x\,\text{m}} = \dfrac{1\,\text{cm}}{500\,\text{m}}$;

   $x = 2.4(500) = 1200$ m

   c.

   $d^2 = 1200^2 + 875^2$;

   $d = \sqrt{2,205,625} \approx 1485$ m

   $\tan\theta = \dfrac{875}{1200}$; $\theta = \tan^{-1}\dfrac{875}{1200} \approx 36.1°$

55. $\tan 42° = \dfrac{h}{500}$

   $h = 500\tan 42° \approx 450$ ft

57. a.   The triangle at the base of the box is isosceles with sides x, so the dotted diagonal on the bottom has length $x\sqrt{2}$ (45-45-90 triangle). The triangle formed by that diagonal, the diagonal across the box, and one edge of the box is right, and we can apply the Pythagorean Theorem.

$\left(x\sqrt{2}\right)^2 + x^2 = 35^2$

$2x^2 + x^2 = 1225$

$3x^2 = 1225$

$x^2 \approx 408.3 \rightarrow x \approx 20.2$ cm

$\cos\theta = \dfrac{20.2\sqrt{2}}{35}$

$$\theta = \cos^{-1}\frac{20.2\sqrt{2}}{35} \approx 35.3°$$

59. $\tan v = \dfrac{h}{d}; \quad d = \dfrac{h}{\tan v}$

$\tan u = \dfrac{h-x}{d}; \quad \tan u = \dfrac{h-x}{\dfrac{h}{\tan v}}$

$\tan u = \dfrac{\tan v(h-x)}{h}$

$h\tan u = h\tan v - x\tan v$

$h\tan u - h\tan v = -x\tan v$

$h\tan v - h\tan u = x\tan v$

$h(\tan v - \tan u) = x\tan v$

$h = \dfrac{x\tan v}{\tan v - \tan u};$

$h = \dfrac{75\tan 50°}{\tan 50° - \tan 40°} \approx 253.45\,\text{m}$

61. $132°42'54'' = \left[132 + 42\left(\dfrac{1}{60}\right) + 54\left(\dfrac{1}{3600}\right)\right]°$

$= 132.715°$

63. If $\tan 22.5° = \sqrt{2}-1,$ then

$\cot 22.5° = \dfrac{1}{\sqrt{2}-1} = \sqrt{2}+1.$

$\sqrt{8}\cot 22.5° = \sqrt{8}\left(\sqrt{2}+1\right)$

$= \sqrt{16}+\sqrt{8}$

$= 4+2\sqrt{2}$

65. For angle β, the opposite side is proportional to 3 and the proportional is similar to 4.

$\sin\beta = \dfrac{\text{opp}}{\text{hyp}} = \dfrac{3}{4} = 0.75$

Mid-Chapter Check

1. $\cos\theta = \dfrac{12}{13} = \dfrac{\text{adj}}{\text{hyp}}$

$\text{opp} = \sqrt{13^2 - 12^2} = \sqrt{25} = 5$

$\sin\theta = \dfrac{5}{13}; \ \csc\theta = \dfrac{13}{5}; \ \sec\theta = \dfrac{13}{12};$

$\tan\theta = \dfrac{5}{12}; \ \cot\theta = \dfrac{12}{5}$

3. $\dfrac{\cos\beta}{\cos\alpha} = \dfrac{\sin(90°-\beta)}{\cos\alpha} = \dfrac{\sin\alpha}{\cos\alpha} = \tan\alpha$

5. $A = 90° - 55° = 35°$

$\sin 55° = \dfrac{24}{c}; \ c\sin 55° = 24;$

$c = \dfrac{24}{\sin 55°} \approx 29.30\,\text{cm}$

$\tan 55° = \dfrac{24}{a}; \ a\tan 55° = 24;$

$a = \dfrac{24}{\tan 55°} \approx 16.80\,\text{cm}$

Angle	Side
$A = 35°$	$a \approx 16.80\,\text{cm}$
$B = 55°$	$b \approx 24\,\text{cm}$
$C = 90°$	$c \approx 29.30\,\text{cm}$

7. $c = \sqrt{7^2 + 14^2} = \sqrt{245} \approx 15.7\,\text{ft}$

$\tan A = \dfrac{7}{14} = \dfrac{1}{2}; \ A = \tan^{-1}\dfrac{1}{2} = 26.6°$

$\tan B = \dfrac{14}{7} = 2; \ B = \tan^{-1}2 = 63.4°$

Angle	Side
$A = 26.6°$	$a \approx 7\,\text{ft}$
$B = 63.4°$	$b \approx 14\,\text{ft}$
$C = 90°$	$c \approx 15.7\,\text{ft}$

9. $\sin\theta = \dfrac{16}{20} = \dfrac{4}{5}; \ \theta = \sin^{-1}\dfrac{4}{5} = 53°$

The acute angle the anchor lines makes with the street is $53°$.

Reinforcing Basic Concepts

1. $A = 28°, b = 20\,\text{cm}, c = 15\,\text{cm}$

    $A = \dfrac{1}{2}bc\sin$

    $\quad = \dfrac{1}{2}(20)(15)\sin 28°$

    $\quad \approx 70.4\,\text{cm}^2$

3. $A = 26.3°, B = 79.6°, a = 45\,\text{in.}$

    $C = 180° - (26.3° + 79.6°) = 74.1°$

    $A = \dfrac{a^2 \sin B \sin C}{2\sin A}$

    $\quad = \dfrac{(45)^2 \sin 79.6° \sin 74.1°}{2\sin 26.3°}$

    $\quad \approx 2161.7\,\text{in.}^2$

2.3 Exercises

1. orientation; parallel

3. calculators; sine; cosine; tangent

5. Answers will vary.

7. $h = 40\tan 15.3763° \approx 11\,\text{m}$

9. $h = 40\tan 19.2900° \approx 14\,\text{m}$

11. $h = 40\tan 23.0255° \approx 17\,\text{m}$

13. $d = 35\sin 45.5847° \approx 25\,\text{ft}$

15. $d = 35\sin 55.9523° \approx 29\,\text{ft}$

17. $d = 35\sin 70.5370° \approx 33\,\text{ft}$

19. a. $63°$

    b. $90° - 63° = 27°$

21. a. $49°$

    b. $90° - 49° = 41°$

23. a. $23°31'$

    b. $90° - 23°31'$
        $= 89°60' - 23°31'$
        $= 66°29'$

25. a. $15°32'49''$

    b. $90° - 15°32'49''$
        $= 89°59'60'' - 15°32'49''$
        $= 74°27'11''$

27. a. $d = \dfrac{80}{\cos 10°} \approx 81.2\,\text{m}$

    b. $81.2 \div 3 = 27.1\,\text{sec}$

29. a. $d = \dfrac{80}{\cos 15°} \approx 82.8\,\text{m}$

    b. $82.8 \div 3 = 27.6\,\text{sec}$

31. a. $d = \dfrac{80}{\cos 20°} \approx 85.1\,\text{m}$

    b. $85.1 \div 3 = 28.4\,\text{sec}$

33. $h = \dfrac{d}{\cot \alpha - \cot \beta}$

    $\quad = \dfrac{50}{\cot 45° - \cot 60°}$

    $\quad \approx 118.3\,\text{ft}$

    The height of the building shown is approximately 118.3 feet.

35.

    $\tan 71.6° = \dfrac{h}{100}$

    $h = 100\tan 71.6° \approx 300.6\,\text{m}$

    The Eiffel Tower is approximately 300.6 meters tall.

37. From #35, we know the height is 300.61 m.

    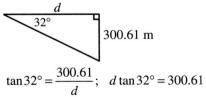

    $\tan 32° = \dfrac{300.61}{d}$; $d\tan 32° = 300.61$

    $d = \dfrac{300.61}{\tan 32°} \approx 481.1\,\text{m}$

    The accident is approximately 481.1 meters from the base of the tower.

39. Let x be the length of the bridge.

$$x = 110 \tan 38°35'15''$$
$$= 110 \tan \left[38 + 35\left(\frac{1}{60}\right) + 15\left(\frac{1}{3600}\right) \right]°$$
$$= 110 \tan 38.5875°$$
$$\approx 87.77 \text{ ft} \approx 87 \text{ ft } 9 \text{ in.}$$

The bridge will be approximately 87 feet 9 inches long.

41. $\tan 83° = \dfrac{d}{50}$; $d = 50 \tan 83° \approx 407.22$ ft

$$\frac{407.22 \text{ ft}}{2.35 \text{ sec}} \cdot \frac{1 \text{ mi}}{5280 \text{ ft}} \cdot \frac{3600 \text{ sec}}{1 \text{ hr}} = 118.1 \text{ mph}$$

The plane is flying at approximately 118.1 miles per hour.

43. First, find the distances $h_s, h_1,$ and h_2 in the diagram below. Then answer the questions.

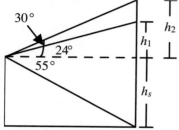

$\tan 55° = \dfrac{h_s}{175}$; $h_s = 175 \tan 55° \approx 250.0$ yd

$\tan 24° = \dfrac{h_1}{175}$; $h_1 = 175 \tan 24° \approx 77.9$ yd

$\tan 30° = \dfrac{h_2}{175}$; $h_2 = 175 \tan 30° \approx 101.0$ yd

a. The southern rim of the canyon is approximately 250.0 yards high.

b. $h_s + h_2 \approx 251.0 + 101.0 = 351.0$ yd

The northern rim of the canyon is approximately 351.0 yards high.

c. $h_2 - h_1 \approx 101.0 - 77.9 = 23.1$ yd

The climber has 23.1 yards to go before reaching the top.

45. Let h_t be the height of the tower and h_r be the height of the restaurant.

$$\tan 74.6° = \frac{h_t}{500}$$
$$h_t = 500 \tan 74.6° \approx 1815.2 \text{ ft}$$

The CNN Tower is approximately 1815.2 feet tall.

$$\tan 66.5° = \frac{h_r}{500}$$
$$h_r = 500 \tan 66.5° \approx 1149.9 \text{ ft}$$

$$1815.2 - 1149.9 = 665.3 \text{ ft}$$

The restaurant is located approximately 665.3 feet below the pinnacle of the tower.

47. The key to solving this exercise are several careful sketches, keeping track of angles and distances, while always maintaining true North.

First Stage

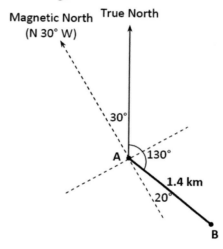

Second Stage
Here our diagram shows us angle B is a right angle.

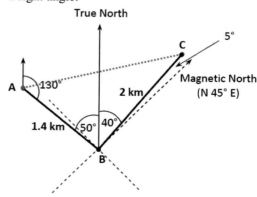

47. (continued)

We can now use our knowledge of right triangles to determine angle C.

$$\tan C = \frac{1.4}{2}$$

$$C = \tan^{-1}\left(\frac{1.4}{2}\right) = \tan^{-1}(0.7) \approx 35°$$

<u>Third Stage</u>
We use one more careful sketch to determine the magnetic direction to return to site **A**.

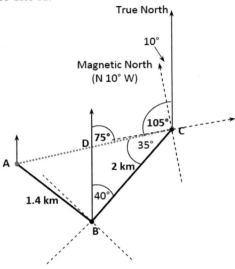

From the properties of triangles, we know $\angle BDC = 105°$. Supplementary angle rules give us the two bold angles of $75°$ and $105°$. To get back to site **A**, the rover needs to turn $105°$ counterclockwise of true north (a $95°$ counterclockwise rotation from magnetic north). This corresponds to a magnetic bearing of S 85° W.

49. $a = \dfrac{c}{2} = \dfrac{14\sqrt{3}}{2} = 7\sqrt{3}$ in.

$b = \sqrt{3}a = \sqrt{3} \cdot 7\sqrt{3} = 21$ in.

51. For $x = 1$, $y = -3(1) = -3$; $(1, -3)$.

$$r = \sqrt{1^2 + (-3)^2} = \sqrt{10}$$

a. $\sin\theta = \dfrac{-3}{\sqrt{10}} = -\dfrac{3\sqrt{10}}{10}$

b. $\cos\theta = \dfrac{1}{\sqrt{10}} = \dfrac{\sqrt{10}}{10}$

13. $-45°$ is a QIV angle:

53. $\sin\alpha = \dfrac{2}{5} = \dfrac{\text{opp}}{\text{hyp}}$

$$\text{adj} = \sqrt{5^2 - 2^2} = \sqrt{21}$$

$$\cos\alpha = \frac{\sqrt{21}}{5}; \ \tan\alpha = \frac{2}{\sqrt{21}} = \frac{2\sqrt{21}}{21};$$

$$\csc\theta = \frac{5}{2}; \ \sec\theta = \frac{5}{\sqrt{21}} = \frac{5\sqrt{21}}{21};$$

$$\cot\theta = \frac{\sqrt{21}}{2}$$

2.4 Exercises

1. coterminal; reference; $80°$

3. integers; $360°k$

5. Answers will vary.

7.

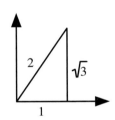

The lengths were obtained using the special triangle relationships for 30-60-90.
The slope of the line is $\sqrt{3}$ since the rise is $\sqrt{3}$ and the run is 1.
The equation is $y = \sqrt{3}x$.
Choose the point $\left(3, 3\sqrt{3}\right)$.

Then $r = \sqrt{3^2 + (3\sqrt{3})^2} = \sqrt{36} = 6$.

$$\sin 60° = \frac{3\sqrt{3}}{6} = \frac{\sqrt{3}}{2}; \ \cos 60° = \frac{3}{6} = \frac{1}{2}$$

$$\tan 60° = \frac{3\sqrt{3}}{3} = \sqrt{3}.$$

These match our known values.

9. $50°$ is a QI angle:
    $\theta_r = 50°$

11. $210°$ is a QIII angle:
    $\theta_r = 210° - 180° = 30°$

$\theta_r = 0° - (-45)° = 45°$

15. $112°$ is a QII angle:
$\theta_r = 180° - 112° = 68°$

17. $404.4°$ is a QI angle:
$\theta_r = 404.4° - 360° = 44.4°$

19. $500°$ is a QII angle:
$\theta_r = 3 \cdot 180° - 500° = 40°$

21. $-168.4°$ is a QIII angle:
$\theta_r = 180° + (-168.4)° = 11.6°$

23. $-382.1°$ is a QI angle:
$\theta_r = -(-382.1°) - 360° = 22.1°$

25. $1361°30'$ is a QIV angle:
$\theta_r = 4 \cdot 360° - 1361°30' = 78°30'$

27. $330°$ is a QIV angle:
$\theta_r = 360° - 330° = 30°$

$\sin\theta = -\dfrac{1}{2}; \quad \cos\theta = \dfrac{\sqrt{3}}{2}; \quad \tan\theta = -\dfrac{1}{\sqrt{3}}$

29. $-45°$ is a QIV angle:
$\theta_r = 0° - (-45)° = 45°$

$\sin\theta = -\dfrac{\sqrt{2}}{2}; \quad \cos\theta = \dfrac{\sqrt{2}}{2}; \quad \tan\theta = -1$

31. $240°$ is a QIII angle:
$\theta_r = 240° - 180° = 60°$

$\sin\theta = -\dfrac{\sqrt{3}}{2}; \quad \cos\theta = -\dfrac{1}{2}; \quad \tan\theta = \sqrt{3}$

33. $-150°$ is a QIII angle:
$\theta_r = 180° + (-150)° = 30°$

$\sin\theta = -\dfrac{1}{2}; \quad \cos\theta = -\dfrac{\sqrt{3}}{2}; \quad \tan\theta = \dfrac{1}{\sqrt{3}}$

35. $600°$ is a QIII angle:
$\theta_r = 600° - 3 \cdot 180° = 60°$

$\sin\theta = -\dfrac{\sqrt{3}}{2}; \quad \cos\theta = -\dfrac{1}{2}; \quad \tan\theta = \sqrt{3}$

37. $-840°$ is a QIII angle:
$\theta_r = -840° + 5 \cdot 180° = 60°$

$\sin\theta = -\dfrac{\sqrt{3}}{2}; \quad \cos\theta = -\dfrac{1}{2}; \quad \tan\theta = \sqrt{3}$

39. $570°$ is a QIII angle:
$\theta_r = 570° - 3 \cdot 180° = 30°$

$\sin\theta = -\dfrac{1}{2}; \quad \cos\theta = -\dfrac{\sqrt{3}}{2}; \quad \tan\theta = \dfrac{1}{\sqrt{3}}$

41. $-1230°$ is a QIII angle:
$\theta_r = -1230° + 7 \cdot 180° = 30°$

$\sin\theta = -\dfrac{1}{2}; \quad \cos\theta = -\dfrac{\sqrt{3}}{2}; \quad \tan\theta = \dfrac{1}{\sqrt{3}}$

43. $52° + 360°k$
$52° + 360°(2) = 772°$
$52° + 360°(1) = 412°$
$52° + 360°(-1) = -308°$
$52° + 360°(-2) = -668°$

45. $87.5° + 360°k$
$87.5° + 360°(2) = 807.5°$
$87.5° + 360°(1) = 447.5°$
$87.5° + 360°(-1) = -272.5°$
$87.5° + 360°(-2) = -632.5°$

47. $225° + 360°k$
$225° + 360°(2) = 945°$
$225° + 360°(1) = 585°$
$225° + 360°(-1) = -135°$
$225° + 360°(-2) = -495°$

49. $-107° + 360°k$
$-107° + 360°(2) = 613°$
$-107° + 360°(1) = 253°$
$-107° + 360°(-1) = -467°$
$-107° + 360°(-2) = -827°$

51. The three angles are coterminal in QII.
$\theta_r = 60°$

$\sin 120° = \dfrac{\sqrt{3}}{2}$

$\cos(-240°) = -\dfrac{1}{2}$

$\tan 480° = -\sqrt{3}$

53. The angles are coterminal in QIV. $\theta_r = 30°$

$$\sin(-30°) = -\frac{1}{2}$$

$$\cos(-390°) = \frac{\sqrt{3}}{2}$$

$$\tan 690° = -\frac{1}{\sqrt{3}}$$

55. QIV; sine is negative
$\theta_r = 2 \cdot 360° - 719° = 1°$
$\sin\theta = -0.0175$
$\sin\theta_r = 0.0175$

57. QIV; tangent is negative
$\theta_r = -360° - (-419°) = 59°$
$\tan\theta = -1.6643$
$\tan\theta_r = 1.6643$

59. QIV; cosecant is negative
$\theta_r = 2 \cdot 360° - 681° = 39°$
$\csc\theta = -1.5890$
$\csc\theta_r = 1.5890$

61. QI; cosine is positive
$\theta_r = 805° - 2 \cdot 360° = 85°$
$\cos\theta = 0.0872$
$\cos\theta_r = 0.0872$

63. a. $A = ab\sin\theta$
    $= (9)(21)\sin 50°$
    $\approx 144.78 \text{ units}^2$

    b. Enter the function $Y_1 = 9 * 21\sin x$ and set up a table with TblStart = 50 and ΔTbl = 1: The first value over 150 is at 53°.
    $$A = ab\sin\theta$$
    $$150 < (9)(21)\sin\theta$$
    $$\frac{150}{(9)(21)} < \sin\theta$$
    $$\theta > \sin^{-1}\frac{150}{(9)(21)} \approx 53°$$

    c. $A = ab\sin\theta$
    $= ab\sin 90°$
    $= ab \cdot 1$
    $= ab$
    The parallelogram is a rectangle whose area is $A = ab$.

    d. Divide the parallelogram in half with a diagonal to form a triangle. The area given two sides and the angle between them is then $A = \frac{1}{2}ab\sin\theta = \frac{ab}{2}\sin\theta$.

65. Cosine is positive in QI and QIV.
$\theta_r = 60°$
$\theta = 60° + 360°k;\quad \theta = 300° + 360°k$

67. Sine is negative in QIII and QIV.
$\theta_r = 60°$
$\theta = 240° + 360°k;\quad \theta = 300° + 360°k$

69. Sine is positive in QI and QII.
$\theta_r = \sin^{-1}0.8754 \approx 61.1°$
$\theta \approx 61.1° + 360°k;\quad \theta \approx 118.9° + 360°k$

71. Tangent is negative in QII and QIV.
$\theta_r = \tan^{-1}(-2.3512) \approx -67.0°$
$\theta \approx 113.0° + 360°k;\quad \theta \approx 293.0° + 360°k$

73. The spinner made five complete turns plus a quarter of another turn.
$5 \cdot 360° + 90° = 1890°$
Coterminal angles: $90° + 360°k$

75. Assuming he was on his feet at the start, after 2.5 revolutions, he'd go in the water head first.
$2 \cdot 360° + 180° = 900°$

77. The angle between the terminal side and the x-axis can be found using a right triangle with opposite 2 and adjacent 6.

$$\tan\theta = \frac{2}{6};\quad \theta = \tan^{-1}\left(\frac{1}{3}\right) \approx 18.4°$$

$720° - 18.4° = 701.6°$
The spiral of Archimedes turned through an angle of $701.6°$.

79. a. 1 o'clock represents 1/3 of the way to 3 o'clock: $1/3(90°) = 30°$
    2 o'clock represents 2/3 of the way to 3 o'clock: $2/3(90°) = 60°$

    b. From part (a), we see that the angle between any two numbers is $30°$.
    At 6:30, the minute hand is on the 6 and the hour hand is halfway between the 6 and the 7. $1/2(30°) = 15°$
    At 7:00, the hour and minute hands are five numbers apart. $5 \cdot 30° = 150°$
    At 7:30, the minute hand is on the 6 and the hour hand is halfway between the 7 and the 8. $3/2(30°) = 45°$

81. a. $3\,\sec \cdot \dfrac{12\,\text{rev}}{\sec} = 36\,\text{rev}$

$36 \cdot 360° = 12{,}960°$

b. $C = 2\pi r = 2\pi(20) = 40\pi \approx 125.66\,\text{in.}$

c. $10\,\sec \cdot \dfrac{12\,\text{rev}}{\sec} = 120\,\text{rev}$

$120\,\text{rev} \cdot \dfrac{125.66\,\text{in.}}{\text{rev}} \approx 15{,}080\,\text{in.}$

d. $\dfrac{15{,}080\,\text{in.}}{10\,\sec} \cdot \dfrac{3600\,\sec}{1\,\text{hr}} \cdot \dfrac{1\,\text{mi}}{12(5280)\,\text{in.}}$

$\approx 85.68\,\text{mph}$

83. Due to the cofunction relationship,

$\cot 50° = \tan(90° - 40°)$

$\qquad = \tan 50°$

$\qquad \approx 0.8391.$

85. Since $c = 2a$, this is a 30-60-90 triangle.

$b = \sqrt{3} \cdot 18 = 18\sqrt{3}\,\text{m}$

Angle	Side
$A = 30°$	$a = 18\,\text{m}$
$B = 60°$	$b = 18\sqrt{3}\,\text{m}$
$C = 90°$	$c = 36\,\text{m}$

87. Complement:

$90° - 12°34'56''$

$= 89°59'60'' - 12°34'56''$

$= (89° - 12°) + (59' - 34') + (60'' - 56'')$

$= 77° + 25' + 04''$

$= 77°25'04''$

Supplement

$180° - 12°34'56''$

$= 179°59'60'' - 12°34'56''$

$= (179° - 12°) + (59' - 34') + (60'' - 56'')$

$= 167° + 25' + 04''$

$= 167°25'04''$

Summary and Concept Review 2.1

1. a. $\sin \alpha = \dfrac{\text{opp}}{\text{hyp}} = \dfrac{2\sqrt{6}}{7}$

b. $\sin \beta = \dfrac{\text{opp}}{\text{hyp}} = \dfrac{5}{7}$

3. a. $\tan \alpha = \dfrac{\text{opp}}{\text{adj}} = \dfrac{2\sqrt{6}}{5}$

b. $\tan \beta = \dfrac{\text{opp}}{\text{adj}} = \dfrac{5}{2\sqrt{6}} = \dfrac{5\sqrt{6}}{12}$

5. a. $\sec \alpha = \dfrac{\text{hyp}}{\text{adj}} = \dfrac{7}{5}$

b. $\sec \beta = \dfrac{\text{hyp}}{\text{adj}} = \dfrac{7}{2\sqrt{6}} = \dfrac{7\sqrt{6}}{12}$

7. $\tan \theta = 3 = \dfrac{3}{1} = \dfrac{\text{opp}}{\text{adj}}$

$\text{hyp} = \sqrt{1^2 + 3^2} = \sqrt{10}$

$\sin \theta = \dfrac{3}{\sqrt{10}} = \dfrac{3\sqrt{10}}{10}$; $\cos \theta = \dfrac{1}{\sqrt{10}} = \dfrac{\sqrt{10}}{10}$

$\csc \theta = \dfrac{\sqrt{10}}{3}$; $\sec \theta = \sqrt{10}$; $\cot \theta = \dfrac{1}{3}$

Summary and Concept Review 2.2

9. a. $A = \cos 37° \approx 0.80$

b. $\cos A = 0.4340$

$A = \cos^{-1} 0.4340 \approx 64.3°$

11. $c = \sqrt{a^2 + b^2} = \sqrt{20^2 + 21^2} = \sqrt{841} = 29$

$\sin A = \dfrac{20}{29}$; $A = \sin^{-1} \dfrac{20}{29} \approx 43.6°$

$B = 90° - 43.6° = 46.4°$

Angle	Side
$A \approx 43.6°$	$a = 20\,\text{m}$
$B° \approx 46.4°$	$b = 21\,\text{m}$
$C = 90°$	$c = 29\,\text{m}$

13. $c = \sqrt{a^2 + b^2} = \sqrt{10^2 + 14^2}$

$\quad = \sqrt{296} = 2\sqrt{74}$

$\sin A = \dfrac{14}{2\sqrt{74}} = \dfrac{7}{\sqrt{74}}$

$A = \sin^{-1} \dfrac{7}{\sqrt{74}} \approx 54.5°$

$B = 90° - 54.5° = 35.5°$

Summary and Concept Review 2.3

15. The four bearings specified are listed.
    N31°E, N31°W, S31°E, S31°W

17. a. Let d_1 be the distance of the nearer boat from Armando.
    $$\theta_1 = 90° - 63.5° = 26.5°$$
    $$\tan 26.5° = \frac{d_1}{480}$$
    $$d_1 = 480 \tan 26.5° \approx 239.32 \text{ m}$$
    The nearer boat is approximately 239.32 meters out to sea.

    Let d_2 be the distance of the further boat from Armando.
    $$\theta_2 = 90° - 45° = 45°$$
    $$\tan 45° = \frac{d_2}{480}$$
    $$d_2 = 480 \tan 45° = 480 \text{ m}$$
    The further boat is 480 meters out to sea.

    b. $480 - 239.32 = 240.68$ m
    The two boats are approximately 240.68 meters apart.

Summary and Concept Review 2.4

19. $-870°$ is a QIII angle:
    $$\theta_r = -870° + 5 \cdot 180° = 30°$$
    $$\sin\theta = -\frac{1}{2}; \quad \cos\theta = -\frac{\sqrt{3}}{2}; \quad \tan\theta = \frac{\sqrt{3}}{3}$$

21. a. Tangent is negative in QII and QIV.
    $$\theta_r = 45°$$
    $$\theta = 135° + 180°k$$

    b. Cosine is positive in QI and QIV.
    $$\theta_r = 30°$$
    $$\theta = 30° + 360°k; \quad \theta = 330° + 360°k$$

    c. Tangent is positive in QI and QIII.
    $$\theta_r = \tan^{-1}(4.0108) \approx 76.0°$$
    $$\theta \approx 76.0° + 180°k$$

    d. Sine is negative in QIII and QIV.
    $$\theta_r = \sin^{-1}(-0.4540) \approx -27.0°$$
    $$\theta \approx -27.0° + 360°k; \quad \theta \approx 207.0° + 360°k$$

13. The clock's hour hand makes $1\frac{3}{4}$ rotations

Mixed Review

1. $$\sin\alpha = \frac{\text{opp}}{\text{hyp}} = \frac{a}{c} = \frac{6}{\sqrt{61}} = \frac{6\sqrt{61}}{61}$$
    $$\tan\beta = \frac{\text{opp}}{\text{adj}} = \frac{b}{a} = \frac{5}{6}$$

3. $1200°$ is a QII angle:
    $$\theta_r = 7 \cdot 180° - 1200° = 60°$$
    $$\sin\theta = \frac{\sqrt{3}}{2}; \quad \cos\theta = -\frac{1}{2}; \quad \tan\theta = -\sqrt{3}$$

5. Let h be the height of the tornado.
    3.2 km = 3200 m
    $$\tan 17.3° = \frac{h}{3200}$$
    $$h = 3200 \tan 17.3° \approx 997 \text{ m}$$
    At that moment, the tornado is approximately 997 meters tall.

7. $$\cos\theta = \frac{36}{85} = \frac{\text{adj}}{\text{hyp}}$$
    $$\text{opp} = \sqrt{85^2 - 36^2} = \sqrt{5929} = 77$$
    $$\sin\theta = \frac{77}{85}; \quad \csc\theta = \frac{85}{77}; \quad \sec\theta = \frac{85}{36};$$
    $$\tan\theta = \frac{77}{36}; \quad \cot\theta = \frac{36}{77}$$

9. The three angles are coterminal in QIV.
    $$\theta_r = 30°$$
    a. $\sin(-30°) = -\dfrac{1}{2}$

    b. $\cos 330° = \dfrac{\sqrt{3}}{2}$

    c. $\tan(-750°) = -\dfrac{\sqrt{3}}{3}$

11. Let d be the distance of the mower from the house.
    $$38°39' = \left[38 + 39\left(\frac{1}{60}\right)\right]° = 38.65°$$
    $$90° - 38.65° = 51.35°$$
    $$\tan 51.35° = \frac{d}{16}$$
    $$d = 16 \tan 51.35° \approx 20 \text{ ft}$$
    The mower is approximately 20 feet from the house.

    in a clockwise (negative) direction.

$$1.75 \cdot (-360°) = -630°$$

15. $\sin\theta = \dfrac{100}{115.47}$

$\theta = \sin^{-1}\dfrac{100}{115.47} \approx 60°$

You should hit the shot at a $60°$ angle.

17. $B = 90° - 11.3° = 78.7°$

$\tan 11.3° = \dfrac{a}{60.5}$

$a = 60.5\tan 11.3° \approx 12.1$ m

$\sin 78.7° = \dfrac{60.5}{c}$; $c\sin 78.7° = 60.5$

$c = \dfrac{60.5}{\sin 78.7°} \approx 61.7$ m

Angle	Side
$A = 11.3°$	$a \approx 12.1\,\text{m}$
$B° = 78.7°$	$b = 60.5\,\text{m}$
$C = 90°$	$c \approx 61.7\,\text{m}$

19. $780°$ is a QI angle:

$\theta_r = 780° - 2\cdot 360° = 60°$

$\tan 780° = \sqrt{3}$

Practice Test

1. $\cos 41° = \dfrac{\text{adj}}{\text{hyp}} = \dfrac{b}{c} = \dfrac{b}{25}$

$b = 25\cos 41° \approx 18.87$ cm

3. $\csc\theta = 4 = \dfrac{4}{1} = \dfrac{\text{hyp}}{\text{opp}}$

$\text{adj} = \sqrt{4^2 - 1^2} = \sqrt{15}$

$\sin\theta = \dfrac{1}{4}$; $\cos\theta = \dfrac{\sqrt{15}}{4}$; $\tan\theta = \dfrac{1}{\sqrt{15}} = \dfrac{\sqrt{15}}{15}$

$\sec\theta = \dfrac{4}{\sqrt{15}} = \dfrac{4\sqrt{15}}{15}$; $\cot\theta = \dfrac{\sqrt{15}}{1} = \sqrt{15}$

5. $c = \sqrt{a^2 + b^2} = \sqrt{138^2 + 174^2}$

$= \sqrt{49{,}320} \approx 222.1$ ft

$\sin A = \dfrac{138}{222.1}$; $A = \sin^{-1}\dfrac{138}{222.1} \approx 38.4°$

$B = 90° - 38.4° = 51.6°$

Angle	Side
$A \approx 38.4°$	$a = 138\,\text{ft}$
$B \approx 51.6°$	$b = 174\,\text{ft}$
$C = 90°$	$c \approx 222.1\,\text{ft}$

7.

θ	$\sin\theta$	$\cos\theta$	$\tan\theta$	$\csc\theta$	$\sec\theta$	$\cot\theta$
$30°$	$\dfrac{1}{2}$	$\dfrac{\sqrt{3}}{2}$	$\dfrac{\sqrt{3}}{3}$	2	$\dfrac{2\sqrt{3}}{3}$	$\sqrt{3}$
$45°$	$\dfrac{\sqrt{2}}{2}$	$\dfrac{\sqrt{2}}{2}$	1	$\sqrt{2}$	$\sqrt{2}$	1
$60°$	$\dfrac{\sqrt{3}}{2}$	$\dfrac{1}{2}$	$\sqrt{3}$	$\dfrac{2\sqrt{3}}{3}$	2	$\dfrac{\sqrt{3}}{3}$
$135°$	$\dfrac{\sqrt{2}}{2}$	$-\dfrac{\sqrt{2}}{2}$	-1	$\sqrt{2}$	$-\sqrt{2}$	-1
$240°$	$-\dfrac{\sqrt{3}}{2}$	$-\dfrac{1}{2}$	$\sqrt{3}$	$-\dfrac{2\sqrt{3}}{3}$	-2	$\dfrac{\sqrt{3}}{3}$
$330°$	$-\dfrac{1}{2}$	$\dfrac{\sqrt{3}}{2}$	$-\dfrac{\sqrt{3}}{3}$	-2	$\dfrac{2\sqrt{3}}{3}$	$-\sqrt{3}$

9. $5.5 \sec \cdot 32 \text{ ft/sec} = 176 \text{ ft}$
    Maya ran down the sideline 176 feet.

    $\tan\theta = \dfrac{176}{160}$; $\theta = \tan^{-1}\dfrac{176}{160} \approx 47.7°$
    Veronica threw the disc at an angle of $47.7°$.

11. $b = \sqrt{88^2 - 57^2} = \sqrt{4495} \approx 67 \text{ cm}$
    The distance from shoulders to toes to about 67 centimeters.

    $\cos\theta = \dfrac{57}{88}$; $\theta = \cos^{-1}\dfrac{57}{88} \approx 49.6°$
    The angle formed at the hips is $49.6°$.

13. $22.1° + 67.9° = 90°$
    There is a right angle between the two flights.
    Let d be the distance between the two planes.

    $\sin 57.1° = \dfrac{2.3}{d}$; $d \sin 57.1° = 2.3$

    $d = \dfrac{2.3}{\sin 57.1°} \approx 2.7$
    The two planes are approximately 2.7 miles apart.

15. a. $\dfrac{b}{a} = \cot\alpha$

    b. $\dfrac{c}{a} = \csc\alpha$

    c. $\dfrac{b}{c} = \cos\alpha$

15. d. $\dfrac{a}{c} = \sin\alpha$

    e. $\dfrac{c}{b} = \sec\alpha$

    f. $\dfrac{a}{b} = \tan\alpha$

17. $\sin\alpha(\sec\beta - \sin\alpha) = \sin^2\beta$
    $\sin\alpha(\csc\alpha - \sin\alpha) = \sin^2\beta$
    $\sin\alpha\left(\dfrac{1}{\sin\alpha} - \sin\alpha\right) = \sin^2\beta$
    $1 - \sin^2\alpha = \sin^2\beta$
    $\cos^2\alpha = \sin^2\beta$
    $\sin^2\beta = \sin^2\beta$

19. All angles have a reference angle of $32°$.
    $\sin 148° \approx 0.53$
    $\sin 212° \approx -0.53$
    $\sin 328° \approx -0.53$

Calculator Exploration and Discovery

Exercise 1:
$\overline{ES} = \overline{EM} \sec 87°$
$\phantom{\overline{ES}} = 240,000 \cdot \sec 87°$
$\phantom{\overline{ES}} \approx 4,586,000 \text{ mi}$

Exercise 3:
Use the table feature of a graphing calculator to find $\angle E \approx 89.852°$.

Strengthening Core Skills

Exercise 1:

θ	0°	30°	45°	60°	90°	120°	135°	150°	180°	210°	225°
$\sin\theta$	0	$\dfrac{1}{2}$	$\dfrac{\sqrt{2}}{2}$	$\dfrac{\sqrt{3}}{2}$	1	$\dfrac{\sqrt{3}}{2}$	$\dfrac{\sqrt{2}}{2}$	$\dfrac{1}{2}$	0	$-\dfrac{1}{2}$	$-\dfrac{\sqrt{2}}{2}$
$\cos\theta$	1	$\dfrac{\sqrt{3}}{2}$	$\dfrac{\sqrt{2}}{2}$	$\dfrac{1}{2}$	0	$-\dfrac{1}{2}$	$-\dfrac{\sqrt{2}}{2}$	$-\dfrac{\sqrt{3}}{2}$	-1	$-\dfrac{\sqrt{3}}{2}$	$-\dfrac{\sqrt{2}}{2}$
$\tan\theta$	0	$\dfrac{\sqrt{3}}{3}$	1	$\sqrt{3}$	$--$	$-\sqrt{3}$	-1	$-\dfrac{\sqrt{3}}{3}$	0	$\dfrac{\sqrt{3}}{3}$	1

Exercise 3:

a. $\sqrt{6}\sin\theta - 2 = 1$

$\quad\quad \sqrt{6}\sin\theta = 3$

$\quad\quad\quad \sin\theta = \dfrac{3}{\sqrt{6}}$

$\quad\quad\quad \sin\theta = \dfrac{\sqrt{6}}{2}$

$\quad\quad\quad\quad \theta = \sin^{-1}\left(\dfrac{\sqrt{6}}{2}\right)$

No solution.

b. $-3\sqrt{2}\cos\theta + \sqrt{2} = 0$

$\quad\quad -3\sqrt{2}\cos\theta = -\sqrt{2}$

$\quad\quad\quad \cos\theta = \dfrac{-\sqrt{2}}{-3\sqrt{2}}$

$\quad\quad\quad \cos\theta = \dfrac{1}{3}$

$\quad\quad\quad\quad \theta = \cos^{-1}\left(\dfrac{1}{3}\right)$

$\quad\quad\quad\quad \theta \approx 70.5°,\ 289.5°$

c. $3\tan\theta + \dfrac{1}{2} = -\dfrac{1}{4}$

$\quad\quad 3\tan\theta = -\dfrac{3}{4}$

$\quad\quad\quad \tan\theta = -\dfrac{1}{4}$

$\quad\quad\quad\quad \theta = \tan^{-1}\left(-\dfrac{1}{4}\right)$

$\quad\quad\quad\quad \theta \approx 166.0°,\ 346.0°$

d. $2\sec\theta = -5$

$\quad\quad \sec\theta = -\dfrac{5}{2}$

$\quad\quad\quad \theta = \sec^{-1}\left(-\dfrac{5}{2}\right)$

$\quad\quad\quad \theta = \cos^{-1}\left(-\dfrac{2}{5}\right)$

$\quad\quad\quad \theta \approx 113.6°,\ 246.4°$

Cumulative Review Chapters 1-2

1.

$c = \sqrt{80^2 + 39^2} = 89$

$\theta = \tan^{-1}\left(\dfrac{80}{39}\right) \approx 64°$

$90° - 64° = 26°$

3. $\alpha = 90° - 29°24'54''$

$\quad = \left(89° + 59' + 60''\right) - 29°24'54''$

$\quad = \left(89° - 29°\right) + \left(59' - 24'\right) + \left(60'' - 54''\right)$

$\quad = 60° + 35' + 06''$

$\quad = 60°35'06''$

$60°35'06'' = \left[60 + 35\left(\dfrac{1}{60}\right) + 6\left(\dfrac{1}{3600}\right)\right]°$

$\quad\quad\quad\quad = 60.585°$

5. Let h be the height of the waterfall.

$\tan 60° = \dfrac{h}{66}$

$h = 66\tan 60° \approx 114.3$ ft

7. $x = -9,\ y = 40,\ r = \sqrt{(-9)^2 + 40^2} = 41$

The angle is in QII.

$\sin\theta = \dfrac{40}{41};\ \csc\theta = \dfrac{41}{40};\ \cos\theta = -\dfrac{9}{41}$

$\sec\theta = -\dfrac{41}{9};\ \tan\theta = -\dfrac{40}{9};\ \cot\theta = -\dfrac{9}{40}$

$\theta = \tan^{-1}\left(-\dfrac{40}{9}\right) \approx -77.3°$

In QII, $180° - 77.3° = 102.7°$.

9. The cofunction of sine is cosine because $\cos(90 - \theta) = \sin\theta$.

11. $\theta = -100°;\ \theta + 360k$

$k = 2;\ -100° + 360°(2) = 620°$

$k = 1;\ -100° + 360°(1) = 260°$

$k = -1;\ -100° + 360°(-1) = -460°$

$k = -2;\ -100° + 360°(-2) = -820°$

13. If $\cos(\theta - 90°) = -1$, then
$\theta - 90° = 180°$ and $\theta = 270°$.

15. If $a = b = 12.1$ in., we have a 45-45-90
triangle, and $\sin \beta = \dfrac{\sqrt{2}}{2}$.

17. $\tan A = \dfrac{a}{b} = \dfrac{11}{10}$; $A = \tan^{-1}\dfrac{11}{10} \approx 47.7°$
$B = 90° - 47.7° = 42.3°$
$c = \sqrt{11^2 + 10^2} = \sqrt{221} \approx 14.87$ m

Angle	Side
$A \approx 47.7°$	$a = 11\,\text{m}$
$B \approx 42.3°$	$b = 10\,\text{m}$
$C = 90°$	$c \approx 14.87\,\text{m}$

19. QIV; sine is negative; cosine is positive;
tangent is negative
$\theta_r = -1 \cdot 360° - (-390°) = 30°$
$\sin(-390°) = -\dfrac{1}{2}$
$\cos(-390°) = \dfrac{\sqrt{3}}{2}$
$\tan(-390°) = -\dfrac{\sqrt{3}}{3}$

21. The triangle is not possible. $a + c < b$

23. $c = \sqrt{7^2 + \left(\sqrt{15}\right)^2} = \sqrt{49 + 15} = \sqrt{64} = 8$
$\sin \beta = \dfrac{\sqrt{15}}{8}$; $\cos \beta = \dfrac{7}{8}$; $\tan \beta = \dfrac{\sqrt{15}}{7}$
$\csc \beta = \dfrac{8}{\sqrt{15}} = \dfrac{8\sqrt{15}}{15}$; $\sec \beta = \dfrac{8}{7}$
$\cot \beta = \dfrac{7}{\sqrt{15}} = \dfrac{7\sqrt{15}}{15}$

25. $a = \dfrac{b}{\sqrt{3}} = \dfrac{5}{\sqrt{3}} \cdot \dfrac{\sqrt{3}}{\sqrt{3}} = \dfrac{5\sqrt{3}}{3}$ in.
$c = 2a = 2 \cdot \dfrac{5\sqrt{3}}{3} = \dfrac{10\sqrt{3}}{3}$ in.

3.1 Exercises

1. central; 5; π

3. π; 3, 4, 6; 1, 2

5. Answers will vary.

7. $\theta = \dfrac{s}{r} = \dfrac{12}{3} = 4$ radians

9. $\theta = \dfrac{s}{r} = \dfrac{5}{5} = 1$ radian

11. $\theta = \dfrac{s}{r} = \dfrac{3}{6} = \dfrac{1}{2}$ radian

13. $\theta = \dfrac{s}{r} = \dfrac{4.2}{1.4} = 3$ radians

15. $\theta = \dfrac{s}{r} = \dfrac{22}{6} = \dfrac{11}{3}$ radians

17. $3 \text{ yd} = 9 \text{ ft}$

$\theta = \dfrac{s}{r} = \dfrac{48}{9} = \dfrac{16}{3}$ radians

19. $\theta = -\dfrac{s}{r} = -\dfrac{21}{7} = -3$ radians

21. $\theta = -\dfrac{s}{r} = -\dfrac{6}{2.5} = -2.4$ radians

23. $\theta = -\dfrac{s}{r} = -\dfrac{3\frac{2}{5}}{\frac{4}{5}} = -\dfrac{\frac{17}{5}}{\frac{4}{5}}$

$\quad = -\dfrac{17}{5} \cdot \dfrac{5}{4} = -\dfrac{17}{4}$ radians

25. $\theta = \dfrac{\pi}{6}$; $\theta + 2\pi k$

$k = 2$; $\dfrac{\pi}{6} + 2\pi(2) = \dfrac{25\pi}{6}$

$k = 1$; $\dfrac{\pi}{6} + 2\pi(1) = \dfrac{13\pi}{6}$

$k = -1$; $\dfrac{\pi}{6} + 2\pi(-1) = -\dfrac{11\pi}{6}$

$k = -2$; $\dfrac{\pi}{6} + 2\pi(-2) = -\dfrac{23\pi}{6}$

27. $\theta = \dfrac{\pi}{3}$; $\theta + 2\pi k$

$k = 2$; $\dfrac{\pi}{3} + 2\pi(2) = \dfrac{13\pi}{3}$

$k = 1$; $\dfrac{\pi}{3} + 2\pi(1) = \dfrac{7\pi}{3}$

$k = -1$; $\dfrac{\pi}{3} + 2\pi(-1) = -\dfrac{5\pi}{3}$

$k = -2$; $\dfrac{\pi}{3} + 2\pi(-2) = -\dfrac{11\pi}{3}$

29. $360° \cdot \dfrac{\pi \text{ rad}}{180°} = 2\pi$ rad

31. $45° \cdot \dfrac{\pi \text{ rad}}{180°} = \dfrac{\pi}{4}$ rad

33. $210° \cdot \dfrac{\pi \text{ rad}}{180°} = \dfrac{7\pi}{6}$ rad

35. $-120° \cdot \dfrac{\pi \text{ rad}}{180°} = -\dfrac{2\pi}{3}$ rad

37. $40° \cdot \dfrac{\pi \text{ rad}}{180°} = \dfrac{2\pi}{9}$ rad

39. $-305° \cdot \dfrac{\pi \text{ rad}}{180°} = -\dfrac{61\pi}{36}$ rad

41. $100°24' = \left[100 + 24 \cdot \dfrac{1}{60} \right]° = 100.4°$

$100.4° \cdot \dfrac{\pi \text{ rad}}{180°} = \dfrac{251\pi}{450}$ rad

43. $27° \cdot \dfrac{\pi \text{ rad}}{180°} \approx 0.4712$ rad

45. $227.9° \cdot \dfrac{\pi \text{ rad}}{180°} \approx 3.9776$ rad

47. $-52°35' = -\left[52 + 35 \cdot \dfrac{1}{60} \right]° = -52.58\overline{3}°$

$-52.58\overline{3}° \cdot \dfrac{\pi \text{ rad}}{180°} \approx -0.9178$ rad

49. $\dfrac{\pi}{3}$ rad $\cdot \dfrac{180°}{\pi \text{ rad}} = 60°$

51. $\dfrac{\pi}{6}$ rad $\cdot \dfrac{180°}{\pi \text{ rad}} = 30°$

53. $\dfrac{2\pi}{3}\,\text{rad}\cdot\dfrac{180^{\circ}}{\pi\,\text{rad}}=120^{\circ}$

55. $4\pi\,\text{rad}\cdot\dfrac{180^{\circ}}{\pi\,\text{rad}}=720^{\circ}$

57. $\dfrac{11\pi}{12}\,\text{rad}\cdot\dfrac{180^{\circ}}{\pi\,\text{rad}}=165^{\circ}$

59. $3.2541\,\text{rad}\cdot\dfrac{180^{\circ}}{\pi\,\text{rad}}\approx186.4^{\circ}$

61. $3\,\text{rad}\cdot\dfrac{180^{\circ}}{\pi\,\text{rad}}\approx171.9^{\circ}$

63. $-2.5\,\text{rad}\cdot\dfrac{180^{\circ}}{\pi\,\text{rad}}\approx-143.2^{\circ}$

65. a. $\theta=2$ corresponds to angle b.

    b. $\theta=5$ corresponds to angle e.

    c. $\theta=3$ corresponds to angle c.

67. $\theta=2.5$ is between $\dfrac{\pi}{2}$ and π; QII

69. $\theta=1.2$ is between 0 and $\dfrac{\pi}{2}$; QI

71. $\theta=-1.9$ is between $-\dfrac{\pi}{2}$ and $-\pi$; QIII

73. $8\text{ in.}=\dfrac{2}{3}\text{ ft}$

$\tau=rF\sin\theta$

$\tau=\dfrac{2}{3}\cdot54\sin\dfrac{\pi}{3}$

$\tau=36\cdot\dfrac{\sqrt{3}}{2}$

$\tau=18\sqrt{3}\text{ ft-lb}$

$F=\dfrac{\tau}{r\sin\theta}=\dfrac{50}{\dfrac{2}{3}\sin\dfrac{\pi}{3}}$

$=\dfrac{50}{\dfrac{2}{3}\cdot\dfrac{\sqrt{3}}{2}}=\dfrac{50}{\dfrac{\sqrt{3}}{3}}$

$=50\cdot\dfrac{3}{\sqrt{3}}=50\sqrt{3}\approx86.6\text{ lb}$

75. $\theta=\dfrac{s}{r}=\dfrac{7}{1.75}=4$ radians

77. $C=2\pi r=2\pi\cdot1.75=3.5\pi$
The distance of one lap is 3.5π miles.

$3.5\pi\cdot45.5=159.25\pi$
The entire length of the race is 159.25π miles.

$\theta=\dfrac{s}{r}=\dfrac{159.25\pi}{1.75}=91\pi$ radians
A car that completes the entire race sweeps out a central angle of 91π radians.

79. $r=\dfrac{1}{2}\cdot300=150\text{ ft}$

$\theta=\dfrac{s}{r}=\dfrac{2000}{150}=13.\overline{3}$ radians

$13.\overline{3}\cdot\dfrac{180^{\circ}}{\pi}\approx764^{\circ}$
The measure of the central angle swept out by the car is 764°.

81. $112.5^{\circ}\cdot\dfrac{\pi\,\text{rad}}{180^{\circ}}=\dfrac{5\pi}{8}\,\text{rad}$

83. $1^{\circ}=1^{\circ}\cdot\dfrac{\pi}{180^{\circ}}\approx0.01745$

$1'=\dfrac{1}{60}^{\circ}\cdot\dfrac{\pi}{180^{\circ}}=\dfrac{\pi}{10,800}\approx0.000291$

$1''=\dfrac{1}{3600}^{\circ}\cdot\dfrac{\pi}{180^{\circ}}=\dfrac{\pi}{648,000}\approx0.00000485$

$67^{\circ}33'18''$
$\approx\left(67\cdot0.01745+33\cdot0.000291+18\cdot0.00000485\right)$
≈1.179

85. 210° is a QIII angle:
$\theta_r=210^{\circ}-180^{\circ}=30^{\circ}$

$\sin\theta=-\dfrac{1}{2};\ \cos\theta=-\dfrac{\sqrt{3}}{2};\ \tan\theta=\dfrac{\sqrt{3}}{3}$

87. $\cos A=0.2525$
$A=\cos^{-1}0.2525\approx75.4^{\circ}$

89. a. 512° is a QII angle:
$\theta_r=3\cdot180^{\circ}-512^{\circ}=28^{\circ}$

    b. -762° is a QII angle:
$\theta_r=-2\cdot360^{\circ}-\left(-762\right)^{\circ}=42^{\circ}$

3.2 Exercises

1. latitude; equator; longitude; Prime Meridian

3. $\omega = \dfrac{\theta}{t}$; $V = r\omega$, radians

5. Answers will vary.

7. $s = r\theta = 280(3.5) = 980$ m

9. $s = r\theta$

   $\theta = \dfrac{s}{r} = \dfrac{2007}{2676} = 0.75$ radians

11. $s = r\theta$

    $r = \dfrac{s}{\theta} = \dfrac{4146.9}{\frac{3\pi}{4}} = 4146.9 \cdot \dfrac{4}{3\pi} \approx 1760$ yd

13. $s = r\theta = \dfrac{4\pi}{3} \cdot 2 = \dfrac{8\pi}{3}$ mi

15. $s = r\theta$

    $\theta = \dfrac{s}{r} = \dfrac{252.35}{980} = 0.2575$ rad

17. $s = r\theta$; $320° \cdot \dfrac{\pi}{180°} = \dfrac{16\pi}{9}$

    $r = \dfrac{s}{\theta} = \dfrac{52.5}{\frac{16\pi}{9}} = 52.5 \cdot \dfrac{9}{16\pi} \approx 9.4$ km

19. $360° = 360° \cdot \dfrac{\pi}{180°} = 2\pi$

    $\omega = \dfrac{\theta}{t} = \dfrac{2\pi}{8} = \dfrac{\pi}{4}$ rad/sec

21. $450° = 450° \cdot \dfrac{\pi}{180°} = \dfrac{5\pi}{2}$

    $\omega = \dfrac{\theta}{t} = \dfrac{\frac{5\pi}{2}}{10} = \dfrac{\pi}{4}$ rad/hr

23. $210° = 210° \cdot \dfrac{\pi}{180°} = \dfrac{7\pi}{6}$

    $\omega = \dfrac{\theta}{t} = \dfrac{\frac{7\pi}{6}}{7} = \dfrac{\pi}{6}$ rad/day

25. $420° = 420° \cdot \dfrac{\pi}{180°} = \dfrac{7\pi}{3}$

    $\omega = \dfrac{\theta}{t} = \dfrac{\frac{7\pi}{3}}{4} = \dfrac{7\pi}{12}$ rad/min

27. $V = r\omega = 8 \cdot 5 = 40$ in./sec

29. $V = r\omega = 3.2 \cdot 14\pi \approx 140.74$ mph

31. $168° = 168° \cdot \dfrac{\pi}{180°} = \dfrac{14\pi}{15}$

    $\omega = \dfrac{\theta}{t} = \dfrac{\frac{14\pi}{15}}{0.28} \approx 10.4720$ rad/sec

    $V = r\omega = 3 \cdot 10.4720 = 31.42$ mm/sec

33. $\omega = \dfrac{\theta}{t} = \dfrac{30}{6} = 5$ rad/hr

    $V = r\omega = 1.2 \cdot 5 = 6$ kph

35. $A = \dfrac{1}{2} r^2 \theta = \left(\dfrac{1}{2}\right)(6.8)^2(5) = 115.6$ km^2

37. $A = \dfrac{1}{2} r^2 \theta$

    $\theta = \dfrac{2A}{r^2} = \dfrac{(2)(1080)}{(60)^2} = 0.6$ rad

39. $A = \dfrac{1}{2} r^2 \theta$

    $r = \sqrt{\dfrac{2A}{\theta}} = \sqrt{\dfrac{(2)(16.5)}{\frac{7\pi}{6}}} \approx 3$ m

41. $\theta = 1.5$ rad; $r = 5$ cm $s = r\theta = 5 \cdot 1.5 = 7.5$ cm

    $A = \dfrac{1}{2} r^2 \theta = \left(\dfrac{1}{2}\right)(5)^2(1.5) = 18.75$ cm^2

43. $r = 10$ m; $s = 43$ m

    $s = r\theta$; $\theta = \dfrac{s}{r} = \dfrac{43}{10} = 4.3$ rad

    $A = \dfrac{1}{2} r^2 \theta = \left(\dfrac{1}{2}\right)(10)^2(4.3) = 215$ m^2

45. $\theta = 3$ rad; $A = 864$ mm^2

$$A = \frac{1}{2}r^2\theta; \quad r = \sqrt{\frac{2A}{\theta}} = \sqrt{\frac{(2)(864)}{3}} = 24 \text{ mm}$$
$$s = r\theta = 24 \cdot 3 = 72 \text{ mm}$$

47. $\alpha_1 = 30° \cdot \dfrac{\pi}{180°} = \dfrac{\pi}{6}$

$\alpha_2 = 38° \cdot \dfrac{\pi}{180°} = \dfrac{19\pi}{90}$

$\beta_1 = 95° \cdot \dfrac{\pi}{180°} = \dfrac{19\pi}{36}$

$\beta_2 = 122° \cdot \dfrac{\pi}{180°} = \dfrac{61\pi}{90}$

$h = \sin^2\left(\dfrac{\alpha_2 - \alpha_1}{2}\right) + \cos\alpha_2 \cos\alpha_1 \sin^2\left(\dfrac{\beta_2 - \beta_1}{2}\right)$

$= \sin^2\left(\dfrac{\frac{19\pi}{90} - \frac{\pi}{6}}{2}\right) + \cos\left(\dfrac{19\pi}{90}\right)\cos\left(\dfrac{\pi}{6}\right)\sin^2\left(\dfrac{\frac{61\pi}{90} - \frac{19\pi}{36}}{2}\right)$

$= \sin^2\left(\dfrac{\pi}{45}\right) + \cos\left(\dfrac{19\pi}{90}\right)\cos\left(\dfrac{\pi}{6}\right)\sin^2\left(\dfrac{3\pi}{40}\right)$

≈ 0.04206

49. $40.3° - 26.4° = 13.9°$

13.9° separate the cities.

$\theta = 13.9° \cdot \dfrac{\pi \text{ rad}}{180°} \approx 0.2426$ rad

$s = r\theta = 3960 \cdot 0.2426 \approx 960.7$ mi

These cities are 960.7 miles apart.

51. a. $\omega = \dfrac{\frac{3}{4}\text{ rev}}{\text{sec}} \cdot \dfrac{2\pi \text{ rad}}{1 \text{ rev}} = 1.5\pi$ rad/sec

 b. $V = (56 \text{ in.})\left(1.5\pi\dfrac{\text{rad}}{\text{sec}}\right) = 84\pi$ in./sec

   Convert to mph.

   $\left(\dfrac{84\pi \text{ in.}}{\text{sec}}\right)\left(\dfrac{1 \text{ mi}}{5280(12)\text{in}}\right)\left(\dfrac{3600 \text{ sec}}{1 \text{ hr}}\right)$

   ≈ 15 mph

53. a. $\omega = \dfrac{20 \text{ rev}}{\text{min}} \cdot \dfrac{2\pi \text{ rad}}{\text{rev}} = 40\pi$ rad/min

 b. $V = (3 \text{ in.})\left(40\pi\dfrac{\text{rad}}{\text{min}}\right) \approx 120\pi$ in./min

   Convert to ft/sec.

   $\left(\dfrac{120\pi \text{ in.}}{\text{sec}}\right)\left(\dfrac{1 \text{ ft}}{12 \text{ in.}}\right)\left(\dfrac{1 \text{ min}}{60 \text{ sec}}\right)$

   $= \dfrac{\pi}{6}$ ft/sec ≈ 0.52 ft/sec

 c. $t = \dfrac{6 \text{ ft}}{0.52 \text{ ft/sec}} \approx 11.5$ sec

55. a. $r = 12$ m; $\theta = 40° \cdot \dfrac{\pi \text{ rad}}{180°} = \dfrac{2\pi}{9}$ rad

   $A = \dfrac{1}{2}r^2\theta = \left(\dfrac{1}{2}\right)(12)^2\left(\dfrac{2\pi}{9}\right) \approx 50.3$ m^2

 b. $A = 2 \cdot 50.3 = 100.6$ m^2

   $A = \dfrac{1}{2}r^2\theta; \quad \theta = \dfrac{2A}{r^2} = \dfrac{(2)(100.6)}{(12)^2} \approx 1.3972$ rad

   $1.3972 \cdot \dfrac{180°}{\pi} \approx 80°$

 c. $A = \dfrac{1}{2}r^2\theta$

   $r = \sqrt{\dfrac{2A}{\theta}} = \sqrt{\dfrac{(2)(100.6)}{\frac{2\pi}{9}}} \approx 17$ m

57. a. $\left(\dfrac{1 \text{ rev}}{7.15 \text{ days}}\right)\left(\dfrac{2\pi \text{ rad}}{1 \text{ rev}}\right) \approx 0.8788$ rad/day

   $\left(\dfrac{0.8788 \text{ rad}}{\text{day}}\right)\left(\dfrac{180°}{\pi \text{ rad}}\right) \approx 50.3°/\text{day}$

 b. $\omega = \dfrac{\theta}{t} = \dfrac{0.8788}{1 \text{ day}} \cdot \dfrac{1 \text{ day}}{24 \text{ hr}} \approx 0.0366$ rad/hr

 c. $V = r\omega$

   $= (656,000 \text{ mi})\left(\dfrac{0.0366 \text{ rad}}{\text{hr}}\right)\left(\dfrac{1 \text{ hr}}{3600 \text{ sec}}\right)$

   ≈ 6.67 mi/sec

59. $V = \dfrac{r\theta}{t} = \dfrac{400 \cdot 2\pi}{3 \text{ days}} \cdot \dfrac{1 \text{ day}}{24 \text{ hr}} \approx 34.9$ m/hr

61. a. If $\theta = 39.5°$, the complementary angle at the bottom of the right triangle is $90° - 39.5° = 50.5°$.

   $\sin 50.5° = \dfrac{r}{3960}$

   $r = 3960 \sin 50.5° \approx 3055.6$ mi

 b. $(180° - 116°) + (180° - 75°) = 169°$

   The closest measure between the longitudes is 169°.

   $s = 3055.6(169°)\left(\dfrac{\pi \text{ rad}}{180°}\right) \approx 9012.8$ mi

 c. $9012.8 \text{ mi} \cdot \dfrac{1 \text{ hr}}{1250 \text{ mi}} = 7.21$ hr, or

   approximately 7 hr, 13 min.

63. $\dfrac{4\pi}{3}\text{rad}\cdot\dfrac{180°}{\pi\text{ rad}}=240°$

65. $a=b=\dfrac{c}{\sqrt{2}}=\dfrac{10}{\sqrt{2}}=\dfrac{10}{\sqrt{2}}\cdot\dfrac{\sqrt{2}}{\sqrt{2}}=5\sqrt{2}$ in.

67. $\csc\alpha=\dfrac{c}{a}=\dfrac{7}{\sqrt{30}}=\dfrac{7}{\sqrt{30}}\cdot\dfrac{\sqrt{30}}{\sqrt{30}}=\dfrac{7\sqrt{30}}{30}$

Mid-Chapter Check

1. $36°06'36''=\left[36+6\left(\dfrac{1}{60}\right)+36\left(\dfrac{1}{3600}\right)\right]°$

$=36.11°\text{N}$

$115°04'48''=\left[115+4\left(\dfrac{1}{60}\right)+48\left(\dfrac{1}{3600}\right)\right]°$

$=115.08°\text{W}$

$s=r\theta=3960\cdot36.11°\cdot\dfrac{\pi}{180°}\approx2495.7$ mi.

3. a. $210°\cdot\dfrac{\pi}{180°}=\dfrac{7\pi}{6}$

b. $-135°\cdot\dfrac{\pi}{180°}=-\dfrac{3\pi}{4}$

c. $480°\cdot\dfrac{\pi}{180°}=\dfrac{8\pi}{3}$

5. $\theta=\dfrac{5\pi}{6};\ \theta+2\pi k$

$k=1;\ \dfrac{5\pi}{6}+2\pi(1)=\dfrac{17\pi}{6}$

$k=-1;\ \dfrac{5\pi}{6}+2\pi(-1)=-\dfrac{7\pi}{6}$

7. a. $105°\cdot\dfrac{\pi}{180°}=\dfrac{7\pi}{12}$

$A=\dfrac{1}{2}r^2\theta=\left(\dfrac{1}{2}\right)(15)^2\left(\dfrac{7\pi}{12}\right)\approx206\text{ in}^2$

b. $\theta=\dfrac{2A}{r^2}=\dfrac{(2)(226)}{(15)^2}\cdot\dfrac{180°}{\pi}\approx115°$

9. $\omega=\dfrac{\theta}{t}=\dfrac{1\text{ rev}}{81\text{ sec}}\cdot\dfrac{2\pi\text{ rad}}{1\text{ rev}}=\dfrac{2\pi}{81}$ rad/sec

$V=r\omega,\ r=\dfrac{V}{\omega}=\dfrac{35}{\frac{2\pi}{81}}=35\cdot\dfrac{81}{2\pi}\approx451$ m

Reinforcing Basic Concepts

Exercise 1:
a. $(0.97,0.24);\ 0.97^2+0.24^2\approx1$
$\cos t=\cos0.25=0.9689124217$
$\sin t=\sin0.25=0.2474039593$

b. $(0.88,0.48);\ 0.88^2+0.48^2\approx1$
$\cos t=\cos0.5=0.8775825619$
$\sin t=\sin0.5=0.4794255386$

c. $(0.73,0.68);\ 0.73^2+0.68^2\approx1$
$\cos t=\cos0.75=0.73168886889$
$\sin t=\sin0.75=0.68163876$

d. $(0.54,0.84);\ 0.54^2+0.84^2\approx1$
$\cos t=\cos1=0.5403023059$
$\sin t=\sin1=0.8414709848$

3.3 Exercises

1. x; y; origin

3. x; y; $\dfrac{y}{x}$; $\sec\theta$; $\csc\theta$; $\cot\theta$

5. Answers will vary.

7. $x^2+(-0.8)^2=1;\ x^2+0.64=1$
$x^2=1-0.64=0.36;\ x=\pm0.6$
QIII, so choose $x=-0.6$: $(-0.6,-0.8)$

9. $\dfrac{5}{13}^2+y^2=1;\ \dfrac{25}{169}+y^2=1$
$y^2=1-\dfrac{25}{169}=\dfrac{144}{169};\ y=\pm\dfrac{12}{13}$
QIV, so choose $y=-\dfrac{12}{13}$: $\dfrac{5}{13},-\dfrac{12}{13}$

11. $\dfrac{\sqrt{11}}{6}^2+y^2=1;\ \dfrac{11}{36}+y^2=1$
$y^2=1-\dfrac{11}{36}=\dfrac{25}{36};\ y=\pm\dfrac{5}{6}$

QI, so choose $y = \dfrac{5}{6}$: $\dfrac{\sqrt{11}}{6}, \dfrac{5}{6}$ 13.

$-\dfrac{\sqrt{11}}{4}^{2} + y^2 = 1;\quad \dfrac{11}{16} + y^2 = 1$

$y^2 = 1 - \dfrac{11}{16} = \dfrac{5}{16};\quad y = \pm\dfrac{\sqrt{5}}{4}$

QII, so choose $y = \dfrac{\sqrt{5}}{4}$: $-\dfrac{\sqrt{11}}{4}, \dfrac{\sqrt{5}}{4}$

15. $x^2 + (-0.2137)^2 = 1$

$x = \pm\sqrt{1 - (-0.2137)^2} = \pm 0.9769$

QIII, so choose $x = -0.9769$

$(-0.9769, -0.2137)$

17. $x^2 + (0.1198)^2 = 1$

$x = \pm\sqrt{1 - (0.1198)^2} \approx \pm 0.9928$

QII, so choose $x = -0.9928$

$(-0.9928, 0.1198)$

19. $-\dfrac{\sqrt{3}}{2}^{2} + \dfrac{1}{2}^{2} = \dfrac{3}{4} + \dfrac{1}{4} = \dfrac{4}{4} = 1$

Other points: $\left(\dfrac{\sqrt{3}}{2}, \dfrac{1}{2}\right)$ QI;

$\left(-\dfrac{\sqrt{3}}{2}, -\dfrac{1}{2}\right)$ QIII; $\left(\dfrac{\sqrt{3}}{2}, -\dfrac{1}{2}\right)$ QIV

21. $\dfrac{\sqrt{11}}{6}^{2} + -\dfrac{5}{6}^{2} = \dfrac{11}{36} + \dfrac{25}{36} = \dfrac{36}{36} = 1$

Other points: $\left(\dfrac{\sqrt{11}}{6}, \dfrac{5}{6}\right)$ QI;

$\left(-\dfrac{\sqrt{11}}{6}, \dfrac{5}{6}\right)$ QII; $\left(-\dfrac{\sqrt{11}}{6}, -\dfrac{5}{6}\right)$ QIII

23. $(0.3325)^2 + (0.9431)^2 = 1$

Other points: $(-0.3325, 0.9431)$ QII
$(-0.3325, -0.9431)$ QIII
$(0.3325, -0.9431)$ QIV

25. $(0.9937)^2 + (-0.1121)^2 = 1$

Other points: $(0.9937, 0.1121)$ QI
$(-0.9937, 0.1121)$ QII
$(-0.9937, -0.1121)$ QIII

27.

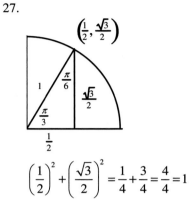

$\left(\dfrac{1}{2}\right)^2 + \left(\dfrac{\sqrt{3}}{2}\right)^2 = \dfrac{1}{4} + \dfrac{3}{4} = \dfrac{4}{4} = 1$

29. $\dfrac{5\pi}{4} - \pi = \dfrac{5\pi}{4} - \dfrac{4\pi}{4} = \dfrac{\pi}{4}$

$\dfrac{5\pi}{4}$ is in QIII, so the point is $-\dfrac{\sqrt{2}}{2}, -\dfrac{\sqrt{2}}{2}$.

31. $-\dfrac{5\pi}{6} - (-\pi) = -\dfrac{5\pi}{6} + \dfrac{6\pi}{6} = \dfrac{\pi}{6}$

$-\dfrac{5\pi}{6}$ is in QIII, so the point is $-\dfrac{\sqrt{3}}{2}, -\dfrac{1}{2}$

33. $3\pi - \dfrac{11\pi}{4} = \dfrac{12\pi}{4} - \dfrac{11\pi}{4} = \dfrac{\pi}{4}$

$\dfrac{11\pi}{4}$ is in QII, so the point is $-\dfrac{\sqrt{2}}{2}, \dfrac{\sqrt{2}}{2}$

35. $\dfrac{25\pi}{6} - 4\pi = \dfrac{25\pi}{6} - \dfrac{24\pi}{6} = \dfrac{\pi}{6}$

$\dfrac{25\pi}{6}$ is in Q1, so the point is $\dfrac{\sqrt{3}}{2}, \dfrac{1}{2}$.

37. The reference angle for each angle is $\dfrac{\pi}{4}$.

   a. $\sin \dfrac{\pi}{4} = \dfrac{\sqrt{2}}{2}$ (QI)

   b. $\sin \dfrac{3\pi}{4} = \dfrac{\sqrt{2}}{2}$ (QII)

   c. $\sin \dfrac{5\pi}{4} = -\dfrac{\sqrt{2}}{2}$ (QIII)

   d. $\sin \dfrac{7\pi}{4} = -\dfrac{\sqrt{2}}{2}$ (QIV)

   e. $\sin \dfrac{9\pi}{4} = \dfrac{\sqrt{2}}{2}$ (QI)

   f. $\sin -\dfrac{\pi}{4} = -\dfrac{\sqrt{2}}{2}$ (QIV)

   g. $\sin -\dfrac{5\pi}{4} = \dfrac{\sqrt{2}}{2}$ (QII)

   h. $\sin -\dfrac{11\pi}{4} = -\dfrac{\sqrt{2}}{2}$ (QIII)

39. Note that these are all quadrantal angles.
   a. $\cos \pi = -1$

   b. $\cos 0 = 1$

   c. $\cos \dfrac{\pi}{2} = 0$

   d. $\cos \dfrac{3\pi}{2} = 0$

41. a.
$$x^2 + y^2 + z^2 = 1$$
$$x^2 + \left(-\dfrac{4}{9}\right)^2 + \left(\dfrac{1}{9}\right)^2 = 1$$
$$x^2 + \dfrac{16}{81} + \dfrac{1}{81} = 1$$
$$x^2 + \dfrac{17}{81} = 1$$
$$x^2 = \dfrac{81}{81} - \dfrac{17}{81}$$
$$x^2 = \dfrac{64}{81}$$
$$x = \pm\dfrac{8}{9}$$

41. b.
$$x^2 + y^2 + z^2 = 1$$
$$\left(\dfrac{2}{11}\right)^2 + y^2 + \left(-\dfrac{9}{11}\right)^2 = 1$$
$$\dfrac{4}{121} + y^2 + \dfrac{81}{121} = 1$$
$$y^2 + \dfrac{85}{121} = 1$$
$$y^2 = \dfrac{121}{121} - \dfrac{85}{121}$$
$$y^2 = \dfrac{36}{121}$$
$$y = \pm\dfrac{6}{11}$$

   c.
$$x^2 + y^2 + z^2 = 1$$
$$\left(\dfrac{2}{7}\right)^2 + \left(\dfrac{3}{7}\right)^2 + z^2 = 1$$
$$\dfrac{4}{49} + \dfrac{9}{49} + z^2 = 1$$
$$\dfrac{13}{49} + z^2 = 1$$
$$z^2 = \dfrac{49}{49} - \dfrac{13}{49}$$
$$z^2 = \dfrac{36}{49}$$
$$z = \pm\dfrac{6}{7}$$

Note: For Exercises 43 through 49, consider that for a unit circle, $x = \cos\theta$ and $y = \sin\theta$.

43. $(\cos 40°, \sin 40°) = (0.7660, 0.6428)$

45. $(\cos 201°, \sin 201°) = (-0.9336, -0.3584)$

47. $(\cos 2, \sin 2) = (-0.4161, 0.9093)$

49. $(\cos 5, \sin 5) = (0.2837, -0.9589)$

51. The distance from Libra's disk to Pisces' disk is twice the horizontal distance from the center to Libra's disk.
$2 \cdot 96.6 = 193.2$ cm

The distance from Libra's disk to Virgo's disk is twice the vertical from the center to Libra's disk.
$2 \cdot 25.9 = 51.8$ cm

53. The point P represents a point 1/6 the way around the circle, measured from the standard positive x-axis.

$$\frac{2\pi}{6} = \frac{\pi}{3} \text{ rad, or } 60°$$

The location of point P is $\left(\cos\frac{\pi}{3}, \sin\frac{\pi}{3}\right)$

$= (\cos 60°, \sin 60°) = (0.5, 0.8660)$.

The point P is 50 cm to the right and 86.6 cm above the center of the circle.

55. Answers will vary.

57. $\omega = \dfrac{\theta}{t} = \dfrac{300 \text{ rev}}{1 \text{ min}} \cdot \dfrac{2\pi \text{ rad}}{1 \text{ rev}} = 600\pi \text{ rad/sec}$

$V = r\omega = 18 \cdot 600\pi = 10{,}800\pi \text{ in./min}$

$V = \dfrac{10{,}800\pi \text{ in.}}{1 \text{ min}} \cdot \dfrac{1 \text{ ft}}{12 \text{ in.}} \cdot \dfrac{1 \text{ mi}}{5280 \text{ ft}} \cdot \dfrac{60 \text{ min}}{1 \text{ hr}}$

$\approx 32 \text{ mph}$

59. a. $s = r\theta$

$\theta = \dfrac{s}{r} = \dfrac{18.5}{5} = 3.7 \text{ rad}$

b. $A = \dfrac{1}{2}r^2\theta = \left(\dfrac{1}{2}\right)(5)^2(3.7) = 46.25 \text{ cm}^2$

61. $\pi - 3$

3.4 Exercises

1. length; equal; radian; t; θ

3. x; y; $\dfrac{y}{x}$; $\sec t$; $\csc t$; $\cot t$

5.

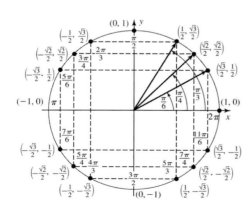

7. The reference arc for each number is $\dfrac{\pi}{6}$.

a. $\cos\dfrac{\pi}{6} = \dfrac{\sqrt{3}}{2}$ (QI)

b. $\cos\dfrac{5\pi}{6} = -\dfrac{\sqrt{3}}{2}$ (QII)

c. $\cos\dfrac{7\pi}{6} = -\dfrac{\sqrt{3}}{2}$ (QIII)

d. $\cos\dfrac{11\pi}{6} = \dfrac{\sqrt{3}}{2}$ (QIV)

e. $\cos\dfrac{13\pi}{6} = \dfrac{\sqrt{3}}{2}$ (QI)

f. $\cos-\dfrac{\pi}{6} = \dfrac{\sqrt{3}}{2}$ (QIV)

g. $\cos-\dfrac{5\pi}{6} = -\dfrac{\sqrt{3}}{2}$ (QIII)

h. $\cos-\dfrac{23\pi}{6} = \dfrac{\sqrt{3}}{2}$ (QI)

9. Note that these are all quadrantal angles.

a. $\tan\pi = \dfrac{0}{-1} = 0$

b. $\tan 0 = \dfrac{0}{1} = 0$

c. $\tan\dfrac{\pi}{2} = \dfrac{1}{0}$ This is undefined.

d. $\tan\dfrac{3\pi}{2} = \dfrac{-1}{0}$ This is undefined.

11. $\sin t = 0.6; \quad \cos t = -0.8;$

$\tan t = \dfrac{0.6}{-0.8} = -0.75; \quad \cot t = \dfrac{-0.8}{0.6} = -1.\overline{3};$

$\csc t = \dfrac{1}{0.6} = 1.\overline{6}; \quad \sec t = \dfrac{1}{-0.8} = -1.25$

13. $\sin t = -\dfrac{12}{13}; \quad \cos t = -\dfrac{5}{13};$

$\tan t = \dfrac{-\dfrac{12}{13}}{-\dfrac{5}{13}} = \dfrac{12}{5}; \quad \cot t = \dfrac{5}{12};$

$\csc t = -\dfrac{13}{12}; \quad \sec t = -\dfrac{13}{5}$

15. $\sin t = \dfrac{\sqrt{11}}{6}$; $\cos t = \dfrac{5}{6}$;

$\tan t = \dfrac{\frac{\sqrt{11}}{6}}{\frac{5}{6}} = \dfrac{\sqrt{11}}{5}$; $\cot t = \dfrac{5}{\sqrt{11}} = \dfrac{5\sqrt{11}}{11}$;

$\csc t = \dfrac{6}{\sqrt{11}} = \dfrac{6\sqrt{11}}{11}$; $\sec t = \dfrac{6}{5}$

17. $\sin t = \dfrac{\sqrt{21}}{5}$; $\cos t = -\dfrac{2}{5}$;

$\tan t = \dfrac{\frac{\sqrt{21}}{5}}{-\frac{2}{5}} = -\dfrac{\sqrt{21}}{2}$;

$\cot t = -\dfrac{2}{\sqrt{21}} = -\dfrac{2\sqrt{21}}{21}$;

$\csc t = \dfrac{5}{\sqrt{21}} = \dfrac{5\sqrt{21}}{21}$; $\sec t = -\dfrac{5}{2}$

19. $\sin t = -\dfrac{2\sqrt{2}}{3}$; $\cos t = -\dfrac{1}{3}$;

$\tan t = \dfrac{-\frac{2\sqrt{2}}{3}}{-\frac{1}{3}} = 2\sqrt{2}$; $\cot t = \dfrac{1}{2\sqrt{2}} = \dfrac{\sqrt{2}}{4}$;

$\csc t = -\dfrac{3}{2\sqrt{2}} = -\dfrac{3\sqrt{2}}{4}$; $\sec t = -3$

21. $\sin t = \dfrac{\sqrt{3}}{2}$; $\cos t = \dfrac{1}{2}$;

$\tan t = \dfrac{\frac{\sqrt{3}}{2}}{\frac{1}{2}} = \sqrt{3}$; $\cot t = \dfrac{1}{\sqrt{3}} = \dfrac{\sqrt{3}}{3}$;

$\csc t = \dfrac{2}{\sqrt{3}} = \dfrac{2\sqrt{3}}{3}$; $\sec t = 2$

23. $\sin t = \dfrac{\sqrt{2}}{2}$; $\cos t = -\dfrac{\sqrt{2}}{2}$;

$\tan t = \dfrac{\frac{\sqrt{2}}{2}}{-\frac{\sqrt{2}}{2}} = -1$; $\cot t = -1$;

$\csc t = \dfrac{2}{\sqrt{2}} = \sqrt{2}$; $\sec t = -\dfrac{2}{\sqrt{2}} = -\sqrt{2}$;

25. QI; $\sin 0.75 \approx 0.7$

27. QIV; $\cos 0.75 \approx 0.7$

29. QI; $\tan 0.8 = \dfrac{\sin 0.8}{\cos 0.8} \approx 1$

31. QII; $\csc 2.0 = \dfrac{1}{\sin 2.0} \approx \dfrac{1}{0.9} \approx 1.1$

33. QII; $\cos\left(\dfrac{5\pi}{8}\right) \approx -0.4$

35. QIV; $\tan\left(\dfrac{8\pi}{5}\right) \approx -3.1$

37. $\sin \dfrac{2\pi}{3} = \dfrac{\sqrt{3}}{2}$

39. $\cos \dfrac{7\pi}{6} = -\dfrac{\sqrt{3}}{2}$

41. $\tan\left(\dfrac{2\pi}{3}\right) = \dfrac{\sin\left(\frac{2\pi}{3}\right)}{\cos\left(\frac{2\pi}{3}\right)} = \dfrac{\frac{\sqrt{3}}{2}}{\frac{-1}{2}} = -\sqrt{3}$

43. $\sin \dfrac{\pi}{2} = 1$

45. $\sec t = -\sqrt{2}$ $\qquad \cos t = -\dfrac{1}{\sqrt{2}} = -\dfrac{\sqrt{2}}{2}$

This occurs at $t = \dfrac{3\pi}{4}$ and $\dfrac{5\pi}{4}$.

47. $\tan t$ undefined $\qquad \cos t = 0$

This occurs at $t = \dfrac{\pi}{2}$ and $\dfrac{3\pi}{2}$.

49. $\cos t = -\dfrac{\sqrt{2}}{2}$ occurs at $t = \dfrac{3\pi}{4}$ and $\dfrac{5\pi}{4}$.

51. $\sin t = 0$ occurs at $t = 0$ and π.

53. $\sin t = 0.3215$; $\cos t > 0 \Rightarrow$ QI

$t = \sin^{-1} 0.3215 \approx 0.3273$

55. $\cos t = -0.1424;\ \tan t > 0 \Rightarrow \text{QIII}$

$t_r = \cos^{-1}\left|-0.1424\right| \approx 1.4279$

$t = \pi + t_r = \pi + 1.4279 \approx 4.5695$

57. $\cot t = -1.2345;\ \sec t < 0 \Rightarrow \text{QII}$

$t_r = \cot^{-1}\left|-1.2345\right| = \tan^{-1}\left|\dfrac{1}{-1.2345}\right|$

$t_r \approx 0.6808$

$t = \pi - t_r = \pi - 0.6808 \approx 2.4608$

59. $\csc t = -1.9709;\ \cot t < 0 \Rightarrow \text{QIV}$

$t_r = \csc^{-1}\left|-1.9709\right| = \sin^{-1}\left|\dfrac{1}{-1.9709}\right|$

$t_r \approx 0.5321$

$t = 2\pi - t_r = 2\pi - 0.5321 \approx 5.7510$

61. 0.8 is in QI

$\sin t > 0$ QII: $\pi - 0.8 \approx 2.3416$

63. 4.5 is in QIII with a reference arc of

$t_r = 4.5 - \pi \approx 1.3584$

$\cos t < 0$ in QII: $\pi - 1.3584 \approx 1.7832$

65. 0.4 is in QI.

$\tan t > 0$ in QIII: $\pi + 0.4 \approx 3.5416$

67. Since $x = \cos t > 0$ and $y = \sin t < 0$,

t is in QIV.

  a. $-t$ is in QI; $\dfrac{3}{4}, \dfrac{4}{5}$

  b. $t + \pi$ is in QII: $-\dfrac{3}{4}, \dfrac{4}{5}$

69. $(2k+1)\dfrac{\pi}{4}$

$k = -3: \left[2(-3)+1\right]\dfrac{\pi}{4} = -5 \cdot \dfrac{\pi}{4} = -\dfrac{5\pi}{4}$

$k = -2: \left[2(-2)+1\right]\dfrac{\pi}{4} = -3 \cdot \dfrac{\pi}{4} = -\dfrac{3\pi}{4}$

$k = -1: \left[2(-1)+1\right]\dfrac{\pi}{4} = -1 \cdot \dfrac{\pi}{4} = -\dfrac{\pi}{4}$

$k = 0: \left[2(0)+1\right]\dfrac{\pi}{4} = 1 \cdot \dfrac{\pi}{4} = \dfrac{\pi}{4}$

$k = 1: \left[2(1)+1\right]\dfrac{\pi}{4} = 3 \cdot \dfrac{\pi}{4} = \dfrac{3\pi}{4}$

$k = 2: \left[2(2)+1\right]\dfrac{\pi}{4} = 5 \cdot \dfrac{\pi}{4} = \dfrac{5\pi}{4}$

71. a. The circumference of the roller is
    $2\pi r = 2\pi(1) = 2\pi$ ft, so 2π ft corresponds to 1
    revolution, or 2π radians.

    $5\,\text{ft} \cdot \dfrac{2\pi\ \text{rad}}{2\pi\ \text{ft}} = 5\ \text{rad}$

  b. 5 radians corresponds to 5 ft, so
    30 radians corresponds to 30 ft.

73. a. The circumference of the spool is
    $2\pi r = 2\pi(1) = 2\pi$ dm, so 2π dm
    corresponds to 1 revolution, or 2π radians.

    $5\,\text{rad} \cdot \dfrac{2\pi\ \text{dm}}{2\pi\ \text{rad}} = 5\ \text{dm}$

  b. If 5 radians corresponds to 5 dm,
    then 2π radians corresponds to
    $2\pi\ (\approx 6.28)$ dm.

75. a. Use $s = r\theta$ with $r = 1 \cdot AU$, $\theta = 2.5$ rad.
    $s = (1\ AU)(2.5\ \text{rad}) = 2.5\ AU$

  b. If 2.5 AU corresponds to 2.5 rad, then
    1 revolution $(2\pi\ \text{rad})$ corresponds to
    2π AU, or about 6.28 AU.

77. Yes, the distance equals the circumference.

79. Since sine and cosine are determined by
    coordinates of points on a circle of radius 1, they
    have to be between –1 and 1, so the range for
    both is [–1, 1].

81. a. $2t \approx 2.2$

  b. $t \approx 1.1$, which is in QI.

  c. $\cos 1.1 \approx 0.5$

  d. $\cos(2t) = \cos(2.2) \approx -0.6;$
    $2\cos t \approx 2 \cdot 0.5 = 0.1$
    No, $\cos(2t) \ne 2\cos t.$

83. The area cleaned is the difference between a
    sector with radius 24 in. and angle $110°$ and a
    sector with radius 4 in. and angle $110°$.

    $110° \cdot \dfrac{\pi\ \text{rad}}{180°} \approx 1.92\ \text{rad}$

    $A_{big} = \dfrac{1}{2}(24)^2(1.92) \approx 553\ \text{in}^2$

    $A_{small} = \dfrac{1}{2}(4)^2(1.92) \approx 15.4\ \text{in}^2$

    $553 - 15.4 = 537.6\ \text{in}^2$

    The area cleaned is approximately $537.6\ \text{in}^2$.

85. $\sin\theta = \dfrac{21}{29} \Rightarrow y = 21,\ r = 29$

   (Since $\cos\theta < 0$, x is negative.)

   The angle θ is in quadrant II.

   $x = -\sqrt{29^2 - 21^2} = \sqrt{400} = 20$

   $\sin\theta = \dfrac{21}{29};\ \cos\theta = -\dfrac{20}{29};\ \tan\theta = -\dfrac{21}{20}$

   $\csc\theta = \dfrac{29}{21};\ \sec\theta = -\dfrac{29}{20};\ \cot\theta = -\dfrac{20}{21}$

87. $\dfrac{11\pi}{6}$ is in QIV.

   $\theta_r = 2\pi - \dfrac{11\pi}{6} = \dfrac{12\pi}{6} - \dfrac{11\pi}{6} = \dfrac{\pi}{6}$

   $\sin\dfrac{11\pi}{6} = -\dfrac{1}{2};\ \cos\dfrac{11\pi}{6} = \dfrac{\sqrt{3}}{2};$

   $\tan\dfrac{11\pi}{6} = \dfrac{-\dfrac{1}{2}}{\dfrac{\sqrt{3}}{2}} = -\dfrac{1}{\sqrt{3}} = -\dfrac{\sqrt{3}}{3};$

   $\csc\dfrac{11\pi}{6} = -2;\ \sec\dfrac{11\pi}{6} = \dfrac{2}{\sqrt{3}} = \dfrac{2\sqrt{3}}{3};$

   $\cot\dfrac{11\pi}{6} = -\dfrac{3}{\sqrt{3}} = -\sqrt{3}$

Summary and Concept Review 3.1

1. $\theta = \dfrac{s}{r} = \dfrac{15}{5} = 3$ radians

3. $-101° \cdot \dfrac{\pi\ \text{rad}}{180°} \approx -1.76$ rad

5. $210° \cdot \dfrac{\pi\ \text{rad}}{180°} = \dfrac{7\pi}{6}$ rad

Summary and Concept Review 3.2

7. $57° \cdot \dfrac{\pi\ \text{rad}}{180°} \approx 0.9948$ rad

   $s = r\theta = 5(0.9948) = 4.97$ units

9. $r = \dfrac{s}{\theta} = \dfrac{96}{2.3} \approx 41.7391 \approx 41.74$ in.

   $A = \dfrac{1}{2}r^2\theta = \left(\dfrac{1}{2}\right)(41.7391)^2(2.3) \approx 2003.48$ in^2

11. a. $\omega = \dfrac{1.5\ \text{rev}}{\sec} \cdot \dfrac{2\pi\ \text{rad}}{1\ \text{rev}}$

      $= 3\pi \approx 9.4248$ rad/sec

   b. $V = (5\ \text{in.})\left(3\pi\dfrac{\text{rad}}{\sec}\right)\left(\dfrac{1\ \text{ft}}{12\ \text{in.}}\right) \approx 3.9$ ft/sec

   c. $\dfrac{60\ \text{ft}}{3.9\ \text{ft/sec}} \approx 15.4$ sec

Summary and Concept Review 3.3

13. $\dfrac{16\pi}{6} = 2\pi + \dfrac{4\pi}{6} = 2\pi + \dfrac{2\pi}{3}$ is in QII.

   Note that we rotate a complete revolution and an

   additional $\dfrac{2\pi}{3}$ radians.

   $\theta_r = \pi - \dfrac{2\pi}{3} = \dfrac{3\pi}{3} - \dfrac{2\pi}{3} = \dfrac{\pi}{3}$

   The associated point is $\left(-\dfrac{1}{2}, \dfrac{\sqrt{3}}{2}\right)$.

15. $(-0.7431)^2 + (-0.6691)^2 \approx 1$

   $\tan\theta = \dfrac{-0.6691}{-0.7431} \approx 0.9004$

Summary and Concept Review 3.4

17. $\sin t = -\dfrac{\sqrt{7}}{4};\ \cos t = \dfrac{3}{4};$

   $\tan t = \dfrac{-\dfrac{\sqrt{7}}{4}}{\dfrac{3}{4}} = -\dfrac{\sqrt{7}}{3};\ \cot t = -\dfrac{3}{\sqrt{7}} = -\dfrac{3\sqrt{7}}{7};$

   $\csc t = -\dfrac{4}{\sqrt{7}} = -\dfrac{4\sqrt{7}}{7};\ \sec t = \dfrac{4}{3}$

19. $\cos t = -0.7641;$ QII

   $t = \cos^{-1}(-0.7641) \approx 2.44$

Mixed Review

1. $\tan t = 1$ occurs at $t = \dfrac{\pi}{4}$ and $\dfrac{5\pi}{4}$.

3. $r = \sqrt{\left(-4\sqrt{3}\right)^2 + \left(-4\right)^2} = \sqrt{48 + 16} = \sqrt{64} = 8$

$\tan\theta = \dfrac{-4}{-4\sqrt{3}} = \dfrac{1}{\sqrt{3}} = \dfrac{\sqrt{3}}{3}$

$\theta = \tan^{-1}\dfrac{\sqrt{3}}{3} = \dfrac{7\pi}{6}$ in QIII.

$s = r\theta = (8)\left(\dfrac{7\pi}{6}\right) = \dfrac{28\pi}{3} \approx 29.3$ units

$A = \dfrac{1}{2}r^2\theta = \left(\dfrac{1}{2}\right)(8)^2\left(\dfrac{7\pi}{6}\right) \approx 117.3$ units^2

5. $\left(-\dfrac{\sqrt{2}}{2}\right)^2 + \left(\dfrac{\sqrt{2}}{2}\right)^2 = \dfrac{2}{4} + \dfrac{2}{4} = \dfrac{4}{4} = 1$

$\sin\theta = \dfrac{\sqrt{2}}{2}; \cos\theta = -\dfrac{\sqrt{2}}{2}; \tan\theta = \dfrac{\frac{\sqrt{2}}{2}}{-\frac{\sqrt{2}}{2}} = -1$

$\csc\theta = \dfrac{2}{\sqrt{2}} = \sqrt{2}; \sec\theta = -\sqrt{2}; \cot\theta = -1$

7. $\dfrac{37\pi}{4} = 4\cdot 2\pi + \dfrac{5\pi}{4}$ is in QIII.

Note that we rotate 4 complete revolutions and an additional $\dfrac{5\pi}{4}$ radians.

$\theta_r = \dfrac{5\pi}{4} - \pi = \dfrac{5\pi}{4} - \dfrac{4\pi}{4} = \dfrac{\pi}{4}$

$\cos\left(\dfrac{37\pi}{4}\right) = -\dfrac{\sqrt{2}}{2}$

9. a. $-135°\cdot\dfrac{\pi\text{ rad}}{180°} = -\dfrac{3\pi}{4}$ rad

b. $258.1°\cdot\dfrac{\pi\text{ rad}}{180°} \approx 4.5047$ rad

11. a. $\dfrac{7\pi}{3}\cdot\dfrac{180°}{\pi\text{ rad}} = 420°$

b. $-\dfrac{1}{2}\cdot\dfrac{180°}{\pi\text{ rad}} \approx -28.6°$

13. $\theta = \dfrac{3\pi}{7}; \theta + 2\pi k$

$k = 2; \dfrac{3\pi}{7} + 2\pi(2) = \dfrac{31\pi}{7}$

$k = 1; \dfrac{3\pi}{7} + 2\pi(1) = \dfrac{17\pi}{7}$

$k = -1; \dfrac{3\pi}{7} + 2\pi(-1) = -\dfrac{11\pi}{7}$

$k = -2; \dfrac{3\pi}{7} + 2\pi(-2) = -\dfrac{25\pi}{7}$

15. 35 of 60 minutes represents an angle of

$\dfrac{35}{60}\cdot 2\pi = \dfrac{7\pi}{6}$ rad

$A = \dfrac{1}{2}r^2\theta = \left(\dfrac{1}{2}\right)(3.5)^2\left(\dfrac{7\pi}{6}\right) \approx 22.45\text{ m}^2$

17. $\omega = \dfrac{10,000\text{ rev}}{\text{min}}\cdot\dfrac{2\pi\text{ rad}}{1\text{ rev}} = 20,000\pi$ rad/min

$V = (6\text{ cm})\left(20,000\pi\ \dfrac{\text{rad}}{\text{min}}\right) = 120,000\pi$ cm/min

Convert to kph.

$\dfrac{120,000\pi\text{ cm}}{\text{min}}\cdot\dfrac{60\text{ min}}{1\text{ hr}}\cdot\dfrac{1\text{ m}}{100\text{ cm}}\cdot\dfrac{1\text{ km}}{1000\text{ m}}$

≈ 226.2 kph

19. $x = \cos 8.25 \approx -0.3857$

$y = \sin 8.25 \approx 0.9226$

$(-0.3857,\ 0.9226)$

Practice Test

1. a. $\dfrac{7\pi}{6}$ is a QIII angle:

$\theta_r = \dfrac{7\pi}{6} - \pi = \dfrac{7\pi}{6} - \dfrac{6\pi}{6} = \dfrac{\pi}{6}$

b. $\dfrac{25\pi}{3} = 4\cdot 2\pi + \dfrac{\pi}{3}$ is in QI.

Note that we rotate 4 complete revolutions and an additional $\dfrac{\pi}{3}$ radians.

$\theta_r = \dfrac{\pi}{3}$

3. $\left(\dfrac{1}{3}\right)^2+\left(-\dfrac{2\sqrt{2}}{3}\right)^2=\dfrac{1}{9}+\dfrac{8}{9}=\dfrac{9}{9}=1$

$\sin\theta=-\dfrac{2\sqrt{2}}{3};\cos\theta=\dfrac{1}{3};$

$\tan\theta=\dfrac{-\dfrac{2\sqrt{2}}{3}}{\dfrac{1}{3}}=-2\sqrt{2};\cot\theta=\dfrac{1}{-2\sqrt{2}}=-\dfrac{\sqrt{2}}{4};$

$\csc\theta=-\dfrac{3}{2\sqrt{2}}=-\dfrac{3\sqrt{2}}{4};\sec\theta=3$

5. a. $\sin\left(\dfrac{7\pi}{6}\right)=-\dfrac{1}{2}$

   b. $\sec\left(\dfrac{11\pi}{6}\right)=\dfrac{1}{\cos\left(\dfrac{11\pi}{6}\right)}=\dfrac{1}{\dfrac{\sqrt{3}}{2}}=\dfrac{2\sqrt{3}}{3}$

   c. $\tan\left(\dfrac{3\pi}{4}\right)=\dfrac{\sin\left(\dfrac{3\pi}{4}\right)}{\cos\left(\dfrac{3\pi}{4}\right)}=\dfrac{\dfrac{\sqrt{2}}{2}}{-\dfrac{\sqrt{2}}{2}}=-1$

7. Point on circle: $\left(\dfrac{20}{29},\dfrac{21}{29}\right)$

   Other points:
   $\left(\dfrac{-20}{29},\dfrac{21}{29}\right),\left(\dfrac{-20}{29},\dfrac{-21}{29}\right),\left(\dfrac{20}{29},\dfrac{-21}{29}\right)$

9. a. $\sin t=-0.7568;$ QIII
   $t=\sin^{-1}(-0.7568)\approx-0.8584$
   In QIII, $\pi-(-0.8584)\approx4$

   b. $\sec t=-1.5;$ QII
   $t=\sec^{-1}(1.5)=\cos^{-1}\theta\left(\dfrac{1}{1.5}\right)\approx0.8411$
   In QII, $\pi-0.8411\approx2.3$

11. a. $9.29\cdot\dfrac{180°}{\pi\text{ rad}}\approx532.3°$

    b. $-\dfrac{3\pi}{2}\cdot\dfrac{180°}{\pi\text{ rad}}=-270°$

    c. $45\cdot\dfrac{180°}{\pi\text{ rad}}\approx2578.3°$

13. $\theta=\dfrac{s}{r}=\dfrac{2.73}{1.3}=2.1$ radians
    $2.1\cdot\dfrac{180°}{\pi\text{ rad}}\approx120.3°$

15. Excluded values include where $\sin t=0$:
    $t=\pi k,k\in\mathbb{Z}$

17. $\theta=\dfrac{s}{r}=\dfrac{2.3}{12.9}\approx0.1783$ radians
    $0.1783\cdot\dfrac{180°}{\pi\text{ rad}}\approx10.2°$

19. $x=\cos(-2.22)\approx-0.6046$
    $y=\sin(-2.22)\approx-0.7966$
    $(-0.6046,-0.7966)$

Calculator Exploration and Discovery

Exercise 1:
   a. $y=x$

   b. $45°$ Vertical angles are equal

   c. $270°-45°=225°$

   d. $y=-x$

   e. $180°-45°=135°$
   $360°-45°=315°$

   f. QI $\left(\dfrac{\sqrt{2}}{2},\dfrac{\sqrt{2}}{2}\right)$; QII $\left(-\dfrac{\sqrt{2}}{2},\dfrac{\sqrt{2}}{2}\right)$;

   QIII $\left(-\dfrac{\sqrt{2}}{2},-\dfrac{\sqrt{2}}{2}\right)$; QIV $\left(\dfrac{\sqrt{2}}{2},-\dfrac{\sqrt{2}}{2}\right)$

   $\sin45°=\dfrac{\sqrt{2}}{2};\sin135°=\dfrac{\sqrt{2}}{2};$

   $\sin225°=-\dfrac{\sqrt{2}}{2};\sin315°=-\dfrac{\sqrt{2}}{2}$

Strengthening Core Skills

1. $x = \cos\left(\dfrac{2\pi}{3}\right) = -\dfrac{1}{2}$

   $y = \sin\left(\dfrac{2\pi}{3}\right) = \dfrac{\sqrt{3}}{2}$

   $\left(-\dfrac{1}{2}, \dfrac{\sqrt{3}}{2}\right)$

3. $t = \dfrac{11\pi}{6}$ is between $\dfrac{3\pi}{2}$ and 2π; QIV

   $\sin t$ would be negative since $y < 0$.

Cumulative Review Chapters 1-3

1. $\sin t = -\dfrac{\sqrt{3}}{2}$

   $t = \sin^{-1}\left(-\dfrac{\sqrt{3}}{2}\right) = \dfrac{7\pi}{6}$ and $\dfrac{11\pi}{6}$

3. $90° - 67°22'39''$
   $= \left(89° + 59' + 60''\right) - 67°22'39''$
   $= \left(89° - 67°\right) + \left(59' - 22'\right) + \left(60'' - 39''\right)$
   $= 22° + 37' + 21''$
   $= 22°37'21''$

5. $\qquad A + B + C = 180$
   $\quad 9x + \left(6x + 4\right) + 7x = 180$
   $\qquad 9x + 6x + 4 + 7x = 180$
   $\qquad\qquad\quad 22x + 4 = 180$
   $\qquad\qquad\qquad 22x = 176$
   $\qquad\qquad\qquad\quad x = 8$

   $A = 9x° \qquad B = \left(6x + 4\right)° \qquad C = 7x°$
   $A = 9\left(8\right)° \quad B = \left[6\left(8\right) + 4\right]° \quad C = 7\left(8\right)°$
   $A = 72° \qquad B = 52° \qquad\quad C = 56°$

7. $90° - 31°15'18''$
   $= \left(89° + 59' + 60''\right) - 31°15'18''$
   $= \left(89° - 31°\right) + \left(59' - 15'\right) + \left(60'' - 18''\right)$
   $= 58° + 44' + 42''$
   $= 58°44'42''$

   $58°44'42'' = \left[58 + 44\left(\dfrac{1}{60}\right) + 42\left(\dfrac{1}{3600}\right)\right]°$
   $\qquad\qquad = 58.745°$

   $58.745° \cdot \dfrac{\pi}{180°} \approx 1.0253$ rad

9. $r = \sqrt{\left(-5\right)^2 + \left(-8\right)^2} = \sqrt{89}$

   $\sin\theta = \dfrac{-8}{\sqrt{89}} = -\dfrac{8\sqrt{89}}{89}; \;\cos\theta = \dfrac{-5}{\sqrt{89}} = -\dfrac{5\sqrt{89}}{89}$

   $\tan\theta = \dfrac{-8}{-5} = \dfrac{8}{5}; \;\cot\theta = \dfrac{5}{8}$

   $\csc\theta = -\dfrac{\sqrt{89}}{8}; \;\sec\theta = -\dfrac{\sqrt{89}}{5}$

11. $b = \sqrt{c^2 - a^2} = \sqrt{14^2 - 7^2} = \sqrt{147} \approx 12.12$ ft

   $\sin A = \dfrac{7}{14} = \dfrac{1}{2}; \;A = \sin^{-1}\dfrac{1}{2} = 30°$

   $B = 90° - 30° = 60°$

Angle	Side
$A = 30°$	$a = 7$ ft
$B = 60°$	$b \approx 12.12$ ft
$C = 90°$	$c = 14$ ft

13. a. $\omega = \dfrac{252\text{ rev}}{\text{min}} \cdot \dfrac{2\pi\text{ rad}}{1\text{ rev}} = 504\pi$ rad/min

   b. $V = \left(2\text{ in.}\right)\left(504\pi\;\dfrac{\text{rad}}{\text{min}}\right) = 1008\pi$ in./min

   Convert to mph.
   $\dfrac{1008\pi\text{ in.}}{\text{min}} \cdot \dfrac{60\text{ min}}{1\text{ hr}} \cdot \dfrac{1\text{ ft}}{12\text{ in.}} \cdot \dfrac{1\text{ mi}}{5280\text{ ft}} \approx 3$ mph

   The groceries are moving approximately 3 mph.

15. $\dfrac{\sin x \cos x + \cos x}{\sin x + \sin^2 x} = \cot x$

   $\dfrac{\cos x\left(\sin x + 1\right)}{\sin x\left(1 + \sin x\right)} = \cot x$

   $\dfrac{\cos x}{\sin x} = \cot x$

   $\cot x = \cot x$

17. a. $s = r\theta = 15\left(1.2\right) = 18$ m

   b. $A = \dfrac{1}{2}\left(15\right)^2\left(1.2\right) = 135$ m^2

19. $\theta = 1000°; \;\theta + 360°k$

   $k = -3; 1000° + 360°\left(-3\right) = -80°$

   $k = -4; 1000° + 360°\left(-4\right) = -440°$

21. $38° - 19° = 19°$

$$19° \cdot \frac{\pi \text{ rad}}{180°} = \frac{19\pi}{180} \text{ rad}$$

$$s = r\theta = 3960\left(\frac{19\pi}{180}\right) \approx 1313 \text{ mi}$$

1313 miles separate the two cities.

23. $(\sin\theta)(\tan\theta) > 0$

Since $(\cos^2\theta)(\sin\theta) < 0 \Rightarrow \sin\theta < 0,$

then $(\sin\theta)(\tan\theta) > 0 \Rightarrow \tan\theta < 0$

$\Rightarrow \cos\theta > 0.$ θ is in QIV.

25. a. $\sec 360° = \dfrac{1}{\cos 360°} = \dfrac{1}{1} = 1$

   b. $\tan 270° = \dfrac{\sin 270°}{\cos 270°} = \dfrac{-1}{0}$ is undefined.

   c. $\csc\pi = \dfrac{1}{\sin\pi} = \dfrac{1}{0}$ is undefined.

   d. $\cot\dfrac{\pi}{2} = \dfrac{\cos\dfrac{\pi}{2}}{\sin\dfrac{\pi}{2}} = \dfrac{0}{1} = 0$

<u>4.1 Exercises</u>

1. increasing

3. $(-\infty,\infty); [-1,1]$

5. Answers will vary.

7.

t	$\cos t$
π	-1
$\dfrac{7\pi}{6}$	$-\dfrac{\sqrt{3}}{2}$
$\dfrac{5\pi}{4}$	$-\dfrac{\sqrt{2}}{2}$
$\dfrac{4\pi}{3}$	$-\dfrac{1}{2}$
$\dfrac{3\pi}{2}$	0
$\dfrac{5\pi}{3}$	$\dfrac{1}{2}$
$\dfrac{7\pi}{4}$	$\dfrac{\sqrt{2}}{2}$
$\dfrac{11\pi}{6}$	$\dfrac{\sqrt{3}}{2}$
2π	1

9. a. $t = \left(\dfrac{\pi}{6}+10\pi\right)$; II

 b. $t = -\dfrac{\pi}{4}$; V

 c. $t = -\dfrac{15\pi}{4}$; IV

 d. $t = 13\pi$; I

 e. $t = \dfrac{21\pi}{2}$; III

11. $y = \sin t$ for $t \in \left[-\dfrac{3\pi}{2}, \dfrac{\pi}{2}\right]$

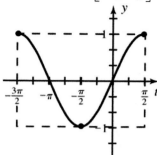

13. $y = \cos t$ for $t \in \left[-\dfrac{\pi}{2}, 2\pi\right]$

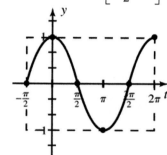

15. $y = 3\sin t$
Amplitude 3, Period 2π

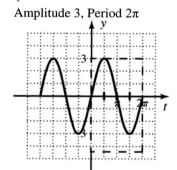

17. $y = -2\cos t$
Amplitude 2, Period 2π

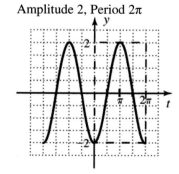

19. $y = \dfrac{1}{2}\sin t$

Amplitude $\dfrac{1}{2}$, Period 2π

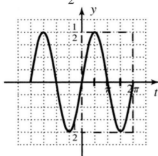

21. $y = -\sin(2t)$

Amplitude 1, Period $\dfrac{2\pi}{2} = \pi$

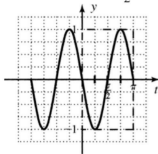

23. $y = 0.8\cos(2t)$

Amplitude 0.8, Period $\dfrac{2\pi}{2} = \pi$

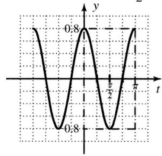

25. $f(t) = 4\cos\left(\dfrac{1}{2}t\right)$

Amplitude 4, Period $\dfrac{2\pi}{\frac{1}{2}} = 4\pi$

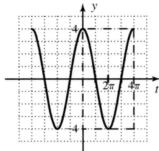

27. $f(t) = 3\sin(4\pi t)$

Amplitude 3, Period $\dfrac{2\pi}{4\pi} = \dfrac{1}{2}$

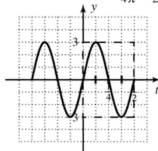

29. $y = 4\sin\left(\dfrac{5\pi}{3}t\right)$

Amplitude 4, Period $\dfrac{2\pi}{\frac{5\pi}{3}} = 2\pi \cdot \dfrac{3}{5\pi} = \dfrac{6}{5}$

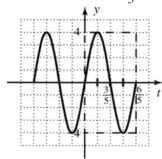

31. $f(t) = 2\sin(256\pi t)$

Amplitude 2, Period $\dfrac{2\pi}{256\pi} = \dfrac{1}{128}$

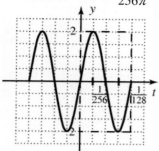

33. $y = -2\cos(4t)$

$|A| = 2,\ P = \dfrac{2\pi}{|4|} = \dfrac{\pi}{2}$ Graph goes through

$(0, -2)$ and matches graph g.

35. $y = 3\sin(2t)$

$|A| = 3,\ P = \dfrac{2\pi}{|2|} = \pi$ Graph goes through $(0, 0)$

and matches graph f.

37. $f(t) = \dfrac{3}{4}\cos(0.4t)$

$|A| = \dfrac{3}{4},\ P = \dfrac{2\pi}{|0.4|} = 5\pi$ Graph goes through

$\left(0, \dfrac{3}{4}\right)$ and matches graph b.

39. $y = 4\sin(144\pi t)$

$|A| = 4,\ P = \dfrac{2\pi}{|144\pi|} = \dfrac{1}{72}$ Graph goes through

$(0, 0)$ and matches graph d.

41. The amplitude is $\dfrac{3}{4}$ and the graph goes through

$\left(0, -\dfrac{3}{4}\right)$, so $A = -\dfrac{3}{4}$.

The period is $\dfrac{\pi}{4}$.

$\dfrac{\pi}{4} = \dfrac{2\pi}{B} \Rightarrow \pi B = 8\pi \Rightarrow B = 8$

$y = -\dfrac{3}{4}\cos(8t)$

43. The amplitude is 6 and the graph goes through $(0, 6)$, so $A = 6$.

The period is 3.

$3 = \dfrac{2\pi}{B} \Rightarrow 3B = 2\pi \Rightarrow B = \dfrac{2\pi}{3}$

$y = 6\cos\dfrac{2\pi}{3}t$

45. The amplitude is 3, and the graph first increases after $(0, 0)$, so $A = 3$.

The period is 10π.

$10\pi = \dfrac{2\pi}{B} \Rightarrow 10\pi B = 2\pi \Rightarrow B = \dfrac{1}{5}$ $y = 3\sin\left(\dfrac{1}{5}t\right)$

47. The amplitude is $\dfrac{3}{22}$, and the graph first

decreases after $(0, 0)$, so $A = -\dfrac{3}{22}$.

The period is 0.2.

$0.2 = \dfrac{2\pi}{B} \Rightarrow 0.2B = 2\pi \Rightarrow B = 10\pi$

$y = -\dfrac{3}{22}\sin(10\pi t)$

49. The red graph is $y = -\cos x$, and the blue graph is $y = \sin x$. The graphs cross at $x = \dfrac{3\pi}{4}$ and $\dfrac{7\pi}{4}$.

51. The red graph is $y = -2\cos x$, and the blue graph is $y = 2\sin(3x)$. The graphs cross at

$x = \dfrac{3\pi}{8}, \dfrac{3\pi}{4}, \dfrac{7\pi}{8}, \dfrac{11\pi}{8}, \dfrac{7\pi}{4}$ and $\dfrac{15\pi}{8}$.

53. a. $A_c = \pi r^2 = \pi(10)^2$
$= 100\pi$ cm$^2 \approx 314.2$ cm^2

b. $A_4 = \dfrac{nr^2}{2}\sin\left(\dfrac{2\pi}{n}\right)$

$= \dfrac{(4)(10)^2}{2}\sin\left(\dfrac{2\pi}{4}\right)$

$= 200\sin\dfrac{\pi}{2}$

$= 200$ cm^2

53. b. (continued)
A four-sided regular polygon is a square.
Since the area of a square is s^2,
$$s^2 = 200 \Rightarrow s = \sqrt{200} = 10\sqrt{2} \text{ cm}$$

Also note that the diagonals of the square are perpendicular and form diameters of the circle. Let r be the radius of the circle and one-half the length of a diagonal.
$$s^2 = r^2 + r^2 = 2r^2, \text{ so}$$
$$s = r\sqrt{2} = 10\sqrt{2} \text{ cm}$$

55. a. The height from crest to trough is 3 ft.

b. The first cycle ends at $x = 80$, so the wavelength is 80 mi.

c. The amplitude is 1.5, so $A = 1.5$.
The period is 80.
$$80 = \frac{2\pi}{B} \Rightarrow 80B = 2\pi \Rightarrow B = \frac{\pi}{40}$$
The equation is $h = 1.5\cos\left(\dfrac{\pi}{40}x\right)$.

57. a. The amplitude is 4 and the graph goes through $(0, -4)$, so $A = -4$.
The period is 24.
$$24 = \frac{2\pi}{B} \Rightarrow 24B = 2\pi \Rightarrow B = \frac{\pi}{12}.$$
The equation is $D = -4\cos\dfrac{\pi}{12}t$.

b. $D(11) = -4\cos\left(\dfrac{\pi}{12} \cdot 11\right) \approx 3.86$

c. Midnight corresponds to $t = 18$.
At $t = 18$, the deviation is 0, so the temperature is 72°.

59. a. The amplitude is 15, so $A = 15$.
The period is 2.
$$2 = \frac{2\pi}{B} \Rightarrow 2B = 2\pi \Rightarrow B = \pi$$
The equation is $D = 15\cos(\pi t)$.

b. The period is 2, so the height at $t = 6.5$ is the same as at $t = 4.5$, which is zero. The tail is at center.

c. Only one cycle is completed every two seconds, so the shark is probably swimming at a leisurely pace.

61. a. Graph a. The energy is highest when closest to the Sun, and this is at $t = 0$ for graph a.

b. This graph is at height 62.5 at about $t = 76$ days.

c. The period is 96 days.

63. a. Wavelength: $\dfrac{2\pi}{\dfrac{\pi}{240}} = 2\pi \cdot \dfrac{240}{\pi} = 480$ nm
This is in the blue range.

b. $\dfrac{2\pi}{\dfrac{\pi}{310}} = 2\pi \cdot \dfrac{310}{\pi} = 620$ nm
This is in the orange range.

65. $A = 30; \quad P = \dfrac{1}{25}$
$$\frac{2\pi}{\omega} = \frac{1}{25} \Rightarrow \omega = 50\pi$$
The equation is $I = 30\sin(50\pi t)$.
$$I(0.045) = 30\sin(50\pi \cdot 0.045) \approx 21.2 \text{ amps}$$

67. All the functions graphed in this section have average value zero.

t	0	$\dfrac{\pi}{2}$	π	$\dfrac{3\pi}{2}$	2π
y	3	5	3	1	3

The average value is $\dfrac{(1+5)}{2} = 3$.
The graph is shifted up by 3 because of the +3 on the end of the function.
The average value of $y = -2\cos t + 1$ is 1.
The amplitude is "centered" on the average value.

69. The function with the largest coefficient of t has the shortest period: $g(t)$.

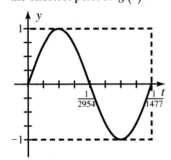

71. First, convert the latitude to decimal degrees, then to radians.

$$46°14'24'' = \left[46 + 14\left(\frac{1}{60}\right) + 24\left(\frac{1}{3600}\right) \right]^{°}$$
$$= 46.24°$$
$$46.24° \cdot \frac{\pi \text{ rad}}{180°} \approx 0.8070 \text{ rad}$$
$$s = r\theta = 3960(0.8070) \approx 3196 \text{ mi}$$

Invercargill is approximately 3196 miles from the equator.

73. This is a 30-60-90 triangle, so the longer leg is $\sqrt{3}$ times the shorter. The shorter leg is $\frac{100}{\sqrt{3}}$ yd.

The hypotenuse is twice as long as the shorter leg, or $\frac{200}{\sqrt{3}} = \frac{200\sqrt{3}}{3} \approx 115.5$ yd.

75. Let h be the height of the pole.

$$\tan 78° = \frac{h}{60}$$
$$h = 60 \tan 78° \approx 282.28 \text{ ft or } 282 \text{ ft, 3 in.}$$

The pole is 282 feet, 3 inches tall.

Technology Highlight

Exercise 1:

There is no asymptotic behavior at these zeroes.

4.2 Exercises

1. π; $P = \dfrac{\pi}{|B|}$

3. odd; $-f(t)$; -0.268

5. a. Use reciprocals of standard values.

   b. Use reciprocals of given values.

7. $y = \csc(2t)$

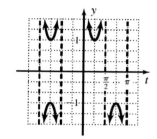

9. $y = \sec\left(\dfrac{1}{2}t\right)$

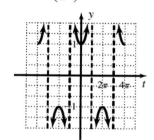

11. $y = 3\csc t$

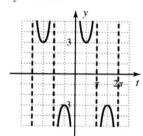

13. $y = 2 \sec t$

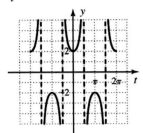

15.

t	π	$\dfrac{7\pi}{6}$	$\dfrac{5\pi}{4}$	$\dfrac{4\pi}{3}$	$\dfrac{3\pi}{2}$
$\tan t = \dfrac{y}{x}$	0	$\dfrac{1}{\sqrt{3}}$	1	$\sqrt{3}$	undef.

17. $\dfrac{\pi}{2} \approx 1.6$; $\dfrac{\pi}{4} \approx 0.8$; $\dfrac{\pi}{6} \approx 0.5$;

   $\sqrt{2} \approx 1.4$; $\dfrac{\sqrt{2}}{2} \approx 0.7$; $\dfrac{2}{\sqrt{3}} \approx 1.2$

19. a. $\tan\left(-\dfrac{\pi}{4}\right) = \dfrac{-\dfrac{\sqrt{2}}{2}}{\dfrac{\sqrt{2}}{2}} = -1$

   b. $\cot\left(\dfrac{\pi}{6}\right) = \dfrac{\dfrac{\sqrt{3}}{2}}{\dfrac{1}{2}} = \sqrt{3}$

   c. $\cot\left(\dfrac{3\pi}{4}\right) = \dfrac{-\dfrac{\sqrt{2}}{2}}{\dfrac{\sqrt{2}}{2}} = -1$

   d. $\tan\left(\dfrac{\pi}{3}\right) = \dfrac{\dfrac{\sqrt{3}}{2}}{\dfrac{1}{2}} = \sqrt{3}$

21. a. $\tan\dfrac{7\pi}{4} = -1$, so $\tan^{-1}(-1) = \dfrac{7\pi}{4}$

   b. $\cot\dfrac{7\pi}{6} = \sqrt{3}$, so $\cot^{-1}\sqrt{3} = \dfrac{7\pi}{6}$

   c. $\cot\dfrac{5\pi}{3} = -\dfrac{1}{\sqrt{3}}$, so $\cot^{-1}-\dfrac{1}{\sqrt{3}} = \dfrac{5\pi}{3}$

   d. $\tan\dfrac{3\pi}{4} = -1$, so $\tan^{-1}(-1) = \dfrac{3\pi}{4}$

23.

t	π	$\dfrac{7\pi}{6}$	$\dfrac{5\pi}{4}$	$\dfrac{4\pi}{3}$	$\dfrac{3\pi}{2}$
$\cot t = \dfrac{x}{y}$	undef.	$\sqrt{3}$	1	$\dfrac{1}{\sqrt{3}}$	0

25. $\dfrac{11\pi}{24} - \pi = -\dfrac{13\pi}{24}$, $\dfrac{11\pi}{24} + \pi = \dfrac{35\pi}{24}$,

   and $\dfrac{11\pi}{24} + 2\pi = \dfrac{59\pi}{24}$.

27. $1.5 - \pi \approx -1.6$, $1.5 + \pi \approx 4.6$,

   and $1.5 + 2\pi \approx 7.8$.

29. $t = \dfrac{\pi}{10}$; $\tan t = \tan\dfrac{\pi}{10} \approx 0.3249$.

   The period is π, so all solutions are given by

   $\dfrac{\pi}{10} + \pi k, k \in Z$.

31. $t = \dfrac{\pi}{12}$; $\cot t = \cot\dfrac{\pi}{12} \approx 3.7321$

   and $2 + \sqrt{3} \approx 3.7321$

   The period is π, so all solutions are given by

   $\dfrac{\pi}{12} + \pi k, k \in Z$.

33. $f(t) = 2\tan t$; $[-2\pi, 2\pi]$

   $P = \pi$

   Asymptotes at $x = -\dfrac{3\pi}{2}, -\dfrac{\pi}{2}, \dfrac{\pi}{2}$ and $\dfrac{3\pi}{2}$.

   Zeros at $x = -2\pi, -\pi, 0, \pi, -2\pi$.

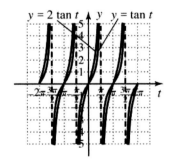

35. $h(t) = 3\cot t;\ [-2\pi, 2\pi]$

Period is π.

Asymptotes at $x = -2\pi, -\pi, 0, \pi, -2\pi$.

Zeros at $x = -\dfrac{3\pi}{2}, -\dfrac{\pi}{2}, \dfrac{\pi}{2}, \dfrac{3\pi}{2}$.

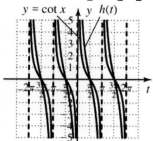

37. $y = \tan(2t);\ \left[-\dfrac{\pi}{2}, \dfrac{\pi}{2}\right]$

Period is $\dfrac{\pi}{2}$.

Asymptotes at $x = -\dfrac{\pi}{4}, \dfrac{\pi}{4}$.

Zeros at $x = -\dfrac{\pi}{2}, 0, \dfrac{\pi}{2}$.

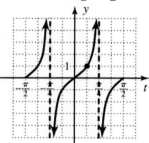

39. $y = \cot(4t);\ \left[-\dfrac{\pi}{4}, \dfrac{\pi}{4}\right]$

Period is $\dfrac{\pi}{4}$.

Asymptotes at $x = -\dfrac{\pi}{4}, 0, \dfrac{\pi}{4}$.

Zeros at $x = -\dfrac{\pi}{8}, \dfrac{\pi}{8}$.

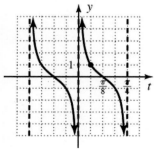

41. $y = 2\tan(4t);\ \left[-\dfrac{\pi}{4}, \dfrac{\pi}{4}\right]$

Period is $\dfrac{\pi}{4}$.

Asymptotes at $x = -\dfrac{\pi}{8}, \dfrac{\pi}{8}$.

Zeros at $x = -\dfrac{\pi}{4}, 0, \dfrac{\pi}{4}$.

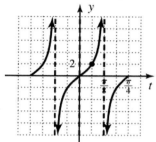

43. $y = 5\cot\left(\dfrac{1}{3}t\right);\ [-3\pi, 3\pi]$

Period is $\dfrac{\pi}{1/3} = 3\pi$.

Asymptotes at $x = -3\pi, 0, 3\pi$.

Zeros at $x = -\dfrac{3\pi}{2}, \dfrac{3\pi}{2}$.

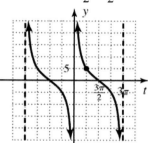

45. $y = 3\tan(2\pi t);\ \left[-\dfrac{1}{2}, \dfrac{1}{2}\right]$

Period is $\dfrac{\pi}{2\pi} = \dfrac{1}{2}$.

Asymptotes at $x = -\dfrac{1}{4}, \dfrac{1}{4}$.

Zeros at $x = -\dfrac{1}{2}, 0, \dfrac{1}{2}$.

45. (continued)

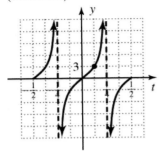

47. $f(t) = 2\cot(\pi t); \; [-1,1]$

Period is $\dfrac{\pi}{\pi} = 1$.

Asymptotes at $x = -1, 0, 1$.

Zeros at $x = -\dfrac{1}{2}, \dfrac{1}{2}$,

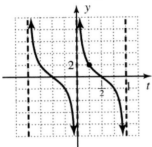

49. $y = 2\csc\left(\dfrac{1}{2}t\right)$

No amplitude; Period is $\dfrac{2\pi}{1/2} = 4\pi$.

Graph has maxs and mins at height 2 and matches graph h.

51. $y = \sec(8\pi t)$

No amplitude; Period is $\dfrac{2\pi}{8\pi} = \dfrac{1}{4}$.

Graph has maxs and mins at height 1 and matches graph d.

53. The maxs and mins are at height 2, so $|A| = 2$.

The first portion to the right of the y-axis is above the x-axis, so $A = 2$.

The period is $\dfrac{2}{5}$.

$\dfrac{2}{5} = \dfrac{2\pi}{B} \Rightarrow 2B = 10\pi \Rightarrow B = 5\pi$

$y = 2\csc(5\pi t)$

55. The period is 2π.

$2\pi = \dfrac{\pi}{B} \Rightarrow 2\pi B = \pi \Rightarrow B = \dfrac{1}{2}$

The equation is $y = A\tan\left(\dfrac{1}{2}t\right)$.

$\dfrac{\pi}{2}, 3$ is on the graph, so

$3 = A\tan\left(\dfrac{1}{2} \cdot \dfrac{\pi}{2}\right) \Rightarrow 3 = A\tan\left(\dfrac{\pi}{4}\right) = A.$

The equation is $y = 3\tan\dfrac{1}{2}t$.

57. The period is $\dfrac{3}{2}$.

$\dfrac{3}{2} = \dfrac{\pi}{B} \Rightarrow 3B = 2\pi \Rightarrow B = \dfrac{2\pi}{3}$

The equation is $y = A\cot\left(\dfrac{2\pi}{3}t\right)$.

$\dfrac{1}{4}, 2\sqrt{3}$ is on the graph, so

$2\sqrt{3} = A\cot\left(\dfrac{2\pi}{3} \cdot \dfrac{1}{4}\right) = A\cot\left(\dfrac{\pi}{6}\right) = A\sqrt{3}$

and $A = 2$.

The equation is $y = 2\cot\left(\dfrac{2\pi}{3}t\right)$.

59. Graphing $Y_1 = \cos(3t)$ and $Y_2 = \tan t$, we see the graphs intersect at $t = \dfrac{\pi}{8} \; (\approx 0.3926)$ and

$\dfrac{3\pi}{8} \; (\approx 1.1781)$.

61. Substitute $u = 40°$, $v = 65°$, and $d = 100$ and solve for h.

$h = \dfrac{d}{\cot u - \cot v}$

$= \dfrac{100}{\cot 40° - \cot 65°}$

≈ 137.8 ft

63. a. Perimeter (circumference) of a circle is
$P = 2\pi r = 2\pi(10) = 20\pi$ cm ≈ 62.8 cm.

b. When $n = 4$, the polygon is a square.
The radius of the circle is half the length of a side, so the sides have length 20 cm and the perimeter is $4(20) = 80$ cm.

c. Substitute $r = 10$ and each value of n into the given formula.

n	10	20	30	100
P	64.984	63.354	63.063	62.853

As n gets larger, the perimeter approaches $20\pi \approx 62.8$ cm.

65. a.

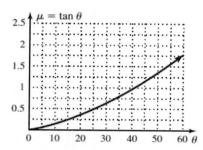

No, the block will not slide at $30°$.
The smallest angle is about $35°$.

b. $\mu = \tan 46.5° = 1.05$

c. This would require an angle steeper than $68.2°$, which is quite steep. Something like soft rubber on sandstone might have a coefficient that high.

67. a. $\tan(80°) \approx 5.67$ units

b. $\theta = \tan^{-1}(16.35) \approx 86.5°$

c. Yes, it can be any length. The range of $\tan\theta$ is $(-\infty, \infty)$.

d. As θ gets close to $90°$, tangent of the angle increases without bound, as does the length of the line segment.

69. a. When $n = 4$, the polygon is a square.
The radius of the circle $(r = 4)$ is half the length of a side, so the sides have length 8 m and the area is $8^2 = 64$ m^2.

$$A = nr^2 \sin\left(\frac{\pi}{n}\right)\sec\left(\frac{\pi}{n}\right)$$
$$= 4 \cdot 4^2 \sin\left(\frac{\pi}{4}\right)\sec\left(\frac{\pi}{4}\right)$$
$$= 64 \cdot \frac{\sqrt{2}}{2} \cdot \frac{2}{\sqrt{2}}$$
$$= 64 \text{ m}^2$$

b. $A = nr^2 \sin\left(\frac{\pi}{n}\right)\sec\left(\frac{\pi}{n}\right)$
$$= 12 \cdot 4^2 \sin\left(\frac{\pi}{12}\right)\sec\left(\frac{\pi}{12}\right)$$
$$\approx 51.45 \text{ m}^2$$

71. $\sin 0.6662394325 \approx 0.6180339887 \approx \dfrac{-1+\sqrt{5}}{2}$

$\cos x = \tan x$ can be rewritten as $\sin^2 x = 1 - \sin x$, which can in turn be converted to $\sin^2(-x) = 1 + \sin(-x)$, which is the basis of the golden ratio.

73. Let d be the distance from the tent to the stake.
$d = \sqrt{4^2 - 2^2} = \sqrt{12} \approx 3.46$ ft

75. $\dfrac{29\pi}{6} - 2 \cdot 2\pi = \dfrac{29\pi}{6} - \dfrac{24\pi}{6} = \dfrac{5\pi}{6}$ (QII)

To get to $\dfrac{29\pi}{6}$, we make two complete revolutions and then continue to $\dfrac{5\pi}{6}$.

$\theta_r = \pi - \dfrac{5\pi}{6} = \dfrac{6\pi}{6} - \dfrac{5\pi}{6} = \dfrac{\pi}{6}$

$\cos\left(\dfrac{29\pi}{6}\right) = -\dfrac{\sqrt{3}}{2}$

77. $\theta_r = 212° - 180° = 32°$ (QIII)
The other solution is $360° - 32° = 328°$ (QIV).

Mid-Chapter Check

1. $y = \cot t$ is decreasing on its domain.

   $y = \cos t$ begins at $(0,1)$ in the interval $t \in [0, 2\pi)$.

3. a. $\cot 60° = \dfrac{\cos 60°}{\sin 60°} = \dfrac{\frac{1}{2}}{\frac{\sqrt{3}}{2}} = \dfrac{1}{\sqrt{3}}$

   b. $\theta_r = 2\pi - \dfrac{7\pi}{4} = \dfrac{8\pi}{4} - \dfrac{7\pi}{4} = \dfrac{\pi}{4}$ (QIV)

   $\sin\left(\dfrac{7\pi}{4}\right) = -\dfrac{\sqrt{2}}{2}$

5. $y = \cos t$ and $y = \sec t$ are even functions.

7. $y = 3\tan\left(\dfrac{\pi}{2}t\right);\ [-2\pi, 2\pi]$

   Period is $\dfrac{\pi}{\pi/2} = 2$.

   Asymptotes at $x = -5, -3, -1, 1, 3, 5$.
   Zeros at $x = -6, -4, -2, 0, 2, 4, 6$.

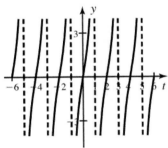

9. a. $\theta = 5.94$ is between $\dfrac{3\pi}{2}$ and 2π; QIV

   b. $2\pi - 5.94 \approx 0.343$

   c. $\sin t$ and $\tan t$ are negative in QIV.

4.3 Exercises

1. $y = A\sin(Bt + C) + D;\ y = A\cos(Bt + C) + D$

3. up; right

5. Answers will vary.

7. $y = 2\sin(4t) + 3;\ [0, \pi]$

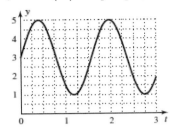

9. $y = 10\cos\left(\dfrac{\pi}{6}t\right) - 5;\ [-6, 18]$

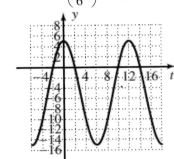

11. $y = -4\sin\left(\dfrac{\pi}{2}t\right) + 4;\ [-4, 4]$

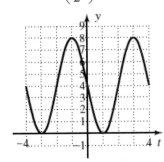

13. $y = \dfrac{1}{2}\cos\left(t - \dfrac{\pi}{2}\right)$; $[0, 3\pi]$

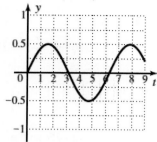

15. $y = 3\sin\left(t + \dfrac{\pi}{3}\right)$; $[-\pi, 2\pi]$

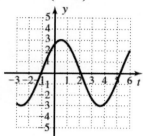

17. $y = 3\sin(4t - \pi)$; $[0, \pi]$

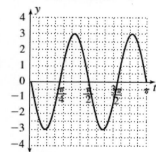

19. $f(t) = 25\sin\left[\dfrac{\pi}{4}(t - 2)\right] + 55$

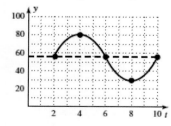

21. $h(t) = 1500\sin\left(\dfrac{\pi}{8}t + \dfrac{\pi}{4}\right) + 7000$

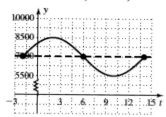

23. $y = 120\sin\left[\dfrac{\pi}{12}(t - 6)\right]$

$|A| = 120$; $P = \dfrac{2\pi}{\dfrac{\pi}{12}} = 24$

HS: 6 units right
VS: none

PI: $0 \le \dfrac{\pi}{12}(t - 6) < 2\pi$

$0 \le t - 6 < 24$

$6 \le t < 30$

25. $h(t) = \sin\left(\dfrac{\pi}{6}t - \dfrac{\pi}{3}\right) = \sin\left[\dfrac{\pi}{6}(t - 2)\right]$

$|A| = 1$; $P = \dfrac{2\pi}{\dfrac{\pi}{6}} = 12$

HS: 2 units right
VS: none

PI: $0 \le \dfrac{\pi}{6}t - \dfrac{\pi}{3} < 2\pi$

$\dfrac{\pi}{3} \le \dfrac{\pi}{6}t < \dfrac{7\pi}{3}$

$2 \le t < 14$

27. $y = \sin\left(\dfrac{\pi}{4}t - \dfrac{\pi}{6}\right) = \sin\left[\dfrac{\pi}{4}\left(t - \dfrac{2}{3}\right)\right]$

$|A| = 1$; $P = \dfrac{2\pi}{\dfrac{\pi}{4}} = 8$

HS: $\dfrac{2}{3}$ unit right
VS: none

PI: $0 \le \dfrac{\pi}{4}t - \dfrac{\pi}{6} < 2\pi$

$\dfrac{\pi}{6} \le \dfrac{\pi}{4}t < \dfrac{13\pi}{6}$

$\dfrac{2}{3} \le t < \dfrac{26}{3}$

29. $f(t) = 24.5 \sin\left[\dfrac{\pi}{10}(t - 2.5)\right] + 15.5$

$|A| = 24.5; \ P = \dfrac{2\pi}{\dfrac{\pi}{10}} = 20$

HS: 2.5 units right

VS: 15.5 units up

PI: $0 \le \dfrac{\pi}{10}(t - 2.5) < 2\pi$

$0 \le t - 2.5 < 20$

$2.5 \le t < 22.5$

31. $g(t) = 28\sin\left(\dfrac{\pi}{6}t - \dfrac{5\pi}{12}\right) + 92$

$= 28\sin\left[\dfrac{\pi}{6}\left(t - \dfrac{5}{2}\right)\right] + 92$

$|A| = 28; \ P = \dfrac{2\pi}{\dfrac{\pi}{6}} = 12$

HS: $\dfrac{5}{2}$ units right

VS: 92 units up

PI: $0 \le \dfrac{\pi}{6}t - \dfrac{5\pi}{12} < 2\pi$

$\dfrac{5\pi}{12} \le \dfrac{\pi}{6}t < \dfrac{29\pi}{12}$

$\dfrac{5}{2} \le t < \dfrac{29}{2}$

33. $y = 2500\sin\left(\dfrac{\pi}{4}t + \dfrac{\pi}{12}\right) + 3150$

$= 2500\sin\left[\dfrac{\pi}{4}\left(t + \dfrac{1}{3}\right)\right] + 3150$

$|A| = 2500; \ P = \dfrac{2\pi}{\dfrac{\pi}{4}} = 8$

HS: $\dfrac{1}{3}$ unit left

VS: 3150 units up

PI: $0 \le \dfrac{\pi}{4}t + \dfrac{\pi}{12} < 2\pi$

$-\dfrac{\pi}{12} \le \dfrac{\pi}{4}t < \dfrac{23\pi}{12}$

$-\dfrac{1}{3} \le t < \dfrac{23}{3}$

35. Max and min are 600 and 100, so

$|A| = \dfrac{600 - 100}{2} = \dfrac{500}{2} = 250.$

Average value is $600 - 250 = 350.$

$P = 24$, so $B = \dfrac{2\pi}{24} = \dfrac{\pi}{12} \quad y = 250\sin\left(\dfrac{\pi}{12}t\right) + 350$

37. Max and min are 18 and 8, so

$|A| = \dfrac{18 - 8}{2} = \dfrac{10}{2} = 5.$

The primary cycle would start at -25, so the horizontal shift is 25 units left.

The average value is $18 - 5 = 13.$

$P = 100$, so $B = \dfrac{2\pi}{100} = \dfrac{\pi}{50}$

$y = 5\sin\left[\dfrac{\pi}{50}(t + 25)\right] + 13$

$= 5\sin\left(\dfrac{\pi}{50}t + \dfrac{\pi}{2}\right) + 13$

39. Max and min are 11 and 3, so

$|A| = \dfrac{11 - 3}{2} = \dfrac{8}{2} = 4.$

The primary cycle begins at -45, so the horizontal shift is 45 units left.

The average value is $11 - 4 = 7.$

$P = 360$, so $B = \dfrac{2\pi}{360} = \dfrac{\pi}{180}$

$y = 4\sin\left[\dfrac{\pi}{180}(t + 45)\right] + 7$

$= 4\sin\left(\dfrac{\pi}{180}t + \dfrac{\pi}{4}\right) + 7$

41. $y = 5\sec\left[\dfrac{1}{3}\left(t + \dfrac{3\pi}{2}\right)\right] + 2; \ [-3\pi, 6\pi]$

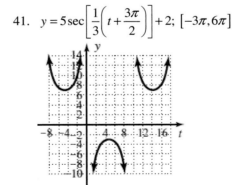

43. $y = 0.7\csc\left(\pi t - \dfrac{\pi}{4}\right) - 1.2;\ [-1.25, 1.75]$

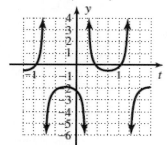

45. $y = 0.5\tan\left[\dfrac{\pi}{4}(t+2)\right]$

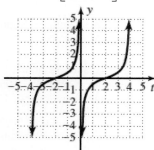

47. $y = 10\cot(2t - 1)$

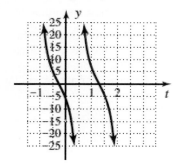

49. a. $A = \dfrac{2A}{B} = \dfrac{2(5)}{4} = \dfrac{5}{2} = 2.5$

   b. $A = \dfrac{2A}{B} = \dfrac{2(4)}{\dfrac{\pi}{3}} = \dfrac{24}{\pi}$

   c. $4\sin\left(\dfrac{\pi}{3}t - \dfrac{2\pi}{3}\right) = 4\sin\left[\dfrac{\pi}{3}(t-2)\right]$

   This is equivalent to the graph of

   $y = 4\sin\left(\dfrac{\pi}{3}t\right)$ moved 2 units to the right.

   So, the area of $y = 4\sin\left(\dfrac{\pi}{3}t - \dfrac{2\pi}{3}\right)$

   between 2 and 5 is equal to the area of

49. c.   (continued)

   $y = 4\sin\left(\dfrac{\pi}{3}t\right)$ between 0 and 3, which

   we found in part b) to be $\dfrac{24}{\pi}$.

51. $T(t) = 4\cos\left(\dfrac{\pi}{12}t + \dfrac{9\pi}{12}\right) + 22$

   a. $P = \dfrac{2\pi}{\dfrac{\pi}{12}} = 24$

   The period is 24 hours.

   b.   Amplitude is 4 and the graph is translated
        22 units up, so the average minimum
        temperature is $22° - 4° = 18°,$ and the
        average maximum temperature is
        $22° + 4° = 26°.$

   c.   Solve to find at what time t the average
        temperature is 18°C.

   $$18 = 4\cos\left(\dfrac{\pi}{12}t + \dfrac{9\pi}{12}\right) + 22$$

   $$-4 = 4\cos\left(\dfrac{\pi}{12}t + \dfrac{9\pi}{12}\right)$$

   $$-1 = \cos\left(\dfrac{\pi}{12}t + \dfrac{9\pi}{12}\right)$$

   $$\cos^{-1}(-1) = \dfrac{\pi}{12}t + \dfrac{9\pi}{12}$$

   $$\pi = \dfrac{\pi}{12}t + \dfrac{9\pi}{12}$$

   $$\dfrac{\pi}{4} = \dfrac{\pi}{12}t$$

   $$3 = t$$

   Solve to find at what time t the average
   temperature is 26°C.

   $$26 = 4\cos\left(\dfrac{\pi}{12}t + \dfrac{9\pi}{12}\right) + 22$$

   $$4 = 4\cos\left(\dfrac{\pi}{12}t + \dfrac{9\pi}{12}\right)$$

   $$1 = \cos\left(\dfrac{\pi}{12}t + \dfrac{9\pi}{12}\right)$$

   $$\cos^{-1}(1) = \dfrac{\pi}{12}t + \dfrac{9\pi}{12}$$

   $$2\pi = \dfrac{\pi}{12}t + \dfrac{9\pi}{12}$$

   $$\dfrac{15\pi}{12} = \dfrac{\pi}{12}t$$

   $$15 = t$$

   The minimum temperature occurs at
   $t = 3$ (3:00 a.m.), and the maximum
   temperature occurs at $t = 15$ (3:00 p.m.).

53. $y = 2.6\sin\left(\dfrac{2\pi}{6}t\right) - 0.6$

 a. $P = \dfrac{2\pi}{\dfrac{2\pi}{6}} = 6$

 The period is 6 seconds.

 b.   Amplitude is 2.6 and the graph is translated 0.6 units down, so the average minimum height is $2.6 - 0.6 = 2$ ft, and the average maximum height is $2.6 + 0.6 = 3.2$ ft.
 $2 + 3.2 = 5.2$
 The wave height from peak to trough is 5.2 feet.

55. $h(t) = 3\tan\left(\dfrac{\pi}{80}t\right)$

 a. $P = \dfrac{\pi}{\dfrac{\pi}{80}} = 80$

 The period is 80 seconds.

 b. $2 = 3\tan\left(\dfrac{\pi}{80}t\right)$

 $\tan^{-1}\left(\dfrac{2}{3}\right) = \dfrac{\pi}{80}t$

 $\dfrac{80}{\pi}\tan^{-1}\left(\dfrac{2}{3}\right) = t$

 $15 \approx t$

 The height is 2 miles after approximately 15 seconds.

 c. $h(20) = 3\tan\left(\dfrac{\pi}{80}\cdot 20\right)$

 $= 3\tan\left(\dfrac{\pi}{4}\right)$

 $= 3 \cdot 1$

 $= 3$

 Height is 3 miles when pitch over begins.

57. a.   Caracas, Venezuela:
 $D = \dfrac{1.3}{2}\sin\left[\dfrac{2\pi}{365}(15 - 79)\right] + 12 \approx 11.4\ \text{hr}$
 Tokyo, Japan:
 $D = \dfrac{4.8}{2}\sin\left[\dfrac{2\pi}{365}(15 - 79)\right] + 12 \approx 9.9\ \text{hr}$

57 b.

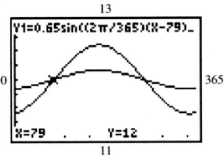

 These cities will have the same number of hours of daylight on the 79th day and 261st day.

 Caracas will have 81 days with 11.5 hours or less of daylight.
 Tokyo will have 158 days with 11.5 hours or less of daylight.

59. a.   The vertical shift of 12 adds 12 hours. The sinusoidal behavior is actually based on hours more/less than an average of 12 hours of light.

 b.   The horizontal (phase) shift of 79 means there are 12 hours of light and dark on March 20 (day 79). This is the solstice.

 c.   The coefficient $\dfrac{K}{2}$ represents additional hours of deviation from the average. In the northern latitudes, the planet is tilted closer toward or farther from the sun, depending on the date. Variations will be greater.

61. $y = 2\sin\left(\dfrac{\pi}{3}t - \dfrac{2\pi}{3}\right)$

 $= 2\sin\left[\dfrac{\pi}{3}(t - 2)\right]$

 $\mathcal{A} = \dfrac{2A}{B} = \dfrac{2(2)}{\dfrac{\pi}{3}} = \dfrac{12}{\pi}$

 $P = \dfrac{2\pi}{\dfrac{\pi}{3}} = 6$

 $|A| = 2$, so the difference between high and low points is 4.
 Note that the area of a "valley" will be equal to one-half the area of the rectangle with length 6 and height 4.
 $A = \dfrac{1}{2}\cdot 6 \cdot 4 = 12$

63. $\theta = \dfrac{s}{r} = \dfrac{168}{67.2} = 2.5$ radians

65. a. Let h_1 be the initial height of the elevator.
    Let h_2 be the final height of the elevator.

    $\tan 20° = \dfrac{h_1}{150}$

    $h_1 = 150 \tan 20° \approx 54.6$ ft

    The initial height of the elevator is approximately 54.6 feet.

    $\tan 52° = \dfrac{h_2}{150}$

    $h_2 = 150 \tan 52° \approx 192.0$ ft

    $192.0 - 54.6 = 137.4$ ft
    The elevator moves 137.4 feet.

    b. $\dfrac{137.4 \text{ ft}}{5 \text{ sec}} \cdot \dfrac{1 \text{ mi}}{5280 \text{ ft}} \cdot \dfrac{3600 \text{ sec}}{1 \text{ hr}} \approx 18.7$ mph

    Average speed of the elevator is 18.7 mph.

67.

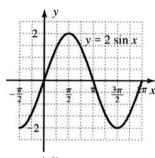

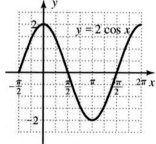

$y = 2 \tan x$

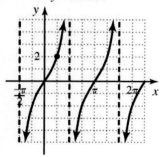

4.4 Exercises

1. $\sin(Bx + C)$; A

3. minimum; maximum

5. Answers will vary.

7. a. $|A| = 50$, $P = 24$

    b. $f(14) \approx -25$

    c. $f(x) \geq 20$ on $[1.6, 10.4]$

9. a. $|A| = 200$, $P = 3$

    b. $f(2) \approx -175$

    c. $f(x) \leq -100$ on $[1.75, 2.75]$

11. $|A| = \dfrac{100 - 20}{2} = 40$; $D = \dfrac{100 + 20}{2} = 60$

    $B = \dfrac{2\pi}{30} = \dfrac{\pi}{15}$; $y = 40 \sin \dfrac{\pi}{15} t + 60$

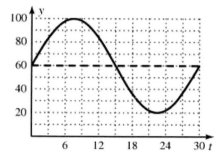

13. $|A| = \dfrac{20 - 4}{2} = 8$; $D = \dfrac{20 + 4}{2} = 12$

    $B = \dfrac{2\pi}{360} = \dfrac{\pi}{180}$; $y = 8 \sin \dfrac{\pi}{180} t + 12$

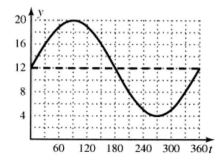

15. $f = \dfrac{B}{2\pi} = \dfrac{\frac{\pi}{2}}{2\pi} = \dfrac{1}{4}$

17. $f = \dfrac{B}{2\pi} = \dfrac{2}{2\pi} = \dfrac{1}{\pi}$

19. $f = \dfrac{B}{2\pi} = \dfrac{\frac{4}{3}}{2\pi} = \dfrac{2}{3\pi}$

21. Since $f = \dfrac{1}{P}$, then $P = \dfrac{1}{f}$.

    Since we also know that $P = \dfrac{2\pi}{B}$,

    then $\dfrac{1}{f} = \dfrac{2\pi}{B} \Rightarrow B = 2\pi f$.

    So $A\sin(Bt) = A\sin\big[(2\pi f)t\big]$.

23. a. $P = \dfrac{2\pi}{\frac{\pi}{2}} = 4$ sec; $f = \dfrac{1}{P} = \dfrac{1}{4}$ cycle/sec

    b. $d(2.5) = 6\sin\left(\dfrac{\pi}{2} \cdot 2.5\right) = -4.24$ cm

    Since 2.5 is just past halfway through the period, it is moving away from the equilibrium point.

    c. $d(3.5) = 6\sin\left(\dfrac{\pi}{2} \cdot 3.5\right) = -4.24$ cm

    Since 3.5 is just short of the end of the period, it is moving toward the equilibrium point.

    d. $\big|d(1.5) - d(1)\big| \approx |4.24 - 6| = 1.76$ cm

    Average velocity is $\dfrac{1.76\,\text{cm}}{0.5\,\text{sec}} = 3.52$ cm/sec.
    We expect a greater velocity for $t = 1.75$ to $t = 2$. The weight reaches the equilibrium point at $t = 2$, so it is still gaining speed during this time.

25. The amplitude is $30 \div 2 = 15$ in. and the period is $0.8 \cdot 2 = 1.6$ sec, so

    $B = \dfrac{2\pi}{1.6} = 1.25\pi = \dfrac{5\pi}{4}$.

    $d(t) = 15\cos\left(\dfrac{5\pi}{4}t\right)$

    Note that we use cosine because the pendulum is at a maximum distance at $t = 0$ sec.

27. Red graph y_1 has a period of about 0.007, so

    $f = \dfrac{1}{P} = \dfrac{1}{0.007} \approx 142.86$; D$_2$.

    Blue graph y_2 has a period of about 0.009, so

    $f = \dfrac{1}{P} = \dfrac{1}{0.009} \approx 111.11$; A$_2$.

29. D$_2$: $y = \sin\big[146.84(2\pi t)\big]$

    $P = \dfrac{2\pi}{B} = \dfrac{2\pi}{146.84(2\pi)} = \dfrac{1}{146.84} \approx 0.0068$ sec

    G$_3$: $y = \sin\big[392(2\pi t)\big]$

    $P = \dfrac{2\pi}{B} = \dfrac{2\pi}{392(2\pi)} = \dfrac{1}{392} \approx 0.00255$ sec

31. a. $|A| = \dfrac{39 - 29}{2} = 5$; $D = \dfrac{39 + 29}{2} = 34$

    P is 24 since there are 24 hours in a day.

    $B = \dfrac{2\pi}{24} = \dfrac{\pi}{12}$; $y = 5\sin\dfrac{\pi}{12}t + 34$

    b.

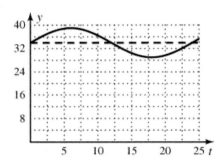

    c. The temperature reaches the freezing point (32°) at $t = 13.5$ (1:30 A.M.) and $t = 22.5$ (10:30 A.M.).

33. a. $|A| = \dfrac{18.8 - 6}{2} = 6.4$; $D = \dfrac{18.8 + 6}{2} = 12.4$

    P is 12 since there are 12 months in a year.

    $B = \dfrac{2\pi}{12} = \dfrac{\pi}{6}$ $y = -6.4\cos\dfrac{\pi}{6}t + 12.4$

    Note that we have a cosine function since the low occurs at $t = 0$.

33. b. (continued)

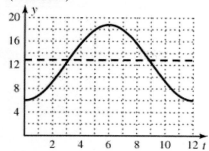

   c. The graph is above 15 from about $t = 3.8$ to $t = 8.2$, which is a span of 4.4 months, or about 134 days.

35. a. $P = \dfrac{2\pi}{\dfrac{2\pi}{11}} = 11$ years

   b.

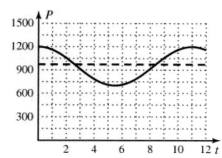

   c. The maximum is 1200 and the minimum is 700.

   d. The height of the graph is below 740 from about $t = 4.5$ to $t = 6.5$, a span of 2 years.

37. The period is 11 years, and the average value occurs one-fourth of the way through a period. This is at $t = 2.75$, so we need to shift the graph 2.75 units to the right.

$$P(t) = 250\cos\left[\dfrac{2\pi}{11}(t - 2.75)\right] + 950 \text{ or}$$

$$P(t) = 250\sin\left(\dfrac{2\pi}{11}t\right) + 950$$

39. The asymptotes occur where the output is infinite. The table shows there are asymptotes at $x = -6$ and $x = 6$, 12 units apart.

$$P = \dfrac{\pi}{B} = 12 \Rightarrow B = \dfrac{\pi}{12}$$

The asymptotes will occur at $6 + 12k,\ k \in Z$.

The equation will look like $y = A\tan\left(\dfrac{\pi}{12}x\right)$.

39. (continued)

We can use the point $(3, 5.2)$ to find $|A|$.

$$5.2 = |A|\tan\left(\dfrac{\pi}{12}\cdot 3\right) = |A|\tan\left(\dfrac{\pi}{4}\right) \Rightarrow |A| = 5.2$$

The equation is $y = 5.2\tan\dfrac{\pi}{12}x$.

At $x = 2$, $y = 5.2\tan\left(\dfrac{\pi}{12}\cdot 2\right) \approx 3.002$.

At $x = -2$, $y = 5.2\tan\left(\dfrac{\pi}{12}\cdot -2\right) \approx -3.002$.

These results agree well with results from the table.

41. The asymptote will be at $90°$.

The zero is at $\theta = 0°$, so the period is $180°$, and

$$\dfrac{180°}{B} = 180° \Rightarrow B = 1.$$

The equation will look like $y = A\tan\theta$.

We can use the point $(30°, 6.9)$ to find $|A|$.

$$6.9 = A\tan 30° = A\cdot\dfrac{1}{\sqrt{3}} \Rightarrow A = 11.95$$

The equation is $y = 11.95\tan\theta$.

Asymptotes will occur at $90° + 180°k,\ k \in Z$.

At $x = 45°$, $y = 11.95\tan 45° = 11.95$.

When the pen is at that angle, it forms a $45°$-$45°$-$90°$ triangle, and the two legs of the pen are of equal length.

The pen is approximately 12 cm long.

43. a. There are 6 hours of daylight; assume those hours are from 9 A.M. to 3 P.M.

$$B = \dfrac{\pi}{6};\quad L(t) = A\csc\left(\dfrac{\pi}{6}t\right)$$

$t = 3$ corresponds to 12:00 noon.

$$L(3) = A\csc\left(\dfrac{\pi}{6}\cdot 3\right)$$

$$10 = A\csc\left(\dfrac{\pi}{2}\right)$$

$$10 = A$$

$$L(t) = 10\csc\left(\dfrac{\pi}{6}t\right)$$

   b. At 2:00 P.M., $t = 5$.

$$L(5) = 10\csc\left(\dfrac{\pi}{6}\cdot 5\right)$$

$$= 10\csc\left(\dfrac{5\pi}{6}\right)$$

$$= 20 \text{ m}$$

45. Answers will vary.

47. $y = \sin(3x)$

The dampening factor is quadratic.

$f(x) \approx 0.02x^2 - 0.32x + 2.28$

$Y_1 = \sin(3x)$

$Y_2 = 0.02x^2 - 0.32x + 2.28$

$x \in [-2\pi, 7\pi], \quad y \in [-5, 5]$

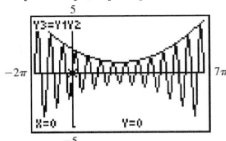

49. $|\cos t| = \dfrac{1}{2}$

$\cos t = \dfrac{1}{2}$ or $\cos t = -\dfrac{1}{2}$

$t = \cos^{-1}\left(\dfrac{1}{2}\right)$ $t = \cos^{-1}\left(-\dfrac{1}{2}\right)$

$t = \dfrac{\pi}{3}, \dfrac{5\pi}{3}$ $t = \dfrac{2\pi}{3}, \dfrac{4\pi}{3}$

51. $y = \sec\left(x - \dfrac{\pi}{3}\right)$

53. $35° \cdot \dfrac{\pi}{180°} = \dfrac{7\pi}{36}$

$A = 2 \cdot \dfrac{1}{2} r^2 \theta = 2 \cdot \dfrac{1}{2}(24)^2\left(\dfrac{7\pi}{36}\right) = 112\pi \text{ in}^2$

The area of the angle's wings is $112\pi \text{ in}^2$.

Summary and Concept Review 4.1

1. $y = 3\sin t;\ |A| = 3;\ P = 2\pi$

Reference Rectangle: $2|A| = 6$ by $P = 2\pi$

Ticmarks $\dfrac{1}{4}(2\pi) = \dfrac{\pi}{2}$ units apart

Rule of fourths: $t = 0, \dfrac{\pi}{2}, \pi, \dfrac{3\pi}{2}, 2\pi$

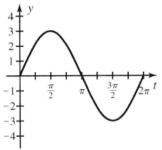

3. $y = 1.7\sin(4t);\ |A| = 1.7;\ P = \dfrac{2\pi}{4} = \dfrac{\pi}{2}$

Reference Rectangle: $2|A| = 3.4$ by $P = \dfrac{\pi}{2}$

Ticmarks $\dfrac{1}{4}\left(\dfrac{\pi}{2}\right) = \dfrac{\pi}{8}$ units apart

Rule of fourths: $t = 0, \dfrac{\pi}{8}, \dfrac{\pi}{4}, \dfrac{3\pi}{8}, \dfrac{\pi}{2}$

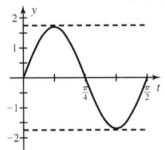

5. $g(t) = 3\sin(398\pi t);\ |A| = 3;\ P = \dfrac{2\pi}{398\pi} = \dfrac{1}{199}$

Reference Rectangle: $2|A| = 6$ by $P = \dfrac{1}{199}$

Ticmarks $\dfrac{1}{4}\left(\dfrac{1}{199}\right) = \dfrac{1}{796}$ units apart

Rule of fourths: $t = 0, \dfrac{1}{796}, \dfrac{1}{398}, \dfrac{3}{796}, \dfrac{1}{199}$

5. (continued)

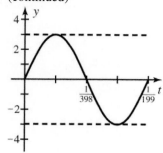

7. $y = \sin\left(\dfrac{\pi}{270}t\right);\quad P = \dfrac{2\pi}{B} = \dfrac{2\pi}{\dfrac{\pi}{270}} = 540$

This equation represents green.

$y = \sin\left(\dfrac{\pi}{320}t\right);\quad P = \dfrac{2\pi}{B} = \dfrac{2\pi}{\dfrac{\pi}{320}} = 640$

This equation represents red.

Summary and Concept Review 4.2

9. $y = A\csc(Bt)$

$|A| = 4$

$B = \dfrac{2\pi}{P} = \dfrac{2\pi}{\dfrac{2}{3}} = 3\pi$

$y = 4\csc(3\pi t)$

11. a. $\tan^{-1}\left(-\sqrt{3}\right) = \dfrac{2\pi}{3}$

   b. $\cot^{-1}\left(-\dfrac{1}{\sqrt{3}}\right) = \dfrac{2\pi}{3}$

13. $y = \dfrac{1}{2}\cos(2\pi t)$

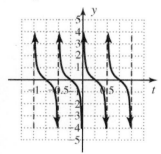

15. Cotangent is also positive in QIII.
    The period is π, so another solution is
    $0.4444 + \pi \approx 3.5860$

Summary and Concept Review 4.3

17. a. $y = 240\sin\left[\dfrac{\pi}{6}(t-3)\right] + 520$

   $|A| = 240;\quad P = \dfrac{2\pi}{\dfrac{\pi}{6}} = 12$

   HS: 3 units right; VS: 520 units up

   b. PI: $0 \le \dfrac{\pi}{6}(t-3) < 2\pi$

   $0 \le t - 3 < 12$

   $3 \le t < 15$

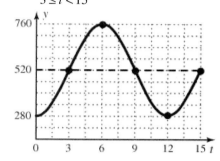

19. $|A| = \dfrac{300 - 50}{2} = 125;\quad P = 2(21-9) = 24$

   HS: 3 units right;VS: $\dfrac{300 + 50}{2} = 175$ units up

   $B = \dfrac{2\pi}{P} = \dfrac{2\pi}{24} = \dfrac{\pi}{12}$

   $y = 125\cos\left[\dfrac{\pi}{12}(t-3)\right] + 175$

Summary and Concept Review 4.4

21. F#₃: $y = \sin\left[370(2\pi t)\right]$

   $P = \dfrac{2\pi}{B} = \dfrac{2\pi}{370(2\pi)} = \dfrac{1}{370} \approx 0.0027$ sec

23. The asymptotes occur where the output is
    infinite. The table shows there are asymptotes at
    $x = -6$ and $x = 6$, 12 units apart.

   $P = \dfrac{\pi}{B} = 12 \Rightarrow B = \dfrac{\pi}{12}$

   The equation will look like $y = A\tan\left(\dfrac{\pi}{12}x\right)$.

   We can use the point $(3, 5.2)$ to find $|A|$.

   $5.2 = |A|\tan\left(\dfrac{\pi}{12}\cdot 3\right) = |A|\tan\left(\dfrac{\pi}{4}\right) \Rightarrow |A| = 5.2$

   The equation is $y = 5.2\tan\dfrac{\pi}{12}x$.

<u>Mixed Review</u>

1. The amplitude is 10, and the graph first increases after $(0,0)$, so $A = 10$.

    The period is π.

    $$\pi = \frac{2\pi}{B} \Rightarrow \pi B = 2\pi \Rightarrow B = 2$$

    $$f(t) = 10\sin(2t)$$

3. a. $|A| = \dfrac{25-5}{2} = \dfrac{20}{2} = 10$

    b. $D = \dfrac{25+5}{2} = \dfrac{30}{2} = 15$

    c. $P = 6$

    d. $f(4) = 20$

5. The period is $\dfrac{2\pi}{3}$.

    $$\frac{2\pi}{3} = \frac{\pi}{B} \Rightarrow 2\pi B = 3\pi \Rightarrow B = \frac{3}{2}$$

    The graph is shifted $\dfrac{\pi}{3}$ units to the left.

    The equation is $g(t) = A\cot\left[\dfrac{3}{2}\left(t + \dfrac{\pi}{3}\right)\right]$.

    $\left(\dfrac{5\pi}{6}, 2\right)$ is on the graph, so

    $$2 = A\cot\left[\frac{3}{2}\left(\frac{5\pi}{6} + \frac{\pi}{3}\right)\right]$$

    $$2 = A\cot\left[\frac{3}{2}\left(\frac{7\pi}{6}\right)\right]$$

    $$2 = A\cot\left(\frac{7\pi}{4}\right)$$

    $$2 = -A$$

    $$-2 = A$$

    The equation is $g(t) = -2\cot\left[\dfrac{3}{2}\left(t + \dfrac{\pi}{3}\right)\right]$.

    Other solutions are possible.

7. $y = -2\csc t$

    Reference Rectangle:

    $2|A| = 4$ by $P = 2\pi$

    Ticmarks $\dfrac{1}{4}(2\pi) = \dfrac{\pi}{2}$ units apart

    Asymptotes at $0, \pi$, and 2π.

    max/min at $t = \dfrac{\pi}{2}$ and $\dfrac{3\pi}{2}$

    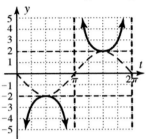

9. $f(t) = \cos(2t) - 1$

    Reference Rectangle:

    $2|A| = 2$ by $P = \dfrac{2\pi}{2} = \pi$

    Ticmarks $\dfrac{1}{4}(\pi) = \dfrac{\pi}{4}$ units apart

    Vertical shift down 1 unit

    Rule of fourths: $t = 0, \dfrac{\pi}{2}, \pi, \dfrac{3\pi}{2}, 2\pi$

    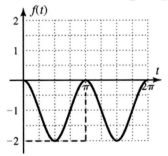

11. $h(t) = \dfrac{3}{2}\sin\left(\dfrac{\pi}{2}t\right)$

   Reference Rectangle:

   $2|A| = 3$ by $P = \dfrac{2\pi}{\dfrac{\pi}{2}} = 4$

   Ticmarks $\dfrac{1}{4}(4) = 1$ unit apart

   Rule of fourths: $t = 0, 1, 2, 3, 4$

   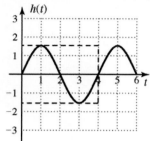

13. a. $|A| = \dfrac{4.05 - 0.79}{2} = 1.63$

   $D = \dfrac{4.05 + 0.79}{2} = 2.42$

   $P = 12$ since there are 12 months in a year.

   $B = \dfrac{2\pi}{P} = \dfrac{2\pi}{12} = \dfrac{\pi}{6}$

   $P(t) = 1.63\sin\left(\dfrac{\pi}{6}t\right) + 2.42$

   b. July:

   $P(3) = 1.63\sin\left(\dfrac{\pi}{6} \cdot 3\right) + 2.42$

   $= 1.63\sin\left(\dfrac{\pi}{2}\right) + 2.42$

   $= 1.63 + 2.42$

   $= 4.05$ in.

   December:

   $P(8) = 1.63\sin\left(\dfrac{\pi}{6} \cdot 8\right) + 2.42$

   $= 1.63\sin\left(\dfrac{4\pi}{3}\right) + 2.42$

   $= 1.63 \cdot \left(-\dfrac{\sqrt{3}}{2}\right) + 2.42$

   ≈ 1.01 in.

15. a. $P = \dfrac{2\pi}{B} = \dfrac{2\pi}{\dfrac{\pi}{6}} = 12$

   $f = \dfrac{1}{P} = \dfrac{1}{12}$

   b. $P = \dfrac{2\pi}{B} = \dfrac{2\pi}{\dfrac{8}{3}} = \dfrac{3\pi}{4}$

   $f = \dfrac{1}{P} = \dfrac{1}{\dfrac{3\pi}{4}} = \dfrac{4}{3\pi}$

17. $y = 5\cos(2t) - 8$

   $|A| = 5; \; P = \dfrac{2\pi}{2} = \pi$

   HS: none
   VS: 8 units down
   PI: $0 \le 2t < 2\pi$
   $\quad\;\; 0 \le t < \pi$

   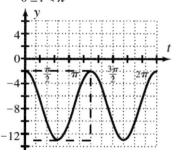

19. $y = 2\tan\left(\dfrac{1}{4}t\right)$

   $P = \dfrac{\pi}{\dfrac{1}{4}} = 4\pi; \;$ HS: none

   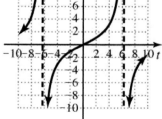

Practice Test

1. $t = 0$
    $\sin t = 0$; $\cos t = 1$; $\tan t = 0$;
    $\csc t$ is undefined; $\sec t = 1$; $\cot t$ is undefined
    $P(x, y) = (1, 0)$

t	sin t	cos t	tan t	csc t	sec t	cot t	P(x, y)
0	0	1	0	--	1	--	(1, 0)
$\frac{\pi}{6}$	$\frac{1}{2}$	$\frac{\sqrt{3}}{2}$	$\frac{\sqrt{3}}{3}$	2	$\frac{2\sqrt{3}}{3}$	$\sqrt{3}$	$\left(\frac{\sqrt{3}}{2}, \frac{1}{2}\right)$
$\frac{\pi}{4}$	$\frac{\sqrt{2}}{2}$	$\frac{\sqrt{2}}{2}$	1	$\sqrt{2}$	$\sqrt{2}$	1	$\left(\frac{\sqrt{2}}{2}, \frac{\sqrt{2}}{2}\right)$
$\frac{\pi}{2}$	1	0	--	1	--	0	(0, 1)
$\frac{2\pi}{3}$	$\frac{\sqrt{3}}{2}$	$-\frac{1}{2}$	$-\sqrt{3}$	$\frac{2\sqrt{3}}{3}$	-2	$-\frac{\sqrt{3}}{3}$	$\left(-\frac{1}{2}, \frac{\sqrt{3}}{2}\right)$
$\frac{5\pi}{6}$	$\frac{1}{2}$	$-\frac{\sqrt{3}}{2}$	$-\frac{\sqrt{3}}{3}$	2	$-\frac{2\sqrt{3}}{3}$	$-\sqrt{3}$	$\left(\frac{1}{2}, -\frac{\sqrt{3}}{2}\right)$
$\frac{5\pi}{4}$	$-\frac{\sqrt{2}}{2}$	$-\frac{\sqrt{2}}{2}$	1	$-\sqrt{2}$	$-\sqrt{2}$	1	$\left(-\frac{\sqrt{2}}{2}, \frac{\sqrt{2}}{2}\right)$
$\frac{4\pi}{3}$	$-\frac{\sqrt{3}}{2}$	$-\frac{1}{2}$	$\sqrt{3}$	$-\frac{2\sqrt{3}}{3}$	2	$\frac{\sqrt{3}}{3}$	$\left(\frac{1}{2}, \frac{\sqrt{3}}{2}\right)$
$\frac{3\pi}{2}$	-1	0	--	-1	--	0	(0, -1)

3. a. $\tan^{-1}\left(\sqrt{3}\right) = \frac{\pi}{3}$ in QI

    b. $\cos^{-1}\left(-\frac{1}{2}\right) = \frac{2\pi}{3}$ in QII

    c. $\sin^{-1}\left(-\frac{\sqrt{3}}{2}\right) = \frac{4\pi}{3}$ in QIII

    d. $\sec^{-1}\left(\sqrt{2}\right) = \frac{7\pi}{4}$ in QIV

5. $y = 2\sec(2t)$, $t \in [0, 2\pi)$

    No amplitude; $P = \frac{2\pi}{2} = \pi$

    Reference Rectangle: $2|A| = 4$ by $P = \pi$

    Ticmarks $\frac{1}{4}(\pi) = \frac{\pi}{4}$ units apart

    Asymptotes at $\frac{\pi}{4}$ and $\frac{3\pi}{4}$,

    max/min at $t = 0$, $\frac{\pi}{2}$, and π

5. (continued)

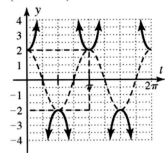

7. $y = 12\sin\left[3\left(t - \frac{\pi}{6}\right)\right] + 19$, $t \in [0, 2\pi)$

    $|A| = 12$; $P = \frac{2\pi}{3}$

    HS: $\frac{\pi}{6}$ units to the right

    VS: 19 units up

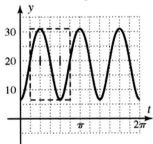

9. $y = 2\cot\left[\frac{1}{3}\pi\left(t - \frac{3}{2}\right)\right]$, $t \in [0, 6)$

    No amplitude; $P = \dfrac{\pi}{\dfrac{\pi}{3}} = 3$

    HS: $\frac{3}{2}$ units to the right

    VS: none

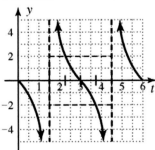

11. The period is π, so two solutions are
    $$4.25 - \pi \approx 1.11$$
    $$4.25 + \pi \approx 7.39$$

13. a. $A = \dfrac{1.06 - 0.24}{2} = 0.41$

$B = \dfrac{2\pi}{P} = \dfrac{2\pi}{12} = \dfrac{\pi}{6}$

The annual low occurs in 8th month (rather than month 6), so the graph is shifted 2 units to the left; $C = 2$.

$D = \dfrac{1.06 + 0.24}{2} = 0.65$

$r(t) = 0.41\sin\left[\dfrac{\pi}{6}(t+2)\right] + 0.65$

b.   The annual high occurs when sine is 1.

$\dfrac{\pi}{6}(t+2) = \dfrac{\pi}{2}$

$t + 2 = 3$

$t = 1$

The annual high occurs in January.

15. Max and min are 20 and 5, so

$|A| = \dfrac{20-5}{2} = \dfrac{15}{2} = 7.5$.

The primary cycle begins at 3, so the horizontal shift is 3 units right.

$D = \dfrac{20+5}{2} = \dfrac{25}{2} = 12.5$

$P = 12$, so $B = \dfrac{2\pi}{12} = \dfrac{\pi}{6}$.

$y = 7.5\sin\left[\dfrac{\pi}{6}(t-3)\right] + 12.5$

$y = 7.5\sin\left(\dfrac{\pi}{6}t - \dfrac{\pi}{2}\right) + 12.5$

17. $y = 3\sin\left[2\left(t - \dfrac{\pi}{6}\right)\right]$; $|A| = 3$; $P = \dfrac{2\pi}{2} = \pi$

HS: $\dfrac{\pi}{6}$ unit to the right

VS: none

The equation corresponds to graph a.

19. $y = -3\sin(\pi t) + 1$; $|A| = 3$; $P = \dfrac{2\pi}{\pi} = 2$

HS: none

VS: 1 unit up

The equation corresponds to graph b.

Calculator Exploration & Discovery

Exercise 1:
   Answers will vary.

Strengthening Core Skills

Exercise 1:

a. $f(t) = \sin\left(t + \dfrac{\pi}{4}\right) - 1$, $g(t) = t + \dfrac{\pi}{4} \Rightarrow$

$h(t) = f[g(t)] = \sin\left(t + \dfrac{\pi}{4} + \dfrac{\pi}{4}\right) - 1$

$h(t) = \sin\left(t + \dfrac{\pi}{2}\right) - 1$

b.   Find a zero of $h(t)$.

$0 = \sin\left(t + \dfrac{\pi}{2}\right) - 1$

$1 = \sin\left(t + \dfrac{\pi}{2}\right)$

$\sin^{-1} 1 = t + \dfrac{\pi}{2}$

$\dfrac{\pi}{2} = t + \dfrac{\pi}{2}$

$0 = t$

The zeros of $f(t)$ can be found by shifting the zeros of $h(t)$ $\dfrac{\pi}{4}$ units right.

$t = \left(0 + \dfrac{\pi}{4}\right) + 2\pi k = \dfrac{\pi}{4} + 2\pi k$

Exercise 3:

a. $f(t) = 3\sin(t - 0.7) + 3$, $g(t) = t + \dfrac{\pi}{2} + 0.7 \Rightarrow$

$h(t) = f[g(t)] = 3\sin\left(t + \dfrac{\pi}{2} + 0.7 - 0.7\right) + 3$

$h(t) = 3\sin\left(t + \dfrac{\pi}{2}\right) + 3$

b.   Find a zero of $h(t)$.

$0 = 3\sin\left(t + \dfrac{\pi}{2}\right) + 3$

$-3 = 3\sin\left(t + \dfrac{\pi}{2}\right)$

$-1 = \sin\left(t + \dfrac{\pi}{2}\right)$

$\sin^{-1}(-1) = t + \dfrac{\pi}{2}$

$\dfrac{3\pi}{2} = t + \dfrac{\pi}{2}$

$\pi = t$

Exercise 3:
b. (continued)
The zeros of $f(t)$ can be found by

shifting the zeros of $h(t)$ $\frac{\pi}{2}+0.7$ units

right.

$$t=\left(\pi+\frac{\pi}{2}+0.7\right)+2\pi k$$

$$=\left(\frac{3\pi}{2}+0.7\right)+2\pi k$$

Cumulative Review Chapters 1-4

1. $y=2.5\sin\left(\frac{\pi}{2}t\right); \ t\in[-2,6)$

Reference Rectangle:

$2|A|=5$ by $P=\dfrac{2\pi}{\dfrac{\pi}{2}}=4$

Ticmarks $\dfrac{1}{4}(4)=1$ unit apart

Rule of fourths: $t=0, 1, 2, 3, 4$

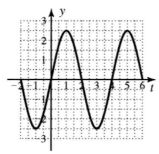

3. $\cot\theta=\dfrac{x}{y}=\dfrac{55}{48}$

$x=55, \ y=48$

$r=\sqrt{55^2+48^2}=\sqrt{5329}=73$

$\theta=\sin^{-1}\dfrac{48}{73}\approx41.1°$

$90°-\theta\approx90°-41.1°=48.9°$

5. Based on similar triangles, we can multiply both coordinates by 3 to clear fractions.

$$x=-\frac{1}{3}\cdot3=-1; \ y=\frac{2\sqrt{2}}{3}\cdot3=2\sqrt{2};$$

$$\left(-1, 2\sqrt{2}\right); \ \sqrt{\left(-1\right)^2+\left(2\sqrt{2}\right)^2}=\sqrt{9}=3$$

$$\sin t=\frac{2\sqrt{2}}{3}; \ \cos t=-\frac{1}{3}; \ \tan t=-2\sqrt{2}$$

$$\csc t=\frac{3}{2\sqrt{2}}=\frac{3\sqrt{2}}{4}; \ \sec t=-3$$

$$\cot t=-\frac{1}{2\sqrt{2}}=-\frac{\sqrt{2}}{4}$$

7. $90°-54°13'03''$
$=\left(89°+59'+60''\right)-54°13'03''$
$=\left(89°-54°\right)+\left(59'-13'\right)+\left(60''-03''\right)$
$=35°+46'+57''$
$=35°46'57''$

a. $35°46'57''=\left[35+46\left(\dfrac{1}{60}\right)+57\left(\dfrac{1}{3600}\right)\right]°$

$=35.7825°$

b. $35.7825°\cdot\dfrac{\pi}{180°}\approx0.6245$ rad

9. $\left(\dfrac{13}{85}\right)^2+\left(\dfrac{84}{85}\right)^2=\dfrac{169}{7225}+\dfrac{7056}{7225}=\dfrac{7225}{7225}=1$

Other points:

$$\left(-\frac{13}{85}, \frac{84}{85}\right); \left(-\frac{13}{85}, -\frac{84}{85}\right); \left(\frac{13}{85}, -\frac{84}{85}\right)$$

11. Let h be the height of the kite.

$\tan69°=\dfrac{h}{10}$

$h=10\tan69°\approx26$ m

13. $\dfrac{4\pi}{3}$ is a QIII angle:

$t_r=\dfrac{4\pi}{3}-\pi=\dfrac{4\pi}{3}-\dfrac{3\pi}{3}=\dfrac{\pi}{3}$

$\sin t=-\dfrac{\sqrt{3}}{2}; \cos t=-\dfrac{1}{2}; \tan t=\sqrt{3}$

$\csc t=-\dfrac{2}{\sqrt{3}}=-\dfrac{2\sqrt{3}}{3}; \sec t=-2$

$\cot t=\dfrac{1}{\sqrt{3}}=\dfrac{\sqrt{3}}{3}$

15. a. $2\pi r = 2\pi \cdot 14 = 28\pi$ in.

In one revolution, the butterfly flies 28π in.

$$\omega = \frac{1\,\text{rev}}{4\,\text{sec}} \cdot \frac{2\pi\,\text{rad}}{1\,\text{rev}} = \frac{\pi}{2}\,\text{rad/sec}$$

b. $V = (14\,\text{in.})\left(\dfrac{\pi}{2}\,\dfrac{\text{rad}}{\text{sec}}\right) = 22\,\text{in./sec}$

17. a. $t = 4.22$ lies in QIII.

b. $t_r = 4.22 - \pi \approx 1.08$

c. $\tan t = \tan 4.22 \approx 1.8641$

19. Max and min are 2 and -1, so

$$|A| = \frac{2-(-1)}{2} = \frac{3}{2}, \quad D = \frac{2+(-1)}{2} = \frac{1}{2}$$

The primary cycle begins at $\dfrac{\pi}{8}$, so the

horizontal shift is $\dfrac{\pi}{8}$ units right.

$P = \dfrac{\pi}{2}$, so $B = \dfrac{2\pi}{\frac{\pi}{2}} = 4$ $y = \dfrac{3}{2}\sin\left[4\left(t - \dfrac{\pi}{8}\right)\right] + \dfrac{1}{2}$

$$= \frac{3}{2}\sin\left(4t - \frac{\pi}{2}\right) + \frac{1}{2}$$

21. False.

$$(\cos t)(\csc t) = (\cos t)\left(\frac{1}{\sin t}\right) = \cot t$$

23. $\csc t = -\dfrac{13}{5} \Rightarrow y = -5,\ r = 13$

Since $\cos t > 0$, x is positive.

The angle t is in quadrant IV.

$$x = \sqrt{13^2 - (-5)^2} = \sqrt{144} = 12$$

$$\sin t = -\frac{5}{13};\ \cos t = \frac{12}{13};\ \tan t = -\frac{5}{12}$$

$$\csc t = -\frac{13}{5};\ \sec t = \frac{13}{12};\ \cot t = -\frac{12}{5}$$

25. a.   Max and min are $14,000$ and 4000.

$$|A| = \frac{14,000 - 4000}{2} = 5000$$

$$D = \frac{14,000 + 4000}{2} = 7000$$

$P = 6$, so $B = \dfrac{2\pi}{6} = \dfrac{\pi}{3}$

The minimum value would ordinarily occur three-fourths of the way through a period.

$$\frac{3}{4} \cdot 6 = \frac{9}{2} = 4.5 \ (\text{or at } -1.5)$$

The minimum value occurs in January $(x = 1.5)$, so the horizontal shift is 3 units right.

$$y = 5000\sin\left[\frac{\pi}{3}(x+3)\right] + 9000$$

$$= 5000\sin\left(\frac{\pi}{3}x + \pi\right) + 9000$$

b.   In August, at $x = 8$,

$$y = 5000\sin\left(\frac{\pi}{3} \cdot 8 + \pi\right) + 9000$$

$$= 5000\sin\left(\frac{11\pi}{3}\right) + 9000$$

$$\approx \$4670$$

c.   Since the period is 6, profits will also peak in month $4.5 + 6 = 10.5$, which corresponds to mid-October.

Technology Highlight

Exercise 1:

$\dfrac{1-\sin^2\theta}{\cos\theta}=\cos\theta$ is an identity.

Let $Y_1=\dfrac{1-\sin^2\theta}{\cos\theta}$.

Let $Y_2=\cos\theta$.

We use a graphing calculator to show that $Y_1=Y_2$.

Exercise 3:

$\dfrac{\cos x}{1+\sin x}=\dfrac{1-\sin x}{\cos x}$ is an identity.

Let $Y_1=\dfrac{\cos x}{1+\sin x}$.

Let $Y_2=\dfrac{1-\sin x}{\cos x}$.

We use a graphing calculator to show that $Y_1=Y_2$.

5.1 Exercises

1. identities; symmetry

3. complicated; simplify; build

5. Because we don't know if the equation is true.

7. $(1+\sin x)\big[1+\sin(-x)\big]=(1+\sin x)(1-\sin x)$
$$=1-\sin^2 x$$
$$=\cos^2 x$$

9. $\sin^2(-x)+\cos^2 x=\left(-\sin^2 x\right)+\cos^2 x$
$$=\sin^2 x+\cos^2 x$$
$$=1$$

11. $\dfrac{1-\sin(-x)}{\cos x+\cos(-x)\sin x}=\dfrac{1+\sin x}{\cos x+\cos x\sin x}$
$$=\dfrac{1+\sin x}{\cos x(1+\sin x)}$$
$$=\dfrac{1}{\cos x}=\sec x$$

13. $\cos^2 x\,\tan^2 x=\cos^2 x\left(\dfrac{\sin^2 x}{\cos^2 x}\right)$
$$=\sin^2 x$$
$$=1-\cos^2 x$$

15. $\tan x+\cot x=\dfrac{\sin x}{\cos x}+\dfrac{\cos x}{\sin x}$
$$=\dfrac{\sin^2 x+\cos^2 x}{\cos x\sin x}$$
$$=\dfrac{1}{\cos x\sin x}$$
$$=\dfrac{1}{\cos x}\cdot\dfrac{1}{\sin x}=\sec x\csc x$$

17. Begin with the right side of the equation.

$\csc x-\sin x=\dfrac{1}{\sin x}-\sin x$
$$=\dfrac{1-\sin^2 x}{\sin x}$$
$$=\dfrac{\cos^2 x}{\sin x}$$
$$=\dfrac{\cos x}{\dfrac{\sin x}{\cos x}}=\dfrac{\cos x}{\tan x}$$

19. Begin with the right side of the equation.

$\sec\theta+\tan\theta=\dfrac{1}{\cos\theta}+\dfrac{\sin\theta}{\cos\theta}$
$$=\dfrac{1+\sin\theta}{\cos\theta}$$
$$=\dfrac{(1+\sin\theta)(1-\sin\theta)}{\cos\theta(1-\sin\theta)}$$
$$=\dfrac{1-\sin^2\theta}{\cos\theta(1-\sin\theta)}$$
$$=\dfrac{\cos^2\theta}{\cos\theta(1-\sin\theta)}=\dfrac{\cos\theta}{1-\sin\theta}$$

21. $\dfrac{1-\sin x}{\cos x}=\dfrac{(1-\sin x)(1+\sin x)}{\cos x(1+\sin x)}$
$$=\dfrac{1-\sin^2 x}{\cos x(1+\sin x)}$$
$$=\dfrac{\cos^2 x}{\cos x(1+\sin x)}=\dfrac{\cos x}{1+\sin x}$$

23. $\dfrac{\csc x}{\cos x}-\dfrac{\cos x}{\csc x}=\dfrac{\csc^2 x-\cos^2 x}{\cos x\csc x}$
$$=\dfrac{\csc^2 x-\left(1-\sin^2 x\right)}{\cos x\left(\dfrac{1}{\sin x}\right)}$$
$$=\dfrac{\csc^2 x-1+\sin^2 x}{\cot x}$$
$$=\dfrac{\cot^2 x+\sin^2 x}{\cot x}$$

25.
$$\frac{\sin x}{1+\sin x} - \frac{\sin x}{1-\sin x}$$
$$= \frac{\sin x(1-\sin x) - \sin x(1+\sin x)}{(1+\sin x)(1-\sin x)}$$
$$= \frac{\sin x - \sin^2 x - \sin x - \sin^2 x}{1-\sin^2 x}$$
$$= \frac{-2\sin^2 x}{\cos^2 x}$$
$$= -2\tan^2 x$$

27.
$$\frac{\cot x}{1+\csc x} - \frac{\cot x}{1-\csc x}$$
$$= \frac{\cot x(1-\csc x) - \cot x(1+\csc x)}{(1+\csc x)(1-\csc x)}$$
$$= \frac{\cot x - \cot x \csc x - \cot x - \cot x \csc x}{1-\csc^2 x}$$
$$= \frac{-2\cot x \csc x}{-\cot^2 x}$$
$$= \frac{2\csc x}{\cot x}$$
$$= \frac{2 \cdot \dfrac{1}{\sin x}}{\dfrac{\cos x}{\sin x}}$$
$$= \frac{2}{\cos x}$$
$$= 2\sec x$$

29.
$$\frac{\sec^2 x}{1+\cot^2 x} = \frac{\sec^2 x}{\csc^2 x}$$
$$= \frac{\dfrac{1}{\cos^2 x}}{\dfrac{1}{\sin^2 x}}$$
$$= \frac{\sin^2 x}{\cos^2 x}$$
$$= \tan^2 x$$

31.
$$\sin^2 x\left(\cot^2 x - \csc^2 x\right)$$
$$= \sin^2 x \cot^2 x - \sin^2 x \csc^2 x$$
$$= \sin^2 x \cdot \frac{\cos^2 x}{\sin^2 x} - \sin^2 x \cdot \frac{1}{\sin^2 x}$$
$$= \cos^2 x - 1$$
$$= -\sin^2 x$$

33.
$$\cos x \cot x + \sin x = \cos x \cdot \frac{\cos x}{\sin x} + \sin x$$
$$= \frac{\cos^2 x}{\sin x} + \sin x$$
$$= \frac{\cos^2 x + \sin^2 x}{\sin x}$$
$$= \frac{1}{\sin x}$$
$$= \csc x$$

35.
$$\frac{\sec x}{\cot x + \tan x} = \frac{\dfrac{1}{\cos x}(\sin x)(\cos x)}{\left(\dfrac{\cos x}{\sin x} + \dfrac{\sin x}{\cos x}\right)(\sin x)(\cos x)}$$
$$= \frac{\sin x}{\cos^2 x + \sin^2 x}$$
$$= \frac{\sin x}{1}$$
$$= \sin x$$

37.
$$\frac{\sin x - \csc x}{\csc x} = \frac{\sin x}{\csc x} - \frac{\csc x}{\csc x}$$
$$= \sin^2 x - 1$$
$$= -\cos^2 x$$

39.
$$\frac{1}{\csc x - \sin x} = \frac{1}{(\csc x - \sin x)} \cdot \frac{\sin x}{\sin x}$$
$$= \frac{\sin x}{1-\sin^2 x}$$
$$= \frac{\sin x}{\cos^2 x}$$
$$= \frac{\sin x}{\cos x} \cdot \frac{1}{\cos x}$$
$$= \tan x \sec x$$

41.
$$\frac{1+\sin x}{1-\sin x} = \frac{(1+\sin x)}{(1-\sin x)} \cdot \frac{(1+\sin x)}{(1+\sin x)}$$
$$= \frac{1+2\sin x + \sin^2 x}{1-\sin^2 x}$$
$$= \frac{1+2\sin x + \sin^2 x}{\cos^2 x}$$
$$= \frac{1}{\cos^2 x} + 2\frac{\sin x}{\cos x} \cdot \frac{1}{\cos x} + \frac{\sin^2 x}{\cos^2 x}$$
$$= \sec^2 x + 2\tan x \sec x + \tan^2 x$$
$$= (\sec x + \tan x)^2$$
$$= (\tan x + \sec x)^2$$

43. $\dfrac{\cos x - \sin x}{1 - \tan x} = \dfrac{(\cos x - \sin x)}{(1 - \tan x)} \cdot \dfrac{(\cos x + \sin x)}{(\cos x + \sin x)}$

$= \dfrac{(\cos x - \sin x)(\cos x + \sin x)}{\cos x + \sin x - \sin x - \dfrac{\sin^2 x}{\cos x}}$

$= \dfrac{(\cos x - \sin x)(\cos x + \sin x)}{\cos x\left(1 - \dfrac{\sin^2 x}{\cos^2 x}\right)}$

$= \dfrac{(\cos x - \sin x)(\cos x + \sin x)}{\cos x\left(1 - \tan^2 x\right)}$

$= \dfrac{(\cos x - \sin x)(\cos x + \sin x)}{\cos x(1 - \tan x)(1 + \tan x)}$

$= \dfrac{(\cos x - \sin x)(\cos x + \sin x)}{(\cos x - \sin x)(1 + \tan x)}$

$= \dfrac{\cos x + \sin x}{1 + \tan x}$

45. $\dfrac{\tan^2 x - \cot^2 x}{\tan x - \cot x} = \dfrac{(\tan x + \cot x)(\tan x - \cot x)}{(\tan x - \cot x)}$

$= \tan x + \cot x$

$= \dfrac{\sin x}{\cos x} + \dfrac{\cos x}{\sin x}$

$= \dfrac{\sin^2 x + \cos^2 x}{\cos x \sin x}$

$= \dfrac{1}{\cos x \sin x}$

$= \dfrac{1}{\cos x} \cdot \dfrac{1}{\sin x}$

$= \sec x \csc x$

$= \csc x \sec x$

47. $\dfrac{\cot x}{\cot x + \tan x} = \dfrac{\dfrac{\cos x}{\sin x}}{\dfrac{\cos x}{\sin x} + \dfrac{\sin x}{\cos x}} \cdot \dfrac{(\cos x)(\sin x)}{(\cos x)(\sin x)}$

$= \dfrac{\cos^2 x}{\cos^2 x + \sin^2 x}$

$= \dfrac{\cos^2 x}{1}$

$= 1 - \sin^2 x$

49. $\dfrac{\sec^4 x - \tan^4 x}{\sec^2 x + \tan^2 x}$

$= \dfrac{(\sec^2 x + \tan^2 x)(\sec^2 x - \tan^2 x)}{(\sec^2 x + \tan^2 x)}$

$= \sec^2 x - \tan^2 x$

$= 1$

51. $\dfrac{\cos^4 x - \sin^4 x}{\cos^2 x}$

$= \dfrac{(\cos^2 x - \sin^2 x)(\cos^2 x + \sin^2 x)}{\cos^2 x}$

$= \dfrac{(\cos^2 x - \sin^2 x)(1)}{\cos^2 x}$

$= \dfrac{\cos^2 x}{\cos^2 x} - \dfrac{\sin^2 x}{\cos^2 x}$

$= 1 - \tan^2 x$

$= 1 - (\sec^2 x - 1)$

$= 1 - \sec^2 x + 1$

$= 2 - \sec^2 x$

53. $(\sec x + \tan x)^2 = \sec^2 x + 2 \sec x \tan x + \tan^2 x$

$= \dfrac{1}{\cos^2 x} + \dfrac{2 \sin x}{\cos^2 x} + \dfrac{\sin^2 x}{\cos^2 x}$

$= \dfrac{1 + 2 \sin x + \sin^2 x}{\cos^2 x}$

$= \dfrac{(1 + \sin x)^2}{\cos^2 x}$

$= \dfrac{(\sin x + 1)^2}{\cos^2 x}$

55. $\dfrac{\cos x}{\sin x} + \dfrac{\sin x}{\cos x} + \dfrac{\csc x}{\sec x}$

$= \dfrac{\cos^2 x \sec x + \sin^2 x \sec x + \csc x \sin x \cos x}{\sin x \cos x \sec x}$

$= \dfrac{\sec x(\cos^2 x + \sin^2 x) + (1)\cos x}{\sin x(1)}$

$= \dfrac{\sec x + \cos x}{\sin x}$

57. Factor numerator as difference of squares, denominator as sum of cubes.

$\dfrac{\sin^4 x - \cos^4 x}{\sin^3 x + \cos^3 x}$

$= \dfrac{(\sin^2 x + \cos^2 x)(\sin^2 x - \cos^2 x)}{(\sin x + \cos x)(\sin^2 x - \sin x \cos x + \cos^2 x)}$

$= \dfrac{(1)(\sin x + \cos x)(\sin x - \cos x)}{(\sin x + \cos x)(\sin^2 x + \cos^2 x - \sin x \cos x)}$

$= \dfrac{\sin x - \cos x}{1 - \sin x \cos x}$

59. $\sin\left(\theta+\dfrac{\pi}{3}\right)\neq\sin\theta+\sin\left(\dfrac{\pi}{3}\right)$

Answers will vary.
We will substitute a convenient value to prove

the equation is false, namely $\theta=\dfrac{\pi}{3}$.

$$\sin\left(\dfrac{\pi}{3}+\dfrac{\pi}{3}\right)\neq\sin\left(\dfrac{\pi}{3}\right)+\sin\left(\dfrac{\pi}{3}\right)$$
$$\sin\left(\dfrac{2\pi}{3}\right)\neq\dfrac{\sqrt{3}}{2}+\dfrac{\sqrt{3}}{2}$$
$$\dfrac{\sqrt{3}}{2}\neq\sqrt{3}$$

61. $\cos(2\theta)\neq2\cos\theta$

Answers will vary.
$\cos(2\theta)$ has an amplitude of 1.
$2\cos\theta$ has an amplitude of 2.
They cannot possibly be equal.

63. $\tan\left(\dfrac{\theta}{4}\right)\neq\dfrac{\tan\theta}{\tan4}$

Answers will vary.
We will substitute a convenient value to prove
the equation is false, namely $\theta=\pi$.

$$\tan\left(\dfrac{\pi}{4}\right)\neq\dfrac{\tan\pi}{\tan4}$$
$$1\neq0$$

65. a. $d^2=(20+x\cos\theta)^2+(20-x\sin\theta)^2$
$$=400+40x\cos\theta+x^2\cos^2\theta$$
$$\quad+400-40x\sin\theta+x^2\sin^2\theta$$
$$=800+40x(\cos\theta-\sin\theta)$$
$$\quad+x^2\left(\cos^2\theta+\sin^2\theta\right)$$
$$=800+40x(\cos\theta-\sin\theta)+x^2$$

b.   The distance between the first row and the
8th row is $3\cdot7=21$ feet.
$$d^2=800+40x(\cos\theta-\sin\theta)+x^2$$
$$=800+40(21)(\cos18°-\sin18°)+(21)^2$$
$$=800+840(\cos18°-\sin18°)+441$$
$$=1241+840(\cos18°-\sin18°)$$

$$d=\sqrt{1241+840(\cos18°-\sin18°)}$$
$$\approx42.2\text{ ft}$$

67. a. $h^2=\left(\sqrt{\cot x}\right)^2+\left(\sqrt{\tan x}\right)^2$
$$=\cot x+\tan x$$
$$h=\sqrt{\cot x+\tan x}$$

Let $x=1.5$ rad.
$$h=\sqrt{\cot(1.5)+\tan(1.5)}\approx3.76\text{ units}$$

b. $h^2=\cot x+\tan x$
$$=\dfrac{\cos x}{\sin x}+\dfrac{\sin x}{\cos x}$$
$$=\dfrac{\cos^2 x+\sin^2 x}{\sin x\cos x}$$
$$=\dfrac{1}{\sin x\cos x}$$
$$=\csc x\sec x$$
$$h=\sqrt{\csc x\sec x}$$

Let $x=1.5$ rad.
$$h=\sqrt{\csc(1.5)\sec(1.5)}\approx3.76\text{ units}$$
Yes, the answers match.

69.   Use Pythagorean Theorem.
$$D^2=(20+x\cos\theta)^2+(x\sin\theta)^2$$
$$=400+40x\cos\theta+x^2\cos^2\theta+x^2\sin^2\theta$$
$$=400+40x\cos\theta+x^2\left(\cos^2\theta+\sin^2\theta\right)$$
$$=400+40x\cos\theta+x^2$$
The opposite side of θ can be represented by
$x\sin\theta$, which is equivalent to the base of the
triangle that contains side D.
$$D^2=400+40x\cos\theta+x^2$$
$$=400+40(21)\cos(18°)+(21)^2$$
$$=400+840\cos(18°)+441$$
$$=841+840\cos(18°)$$
$$D=\sqrt{841+840\cos(18°)}\approx40.5\text{ ft}$$

71. $\sin\alpha=\dfrac{I_1\cos\theta}{\sqrt{(I_1\cos\theta)^2+(I_2\sin\theta)^2}}$
$$=\dfrac{I_1\cos\theta}{\sqrt{(I_1\cos\theta)^2+(I_1\sin\theta)^2}}$$
$$=\dfrac{I_1\cos\theta}{\sqrt{I_1^{\,2}\cos^2\theta+I_1^{\,2}\sin^2\theta}}$$
$$=\dfrac{I_1\cos\theta}{\sqrt{I_1^{\,2}\left(\cos^2\theta+\sin^2\theta\right)}}$$
$$=\dfrac{I_1\cos\theta}{\sqrt{I_1^{\,2}(1)}}=\dfrac{I_1\cos\theta}{I_1}=\cos\theta$$

73. Answers will vary.

75. $\sin^4 x + 2\sin^2 x \cos^2 x + \cos^4 x$

$= \left(\sin^2 x + \cos^2 x\right)^2$

$= (1)^2$

$= 1$

77. Le h be the height of the tower.

$\tan 77° = \dfrac{h}{265}$

$h = 265 \tan 77° \approx 1148$ ft

79. $P(-16, -63); \ x = -16, \ y = -63$

$r = \sqrt{(-16)^2 + (-63)^2} = \sqrt{4225} = 65$

$\sin\theta = \dfrac{-63}{65}; \ \csc\theta = \dfrac{-65}{63}; \ \cos\theta = \dfrac{-16}{65};$

$\sec\theta = \dfrac{-65}{16}; \ \tan\theta = \dfrac{63}{16}; \ \cot\theta = \dfrac{16}{63};$

81. $y = 2\sin(2t)$ for $t \in [0, 2\pi)$

$|A| = 2; \ P = \dfrac{2\pi}{2} = \pi$

Reference Rectangle: $2|A| = 4$ by $P = \pi$

Ticmarks $\dfrac{1}{4}(\pi) = \dfrac{\pi}{4}$ units apart

Rule of fourths: $t = 0, \dfrac{\pi}{4}, \dfrac{\pi}{2}, \dfrac{3\pi}{4}, \pi$

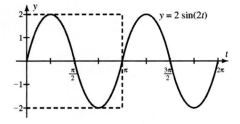

Technology Highlight

Exercise 1:

$\tan\alpha = \dfrac{40}{9} \ (\text{QIII}) \Rightarrow$

$r_\alpha = \sqrt{(-9)^2 + (-40)^2} = 41$

$\cos\alpha = -\dfrac{9}{41}; \ \sin\alpha = -\dfrac{40}{41}$

$\cos\beta = \dfrac{12}{37} \ (\text{QIV}) \Rightarrow$

$y_\beta = -\sqrt{37^2 - 12^2} = -35$

$\sin\beta = -\dfrac{35}{37}; \ \tan\beta = -\dfrac{35}{12}$

$\cos(\alpha - \beta) = \cos\alpha\cos\beta + \sin\alpha\sin\beta$

$\quad = \left(-\dfrac{9}{41}\right)\left(\dfrac{12}{37}\right) + \left(-\dfrac{40}{41}\right)\left(-\dfrac{35}{37}\right)$

$\quad = -\dfrac{108}{1517} + \dfrac{1400}{1517}$

$\quad = \dfrac{1292}{1517}$

$\sin(\alpha - \beta) = \sin\alpha\cos\beta - \cos\alpha\sin\beta$

$\quad = \left(-\dfrac{40}{41}\right)\left(\dfrac{12}{37}\right) - \left(-\dfrac{9}{41}\right)\left(-\dfrac{35}{37}\right)$

$\quad = -\dfrac{480}{1517} - \dfrac{315}{1517}$

$\quad = -\dfrac{795}{1517}$

$\tan(\alpha - \beta) = \dfrac{\tan\alpha - \tan\beta}{1 + \tan\alpha\tan\beta}$

$\quad = \dfrac{\dfrac{40}{9} - \left(-\dfrac{35}{12}\right)}{1 + \left(\dfrac{40}{9}\right)\left(-\dfrac{35}{12}\right)}$

$\quad = \dfrac{\dfrac{40}{9} - \left(-\dfrac{35}{12}\right)}{1 + \left(\dfrac{40}{9}\right)\left(-\dfrac{35}{12}\right)} \cdot \dfrac{108}{108}$

$\quad = \dfrac{480 + 315}{108 - 1400}$

$\quad = -\dfrac{795}{1292}$

5.2 Exercises

1. false; QII

3. repeat; opposite

5. Answers will vary.

7. $\cos 105° = \cos\left(45° + 60°\right)$
$$= \cos 45° \cos 60° - \sin 45° \sin 60°$$
$$= \left(\frac{\sqrt{2}}{2}\right)\left(\frac{1}{2}\right) - \left(\frac{\sqrt{2}}{2}\right)\left(\frac{\sqrt{3}}{2}\right)$$
$$= \frac{\sqrt{2} - \sqrt{6}}{4}$$

9. $\cos\left(\frac{7\pi}{12}\right) = \cos\left(\frac{\pi}{3} + \frac{\pi}{4}\right)$
$$= \cos\left(\frac{\pi}{3}\right)\cos\left(\frac{\pi}{4}\right) - \sin\left(\frac{\pi}{3}\right)\sin\left(\frac{\pi}{4}\right)$$
$$= \left(\frac{1}{2}\right)\left(\frac{\sqrt{2}}{2}\right) - \left(\frac{\sqrt{3}}{2}\right)\left(\frac{\sqrt{2}}{2}\right)$$
$$= \frac{\sqrt{2} - \sqrt{6}}{4}$$

11. a. $\cos\left(45° + 30°\right)$
$$= \cos 45° \cos 30° - \sin 45° \sin 30°$$
$$= \left(\frac{\sqrt{2}}{2}\right)\left(\frac{\sqrt{3}}{2}\right) - \left(\frac{\sqrt{2}}{2}\right)\left(\frac{1}{2}\right)$$
$$= \frac{\sqrt{6} - \sqrt{2}}{4}$$

    b. $\cos\left(120° - 45°\right)$
$$= \cos 120° \cos 45° + \sin 120° \sin 45°$$
$$= \left(-\frac{1}{2}\right)\left(\frac{\sqrt{2}}{2}\right) + \left(\frac{\sqrt{3}}{2}\right)\left(\frac{\sqrt{2}}{2}\right)$$
$$= \frac{-\sqrt{2} + \sqrt{6}}{4}$$
$$= \frac{\sqrt{6} - \sqrt{2}}{4}$$

13. $\cos\left(7\theta\right)\cos\left(2\theta\right) + \sin\left(7\theta\right)\sin\left(2\theta\right)$
$$= \cos\left(7\theta - 2\theta\right)$$
$$= \cos\left(5\theta\right)$$

15. $\cos 183° \cos 153° + \sin 183° \sin 153°$
$$= \cos\left(183° - 153°\right)$$
$$= \cos 30°$$
$$= \frac{\sqrt{3}}{2}$$

17. $\sin \alpha = -\frac{4}{5}$ (QIV) $\Rightarrow x_\alpha = \sqrt{5^2 - \left(-4\right)^2} = 3$
$$\cos \alpha = \frac{3}{5}; \ \tan \alpha = -\frac{4}{3}$$
$$\tan \beta = -\frac{5}{12} \text{ (QII)} \Rightarrow r_\beta = \sqrt{12^2 + \left(-5\right)^2} = 13$$
$$\sin \beta = \frac{5}{13}; \ \cos \beta = -\frac{12}{13}$$
$$\cos\left(\alpha + \beta\right) = \cos \alpha \cos \beta - \sin \alpha \sin \beta$$
$$= \left(\frac{3}{5}\right)\left(-\frac{12}{13}\right) - \left(-\frac{4}{5}\right)\left(\frac{5}{13}\right)$$
$$= -\frac{36}{65} + \frac{20}{65}$$
$$= -\frac{16}{65}$$

19. $\cos 57° = \sin\left(90° - 57°\right) = \sin 33°$

    Recall: $\left(\sin \frac{\pi}{2} - t\right) = \cos t$

21. $\tan\left(\frac{5\pi}{12}\right) = \cot\left(\frac{\pi}{2} - \frac{5\pi}{12}\right) = \cot\left(\frac{\pi}{12}\right)$

    Recall: $\left(\cot \frac{\pi}{2} - t\right) = \tan t$

23. $\sin\left(\frac{\pi}{6} - \theta\right) = \cos\left(\frac{\pi}{2} - \left(\frac{\pi}{6} - \theta\right)\right)$
$$= \cos\left(\frac{\pi}{2} - \frac{\pi}{6} + \theta\right)$$
$$= \cos\left(\frac{\pi}{3} + \theta\right)$$

25. $\sin\left(3x\right)\cos\left(5x\right) + \cos\left(3x\right)\sin\left(5x\right)$
$$= \sin\left(3x + 5x\right)$$
$$= \sin\left(8x\right)$$

27. $\dfrac{\tan\left(5\theta\right) - \tan\left(2\theta\right)}{1 + \tan\left(5\theta\right)\tan\left(2\theta\right)} = \tan\left(5\theta - 2\theta\right)$
$$= \tan\left(3\theta\right)$$

29. $\sin 137° \cos 47° - \cos 137° \sin 47°$
 $= \sin(137° - 47°)$
 $= \sin 90°$
 $= 1$

31. $\dfrac{\tan\left(\dfrac{11\pi}{21}\right) - \tan\left(\dfrac{4\pi}{21}\right)}{1 + \tan\left(\dfrac{11\pi}{21}\right)\tan\left(\dfrac{4\pi}{21}\right)}$

 $= \tan\left(\dfrac{11\pi}{21} - \dfrac{4\pi}{21}\right)$

 $= \tan\left(\dfrac{\pi}{3}\right)$

 $= \sqrt{3}$

33. $\cos\alpha = -\dfrac{7}{25}$ (QII) $\Rightarrow y_\alpha = \sqrt{25^2 - (-7)^2} = 24$

 $\sin\alpha = \dfrac{24}{25}; \quad \tan\alpha = -\dfrac{24}{7}$

 $\cot\beta = \dfrac{15}{8}$ (QIII) $\Rightarrow r_\beta = \sqrt{15^2 + 8^2} = 17$

 $\sin\beta = -\dfrac{8}{17}; \quad \cos\beta = -\dfrac{15}{17}; \quad \tan\beta = \dfrac{8}{15}$

 a. $\sin(\alpha + \beta) = \sin\alpha\cos\beta + \cos\alpha\sin\beta$

 $= \left(\dfrac{24}{25}\right)\left(-\dfrac{15}{17}\right) + \left(-\dfrac{7}{25}\right)\left(-\dfrac{8}{17}\right)$

 $= -\dfrac{360}{425} + \dfrac{56}{425}$

 $= -\dfrac{304}{425}$

 b. $\tan(\alpha + \beta) = \dfrac{\tan\alpha + \tan\beta}{1 + \tan\alpha\tan\beta}$

 $= \dfrac{-\dfrac{24}{7} + \dfrac{8}{15}}{1 - \left(-\dfrac{24}{7}\right)\left(\dfrac{8}{15}\right)}$

 $= \dfrac{-\dfrac{24}{7} + \dfrac{8}{15}}{1 - \left(-\dfrac{24}{7}\right)\left(\dfrac{8}{15}\right)} \cdot \dfrac{105}{105}$

 $= \dfrac{-360 + 56}{105 + 192}$

 $= -\dfrac{304}{297}$

35. $\sin 105° = \sin(45° + 60°)$
 $= \sin 45° \cos 60° + \cos 45° \sin 60°$

 $= \left(\dfrac{\sqrt{2}}{2}\right)\left(\dfrac{1}{2}\right) + \left(\dfrac{\sqrt{2}}{2}\right)\left(\dfrac{\sqrt{3}}{2}\right)$

 $= \dfrac{\sqrt{2} + \sqrt{6}}{4}$

 $= \dfrac{\sqrt{6} + \sqrt{2}}{4}$

37. $\sin\left(\dfrac{5\pi}{12}\right) = \sin\left(\dfrac{\pi}{6} + \dfrac{\pi}{4}\right)$

 $= \sin\left(\dfrac{\pi}{6}\right)\cos\left(\dfrac{\pi}{4}\right) + \cos\left(\dfrac{\pi}{6}\right)\sin\left(\dfrac{\pi}{4}\right)$

 $= \left(\dfrac{1}{2}\right)\left(\dfrac{\sqrt{2}}{2}\right) + \dfrac{\sqrt{3}}{2}\left(\dfrac{\sqrt{2}}{2}\right)$

 $= \dfrac{\sqrt{2} + \sqrt{6}}{4}$

 $= \dfrac{\sqrt{6} + \sqrt{2}}{4}$

39. $\tan 150° = \tan(180° - 30°)$

 $= \dfrac{\tan 180° - \tan 30°}{1 + \tan 180° \tan 30°}$

 $= \dfrac{0 - \dfrac{\sqrt{3}}{3}}{1 + (0)\left(\dfrac{\sqrt{3}}{3}\right)}$

 $= -\dfrac{\sqrt{3}}{3}$

41. $\tan\left(\dfrac{2\pi}{3}\right) = \tan\left(\dfrac{\pi}{3} + \dfrac{\pi}{3}\right)$

 $= \dfrac{\tan\left(\dfrac{\pi}{3}\right) + \tan\left(\dfrac{\pi}{3}\right)}{1 - \tan\left(\dfrac{\pi}{3}\right)\tan\left(\dfrac{\pi}{3}\right)}$

 $= \dfrac{\sqrt{3} + \sqrt{3}}{1 - \left(\sqrt{3}\right)\left(\sqrt{3}\right)}$

 $= \dfrac{2\sqrt{3}}{-2}$

 $= -\sqrt{3}$

43. a. $\sin(45° - 30°)$

$= \sin 45° \cos 30° - \cos 45° \sin 30°$

$= \left(\dfrac{\sqrt{2}}{2}\right)\left(\dfrac{\sqrt{3}}{2}\right) - \left(\dfrac{\sqrt{2}}{2}\right)\left(\dfrac{1}{2}\right)$

$= \dfrac{\sqrt{6} - \sqrt{2}}{4}$

    b. $\sin(135° - 120°)$

$= \sin 135° \cos 120° - \cos 135° \sin 120°$

$= \left(\dfrac{\sqrt{2}}{2}\right)\left(\dfrac{-1}{2}\right) - \left(-\dfrac{\sqrt{2}}{2}\right)\left(\dfrac{\sqrt{3}}{2}\right)$

$= \dfrac{-\sqrt{2} + \sqrt{6}}{4}$

$= \dfrac{\sqrt{6} - \sqrt{2}}{4}$

45. In Exercise 7 and 35, we evaluated

$\cos 105° = \dfrac{\sqrt{2} - \sqrt{6}}{4}$ and $\sin 105° = \dfrac{\sqrt{6} + \sqrt{2}}{4}$.

$\sin 255° = \sin(150° + 105°)$

$= \sin 150° \cos 105° + \cos 150° \sin 105°$

$= \left(\dfrac{1}{2}\right)\left(\dfrac{\sqrt{2} - \sqrt{6}}{4}\right) + \left(\dfrac{-\sqrt{3}}{2}\right)\left(\dfrac{\sqrt{6} + \sqrt{2}}{4}\right)$

$= \dfrac{\sqrt{2} - \sqrt{6}}{8} - \dfrac{\sqrt{18} + \sqrt{6}}{8}$

$= \dfrac{\sqrt{2} - \sqrt{6} - 3\sqrt{2} - \sqrt{6}}{8}$

$= \dfrac{-2\sqrt{2} - 2\sqrt{6}}{8}$

$= \dfrac{-\sqrt{2} - \sqrt{6}}{4}$

47. $\sin \alpha = \dfrac{12}{13} \Rightarrow x_\alpha = \sqrt{13^2 - 12^2} = 5$

$\cos \alpha = \dfrac{5}{13}$; $\tan \alpha = \dfrac{12}{5}$

$\tan \beta = \dfrac{35}{12} \Rightarrow r_\beta = \sqrt{12^2 + 35^2} = 37$

$\sin \beta = \dfrac{35}{37}$; $\cos \beta = \dfrac{12}{37}$

    a. $\sin(\alpha + \beta) = \sin \alpha \cos \beta + \cos \alpha \sin \beta$

$= \left(\dfrac{12}{13}\right)\left(\dfrac{12}{37}\right) + \left(\dfrac{5}{13}\right)\left(\dfrac{35}{37}\right)$

$= \dfrac{144}{481} + \dfrac{175}{481}$

$= \dfrac{319}{481}$

47. b. $\cos(\alpha - \beta) = \cos \alpha \cos \beta + \sin \alpha \sin \beta$

$= \left(\dfrac{5}{13}\right)\left(\dfrac{12}{37}\right) + \left(\dfrac{12}{13}\right)\left(\dfrac{35}{37}\right)$

$= \dfrac{60}{481} + \dfrac{420}{481}$

$= \dfrac{480}{481}$

    c. $\tan(\alpha + \beta) = \dfrac{\tan \alpha + \tan \beta}{1 - \tan \alpha \tan \beta}$

$= \dfrac{\dfrac{12}{5} + \dfrac{35}{12}}{1 - \left(\dfrac{12}{5}\right)\left(\dfrac{35}{12}\right)}$

$= \dfrac{\dfrac{12}{5} + \dfrac{35}{12}}{1 - \left(\dfrac{12}{5}\right)\left(\dfrac{35}{12}\right)} \cdot \dfrac{60}{60}$

$= \dfrac{144 + 175}{60 - 420}$

$= -\dfrac{319}{360}$

49. $\sin \alpha = \dfrac{28}{53} \Rightarrow x_\alpha = -\sqrt{53^2 - 28^2} = -45$

$\cos \alpha = -\dfrac{45}{53}$; $\tan \alpha = -\dfrac{28}{45}$

$\cos \beta = -\dfrac{13}{85} \Rightarrow y_\beta = \sqrt{85^2 - (-13)^2} = 84$

$\sin \beta = \dfrac{84}{85}$; $\tan \beta = -\dfrac{84}{13}$

    a. $\sin(\alpha - \beta) = \sin \alpha \cos \beta - \cos \alpha \sin \beta$

$= \left(\dfrac{28}{53}\right)\left(-\dfrac{13}{85}\right) - \left(-\dfrac{45}{53}\right)\left(\dfrac{84}{85}\right)$

$= -\dfrac{364}{4505} + \dfrac{3780}{4505}$

$= \dfrac{3416}{4505}$

    b. $\cos(\alpha + \beta) = \cos \alpha \cos \beta - \sin \alpha \sin \beta$

$= \left(-\dfrac{45}{53}\right)\left(-\dfrac{13}{85}\right) - \left(\dfrac{28}{53}\right)\left(\dfrac{84}{85}\right)$

$= \dfrac{585}{4505} - \dfrac{2352}{4505}$

$= -\dfrac{1767}{4505}$

49. c. $\tan(\alpha-\beta) = \dfrac{\tan\alpha - \tan\beta}{1+\tan\alpha\tan\beta}$

$= \dfrac{\dfrac{28}{45} - -\dfrac{84}{13}}{1+\dfrac{-28}{45}\cdot\dfrac{-84}{13}}$

$= \dfrac{\dfrac{28}{45} - -\dfrac{84}{13}}{1+\dfrac{-28}{45}\cdot\dfrac{-84}{13}} \cdot \dfrac{585}{585}$

$= \dfrac{-364+3780}{585+2352}$

$= \dfrac{3416}{2937}$

51. Let h be the hypotenuse of the smaller triangle with angle θ. $h = \sqrt{12^2+5^2} = 13$

a. $\sin A = \sin(30°+\theta)$

$= \sin30°\cos\theta + \cos30°\sin\theta$

$= \left(\dfrac{1}{2}\right)\left(\dfrac{12}{13}\right) + \left(\dfrac{\sqrt{3}}{2}\right)\left(\dfrac{5}{13}\right)$

$= \dfrac{12+5\sqrt{3}}{26}$

b. $\cos A = \cos(30°+\theta)$

$= \cos30°\cos\theta - \sin30°\sin\theta$

$= \left(\dfrac{\sqrt{3}}{2}\right)\left(\dfrac{12}{13}\right) - \left(\dfrac{1}{2}\right)\left(\dfrac{5}{13}\right)$

$= \dfrac{12\sqrt{3}-5}{26}$

c. $\tan A = \dfrac{\sin A}{\cos A}$

$= \dfrac{\dfrac{12+5\sqrt{3}}{26}}{\dfrac{12\sqrt{3}-5}{26}}$

$= \dfrac{12+5\sqrt{3}}{12\sqrt{3}-5}$

53. Third angle of 1st triangle: $90-\alpha$
Third angle of the 3rd triangle: $90-\beta$
Supplementary angles:
$90-\alpha+\theta+90-\beta = 180 \Rightarrow \theta = \alpha+\beta$
Let h_1 be the hypotenuse of the 1st triangle.

$h_1 = \sqrt{32^2+24^2} = 40$

Let h_2 be the hypotenuse of the 3rd triangle.

$h_2 = \sqrt{45^2+28^2} = 53$

$\sin\alpha = \dfrac{24}{40}; \cos\alpha = \dfrac{32}{40}$

$\sin\beta = \dfrac{28}{53}; \cos\beta = \dfrac{45}{53}$

a. $\sin\theta = \sin(\alpha+\beta)$

$= \sin\alpha\cos\beta + \cos\alpha\sin\beta$

$= \left(\dfrac{24}{40}\right)\left(\dfrac{45}{53}\right) + \left(\dfrac{32}{40}\right)\left(\dfrac{28}{53}\right)$

$= \dfrac{1080}{2120} + \dfrac{896}{2120}$

$= \dfrac{1976}{2120} = \dfrac{247}{265}$

b. $\cos\theta = \cos(\alpha+\beta)$

$= \cos\alpha\cos\beta - \sin\alpha\sin\beta$

$= \left(\dfrac{32}{40}\right)\left(\dfrac{45}{53}\right) - \left(\dfrac{24}{40}\right)\left(\dfrac{28}{53}\right)$

$= \dfrac{1440}{2120} - \dfrac{672}{2120}$

$= \dfrac{768}{2120} = \dfrac{96}{265}$

c. $\tan\theta = \dfrac{\sin\theta}{\cos\theta}$

$= \dfrac{\dfrac{247}{265}}{\dfrac{96}{265}}$

$= \dfrac{247}{96}$

55. $\sin(\pi-\alpha) = \sin\pi\cos\alpha - \cos\pi\sin\alpha$

$= (0)\cos\alpha - (-1)\sin\alpha$

$= \sin\alpha$

57. $\cos\left(x+\dfrac{\pi}{4}\right) = \cos x\cos\left(\dfrac{\pi}{4}\right) - \sin x\sin\left(\dfrac{\pi}{4}\right)$

$= \cos x\left(\dfrac{\sqrt{2}}{2}\right) - \sin x\left(\dfrac{\sqrt{2}}{2}\right)$

$= \dfrac{\sqrt{2}}{2}(\cos x - \sin x)$

59. $\tan\left(x+\dfrac{\pi}{4}\right)=\dfrac{\tan x+\tan\left(\dfrac{\pi}{4}\right)}{1-\tan x\tan\left(\dfrac{\pi}{4}\right)}$

$=\dfrac{\tan x+1}{1-\tan x}$

$=\dfrac{1+\tan x}{1-\tan x}$

61. $\cos(\alpha+\beta)+\cos(\alpha-\beta)$

$=\cos\alpha\cos\beta-\sin\alpha\sin\beta+\cos\alpha\cos\beta+\sin\alpha\sin\beta$

$=2\cos\alpha\cos\beta$

63. $\cos(2t)=\cos(t+t)$

$=\cos t\cos t-\sin t\sin t$

$=\cos^2 t-\sin^2 t$

65. $\sin(3t)=\sin(2t+t)$

$=\sin(2t)\cos t+\cos(2t)\sin t$

$=(2\sin t\cos t)\cos t+\left(\cos^2 t-\sin^2 t\right)\sin t$

$=2\sin t\cos^2 t+\sin t\cos^2 t-\sin^3 t$

$=3\sin t\cos^2 t-\sin^3 t$

$=3\sin t\left(1-\sin^2 t\right)-\sin^3 t$

$=3\sin t-3\sin^3 t-\sin^3 t$

$=-4\sin^3 t+3\sin t$

67. $\cos\left(x-\dfrac{\pi}{4}\right)=\cos x\cos\left(\dfrac{\pi}{4}\right)+\sin x\sin\left(\dfrac{\pi}{4}\right)$

$=\cos x\left(\dfrac{\sqrt{2}}{2}\right)+\sin x\left(\dfrac{\sqrt{2}}{2}\right)$

$=\dfrac{\sqrt{2}}{2}(\cos x+\sin x)$

69. $F=\dfrac{Wk}{c}\tan(p-\theta)$

$=\dfrac{Wk}{c}\tan\left(\dfrac{\pi}{6}-\dfrac{\pi}{4}\right)$

$=\dfrac{Wk}{c}\cdot\dfrac{\tan\left(\dfrac{\pi}{6}\right)-\tan\left(\dfrac{\pi}{4}\right)}{1+\tan\left(\dfrac{\pi}{6}\right)\tan\left(\dfrac{\pi}{4}\right)}$

$=\dfrac{Wk}{c}\cdot\dfrac{\dfrac{1}{\sqrt{3}}-1}{1+\left(\dfrac{1}{\sqrt{3}}\right)(1)}$

$=\dfrac{Wk}{c}\cdot\dfrac{1-\sqrt{3}}{\sqrt{3}+1}$

$=\dfrac{Wk}{c}\cdot\dfrac{1-\sqrt{3}}{1+\sqrt{3}}$

71. $R=\dfrac{\cos s\cos t}{\omega C\sin(s+t)}$

$=\dfrac{\cos s\cos t}{\omega C(\sin s\cos t+\cos s\sin t)}$

$=\dfrac{\cos s\cos t\cdot\dfrac{1}{\cos s\cos t}}{\omega C(\sin s\cos t+\cos s\sin t)\cdot\dfrac{1}{\cos s\cos t}}$

$=\dfrac{1}{\omega C\left(\dfrac{\sin s\cos t}{\cos s\cos t}+\dfrac{\cos s\sin t}{\cos s\cos t}\right)}$

$=\dfrac{1}{\omega C\left(\dfrac{\sin s}{\cos s}+\dfrac{\sin t}{\cos t}\right)}$

$=\dfrac{1}{\omega C(\tan s+\tan t)}$

73. $\dfrac{A}{B}=\dfrac{\tan\theta}{\tan(90°-\theta)}$

$=\dfrac{\dfrac{\sin\theta}{\cos\theta}}{\dfrac{\sin(90°-\theta)}{\cos(90°-\theta)}}$

$=\dfrac{\sin\theta\cos(90°-\theta)}{\cos\theta\sin(90°-\theta)}$

$=\dfrac{\sin\theta(\cos 90°\cos\theta+\sin 90°\sin\theta)}{\cos\theta(\sin 90°\cos\theta-\cos 90°\sin\theta)}$

$=\dfrac{\sin\theta(0+\sin\theta)}{\cos\theta(\cos\theta-0)}$

$=\dfrac{\sin^2\theta}{\cos^2\theta}$

$=\tan^2\theta$

75. This is verified using sum identity for sine.

$P_1(t)+P_2(t)$

$=A\sin(2\pi ft)+A\sin\left(2\pi ft+\dfrac{\pi}{2}\right)$

$=A\sin(2\pi ft)$

$\quad+A\left[\sin(2\pi ft)\cos\left(\dfrac{\pi}{2}\right)+\cos(2\pi ft)\sin\left(\dfrac{\pi}{2}\right)\right]$

$=A\sin(2\pi ft)+A\left[\sin(2\pi ft)(0)+\cos(2\pi ft)(1)\right]$

$=A\sin(2\pi ft)+A\cos(2\pi ft)$

$=A\left[\sin(2\pi ft)+\cos(2\pi ft)\right]$

77. $f(x) = \sin x$

$$\frac{f(x+h)-f(x)}{h} = \frac{\sin(x+h)-\sin x}{h}$$

$$= \frac{\sin x \cos h + \cos x \sin h - \sin x}{h}$$

$$= \frac{\sin x \cos h - \sin x + \cos x \sin h}{h}$$

$$= \frac{\sin x(\cos h - 1) + \cos x \sin h}{h}$$

$$= \sin x \left(\frac{\cos h - 1}{h} \right) + \cos x \frac{(\sin h)}{h}$$

79. $\cos 1665° = \cos(225° + 360° \cdot 4)$

$$= \cos(225°)$$

$$= -\frac{\sqrt{2}}{3}$$

81. $\sin\left(\dfrac{41\pi}{6} \right) = \sin\left(\dfrac{5\pi}{6} + 2\pi \cdot 3 \right)$

$$= \sin\left(\frac{5\pi}{6} \right)$$

$$= \frac{1}{2}$$

83. $D = d$, so $D^2 = d^2$, and

$$D^2 = (\cos\alpha - \cos\beta)^2 + (\sin\alpha - \sin\beta)^2$$

$$= \cos^2\alpha - 2\cos\alpha\cos\beta + \cos^2\beta$$

$$+ \sin^2\alpha - 2\sin\alpha\sin\beta + \sin^2\beta$$

$$= 2 - 2\cos\alpha\cos\beta - 2\sin\alpha\sin\beta$$

$$d^2 = \sin^2(\alpha-\beta) + \left[\cos(\alpha-\beta) - 1 \right]^2$$

$$= \sin^2(\alpha-\beta) + \cos^2(\alpha-\beta) - 2\cos(\alpha-\beta) + 1$$

$$= 2 - 2\cos(\alpha-\beta)$$

$D^2 = d^2$ so

$$2 - 2\cos\alpha\cos\beta - 2\sin\alpha\sin\beta = 2 - 2\cos(\alpha-\beta)$$

$$\frac{-2\cos\alpha\cos\beta - 2\sin\alpha\sin\beta}{-2} = \frac{-2\cos(\alpha-\beta)}{-2}$$

Since this is an identity, we know that
$\cos\alpha\cos\beta + \sin\alpha\sin\beta = \cos(\alpha-\beta)$.

85. $\left(\dfrac{\sqrt{7}}{4}, \dfrac{3}{4} \right)$

$$\left(\frac{\sqrt{7}}{4} \right)^2 + \left(\frac{3}{4} \right)^2 = \frac{7}{16} + \frac{9}{16} = \frac{16}{16} = 1$$

$$\sin\theta = \frac{3}{4}; \ \cos\theta = \frac{\sqrt{7}}{4}; \ \tan\theta = \frac{3}{\sqrt{7}}$$

87. For a 45-45-90 triangle, the standard ratio of the sides is 1, 1, $\sqrt{2}$.

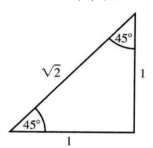

For a 30-60-90 triangle, the standard ratio of the sides is 1, $\sqrt{3}$, 2.

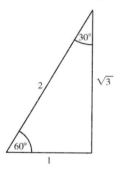

89. $y = -2\cos\left(t + \dfrac{\pi}{4} \right); \ t \in [0, 2\pi)$

$|A| = 2; \ P = 2\pi$

HS: $\dfrac{\pi}{4}$ units left

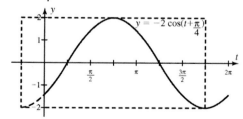

<u>Mid-Chapter Check</u>

1. $\cos^2 x - \cot^2 x = \cos^2 x - \dfrac{\cos^2 x}{\sin^2 x}$

    $\qquad = \cos^2 x \left(1 - \dfrac{1}{\sin^2 x}\right)$

    $\qquad = \cos^2 x \left(1 - \csc^2 x\right)$

    $\qquad = \cos^2 x \left(-\cot^2 x\right)$

    $\qquad = -\cos^2 x \cot^2 x$

3. $\dfrac{2\sin x}{\sec x} - \dfrac{\cos x}{\csc x} = \dfrac{2\sin x \csc x - \cos x \sec x}{\sec x \csc x}$

    $\qquad = \dfrac{2(1) - 1}{\sec x \csc x}$

    $\qquad = \dfrac{1}{\sec x \csc x}$

    $\qquad = \cos x \sin x$

5. $1 + \sec^2 x \neq \tan^2 x$
    Answers will vary.
    We will substitute a convenient value to prove
    the equation is false, namely $\theta = 0$.
    $1 + \sec^2(0) \neq \tan^2(0)$
    $\qquad 1 + 1^2 \neq 0^2$
    $\qquad\quad 2 \neq 0$

7. $\cos(6\alpha)\cos(2\alpha) + \sin(6\alpha)\sin(2\alpha)$
    $= \cos(6\alpha - 2\alpha)$
    $= \cos(4\alpha)$

9. $\cos\alpha = \dfrac{3}{5} \Rightarrow y_\alpha = \sqrt{5^2 - 3^2} = 4$

    $\sin\alpha = \dfrac{4}{5}$; $\tan\alpha = \dfrac{4}{3}$

    $\cot\beta = \dfrac{5}{12} \Rightarrow r_\beta = \sqrt{5^2 + 12^2} = 13$

    $\sin\beta = \dfrac{12}{13}$; $\cos\beta = \dfrac{5}{13}$; $\tan\beta = \dfrac{12}{5}$

    a. $\sin(\alpha + \beta) = \sin\alpha\cos\beta + \cos\alpha\sin\beta$

    $\qquad = \left(\dfrac{4}{5}\right)\left(\dfrac{5}{13}\right) + \left(\dfrac{3}{5}\right)\left(\dfrac{12}{13}\right)$

    $\qquad = \dfrac{20}{65} + \dfrac{36}{65}$

    $\qquad = \dfrac{56}{65}$

    b. $\cos(\alpha - \beta) = \cos\alpha\cos\beta + \sin\alpha\sin\beta$

    $\qquad = \left(\dfrac{3}{5}\right)\left(\dfrac{5}{13}\right) + \left(\dfrac{4}{5}\right)\left(\dfrac{12}{13}\right)$

    $\qquad = \dfrac{15}{65} + \dfrac{48}{65}$

    $\qquad = \dfrac{63}{65}$

    c. $\tan(\alpha + \beta) = \dfrac{\tan\alpha + \tan\beta}{1 - \tan\alpha\tan\beta}$

    $\qquad = \dfrac{\dfrac{4}{3} + \dfrac{12}{5}}{1 - \left(\dfrac{4}{3}\right)\left(\dfrac{12}{5}\right)}$

    $\qquad = \dfrac{\dfrac{4}{3} + \dfrac{12}{5}}{1 - \left(\dfrac{4}{3}\right)\left(\dfrac{12}{5}\right)} \cdot \dfrac{15}{15}$

    $\qquad = \dfrac{20 + 36}{15 - 48}$

    $\qquad = -\dfrac{56}{33}$

Reinforcing Basic Concepts

Exercise 1:

For α, $a \approx 34$ mm, $b \approx 18.5$ mm.

$34^2 + 18.5^2 = h^2$

$\sqrt{1498.25} = h$

$38.7 \approx h$

38.5 versus 38.7; 0.5%

For β, $a \approx 34$ mm, $b \approx 23.5$ mm.

$34^2 + 23.5^2 = h^2$

$\sqrt{1708.25} = h$

$41.3 \approx h$

41.5 vs 41.3; 0.4%

Exercise 3:

$\tan \alpha = \dfrac{\sin \alpha}{\cos \alpha}$; yes

$\tan \beta = \dfrac{\sin \beta}{\cos \beta}$; yes

5.3 Exercises

1. sum; $\alpha = \beta$

3. $2x$; x

5. Answers will vary.

7. $\sin \theta = \dfrac{5}{13}$; θ in QII

$x = -\sqrt{13^2 - 5^2} = -12$; $\cos \theta = -\dfrac{12}{13}$

$\sin(2\theta) = 2\sin\theta\cos\theta$

$= 2\left(\dfrac{5}{13}\right)\left(-\dfrac{12}{13}\right)$

$= -\dfrac{120}{169}$

$\cos(2\theta) = \cos^2\theta - \sin^2\theta$

$= \left(-\dfrac{12}{13}\right)^2 - \left(\dfrac{5}{13}\right)^2$

$= \dfrac{144}{169} - \dfrac{25}{169}$

$= \dfrac{119}{169}$

7. (continued)

$\tan(2\theta) = \dfrac{2\tan\theta}{1 - \tan^2\theta}$

$= \dfrac{2\left(-\dfrac{5}{12}\right)}{1 - \left(-\dfrac{5}{12}\right)^2}$

$= \dfrac{-\dfrac{10}{12}}{1 - \dfrac{25}{144}}$

$= \dfrac{-\dfrac{10}{12}}{\dfrac{119}{144}}$

$= -\dfrac{120}{119}$

9. $\cos\theta = -\dfrac{9}{41}$; θ in QII

$y = \sqrt{41^2 - (-9)^2} = 40$; $\sin\theta = \dfrac{40}{41}$

$\sin(2\theta) = 2\sin\theta\cos\theta$

$= 2\left(\dfrac{40}{41}\right)\left(-\dfrac{9}{41}\right)$

$= -\dfrac{720}{1681}$

$\cos(2\theta) = \cos^2\theta - \sin^2\theta$

$= \left(-\dfrac{9}{41}\right)^2 - \left(\dfrac{40}{41}\right)^2$

$= \dfrac{81}{1681} - \dfrac{1600}{1681}$

$= -\dfrac{1519}{1681}$

$\tan(2\theta) = \dfrac{\sin(2\theta)}{\cos(2\theta)}$

$= \dfrac{-\dfrac{720}{1681}}{-\dfrac{1519}{1681}} = \dfrac{720}{1519}$

11. $\tan\theta = \dfrac{13}{84}$; θ in QIII

$r = \sqrt{(-84)^2 + (-13)^2} = 85$

$\sin\theta = -\dfrac{13}{85}$; $\cos\theta = -\dfrac{84}{85}$

$\sin(2\theta) = 2\sin\theta\cos\theta$

$\qquad = 2\left(-\dfrac{13}{85}\right)\left(-\dfrac{84}{85}\right)$

$\qquad = \dfrac{2184}{7225}$

$\cos(2\theta) = \cos^2\theta - \sin^2\theta$

$\qquad = \left(-\dfrac{84}{85}\right)^2 - \left(-\dfrac{13}{85}\right)^2$

$\qquad = \dfrac{7056}{7225} - \dfrac{169}{7225}$

$\qquad = \dfrac{6887}{7225}$

$\tan(2\theta) = \dfrac{\sin(2\theta)}{\cos(2\theta)}$

$\qquad = \dfrac{\frac{2184}{7225}}{\frac{6887}{7225}} = \dfrac{2184}{6887}$

13. $\sin\theta = \dfrac{48}{73}$; $\cos\theta < 0$, so θ in QII

$x = -\sqrt{73^2 - 48^2} = -55$; $\cos\theta = -\dfrac{55}{73}$

$\sin(2\theta) = 2\sin\theta\cos\theta$

$\qquad = 2\left(\dfrac{48}{73}\right)\left(-\dfrac{55}{73}\right)$

$\qquad = -\dfrac{5280}{5329}$

$\cos(2\theta) = \cos^2\theta - \sin^2\theta$

$\qquad = \left(-\dfrac{55}{73}\right)^2 - \left(\dfrac{48}{73}\right)^2$

$\qquad = \dfrac{3025}{5329} - \dfrac{2304}{5329}$

$\qquad = \dfrac{721}{5329}$

$\tan(2\theta) = \dfrac{\sin(2\theta)}{\cos(2\theta)}$

$\qquad = \dfrac{-\frac{5280}{5329}}{\frac{721}{5329}} = -\dfrac{5280}{721}$

15. $\csc\theta = \dfrac{5}{3}$; $\sec\theta < 0$, so θ in QII

$x = -\sqrt{5^2 - 3^2} = -4$

$\sin\theta = \dfrac{3}{5}$; $\cos\theta = -\dfrac{4}{5}$

$\sin(2\theta) = 2\sin\theta\cos\theta$

$\qquad = 2\left(\dfrac{3}{5}\right)\left(-\dfrac{4}{5}\right)$

$\qquad = -\dfrac{24}{25}$

$\cos(2\theta) = \cos^2\theta - \sin^2\theta$

$\qquad = \left(-\dfrac{4}{5}\right)^2 - \left(\dfrac{3}{5}\right)^2$

$\qquad = \dfrac{16}{25} - \dfrac{9}{25}$

$\qquad = \dfrac{7}{25}$

$\tan(2\theta) = \dfrac{\sin(2\theta)}{\cos(2\theta)}$

$\qquad = \dfrac{-\frac{24}{25}}{\frac{7}{25}} = -\dfrac{24}{7}$

17. $\sin(2\theta) = \dfrac{24}{25}$; 2θ in QII

$x = -\sqrt{25^2 - 24^2} = -7$; $\cos(2\theta) = -\dfrac{7}{25}$

$\dfrac{\pi}{2} < 2\theta < \pi \ \Rightarrow\ \dfrac{\pi}{4} < \theta < \dfrac{\pi}{2}$; θ in QI

$\sin\theta = \sin\left(\dfrac{2\theta}{2}\right) = \sqrt{\dfrac{1 - \cos(2\theta)}{2}}$

$\qquad = \sqrt{\dfrac{1 - \left(-\frac{7}{25}\right)}{2}} = \sqrt{\dfrac{\frac{32}{25}}{2}} = \sqrt{\dfrac{16}{25}} = \dfrac{4}{5}$

$\cos\theta = \cos\left(\dfrac{2\theta}{2}\right) = \sqrt{\dfrac{1 + \cos(2\theta)}{2}}$

$\qquad = \sqrt{\dfrac{1 + \left(-\frac{7}{25}\right)}{2}} = \sqrt{\dfrac{\frac{18}{25}}{2}} = \sqrt{\dfrac{9}{25}} = \dfrac{3}{5}$

$\tan(\theta) = \dfrac{\sin(\theta)}{\cos(\theta)}$

$\qquad = \dfrac{\frac{4}{5}}{\frac{3}{5}} = \dfrac{4}{3}$

19. $\cos(2\theta) = -\dfrac{41}{841}$; 2θ in QII

$\dfrac{\pi}{2} < 2\theta < \pi \Rightarrow \dfrac{\pi}{4} < \theta < \dfrac{\pi}{2}$; θ in QI

$\sin\theta = \sin\left(\dfrac{2\theta}{2}\right) = \sqrt{\dfrac{1-\cos(2\theta)}{2}}$

$= \sqrt{\dfrac{1-\left(-\dfrac{41}{841}\right)}{2}} = \sqrt{\dfrac{\dfrac{882}{841}}{2}} = \sqrt{\dfrac{441}{841}} = \dfrac{21}{29}$

$\cos\theta = \cos\left(\dfrac{2\theta}{2}\right) = \sqrt{\dfrac{1+\cos(2\theta)}{2}}$

$= \sqrt{\dfrac{1+\left(-\dfrac{41}{841}\right)}{2}} = \sqrt{\dfrac{\dfrac{800}{841}}{2}} = \sqrt{\dfrac{400}{841}} = \dfrac{20}{29}$

$\tan(\theta) = \dfrac{\sin(\theta)}{\cos(\theta)}$

$= \dfrac{\dfrac{21}{29}}{\dfrac{20}{29}} = \dfrac{21}{20}$

21. $\sin(3\theta) = \sin(2\theta + \theta)$
$= \sin(2\theta)\cos\theta + \cos(2\theta)\sin\theta$
$= (2\sin\theta\cos\theta)\cos\theta + (1-2\sin^2\theta)\sin\theta$
$= 2\sin\theta\cos^2\theta + \sin\theta - 2\sin^3\theta$
$= 2\sin\theta(1-\sin^2\theta) + \sin\theta - 2\sin^3\theta$
$= 2\sin\theta - 2\sin^3\theta + \sin\theta - 2\sin^3\theta$
$= 3\sin\theta - 4\sin^3\theta$

23. $2\sin\alpha\cos\alpha = \sin(2\alpha) \Rightarrow$
$\cos\alpha\sin\alpha = \dfrac{1}{2}\sin(2\alpha)$
$\cos 75°\sin 75° = \dfrac{1}{2}\sin(2\cdot 75°)$
$= \dfrac{1}{2}\sin(150°)$
$= \dfrac{1}{2}\cdot\dfrac{1}{2} = \dfrac{1}{4}$

25. $1-2\sin^2\alpha = \cos(2\alpha) \Rightarrow$
$1-2\sin^2\left(\dfrac{\pi}{8}\right) = \cos\left(2\cdot\dfrac{\pi}{8}\right)$
$= \cos\left(\dfrac{\pi}{4}\right)$
$= \dfrac{\sqrt{2}}{2}$

27. $\dfrac{2\tan\alpha}{1-\tan^2\alpha} = \tan(2\alpha) \Rightarrow$
$\dfrac{2\tan 22.5°}{1-\tan^2 22.5°} = \tan(2\cdot 22.5°)$
$= \tan(45°)$
$= 1$

29. $9\sin(3x)\cos(3x) = \dfrac{9}{2}\left[2\sin(3x)\cos(3x)\right]$
$= \dfrac{9}{2}\sin\left[2(3x)\right]$
$= 4.5\sin(6x)$

31. $\sin^2 x\cos^2 x = \dfrac{1-\cos(2x)}{2}\cdot\dfrac{1+\cos(2x)}{2}$
$= \dfrac{1-\cos^2(2x)}{4}$
$= \dfrac{1}{4}(1-\cos^2(2x))$
$= \dfrac{1}{4}\left(1-\dfrac{1+\cos(4x)}{2}\right)$
$= \dfrac{1}{4}-\dfrac{1+\cos(4x)}{8}$
$= \dfrac{1}{4}-\dfrac{1}{8}-\dfrac{\cos(4x)}{8}$
$= \dfrac{1}{8}-\dfrac{\cos(4x)}{8}$
$= \dfrac{1}{8}-\dfrac{1}{8}\cos(4x)$

33. $3\cos^4 x = 3\left[\dfrac{1+\cos(2x)}{2}\right]^2$
$= \dfrac{3}{4}\left[1+2\cos(2x)+\cos^2(2x)\right]$
$= \dfrac{3}{4}\left[1+2\cos(2x)+\dfrac{1+\cos(4x)}{2}\right]$
$= \dfrac{3}{4}+\dfrac{3}{2}\cos(2x)+\dfrac{3}{8}+\dfrac{3\cos(4x)}{8}$
$= \dfrac{9}{8}+\dfrac{3}{2}\cos(2x)+\dfrac{3}{8}\cos(4x)$

35. $2\sin^6 x = 2\left[\dfrac{1-\cos(2x)}{2}\right]^3$

$= \dfrac{1}{4}\left[1-\cos(2x)\right]\left[1-\cos(2x)\right]\left[1-\cos(2x)\right]$

$= \dfrac{1}{4}\left[1-2\cos(2x)+\cos^2(2x)\right]\left[1-\cos(2x)\right]$

$= \dfrac{1}{4}\left[1-2\cos(2x)+\dfrac{1+\cos(4x)}{2}\right]\left[1-\cos(2x)\right]$

$= \dfrac{1}{4}\left[\dfrac{3}{2}-2\cos(2x)+\dfrac{1}{2}\cos(4x)\right]\left[1-\cos(2x)\right]$

$= \dfrac{1}{4}\left[\dfrac{3}{2}-2\cos(2x)+\dfrac{1}{2}\cos(4x)-\dfrac{3}{2}\cos(2x)+2\cos^2(2x)-\dfrac{1}{2}\cos(2x)\cos(4x)\right]$

$= \dfrac{1}{4}\left[\dfrac{3}{2}-\dfrac{7}{2}\cos(2x)+\dfrac{1}{2}\cos(4x)+\dfrac{2(1+\cos(4x))}{2}-\dfrac{1}{2}\cos(2x)\cos(4x)\right]$

$= \dfrac{1}{4}\left[\dfrac{5}{2}-\dfrac{7}{2}\cos(2x)+\dfrac{3}{2}\cos(4x)-\dfrac{1}{2}\cos(2x)\cos(4x)\right]$

$= \dfrac{5}{8}-\dfrac{7}{8}\cos(2x)+\dfrac{3}{8}\cos(4x)-\dfrac{1}{8}\cos(2x)\cos(4x)$

37. $\theta = 22.5°$

$\sin 22.5° = \sin\left(\dfrac{45°}{2}\right) = \sqrt{\dfrac{1-\cos 45°}{2}}$

$= \sqrt{\dfrac{1-\dfrac{\sqrt{2}}{2}}{2}} = \dfrac{\sqrt{2-\sqrt{2}}}{2}$

$\cos 22.5° = \cos\left(\dfrac{45°}{2}\right) = \sqrt{\dfrac{1+\cos 45°}{2}}$

$= \sqrt{\dfrac{1+\dfrac{\sqrt{2}}{2}}{2}} = \dfrac{\sqrt{2+\sqrt{2}}}{2}$

$\tan 22.5° = \tan\left(\dfrac{45°}{2}\right) = \dfrac{1-\cos 45°}{\sin 45°}$

$= \dfrac{1-\dfrac{\sqrt{2}}{2}}{\dfrac{\sqrt{2}}{2}} = \dfrac{2-\sqrt{2}}{\sqrt{2}}$

$= \dfrac{2\sqrt{2}-2}{2} = \sqrt{2}-1$

39. $\theta = \dfrac{\pi}{12}$

$\sin\left(\dfrac{\pi}{12}\right) = \sin\left(\dfrac{\dfrac{\pi}{6}}{2}\right) = \sqrt{\dfrac{1-\cos\left(\dfrac{\pi}{6}\right)}{2}}$

$= \sqrt{\dfrac{1-\dfrac{\sqrt{3}}{2}}{2}} = \dfrac{\sqrt{2-\sqrt{3}}}{2}$

$\cos\left(\dfrac{\pi}{12}\right) = \cos\left(\dfrac{\dfrac{\pi}{6}}{2}\right) = \sqrt{\dfrac{1+\cos\left(\dfrac{\pi}{6}\right)}{2}}$

$= \sqrt{\dfrac{1+\dfrac{\sqrt{3}}{2}}{2}} = \dfrac{\sqrt{2+\sqrt{3}}}{2}$

$\tan\left(\dfrac{\pi}{12}\right) = \tan\left(\dfrac{\dfrac{\pi}{6}}{2}\right) = \dfrac{1-\cos\left(\dfrac{\pi}{6}\right)}{\sin\left(\dfrac{\pi}{6}\right)}$

$= \dfrac{1-\dfrac{\sqrt{3}}{2}}{\dfrac{1}{2}} = 2-\sqrt{3}$

41. $\theta = 67.5°$

$$\sin 67.5° = \sin\left(\frac{135°}{2}\right) = \sqrt{\frac{1-\cos 135°}{2}}$$

$$= \sqrt{\frac{1-\left(-\frac{\sqrt{2}}{2}\right)}{2}} = \frac{\sqrt{2+\sqrt{2}}}{2}$$

$$\cos 67.5° = \cos\left(\frac{135°}{2}\right) = \sqrt{\frac{1+\cos 135°}{2}}$$

$$= \sqrt{\frac{1+\left(-\frac{\sqrt{2}}{2}\right)}{2}} = \frac{\sqrt{2-\sqrt{2}}}{2}$$

$$\tan 67.5° = \tan\left(\frac{135°}{2}\right) = \frac{1-\cos 135°}{\sin 135°}$$

$$= \frac{1-\left(-\frac{\sqrt{2}}{2}\right)}{\frac{\sqrt{2}}{2}} = \frac{2+\sqrt{2}}{\sqrt{2}}$$

$$= \frac{2\sqrt{2}+2}{2} = \sqrt{2}+1$$

43. $\theta = \dfrac{3\pi}{8}$

$$\sin\left(\frac{3\pi}{8}\right) = \sin\left(\frac{\frac{3\pi}{4}}{2}\right) = \sqrt{\frac{1-\cos\left(\frac{3\pi}{4}\right)}{2}}$$

$$= \sqrt{\frac{1-\left(-\frac{\sqrt{2}}{2}\right)}{2}} = \frac{\sqrt{2+\sqrt{2}}}{2}$$

$$\cos\left(\frac{3\pi}{8}\right) = \cos\left(\frac{\frac{3\pi}{4}}{2}\right) = \sqrt{\frac{1+\cos\left(\frac{3\pi}{4}\right)}{2}}$$

$$= \sqrt{\frac{1+\left(-\frac{\sqrt{2}}{2}\right)}{2}} = \frac{\sqrt{2-\sqrt{2}}}{2}$$

43. (continued)

$$\tan\left(\frac{3\pi}{8}\right) = \tan\left(\frac{\frac{3\pi}{4}}{2}\right) = \frac{1-\cos\left(\frac{3\pi}{4}\right)}{\sin\left(\frac{3\pi}{4}\right)}$$

$$= \frac{1-\left(-\frac{\sqrt{2}}{2}\right)}{\frac{\sqrt{2}}{2}} = \frac{2+\sqrt{2}}{\sqrt{2}}$$

$$= \frac{2\sqrt{2}+2}{2} = \sqrt{2}+1$$

45. Recall from Exercise 37 that

$$\cos 22.5° = \frac{\sqrt{2+\sqrt{2}}}{2}.$$

$$\sin 11.25° = \sin\left(\frac{22.5°}{2}\right) = \sqrt{\frac{1-\cos 22.5°}{2}}$$

$$= \sqrt{\frac{1-\frac{\sqrt{2+\sqrt{2}}}{2}}{2}} = \frac{\sqrt{2-\sqrt{2+\sqrt{2}}}}{2}$$

47. Recall from Exercise 39 that

$$\cos\left(\frac{\pi}{12}\right) = \frac{\sqrt{2+\sqrt{3}}}{2}.$$

$$\sin\left(\frac{\pi}{24}\right) = \sin\left(\frac{\frac{\pi}{12}}{2}\right) = \sqrt{\frac{1-\cos\left(\frac{\pi}{12}\right)}{2}}$$

$$= \sqrt{\frac{1-\frac{\sqrt{2+\sqrt{3}}}{2}}{2}} = \frac{\sqrt{2-\sqrt{2+\sqrt{3}}}}{2}$$

49. $\sqrt{\dfrac{1+\cos 30°}{2}} = \cos\left(\dfrac{30°}{2}\right) = \cos 15°$

51. $\sqrt{\dfrac{1-\cos(4\theta)}{1+\cos(4\theta)}} = \tan\left(\dfrac{4\theta}{2}\right) = \tan(2\theta)$

53. $\dfrac{\sin(2x)}{1+\cos(2x)} = \tan\left(\dfrac{2x}{2}\right) = \tan x$

55. $\sin\theta = \dfrac{12}{13}$; θ is obtuse

$x = -\sqrt{13^2 - 12^2} = -5$; $\cos\theta = -\dfrac{5}{13}$

$$\sin\left(\frac{\theta}{2}\right) = \sqrt{\frac{1-\cos\theta}{2}} = \sqrt{\frac{1-\left(-\frac{5}{13}\right)}{2}}$$
$$= \sqrt{\frac{\frac{18}{13}}{2}} = \sqrt{\frac{9}{13}} = \frac{3}{\sqrt{13}}$$

$$\cos\left(\frac{\theta}{2}\right) = \sqrt{\frac{1+\cos\theta}{2}} = \sqrt{\frac{1+\left(-\frac{5}{13}\right)}{2}}$$
$$= \sqrt{\frac{\frac{8}{13}}{2}} = \sqrt{\frac{4}{13}} = \frac{2}{\sqrt{13}}$$

$$\tan\left(\frac{\theta}{2}\right) = \frac{\sin\left(\frac{\theta}{2}\right)}{\cos\left(\frac{\theta}{2}\right)} = \frac{\frac{3}{\sqrt{13}}}{\frac{2}{\sqrt{13}}} = \frac{3}{2}$$

57. $\cos\theta = -\dfrac{4}{5}$; θ in QII

$\dfrac{\pi}{2} < \theta < \pi \Rightarrow \dfrac{\pi}{4} < \dfrac{\theta}{2} < \dfrac{\pi}{2}$; $\dfrac{\theta}{2}$ in QI

$$\sin\left(\frac{\theta}{2}\right) = \sqrt{\frac{1-\cos\theta}{2}} = \sqrt{\frac{1-\left(-\frac{4}{5}\right)}{2}}$$
$$= \sqrt{\frac{\frac{9}{5}}{2}} = \sqrt{\frac{9}{10}} = \frac{3}{\sqrt{10}}$$

$$\cos\left(\frac{\theta}{2}\right) = \sqrt{\frac{1+\cos\theta}{2}} = \sqrt{\frac{1+\left(-\frac{4}{5}\right)}{2}}$$
$$= \sqrt{\frac{\frac{1}{5}}{2}} = \sqrt{\frac{1}{10}} = \frac{1}{\sqrt{10}}$$

$$\tan\left(\frac{\theta}{2}\right) = \frac{\sin\left(\frac{\theta}{2}\right)}{\cos\left(\frac{\theta}{2}\right)} = \frac{\frac{3}{\sqrt{10}}}{\frac{1}{\sqrt{10}}} = 3$$

59. $\tan\theta = -\dfrac{35}{12}$; θ in QII

$r = \sqrt{(-12)^2 + 35^2} = 37$; $\cos\theta = -\dfrac{12}{37}$

$\dfrac{\pi}{2} < \theta < \pi \Rightarrow \dfrac{\pi}{4} < \dfrac{\theta}{2} < \dfrac{\pi}{2}$; $\dfrac{\theta}{2}$ in QI

$$\sin\left(\frac{\theta}{2}\right) = \sqrt{\frac{1-\cos\theta}{2}} = \sqrt{\frac{1-\left(-\frac{12}{37}\right)}{2}}$$
$$= \sqrt{\frac{\frac{49}{37}}{2}} = \sqrt{\frac{49}{74}} = \frac{7}{\sqrt{74}}$$

$$\cos\left(\frac{\theta}{2}\right) = \sqrt{\frac{1+\cos\theta}{2}} = \sqrt{\frac{1+\left(-\frac{12}{37}\right)}{2}}$$
$$= \sqrt{\frac{\frac{25}{37}}{2}} = \sqrt{\frac{25}{74}} = \frac{5}{\sqrt{74}}$$

$$\tan\left(\frac{\theta}{2}\right) = \frac{\sin\left(\frac{\theta}{2}\right)}{\cos\left(\frac{\theta}{2}\right)} = \frac{\frac{7}{\sqrt{74}}}{\frac{5}{\sqrt{74}}} = \frac{7}{5}$$

61. $\sin\theta = \dfrac{15}{113}$; θ is acute

$x = \sqrt{113^2 - 15^2} = 112$; $\cos\theta = \dfrac{112}{113}$

$$\sin\left(\frac{\theta}{2}\right) = \sqrt{\frac{1-\cos\theta}{2}} = \sqrt{\frac{1-\frac{112}{113}}{2}}$$
$$= \sqrt{\frac{\frac{1}{113}}{2}} = \sqrt{\frac{1}{226}} = \frac{1}{\sqrt{226}}$$

$$\cos\left(\frac{\theta}{2}\right) = \sqrt{\frac{1+\cos\theta}{2}} = \sqrt{\frac{1+\frac{112}{113}}{2}}$$
$$= \sqrt{\frac{\frac{225}{113}}{2}} = \sqrt{\frac{225}{226}} = \frac{15}{\sqrt{226}}$$

$$\tan\left(\frac{\theta}{2}\right) = \frac{\sin\left(\frac{\theta}{2}\right)}{\cos\left(\frac{\theta}{2}\right)} = \frac{\frac{1}{\sqrt{226}}}{\frac{15}{\sqrt{226}}} = \frac{1}{15}$$

63. $\cot\theta = \dfrac{21}{20}$; $\pi < \theta < \dfrac{3\pi}{2}$

$r = \sqrt{(-21)^2 + (-20)^2} = 29$; $\cos\theta = -\dfrac{21}{29}$

$\pi < \theta < \dfrac{3\pi}{2} \;\Rightarrow\; \dfrac{\pi}{2} < \dfrac{\theta}{2} < \dfrac{3\pi}{4}$; $\dfrac{\theta}{2}$ in QII

$\sin\left(\dfrac{\theta}{2}\right) = \sqrt{\dfrac{1-\cos\theta}{2}} = \sqrt{\dfrac{1-\left(-\dfrac{21}{29}\right)}{2}}$

$= \sqrt{\dfrac{\dfrac{50}{29}}{2}} = \sqrt{\dfrac{25}{29}} = \dfrac{5}{\sqrt{29}}$

$\cos\left(\dfrac{\theta}{2}\right) = -\sqrt{\dfrac{1+\cos\theta}{2}} = -\sqrt{\dfrac{1+\left(-\dfrac{21}{29}\right)}{2}}$

$= -\sqrt{\dfrac{\dfrac{8}{29}}{2}} = -\sqrt{\dfrac{4}{29}} = -\dfrac{2}{\sqrt{29}}$

$\tan\left(\dfrac{\theta}{2}\right) = \dfrac{\sin\left(\dfrac{\theta}{2}\right)}{\cos\left(\dfrac{\theta}{2}\right)} = \dfrac{\dfrac{5}{\sqrt{29}}}{-\dfrac{2}{\sqrt{29}}} = -\dfrac{5}{2}$

65. $\dfrac{2\sin x\cos x}{\cos^2 x - \sin^2 x} = \dfrac{\sin(2x)}{\cos(2x)} = \tan(2x)$

67. $(\sin x + \cos x)^2 = \sin^2 x + 2\sin x\cos x + \cos^2 x$

$= \sin^2 x + \cos^2 x + 2\sin x\cos x$

$= 1 + 2\sin x\cos x$

$= 1 + \sin(2x)$

69. $\cos(8\theta) = \cos(2\cdot4\theta) = \cos^2(4\theta) - \sin^2(4\theta)$

71. $\dfrac{\cos(2\theta)}{\sin^2\theta} = \dfrac{\cos^2\theta - \sin^2\theta}{\sin^2\theta}$

$= \dfrac{\cos^2\theta}{\sin^2\theta} - 1$

$= \cot^2\theta - 1$

73. $\tan(2\theta) = \dfrac{2\tan\theta}{1-\tan^2\theta}$

$= \dfrac{(2\tan\theta)\dfrac{1}{\tan\theta}}{(1-\tan^2\theta)\dfrac{1}{\tan\theta}}$

$= \dfrac{2}{\dfrac{1}{\tan\theta} - \tan\theta} = \dfrac{2}{\cot\theta - \tan\theta}$

75. Begin with the right side of the equation.

$2\csc(2x) = \dfrac{2}{\sin(2x)}$

$= \dfrac{2}{2\sin x\cos x}$

$= \dfrac{1}{\sin x\cos x}$

$= \dfrac{\sin^2 x + \cos^2 x}{\sin x\cos x}$

$= \dfrac{\sin^2 x}{\sin x\cos x} + \dfrac{\cos^2 x}{\sin x\cos x}$

$= \dfrac{\sin x}{\cos x} + \dfrac{\cos x}{\sin x}$

$= \tan x + \cot x$

77. $\cos^2\left(\dfrac{x}{2}\right) - \sin^2\left(\dfrac{x}{2}\right) = \cos\left(2\cdot\dfrac{x}{2}\right)$

$= \cos x$

79. Begin with the right side of the equation.

$1 - 4\sin^2\theta + 4\sin^4\theta = \left(1 - 2\sin^2\theta\right)^2$

$= \left[\cos(2\theta)\right]^2$

$= \cos^2(2\theta)$

$= 1 - \sin^2(2\theta)$

81. $\sin^2\alpha + (1-\cos\alpha)^2$

$= \sin^2\alpha + 1 - 2\cos\alpha + \cos^2\alpha$

$= \sin^2\alpha + \cos^2\alpha + 1 - 2\cos\alpha$

$= 1 + 1 - 2\cos\alpha$

$= 2 - 2\cos\alpha$

$= 2(1 - \cos\alpha)$

$= 4\left(\dfrac{1-\cos\alpha}{2}\right)$

$= 4\sin^2\left(\dfrac{\alpha}{2}\right)$

$= \left[2\sin\left(\dfrac{\alpha}{2}\right)\right]^2$

83. $\sin(2\alpha) = \sin(\alpha+\alpha)$

$= \sin\alpha\cos\alpha + \cos\alpha\sin\alpha$

$= \sin\alpha\cos\alpha + \sin\alpha\cos\alpha$

$= 2\sin\alpha\cos\alpha$

$\tan(2\alpha) = \tan(\alpha+\alpha)$

$= \dfrac{\tan\alpha + \tan\alpha}{1 - \tan\alpha\tan\alpha}$

$= \dfrac{2\tan\alpha}{1 - \tan^2\alpha}$

85. $M = \csc\left(\dfrac{\theta}{2}\right)$

 a. $M = \csc\left(\dfrac{30°}{2}\right) = \dfrac{1}{\sin\left(\dfrac{30°}{2}\right)}$

 $= \dfrac{1}{\sqrt{\dfrac{1-\dfrac{\sqrt{3}}{2}}{2}}} = \dfrac{1}{\dfrac{\sqrt{2-\sqrt{3}}}{2}}$

 $= \dfrac{2}{\sqrt{2-\sqrt{3}}} \approx 3.9$

 b. $M = \csc\left(\dfrac{45°}{2}\right) = \dfrac{1}{\sin\left(\dfrac{45°}{2}\right)}$

 $= \dfrac{1}{\sqrt{\dfrac{1-\dfrac{\sqrt{2}}{2}}{2}}} = \dfrac{1}{\dfrac{\sqrt{2-\sqrt{2}}}{2}}$

 $= \dfrac{2}{\sqrt{2-\sqrt{2}}} \approx 2.6$

 c. $2 = \csc\left(\dfrac{\theta}{2}\right)$

 $2 = \dfrac{1}{\sin\left(\dfrac{\theta}{2}\right)}$

 $\sin\left(\dfrac{\theta}{2}\right) = \dfrac{1}{2}$

 $\sqrt{\dfrac{1-\cos\theta}{2}} = \dfrac{1}{2}$

 $\dfrac{1-\cos\theta}{2} = \dfrac{1}{4}$

 $1-\cos\theta = \dfrac{1}{2}$

 $-\cos\theta = -\dfrac{1}{2}$

 $\cos\theta = \dfrac{1}{2}$

 $\theta = \cos^{-1}\left(\dfrac{1}{2}\right)$

 $\theta = 60°$

87. $d(t) = \left|6\sin\left(\dfrac{\pi t}{60}\right)\right| = \left|6\sin\left(\dfrac{1}{2}\cdot\dfrac{\pi t}{30}\right)\right|$

 $= \left|6\left(\pm\sqrt{\dfrac{1-\cos\left(\dfrac{\pi t}{30}\right)}{2}}\right)\right|$

 $= 6\left(\sqrt{\dfrac{1-\cos\left(\dfrac{\pi t}{30}\right)}{2}}\right)$

 $= \sqrt{36\cdot\dfrac{1-\cos\left(\dfrac{\pi t}{30}\right)}{2}}$

 $= \sqrt{18\left[1-\cos\left(\dfrac{\pi t}{30}\right)\right]}$

89. a. $\sin(2\theta-90°)+1$
  $= \sin(2\theta)\cos 90° - \cos(2\theta)\sin(90°)+1$
  $= 0 - \cos(2\theta)+1$
  $= 1-\cos(2\theta)$

 b. $2\sin^2\theta = \sin^2\theta + \sin^2\theta$
  $= 1-\cos^2\theta + \sin^2\theta$
  $= 1-\left(\cos^2\theta - \sin^2\theta\right)$
  $= 1-\cos(2\theta)$

 c. $1+\sin^2\theta - \cos^2\theta = 1-\left(\cos^2\theta - \sin^2\theta\right)$
  $= 1-\cos(2\theta)$

 d. $1-\cos(2\theta) = 1-\cos(2\theta)$

91. Half-angle identity:

 $\cos 15° = \cos\left(\dfrac{30°}{2}\right) = \sqrt{\dfrac{1+\cos 30°}{2}}$

 $= \sqrt{\dfrac{1+\dfrac{\sqrt{3}}{2}}{2}} = \dfrac{\sqrt{2+\sqrt{3}}}{2}$

 Difference identity:

 $\cos 15° = \cos(45° - 30°)$
 $= \cos 45°\cos 30° + \sin 45°\sin 30°$
 $= \left(\dfrac{\sqrt{2}}{2}\right)\left(\dfrac{\sqrt{3}}{2}\right) + \left(\dfrac{\sqrt{2}}{2}\right)\left(\dfrac{1}{2}\right)$
 $= \dfrac{\sqrt{6}}{4} + \dfrac{\sqrt{2}}{4} = \dfrac{\sqrt{6}+\sqrt{2}}{4}$

91. a. $\dfrac{\sqrt{2-\sqrt{3}}}{2} \approx 0.2588$

$\dfrac{\sqrt{6}-\sqrt{2}}{4} \approx 0.2588$

b. Show $\left(\dfrac{\sqrt{2+\sqrt{3}}}{2}\right)^2 \overset{?}{=} \left(\dfrac{\sqrt{6}+\sqrt{2}}{4}\right)^2$

$\dfrac{2+\sqrt{3}}{4} \overset{?}{=} \dfrac{6+2\sqrt{12}+2}{16}$

$\dfrac{2+\sqrt{3}}{4} \overset{?}{=} \dfrac{8+2\sqrt{4\cdot 3}}{16}$

$\dfrac{2+\sqrt{3}}{4} \overset{?}{=} \dfrac{8+4\sqrt{3}}{16}$

$\dfrac{2+\sqrt{3}}{4} \overset{?}{=} \dfrac{2+\sqrt{3}}{4}$

93. $\cos 15° = \dfrac{\sqrt{2+\sqrt{3}}}{2}$

$\cos 7.5° = \dfrac{\sqrt{2+\sqrt{2+\sqrt{3}}}}{2}$

$\cos 3.75° = \dfrac{\sqrt{2+\sqrt{2+\sqrt{2+\sqrt{3}}}}}{2} \approx 0.9979$

$\cos 1.875° = \dfrac{\sqrt{2+\sqrt{2\sqrt{2+\sqrt{2+\sqrt{3}}}}}}{2}$

≈ 0.9995

They are getting close to 1.

95. $\sin^2 x + \cos^2 x = 1$

$\tan^2 x + 1 = \sec^2 x$

$1 + \cot^2 x = \csc^2 x$

97. Let h be the height of the end of the cannon.

$\sin 40° = \dfrac{h}{30}$

$h = 30\sin 40° \approx 19.3$ ft

99. $(1, 58°),\ (7, 110°)$

Amplitude: $|A| = \dfrac{110-58}{2} = 26;\ \ P = \dfrac{2\pi}{12} = \dfrac{\pi}{6}$

Phase Shift: $\dfrac{1+7}{2} = 4$ to the right

Vertical Shift: $\dfrac{110+58}{2} = 84$

$y = 26\sin\left[\dfrac{\pi}{6}(x-4)\right] + 84$

Technology Highlight

Exercise 1:
  Only one graph appears. No.

5.4 Exercises

1. product; sum; sum; difference

3. $\dfrac{1}{16}v^2 \sin\theta\cos\theta$; range; air resistance

5. Answers will vary.

7. $\sin(-4\theta)(8\theta)$

$= \dfrac{1}{2}\left[\cos(-4\theta-8\theta) - \cos(-4\theta+8\theta)\right]$

$= \dfrac{1}{2}\left[\cos(-12\theta) - \cos(4\theta)\right]$

$= \dfrac{1}{2}\left[\cos(12\theta) - \cos(4\theta)\right]$

9. $2\cos\left(\dfrac{7t}{2}\right)\sin\left(\dfrac{3t}{2}\right)$

$= 2\cdot\dfrac{1}{2}\left[\sin\left(\dfrac{7t}{2}+\dfrac{3t}{2}\right) - \sin\left(\dfrac{7t}{2}-\dfrac{3t}{2}\right)\right]$

$= \sin(5t) - \sin(2t)$

11. $2\cos(1979\pi t)\cos(439\pi t)$

$= 2\cdot\dfrac{1}{2}\left[\cos(1979\pi t - 439\pi t)\right.$

$\left.+\cos(1979\pi t + 439\pi t)\right]$

$= \cos(1540\pi t) + \cos(2418\pi t)$

13. $2\sin(x+2y)\cos(x-2y)$

$= 2\sin\left(\dfrac{2x+4y}{2}\right)\cos\left(\dfrac{2x-4y}{2}\right)$

$= \sin(2x) + \sin(4y)$

15. $2\cos 15° \sin 135°$

$= 2\cdot\dfrac{1}{2}\left[\sin(15°+135°) - \sin(15°-135°)\right]$

$= \sin(150°) - \sin(-120°)$

$= \sin(150°) + \sin(120°)$

$= \dfrac{1}{2} + \dfrac{\sqrt{3}}{2} = \dfrac{1+\sqrt{3}}{2}$

17. $\sin\left(\dfrac{7\pi}{8}\right)\cos\left(\dfrac{\pi}{8}\right)$

$= \dfrac{1}{2}\left[\sin\left(\dfrac{7\pi}{8}+\dfrac{\pi}{8}\right)+\sin\left(\dfrac{7\pi}{8}-\dfrac{\pi}{8}\right)\right]$

$= \dfrac{1}{2}\left[\sin(\pi)+\sin\left(\dfrac{3\pi}{4}\right)\right]$

$= \dfrac{1}{2}\left[0+\dfrac{\sqrt{2}}{2}\right]=\dfrac{\sqrt{2}}{4}$

19. $\cos(9h)+\cos(4h)$

$= 2\cos\left(\dfrac{9h+4h}{2}\right)\cos\left(\dfrac{9h-4h}{2}\right)$

$= 2\cos\left(\dfrac{13h}{2}\right)\cos\left(\dfrac{5h}{2}\right)$

21. $\sin\left(\dfrac{11x}{8}\right)-\sin\left(\dfrac{5x}{8}\right)$

$= 2\cos\left(\dfrac{\dfrac{11x}{8}+\dfrac{5x}{8}}{2}\right)\sin\left(\dfrac{\dfrac{11x}{8}-\dfrac{5x}{8}}{2}\right)$

$= 2\cos\left(\dfrac{16x}{16}\right)\sin\left(\dfrac{6x}{16}\right)$

$= 2\cos x\sin\left(\dfrac{3x}{8}\right)$

23. $\cos(697\pi t)-\cos(1447\pi t)$

$= -2\sin\left(\dfrac{697\pi t+1447\pi t}{2}\right)\sin\left(\dfrac{697\pi t-1447\pi t}{2}\right)$

$= -2\sin\left(\dfrac{2144\pi t}{2}\right)\sin\left(\dfrac{-750\pi t}{2}\right)$

$= -2\sin(1072\pi t)\sin(-375\pi t)$

$= 2\sin(1072\pi t)\sin(375\pi t)$

25. $\sin(3x+y)+\sin(3x+5y)$

$= 2\sin\left[\dfrac{(3x+y)+(3x+5y)}{2}\right]$

$\qquad \cdot\cos\left[\dfrac{(3x+y)-(3x+5y)}{2}\right]$

$= 2\sin\left(\dfrac{6x+6y}{2}\right)\cos\left(-\dfrac{4y}{2}\right)$

$= 2\sin(3x+3y)\cos(-2y)$

27. $\cos 75°+\cos 15°$

$= 2\cos\left(\dfrac{75°+15°}{2}\right)\cos\left(\dfrac{75°-15°}{2}\right)$

$= 2\cos\left(\dfrac{90°}{2}\right)\cos\left(\dfrac{60°}{2}\right)$

$= 2\cos(45°)\cos(30°)$

$= 2\left(\dfrac{\sqrt{2}}{2}\right)\left(\dfrac{\sqrt{3}}{2}\right)=\dfrac{\sqrt{6}}{2}$

29. $\sin\left(\dfrac{17}{12}\pi\right)-\sin\left(\dfrac{13\pi}{12}\right)$

$= 2\cos\left(\dfrac{\dfrac{17}{12}\pi+\dfrac{13}{12}\pi}{2}\right)\sin\left(\dfrac{\dfrac{17}{12}\pi-\dfrac{13}{12}\pi}{2}\right)$

$= 2\cos\left(\dfrac{5}{4}\pi\right)\sin\left(\dfrac{1}{6}\pi\right)$

$= 2\left(-\dfrac{\sqrt{2}}{2}\right)\left(\dfrac{1}{2}\right)=-\dfrac{\sqrt{2}}{2}$

31. $\dfrac{\sin m+\sin n}{\cos m+\cos n}$

$= \dfrac{2\sin\left(\dfrac{m+n}{2}\right)\cos\left(\dfrac{m-n}{2}\right)}{2\cos\left(\dfrac{m+n}{2}\right)\cos\left(\dfrac{m-n}{2}\right)}$

$= \dfrac{\sin\left(\dfrac{m+n}{2}\right)}{\cos\left(\dfrac{m+n}{2}\right)}$

$= \tan\left(\dfrac{m+n}{2}\right)$

33. $\dfrac{2\sin 2t\cos t-\sin 3t}{\cos t}$

$= \dfrac{2\left[\dfrac{1}{2}(\sin 3t+\sin t)\right]-\sin 3t}{\cos t}$

$= \dfrac{\sin 3t+\sin t-\sin 3t}{\cos t}$

$= \dfrac{\sin t}{\cos t}$

$= \tan t$

35. $\dfrac{2\cos 2t}{\sin 3t - \sin t} = \dfrac{2\cos 2t}{2\cos 2t \sin t}$

$= \dfrac{1}{\sin t}$

$= \csc t$

37. $\dfrac{\sin(120\pi t) + \sin(80\pi t)}{\cos(120\pi t) - \cos(80\pi t)}$

$= \dfrac{2\sin(100\pi t)\cos(20\pi t)}{-2\sin(100\pi t)\sin(20\pi t)}$

$= \dfrac{\cos(20\pi t)}{-\sin(20\pi t)}$

$= -\cot(20\pi t)$

39. Subtract the identities.

$\cos\alpha\cos\beta + \sin\alpha\sin\beta = \cos(\alpha-\beta)$

$\cos\alpha\cos\beta - \sin\alpha\sin\beta = \cos(\alpha+\beta)$

$2\sin\alpha\sin\beta = \cos(\alpha-\beta) - \cos(\alpha+\beta)$

$\sin\alpha\sin\beta = \dfrac{1}{2}\left[\cos(\alpha-\beta) - \cos(\alpha+\beta)\right]$

41. $\sin\alpha\cos\beta = \sin\left(\dfrac{5\pi}{6}\right)\cos\left(\dfrac{2\pi}{3}\right)$

$= \left(\dfrac{1}{2}\right)\left(-\dfrac{1}{2}\right) = -\dfrac{1}{4}$

$\dfrac{1}{2}\sin(\alpha\ \beta)\ \sin(\alpha\ \beta)$

$= \dfrac{1}{2}\left[\sin\left(\dfrac{5\pi}{6}+\dfrac{2\pi}{3}\right) + \sin\left(\dfrac{5\pi}{6}-\dfrac{2\pi}{3}\right)\right]$

$= \dfrac{1}{2}\left[\sin\dfrac{9\pi}{6} + \sin\dfrac{\pi}{6}\right]$

$= \dfrac{1}{2}\left[\sin\dfrac{3\pi}{2} + \sin\dfrac{\pi}{6}\right]$

$= \dfrac{1}{2}\left[-1+\dfrac{1}{2}\right] = \dfrac{1}{2}\left[-\dfrac{1}{2}\right] = -\dfrac{1}{4}$

43. $y_1 = \cos(2\pi\,1477t) = \cos(2954\pi t)$

$y_2 = \cos(2\pi\,697t) = \cos(1394\pi t)$

$u = 2954\pi t;\ v = 1394\pi t$

$\dfrac{u+v}{2} = \dfrac{2954\pi + 1394\pi t}{2} = 2174\pi t$

$\dfrac{u-v}{2} = \dfrac{2954\pi - 1394\pi t}{2} = 780\pi t$

$y(t) = 2\cos\left(\dfrac{u+v}{2}\right)\cos\left(\dfrac{u-v}{2}\right)$

$= 2\cos(2174\pi t)\cos(780\pi t)$

45. $y(t) = 2\cos(2150\pi t)\cos(268\pi t)$

$= 2\cdot\dfrac{1}{2}\left[\cos(2150\pi t - 268\pi t)\right.$

$\left. + \cos(2150\pi t + 268\pi t)\right]$

$= \cos(1882\pi t) + \cos(2418\pi t)$

$= \cos(2418\pi t) + \cos(1882\pi t)$

$= \cos\left[2\pi(1209)t\right] + \cos\left[2\pi(941)t\right]$

the $\boxed{*}$ key

47. a. $r(\theta) = \dfrac{1}{32}v^2\sin(2\theta)$

$r(45°) = \dfrac{1}{32}(96)^2\sin(2\cdot 45°)$

$= \dfrac{1}{32}(9216)\sin 90°$

$= 288$ ft

$r(22.5°) = \dfrac{1}{32}(96)^2\sin(2\cdot 22.5°)$

$= \dfrac{1}{32}(9216)\sin 45°$

$= 288\sin 45°$

$= 288\left(\dfrac{1}{\sqrt{2}}\right) = 144\sqrt{2}$ ft

$288 - 144\sqrt{2} \approx 84.3$ ft
The projectile will fall 84.3 feet short of the maximum.

b. $r(\theta) = \dfrac{1}{32}v^2\sin(2\theta)$

$r(45°) = \dfrac{1}{32}(96)^2\sin(2\cdot 45°)$

$= \dfrac{1}{32}(9216)\sin 90°$

$= 288$ ft

$r(67.5°) = \dfrac{1}{32}(96)^2\sin(2\cdot 67.5°)$

$= \dfrac{1}{32}(9216)\sin 135°$

$= 288\sin 135°$

$= 288\left(\dfrac{1}{\sqrt{2}}\right) = 144\sqrt{2}$ ft

$288 - 144\sqrt{2} \approx 84.3$ ft
The projectile will fall 84.3 feet short of the maximum.

49. $y = y_i + y_o$

$y = 2\sin(1.1x - 0.6t) + 2\sin(1.1x + 0.6t)$

$y = 2\left[\sin(1.1x + 0.6t) + \sin(1.1x - 0.6t)\right]$

$y = 4 \cdot \dfrac{1}{2}\left[\sin(1.1x + 0.6t) + \sin(1.1x - 0.6t)\right]$

$y = 4\sin(1.1x)\cos(0.6t)$

51. $\sin a \sin b \sin c$

$= (\sin a \sin b)\sin c$

$= \dfrac{1}{2}\left[\cos(a-b)(\sin c) - \cos(a+b)(\sin c)\right]$

$= \dfrac{1}{2}\left\{\dfrac{1}{2}\left[\sin(a-b+c) - (\sin a - b - c)\right]\right.$

$\left. - \dfrac{1}{2}\left[\sin(a+b+c) - \sin(a+b-c)\right]\right\}$

$= \dfrac{1}{4}\left[\sin(a+b-c) + \sin(b+c-a)\right.$

$\left. + \sin(c+a-b) - \sin(a+b+c)\right]$

53. Y_1 is increasing;

Y_2 is defined on $(0, \pi)$.

55. $\left(\dfrac{16}{65}\right)^2 + \left(\dfrac{63}{65}\right)^2 = \dfrac{256}{4225} + \dfrac{3969}{4225} = \dfrac{4225}{4225} = 1$

$\tan\theta = \dfrac{63}{16};\ \sec\theta = \dfrac{65}{16}$

$1 + \tan^2\theta = \sec^2\theta$

$1 + \left(\dfrac{63}{16}\right)^2 = \left(\dfrac{65}{16}\right)^2$

$1 + \dfrac{3969}{256} = \dfrac{4225}{256}$

$\dfrac{256}{256} + \dfrac{3969}{256} = \dfrac{4225}{256}$

57. $\cos(105°) = \cos(45° + 60°)$

$= \cos 45°\cos 60° - \sin 45°\sin 60°$

$= \dfrac{\sqrt{2}}{2} \cdot \dfrac{1}{2} - \dfrac{\sqrt{2}}{2} \cdot \dfrac{\sqrt{3}}{2}$

$= \dfrac{\sqrt{2} - \sqrt{6}}{4}$

Summary and Concept Review 5.1

1. $\dfrac{\csc^2 x(1 - \cos^2 x)}{\tan^2 x} = \dfrac{\csc^2 x(\sin^2 x)}{\tan^2 x}$

$= \dfrac{1}{\tan^2 x}$

$= \cot^2 x$

3. $\dfrac{\sin^4 x - \cos^4 x}{\sin x \cos x} = \dfrac{(\sin^2 x - \cos^2 x)(\sin^2 x + \cos^2 x)}{\sin x \cos x}$

$= \dfrac{(\sin^2 x - \cos^2 x)(1)}{\sin x \cos x}$

$= \dfrac{\sin x \sin x}{\sin x \cos x} - \dfrac{\cos x \cos x}{\sin x \cos x}$

$= \dfrac{\sin x}{\cos x} - \dfrac{\cos x}{\sin x}$

$= \tan x - \cot x$

Summary and Concept Review 5.2

5. a. $\cos 75° = \cos(30° + 45°)$

$= \cos 30°\cos 45° - \sin 30°\sin 45°$

$= \dfrac{\sqrt{3}}{2}\,\dfrac{\sqrt{2}}{2} - \dfrac{1}{2}\,\dfrac{\sqrt{2}}{2}$

$= \dfrac{\sqrt{6}}{4} - \dfrac{\sqrt{2}}{4} = \dfrac{\sqrt{6} - \sqrt{2}}{4}$

b. $\tan\left(\dfrac{\pi}{12}\right) = \tan\left(\dfrac{\pi}{3} - \dfrac{\pi}{4}\right)$

$= \dfrac{\tan\dfrac{\pi}{3} - \tan\dfrac{\pi}{4}}{1 + \tan\dfrac{\pi}{3}\,\tan\dfrac{\pi}{4}}$

$= \dfrac{\sqrt{3} - 1}{1 + (\sqrt{3})(1)} \cdot \dfrac{1 - \sqrt{3}}{1 - \sqrt{3}}$

$= \dfrac{4 - 2\sqrt{3}}{2} = 2 - \sqrt{3}$

7. a. $\cos 109°\cos 71° - \sin 109°\sin 71°$

$= \cos(109° + 71°)$

$= \cos 180°$

$= -1$

b. $\sin 139°\cos 19° - \cos 139°\sin 19°$

$= \sin(139° - 19°)$

$= \sin 120°$

$= \dfrac{\sqrt{3}}{2}$

9. a. $1170° - 3(360°) = 1170° - 1080° = 90°$

$\cos 1170°$

$= \cos(1080° + 90°)$

$= \cos(1080°)\cos(90°) - \sin 1080° \sin 90°$

$= (1)\cos(90°) - (0)\sin 90°$

$= \cos 90°$

$= 0$

b. $\dfrac{57\pi}{4} = \dfrac{56\pi}{4} + \dfrac{\pi}{4} = 7(2\pi) + \dfrac{\pi}{4}$

$\sin\left(14\pi + \dfrac{\pi}{4}\right)$

$= \sin(14\pi)\cos\left(\dfrac{\pi}{4}\right) + \cos(14\pi)\sin\left(\dfrac{\pi}{4}\right)$

$= (0)\cos\left(\dfrac{\pi}{4}\right) + (1)\sin\left(\dfrac{\pi}{4}\right)$

$= \sin\dfrac{\pi}{4}$

$= \dfrac{\sqrt{2}}{2}$

11. $\tan 15° = \tan(45° - 30°)$

$= \dfrac{\tan 45° - \tan 30°}{1 + \tan 45° \tan 30°}$

$= \dfrac{1 - \dfrac{\sqrt{3}}{3}}{1 + (1)\left(\dfrac{\sqrt{3}}{3}\right)} = \dfrac{3 - \sqrt{3}}{3 + \sqrt{3}}$

$= \dfrac{\sqrt{3}(\sqrt{3} - 1)}{\sqrt{3}(\sqrt{3} + 1)} = \dfrac{\sqrt{3} - 1}{\sqrt{3} + 1}$

$\tan 15° = \tan(135° - 120°)$

$= \dfrac{\tan 135° - \tan 120°}{1 + \tan 135° \tan 120°}$

$= \dfrac{-1 - (-\sqrt{3})}{1 + (-1)(-\sqrt{3})}$

$= \dfrac{-1 + \sqrt{3}}{1 + \sqrt{3}}$

$= \dfrac{\sqrt{3} - 1}{\sqrt{3} + 1}$

Both expressions yield the same results.

Summary and Concept Review 5.3

13. a. $\cos\theta = \dfrac{13}{85};\ \theta$ in QIV

$y = -\sqrt{85^2 - 13^2} = -84;\ \sin\theta = -\dfrac{84}{85}$

$\sin(2\theta) = 2\sin\theta\cos\theta$

$= 2\left(-\dfrac{84}{85}\right)\left(\dfrac{13}{85}\right) = -\dfrac{2184}{7225}$

$\cos(2\theta) = \cos^2\theta - \sin^2\theta$

$= \left(\dfrac{13}{85}\right)^2 - \left(-\dfrac{84}{85}\right)^2$

$= \dfrac{169}{7225} - \dfrac{7056}{7225} = -\dfrac{6887}{7225}$

$\tan(2\theta) = \dfrac{\sin(2\theta)}{\cos(2\theta)}$

$= \dfrac{-\dfrac{2184}{7225}}{-\dfrac{6887}{7225}} = \dfrac{2184}{6887}$

b. $\csc\theta = -\dfrac{29}{20};\ \theta$ in QIII

$x = -\sqrt{29^2 - (-20)^2} = -21;\ \cos\theta = -\dfrac{21}{29}$

$\sin(2\theta) = 2\sin\theta\cos\theta$

$= 2\left(-\dfrac{20}{29}\right)\left(-\dfrac{21}{29}\right) = \dfrac{840}{841}$

$\cos(2\theta) = \cos^2\theta - \sin^2\theta$

$= \left(-\dfrac{21}{29}\right)^2 - \left(-\dfrac{20}{29}\right)^2$

$= \dfrac{441}{841} - \dfrac{400}{841} = \dfrac{41}{841}$

$\tan(2\theta) = \dfrac{\sin(2\theta)}{\cos(2\theta)}$

$= \dfrac{\dfrac{840}{841}}{\dfrac{41}{841}} = \dfrac{840}{41}$

15. a. $\cos^2 22.5^\circ - \sin^2 22.5^\circ = \cos\ 2(22.5^\circ)$

$= \cos 45^\circ = \dfrac{\sqrt{2}}{2}$

b. $1 - 2\sin^2\dfrac{\pi}{12} = \cos\ 2\cdot\dfrac{\pi}{12}$

$= \cos\dfrac{\pi}{6} = \dfrac{\sqrt{3}}{2}$

17. a. $\cos\theta = \dfrac{24}{25};\ 0^\circ < \theta < 360^\circ;\ \theta$ in QIV

$270^\circ < \theta < 360^\circ \Rightarrow 135^\circ < \dfrac{\theta}{2} < 180^\circ;\ \dfrac{\theta}{2}$ in QII

$\sin\left(\dfrac{\theta}{2}\right) = \sqrt{\dfrac{1-\cos\theta}{2}} = \sqrt{\dfrac{1-\dfrac{24}{25}}{2}}$

$= \sqrt{\dfrac{\dfrac{1}{25}}{2}} = \sqrt{\dfrac{1}{50}} = \dfrac{1}{5\sqrt{2}}$

$\cos\left(\dfrac{\theta}{2}\right) = -\sqrt{\dfrac{1+\cos\theta}{2}} = -\sqrt{\dfrac{1+\dfrac{24}{25}}{2}}$

$= -\sqrt{\dfrac{\dfrac{49}{25}}{2}} = -\sqrt{\dfrac{49}{50}} = -\dfrac{7}{5\sqrt{2}}$

b. $\csc\theta = -\dfrac{65}{33};\ -90^\circ < \theta < 0^\circ;\ \theta$ in QIV

$x = \sqrt{65^2 - (-33)^2} = 56;\ \cos\theta = \dfrac{56}{65}$

$-90^\circ < \theta < 0^\circ \Rightarrow -45^\circ < \dfrac{\theta}{2} < 0^\circ;\ \dfrac{\theta}{2}$ in QIV

$\sin\left(\dfrac{\theta}{2}\right) = -\sqrt{\dfrac{1-\cos\theta}{2}} = -\sqrt{\dfrac{1-\dfrac{56}{65}}{2}}$

$= -\sqrt{\dfrac{\dfrac{9}{65}}{2}} = -\sqrt{\dfrac{9}{130}} = -\dfrac{3}{\sqrt{130}}$

$\cos\left(\dfrac{\theta}{2}\right) = \sqrt{\dfrac{1+\cos\theta}{2}} = \sqrt{\dfrac{1+\dfrac{56}{65}}{2}}$

$= \sqrt{\dfrac{\dfrac{121}{65}}{2}} = \sqrt{\dfrac{121}{130}} = \dfrac{11}{\sqrt{130}}$

Summary and Concept Review 5.4

19. $\cos(3t)\sin(-9t)$

$= \dfrac{1}{2}\Big[\sin\big(3t+(-9t)\big) - \sin\big(3t-(-9t)\big)\Big]$

$= \dfrac{1}{2}\Big[\sin(-6t) - \sin(12t)\Big]$

21. $\cos t + \cos(3t)$

$= 2\cos\left(\dfrac{t+3t}{2}\right)\cos\left(\dfrac{t-3t}{2}\right)$

$= 2\cos(2t)\cos(-t)$

23. $2\cos\left(\dfrac{11\pi}{12}\right)\cos\left(\dfrac{\pi}{12}\right)$

$= 2\cdot\dfrac{1}{2}\left[\cos\left(\dfrac{11\pi}{12}-\dfrac{\pi}{12}\right) + \cos\left(\dfrac{11\pi}{12}+\dfrac{\pi}{12}\right)\right]$

$= \cos\left(\dfrac{5\pi}{6}\right) + \cos(\pi)$

$= -\dfrac{\sqrt{3}}{2} - 1$

25. $\dfrac{\cos(3\alpha) - \cos\alpha}{\cos(3\alpha) + \cos\alpha}$

$= \dfrac{-2\sin\left(\dfrac{3\alpha+\alpha}{2}\right)\sin\left(\dfrac{3\alpha-\alpha}{2}\right)}{2\cos\left(\dfrac{3\alpha+\alpha}{2}\right)\cos\left(\dfrac{3\alpha-\alpha}{2}\right)}$

$= \dfrac{-\sin(2\alpha)\sin(\alpha)}{\cos(2\alpha)\cos(\alpha)}$

$= -\dfrac{2\sin\alpha\cos\alpha\sin\alpha}{(2\cos^2\alpha-1)\cos\alpha}$

$= -\dfrac{2\sin^2\alpha}{2\cos^2\alpha-1}$

$= \dfrac{2\sin^2\alpha}{1-2\cos^2\alpha}$

$= \dfrac{\dfrac{2\sin^2\alpha}{\cos^2\alpha}}{\dfrac{1-2\cos^2\alpha}{\cos^2\alpha}}$

$= \dfrac{2\tan^2\alpha}{\dfrac{1}{\cos^2\alpha}-2}$

$= \dfrac{2\tan^2\alpha}{\sec^2\alpha-2}$

Mixed Review

1. $\sin(-\theta)\tan(-\theta)+\cos\theta$
    $=(-\sin\theta)(-\tan\theta)+\cos\theta$
    $=\sin\theta\tan\theta+\cos\theta$
    $=\dfrac{\sin^2\theta}{\cos\theta}+\cos\theta$
    $=\dfrac{\sin^2\theta}{\cos\theta}+\dfrac{\cos^2\theta}{\cos\theta}$
    $=\dfrac{1}{\cos\theta}$
    $=\sec\theta$
    $=\sec(-\theta)$

3. $\tan255°=\tan(225°+30°)$
    $=\dfrac{\tan225°+\tan30°}{1-\tan225°\tan30°}$
    $=\dfrac{1+\dfrac{\sqrt{3}}{3}}{1-(1)\left(\dfrac{\sqrt{3}}{3}\right)}=\dfrac{3+\sqrt{3}}{3-\sqrt{3}}\cdot\dfrac{3+\sqrt{3}}{3+\sqrt{3}}$
    $=\dfrac{12+6\sqrt{3}}{6}=2+\sqrt{3}$

5. $2\cos^2\left(\dfrac{\pi}{12}\right)-1=\cos\left[2\left(\dfrac{\pi}{12}\right)\right]$
    $=\cos\left(\dfrac{\pi}{6}\right)$
    $=\dfrac{\sqrt{3}}{2}$

7. $\dfrac{1-\cos^2\theta+\sin^2\theta}{\tan^2\theta}$
    $=\dfrac{1-\left(\cos^2\theta-\sin^2\theta\right)}{\tan^2\theta}$
    $=\dfrac{1-\cos(2\theta)}{\dfrac{1-\cos(2\theta)}{1+\cos(2\theta)}}$
    $=\left[1-\cos(2\theta)\right]\left[\dfrac{1+\cos(2\theta)}{1-\cos(2\theta)}\right]$
    $=1+\cos(2\theta)$

9. $\sin x=-\dfrac{6}{7.5};\ 540°<\theta<630°;\ \theta$ in QIII
    $x=-\sqrt{7.5^2-(-6)^2}=-4.5;\ \cos\theta=-\dfrac{4.5}{7.5}$
    $540°<x<630°\Rightarrow270°<\dfrac{x}{2}<315°;\ \dfrac{x}{2}$ in QIV

9. (continued)
    $\sin\left(\dfrac{x}{2}\right)=-\sqrt{\dfrac{1-\cos x}{2}}=-\sqrt{\dfrac{1-\left(-\dfrac{4.5}{7.5}\right)}{2}}$
    $=-\sqrt{\dfrac{\dfrac{12}{7.5}}{2}}=-\sqrt{\dfrac{12}{15}}=-\dfrac{2}{\sqrt{5}}$

    $\cos\left(\dfrac{x}{2}\right)=-\sqrt{\dfrac{1+\cos x}{2}}=\sqrt{\dfrac{1+\left(-\dfrac{4.5}{7.5}\right)}{2}}$
    $=\sqrt{\dfrac{\dfrac{3}{7.5}}{2}}=\sqrt{\dfrac{3}{15}}=\dfrac{1}{\sqrt{5}}$

11. $\sin(2\alpha)=\sin(\alpha+\alpha)$
    $=\sin\alpha\cos\alpha+\cos\alpha\sin\alpha$
    $=2\sin\alpha\cos\alpha$

13. $\sin172.5°-\sin52.5°$
    $=2\cos\left(\dfrac{172.5°+52.5°}{2}\right)\sin\left(\dfrac{172.5°-52.5°}{2}\right)$
    $=2\cos\left(\dfrac{225°}{2}\right)\sin(60°)$
    $=2\left(-\sqrt{\dfrac{1+\cos225°}{2}}\right)\left(\dfrac{\sqrt{3}}{2}\right)$
    $=\sqrt{3}\left(-\sqrt{\dfrac{1+\left(-\dfrac{\sqrt{2}}{2}\right)}{2}}\right)$
    $=\sqrt{3}\left(-\dfrac{\sqrt{2-\sqrt{2}}}{2}\right)$
    $=-\dfrac{\sqrt{3}\sqrt{2-\sqrt{2}}}{2}$

15. $\sin\left(\dfrac{13\pi}{24}\right)\cos\left(\dfrac{7\pi}{24}\right)$
    $=\dfrac{1}{2}\left[\sin\left(\dfrac{13\pi}{24}+\dfrac{7\pi}{24}\right)+\sin\left(\dfrac{13\pi}{24}-\dfrac{7\pi}{24}\right)\right]$
    $=\dfrac{1}{2}\left[\sin\left(\dfrac{5\pi}{6}\right)+\sin\left(\dfrac{\pi}{4}\right)\right]$
    $=\dfrac{1}{2}\left[\dfrac{1}{2}+\dfrac{\sqrt{2}}{2}\right]=\dfrac{1+\sqrt{2}}{4}$

17. $\sin(\alpha+\beta)\sin(\alpha-\beta)$
$= (\sin\alpha\cos\alpha + \cos\alpha\sin\beta)$
$\quad (\sin\alpha\cos\beta - \cos\alpha\sin\beta)$
$= \sin^2\alpha\cos^2\beta - \cos^2\alpha\sin^2\beta$
$= \sin^2\alpha(1-\sin^2\beta) - (1-\sin^2\alpha)\sin^2\beta$
$= \sin^2\alpha - \sin^2\alpha\sin^2\beta - \sin^2\beta + \sin^2\alpha\sin^2\beta$
$= \sin^2\alpha - \sin^2\beta$

19. $R = \dfrac{1}{16}v^2\sin\theta\cos\theta$
$= \dfrac{1}{2}\cdot\dfrac{1}{16}v^2(2)\sin\theta\cos\theta$
$= \dfrac{1}{32}v^2\sin(2\theta)$

Practice Test

1. $\dfrac{(\csc x - \cot x)(\csc x + \cot x)}{\sec x}$
$= \dfrac{\csc^2 x + \csc x\cot x - \csc x\cot x - \cot^2 x}{\sec x}$
$= \dfrac{\csc^2 x - \cot^2 x}{\sec x}$
$= \dfrac{(1+\cot^2 x) - \cot^2 x}{\sec x}$
$= \dfrac{1}{\sec x}$
$= \cos x$

3. $\cos = \dfrac{48}{73};\ \theta$ in QIV
$x = 48;\ r = 73;\ y = -\sqrt{73^2-48^2} = -55$
$\sin\theta = -\dfrac{55}{73};\ \sec\theta = \dfrac{73}{48};\ \cot\theta = -\dfrac{48}{55}$
$\tan\theta = -\dfrac{55}{48};\ \csc\theta = -\dfrac{73}{55}$

5. $\cos 81°\cos 36° + \sin 81°\sin 36°$
$= \cos(81°-36°)$
$= \cos(45°)$
$= \dfrac{\sqrt{2}}{2}$

7. $\sin\left(x+\dfrac{\pi}{4}\right) - \sin\left(x-\dfrac{\pi}{4}\right)$
$= \left[\sin x\cos\left(\dfrac{\pi}{4}\right) + \cos x\sin\left(\dfrac{\pi}{4}\right)\right]$
$\quad - \left[\sin x\cos\left(\dfrac{\pi}{4}\right) - \cos x\sin\left(\dfrac{\pi}{4}\right)\right]$
$= \sin x\cos\dfrac{\pi}{4} + \cos x\sin\dfrac{\pi}{4}$
$\quad -\sin x\cos\dfrac{\pi}{4} + \cos x\sin\dfrac{\pi}{4}$
$= \cos x\sin\dfrac{\pi}{4} + \cos x\sin\dfrac{\pi}{4}$
$= 2\sin\dfrac{\pi}{4}\cos x$
$= 2\dfrac{\sqrt{2}}{2}\cos x = \sqrt{2}\cos x$

9. $2\cos^2 75° - 1 = \cos 2(75°)$
$= \cos 150°$
$= -\dfrac{\sqrt{3}}{2}$

11. $A = \dfrac{1}{2}bc\sin\alpha$
$A = \dfrac{1}{2}(8)(10)\sin 22.5°$
$= 40\sin\left(\dfrac{45°}{2}\right)$
$= 40\sqrt{\dfrac{1-\cos 45°}{2}}$
$= 40\sqrt{\dfrac{1-\dfrac{\sqrt{2}}{2}}{2}}$
$= 40\dfrac{\sqrt{2-\sqrt{2}}}{2}$
$= 20\sqrt{2-\sqrt{2}}$

13. $\dfrac{\tan\theta+\cot\theta}{\sin\theta\cos\theta} = \dfrac{\dfrac{\sin\theta}{\cos\theta}+\dfrac{\cos\theta}{\sin\theta}}{\sin\theta\cos\theta}$
$= \dfrac{\dfrac{\sin^2\theta+\cos^2\theta}{\sin\theta\cos\theta}}{\sin\theta\cos\theta}$
$= \dfrac{1}{\sin\theta\cos\theta}\cdot\dfrac{1}{\sin\theta\cos\theta}$
$= \dfrac{1}{\sin^2\theta}\cdot\dfrac{1}{\cos^2\theta}$
$= \csc^2\theta\sec^2\theta$

15. $\tan(15°) = \tan(45° - 30°)$

$$= \frac{\tan 45° - \tan 30°}{1 + \tan 45° \tan 30°}$$

$$= \frac{1 - \dfrac{\sqrt{3}}{3}}{1 + 1\left(\dfrac{\sqrt{3}}{3}\right)} = \frac{3 - \sqrt{3}}{3 + \sqrt{3}}$$

17. $\sin\theta = -\dfrac{12}{37};\ \theta$ in QIII

$$x = -\sqrt{37^2 - (-12)^2} = -35;\ \cos\theta = -\frac{35}{37}$$

$$\sin(2\theta) = 2\sin\theta\cos\theta$$

$$= 2\left(-\frac{12}{37}\right)\left(-\frac{35}{37}\right)$$

$$= \frac{840}{1369}$$

$$\cos(2\theta) = \cos^2\theta - \sin^2\theta$$

$$= \left(-\frac{35}{37}\right)^2 - \left(-\frac{12}{37}\right)^2$$

$$= \frac{1225}{1369} - \frac{144}{1369}$$

$$= \frac{1081}{1369}$$

$$\tan(2\theta) = \frac{\sin(2\theta)}{\cos(2\theta)}$$

$$= \frac{\dfrac{840}{1369}}{\dfrac{1081}{1369}} = \frac{840}{1081}$$

19. $y(t) = \cos(2\pi 1336t) + \cos(2\pi 941t)$

   a. The zero "0" was pressed.

   b. $\cos(2\pi 1336t) + \cos(2\pi 941t)$

$$= 2\cos\left(\frac{2\pi 1336t + 2\pi 941t}{2}\right)$$

$$\cdot\cos\left(\frac{2\pi 1336t - 2\pi 941t}{2}\right)$$

$$= 2\cos(2277\pi t)\cos(395\pi t)$$

Calculator Exploration and Discovery

Exercise 1:
$$Y_1 = \cos(14t);\ Y_2 = \cos(8t)$$

   a. $Y_R = Y_1 + Y_2 = \cos(14t) + \cos(8t)$

$$= 2\cos\left(\frac{14t + 8t}{2}\right)\cos\left(\frac{14t - 8t}{2}\right)$$

$$= 2\cos(11t)\cos(3t)$$

   b. $14 - 8 = 6$ beats

   c. $\dfrac{k}{2} = \dfrac{14 - 8}{2} = 3;\ y = \pm 2\cos(3x)$

Exercise 3:
$$Y_1 = \cos(14t);\ Y_2 = \cos(6t)$$

   a. $Y_R = Y_1 + Y_2 = \cos(14t) + \cos(6t)$

$$= 2\cos\left(\frac{14t + 6t}{2}\right)\cos\left(\frac{14t - 6t}{2}\right)$$

$$= 2\cos(10t)\cos(4t)$$

   b. $14 - 6 = 8$ beats

   c. $\dfrac{k}{2} = \dfrac{14 - 6}{2} = 4;\ y = \pm 2\cos(4x)$

Strengthening Core Skills

Exercise 1:
$$\sin^2 x + \cos^2 x = 1$$

$$\frac{\sin^2 x}{\sin^2 x} + \frac{\cos^2 x}{\sin^2 x} = \frac{1}{\sin^2 x}$$

$$1 + \cot^2 x = \csc^2 x$$

$$\sin^2 x + \cos^2 x = 1$$

$$\frac{\sin^2 x}{\cos^2 x} + \frac{\cos^2 x}{\cos^2 x} = \frac{1}{\cos^2 x}$$

$$\tan^2 x + 1 = \sec^2 x$$

Cumulative Review Chapters 1-5

1. $\beta = 90° - 30° = 60°$

    $b = \sqrt{3}a = \sqrt{3} \cdot 20 = 20\sqrt{3}$ m
    $c = 2a = 2 \cdot 20 = 40$ m

Angles	Sides
$\alpha = 30°$	$a = 20$ m
$\beta = 60°$	$b = 20\sqrt{3}$ m
$\gamma = 90°$	$c = 40$ m

3. $\sin^2 x + \cos^2 x = 1$
    $1 + \cot^2 x = \csc^2 x$
    $\tan^2 x + 1 = \sec^2 x$

5. $V = r\theta$

    $V = 6 \cdot \dfrac{300 \text{ rev}}{1 \text{ min}} \cdot \dfrac{2\pi \text{ rad}}{1 \text{ rev}} = 3600\pi \text{ rad/min}$

    $\left(\dfrac{3600\pi \text{ rad}}{1 \text{ min}}\right)\left(\dfrac{1 \text{ min}}{60 \text{ sec}}\right)\left(\dfrac{1 \text{ ft}}{12 \text{ in}}\right) \approx 15.7 \text{ ft/sec}$

7. $y = 3\cos\left(2x - \dfrac{\pi}{4}\right) = 3\cos\left[2\left(x - \dfrac{\pi}{8}\right)\right]$

    $|A| = 3;\ P = \dfrac{2\pi}{2} = \pi$

    HS: $\dfrac{\pi}{8}$ units right; VS: none

    Ref Rect: $2|A| = 6$ by $P = \pi$ units

    Rule of Fourths: $t = \dfrac{\pi}{8}, \dfrac{3\pi}{8}, \dfrac{5\pi}{8}, \dfrac{7\pi}{8}, \text{and} \dfrac{9\pi}{8}$

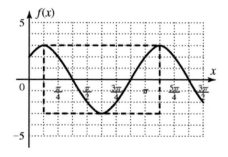

9. Begin on the right side of the equation.

    $\cos^2\left(\dfrac{\alpha}{2}\right) = \dfrac{\sec\alpha + 2 + \cos\alpha}{2\sec\alpha + 2}$

    $\quad = \dfrac{\sec\alpha + 2 + \cos\alpha}{2\sec\alpha + 2} \cdot \dfrac{\cos\alpha}{\cos\alpha}$

    $\quad = \dfrac{1 + 2\cos\alpha + \cos^2\alpha}{2 + 2\cos\alpha}$

    $\quad = \dfrac{(1 + \cos\alpha)(1 + \cos\alpha)}{2(1 + \cos\alpha)}$

    $\quad = \left(\dfrac{1 + \cos\alpha}{2}\right);$ let $\alpha = 2\theta$

11. $\sin(2x) = 2\sin x\cos x$;
    $\cos(2x) = \cos^2 x - \sin^2 x$
    $\cos(2x) = 2\cos^2 x - 1$
    $\cos(2x) = 1 - 2\sin^2 x$

13. $\sin 195° = \sin(150° + 45°)$
    $\quad = \sin 150°\cos 45° + \cos 150°\sin 45°$

    $\quad = \left(\dfrac{1}{2}\right)\left(\dfrac{\sqrt{2}}{2}\right) + \left(-\dfrac{\sqrt{3}}{2}\right)\left(\dfrac{\sqrt{2}}{2}\right)$

    $\quad = \dfrac{\sqrt{2} - \sqrt{6}}{4}$

    $\cos 195° = \cos(150° + 45°)$
    $\quad = \cos 150°\cos 45° - \sin 150°\sin 45°$

    $\quad = \left(-\dfrac{\sqrt{3}}{2}\right)\left(\dfrac{\sqrt{2}}{2}\right) - \left(\dfrac{1}{2}\right)\left(\dfrac{\sqrt{2}}{2}\right)$

    $\quad = \dfrac{-\sqrt{6} - \sqrt{2}}{4}$

15. $f(t) = 6.7547\sin(0.4351t - 1.3721) + 11.3216$

    a.   just over 15 hours

    b.   April 15 to September 1 or 2

17. $\cot x \ \tan x - \dfrac{\sin x}{\cos^3 x} = 1 - \dfrac{\cos x}{\sin x} \cdot \dfrac{\sin x}{\cos^3 x}$

    $\quad = 1 - \dfrac{1}{\cos^2 x}$

    $\quad = 1 - \sec^2 x = \tan^2 x$

19. $59.6° - 50.3° = 9.3°$

    $9.3° \cdot \dfrac{\pi \text{ rad}}{180°} = \dfrac{31\pi}{600} \text{ rad}$

    $s = r\theta = 6372\left(\dfrac{31\pi}{600}\right) \approx 1034 \text{ km}$

    Approximate 1034 kilometers separate the two cities.

Technology Highlight

1. a. $f(x) = 2x + 1$

    $\quad\quad y = 2x + 1$

    $\quad\quad x = 2y + 1$

    $\quad\quad x - 1 = 2y$

    $\quad\quad y = \dfrac{x-1}{2}$

    $\quad f^{-1}(x) = \dfrac{x-1}{2}$

    b. This can be verified using a graphing calculator.

    c. This can be verified using a graphing calculator.

    d.

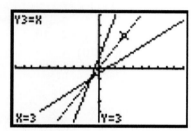

3. a. $h(x) = \dfrac{x}{x+1}$

    $\quad\quad y = \dfrac{x}{x+1}$

    $\quad\quad x = \dfrac{y}{y+1}$

    $\quad x(y+1) = y$

    $\quad xy + x = y$

    $\quad xy - y = -x$

    $\quad y(x-1) = -x$

    $\quad\quad y = \dfrac{-x}{x-1}$

    $\quad h^{-1}(x) = \dfrac{-x}{x-1} = \dfrac{x}{1-x}$

    b. This can be verified using a graphing calculator.

    c. This can be verified using a graphing calculator.

3. d.

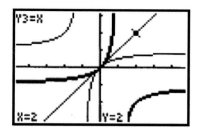

6.1 Exercises

1. second; one

3. $(-11, -2), (-5, 0), (1, 2), (19, 4)$

5. False, answers will vary.

7. one-to-one

9. one-to-one

11. not a function

13. one-to-one

15. not one-to-one; fails horizontal line test; $x = -3$ and $x = 3$ are each paired with $y = 1$

17. not one-to-one; $y = 7$ is paired with $x = -2$ and $x = 2$

19. one-to-one

21. one-to-one

23. not one-to-one; $p(t) > 5$, corresponds to two x-values.

25. one-to-one

27. one-to-one

29. $f(x)=\{(-2,1),(-1,4),(0,5),$
$(2,9),(5,15)\}$

$f^{-1}(x)=\{(1,-2),(4,-1),(5,0),$
$(9,2),(15,5)\}$

31. $v(x)=\{(-4,3),(-3,2)(0,1),(5,0),$
$(12,-1),(21,-2),(32,-3)\}$

$v^{-1}(x)=\{(3,-4),(2,-3)(1,0),(0,5),$
$(-1,12),(-2,21),(-3,32)\}$

33. $f(x)=x+5$
$y=x+5$
$x=y+5$
$y=x-5$
$f^{-1}(x)=x-5$

35. $p(x)=2x-3$
$y=-\dfrac{4}{5}x$
$x=-\dfrac{4}{5}y$
$y=-\dfrac{5}{4}x$
$p^{-1}(x)=-\dfrac{5}{4}x$

37. $f(x)=4x+3$
$y=4x+3$
$x=4y+3$
$4y=x-3$
$y=\dfrac{x-3}{4}$
$f^{-1}(x)=\dfrac{x-3}{4}$

39. $Y_1=\sqrt[3]{x-4}$
$y=\sqrt[3]{x-4}$
$x=\sqrt[3]{y-4}$
$x^3=y-4$
$y=x^3+4$
$Y_1^{-1}=x^3+4$

41. $f(x)=\sqrt[3]{x-2}$

a.   Answers will vary.
$f(1)=\sqrt[3]{1-2}=\sqrt[3]{-1}=-1$
$f(2)=\sqrt[3]{2-2}=\sqrt[3]{0}=0$
$f(10)=\sqrt[3]{10-2}=\sqrt[3]{8}=2$
$(1,-1),(2,0),(10,2)$

b. $f(x)=\sqrt[3]{x-2}$
$y=\sqrt[3]{x-2}$
$x=\sqrt[3]{y-2}$
$x^3=y-2$
$y=x^3+2$
$f^{-1}(x)=x^3+2$

c. $f(-1)=x^3+2=(-1)^3+2=1$
$f(0)=x^3+2=(0)^3+2=2$
$f(2)=x^3+2=(2)^3+2=10$
$(-1,1),(0,2),(2,10)$

43. $f(x)=x^3+1$

a.   Answers will vary.
$f(-2)=(-2)^3+1=-8+1=-7$
$f(0)=0^3+1=0+1=1$
$f(1)=1^3+1=1+1=2$
$(-2,-7),(0,1),(1,2)$

b. $f(x)=x^3+1$
$y=x^3+1$
$x=y^3+1$
$y^3=x-1$
$y=\sqrt[3]{x-1}$
$f^{-1}(x)=\sqrt[3]{x-1}$

c. $f^{-1}(-7)=\sqrt[3]{-7-1}=\sqrt[3]{-8}=-2$
$f^{-1}(1)=\sqrt[3]{1-1}=\sqrt[3]{0}=0$
$f^{-1}(2)=\sqrt[3]{2-1}=\sqrt[3]{1}=1$
$(-7,-2),(1,0),(2,1)$

45. $f(x) = \dfrac{8}{x+2}$

 a. Answers will vary.

 $$f(0) = \dfrac{8}{0+2} = \dfrac{8}{2} = 4$$

 $$f(-1) = \dfrac{8}{-1+2} = \dfrac{8}{1} = 8$$

 $$f(2) = \dfrac{8}{2+2} = \dfrac{8}{4} = 2$$

 $(0,4), (-1,8), (2,2)$

 b. $f(x) = \dfrac{8}{x+2}$

 $$y = \dfrac{8}{x+2}$$

 $$x = \dfrac{8}{y+2}$$

 $$y+2 = \dfrac{8}{x}$$

 $$y = \dfrac{8}{x} - 2$$

 $$f^{-1}(x) = \dfrac{8}{x} - 2$$

 c. $f^{-1}(4) = \dfrac{8}{4} - 2 = 2 - 2 = 0$

 $$f^{-1}(8) = \dfrac{8}{8} - 2 = 1 - 2 = -1$$

 $$f^{-1}(2) = \dfrac{8}{2} - 2 = 4 - 2 = 2$$

 $(4,0), (8,-1), (2,2)$

47. $f(x) = \dfrac{x}{x+1}$

 a. Answers will vary.

 $$f(-2) = \dfrac{-2}{-2+1} = \dfrac{-2}{-1} = 2$$

 $$f(0) = \dfrac{0}{0+1} = \dfrac{0}{1} = 0$$

 $$f(1) = \dfrac{1}{1+1} = \dfrac{1}{2}$$

 $(-2,2), (0,0), \left(1, \dfrac{1}{2}\right)$

47. b. $f(x) = \dfrac{x}{x+1}$

 $$y = \dfrac{x}{x+1}$$

 $$x = \dfrac{y}{y+1}$$

 $$x(y+1) = y$$

 $$xy + x = y$$

 $$xy - y = -x$$

 $$y(x-1) = -x$$

 $$y = \dfrac{-x}{x-1}$$

 $$y = \dfrac{x}{1-x}$$

 $$f^{-1}(x) = \dfrac{x}{1-x}$$

 c. $f^{-1}(2) = \dfrac{2}{1-2} = \dfrac{2}{-1} = -2$

 $$f^{-1}(0) = \dfrac{0}{1-0} = 0$$

 $$f^{-1}\left(\dfrac{1}{2}\right) = \dfrac{\frac{1}{2}}{1-\frac{1}{2}} = \dfrac{\frac{1}{2}}{\frac{1}{2}} = 1$$

 $(2,-2), (0,0), \left(\dfrac{1}{2}, 1\right)$

49. $f(x) = (x+5)^2$

 a. Restrict domain to $x \ge -5$.
 Range: $y \ge 0$

 b. $f(x) = (x+5)^2$

 $$y = (x+5)^2$$

 $$x = (y+5)^2$$

 $$y+5 = \pm\sqrt{x}$$

 $$y = \sqrt{x} - 5 \qquad \text{Use } \sqrt{x} \text{ since } x \ge -5.$$

 $$f^{-1}(x) = \sqrt{x} - 5$$

 Domain: $x \ge 0$
 Range: $y \ge -5$

51. $v(x) = \dfrac{8}{(x-3)^2}$

    a. Restrict domain to $x > 3$.
        Range: $y > 0$

    b. $v(x) = \dfrac{8}{(x-3)^2}$

        $y = \dfrac{8}{(x-3)^2}$

        $x = \dfrac{8}{(y-3)^2}$

        $(y-3)^2 = \dfrac{8}{x}$

        $y - 3 = \pm\sqrt{\dfrac{8}{x}}$

        $y = \sqrt{\dfrac{8}{x}} + 3$ Use $\sqrt{\dfrac{8}{x}}$ since $x > 3$.

        $v^{-1}(x) = \sqrt{\dfrac{8}{x}} + 3$

        Domain: $x > 0$
        Range: $y > 3$

53. $p(x) = (x+4)^2 - 2$

    a. Restrict domain to $x \geq -4$.
        Range: $y \geq -2$

    b. $p(x) = (x+4)^2 - 2$

        $y = (x+4)^2 - 2$

        $x = (y+4)^2 - 2$

        $x + 2 = (y+4)^2$

        $y + 4 = \pm\sqrt{x+2}$

        $y = \sqrt{x+2} - 4$ Use $\sqrt{x+2}$ since $x \geq -2$.

    $p^{-1}(x) = \sqrt{x+2} - 4$

    Domain: $x \geq -2$
    Range: $y \geq -4$

55. $f(x) = -2x + 5$, $g(x) = \dfrac{x-5}{-2}$

    $(f \circ g)(x) = f\big[g(x)\big]$

              $= -2\big[g(x)\big] + 5$

              $= -2\left(\dfrac{x-5}{-2}\right) + 5$

              $= x - 5 + 5$

              $= x$

    $(g \circ f)(x) = g\big[f(x)\big]$

              $= \dfrac{f(x) - 5}{-2}$

              $= \dfrac{-2x + 5 - 5}{-2}$

              $= \dfrac{-2x}{-2}$

              $= x$

57. $f(x) = \sqrt[3]{x+5}$, $g(x) = x^3 - 5$

    $(f \circ g)(x) = f\big[g(x)\big]$

              $= \sqrt[3]{g(x) + 5}$

              $= \sqrt[3]{x^3 - 5 + 5}$

              $= \sqrt[3]{x^3}$

              $= x$

    $(g \circ f)(x) = g\big[f(x)\big]$

              $= \big[f(x)\big]^3 - 5$

              $= \left(\sqrt[3]{x+5}\right)^3 - 5$

              $= x + 5 - 5$

              $= x$

59. $f(x) = \dfrac{2}{3}x - 6$, $g(x) = \dfrac{3}{2}x + 9$

    $(f \circ g)(x) = f\big[g(x)\big]$

              $= \dfrac{2}{3}g(x) - 6$

              $= \dfrac{2}{3}\left(\dfrac{3}{2}x + 9\right) - 6$

              $= x + 6 - 6$

              $= x$

    $(g \circ f)(x) = g\big[f(x)\big]$

              $= \dfrac{3}{2}f(x) + 9$

              $= \dfrac{3}{2}\left(\dfrac{2}{3}x - 6\right) + 9$

              $= x - 9 + 9$

              $= x$

61. $f(x) = x^2 - 3; \; x \geq 0, \; g(x) = \sqrt{x+3}$

$$(f \circ g)(x) = f[g(x)]$$
$$= [g(x)]^2 - 3$$
$$= (\sqrt{x+3})^2 - 3$$
$$= x + 3 - 3$$
$$= x$$

$$(g \circ f)(x) = g[f(x)]$$
$$= \sqrt{f(x) + 3}$$
$$= \sqrt{x^2 - 3 + 3}$$
$$= \sqrt{x^2}$$
$$= x$$

63. $f(x) = 3x - 5$
$$y = 3x - 5$$
$$x = 3y - 5$$
$$3y = x + 5$$
$$y = \frac{x+5}{3}$$
$$f^{-1}(x) = \frac{x+5}{3}$$

$$(f \circ f^{-1})(x) = f[f^{-1}(x)]$$
$$= 3[f^{-1}(x)] - 5$$
$$= 3\left(\frac{x+5}{3}\right) - 5$$
$$= x + 5 - 5$$
$$= x$$

$$(f^{-1} \circ f)(x) = f^{-1}[f(x)]$$
$$= \frac{f(x) + 5}{3}$$
$$= \frac{3x - 5 + 5}{3}$$
$$= \frac{3x}{3}$$
$$= x$$

65. $f(x) = \dfrac{x-5}{2}$

$$y = \frac{x-5}{2}$$
$$x = \frac{y-5}{2}$$
$$y - 5 = 2x$$
$$y = 2x + 5$$
$$f^{-1}(x) = 2x + 5$$

$$(f \circ f^{-1})(x) = f[f^{-1}(x)]$$
$$= \frac{f^{-1}(x) - 5}{2}$$
$$= \frac{2x + 5 - 5}{2}$$
$$= \frac{2x}{2}$$
$$= x$$

$$(f^{-1} \circ f)(x) = f^{-1}[f(x)]$$
$$= 2[f(x)] + 5$$
$$= 2\left(\frac{x-5}{2}\right) + 5$$
$$= x - 5 + 5$$
$$= x$$

67. $f(x) = \dfrac{1}{2}x - 3$

$$y = \frac{1}{2}x - 3$$
$$x = \frac{1}{2}y - 3$$
$$\frac{1}{2}y = x + 3$$
$$y = 2x + 6$$
$$f^{-1}(x) = 2x + 6$$

$$(f \circ f^{-1})(x) = f[f^{-1}(x)]$$
$$= \frac{1}{2}[f^{-1}(x)] - 3$$
$$= \frac{1}{2}(2x + 6) - 3$$
$$= x + 3 - 3 = x$$

$$(f^{-1} \circ f)(x) = f^{-1}[f(x)]$$
$$= 2[f(x)] + 6$$
$$= 2\left(\frac{1}{2}x - 3\right) + 6$$
$$= x - 6 + 6 = x$$

69. $f(x) = x^3 + 3$

$\qquad y = x^3 + 3$

$\qquad x = y^3 + 3$

$\qquad y^3 = x - 3$

$\qquad y = \sqrt[3]{x-3}$

$f^{-1}(x) = \sqrt[3]{x-3}$

$(f \circ f^{-1})(x) = f\left[f^{-1}(x)\right]$

$\qquad = \left[f^{-1}(x)\right]^3 + 3$

$\qquad = \left(\sqrt[3]{x-3}\right)^3 + 3$

$\qquad = x - 3 + 3$

$\qquad = x$

$(f^{-1} \circ f)(x) = f^{-1}\left[f(x)\right]$

$\qquad = \sqrt[3]{f(x) - 3}$

$\qquad = \sqrt[3]{x^3 + 3 - 3}$

$\qquad = \sqrt[3]{x^3}$

$\qquad = x$

71. $f(x) = \sqrt[3]{2x+1}$

$\qquad y = \sqrt[3]{2x+1}$

$\qquad x = \sqrt[3]{2y+1}$

$\qquad x^3 = 2y + 1$

$\qquad 2y = x^3 - 1$

$\qquad y = \dfrac{x^3 - 1}{2}$

$f^{-1}(x) = \dfrac{x^3 - 1}{2}$

$(f \circ f^{-1})(x) = f\left[f^{-1}(x)\right]$

$\qquad = \sqrt[3]{2\left[f^{-1}(x)\right]+1}$

$\qquad = \sqrt[3]{2\left(\dfrac{x^3-1}{2}\right)+1}$

$\qquad = \sqrt[3]{x^3 - 1 + 1}$

$\qquad = \sqrt[3]{x^3}$

$\qquad = x$

71.   (continued)

$(f^{-1} \circ f)(x) = f^{-1}\left[f(x)\right]$

$\qquad = \dfrac{\left[f(x)\right]^3 - 1}{2}$

$\qquad = \dfrac{\left(\sqrt[3]{2x+1}\right)^3 - 1}{2}$

$\qquad = \dfrac{2x + 1 - 1}{2}$

$\qquad = \dfrac{2x}{2}$

$\qquad = x$

73. $f(x) = \dfrac{(x-1)^3}{8}$

$\qquad y = \dfrac{(x-1)^3}{8}$

$\qquad x = \dfrac{(y-1)^3}{8}$

$\qquad 8x = (y-1)^3$

$\qquad \sqrt[3]{8x} = y - 1$

$\qquad y = 2\sqrt[3]{x} + 1$

$f^{-1}(x) = 2\sqrt[3]{x} + 1$

$(f \circ f^{-1})(x) = f\left[f^{-1}(x)\right]$

$\qquad = \dfrac{\left(f^{-1}(x)-1\right)^3}{8}$

$\qquad = \dfrac{\left(2\sqrt[3]{x} + 1 - 1\right)^3}{8}$

$\qquad = \dfrac{\left(2\sqrt[3]{x}\right)^3}{8}$

$\qquad = \dfrac{8x}{8}$

$\qquad = x$

$(f^{-1} \circ f)(x) = f^{-1}\left[f(x)\right]$

$\qquad = 2\sqrt[3]{f(x)} + 1$

$\qquad = 2\sqrt[3]{\dfrac{(x-1)^3}{8}} + 1$

$\qquad = 2\left(\dfrac{x-1}{2}\right) + 1$

$\qquad = x - 1 + 1$

$\qquad = x$

75. $f(x) = \sqrt{3x+2}; \ x \in \left[-\dfrac{2}{3}, \infty\right), \ y \geq 0$

$$y = \sqrt{3x+2}$$
$$x = \sqrt{3y+2}$$
$$x^2 = 3y+2$$
$$3y = x^2-2$$
$$y = \dfrac{x^2-2}{3}$$
$$f^{-1}(x) = \dfrac{x^2-2}{3}; \ x \geq 0, \ y \in \left[-\dfrac{2}{3}, \infty\right)$$

$(f \circ f^{-1})(x) = f(f^{-1}(x))$
$$= \sqrt{3\left[f^{-1}(x)\right]+2}$$
$$= \sqrt{3\left(\dfrac{x^2-2}{3}\right)+2}$$
$$= \sqrt{x^2-2+2}$$
$$= \sqrt{x^2}$$
$$= |x|$$
$$= x \qquad \text{since } x \geq 0$$

$(f^{-1} \circ f)(x) = f^{-1}[f(x)]$
$$= \dfrac{(f(x))^2-2}{3}$$
$$= \dfrac{(\sqrt{3x+2})^2-2}{3}$$
$$= \dfrac{3x+2-2}{3}$$
$$= \dfrac{3x}{3}$$
$$= x$$

77. $p(x) = 2\sqrt{x-3}; \ x \in [3, \infty), \ y \geq 0$

$$y = 2\sqrt{x-3}$$
$$x = 2\sqrt{y-3}$$
$$\dfrac{x}{2} = \sqrt{y-3}$$
$$\dfrac{x^2}{4} = y-3$$
$$y = \dfrac{x^2}{4}+3$$
$$p^{-1}(x) = \dfrac{x^2}{4}+3; \ x \geq 0, \ y \in [3, \infty)$$

77. (continued)
$(p \circ p^{-1})(x) = p(p^{-1}(x))$
$$= 2\sqrt{p^{-1}(x)-3}$$
$$= 2\sqrt{\dfrac{x^2}{4}+3-3}$$
$$= 2\sqrt{\dfrac{x^2}{4}}$$
$$= 2\left(\dfrac{x}{2}\right)$$
$$= x$$

$(p^{-1} \circ p)(x) = p^{-1}[p(x)]$
$$= \dfrac{[p(x)]^2}{4}+3$$
$$= \dfrac{(2\sqrt{x-3})^2}{4}+3$$
$$= \dfrac{4(x-3)}{4}+3$$
$$= x-3+3$$
$$= x$$

79. $v(x) = x^2+3; \ x \geq 0, \ y \in [3, \infty)$

$$y = x^2+3$$
$$x = y^2+3$$
$$y^2 = x-3$$
$$y = \sqrt{x-3}$$
$$v^{-1}(x) = \sqrt{x-3}; \ x \geq 3, \ y \in [0, \infty)$$

$(v \circ v^{-1})(x) = v[v^{-1}(x)]$
$$= [v^{-1}(x)]^2+3$$
$$= (\sqrt{x-3})^2+3$$
$$= x-3+3$$
$$= x$$

$(v^{-1} \circ v)(x) = v^{-1}[v(x)]$
$$= \sqrt{v(x)-3}$$
$$= \sqrt{x^2+3-3}$$
$$= \sqrt{x^2}$$
$$= |x|$$
$$= x \qquad \text{since } x \geq 0$$

81. $f(x) = 4x + 1$; $f^{-1}(x) = \dfrac{x-1}{4}$

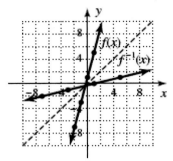

$$(f \circ f^{-1})(x) = f\left[f^{-1}(x)\right]$$
$$= 4\left[f^{-1}(x)\right] + 1$$
$$= 4\left(\dfrac{x-1}{4}\right) + 1$$
$$= x - 1 + 1$$
$$= x$$

$$(f^{-1} \circ f)(x) = f^{-1}\left[f(x)\right]$$
$$= \dfrac{f(x) - 1}{4}$$
$$= \dfrac{4x + 1 - 1}{4}$$
$$= \dfrac{4x}{4}$$
$$= x$$

83. $f(x) = \sqrt[3]{x+2}$; $f^{-1}(x) = x^3 - 2$

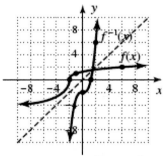

$$(f \circ f^{-1})(x) = f\left[f^{-1}(x)\right]$$
$$= \sqrt[3]{f^{-1}(x) + 2}$$
$$= \sqrt[3]{x^3 - 2 + 2}$$
$$= \sqrt[3]{x^3}$$
$$= x$$

$$(f^{-1} \circ f)(x) = f^{-1}\left[f(x)\right]$$
$$= \left[f(x)\right]^3 - 2$$
$$= \left(\sqrt[3]{x+2}\right)^3 - 2$$
$$= x + 2 - 2$$
$$= x$$

85. $f(x) = 0.2x + 1$; $f^{-1}(x) = 5x - 5$

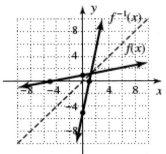

$$(f \circ f^{-1})(x) = f\left[f^{-1}(x)\right]$$
$$= 0.2\left[f^{-1}(x)\right] + 1$$
$$= 0.2(5x - 5) + 1$$
$$= x - 1 + 1$$
$$= x$$

$$(f^{-1} \circ f)(x) = f^{-1}\left[f(x)\right]$$
$$= 5\left[f(x)\right] - 5$$
$$= 5(0.2x + 1) - 5$$
$$= x + 5 - 5$$
$$= x$$

87. $f(x) = (x+2)^2$, $x \geq -2$; $f^{-1}(x) = \sqrt{x} - 2$

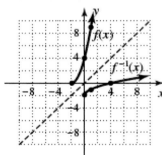

$$(f \circ f^{-1})(x) = f\left(f^{-1}(x)\right)$$
$$= \left(f^{-1}(x) + 2\right)^2$$
$$= \left(\sqrt{x} - 2 + 2\right)^2$$
$$= \left(\sqrt{x}\right)^2$$
$$= x$$

$$(f^{-1} \circ f)(x) = f^{-1}\left[f(x)\right]$$
$$= \sqrt{f(x)} - 2$$
$$= \sqrt{(x+2)^2} - 2$$
$$= x + 2 - 2$$
$$= x$$

89. $f(x)$: $D: x \in [0,\infty)$, $R: y \in [-2,\infty)$
    $f^{-1}(x)$: $D: x \in [-2,\infty)$, $R: y \in [0,\infty)$

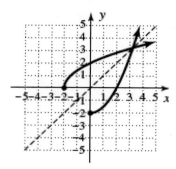

91. $f(x)$: $D: x \in (0,\infty)$, $R: y \in (-\infty,\infty)$
    $f^{-1}(x)$: $D: x \in (-\infty,\infty)$, $R: y \in (0,\infty)$

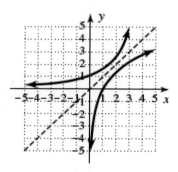

93. $f(x)$: $D: x \in (-\infty,4]$, $R: y \in (-\infty,4]$
    $f^{-1}(x)$: $D: x \in (-\infty,4]$, $R: y \in (-\infty,4]$

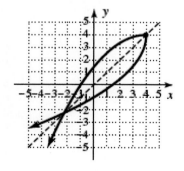

95. $f(x) = \dfrac{1}{2}x - 8.5$

a. $f(80) = \dfrac{1}{2}(80) - 8.5 = 31.5 \, \text{cm}$

$$y = \dfrac{1}{2}x - 8.5$$

$$x = \dfrac{1}{2}y - 8.5$$

b. $\dfrac{1}{2}y = x + 8.5$

$y = 2x + 17$

$f^{-1}(x) = 2x + 17$

$f^{-1}(31.5) = 2(31.5) + 17 = 80 \, \text{cm}$

The inverse function gives the distance of the projector from screen.

97. $f(x) = -\dfrac{7}{2}x + 59$

a. $f(35) = -\dfrac{7}{2}(35) + 59$

$= -63.5°\text{F}$

b. $y = -\dfrac{7}{2}x + 59$

$x = -\dfrac{7}{2}y + 59$

$-\dfrac{7}{2}y = x - 59$

$y = -\dfrac{2}{7}(x - 59)$

$f^{-1}(x) = -\dfrac{2}{7}(x - 59)$

independent: temperature
dependent: altitude

c. $f^{-1}(-18) = -\dfrac{2}{7}(-18 - 59)$

$= -\dfrac{2}{7}(-77)$

$= 22 \, \text{ft}$

The approximate altitude is 22,000 feet.

99. $f(x) = 16x^2, \ x \geq 0$

a. $f(3) = 16(3)^2$
$= 16(9)$
$= 144$ ft

b. $y = 16x^2$
$x = 16y^2$
$y^2 = \dfrac{x}{16}$
$y = \dfrac{\sqrt{x}}{4}$
$f^{-1}(x) = \dfrac{\sqrt{x}}{4}$

independent: distance fallen
dependent: time fallen

c. $f^{-1}(784) = \dfrac{\sqrt{784}}{4}$
$= \dfrac{28}{4}$
$= 7$ sec

101. $f(x) = \dfrac{1}{3}\pi x^3$

a. $f(30) = \dfrac{1}{3}(3.14)(30)^3$
$= \dfrac{1}{3}(3.14)(27{,}000)$
$= 28{,}260$ ft^3

b. $y = \dfrac{1}{3}\pi x^3$
$x = \dfrac{1}{3}\pi y^3$
$3x = \pi y^3$
$y^3 = \dfrac{3x}{\pi}$
$y = \sqrt[3]{\dfrac{3x}{\pi}}$
$f^{-1}(x) = \sqrt[3]{\dfrac{3x}{\pi}}$

independent: volume
dependent: height

c. $f^{-1}(763.02) = \sqrt[3]{\dfrac{3(763.02)}{\pi}}$
≈ 9 ft

103. Answers will vary.

105. By inspection, we see that the function in d.,
$f^{-1}(x) = \sqrt[5]{\dfrac{3}{2}\left(x - \dfrac{4}{5}\right)} + \dfrac{1}{2}$ is the inverse, since
the operations are the opposite of those in $f(x)$.

$f(x) = \dfrac{2}{3}\left(x - \dfrac{1}{2}\right)^5 + \dfrac{4}{5}$

$y = \dfrac{2}{3}\left(x - \dfrac{1}{2}\right)^5 + \dfrac{4}{5}$

$x = \dfrac{2}{3}\left(y - \dfrac{1}{2}\right)^5 + \dfrac{4}{5}$

$x - \dfrac{4}{5} = \dfrac{2}{3}\left(y - \dfrac{1}{2}\right)^5$

$\dfrac{3}{2}\left(x - \dfrac{4}{5}\right) = \left(y - \dfrac{1}{2}\right)^5$

$\sqrt[5]{\dfrac{3}{2}\left(x - \dfrac{4}{5}\right)} = y - \dfrac{1}{2}$

$\sqrt[5]{\dfrac{3}{2}\left(x - \dfrac{4}{5}\right)} + \dfrac{1}{2} = y$

d. $f^{-1}(x) = \sqrt[5]{\dfrac{3}{2}\left(x - \dfrac{4}{5}\right)} + \dfrac{1}{2}$

107. Begin on the right side of the equation.

$\tan^2\theta - \sin^2\theta = \dfrac{\sin^2\theta}{\cos^2\theta} - \sin^2\theta$

$= \dfrac{\sin^2\theta}{\cos^2\theta} - \dfrac{\sin^2\theta\cos^2\theta}{\cos^2\theta}$

$= \dfrac{\sin^2\theta - \sin^2\theta\cos^2\theta}{\cos^2\theta}$

$= \dfrac{\sin^2\theta}{\cos^2\theta}\left(1 - \cos^2\theta\right)$

$= \tan^2\theta\sin^2\theta$

109. $|A| = 2; \ B = \dfrac{2\pi}{2\pi} = 1$

HS: $\dfrac{\pi}{4}$ units to the right

$y = 2\sin\left(x - \dfrac{\pi}{4}\right)$

$|A| = 2; \ B = \dfrac{2\pi}{2\pi} = 1$

HS: $\dfrac{3\pi}{4}$ units to the right

$y = 2\cos\left(x - \dfrac{3\pi}{4}\right)$

111. $\tan 22°46' = \dfrac{h}{9000}$

$h = 9000\tan 22°46'$

$h \approx 3777$ m

Yes, Mt. Fuji is taller than Mount Hood.

Technology Highlight

Exercise 1:

Use a graphing calculator.

$Y_1 = \cos x$

$Y_2 = \cos^{-1} x$

6.2 Exercises

1. horizontal line; one; one

3. $[-1, 1];\ \left[-\dfrac{\pi}{2}, \dfrac{\pi}{2}\right]$

5. $\cos^{-1}\left(\dfrac{1}{5}\right)$

7. $\sin^{-1} 0 = 0$

$\sin\left(\dfrac{\pi}{6}\right) = \sin 30° = \dfrac{1}{2}$

$\sin^{-1}\left(-\dfrac{1}{2}\right) = -\dfrac{\pi}{6}$

$\sin^{-1}(-1) = -\dfrac{\pi}{2}$

9. $\sin^{-1}\left(\dfrac{\sqrt{2}}{2}\right) = y$ where $-\dfrac{\pi}{2} \le y \le \dfrac{\pi}{2}$

y is the number or angle whose sine is $\dfrac{\sqrt{2}}{2}$.

$\sin y = \dfrac{\sqrt{2}}{2};\ \ \sin^{-1}\left(\dfrac{\sqrt{2}}{2}\right) = \dfrac{\pi}{4}$

11. $\sin^{-1} 1 = y$ where $-\dfrac{\pi}{2} \le y \le \dfrac{\pi}{2}$

y is the number or angle whose sine is 1.

$\sin y = 1;\ \ \sin^{-1} 1 = \dfrac{\pi}{2}$

13. $\arcsin 0.8892 \approx 1.0956$

$1.0956\left(\dfrac{180°}{\pi}\right) \approx 62.8°$

15. $\sin^{-1}\left(\dfrac{1}{\sqrt{7}}\right) \approx 0.3876$

$0.3876\left(\dfrac{180°}{\pi}\right) = 22.2°$

17. $\sin\left[\sin^{-1}\left(\dfrac{\sqrt{2}}{2}\right)\right] = \dfrac{\sqrt{2}}{2}$

since $\dfrac{\sqrt{2}}{2} \in [-1, 1]$.

19. $\arcsin\left[\sin\left(\dfrac{\pi}{3}\right)\right] = \dfrac{\pi}{3}$

since $\dfrac{\pi}{3} \in \left[-\dfrac{\pi}{2}, \dfrac{\pi}{2}\right]$.

21. $\sin^{-1}(\sin 135°) = 45°$, since $\sin 135° = \sin 45°$

and $45° \in [-90°, 90°]$.

23. $\sin\left(\sin^{-1} 0.8205\right) = 0.8205$

since $0.8205 \in [-1, 1]$.

25. $\cos^{-1} 1 = 0$

$\cos\left(\dfrac{\pi}{6}\right) = \dfrac{\sqrt{3}}{2}$

$\arccos\left(-\dfrac{1}{2}\right) = 120°$

$\cos^{-1}(-1) = \pi$

27. $\cos^{-1}\left(\dfrac{1}{2}\right) = y$ where $0 \le y \le \pi$

y is the number or angle whose cosine is $\dfrac{1}{2}$.

$\cos y = \dfrac{1}{2};\ \ \cos^{-1}\left(\dfrac{1}{2}\right) = \dfrac{\pi}{3}$

29. $\cos^{-1}(-1) = y$ where $0 \le y \le \pi$

y is the number or angle whose cosine is -1.

$\cos y = -1;\ \ \cos^{-1}\left(\dfrac{1}{2}\right) = \dfrac{\pi}{3}$

31. $\arccos 0.1352 \approx 1.4352$

$1.4352\left(\dfrac{180°}{\pi}\right) \approx 82.2°$

33. $\cos^{-1}\left(\dfrac{\sqrt{5}}{3}\right) \approx 0.7297$

$0.7297\left(\dfrac{180°}{\pi}\right) \approx 41.8°$

35. $\arccos\left[\cos\left(\dfrac{\pi}{4}\right)\right] = \dfrac{\pi}{4}$

since $\dfrac{\pi}{4} \in [0, \pi]$.

37. $\cos^{-1}(\cos 0.5560) = 0.5560$

since $0.5560 \in [0, \pi]$.

39. $\cos\left[\cos^{-1}\left(-\dfrac{\sqrt{2}}{2}\right)\right] = -\dfrac{\sqrt{2}}{2}$

since $-\dfrac{\sqrt{2}}{2} \in [-1, 1]$.

41. $\cos^{-1}\left[\cos\left(\dfrac{5\pi}{4}\right)\right] = \dfrac{3\pi}{4}$, since $\cos\dfrac{5\pi}{4} = \cos\dfrac{3\pi}{4}$

and $\dfrac{3\pi}{4} \in [0, \pi]$.

43. $\tan^{-1} 0 = 0$

$\tan\left(-\dfrac{\pi}{3}\right) = -\sqrt{3}$

$\arctan\left(\dfrac{\sqrt{3}}{3}\right) = 30°$

$\tan\left(\dfrac{\pi}{3}\right) = \sqrt{3}$

$\tan^{-1}\left(\sqrt{3}\right) = \dfrac{\pi}{3}$

45. $\tan^{-1}\left(-\dfrac{\sqrt{3}}{3}\right) = -\dfrac{\pi}{6}$

47. $\arctan\left(\sqrt{3}\right) = \dfrac{\pi}{3}$

49. $\tan^{-1}(-2.05) \approx -1.1170$

$-1.1170\left(\dfrac{180°}{\pi}\right) \approx -64.0°$

51. $\arctan\left(\dfrac{29}{21}\right) \approx 0.9441$

$0.9441\left(\dfrac{180°}{\pi}\right) \approx 54.1°$

53. $\sin^{-1}\left[\cos\left(\dfrac{2\pi}{3}\right)\right] = -\dfrac{\pi}{6}$

$\cos\left(\dfrac{2\pi}{3}\right) = -\dfrac{1}{2}$

$\sin^{-1}\left(-\dfrac{1}{2}\right) = -\dfrac{\pi}{6}$

55. $\tan\left[\arccos\left(\dfrac{\sqrt{3}}{2}\right)\right] = \dfrac{\sqrt{3}}{3}$

$\arccos\left(\dfrac{\sqrt{3}}{2}\right) = \dfrac{\pi}{6}$

$\tan\left(\dfrac{\pi}{6}\right) = \dfrac{\sqrt{3}}{3}$

57. $\csc\left[\sin^{-1}\left(\dfrac{\sqrt{2}}{2}\right)\right] = \sqrt{2}$

$\sin^{-1}\left(\dfrac{\sqrt{2}}{2}\right) = 45°$ or $\dfrac{\pi}{4}$

$\csc\left(\dfrac{\pi}{4}\right) = \dfrac{1}{\sin\left(\dfrac{\pi}{4}\right)} = \sqrt{2}$

59. $\arccos\left[\sin(-30°)\right] = 120°$

$\sin(-30°) = -\dfrac{1}{2}$

$\arccos\left(-\dfrac{1}{2}\right) = 120°$

61. $\tan\left(\sin^{-1} 1\right)$

$\sin^{-1} 1 = \dfrac{\pi}{2}$

$\tan\left(\dfrac{\pi}{2}\right)$ cannot be evaluated because

$x = \dfrac{\pi}{2}$ is a vertical asymptote for $\tan x$.

$\dfrac{\pi}{2}$ is not in the domain of $\tan x$.

63. $\sin^{-1}\left(\csc\dfrac{\pi}{4}\right)$; $\csc\dfrac{\pi}{4}=\sqrt{2}>1$

Since $-1\le\sin x\le 1,$ this value is not in the

domain of $\sin^{-1}x$.

65. a. $\sin\theta=\dfrac{0.3}{0.5}=\dfrac{3}{5}$

b. $\cos\theta=\dfrac{0.4}{0.5}=\dfrac{4}{5}$

c. $\tan\theta=\dfrac{0.3}{0.4}=\dfrac{3}{4}$

67. a. $\sin\theta=\dfrac{\sqrt{x^2-36}}{x}$

b. $\cos\theta=\dfrac{6}{x}$

c. $\tan\theta=\dfrac{\sqrt{x^2-36}}{6}$

69. $\sin\left[\cos^{-1}\left(-\dfrac{7}{25}\right)\right]=\dfrac{24}{25}$

$y=\sqrt{25^2-(-7)^2}=\sqrt{576}=24$

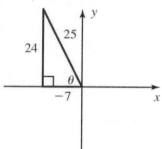

71. $\sin\left[\tan^{-1}\left(\dfrac{\sqrt{5}}{2}\right)\right]=\dfrac{\sqrt{5}}{3}$

$r=\sqrt{2^2+\left(\sqrt{5}\right)^2}$

$=\sqrt{9}=3$

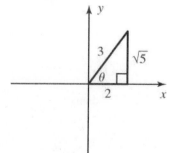

73. $\cot\left[\arcsin\left(\dfrac{3x}{5}\right)\right]=\dfrac{\sqrt{25-9x^2}}{3x}$

$x_t=\sqrt{5^2-(3x)^2}$

$=\sqrt{25-9x^2}$

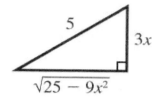

75. $\cos\left[\sin^{-1}\left(\dfrac{x}{\sqrt{12+x^2}}\right)\right]=\dfrac{\sqrt{12}}{\sqrt{25+x^2}}$

$=\sqrt{\dfrac{12}{12+x^2}}$

$x_t=\sqrt{\left(\sqrt{12+x^2}\right)^2-x^2}$

$=\sqrt{12+x^2-x^2}=\sqrt{12}$

77. $\sec^{-1}1=0$

$\sec\left(\dfrac{\pi}{3}\right)=2$

$\operatorname{arc\,sec}\left(\dfrac{2}{\sqrt{3}}\right)=30°$

$\sec(\pi)=-1$

79. $\operatorname{arc\,csc}2=\sin^{-1}\left(\dfrac{1}{2}\right)=30°=\dfrac{\pi}{6}$

81. $\cot^{-1}\sqrt{3}=\tan^{-1}\left(\dfrac{1}{\sqrt{3}}\right)=30°=\dfrac{\pi}{6}$

83. $\operatorname{arc\,sec}5.789=\cos^{-1}\left(\dfrac{1}{5.789}\right)\approx 80.1°$

85. $\sec^{-1}\sqrt{7}=\cos^{-1}\dfrac{1}{\sqrt{7}}=67.8°$

87. $F_N = mg \cos \theta$

    $m = 225 \text{ g} = 0.225 \text{ kg}$

    a. Find F_N for $\theta = 15°$ and $\theta = 45°$

    $\theta = 15°$

    $F_N = mg \cos \theta$
    $= (0.225)(9.8) \cos 15°$
    $\approx 2.13 \text{ N}$

    $\theta = 45°$

    $F_N = mg \cos \theta$
    $= (0.225)(9.8) \cos 45°$
    $\approx 1.56 \text{ N}$

    b. Find θ for F_N for $F_N = 1 \text{ N}$ and

    $F_N = 2 \text{ N}$

    $F_N = 1 \text{ N}$

    $1 = 0.225(9.8) \cos \theta$
    $1 = 2.205 \cos \theta$

    $\dfrac{1}{2.205} = \cos \theta$

    $\theta = \cos^{-1}\left(\dfrac{1}{2.205}\right)$

    $\theta \approx 63.0°$

    $F_N = 2 \text{ N}$

    $2 = 0.225(9.8) \cos \theta$
    $2 = 2.205 \cos \theta$

    $\dfrac{2}{2.205} = \cos \theta$

    $\theta = \cos^{-1}\left(\dfrac{2}{2.205}\right)$

    $\theta \approx 24.9°$

89. $\tan \theta = \dfrac{5.35}{20}$

    $\theta = \tan^{-1}\left(\dfrac{5.35}{20}\right)$

    $\theta \approx 14.98°$

    $2\theta \approx 30°$

    The angle formed by a cross-section of the cup is $30°$.

91. $\tan \theta = \dfrac{150}{48}$

    $\theta = \tan^{-1}\left(\dfrac{150}{48}\right)$

    $\theta \approx 72.3°$

    The angle to the hole is $72.3°$.

    Let d be the straight-line distance from the hole.

    $d = \sqrt{48^2 + 150^2}$
    $= \sqrt{2304 + 22{,}500}$
    $= \sqrt{24{,}804}$
    $\approx 157.5 \text{ yd}$

93. a. $\tan \alpha = \dfrac{75}{d}$

    $\alpha = \tan^{-1}\left(\dfrac{75}{d}\right)$

    $\tan \beta = \dfrac{50}{d}$

    $\beta = \tan^{-1}\left(\dfrac{50}{d}\right)$

    $\theta = \alpha - \beta = \tan^{-1}\left(\dfrac{75}{d}\right) - \tan^{-1}\left(\dfrac{50}{d}\right)$

    b. $d \in (39.2, 95.7)$

    c. $\theta \approx 11.5°$ at $d \approx 61.2 \text{ ft}$

95. a. $\tan \alpha = \dfrac{94}{d}$

    $\alpha = \tan^{-1}\left(\dfrac{94}{d}\right)$

    $\tan \beta = \dfrac{70}{d}$

    $\beta = \tan^{-1}\left(\dfrac{70}{d}\right)$

    $\theta = \alpha - \beta = \tan^{-1}\left(\dfrac{94}{d}\right) - \tan^{-1}\left(\dfrac{70}{d}\right)$

    b. $\theta \approx 8.4°$ at $d \approx 81.1 \text{ ft}$

97. $\cos \theta = \dfrac{3960}{150 + 3960}$

    a. $\theta = \cos^{-1}\left(\dfrac{3960}{150 + 3960}\right)$
    $= 15.5° \approx 0.2705 \text{ radians}$

97. b. $d = \sqrt{2xr + x^2}$

$= \sqrt{2(150)(3960) + (150)^2}$

$= \sqrt{1,188,000 + 22,500}$

$= \sqrt{1,210,500}$

≈ 1100 mi

$s = r\theta$

$\approx 0.2705(3960)$

≈ 1071 mi

$d - s \approx 29$ miles

99. $x = v_0 \cos\theta t$

$y = y_0 + v_0 \sin\theta t - 16t^2$

a. $x = 70\cos 10° t$

$= 70\cos 10°(6)$

$= 420\cos 10°$

≈ 413.6 ft away

b. $y = 0 + 70\sin 10° t - 16t^2$

$= 0 + 70\sin 10°(6) - 16(6)^2$

$= 420\sin 10° - 576$

≈ -503 ft

c. $d = \sqrt{413.6^2 + (-503)^2}$

$= \sqrt{171,064.96 + 253,009}$

$= \sqrt{424,073.96}$

≈ 651.2 ft

101. $\sin 2\theta = 2\sin\theta\cos\theta$

$= 2\left(\dfrac{6}{\sqrt{85}}\right)\left(\dfrac{7}{\sqrt{85}}\right)$

$= \dfrac{84}{85}$

103. $\omega = \dfrac{3.5 \text{ rev}}{1 \text{ sec}} \cdot \dfrac{2\pi \text{ rad}}{1 \text{ rev}} = 7\pi$ rad/sec

$V = r\omega$

$= 4(7\pi)$

≈ 87.96 in./sec

Convert to mph.

$\dfrac{87.96 \text{ in.}}{\text{sec}} \cdot \left(\dfrac{3600 \text{ sec}}{1 \text{ hr}}\right) \cdot \left(\dfrac{1 \text{ mile}}{63,360 \text{ in.}}\right) \approx 5$ mph

105. $x = 5$, $y = 12$

$r = \sqrt{5^2 + 12^2} = 13$

$\sin\theta = \dfrac{12}{13}$; $\cos\theta = \dfrac{5}{13}$; $\tan\theta = \dfrac{12}{5}$

Mid-Chapter Check

1. implicit; explicit

3. $f^{-1}(x) = \{(-14, -3), (-8, -1),$
    $(10, 5), (-11, -2), (-2, 1)\}$

5. a. $g(x)$ fails the horizontal line test.

    b. $D = [-3, \infty)$

    c. $y = x - 1$, $D = [-2, \infty)$, $R = [-3, \infty)$

7. a. $\sec^{-1}\left(\sqrt{2}\right) = \cos^{-1}\left(\dfrac{\sqrt{2}}{2}\right) = \dfrac{\pi}{4}$

    b. $\csc^{-1}\left(\dfrac{2}{\sqrt{3}}\right) = \sin^{-1}\left(\dfrac{\sqrt{3}}{2}\right) = \dfrac{\pi}{3}$

9. a. $\sin^{-1}(\sin 2.2) \approx 0.9$

    b. $\cos^{-1}(\cos 5.1) \approx 1.2$

Reinforcing Basic Concepts

1. a. $D = (-\infty, -1] \cup [1, \infty)$
    $R = \left[-\dfrac{\pi}{2}, 0\right) \cup \left(0, \dfrac{\pi}{2}\right]$

    b. $D = [-1, 1]$
    $R = [0, \pi]$

6.3 Exercises

1. principal; $[0, 2\pi)$; real

3. $\dfrac{\pi}{4}$; $\dfrac{\pi}{4}$; $\dfrac{3\pi}{4}$; $\dfrac{\pi}{4} + 2\pi k$; $\dfrac{3\pi}{4} + 2\pi k$

5. Answers will vary.

7. $\sin x = -\dfrac{3}{4}$

    $y = \sin x$; $y = -\dfrac{3}{4}$
    a. Principal root: QIV
    b. 2 roots

9. $y = \tan x$
    $y = -1.5$; $\tan x = -1.5$
    a. Principal root: QIV
    b. 2 roots

11.

θ	$\sin\theta$	$\cos\theta$	$\tan\theta$
0	0	1	0
$\dfrac{\pi}{6}$	$\dfrac{1}{2}$	$\dfrac{\sqrt{3}}{2}$	$\dfrac{\sqrt{3}}{3}$
$\dfrac{\pi}{3}$	$\dfrac{\sqrt{3}}{2}$	$\dfrac{1}{2}$	$\sqrt{3}$
$\dfrac{\pi}{2}$	1	0	undef
$\dfrac{2\pi}{3}$	$\dfrac{\sqrt{3}}{2}$	$-\dfrac{1}{2}$	$-\sqrt{3}$
$\dfrac{5\pi}{6}$	$\dfrac{1}{2}$	$-\dfrac{\sqrt{3}}{2}$	$-\dfrac{\sqrt{3}}{3}$
π	0	-1	0
$\dfrac{7\pi}{6}$	$-\dfrac{1}{2}$	$-\dfrac{\sqrt{3}}{2}$	$\dfrac{\sqrt{3}}{3}$
$\dfrac{4\pi}{3}$	$-\dfrac{\sqrt{3}}{2}$	$-\dfrac{1}{2}$	$\sqrt{3}$

13. $2\cos x = \sqrt{2}$

$$\cos x = \dfrac{\sqrt{2}}{2}$$

$$\cos^{-1}(\cos x) = \cos^{-1}\left(\dfrac{\sqrt{2}}{2}\right)$$

$$x = \dfrac{\pi}{4}$$

15. $-4\sin x = 2\sqrt{2}$

$$\sin x = -\dfrac{\sqrt{2}}{2}$$

$$\sin^{-1}(\sin x) = \sin^{-1}\left(-\dfrac{\sqrt{2}}{2}\right)$$

$$x = -\dfrac{\pi}{4}$$

17. $\sqrt{3}\tan x = 1$

$$\tan x = \dfrac{1}{\sqrt{3}}$$

$$\tan^{-1}(\tan x) = \tan^{-1}\left(\dfrac{1}{\sqrt{3}}\right)$$

$$x = \dfrac{\pi}{6}$$

19. $2\sqrt{3}\sin x = -3$

$$\sin x = -\dfrac{3}{2\sqrt{3}}$$

$$\sin x = -\dfrac{\sqrt{3}}{2}$$

$$\sin^{-1}(\sin x) = \sin^{-1}\left(-\dfrac{\sqrt{3}}{2}\right)$$

$$x = -\dfrac{\pi}{3}$$

21. $-6\cos x = 6$

$$\cos x = -1$$

$$\cos^{-1}(\cos x) = \cos^{-1}(-1)$$

$$x = \pi$$

23. $\dfrac{7}{8}\cos x = \dfrac{7}{16}$

$$\cos x = \dfrac{8}{7}\cdot\dfrac{7}{16}$$

$$\cos x = \dfrac{1}{2}$$

$$\cos^{-1}(\cos x) = \cos^{-1}\left(\dfrac{1}{2}\right)$$

$$x = \dfrac{\pi}{3}$$

25. $2 = 4\sin\theta$

$$\dfrac{1}{2} = \sin\theta$$

$$\sin^{-1}\left(\dfrac{1}{2}\right) = \sin^{-1}(\sin\theta)$$

$$\dfrac{\pi}{6} = \theta$$

27. $-5\sqrt{3} = 10\cos\theta$

$$-\frac{\sqrt{3}}{2} = \cos\theta$$

$$\cos^{-1}\left(-\frac{\sqrt{3}}{2}\right) = \cos^{-1}(\cos\theta)$$

$$\frac{5\pi}{6} = \theta$$

29. $9\sin x - 3.5 = 1$

$\quad 9\sin x = 4.5$

$$\sin x = \frac{1}{2}$$

Sine is positive in QI or QII.

$$x = \sin^{-1}\left(\frac{1}{2}\right)$$

$$x = \frac{\pi}{6} \text{ or } \pi - \frac{\pi}{6} = \frac{5\pi}{6}$$

$$x = \frac{\pi}{6}, \frac{5\pi}{6}$$

31. $8\tan x + 7\sqrt{3} = -\sqrt{3}$

$\quad 8\tan x = -8\sqrt{3}$

$\quad \tan x = -\sqrt{3}$

Tangent is negative in QII or QIV.

$$x = \tan^{-1}\left(-\sqrt{3}\right)$$

$$x = \pi - \frac{\pi}{3} = \frac{2\pi}{3} \text{ or } 2\pi - \frac{\pi}{3} = \frac{5\pi}{3}$$

$$x = \frac{2\pi}{3}, \frac{5\pi}{3}$$

33. $\dfrac{2}{3}\cot x - \dfrac{5}{6} = -\dfrac{3}{2}$

$$\frac{2}{3}\cot x = \frac{-2}{3}$$

$$\cot x = -1$$

Cotangent is negative in QII or QIV.

$$x = \cot^{-1}(-1)$$

$$x = \pi - \frac{\pi}{4} = \frac{3\pi}{4} \text{ or } x = 2\pi - \frac{\pi}{4} = \frac{7\pi}{4}$$

$$x = \frac{3\pi}{4}, \frac{7\pi}{4}$$

35. $4\cos^2 x = 3$

$$\cos^2 x = \frac{3}{4}$$

$$\cos x = \frac{\pm\sqrt{3}}{2}$$

$$x = \cos^{-1}\left(\pm\frac{\sqrt{3}}{2}\right)$$

$$x = \frac{\pi}{6}, \frac{5\pi}{6}, \frac{7\pi}{6}, \frac{11\pi}{6}$$

37. $-7\tan^2 x = -21$

$\quad \tan^2 x = 3$

$\quad \tan x = \pm\sqrt{3}$

$$x = \tan^{-1}\left(\pm\sqrt{3}\right)$$

$$x = \frac{\pi}{3}, \frac{2\pi}{3}, \frac{4\pi}{3}, \frac{5\pi}{3}$$

39. $-4\csc^2 x = -8$

$\quad \csc^2 x = 2$

$\quad \csc x = \pm\sqrt{2}$

$$x = \csc^{-1}\left(\pm\sqrt{2}\right)$$

$$x = \frac{\pi}{4}, \frac{3\pi}{4}, \frac{5\pi}{4}, \frac{7\pi}{4}$$

41. $4\sqrt{2}\sin^2 x = 4\sqrt{2}$

$\quad \sin^2 x = 1$

$\quad \sin x = \pm 1$

$$x = \sin^{-1}(\pm 1)$$

$$x = \frac{\pi}{2}, \frac{3\pi}{2}$$

43. $3\cos^2\theta + 14\cos\theta - 5 = 0$

Let $u = \cos\theta$, $u^2 = \cos^2\theta$.

$$3u^2 + 14u - 5 = 0$$

$$(3u - 1)(u + 5) = 0$$

$$u = \frac{1}{3} \qquad\qquad u = -5$$

$$\qquad\qquad\qquad\qquad \cos\theta = -5$$

$$\cos\theta = \frac{1}{3} \qquad \text{Extraneous because}$$

$$\qquad\qquad\qquad -1 \le \cos\theta \le 1.$$

$$\theta = \cos^{-1}\left(\frac{1}{3}\right)$$

$$\theta = 1.2310 + 2\pi k \ \text{ or } \ 5.0522 + 2\pi k$$

45. $2\cos x \sin x - \cos x = 0$

$\cos x(2\sin x - 1) = 0$

$\cos x = 0 \qquad\qquad 2\sin x - 1 = 0$

$x = \cos^{-1} 0 \qquad\qquad 2\sin x = 1$

$x = \dfrac{\pi}{2}, \dfrac{3\pi}{2} \qquad\qquad \sin x = \dfrac{1}{2}$

$\qquad\qquad\qquad\qquad x = \sin^{-1}\left(\dfrac{1}{2}\right)$

$\qquad\qquad\qquad\qquad x = \dfrac{\pi}{6}, \dfrac{5\pi}{6}$

$x = \dfrac{\pi}{2} + \pi k$ or $\dfrac{\pi}{6} + 2\pi k$ or $\dfrac{5\pi}{6} + 2\pi k$

47. $\sec^2 x - 6\sec x = 16$

$\sec^2 x - 6\sec x - 16 = 0$

$(\sec x + 2)(\sec x - 8) = 0$

$\sec x + 2 = 0 \qquad\qquad \sec x - 8 = 0$

$\sec x = -2 \qquad\qquad\quad \sec x = 8$

$x = \sec^{-1}(-2) \qquad\quad x = \sec^{-1}(8)$

$x = \cos^{-1}\left(-\dfrac{1}{2}\right) \qquad x = \cos^{-1}\left(\dfrac{1}{8}\right)$

$x = \dfrac{2\pi}{3}, \dfrac{4\pi}{3} \qquad\qquad x \approx 1.4455, 4.8377$

$x = \dfrac{2\pi}{3} + 2\pi k$ or $\dfrac{4\pi}{3} + 2\pi k$ or

$x \approx 1.4455 + 2\pi k$ or $\approx 4.8377 + 2\pi k$

49. $4\sin^2 x - 1 = 0$

$(2\sin x - 1)(2\sin x + 1) = 0$

$2\sin x - 1 = 0 \qquad\qquad 2\sin x + 1 = 0$

$2\sin x = 1 \qquad\qquad\quad 2\sin x = -1$

$\sin x = \dfrac{1}{2} \qquad\qquad\quad \sin x = -\dfrac{1}{2}$

$x = \sin^{-1}\left(\dfrac{1}{2}\right) \qquad\quad x = \sin^{-1}\left(-\dfrac{1}{2}\right)$

$x = \dfrac{\pi}{6}, \dfrac{5\pi}{6} \qquad\qquad x = \dfrac{7\pi}{6}, \dfrac{11\pi}{6}$

$x = \dfrac{\pi}{6} + \pi k$ or $\dfrac{5\pi}{6} + \pi k$

51. $-2\sin x = \sqrt{2}$

$\sin x = -\dfrac{\sqrt{2}}{2}$

$\sin^{-1}(\sin x) = \sin^{-1}\left(-\dfrac{\sqrt{2}}{2}\right)$

$x = \sin^{-1}\left(-\dfrac{\sqrt{2}}{2}\right)$

$x = \dfrac{5\pi}{4} + 2\pi k$ or $\dfrac{7\pi}{4} + 2\pi k$

53. $-4\cos x = 2\sqrt{2}$

$\cos x = -\dfrac{\sqrt{2}}{2}$

$\cos^{-1}(\cos x) = \cos^{-1}\left(-\dfrac{\sqrt{2}}{2}\right)$

$x = \cos^{-1}\left(-\dfrac{\sqrt{2}}{2}\right)$

$x = \dfrac{3\pi}{4} + 2\pi k$ or $\dfrac{5\pi}{4} + 2\pi k$

55. $\sqrt{3}\tan x = -\sqrt{3}$

$\tan x = -1$

$\tan^{-1}(\tan x) = \tan^{-1}(-1)$

$x = \tan^{-1}(-1)$

$x = \dfrac{3\pi}{4} + \pi k$

57. $6\cos(2x) = -3$

$\cos(2x) = -\dfrac{1}{2}$

$\cos^{-1}(\cos 2x) = \cos^{-1}\left(-\dfrac{1}{2}\right)$

$2x = \cos^{-1}\left(-\dfrac{1}{2}\right)$

$2x = \dfrac{2\pi}{3} + 2\pi k$ or $\dfrac{4\pi}{3} + 2\pi k$

$x = \dfrac{\pi}{3} + \pi k$ or $\dfrac{2\pi}{3} + \pi k$

59. $\sqrt{3}\tan 2x = -\sqrt{3}$

$\tan 2x = -1$

$\tan^{-1}(\tan 2x) = \tan^{-1}(-1)$

$2x = \tan^{-1}(-1)$

$2x = \dfrac{3\pi}{4} + \pi k$

$x = \dfrac{3\pi}{8} + \dfrac{\pi}{2}k$

61. $-2\sqrt{3}\cos\left(\dfrac{1}{3}x\right) = 2\sqrt{3}$

$\cos\left(\dfrac{1}{3}x\right) = -1$

$\cos^{-1}\left[\cos\left(\dfrac{1}{3}x\right)\right] = \cos^{-1}(-1)$

$\dfrac{1}{3}x = \cos^{-1}(-1)$

$\dfrac{1}{3}x = \pi + 2\pi k$

$x = 3\pi + 6\pi k$

63. $\sqrt{2}\cos x\sin(2x)-3\cos x=0$

$\cos x\left[\sqrt{2}\sin(2x)-3\right]=0$

$\cos x=0$ $\qquad$ $\sqrt{2}\sin(2x)-3=0$

$x=\cos^{-1}(0)$ $\qquad$ $\sqrt{2}\sin(2x)=3$

$x=\dfrac{\pi}{2},\dfrac{3\pi}{2}$ $\qquad$ $\sin(2x)=\dfrac{3}{\sqrt{2}}>1$

$\qquad\qquad\qquad$ Extraneous

$x=\dfrac{\pi}{2}+\pi k$

65. $\cos(3x)\csc(2x)-2\cos(3x)=0$

$\cos(3x)\left[\csc(2x)-2\right]=0$

$\cos(3x)=0$ $\qquad$ $\csc(2x)-2=0$

$3x=\cos^{-1}(0)$ $\qquad$ $\csc(2x)=2$

$3x=\dfrac{\pi}{2},\dfrac{3\pi}{2}$ $\qquad$ $\dfrac{1}{\sin(2x)}=2$

$x=\dfrac{\pi}{6},\dfrac{\pi}{2}$ $\qquad$ $\sin(2x)=\dfrac{1}{2}$

$\qquad\qquad\qquad$ $2x=\sin^{-1}\left(\dfrac{1}{2}\right)$

$\qquad\qquad\qquad$ $2x=\dfrac{\pi}{6},\dfrac{5\pi}{6}$

$\qquad\qquad\qquad$ $x=\dfrac{\pi}{12},\dfrac{5\pi}{12}$

$x=\dfrac{\pi}{6}+\dfrac{\pi}{3}k$ or $\dfrac{\pi}{12}+\pi k$ or $\dfrac{5\pi}{12}+\pi k$

67. $\qquad$ $3\cos x=1$

$\cos x=\dfrac{1}{3}$

$\cos^{-1}(\cos x)=\cos^{-1}\left(\dfrac{1}{3}\right)$

$x=\cos^{-1}\left(\dfrac{1}{3}\right)$

a. $x\approx1.2310$

b. $x\approx1.2310+2\pi k$

$\qquad$ $x\approx(2\pi-1.2310)+2\pi k\approx5.0522+2\pi k$

69. $\sqrt{2}\sec x+3=7$

$\sec x=\dfrac{4}{\sqrt{2}}$

$\cos x=\dfrac{\sqrt{2}}{4}$

$\cos^{-1}(\cos x)=\cos^{-1}\left(\dfrac{\sqrt{2}}{4}\right)$

$x=\cos^{-1}\left(\dfrac{\sqrt{2}}{4}\right)$

69. a. $x\approx1.2094$

b. $x\approx1.2094+2\pi k$

$\qquad$ $x\approx(2\pi-1.2094)+2\pi k\approx5.0738+2\pi k$

71. $\qquad$ $\dfrac{1}{2}\sin(2\theta)=\dfrac{1}{3}$

$\sin(2\theta)=\dfrac{2}{3}$

$\sin^{-1}\left[\sin(2\theta)\right]=\sin^{-1}\left(\dfrac{2}{3}\right)$

$2\theta=\sin^{-1}\left(\dfrac{2}{3}\right)$

a. $2\theta\approx0.7297$

$\qquad$ $\theta\approx0.3649$

b. $2\theta\approx0.7297+2\pi k$

$\qquad$ $\theta\approx0.3649+\pi k$

$\qquad$ $2\theta\approx(\pi-0.7297)+2\pi k\approx2.4119+2\pi k$

$\qquad$ $\theta\approx1.2059+\pi k$

73. $-5\cos(2\theta)-1=0$

$\cos(2\theta)=-\dfrac{1}{5}$

$\cos^{-1}\left[\cos(2\theta)\right]=\cos^{-1}\left(-\dfrac{1}{5}\right)$

$2\theta=\cos^{-1}\left(-\dfrac{1}{5}\right)$

a. $\cos<0$ in QII and QIII.

$\qquad$ $2\theta\approx1.7722$

$\qquad$ $\theta\approx0.8861$

b. $2\theta\approx1.7722+2\pi k$

$\qquad$ $\theta\approx0.8861+\pi k$

$\qquad$ $2\theta\approx(2\pi-1.7722)+2\pi k\approx4.5110+2\pi k$

$\qquad$ $\theta\approx2.2555+\pi k$

75. $\cos^2 x-\sin^2 x=\dfrac{1}{2}$

$\cos(2x)=\dfrac{1}{2}$

$\cos^{-1}(\cos2x)=\cos^{-1}\left(\dfrac{1}{2}\right)$

$2x=\cos^{-1}\left(\dfrac{1}{2}\right)$

$2x=\dfrac{\pi}{3}+2\pi k$ or $\dfrac{5\pi}{3}+2\pi k$

$x=\dfrac{\pi}{6}+\pi k$ or $\dfrac{5\pi}{6}+\pi k$

77. $2\cos\left(\dfrac{1}{2}x\right)\cos x - 2\sin\left(\dfrac{1}{2}x\right)\sin x = 1$

$2\left[\cos\left(\dfrac{1}{2}x\right)\cos x - \sin\left(\dfrac{1}{2}x\right)\sin x\right] = 1$

$2\cos\left(\dfrac{1}{2}x + x\right) = 1$

$\cos\left(\dfrac{3}{2}x\right) = \dfrac{1}{2}$

$\cos^{-1}\left[\cos\left(\dfrac{3}{2}x\right)\right] = \cos^{-1}\left(\dfrac{1}{2}\right)$

$\dfrac{3}{2}x = \cos^{-1}\left(\dfrac{1}{2}\right)$

$\dfrac{3}{2}x = \dfrac{\pi}{3} + 2\pi k \ \text{ or } \ \dfrac{5\pi}{3} + 2\pi k$

$x = \dfrac{2\pi}{9} + \dfrac{4\pi}{3}k \ \text{ or } \ \dfrac{10\pi}{9} + \dfrac{4\pi}{3}k$

79. $(\cos\theta + \sin\theta)^2 = 1$

$\cos^2\theta + 2\sin\theta\cos\theta + \sin^2\theta = 1$

$1 + 2\sin\theta\cos\theta = 1$

$2\sin\theta\cos\theta = 0$

$\sin(2\theta) = 0$

$\sin^{-1}\left[\sin(2\theta)\right] = \sin^{-1}(0)$

$2\theta = \sin^{-1}(0)$

$2\theta = 0 + 2\pi k \ \text{ or } \ \pi + 2\pi k$

$\theta = 0 + \pi k \ \text{ or } \ \dfrac{\pi}{2} + \pi k \ \Rightarrow \ \theta = \dfrac{\pi}{2}k$

81. $\cos(2\theta) + 2\sin^2\theta - 3\sin\theta = 0$

$1 - 2\sin^2\theta + 2\sin^2\theta - 3\sin\theta = 0$

$-3\sin\theta = -1$

$\sin\theta = \dfrac{1}{3}$

$\sin^{-1}(\sin\theta) = \sin^{-1}\left(\dfrac{1}{3}\right)$

$\theta = \sin^{-1}\left(\dfrac{1}{3}\right)$

$\theta \approx 0.3398 + 2\pi k$

$\theta \approx \pi - 0.3398 + 2\pi k \approx 2.8018 + 2\pi k$

83. $5\cos x - x = 3$

$Y_1 = 5\cos x - x$

$Y_2 = 3$

$x \approx 0.7290$

85. $\cos^2(2x) + x = 3$

$Y_1 = \cos^2(2x) + x$

$Y_2 = 3$

$x \approx 2.6649$

87. $x^2 + \sin(2x) = 1$

$Y_1 = x^2 + \sin(2x)$

$Y_2 = 1$

$x \approx 0.4566$

89. $R = \dfrac{5}{49}v^2\sin(2\theta)$

$16 = \dfrac{5}{49}(15)^2\sin(2\theta)$

$\dfrac{784}{1125} = \sin(2\theta)$

$\sin^{-1}\left(\dfrac{784}{1125}\right) = \sin^{-1}(\sin(2\theta))$

$\sin^{-1}\left(\dfrac{784}{1125}\right) = 2\theta$

$2\theta \approx 44.2°$

$\theta \approx 22.1°$

$2\theta \approx 180° - 44.2° = 135.8°$

$\theta \approx 67.9°$

91. $A(\theta) = 9.8\sin\theta$

$0 = 9.8\sin\theta$

$0 = \sin\theta$

$\sin^{-1}(0) = \sin^{-1}(\sin\theta)$

$0° = \theta$

The ramp is horizontal.

93. $A(\theta) = 9.8\sin\theta$

$5 = 9.8\sin\theta$

$\dfrac{5}{9.8} = \sin\theta$

$\sin^{-1}\left(\dfrac{5}{9.8}\right) = \sin^{-1}(\sin\theta)$

$30.7° \approx \theta$

$A(\theta) = 9.8\sin\theta$

$4.5 = 9.8\sin\theta$

$\dfrac{4.5}{9.8} = \sin\theta$

$\sin^{-1}\left(\dfrac{4.5}{9.8}\right) = \sin^{-1}(\sin\theta)$

$27.3° \approx \theta$

The angle will be smaller.

95. $\sin\alpha = k\sin\beta$

$\alpha = 90° - 55° = 35°$

$\sin 35° = 1.33\sin\beta$

$0.5736 = 1.33\sin\beta$

$0.4313 \approx \sin\beta$

$\sin^{-1}(0.4313) \approx \sin^{-1}(\sin\beta)$

$25.5° \approx \beta$

97. $\sin\alpha = k\sin\beta$

$\alpha = 90° - 40° = 50°$

$\sin 50° = k\sin 34.3°$

$1.36 \approx k$

$\sin\alpha = 1.36\sin 15°$

$\sin\alpha \approx 0.3520$

$\sin^{-1}(\sin\alpha) \approx \sin^{-1}(0.3520)$

$\alpha = 20.6°$

99. $y = 5\sin\left(\dfrac{1}{2}x\right) + 7$

a. Evaluate y at $x = 0$.

$y = 5\sin\left(\dfrac{1}{2}\cdot 0\right) + 7$

$= 5\sin(0) + 7$

$= 7$ in.

The platform is 7 inches high.

b. Let $y = 9.5$ and solve for x.

$9.5 = 5\sin\left(\dfrac{1}{2}x\right) + 7$

$2.5 = 5\sin\left(\dfrac{1}{2}x\right)$

$\dfrac{1}{2} = \sin\left(\dfrac{1}{2}x\right)$

$\sin^{-1}\left(\dfrac{1}{2}\right) = \sin^{-1}\left[\sin\left(\dfrac{1}{2}x\right)\right]$

$\dfrac{1}{2}x = \dfrac{\pi}{6}$ $\dfrac{1}{2}x = \dfrac{5\pi}{6}$

$x = \dfrac{\pi}{3}$ $x = \dfrac{5\pi}{3}$

$x \approx 1.05$ in. $x \approx 5.24$ in.

101. $A = \dfrac{1}{2}r^2(\theta - \sin\theta)$

$12 = \dfrac{1}{2}(10)^2(\theta - \sin\theta)$

$Y_1 = 12$; $Y_2 = \dfrac{1}{2}(10)^2(\theta - \sin\theta)$

$\theta \approx 1.1547$

103. $5\cos x - x = -x$

$Y_1 = 5\cos x - x$

$Y_2 = -x$

$x = \dfrac{\pi}{2} + \pi k$

$5\cos x - x = -x$

$5\cos x = 0$

$\cos x = 0$

$\cos^{-1}(\cos x) = \cos^{-1}(0)$

$x = \dfrac{\pi}{2} + \pi k$

Intersection method; zero method. Explanations will vary.

105. $\cos\theta = -\dfrac{5}{13} \Rightarrow x = -5,\ r = 13$

Since $\tan\theta > 0$, y is negative.

The angle θ is in quadrant III.

$y = -\sqrt{13^2 - 5^2} = -\sqrt{144} = -12$

$\cos\theta = -\dfrac{5}{13}$; $\sec\theta = -\dfrac{13}{5}$; $\sin\theta = -\dfrac{12}{13}$

$\csc\theta = -\dfrac{13}{12}$; $\tan\theta = \dfrac{12}{5}$; $\cot\theta = \dfrac{5}{12}$

107. $\tan\theta = -0.12$

$\theta = \tan^{-1}(-0.12)$

$\theta \approx -6.8°$

109. $|A| = 1$; $P = 2\pi$

HS: $\dfrac{\pi}{4}$ units to the right

$y = \sec\left(x - \dfrac{\pi}{4}\right)$

$|A| = 1$; $P = 2\pi$

HS: $\dfrac{\pi}{4}$ units to the left

$y = \csc\left(x + \dfrac{\pi}{4}\right)$

Technology Highlight

Exercise 1:

This can be verified using a graphing calculator.

6.4 Exercises

1. $\sin^2 x + \cos^2 x = 1$;
    $1 + \tan^2 x = \sec^2 x$;
    $1 + \cot^2 x = \csc^2 x$

3. factor; grouping

5. Answers will vary.

7.
$$\sin x + \cos x = \frac{\sqrt{6}}{2}$$
$$(\sin x + \cos x)^2 = \left(\frac{\sqrt{6}}{2}\right)^2$$
$$\sin^2 x + 2\sin x \cos x + \cos^2 x = \frac{3}{2}$$
$$1 + 2\sin x \cos x = \frac{3}{2}$$
$$2\sin x \cos x = \frac{1}{2}$$
$$\sin 2x = \frac{1}{2}$$
$$2x = \sin^{-1}\left(\frac{1}{2}\right)$$

$\sin > 0$ in QI and QII
$0 \le x < 2\pi \Rightarrow 0 \le 2x < 4\pi$
$$2x = \frac{\pi}{6}, \frac{5\pi}{6}, \frac{13\pi}{6}, \frac{17\pi}{6}$$
The solutions are $x = \frac{\pi}{12}, \frac{5\pi}{12}$.

Note that $x = \frac{13\pi}{12}, \frac{17\pi}{12}$ are extraneous.

9. $\tan x - \sec x = -1$
    $\tan x = \sec x - 1$
    $\tan^2 x = (\sec x - 1)^2$
    $\tan^2 x = \sec^2 x - 2\sec x + 1$
    $\tan^2 x = 1 + \tan^2 x - 2\sec x + 1$
    $2\sec x = 2$
    $\sec x = 1$
    $\cos x = 1$
    $x = 0$

11.
$$\cos x + \sin x = \frac{4}{3}$$
$$(\cos x + \sin x)^2 = \left(\frac{4}{3}\right)^2$$
$$\cos^2 x + 2\cos x \sin x + \sin^2 x = \frac{16}{9}$$
$$1 + 2\cos x \sin x = \frac{16}{9}$$
$$2\cos x \sin x = \frac{7}{9}$$
$$\sin 2x = \frac{7}{9}$$
$$2x = \sin^{-1}\left(\frac{7}{9}\right)$$

$\sin > 0$ in QI and QII
$0 \le x < 2\pi \Rightarrow 0 \le 2x < 4\pi$
$2x = 0.8911; \ x = 0.4456$
$2x = \pi - 0.8911 \approx 2.2505; \ x \approx 1.1252$

13. $\cot x \csc x - 2\cot x - \csc x + 2 = 0$
$(\cot x \csc x - 2\cot x) - (\csc x - 2) = 0$
$\cot x(\csc x - 2) - 1(\csc x - 2) = 0$
$(\cot x - 1)(\csc x - 2) = 0$

$\cot x - 1 = 0$	$\csc x - 2 = 0$
$\cot x = 1$	$\csc x = 2$
$\tan x = 1$	$\sin x = \frac{1}{2}$
$x = \tan^{-1}(1)$	$x = \sin^{-1}\left(\frac{1}{2}\right)$

$\tan > 0$ in QI and QIII. $x = \frac{\pi}{4}, \frac{5\pi}{4}$

$\sin > 0$ in QI and QII. $x = \frac{\pi}{6}, \frac{5\pi}{6}$

The solutions are $\frac{\pi}{4}, \frac{5\pi}{4}, \frac{\pi}{6}, \frac{5\pi}{6}$.

15. $3\tan^2 x \cos x - 3\cos x + 2 = 2\tan^2 x$
$3\tan^2 x \cos x - 3\cos x + 2 - 2\tan^2 x = 0$
$3\cos x(\tan^2 x - 1) + 2(1 - \tan^2 x) = 0$
$3\cos x(\tan^2 x - 1) - 2(\tan^2 x - 1) = 0$
$(\tan^2 x - 1)(3\cos x - 2) = 0$

$\tan^2 x - 1 = 0$	$3\cos x - 2 = 0$
$\tan^2 x = 1$	$3\cos x = 2$
$\tan x = \pm 1$	$\cos x = \frac{2}{3}$
$x = \tan^{-1}(\pm 1)$	$x = \cos^{-1}\left(\frac{2}{3}\right)$

$$x = \frac{\pi}{4}, \frac{3\pi}{4}, \frac{5\pi}{4}, \frac{7\pi}{4}$$

15. (continued)

cos > 0 in QI and QIV

$x = 0.8411$

$x = 2\pi - 0.8411 \approx 5.4421$

The solutions are

$x = \dfrac{\pi}{4}, \dfrac{3\pi}{4}, \dfrac{5\pi}{4}, \dfrac{7\pi}{4}, 0.8411, 5.4421.$

17. $\dfrac{1 + \cot^2 x}{\cot^2 x} = 2$

$\dfrac{\csc^2 x}{\cot^2 x} = 2$

$\dfrac{\csc x}{\cot x} = \pm\sqrt{2}$

$\dfrac{\frac{1}{\sin x}}{\frac{\cos x}{\sin x}} = \pm\sqrt{2}$

$\dfrac{1}{\cos x} = \pm\sqrt{2}$

$\cos x = \pm\dfrac{\sqrt{2}}{2}$

$x = \cos^{-1}\left(\pm\dfrac{\sqrt{2}}{2}\right)$

The solutions are $x = \dfrac{\pi}{4}, \dfrac{3\pi}{4}, \dfrac{5\pi}{4}, \dfrac{7\pi}{4}.$

19. $3\cos(2x) + 7\sin x - 5 = 0$

$3(1 - 2\sin^2 x) + 7\sin x - 5 = 0$

$3 - 6\sin^2 x + 7\sin x - 5 = 0$

$-6\sin^2 x + 7\sin x - 2 = 0$

$6\sin^2 x - 7\sin x + 2 = 0$

$(2\sin x - 1)(3\sin x - 2) = 0$

$\begin{array}{ll} 2\sin x - 1 = 0 & 3\sin x - 2 = 0 \\ 2\sin x = 1 & 3\sin x = 2 \\ \sin x = \dfrac{1}{2} & \sin x = \dfrac{2}{3} \\ x = \sin^{-1}\left(\dfrac{1}{2}\right) & x = \sin^{-1}\left(\dfrac{2}{3}\right) \end{array}$

sin > 0 in QI and QII.

The solutions are $x = \dfrac{\pi}{6}, \dfrac{5\pi}{6}, 0.7297, 2.4119.$

21. $2\sin^2\left(\dfrac{x}{2}\right) - 3\cos\left(\dfrac{x}{2}\right) = 0$

$2\left[1 - \cos^2\left(\dfrac{x}{2}\right)\right] - 3\cos\left(\dfrac{x}{2}\right) = 0$

$2 - 2\cos^2\left(\dfrac{x}{2}\right) - 3\cos\left(\dfrac{x}{2}\right) = 0$

$2\cos^2\left(\dfrac{x}{2}\right) + 3\cos\left(\dfrac{x}{2}\right) - 2 = 0$

$\left[2\cos\left(\dfrac{x}{2}\right) - 1\right]\left[\cos\left(\dfrac{x}{2}\right) + 2\right] = 0$

$\begin{array}{ll} 2\cos\left(\dfrac{x}{2}\right) - 1 = 0 & \cos\left(\dfrac{x}{2}\right) + 2 = 0 \\ 2\cos\left(\dfrac{x}{2}\right) = 1 & \cos\left(\dfrac{x}{2}\right) = -2 \\ \cos\left(\dfrac{x}{2}\right) = \dfrac{1}{2} & \text{Undefined.} \end{array}$

$\dfrac{x}{2} = \cos^{-1}\left(\dfrac{1}{2}\right)$

$0 \le x < 2\pi \Rightarrow 0 \le \dfrac{x}{2} < \pi$

cos > 0 in QI.

$\dfrac{x}{2} = \dfrac{\pi}{3} \Rightarrow x = \dfrac{2\pi}{3}$ The solution is $x = \dfrac{2\pi}{3}.$

23. $\cos(3x) + \cos(5x)\cos(2x)$
$\quad + \sin(5x)\sin(2x) - 1 = 0$

$\cos(3x) + \cos(5x - 2x) - 1 = 0$

$\cos(3x) + \cos(3x) - 1 = 0$

$2\cos(3x) = 1$

$\cos(3x) = \dfrac{1}{2}$

$3x = \cos^{-1}\left(\dfrac{1}{2}\right)$

$0 \le x < 2\pi \Rightarrow 0 \le 3x < 6\pi$

cos > 0 in QI and QIV.

$3x = \dfrac{\pi}{3} + 2\pi k, \dfrac{5\pi}{3} + 2\pi k, \ k = 0, 1, 2$

$x = \dfrac{\pi}{9} + \dfrac{2\pi}{3}k, \dfrac{5\pi}{9} + \dfrac{2\pi}{3}k, \ k = 0, 1, 2$

25. $\sec^4 x - 2\sec^2 x\tan^2 x + \tan^4 x = \tan^2 x$

$\left(\sec^2 x - \tan^2 x\right)^2 = \tan^2 x$

$1^2 = \tan^2 x$

$\pm 1 = \tan x$

$\tan^{-1}(\pm 1) = x$

The solutions are $x = \dfrac{\pi}{4}, \dfrac{3\pi}{4}, \dfrac{5\pi}{4}, \dfrac{7\pi}{4}.$

27. $P = \dfrac{2\pi}{\dfrac{\pi}{6}} = 12 \to [0,\, 12)$

$$250\sin\left(\frac{\pi}{6}x + \frac{\pi}{3}\right) - 125 = 0$$

$$250\sin\left(\frac{\pi}{6}x + \frac{\pi}{3}\right) = 125$$

$$\sin\left(\frac{\pi}{6}x + \frac{\pi}{3}\right) = \frac{1}{2}$$

Let $u = \dfrac{\pi}{6}x + \dfrac{\pi}{3}$.

$\sin u > 0$ in QI and QII.

$$u = \sin^{-1}\left(\frac{1}{2}\right) \Rightarrow u = \frac{\pi}{6} + 2\pi k$$

$$u = \frac{5\pi}{6} + 2\pi k$$

Consider $k = 0$.

$$u = \frac{\pi}{6} + 2\pi(0) = \frac{\pi}{6}$$

$$\frac{\pi}{6}x + \frac{\pi}{3} = \frac{\pi}{6}$$

$$\frac{\pi}{6}x = -\frac{\pi}{6}$$

$$x = -1 \quad \text{not in interval}$$

$$u = \frac{5\pi}{6} + 2\pi(0) = \frac{5\pi}{6}$$

$$\frac{\pi}{6}x + \frac{\pi}{3} = \frac{5\pi}{6}$$

$$\frac{\pi}{6}x = \frac{\pi}{2}$$

$$x = 3$$

Consider $k = 1$.

$$u = \frac{\pi}{6} + 2\pi(1) = \frac{13\pi}{6}$$

$$\frac{\pi}{6}x + \frac{\pi}{3} = \frac{13\pi}{6}$$

$$\frac{\pi}{6}x = \frac{11\pi}{6}$$

$$x = 11$$

$$u = \frac{5\pi}{6} + 2\pi(1) = \frac{17\pi}{6}$$

$$\frac{\pi}{6}x + \frac{\pi}{3} = \frac{17\pi}{6}$$

$$\frac{\pi}{6}x = \frac{5\pi}{2}$$

$$x = 15 \quad \text{not in interval}$$

The solutions are $x = 3, 11$.

29. $P = \dfrac{2\pi}{\dfrac{\pi}{12}} = 24 \to [0,\, 24)$

$$1235\cos\left(\frac{\pi}{12}x - \frac{\pi}{4}\right) + 772 = 1750$$

$$1235\cos\left(\frac{\pi}{12}x - \frac{\pi}{4}\right) = 978$$

$$\cos\left(\frac{\pi}{12}x - \frac{\pi}{4}\right) = 0.7919$$

Let $u = \dfrac{\pi}{12}x - \dfrac{\pi}{4}$.

$\cos u > 0$ in QI and QIV.

$$u = \cos^{-1}(0.7919) \Rightarrow u \approx -0.6569 + 2\pi k$$

$$u \approx 0.6569 + 2\pi k$$

Consider $k = 0$.

$$u \approx -0.6569 + 2\pi(0) = -0.6569$$

$$\frac{\pi}{12}x - \frac{\pi}{4} \approx -0.6569$$

$$\frac{\pi}{12}x \approx 0.1285$$

$$x \approx 0.4908$$

$$u \approx 0.6569 + 2\pi(0) = 0.6569$$

$$\frac{\pi}{12}x - \frac{\pi}{4} \approx 0.6569$$

$$\frac{\pi}{12}x \approx 1.4423$$

$$x \approx 5.5091$$

31.
$$\cos x - \sin x = \frac{\sqrt{2}}{2}$$

$$(\cos x - \sin x)^2 = \left(\frac{\sqrt{2}}{2}\right)^2$$

$$\cos^2 x - 2\sin x \cos x + \sin^2 x = \frac{1}{2}$$

$$1 - 2\sin x \cos x = \frac{1}{2}$$

$$-2\sin x \cos x = -\frac{1}{2}$$

$$2\sin x \cos x = \frac{1}{2}$$

$$\sin 2x = \frac{1}{2}$$

$$0 \le x < 2\pi \Rightarrow 0 \le 2x < 4\pi$$

$\sin > 0$ in QI and QII.

$$2x = \sin^{-1}\left(\frac{1}{2}\right) = \frac{\pi}{6} + 2\pi k, \frac{5\pi}{6} + 2\pi k$$

$$x = \frac{\pi}{12} + \pi k, \frac{5\pi}{12} + \pi k$$

31. (continued)

Consider $k = 0$.

$$x = \frac{\pi}{12} + \pi(0) = \frac{\pi}{12}$$

$$x = \frac{5\pi}{12} + \pi(0) = \frac{5\pi}{12} \text{ is extraneous.}$$

Consider $k = 0$.

$$x = \frac{\pi}{12} + \pi(1) = \frac{13\pi}{12} \text{ is extraneous.}$$

$$x = \frac{5\pi}{12} + \pi(1) = \frac{17\pi}{12}$$

The solutions are $x = \dfrac{\pi}{12}, \dfrac{17\pi}{12}$.

33.
$$\frac{1 - \cos^2 x}{\tan^2 x} = \frac{\sqrt{3}}{2}$$

$$\frac{\sin^2 x}{\tan^2 x} = \frac{\sqrt{3}}{2}$$

$$\frac{\sin^2 x}{\dfrac{\sin^2 x}{\cos^2 x}} = \frac{\sqrt{3}}{2}$$

$$\cos^2 x = \frac{\sqrt{3}}{2}$$

$$\cos x = \pm\sqrt{\frac{\sqrt{3}}{2}}$$

$$x = \cos^{-1}\left[\pm\sqrt{\frac{\sqrt{3}}{2}}\right]$$

The solutions are

$x \approx 0.3747$

$x \approx \pi - 0.3747 \approx 2.7669$

$x \approx \pi + 0.3747 \approx 3.5163$

$x \approx 2\pi - 0.3747 \approx 5.9085$.

35. $\csc x + \cot x = 1$

$$\csc x = 1 - \cot x$$

$$(\csc x)^2 = (1 - \cot x)^2$$

$$\csc^2 x = 1 - 2\cot x + \cot^2 x$$

$$1 + \cot^2 x = 1 - 2\cot x + \cot^2 x$$

$$0 = -2\cot x$$

$$2\cot x = 0$$

$$\cot x = 0$$

This implies that $\cos x = 0$

$$x = \cos^{-1}(0).$$

The solutions is $x = \dfrac{\pi}{2}$.

Note that $x = \dfrac{3\pi}{2}$ is extraneous.

37. $\sec x \cos\left(\dfrac{\pi}{2} - x\right) = -1$

$$\sec x \sin x = -1$$

$$\frac{1}{\cos x} \cdot \sin x = -1$$

$$\tan x = -1$$

$$x = \tan^{-1}(-1)$$

$\tan < 0$ in QII and QIV.

The solutions are $x = \dfrac{3\pi}{4}, \dfrac{7\pi}{4}$.

39. $\sec^2 x \tan\left(\dfrac{\pi}{2} - x\right) = 4$

$$\sec^2 x \cot x = 4$$

$$\frac{1}{\cos^2 x} \cdot \cot x = 4$$

$$\frac{1}{\cos^2 x} \cdot \frac{\cos x}{\sin x} = 4$$

$$\frac{1}{\cos x \sin x} = 4$$

$$\cos x \sin x = \frac{1}{4}$$

$$2\cos x \sin x = \frac{1}{2}$$

$$\sin 2x = \frac{1}{2}$$

$$2x = \sin^{-1}\left(\frac{1}{2}\right)$$

$\sin > 0$ in QI and QII.

$0 \le x < 2\pi \Rightarrow 0 \le 2x < 4\pi$

$$2x = \frac{\pi}{6}, \frac{5\pi}{6}, \frac{13\pi}{6}, \frac{17\pi}{6}$$

The solutions are $x = \dfrac{\pi}{12}, \dfrac{5\pi}{12}, \dfrac{13\pi}{12}, \dfrac{17\pi}{12}$.

41. $y = \dfrac{D - x\cos\theta}{\sin\theta}$

I. $L_1 : y = -x + 5$

$\quad L_2 : y = x$

a. Point of intersection: $\left(\dfrac{5}{2}, \dfrac{5}{2}\right)$

b. $D = \sqrt{2.5^2 + 2.5^2}$

$\quad = \sqrt{6.25 + 6.25} = \sqrt{12.5}$

$\theta = \tan^{-1}\left(\dfrac{2.5}{2.5}\right) = \tan^{-1}(1) = \dfrac{\pi}{4}$

$$y = \frac{\sqrt{12.5} - x\cos\left(\dfrac{\pi}{4}\right)}{\sin\left(\dfrac{\pi}{4}\right)}$$

41. I   c.   Verified.

    II. $L_1 : y = -\dfrac{1}{2}x + 5$

    $L_2 : y = 2x$

    a.   Point of intersection: $(2, 4)$

    b. $D = \sqrt{2^2 + 4^2} = \sqrt{4 + 16} = \sqrt{20} = 2\sqrt{5}$

    $\theta = \tan^{-1}\left(\dfrac{4}{2}\right) = \tan^{-1}(2) \approx 1.1071$

    $y = \dfrac{2\sqrt{5} - x\cos 1.1071}{\sin 1.1071}$

    c.   Verified.

    III. $L_1 : y = -\dfrac{\sqrt{3}}{3}x + \dfrac{4\sqrt{3}}{3}$

    $L_2 : y = \sqrt{3}x$

    a.   Point of intersection: $\left(1, \sqrt{3}\right)$

    b. $D = \sqrt{(1)^2 + \left(\sqrt{3}\right)^2} = \sqrt{1 + 3} = \sqrt{4} = 2$

    $\theta = \tan^{-1}\left(\dfrac{\sqrt{3}}{1}\right) = \dfrac{\pi}{3}$

    $y = \dfrac{2 - x\cos\left(\dfrac{\pi}{3}\right)}{\sin\left(\dfrac{\pi}{3}\right)}$

    c.   Verified.

43. $V = \pi r^2 h \sin\theta$
    $r = 10$ ft, $h = 25$ ft

    a. $V = \pi r^2 h \sin\theta$

    $V = \pi (10)^2 (25)\sin\left(\dfrac{\pi}{2}\right)$

    $= 2500\pi \sin\left(\dfrac{\pi}{2}\right)$

    $= 2500\pi$ ft$^3 \approx 7853.98$ ft^3

    b. $\theta = 90° - 5° = 85°$

    $V = \pi (10)^2 (25)\sin(85°)$

    $= 2500\pi \sin(85°)$

    ≈ 7824.09 ft^3

    c.   The new volume will be 98% of the original volume.

    98% of $7853.98 = 0.98 \cdot 7853.98$

    ≈ 7696.90

    $7696.90 = 2500\pi \sin\theta$

    $0.98 = \sin(\theta)$

    $\sin^{-1}(0.98) = \theta$

    $78.5° \approx \theta$

45. $D(t) = 36\sin\left(\dfrac{\pi}{4}t - \dfrac{9}{4}\right) + 44$

    a.   Mid-September corresponds to $t = 4.5$.

    $D(4.5) = 36\sin\left[\dfrac{\pi}{4}(4.5) - \dfrac{9}{4}\right] + 44$

    ≈ 78.53 m^3/sec

    b.   A graphing calculator may be used. An algebraic solution is shown.

    $P = \dfrac{2\pi}{\dfrac{\pi}{4}} = 8 \rightarrow [0, 8)$

    $50 = 36\sin\left(\dfrac{\pi}{4}t - \dfrac{9}{4}\right) + 44$

    $6 = 36\sin\left(\dfrac{\pi}{4}t - \dfrac{9}{4}\right)$

    $\dfrac{1}{6} = \sin\left(\dfrac{\pi}{4}t - \dfrac{9}{4}\right)$

    Let $u = \dfrac{\pi}{4}t - \dfrac{9}{4}$.

    $\sin u > 0$ in QI and QII.

    $u = \sin^{-1}\left(\dfrac{1}{6}\right) \Rightarrow u \approx 0.1674,\ 2.9741$

    $u = \dfrac{\pi}{4}t - \dfrac{9}{4} \approx 0.1674$

    $\dfrac{\pi}{4}t \approx 2.4174$

    $t \approx 3.0779$

    $u = \dfrac{\pi}{4}t - \dfrac{9}{4} \approx 2.9741$

    $\dfrac{\pi}{4}t \approx 5.2241$

    $t \approx 6.6515$

    Discharge rate is over 50 m^3/sec in August, September, October, and November.

47. $S(x) = 1600\cos\left(\dfrac{\pi}{6}x - \dfrac{\pi}{12}\right) + 5100$

    a.   July corresponds to $x = 7$.

    $S(7) = 1600\cos\left[\dfrac{\pi}{6}(7) - \dfrac{\pi}{12}\right] + 5100$

    $\approx \$3554.52$

47. b. A graphing calculator may be used.
An algebraic solution is shown.

$$4000 = 1600\cos\left(\frac{\pi}{6}x - \frac{\pi}{12}\right) + 5100$$

$$-1100 = 1600\cos\left(\frac{\pi}{6}x - \frac{\pi}{12}\right)$$

$$-\frac{11}{16} = \cos\left(\frac{\pi}{6}x - \frac{\pi}{12}\right)$$

Let $u = \frac{\pi}{6}x - \frac{\pi}{12}$.

$\cos u < 0$ in QII and QIII.

$$u = \cos^{-1}\left(-\frac{11}{16}\right) \Rightarrow u \approx 2.3288, 3.9543$$

$$u = \frac{\pi}{6}x - \frac{\pi}{12} \approx 2.3288$$

$$\frac{\pi}{6}x \approx 2.5906$$

$$t \approx 4.9477$$

$$u = \frac{\pi}{6}x - \frac{\pi}{12} \approx 3.9543$$

$$\frac{\pi}{6}x \approx 4.2161$$

$$t \approx 8.0522$$

Sales are less than $4000 during May, June, July, and August.

49. $T(x) = 9\cos\left(\frac{\pi}{6}x\right) + 15$

a. Mid-March corresponds to $x = 3.5$.

$$T(3.5) = 9\cos\left[\frac{\pi}{6}(3.5)\right] + 15 \approx 12.67 \text{ in.}$$

b. A graphing calculator may be used.
An algebraic solution is shown.

$$10.5 = 9\cos\left(\frac{\pi}{6}x\right) + 15$$

$$-4.5 = 9\cos\left(\frac{\pi}{6}x\right)$$

$$-\frac{1}{2} = \cos\left(\frac{\pi}{6}x\right)$$

Let $u = \frac{\pi}{6}x$.

$\cos u < 0$ in QII and QIII.

$$u = \cos^{-1}\left(-\frac{1}{2}\right) \Rightarrow u = \frac{2\pi}{3}, \frac{4\pi}{3}$$

$$u = \frac{\pi}{6}x = \frac{2\pi}{3} \qquad u = \frac{\pi}{6}x = \frac{4\pi}{3}$$

$$x = 4 \qquad\qquad x = 8$$

The ice is at most 10.5 inches thick in April, May, June, July and August.

51. $G(x) = 21\cos\left(\frac{2\pi}{365}x + \frac{\pi}{2}\right) + 29$

a. March 21 corresponds to $x = 80$.

$$G(80) = 21\cos\left[\frac{2\pi}{365}(80) + \frac{\pi}{2}\right] + 29$$

$$\approx 8.39 \text{ gallons}$$

b. A graphing calculator may be used.
An algebraic solution is shown.

$$40 = 21\cos\left(\frac{2\pi}{365}x + \frac{\pi}{2}\right) + 29$$

$$11 = 21\cos\left(\frac{2\pi}{365}x + \frac{\pi}{2}\right)$$

$$\frac{11}{21} = \cos\left(\frac{2\pi}{365}x + \frac{\pi}{2}\right)$$

Let $u = \frac{2\pi}{365}x + \frac{\pi}{2}$.

$\cos u > 0$ in QI and QIV.

$$u = \cos^{-1}\left(\frac{11}{21}\right) \Rightarrow u \approx 1.0195 + 2\pi k$$

$$u \approx 5.2637 + 2\pi k$$

Consider $k = 0$.

$$u \approx 1.0195 + 2\pi(0) \approx 1.0195$$

$$\frac{2\pi}{365}x + \frac{\pi}{2} \approx 1.0195$$

$$\frac{2\pi}{365}x \approx -0.5513$$

$$x \approx -32.0257$$

out of interval

$$u \approx 5.2637 + 2\pi(0) \approx 5.2637$$

$$\frac{2\pi}{365}x + \frac{\pi}{2} \approx 5.2637$$

$$\frac{2\pi}{365}x \approx 3.6929$$

$$x \approx 214.5265$$

Consider $k = 1$.

$$u \approx 1.0195 + 2\pi(1) \approx 7.3027$$

$$\frac{2\pi}{365}x + \frac{\pi}{2} \approx 7.3027$$

$$\frac{2\pi}{365}x \approx 5.7319$$

$$x \approx 332.9743$$

$$u \approx 5.2637 + 2\pi(1) \approx 11.5469$$

$$\frac{2\pi}{365}x + \frac{\pi}{2} \approx 11.5469$$

$$\frac{2\pi}{365}x \approx 9.9761$$

$$x \approx 579.5265$$

out of interval

More than 40 gallons of coffee are sold from day 214 to day 333.

53. $B(x) = 58\cos\left(\dfrac{\pi}{6}x + \pi\right) + 126$

  a. $B(0) = 58\cos\left[\dfrac{\pi}{6}(0) + \pi\right] + 126$
  $= 58\cos(0 + \pi) + 126$
  $= 58\cos\pi + 126$
  $= 58(-1) + 126$
  $= 68 \text{ bpm}$

  b. $B(5) = 58\cos\left[\dfrac{\pi}{6}(5) + \pi\right] + 126$
  $= 58\cos\left(\dfrac{5\pi}{6} + \pi\right) + 126$
  $= 58\cos\left(\dfrac{11\pi}{6}\right) + 126$
  $= 58\left(\dfrac{\sqrt{3}}{2}\right) + 126$
  $\approx 176.2 \text{ bpm}$

  c. Use a graphing calculator.
  $Y_1 = 58\cos\left(\dfrac{\pi}{6}x + \pi\right) + 126$

  $Y_2 = 170$

  His heart rate was over 170 bpm from about 4.6 min to 7.4 min.

55. Answers will vary.

  a. Example: $y = 19\cos\left(\pi - \dfrac{\pi}{6}x\right) + 53$

  b. Example: $y = -21\sin\left(\dfrac{2\pi}{365}x\right) + 29$

57. Option I:
  Let h be the height (side opposite θ).
  Let x be the length and width (of square ends).
  Write a formula for the surface area.
  $2x^2 + 4xh = 1288$
  $x^2 + 2xh = 644$

  Write a formula for the sum of all edges.
  $4h + 4x + 4x = 176$
  $4h + 8x = 176$
  $h + 2x = 44$
  $h = 44 - 2x$

57. (continued)
  Substitute the expression for h into the formula for surface area.
  $x^2 + 2x(44 - 2x) = 644$
  $x^2 + 88x - 4x^2 = 644$
  $-3x^2 + 88x = 644$
  $0 = 3x^2 - 88x + 644$
  $0 = (3x - 46)(x - 14)$

  $3x - 46 = 0 \qquad\qquad x - 14 = 0$
  $3x = 46 \qquad\qquad\quad x = 14$
  $x = \dfrac{46}{3}$

  $x = \dfrac{46}{3}$ cm yields $h = 44 - 2\left(\dfrac{46}{3}\right) = \dfrac{40}{3}$ cm
  $x = 14$ cm yields $h = 44 - 2(14) = 16$ cm
  Choose dimensions 14 cm×14 cm×16 cm.

  a. Find the length of the diagonal.
  Consider the base to be the bottom of the figure.
  $\sqrt{14^2 + 14^2} = 14\sqrt{2}$ cm
  The length of the diagonal of the base is $14\sqrt{2}$ cm.
  $L = \sqrt{\left(14\sqrt{2}\right)^2 + 16^2} = \sqrt{648} = 18\sqrt{2}$ cm
  The length of the diagonal of the parallelepiped is $18\sqrt{2}$ cm ≈ 25.5 cm.

  b. Consider the base to be the bottom of the figure.
  $\cos\theta = \dfrac{14\sqrt{2}}{18\sqrt{2}}$
  $\cos\theta = \dfrac{7}{9}$
  $\theta = \cos^{-1}\left(\dfrac{7}{9}\right)$
  $\theta \approx 38.9°$

  Consider the base to be a side of the figure.
  $\sqrt{14^2 + 16^2} = \sqrt{452} = 2\sqrt{113}$
  $\cos\theta = \dfrac{2\sqrt{113}}{18\sqrt{2}}$
  $\cos\theta = \dfrac{\sqrt{113}}{9\sqrt{2}}$
  $\theta = \cos^{-1}\left(\dfrac{\sqrt{113}}{9\sqrt{2}}\right)$
  $\theta \approx 33.4°$

59. $\theta = \tan^{-1}\left(\dfrac{x}{6}\right)$, $\cos\theta = \dfrac{6}{\sqrt{x^2 + 6}}$

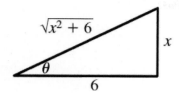

61. $\sin\alpha = \dfrac{\sqrt{2}}{2}$ $\qquad \cos\beta = \dfrac{\sqrt{3}}{2}$

$\alpha = \sin^{-1}\left(\dfrac{\sqrt{2}}{2}\right)$ $\qquad \beta = \cos^{-1}\left(\dfrac{\sqrt{3}}{2}\right)$

$\alpha = \dfrac{\pi}{4}$ $\qquad\qquad \beta = \dfrac{\pi}{6}$

$\sin(\alpha + \beta) = \sin\alpha\cos\beta + \cos\alpha\sin\beta$

$\qquad = \left(\dfrac{\sqrt{2}}{2}\right)\left(\dfrac{\sqrt{3}}{2}\right) + \left(\dfrac{\sqrt{2}}{2}\right)\left(\dfrac{1}{2}\right)$

$\qquad = \dfrac{\sqrt{6} + \sqrt{2}}{4}$

$\cos(\alpha + \beta) = \cos\alpha\cos\beta - \sin\alpha\sin\beta$

$\qquad = \left(\dfrac{\sqrt{2}}{2}\right)\left(\dfrac{\sqrt{3}}{2}\right) - \left(\dfrac{\sqrt{2}}{2}\right)\left(\dfrac{1}{2}\right)$

$\qquad = \dfrac{\sqrt{6} - \sqrt{2}}{4}$

63. Let β represent the angle formed from the base of the tower to the top of the tower.

$\tan\beta = \dfrac{1450}{1000}$

$\beta = \tan^{-1}\left(\dfrac{1450}{1000}\right)$

$\beta \approx 55.41°$

Let α represent the angle formed from the base of the tower to the top of the antenna.

$\tan\alpha = \dfrac{1450 + 280}{1000}$

$\alpha = \tan^{-1}\left(\dfrac{1730}{1000}\right)$

$\alpha = 59.97°$

$\theta = \alpha - \beta = 59.97° - 55.41° = 4.56°$

Summary and Concept Review 6.1

1. $h(x) = -|x - 2| + 3$

   No, the function is not one-to-one.

3. $s(x) = \sqrt{x - 1} + 5$

   Yes, the function is one-to-one.

5. $f(x) = x^2 - 2,\ x \geq 0$

   $\qquad y = x^2 - 2$

   $\qquad x = y^2 - 2$

   $\qquad y^2 = x + 2$

   $\qquad y = \pm\sqrt{x + 2}$

   $f^{-1}(x) = \sqrt{x + 2}$ since $x \geq 0$.

   $\left(f \circ f^{-1}\right)(x) = f\left[f^{-1}(x)\right]$

   $\qquad\qquad = \left[f^{-1}(x)\right]^2 - 2$

   $\qquad\qquad = \left(\sqrt{x + 2}\right)^2 - 2$

   $\qquad\qquad = x + 2 - 2$

   $\qquad\qquad = x$

   $\left(f^{-1} \circ f\right)(x) = f^{-1}\left[f(x)\right]$

   $\qquad\qquad = \sqrt{f(x) + 2}$

   $\qquad\qquad = \sqrt{x^2 - 2 + 2}$

   $\qquad\qquad = \sqrt{x^2}$

   $\qquad\qquad = x$

7. $f(x)$: $D: x \in [-4, \infty)$, $R: y \in [0, \infty)$

   $f^{-1}(x)$: $D: x \in [0, \infty)$, $R: y \in [-4, \infty)$

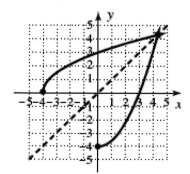

9. $f(x):\ D:x\in(-\infty,\infty),\ R:y\in(0,\infty)$

$f^{-1}(x):\ D:x\in(0,\infty),\ R:y\in(-\infty,\infty)$

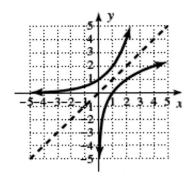

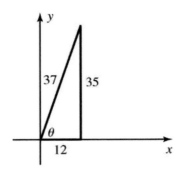

Summary and Concept Review 6.2

11. $y=\sin^{-1}\left(\dfrac{\sqrt{2}}{2}\right)$

$=\dfrac{\pi}{4}$ or $45°$

13. $y=\arccos\left(-\dfrac{\sqrt{3}}{2}\right)$

$=\dfrac{5\pi}{6}$ or $150°$

15. $y=\sin^{-1}(0.8892)$

≈1.0956 or $62.8°$

17. $\sin\left[\sin^{-1}\left(\dfrac{1}{2}\right)\right]=\dfrac{1}{2}$

19. $\cos\left[\cos^{-1}(2)\right]$ is undefined.

21. $\arccos\left[\cos(-60°)\right]=\arccos\left(\dfrac{1}{2}\right)$

$=60°$

23. $\sin\left[\cos^{-1}\left(\dfrac{12}{37}\right)\right]=\dfrac{35}{37}$

$y=\sqrt{37^2-12^2}=\sqrt{1225}=35$

25. $\cot\left[\sin^{-1}\left(\dfrac{x}{\sqrt{81+x^2}}\right)\right]=\dfrac{9}{x}$

$x_t=\sqrt{\left(\sqrt{81+x^2}\right)^2-x^2}$

$=\sqrt{81+x^2-x^2}$

$=\sqrt{81}=9$

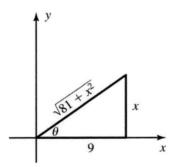

27. $7\sqrt{3}\sec\theta=x$

$\sec\theta=\dfrac{x}{7\sqrt{3}}$

$\theta=\sec^{-1}\left(\dfrac{x}{7\sqrt{3}}\right)$

Summary and Concept Review 6.3

29. $2\sin x = \sqrt{2}$

$\qquad \sin x = \dfrac{\sqrt{2}}{2}$

   a. $x = \sin^{-1}\left(\dfrac{\sqrt{2}}{2}\right) = \dfrac{\pi}{4}$

   b. $\sin > 0$ in QI and QII.

$\qquad \dfrac{\pi}{4}, \dfrac{3\pi}{4}$

   c. $x = \dfrac{\pi}{4} + 2\pi k$ or $x = \dfrac{3\pi}{4} + 2\pi k,\ k \in \mathbb{Z}$

31. $8\tan x + 7\sqrt{3} = -\sqrt{3}$

$\qquad 8\tan x = -8\sqrt{3}$

$\qquad \tan x = -\dfrac{8\sqrt{3}}{8}$

$\qquad \tan x = -\sqrt{3}$

   a. $x = \tan^{-1}\left(-\sqrt{3}\right) = -\dfrac{\pi}{3}$

   b. $\tan < 0$ in QII and QIV.

$\qquad \dfrac{2\pi}{3}, \dfrac{5\pi}{3}$

   c. $\dfrac{2\pi}{3} + k\pi,\ k \in \mathbb{Z}$

33. $\dfrac{2}{5}\sin(2\theta) = \dfrac{1}{4}$

$\qquad \sin(2\theta) = \dfrac{5}{8}$

   a. $2\theta = \sin^{-1}\left(\dfrac{5}{8}\right) \approx 0.6751$

$\qquad \theta \approx 0.3376$

   b. $\sin > 0$ in QI and QII.

$\qquad 0 \le \theta < 2\pi \ \Rightarrow\ 0 \le 2\theta < 4\pi$

$\qquad 2\theta \approx 0.6751$

$\qquad 2\theta \approx \pi - 0.6751 \approx 2.4665$

$\qquad 2\theta \approx 2\pi + 0.6751 \approx 6.9583$

$\qquad 2\theta \approx 3\pi - 0.6751 \approx 8.7497$

$\qquad \theta \approx 0.6751 \div 2 \approx 0.3376$

$\qquad \theta \approx 2.4665 \div 2 \approx 1.2332$

$\qquad \theta \approx 6.9583 \div 2 \approx 3.4792$

$\qquad \theta \approx 8.7497 \div 2 \approx 4.3748$

   c. $x \approx 0.3376 + \pi k$ or $1.2332 + xk,\ k \in \mathbb{Z}$

35. $A = \dfrac{1}{2}r^2(\theta - \sin\theta)$

$\qquad 12 = \dfrac{1}{2}(10)^2(\theta - \sin\theta)$

$\qquad 12 = 50(\theta - \sin\theta)$

$\qquad \dfrac{6}{25} = \theta - \sin\theta$

Using a graphing calculator, we see that
$\theta \approx 1.1547$.

Summary and Concept Review 6.4

37. $3\cos(2x) + 7\sin x - 5 = 0$

$\qquad 3\left(1 - 2\sin^2 x\right) + 7\sin x - 5 = 0$

$\qquad 3 - 6\sin^2 x + 7\sin x - 5 = 0$

$\qquad -6\sin^2 x + 7\sin x - 2 = 0$

$\qquad 6\sin^2 x - 7\sin x + 2 = 0$

$\qquad (2\sin x - 1)(3\sin x - 2) = 0$

$\quad 2\sin x - 1 = 0 \qquad\quad 3\sin x - 2 = 0$

$\quad 2\sin x = 1 \qquad\qquad 3\sin x = 2$

$\quad \sin x = \dfrac{1}{2} \qquad\qquad \sin x = \dfrac{2}{3}$

$\quad x = \sin^{-1}\left(\dfrac{1}{2}\right) \qquad x = \sin^{-1}\left(\dfrac{2}{3}\right)$

$\sin > 0$ in QI and QII.

The solutions are $x = \dfrac{\pi}{6}, \dfrac{5\pi}{6}, 0.7297, 2.4119$.

39. $\csc x + \cot x = 1$

$\qquad \csc x = 1 - \cot x$

$\qquad (\csc x)^2 = (1 - \cot x)^2$

$\qquad \csc^2 x = 1 - 2\cot x + \cot^2 x$

$\qquad 1 + \cot^2 x = 1 - 2\cot x + \cot^2 x$

$\qquad\qquad 0 = -2\cot x$

$\qquad\qquad 2\cot x = 0$

$\qquad\qquad \cot x = 0$

This implies that $\cos x = 0$

$\qquad\qquad x = \cos^{-1}(0)$.

The solutions is $x = \dfrac{\pi}{2}$.

Note that $x = \dfrac{3\pi}{2}$ is extraneous.

41. $P=\dfrac{2\pi}{\frac{\pi}{3}}=6\rightarrow[0,\ 6)$

$80\cos\left(\dfrac{\pi}{3}x+\dfrac{\pi}{4}\right)-40\sqrt{2}=0$

$80\cos\left(\dfrac{\pi}{3}x+\dfrac{\pi}{4}\right)=40\sqrt{2}$

$\cos\left(\dfrac{\pi}{3}x+\dfrac{\pi}{4}\right)=\dfrac{\sqrt{2}}{2}$

Let $u=\dfrac{\pi}{3}x+\dfrac{\pi}{4}$.

$\cos u>0$ in QI and QIV.

$u=\cos^{-1}\left(\dfrac{\sqrt{2}}{2}\right)\Rightarrow u=\dfrac{\pi}{4}+2\pi k$

$u=\dfrac{7\pi}{4}+2\pi k$

Consider $k=0$.

$u=\dfrac{\pi}{4}+2\pi(0)=\dfrac{\pi}{4}$

$\dfrac{\pi}{3}x+\dfrac{\pi}{4}=\dfrac{\pi}{4}$

$\dfrac{\pi}{3}x=0$

$x=0$

$u=\dfrac{7\pi}{4}+2\pi(0)=\dfrac{7\pi}{4}$

$\dfrac{\pi}{3}x+\dfrac{\pi}{4}=\dfrac{7\pi}{4}$

$\dfrac{\pi}{3}x=\dfrac{3\pi}{2}$

$x=\dfrac{9}{2}$

Mixed Review

1. $f(x)=\dfrac{1}{(x+2)^2},\ x>-2$

a. $y=\dfrac{1}{(x+2)^2}$

$x=\dfrac{1}{(y+2)^2}$

$(y+2)^2=\dfrac{1}{x}$

$y+2=\sqrt{\dfrac{1}{x}}$

$y=\sqrt{\dfrac{1}{x}}-2$

$f^{-1}(x)=\sqrt{\dfrac{1}{x}}-2$

b. $f^{-1}(x):\ D:x\in(0,\infty),\ R:y\in(-2,\infty)$

c. $(f\circ f^{-1})(x)=f\left[f^{-1}(x)\right]$

$=\dfrac{1}{\left[f^{-1}(x)+2\right]^2}$

$=\dfrac{1}{\left(\sqrt{\dfrac{1}{x}}-2+2\right)^2}$

$=\dfrac{1}{\left(\sqrt{\dfrac{1}{x}}\right)^2}$

$=\dfrac{1}{\dfrac{1}{x}}$

$=x$

$(f^{-1}\circ f)(x)=f^{-1}\left[f(x)\right]$

$=\sqrt{\dfrac{1}{f(x)}}-2$

$=\sqrt{\dfrac{1}{\dfrac{1}{(x+2)^2}}}-2$

$=\sqrt{(x+2)^2}-2$

$=x+2-2$

$=x$

3. $-12\sin x + 5 = 11$

    $-12\sin x = 6$

    $\sin x = -\dfrac{1}{2}$

    $\sin < 0$ in QIII and QIV.

    $x = \sin^{-1}\left(-\dfrac{1}{2}\right) = \dfrac{7\pi}{6}, \dfrac{11\pi}{6}$

5. $\tan\left[\operatorname{arccsc}\left(\dfrac{10}{x}\right)\right] = \dfrac{x}{\sqrt{100 - x^2}}$

    $x_t = \sqrt{10^2 - x^2}$

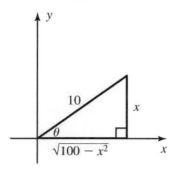

7. $P = \dfrac{2\pi}{\dfrac{\pi}{4}} = 8 \to [0,\ 8)$

    $-100\sin\left(\dfrac{\pi}{4}x - \dfrac{\pi}{6}\right) + 80 = 100$

    $-100\sin\left(\dfrac{\pi}{4}x - \dfrac{\pi}{6}\right) = 20$

    $\sin\left(\dfrac{\pi}{4}x - \dfrac{\pi}{6}\right) = -\dfrac{1}{5}$

Let $u = \dfrac{\pi}{4}x - \dfrac{\pi}{6}$.

$\sin u < 0$ in QIII and QIV.

$u = \sin^{-1}\left(-\dfrac{1}{5}\right) \Rightarrow u = -0.2014 + 2\pi k$

    $u = 3.3430 + 2\pi k$

Consider $k = 0$.

$u \approx -0.2014 + 2\pi(0) \approx -0.2014$

    $\dfrac{\pi}{4}x - \dfrac{\pi}{6} \approx -0.2014$

        $\dfrac{\pi}{4}x \approx 0.3222$

            $x \approx 0.4103$

$u \approx 3.3430 + 2\pi(0) \approx 3.3430$

    $\dfrac{\pi}{4}x - \dfrac{\pi}{6} \approx 3.3430$

        $\dfrac{\pi}{4}x \approx 3.8666$

            $x \approx 4.9230$

9. $g(x) = \sqrt{x - 1} + 2$

  a. $D: x \in [1, \infty),\ R: y \in [2, \infty)$

  b. $y = \sqrt{x - 1} + 2$

       $x = \sqrt{y - 1} + 2$

      $x - 2 = \sqrt{y - 1}$

     $(x - 2)^2 = y - 1$

         $y = (x - 2)^2 + 1$

      $g^{-1}(x) = (x - 2)^2 + 1$

      $D: x \in [2, \infty),\ R: y \in [1, \infty)$

  c. Answers will vary.

11. $y = \operatorname{arcsec}\left(-\sqrt{2}\right)$

    $= \arccos\left(-\dfrac{\sqrt{2}}{2}\right)$

    $= \dfrac{3\pi}{4}$ or $135°$

13. $y = \arctan\sqrt{3} = \dfrac{\pi}{3}$ or $60°$

15. $2\sqrt{2}\csc\ \theta - \dfrac{\pi}{4} = x$

    $\csc\ \theta - \dfrac{\pi}{4} = \dfrac{x}{2\sqrt{2}}$

      $\theta - \dfrac{\pi}{4} = \csc^{-1}\ \dfrac{x}{2\sqrt{2}}$

         $\theta = \csc^{-1}\ \dfrac{x}{2\sqrt{2}} + \dfrac{\pi}{4}$

17. $3.2^2 = 11^2 + 9.4^2 - 2(11)(9.4)\cos\theta$

    $10.24 = 121 + 88.36 - 206.8\cos\theta$

    $-199.12 = -206.8\cos\theta$

    $0.9629 = \cos\theta$

    $\cos^{-1}(0.9629) \approx \theta$

    $15.7° \approx \theta$

19. $\cos(2\theta) + 2\sin^2\theta = -2\sin\theta$

    $1 - 2\sin^2\theta + 2\sin^2\theta = -2\sin\theta$

              $1 = -2\sin\theta$

         $-\dfrac{1}{2} = \sin\theta$

        $\theta = \sin^{-1}\left(-\dfrac{1}{2}\right)$

  $\theta = \dfrac{7\pi}{6} + 2\pi k$ or $\dfrac{11\pi}{6} + 2\pi k,\ k \in \mathbb{Z}$

Practice Test

1. $f(x) = x^3$ is a one-to-one function, $f(x) = x^2$ is not.

3. $y = \cos^{-1} x$

$D : x \in [-1,1], \ R : y \in [0,\pi]$

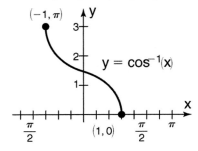

5. $y = \tan^{-1}\left(\dfrac{1}{\sqrt{3}}\right) = 30°$

7. $y = \arccos(\cos 30°) = 30°$

9. $y = \arctan(\tan 78.5°) = 78.5°$ or $\dfrac{157\pi}{360}$ rad

11. $\cos\left[\tan^{-1}\left(\dfrac{56}{33}\right)\right] = \dfrac{33}{65}$

$r = \sqrt{33^2 + 56^2} = \sqrt{4225} = 65$

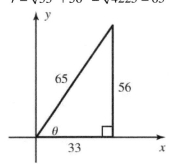

13. $8\cos x = -4\sqrt{2}$

$\cos x = -\dfrac{\sqrt{2}}{2}$

a. $x = \cos^{-1}\left(-\dfrac{\sqrt{2}}{2}\right) = \dfrac{3\pi}{4}$

b. $\cos < 0$ in QII and QIII.

$x = \dfrac{3\pi}{4}, \dfrac{5\pi}{4}$

c. $x = \dfrac{3\pi}{4} + 2\pi k$ or $\dfrac{5\pi}{4} + 2\pi k, \ k \in \mathbb{Z}$

15. $\dfrac{2}{3}\sin(2x) = \dfrac{1}{4}$

$\sin(2x) = \dfrac{3}{8}$

a. $2x = \sin^{-1}\left(\dfrac{3}{8}\right) \approx 0.3844$

$x \approx 0.1922$

b. $\sin > 0$ in QI and QII.

$0 \le x < 2\pi \ \Rightarrow \ 0 \le 2x < 4\pi$

$2x \approx 0.3844$

$2x \approx \pi - 0.3844 \approx 2.7572$

$2x \approx 2\pi + 0.3844 \approx 6.6676$

$2x \approx 3\pi - 0.3844 \approx 9.0404$

$x \approx 0.3844 \div 2 \approx 0.1922$

$x \approx 2.7572 \div 2 \approx 1.3786$

$x \approx 6.6676 \div 2 \approx 3.3338$

$x \approx 9.0404 \div 2 \approx 4.5202$

c. $x \approx 0.1922 + \pi k$ or $1.3786 + \pi k, \ k \in \mathbb{Z}$

17. $Y_1 = 3\cos(2x - 1)$

$Y_2 = \sin x$

$x \in [-\pi, \pi]$

$x \approx -1.6875, \ -0.3413, \ 1.1321, \ 2.8967$

19. $2\sin x \sin(2x) + \sin(2x) = 0$

$\sin(2x)[2\sin x + 1] = 0$

$\sin(2x) = 0 \qquad\qquad 2\sin x + 1 = 0$

$\qquad\qquad\qquad\qquad\quad 2\sin x = -1$

$\qquad\qquad\qquad\qquad\quad \sin x = -\dfrac{1}{2}$

$0 \le x < 2\pi \ \Rightarrow \ 0 \le 2x < 4\pi$

$2x = \sin^{-1}(0) \qquad x = \sin^{-1}\left(-\dfrac{1}{2}\right)$

$2x = 0, \pi, 2\pi, 3\pi$

$x = 0, \dfrac{\pi}{2}, \pi, \dfrac{3\pi}{2} \qquad x = \dfrac{7\pi}{6}, \dfrac{11\pi}{6}$

The solutions are $x = 0, \dfrac{\pi}{2}, \pi, \dfrac{3\pi}{2}, \dfrac{7\pi}{6}, \dfrac{11\pi}{6}$.

21.
$$3\sin(2x)+\cos x=0$$
$$3(2\sin x\cos x)+\cos x=0$$
$$6\sin x\cos x+\cos x=0$$
$$\cos x(6\sin x+1)=0$$

$$\cos x=0 \qquad\qquad 6\sin x+1=0$$
$$x=\cos^{-1}(0) \qquad 6\sin x=-1$$
$$x=\frac{\pi}{2},\frac{3\pi}{2} \qquad\quad \sin x=-\frac{1}{6}$$
$$x=\sin^{-1}\left(-\frac{1}{6}\right)$$
$$x\approx 3.3090,\ 6.1157$$

Solutions are $x=\dfrac{\pi}{2},\dfrac{3\pi}{2};\ x\approx 3.3090,\ 6.1157.$

23. $R(x)=7.5\cos\left(\dfrac{\pi}{6}x+\dfrac{4\pi}{3}\right)+12.5$

a. September corresponds to $x=9$.
$$R(9)=7.5\cos\left[\frac{\pi}{6}(9)+\frac{4\pi}{3}\right]+12.5$$
$$=7.5\cos\left(\frac{3\pi}{2}+\frac{4\pi}{3}\right)+12.5$$
$$=7.5\cos\left(\frac{17\pi}{6}\right)+12.5$$
$$=7.5\left(-\frac{\sqrt{3}}{2}\right)+12.5$$
$$\approx 6\text{ thousand}\ (\$6000)$$

b. A graphing calculator may be used. An algebraic solution is shown.
$$P=\frac{2\pi}{\frac{\pi}{6}}=12\to[0,12)$$
$$12.5=7.5\cos\left(\frac{\pi}{6}x+\frac{4\pi}{3}\right)+12.5$$
$$0=7.5\cos\left(\frac{\pi}{6}x+\frac{4\pi}{3}\right)$$
$$0=\cos\left(\frac{\pi}{6}x+\frac{4\pi}{3}\right)$$

Let $u=\dfrac{\pi}{6}x+\dfrac{4\pi}{3}$.

$\cos u=0$ at $\dfrac{\pi}{2}+\pi k$.

23. b. (continued)
Consider $k=0$.
$$u=\frac{\pi}{2}+\pi(0)=\frac{\pi}{2}$$
$$\frac{\pi}{6}x+\frac{4\pi}{3}=\frac{\pi}{2}$$
$$\frac{\pi}{6}x=-\frac{5\pi}{6}$$
$$x=-5 \qquad\text{not in interval}$$

Consider $k=1$.
$$u=\frac{\pi}{2}+\pi(1)=\frac{3\pi}{2}$$
$$\frac{\pi}{6}x+\frac{4\pi}{3}=\frac{3\pi}{2}$$
$$\frac{\pi}{6}x=\frac{\pi}{6}$$
$$x=1$$

Consider $k=2$.
$$u=\frac{\pi}{2}+\pi(2)=\frac{5\pi}{2}$$
$$\frac{\pi}{6}x+\frac{4\pi}{3}=\frac{5\pi}{2}$$
$$\frac{\pi}{6}x=\frac{7\pi}{6}$$
$$x=7$$

The revenue is at least \$12,500 from January through July.

25. $\sin\left[\tan^{-1}\left\{\tan\left[\sec^{-1}\left(-\frac{2}{\sqrt{3}}\right)\right]\right\}\right]$
$$=\sin\left[\tan^{-1}\left\{\tan\left[\cos^{-1}\left(-\frac{\sqrt{3}}{2}\right)\right]\right\}\right]$$
$$=\sin\left[\tan^{-1}\left\{\tan\left[\frac{5\pi}{6}\right]\right\}\right]$$
$$=\sin\left[\tan^{-1}\left\{-\frac{\sqrt{3}}{3}\right\}\right]$$
$$=\sin\left(-\frac{\pi}{6}\right)$$
$$=-\frac{1}{2}$$

Calculator Exploration and Discovery

Exercise 1:

$$Y_1 = (1+\sin x)^2 + \cos(2x)$$

$$Y_2 = 4\cos x(1+\sin x)$$

$$x \approx 1.1706 + 2\pi k, \ 4.1287 + 2\pi k$$

Strengthening Core Skills

Exercise 1:

$$f(x) = 3\sin x + 2;$$

$$f(x) > 3.7; \ x \in [0, 2\pi)$$

$$3\sin x + 2 = 3.7$$

$$3\sin x = 1.7$$

$$\sin x = \frac{1.7}{3}$$

$\sin > 0$ in QI and QII.

$$x = \sin^{-1}\left(\frac{1.7}{3}\right)$$

$$x \approx 0.6025, -2.5391$$

Since $3\sin x + 2 > 3.7$, the solution is

$$x \in (0.6025, 2.5391).$$

Exercise 3:

$$h(x) = 125\sin\left(\frac{\pi}{6}x - \frac{\pi}{2}\right) + 175;$$

$$h(x) \le 150; \ x \in [0, 12)$$

$$125\sin\left(\frac{\pi}{6}x - \frac{\pi}{2}\right) + 175 = 150$$

$$125\sin\left(\frac{\pi}{6}x - \frac{\pi}{2}\right) = -25$$

$$\sin\left(\frac{\pi}{6}x - \frac{\pi}{2}\right) = -\frac{1}{5}$$

Let $u = \frac{\pi}{6}x - \frac{\pi}{2}$.

$\sin u < 0$ in QIII and QIV.

$$x = \sin^{-1}\left(-\frac{1}{5}\right)$$

$$x \approx -0.2014, \ 3.3430$$

$$u = \frac{\pi}{6}x - \frac{\pi}{2} \approx -0.2014$$

$$\frac{\pi}{6}x \approx 1.3694$$

$$x \approx 2.6154$$

$$u = \frac{\pi}{6}x - \frac{\pi}{2} \approx 3.3430$$

$$\frac{\pi}{6}x \approx 4.9138$$

$$x \approx 9.3847$$

Since $125\sin\left(\frac{\pi}{6}x - \frac{\pi}{2}\right) + 175 \le 150$, the

solution is $x \in [0, 2.6154] \cup [9.3847, 12)$.

Cumulative Review Chapters 1-6

1. $x = -13, \ y = 84, \ r = \sqrt{(-13)^2 + 84^2} = 85$

$$\sin\theta = \frac{84}{85}; \ \csc\theta = \frac{85}{84}; \ \cos\theta = -\frac{13}{85}$$

$$\sec\theta = -\frac{85}{13}; \ \tan\theta = -\frac{84}{13}; \ \cot\theta = -\frac{13}{84}$$

3.   a. $56°20'06'' = \left[56 + 20\left(\frac{1}{60}\right) + 6\left(\frac{1}{3600}\right)\right]°$

$$= 56.335°$$

b. $56.335° \cdot \frac{\pi}{180°} \approx 0.9832$ radians

5. $\tan(36°56') = \dfrac{x}{26,400}$

$$x = 26,400\tan(36°56')$$

$$x \approx 19,846 \text{ ft}$$

$20,320 - 19,846 = 474$ ft

Mt McKinley is about 474 ft taller.

7.
$$3\sin(2x)+\cos x=0$$
$$3(2\sin x\cos x)+\cos x=0$$
$$6\sin x\cos x+\cos x=0$$
$$\cos x(6\sin x+1)=0$$

$$\cos x=0 \qquad\qquad 6\sin x+1=0$$
$$x=\cos^{-1}(0) \qquad\quad 6\sin x=-1$$
$$x=\frac{\pi}{2},\frac{3\pi}{2} \qquad\qquad \sin x=-\frac{1}{6}$$
$$x=\sin^{-1}\left(-\frac{1}{6}\right)$$
$$x\approx 3.3090,\ 6.1157$$

Solutions are $x=\dfrac{\pi}{2},\dfrac{3\pi}{2}$; $x\approx 3.3090,\ 6.1157$.

9.
$$\omega=\frac{5\ \text{rev}}{1\ \text{sec}}\cdot\frac{2\pi\ \text{rad}}{1\ \text{rev}}=10\pi\ \text{rad/sec}$$
$$V=r\omega$$
$$=45(10\pi)$$
$$\approx 450\pi\ \text{cm/sec}$$

Convert to kph.
$$\frac{450\pi\ \text{cm}}{\text{sec}}\cdot\left(\frac{3600\ \text{sec}}{1\ \text{hr}}\right)\cdot\left(\frac{1\ \text{km}}{100{,}000\ \text{cm}}\right)$$
$$\approx 50.89\ \text{kph}$$

11. $\cos\left[\sin^{-1}\left(\dfrac{1}{2}\right)\right]=\cos\left(\dfrac{\pi}{6}\right)=\dfrac{\sqrt{3}}{2}$

13. a. $Y_1=48.778\sin(0.213x-1.106)+51.642$

   b. $x=31+7=38$
   June 7th is day 38.
   One this day, about 83.2% of the Moon
   will be illuminated.

15. $f(x)=325\cos\left(\dfrac{\pi}{6}x-\dfrac{\pi}{2}\right)+168;$

   $f(x)>330.5,\ x\in[0,\ 2\pi)$

   $$325\cos\left(\frac{\pi}{6}x-\frac{\pi}{2}\right)+168=330.5$$
   $$325\cos\left(\frac{\pi}{6}x-\frac{\pi}{2}\right)=162.5$$
   $$\cos\left(\frac{\pi}{6}x-\frac{\pi}{2}\right)=\frac{1}{2}$$

   Let $u=\dfrac{\pi}{6}x-\dfrac{\pi}{2}$.

   $\cos u>0$ in QI and QIV.

   $$x=\cos^{-1}\left(\frac{1}{2}\right)=-\frac{\pi}{3},\frac{\pi}{3}$$

   $$u=\frac{\pi}{6}x-\frac{\pi}{2}=-\frac{\pi}{3} \qquad u=\frac{\pi}{6}x-\frac{\pi}{2}=\frac{\pi}{3}$$
   $$\frac{\pi}{6}x=\frac{\pi}{6} \qquad\qquad \frac{\pi}{6}x=\frac{5\pi}{6}$$
   $$x=1 \qquad\qquad\qquad x=5$$

   Since $325\cos\left(\dfrac{\pi}{6}x-\dfrac{\pi}{2}\right)+168>330.5,$

   the solution is $x\in(1,\ 5)$.

17. $\sin(2\theta)=\sin(\theta+\theta)$
   $$=\sin\theta\cos\theta+\cos\theta\sin\theta$$
   $$=\left(\frac{11}{\sqrt{202}}\right)\left(\frac{9}{\sqrt{202}}\right)+\left(\frac{9}{\sqrt{202}}\right)\left(\frac{11}{\sqrt{202}}\right)$$
   $$=\frac{198}{202}=\frac{99}{101}$$

19. Begin on the right side of equation.
   $$\frac{\cos x}{\sec x-1}=\frac{\cos x(\sec x+1)}{(\sec x-1)(\sec x+1)}$$
   $$=\frac{1+\cos x}{\sec^2 x-1}$$
   $$=\frac{\cos x+1}{\tan^2 x}$$

Technology Highlight

Exercise 1:

$\angle A = 35°$, side $c = 25$ mm

$$\sin \angle A = \frac{a}{c}$$

$$\sin 35° = \frac{a}{25}$$

$$a = 25\sin 35° \approx 14.3 \text{ mm}$$

When $a \geq 25$, one obtuse triangle is formed.
When $14.34 < a < 25$, two triangles are formed.
When $a \approx 14.34$, one right triangle is formed.

Exercise 3:

$\angle C = 52°$, side $a = 27.5$ cm

$$\sin \angle C = \frac{c}{a}$$

$$\sin 52° = \frac{c}{27.5}$$

$$c = 27.5\sin 52° \approx 21.67 \text{ cm}$$

When $c \geq 27.5$, one obtuse triangle is formed.
When $21.67 < c < 27.5$, two triangles are formed.
When $c \approx 21.67$, one right triangle is formed.

7.1 Exercises

1. ambiguous

3. I; II

5. Answers will vary.

7.
$$\frac{\sin 32°}{15} = \frac{\sin 18.5°}{a}$$
$$a\sin 32° = 15\sin 18.5°$$
$$a = \frac{15\sin 18.5°}{\sin 32°} \approx 8.98$$

9.
$$\frac{\sin 63°}{21.9} = \frac{\sin C}{18.6}$$
$$21.9\sin C = 18.6\sin 63°$$
$$\sin C = \frac{18.6\sin 63°}{21.9}$$
$$C = \sin^{-1}\left(\frac{18.6\sin 63°}{21.9}\right) \approx 49.2°$$

11.
$$\frac{\sin C}{48.5} = \frac{\sin 19°}{43.2}$$
$$43.2\sin C = 48.5\sin 19°$$
$$\sin C = \frac{48.5\sin 19°}{43.2}$$
$$C = \sin^{-1}\left(\frac{48.5\sin 19°}{43.2}\right) \approx 21.4°$$

13. $\angle C = 180° - (38° + 64°) = 78°$
$$\frac{\sin 38°}{75} = \frac{\sin 64°}{b}$$
$$b\sin 38° = 75\sin 64°$$
$$b = \frac{75\sin 64°}{\sin 38°} \approx 109.5 \text{ cm}$$

$$\frac{\sin 78°}{c} = \frac{\sin 38°}{75}$$
$$c\sin 38° = 75\sin 78°$$
$$c = \frac{75\sin 78°}{\sin 38°} \approx 119.2 \text{ cm}$$

15. $\angle C = 180° - (30° + 60°) = 90°$
$$\frac{\sin 60°}{10\sqrt{3}} = \frac{\sin 30°}{a}$$
$$a\sin 60° = 10\sqrt{3}\sin 30°$$
$$a = \frac{10\sqrt{3}\sin 30°}{\sin 60°} = 10 \text{ in.}$$

$$\frac{\sin 60°}{10\sqrt{3}} = \frac{\sin 90°}{c}$$
$$c\sin 60° = 10\sqrt{3}\sin 90°$$
$$c = \frac{10\sqrt{3}\sin 90°}{\sin 60°} = 20 \text{ in.}$$

17. $\angle A = 33°$, $\angle B = 102°$, $b = 19$ in.
$\angle C = 180° - (33° + 102°) = 45°$
$$\frac{\sin 102°}{19} = \frac{\sin 33°}{a}$$
$$a\sin 102° = 19\sin 33°$$
$$a = \frac{19\sin 33°}{\sin 102°} \approx 10.6 \text{ in.}$$

$$\frac{\sin 102°}{19} = \frac{\sin 45°}{c}$$
$$c\sin 102° = 19\sin 45°$$
$$c = \frac{19\sin 45°}{\sin 102°} \approx 13.7 \text{ in.}$$

17. (continued)

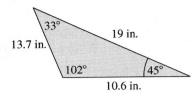

19. $\angle C = 180° - (45° + 45°) = 90°$

$$\frac{\sin 90°}{15\sqrt{2}} = \frac{\sin 45°}{a}$$

$$a\sin 90° = 15\sqrt{2}\sin 45°$$

$$a = \frac{15\sqrt{2}\sin 45°}{\sin 90°} = 15 \text{ mi}$$

$b = 15$ mi

21. $\angle A = 180° - (103.4° + 19.6°) = 57°$

$$\frac{\sin 57°}{42.7} = \frac{\sin 103.4°}{b}$$

$$b\sin 57° = 42.7\sin 103.4°$$

$$b = \frac{42.7\sin 103.4°}{\sin 57°} \approx 49.5 \text{ km}$$

$$\frac{\sin 57°}{42.7} = \frac{\sin 19.6°}{c}$$

$$c\sin 57° = 42.7\sin 19.6°$$

$$c = \frac{42.7\sin 19.6°}{\sin 57°} \approx 17.1 \text{ km}$$

23. $\angle A = 56°,\ \angle B = 112°,\ c = 0.8$ cm
$\angle C = 180° - (56° + 112°) = 12°$

$$\frac{\sin 12°}{0.8} = \frac{\sin 56°}{a}$$

$$a\sin 12° = 0.8\sin 56°$$

$$a = \frac{0.8\sin 56°}{\sin 12°} \approx 3.2 \text{ cm}$$

$$\frac{\sin 12°}{0.8} = \frac{\sin 112°}{b}$$

$$b\sin 12° = 0.8\sin 112°$$

$$b = \frac{0.8\sin 112°}{\sin 12°} \approx 3.6 \text{ cm}$$

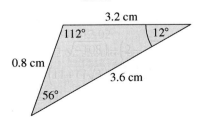

25. a.

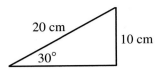

The right triangle is a 30°-60°-90° triangle, so the short side is half the hypotenuse, or 10 cm.

b. If $a = 8$ cm, the vertical side is too short to reach the base, so none is possible.

c.

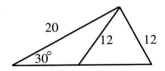

If $a = 12$ cm, two triangles are possible.

d.

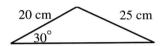

If $a = 25$ cm, only one triangle is possible.

27. $$\frac{\sin 67°}{385} = \frac{\sin A}{490}$$

$$385\sin A = 490\sin 67°$$

$$\sin A = \frac{490\sin 67°}{385} \approx 1.17$$

not possible

29. $$\frac{\sin 30°}{12.9} = \frac{\sin C}{25.8}$$

$$12.9\sin C = 25.8\sin 30°$$

$$\sin C = \frac{25.8\sin 30°}{12.9}$$

$$\sin C = 1$$

$$C = 90°$$

There is only one possible triangle.

$B = 180° - (30° + 90°) = 60°$
This is a 30°-60°-90° triangle, so
$b = 12.9\sqrt{3}$ mi.

31. $\dfrac{\sin B}{67} = \dfrac{\sin 59°}{58}$

$58\sin B = 67\sin 59°$

$\sin B = \dfrac{67\sin 59°}{58}$

$\sin B \approx 0.9902$

$B = \sin^{-1}(0.9902)$

$B \approx 82°$

or $B = 180° - 82° = 98°.$

Consider $B = 82°.$

$A = 180° - (59° + 82°) = 39°$

$\dfrac{\sin 39°}{a} = \dfrac{\sin 59°}{58}$

$a\sin 59° = 58\sin 39°$

$a = \dfrac{58\sin 39°}{\sin 59°} \approx 42.6 \text{ mi}$

Consider $B = 98°.$

$A = 180° - (98° + 59°) = 23°$

$\dfrac{\sin 23°}{a} = \dfrac{\sin 59°}{58}$

$a\sin 59° = 58\sin 23°$

$a = \dfrac{58\sin 23°}{\sin 59°} \approx 26.4 \text{ mi}$

33. $\dfrac{\sin 59°}{58} = \dfrac{\sin B}{67}$

$58\sin B = 67\sin 59°$

$\sin B = \dfrac{67\sin 59°}{58}$

$\sin B \approx 0.9902$

$B = \sin^{-1}(0.9902)$

$B \approx 82°$

or $B = 180° - 82° = 98°.$

Consider $B = 82°.$

$A = 180° - (59° + 82°) = 39°$

$\dfrac{\sin 39°}{a} = \dfrac{\sin 59°}{58}$

$a\sin 59° = 58\sin 39°$

$a = \dfrac{58\sin 39°}{\sin 59°} \approx 42.6 \text{ ft}$

Consider $B = 98°.$

$A = 180° - (98° + 59°) = 23°$

$\dfrac{\sin 23°}{a} = \dfrac{\sin 59°}{58}$

$a\sin 59° = 58\sin 23°$

$a = \dfrac{58\sin 23°}{\sin 59°} \approx 26.4 \text{ ft}$

35. $\dfrac{\sin 38°}{6.7} = \dfrac{\sin A}{10.9}$

$6.7\sin A = 10.9\sin 38°$

$\sin A = \dfrac{10.9\sin 38°}{6.7} \approx 1.002$

not possible

37. $\dfrac{\sin 62°}{2.6\times10^{25}} = \dfrac{\sin A}{2.9\times10^{25}}$

$(2.6\times10^{25})\sin A = (2.9\times10^{25})\sin 62°$

$\sin A = \dfrac{(2.9\times10^{25})\sin 62°}{(2.6\times10^{25})}$

$\sin A \approx 0.9848$

$A \approx \sin^{-1}(0.9848)$

$A \approx 80.0°$

$B \approx 180° - (80.0° + 62°) = 38.0°$

$\dfrac{\sin 62°}{2.6\times10^{25}} = \dfrac{\sin 38°}{b}$

$b\sin 62° = (2.6\times10^{25})\sin 38°$

$b = \dfrac{(2.6\times10^{25})\sin 38°}{\sin 62°}$

$b \approx 1.8\times10^{25} \text{ mi}$

39. $\dfrac{\sin A}{12} = \dfrac{\sin 48°}{27}$

$27\sin A = 12\sin 48°$

$\sin A = \dfrac{12\sin 48°}{27}$

$A = \sin^{-1}\left(\dfrac{12\sin 48°}{27}\right)$

$A \approx 19.3°$

or $A = 180° - 19.3° = 160.7°$

$160.7° + 48° = 208.7° > 180°$

no second solution possible

41. $\dfrac{\sin 57°}{35.6} = \dfrac{\sin C}{40.2}$

$35.6\sin C = 40.2\sin 57°$

$\sin C = \dfrac{40.2\sin 57°}{35.6}$

$C = \sin^{-1}\left(\dfrac{40.2\sin 57°}{35.6}\right)$

$C \approx 71.3°$

or $C = 180° - 71.3° = 108.7°$

$108.7° + 57° = 165.7° < 180°$

two solutions possible

43. $$\frac{\sin A}{280} = \frac{\sin 15°}{52}$$

$$52 \sin A = 280 \sin 15°$$

$$\sin A = \frac{280 \sin 15°}{52} \approx 1.39$$

not possible

45. $\sin(3\theta) = 3\sin\theta - 4\sin^3\theta$

$\sin 135° = \sin(3 \cdot 45°)$

$\qquad = 3\sin 45° - 4\sin^3 45°$

$\qquad = 3 \cdot \frac{\sqrt{2}}{2} - 4\left(\frac{\sqrt{2}}{2}\right)^3$

$\qquad = \frac{3\sqrt{2}}{2} - 4\left(\frac{2\sqrt{2}}{8}\right)$

$\qquad = \frac{3\sqrt{2}}{2} - \frac{2\sqrt{2}}{2}$

$\qquad = \frac{\sqrt{2}}{2}$

The reference angle for 135° is 45°, and 135° is in QII, so $\sin 135° = \frac{\sqrt{2}}{2}$.

47. We are given $\theta = 20°$. Let α be the angle with vertex at Sorus and β be the angle with vertex at the Sun.

$$\frac{\sin 20°}{51} = \frac{\sin\alpha}{82}$$

$$82 \sin 20° = 51 \sin\alpha$$

$$\sin\alpha = \frac{82\sin 20°}{51}$$

$$\sin\alpha \approx 0.5499$$

$$\alpha = \sin^{-1}(0.5499)$$

$$\alpha = 33.4°$$

or $\alpha = 180° - 33.4° = 146.6°$

When $\alpha = 33.4°$, the distance is the further of the two. Let d_1 represent this distance.

$\beta = 180° - (33.4° + 20°) = 126.6°$

$$\frac{\sin 126.6°}{d_1} = \frac{\sin 20°}{51}$$

$$d_1 \sin 20° = 51 \sin 126.6°$$

$$d_1 = \frac{51 \sin 126.6°}{\sin 20°} \approx 119.7 \text{ million miles}$$

$$d_1 \approx 119.7 \text{ million miles}$$

47. (continued)

When $\alpha = 146.6°$, the distance is the closer of the two. Let d_2 represent this distance.

$\beta = 180° - (146.6° + 20°) = 13.4°$

$$\frac{\sin 13.4°}{d_2} = \frac{\sin 20°}{51}$$

$$d_2 \sin 20° = 51 \sin 13.4°$$

$$d_2 = \frac{51 \sin 13.4°}{\sin 20°} \approx 34.6 \text{ million miles}$$

$$d_2 \approx 34.6 \text{ million miles}$$

49. a. $$\frac{\sin 35°}{8} = \frac{\sin B}{15}$$

$$8 \sin B = 15 \sin 35°$$

$$\sin B = \frac{15 \sin 35°}{8} \approx 1.08$$

No, a radar with a range of 8.0 miles will not detect the ship.

b. $$\frac{\sin 35°}{12} = \frac{\sin B}{15}$$

$$12 \sin B = 15 \sin 35°$$

$$\sin B = \frac{15 \sin 35°}{12}$$

$$\sin B \approx 0.7170$$

$$B = \sin^{-1}(0.7170)$$

$$B \approx 45.8°$$

or $B = 180° - 4.8° = 134.2°$

The closest point of detection will be when $B = 134.2°$, in which case the third angle is $180° - (35° + 134.2°) = 10.8°$.

$$\frac{\sin 10.8°}{d} = \frac{\sin 35°}{12}$$

$$d \sin 35° = 12 \sin 10.8°$$

$$d = \frac{12 \sin 10.8°}{\sin 35°}$$

$$d \approx 3.9 \text{ mi}$$

51. Segment SR is 55 km.

$$\frac{\sin 40°}{55} = \frac{\sin \angle P}{80}$$
$$55 \sin \angle P = 80 \sin 40°$$
$$\sin \angle P = \frac{80 \sin 40°}{55}$$
$$\sin \angle P \approx 0.9350$$
$$\angle P \approx 69.2°$$
$$\angle VRP = 180° - (40° + 69.2°) = 70.8°$$
$$\angle VSR = 180° - 69.2° = 110.8°$$
$$\angle VRS = 180° - (110.8° + 40°) = 29.2°$$

Let d_1 be the distance from V to P.

$$\frac{\sin 70.8°}{d_1} = \frac{\sin 40°}{55}$$
$$d_1 \sin 40° = 55 \sin 70.8°$$
$$d_1 = \frac{55 \sin 70.8°}{\sin 40°}$$
$$d_1 \approx 80.8 \text{ km}$$

Let d_2 be the distance from V to S.

$$\frac{\sin 29.2°}{d_2} = \frac{\sin 40°}{55}$$
$$d_2 \sin 40° = 55 \sin 29.2°$$
$$d_2 = \frac{55 \sin 29.2°}{\sin 40°}$$
$$d_2 \approx 41.7 \text{ km}$$

53. Let B be the angle at the target.

a. $$\frac{\sin 55°}{180} = \frac{\sin B}{246}$$
$$180 \sin B = 246 \sin 55°$$
$$\sin B = \frac{246 \sin 55°}{180} \approx 1.1$$
No, the target will not be hit.

b. $$\frac{\sin 55°}{a} = \frac{\sin 90°}{246}$$
$$a \sin 90° = 246 \sin 55°$$
$$a = \frac{246 \sin 55°}{\sin 90°}$$
$$a \approx 201.5 \text{ ft}$$

53. c. We need to find the distance $d_2 - d_1$ in the diagram below.

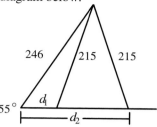

Let C be the angle at the archer.

$$\frac{\sin 55°}{215} = \frac{\sin B}{246}$$
$$215 \sin B = 246 \sin 55°$$
$$\sin B = \frac{246 \sin 55°}{215}$$
$$\sin B \approx 0.9373$$
$$B = \sin^{-1}(0.9373)$$
$$B \approx 69.6°$$
or $B = 180° - 69.6° = 110.4°$

Consider $B = 69.6°$.
$$C = 180° - (69.6° + 55°) = 55.4°$$
$$\frac{\sin 55°}{215} = \frac{\sin 55.4°}{d_2}$$
$$d_2 \sin 55° = 215 \sin 55.4°$$
$$d_2 = \frac{215 \sin 55.4°}{\sin 55°}$$
$$d_2 \approx 216 \text{ ft}$$

Consider $B = 110.4°$.
$$C = 180° - (110.4° + 55°) = 14.6°$$
$$\frac{\sin 55°}{215} = \frac{\sin 14.6°}{d_1}$$
$$d_1 \sin 55° = 215 \sin 14.6°$$
$$d_1 = \frac{215 \sin 14.6°}{\sin 55°}$$
$$d_1 \approx 66 \text{ ft}$$

$$d_2 - d_1 = 216 - 66 = 150 \text{ ft}$$
$$\frac{150 \text{ ft}}{10 \text{ ft/sec}} = 15 \text{ sec}$$
The target is within range for 15 seconds.

55. $\dfrac{\sin 26°}{8} = \dfrac{\sin A}{12}$

$8 \sin A = 12 \sin 26°$

$\sin A = \dfrac{12 \sin 26°}{8}$

$\sin A \approx 0.6576$

$A = \sin^{-1}(0.6576)$

$A \approx 41.1°$

or $A = 180° - 41.1° = 138.9°$

Two triangles are possible.

Consider $A = 41.1°$.

$C_1 = 180° - (41.1° + 26°) = 112.9°$

$\dfrac{\sin 112.9°}{c_1} = \dfrac{\sin 26°}{8}$

$c_1 \sin 26° = 8 \sin 112.9°$

$c_1 = \dfrac{8 \sin 112.9°}{\sin 26°}$

$c_1 \approx 16.8 \text{ cm}$

Angles	Sides
$A_1 \approx 41.1°$	$a = 12 \text{ cm}$
$B = 26°$	$b = 8 \text{ cm}$
$C_1 \approx 112.9°$	$c_1 \approx 16.8 \text{ cm}$

Consider $A = 138.9°$.

$C_1 = 180° - (138.9° + 26°) = 15.1°$

$\dfrac{\sin 15.1°}{c_2} = \dfrac{\sin 26°}{8}$

$c_2 \sin 26° = 8 \sin 15.1°$

$c_2 = \dfrac{8 \sin 15.1°}{\sin 26°}$

$c_2 \approx 4.8 \text{ cm}$

Angles	Sides
$A_2 \approx 138.9°$	$a = 12 \text{ cm}$
$B = 26°$	$b = 8 \text{ cm}$
$C_2 \approx 15.1°$	$c_2 \approx 4.8 \text{ cm}$

57. From the grid, $a = 9$, $c = 4$.

Consider the right triangle in the diagram as drawn. The shorter leg has length 4.

$\tan C = \dfrac{4}{9}$

$C = \tan^{-1}\left(\dfrac{4}{9}\right)$

$C \approx 24°$

Now use the Law of Sines with $a = 9$, $c = 5$, and $C = 24°$.

$\dfrac{\sin 24°}{5} = \dfrac{\sin A}{9}$

$5 \sin A = 9 \sin 24°$

$\sin A = \dfrac{9 \sin 24°}{5}$

$\sin A \approx 0.7321$

$A \approx \sin^{-1}(0.7321)$

$A \approx 47.0°$

or $A = 180° - 47.0° = 133.0°$

Consider $A = 47.0°$.

$C_1 = 180° - (47.0° + 24°) = 109.0°$

$\dfrac{\sin 109.0°}{b} = \dfrac{\sin 24°}{5}$

$b \sin 24° = 5 \sin 109.0°$

$b = \dfrac{5 \sin 109.0°}{\sin 24°}$

$b \approx 11.6$

Angles	Sides
$A_1 \approx 47.0°$	$a = 9$
$B_1 \approx 109.0°$	$b_1 \approx 11.6$
$C \approx 24°$	$c = 5$

Consider $A = 133.0°$.

$C_1 = 180° - (133.0° + 24°) = 23.0°$

$\dfrac{\sin 23.0°}{b} = \dfrac{\sin 24°}{5}$

$b \sin 24° = 5 \sin 23.0°$

$b = \dfrac{5 \sin 23.0°}{\sin 24°}$

$b \approx 4.8$

Angles	Sides
$A_2 \approx 133.0°$	$a = 9$
$B_2 \approx 23.0°$	$b_2 \approx 4.8$
$C \approx 24°$	$c = 5$

59. $\angle B = 180° - (32° + 53°) = 95°$

$$\frac{\sin 95°}{42} = \frac{\sin 53°}{a}$$
$$a\sin 95° = 42\sin 53°$$
$$a = \frac{42\sin 53°}{\sin 95°}$$
$$a \approx 33.7 \text{ ft}$$

$$\frac{\sin 95°}{42} = \frac{\sin 32°}{c}$$
$$c\sin 95° = 42\sin 32°$$
$$c = \frac{42\sin 32°}{\sin 95°}$$
$$c \approx 22.3 \text{ ft}$$

61. The third angle is $180° - (96° + 58°) = 26°$.

Rhymes to Tarryson:
$$\frac{\sin 26°}{27.2} = \frac{\sin 96°}{\overline{RT}}$$
$$\overline{RT}\sin 26° = 27.2\sin 96°$$
$$\overline{RT} = \frac{27.2\sin 96°}{\sin 26°}$$
$$\overline{RT} \approx 61.7 \text{ km}$$

Sexton to Tarryson:
$$\frac{\sin 26°}{27.2} = \frac{\sin 58°}{\overline{ST}}$$
$$\overline{ST}\sin 26° = 27.2\sin 58°$$
$$\overline{ST} = \frac{27.2\sin 58°}{\sin 26°}$$
$$\overline{ST} \approx 52.6 \text{ km}$$

63. The third angle is $180° - (39° + 58°) = 83°$.

The shortest side is across from the 39° angle, so let d be that distance.
$$\frac{\sin 83°}{5} = \frac{\sin 39°}{d}$$
$$d\sin 83° = 5\sin 39°$$
$$d = \frac{5\sin 39°}{\sin 83°}$$
$$d \approx 3.2 \text{ mi}$$

65. The third angle is $180° - (70° + 62°) = 48°$.

In the diagram provided, we need to find h.

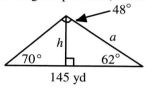

First, find a.
$$\frac{\sin 48°}{145} = \frac{\sin 70°}{a}$$
$$a\sin 48° = 145\sin 70°$$
$$a = \frac{145\sin 70°}{\sin 48°}$$
$$a \approx 183.35 \text{ yd}$$

Now, use the triangle on the right to find h.
$$\sin 62° = \frac{h}{183.35}$$
$$h = 183.35\sin 62°$$
$$h \approx 161.9 \text{ yd}$$

67. Let a be the side across from the 63° angle and d be the base of the triangle.
$$\frac{\sin 27°}{5} = \frac{\sin 63°}{a}$$
$$a\sin 27° = 5\sin 63°$$
$$a = \frac{5\sin 63°}{\sin 27°}$$
$$a \approx 9.8 \text{ cm}$$

$$\frac{\sin 27°}{5} = \frac{\sin 90°}{d}$$
$$d\sin 27° = 5\sin 90°$$
$$d = \frac{5\sin 90°}{\sin 27°}$$
$$d \approx 11 \text{ cm}$$

The diameter of the circle is 11 cm, the base of the triangle. It is a right triangle.

69.

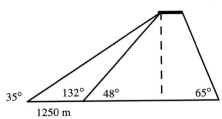

1250 m

a. The small angle at the top of the left-hand triangle is $180° - (35° + 132°) = 13°$.

Let s_w be the slant height of the west side.

$$\frac{\sin 13°}{1250} = \frac{\sin 35°}{s_w}$$

$$s_w \sin 13° = 1250 \sin 35°$$

$$s_w = \frac{1250 \sin 35°}{\sin 13°}$$

$$s_w \approx 3187 \text{ m}$$

The slant height of the west side of the mountain is about 3187 meters.

b. Let s_e be the slant height of the east side of the mountain.

$$\frac{\sin 65°}{3187} = \frac{\sin 48°}{s_e}$$

$$s_e \sin 65° = 3187 \sin 48°$$

$$s_e = \frac{3187 \sin 48°}{\sin 65°}$$

$$s_e \approx 2613 \text{ m}$$

The slant height of the east side of the mountain is about 2613 meters.

c. Let h be the vertical height (dashed line).

$$\sin 48° = \frac{h}{3187}$$

$$h = 3187 \sin 48°$$

$$h \approx 2368 \text{ m}$$

The mountain is 2368 meters high.

71. This is a 30-60-90 triangle. The base of the triangle is $10.2\sqrt{3}$ cm, and the hypotenuse is 20.4 cm. Sine is defined as opposite over hypotenuse, so we have the following.

$$\sin 60° = \frac{10.2\sqrt{3}}{20.4} \text{ and } \sin 30° = \frac{10.2}{20.4},$$

$$\frac{\sin 60°}{\sin 30°} = \frac{\frac{10.2\sqrt{3}}{20.4}}{\frac{10.2}{20.4}} = \sqrt{3}$$

We know that $\sin 45° = \dfrac{1}{\sqrt{2}}$ and $\sin 90° = 1$, so

$$\frac{\sin 90°}{\sin 45°} = \frac{1}{\frac{1}{\sqrt{2}}} = \sqrt{2}$$

71. (continued)

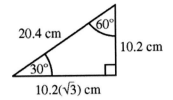

20.4 cm   60°

10.2 cm

30°

10.2(√3) cm

73. $$\frac{a+b}{a-b} = \frac{\tan\left[\frac{1}{2}(A+B)\right]}{\tan\left[\frac{1}{2}(A-B)\right]}$$

Substitute $a = 45$ cm, $A = 19°$, $B = 31°$.

$$\frac{45+b}{45-b} = \frac{\tan\left[\frac{1}{2}(19+31)\right]}{\tan\left[\frac{1}{2}(19-31)\right]}$$

$$= \frac{\tan 25}{\tan(-6)} \approx -4.44$$

Solve for b.

$$\frac{45+b}{45-b} = -4.4366$$

$$45+b = -4.4366(45-b)$$

$$45+b = -199.647 + 4.4366b$$

$$-3.4366b = -244.647$$

$$b \approx 71.2 \text{ cm}$$

Note that $C = 180° - (19° + 31°) = 130°$.

Substitute $a = 45$ cm, $A = 19°$, $C = 130°$.

$$\frac{45+c}{45-c} = \frac{\tan\left[\frac{1}{2}(19° + 130°)\right]}{\tan\left[\frac{1}{2}(19° - 130°)\right]}$$

$$= \frac{\tan 74.5°}{\tan(-55.5°)} \approx -2.48$$

Solve for c.

$$\frac{45+c}{45-c} = -2.4783$$

$$45+c = -2.4783(45-c)$$

$$45+c = -111.5235 + 2.4783c$$

$$-1.4783c = -156.5235$$

$$c \approx 105.9 \text{ cm}$$

75. A diagram of the first sighting is given.

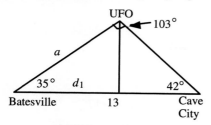

We can find side a using the Law of Sines, then use it to find d_1, which is the distance from the UFO's initial location to Batesville.

$$\frac{\sin 103°}{13} = \frac{\sin 42°}{a}$$
$$a\sin 103° = 13\sin 42°$$
$$a = \frac{13\sin 42°}{\sin 103°}$$
$$a \approx 8.9275 \text{ mi}$$

$$\cos 35° = \frac{d_1}{8.9275}$$
$$d_1 = 8.9275\cos 35°$$
$$d_1 \approx 7.3130 \text{ mi}$$

It will be helpful later to find the height:

$$\sin 35° = \frac{h}{8.9275}$$
$$h = 8.9275\sin 35°$$
$$h \approx 5.1206$$

Second sighting:
$$\tan 24° = \frac{5.1206}{d_2}$$
$$d_2 = \frac{5.1206}{\tan 24°}$$
$$d_2 \approx 11.5011 \text{ mi}$$

$11.5011 - 7.3130 = 4.1881 \text{ mi}$
$$\frac{4.1881 \text{ mi}}{1.2 \text{ sec}} \cdot \frac{3600 \text{ sec}}{1 \text{ hr}} \approx 12,564 \text{ mph}$$
The UFO traveled at an average speed of approximately 12,564 mph.

77. $\tan^2 x - \sin^2 x = \dfrac{\sin^2 x}{\cos^2 x} - \sin^2 x$

$$= \frac{\sin^2 x}{\cos^2 x} - \frac{\sin^2 x\cos^2 x}{\cos^2 x}$$
$$= \frac{\sin^2 x - \sin^2 x\cos^2 x}{\cos^2 x}$$
$$= \frac{\sin^2 x\left(1 - \cos^2 x\right)}{\cos^2 x}$$
$$= \frac{\sin^2 x\sin^2 x}{\cos^2 x}$$
$$= \sin^2 x\frac{\sin^2 x}{\cos^2 x}$$
$$= \tan^2 x\sin^2 x$$

79. $\quad 2\sin^2 x - 7\sin x = -3$
$$2\sin^2 x - 7\sin x + 3 = 0$$
$$\left(2\sin x - 1\right)\left(\sin x - 3\right) = 0$$

$2\sin x - 1 = 0 \qquad$ or $\qquad \sin x - 3 = 0$

$\sin x = \dfrac{1}{2} \qquad\qquad\qquad \sin x = 3$

$x = \sin^{-1}\left(\dfrac{1}{2}\right) \qquad\qquad x = \sin^{-1}(3)$

$x = \dfrac{\pi}{6} \qquad\qquad\qquad$ no solution

QI: $x = \dfrac{\pi}{6}$; QII: $x = \pi - \dfrac{\pi}{6} = \dfrac{5\pi}{6}$

81. Period: $P = 2\pi$; $B = \dfrac{\pi}{2\pi} = \dfrac{1}{2}$

HS: π units right; VS: None;

Substitute the point $\left(\dfrac{3\pi}{2}, 2\right)$ and solve for A.

$$2 = A\tan\left[\frac{1}{2}\left(\frac{3\pi}{2} - \pi\right)\right]$$
$$2 = A\tan\left[\frac{3\pi}{4} - \frac{\pi}{2}\right]$$
$$2 = A\tan\left(\frac{\pi}{4}\right)$$
$$2 = A$$
$$y = 2\tan\left(\frac{1}{2}x - \frac{\pi}{2}\right)$$

Technology Highlight

Displays *PLEASE ENTER*

Displays *THE LONGEST*

Displays SIDE AS SIDE *A*

Pauses execution, allows user to view results until
ENTER is pressed

Clears the home screen, places cursor in upper left
position

Pauses execution, allows user to view results until
ENTER is pressed

Computes the value of $\angle B$ and stores it in
memory location E

Displays *ANGLE B IS*

Rounds the value stored in E to one decimal place,
restores it in E

Displays the value now stored in memory location
E

Pauses execution, allows user to view results until
ENTER is pressed

Computes the value of the remaining angle C

Displays *ANGLE C IS*

Rounds the value stored in F to one decimal place,
restores it in F

Displays the value now stored in memory location
F

7.2 Exercises

1. cosines

3. Pythagorean

5. Law of Cosines:
    $b = 37$ m, $c = 52$ m, $A = 17°$
    $$a^2 = 37^2 + 52^2 - 2(37)(52)\cos 17°$$
    $$a^2 = 1369 + 2704 - 3848\cos 17°$$
    $$a = 393.1$$
    $$a \approx 19.8 \text{ m}$$

    $a = 19.8$ m, $b = 37$ m, $c = 52$ m
    $$52^2 = 19.8^2 + 37^2 - 2(19.8)(37)\cos C$$
    $$2704 = 392.04 + 1369 - 1465.2\cos C$$
    $$942.96 = -1465.2\cos C$$
    $$\cos C = -\frac{942.96}{1465.2}$$
    $$C = \cos^{-1}\left(-\frac{942.96}{1465.2}\right)$$
    $$C \approx 130°$$
    $$B = 180° - (130° + 17°) = 33°.$$

    Law of Sines:
    $a = 19.8$ m, $b = 37$ m, $A = 17°$
    $$\frac{\sin B}{37} = \frac{\sin 17°}{19.8}$$
    $$19.8\sin B = 37\sin 17°$$
    $$\sin B = \frac{37\sin 17°}{19.8}$$
    $$B = \sin^{-1}\left(\frac{37\sin 17°}{19.8}\right)$$
    $$B \approx 33.1°$$
    $$C = 180° - (33.1° + 17°) = 129.9°.$$

    The second method, using the Law of Sines,
    is more efficient.

7. Yes

9. No; there will be two unknowns in any of the
    three forms.

11. Yes

13. $a^2 = b^2 + c^2 - 2bc \cos A$
$52.4^2 = 50^2 + 26.6^2 - 2(50)(26.6)\cos 80°$
$2745.76 = 2500 + 707.56 - 2660 \cos 80°$
$2745.76 \approx 2745.66$
$b^2 = a^2 + c^2 - 2ac \cos B$
$50^2 = 52.4^2 + 26.6^2 - 2(52.4)(26.6)\cos 70°$
$2500 = 2745.76 + 707.56 - 2787.68 \cos 70°$
$2500 \approx 2499.88$

$c^2 = a^2 + b^2 - 2ab \cos C$
$26.6^2 = 50^2 + 52.4^2 - 2(50)(52.4)\cos 30°$
$707.56 = 2500 + 2745.76 - 5240 \cos 30°$
$707.56 \approx 707.79$
With some rounding, all result in equality.

15. $4^2 = 5^2 + 6^2 - 2(5)(6)\cos B$
$16 = 25 + 36 - 60 \cos B$
$-45 = -60 \cos B$
$\cos B = \dfrac{45}{60}$
$B = \cos^{-1}\left(\dfrac{3}{4}\right)$
$B \approx 41.4°$

17. $a^2 = 9^2 + 7^2 - 2(9)(7)\cos 52°$
$a^2 = 81 + 49 - 126 \cos 52°$
$a^2 \approx 52.43$
$a \approx 7.24$

19. $10^2 = 12^2 + 15^2 - 2(12)(15)\cos A$
$100 = 144 + 225 - 360 \cos A$
$-269 = -360 \cos A$
$\cos A = \dfrac{-269}{-360}$
$A = \cos^{-1}\left(\dfrac{269}{360}\right)$
$A \approx 41.6°$

21. $c^2 = 75^2 + 32^2 - 2(75)(32)\cos 38°$
$c^2 = 5625 + 1024 - 4800 \cos 38°$
$c^2 \approx 2866.5$
$c \approx 53.5$ cm
$\dfrac{\sin 38°}{53.5} = \dfrac{\sin B}{32}$
$53.5 \sin B = 32 \sin 38°$
$\sin B = \dfrac{32 \sin 38°}{53.5}$
$B = \sin^{-1}\left(\dfrac{32 \sin 38°}{53.5}\right)$
$B \approx 21.6°$
$A = 180° - (21.6° + 38°) = 120.4°$

23. $b^2 = 12.9^2 + 25.8^2 - 2(12.9)(25.8)\cos 30°$
$b^2 = 166.41 + 665.64 - 665.64 \cos 30°$
$b^2 \approx 255.59$
$b \approx 16.0$ mi

$\dfrac{\sin 30°}{16.0} = \dfrac{\sin A}{12.9}$
$16.0 \sin A = 12.9 \sin 30°$
$\sin A = \dfrac{12.9 \sin 30°}{16.0}$
$A = \sin^{-1}\left(\dfrac{12.9 \sin 30°}{16.0}\right)$
$A \approx 23.8°$

$C = 180° - (23.8° + 30°) = 126.2°$

25. $c^2 = 538^2 + 465^2 - 2(538)(465)\cos 29°$
$c^2 = 289,444 + 216,225 - 500,340 \cos 29°$
$c^2 \approx 68,061.8$
$c \approx 260.9$ mm

$\dfrac{\sin 29°}{260.9} = \dfrac{\sin B}{465}$
$260.9 \sin B = 465 \sin 29°$
$\sin B = \dfrac{465 \sin 29°}{260.9}$
$B = \sin^{-1}\left(\dfrac{465 \sin 29°}{260.9}\right)$
$B \approx 59.8°$

$A = 180° - (59.8° + 29°) = 91.2°$

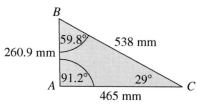

27. $a^2 = b^2 + c^2 - 2bc \cos A$
$\left(15\sqrt{3}\right)^2 = \left(6\sqrt{3}\right)^2 + \left(10\sqrt{3}\right)^2 - 2\left(6\sqrt{3}\right)\left(10\sqrt{3}\right)\cos A$
$675 = 108 + 300 - 360 \cos A$
$267 = -360 \cos A$
$\cos A = \dfrac{267}{-360}$
$A = \cos^{-1}\left(-\dfrac{89}{120}\right)$
$A \approx 137.9°$

27. (continued)

$$\frac{\sin 137.9°}{15\sqrt{3}} = \frac{\sin B}{6\sqrt{3}}$$

$$15\sqrt{3}\sin B = 6\sqrt{3}\sin 137.9°$$

$$\sin B = \frac{6\sqrt{3}\sin 137.9°}{15\sqrt{3}}$$

$$B = \sin^{-1}\left(\frac{6\sqrt{3}\sin 137.9°}{15\sqrt{3}}\right)$$

$$B \approx 15.6°$$

$$C = 180° - (15.6° + 137.9°) = 26.5°$$

29.

$$a^2 = b^2 + c^2 - 2bc\cos A$$

$$32.8^2 = 24.9^2 + 12.4^2 - 2(24.9)(12.4)\cos A$$

$$1075.84 = 620.01 + 153.76 - 617.52\cos A$$

$$302.07 = -617.52\cos A$$

$$\cos A = \frac{302.07}{-617.52}$$

$$A = \cos^{-1}\left(-\frac{302.07}{617.52}\right)$$

$$A \approx 119.3°$$

$$\frac{\sin 119.3°}{32.8} = \frac{\sin B}{24.9}$$

$$32.8\sin B = 24.9\sin 119.3°$$

$$\sin B = \frac{24.9\sin 119.3°}{32.8}$$

$$B = \sin^{-1}\left(\frac{24.9\sin 119.3°}{32.8}\right)$$

$$B \approx 41.5°$$

$$C = 180° - (41.5° + 119.3°) = 19.2°$$

31.

$$a^2 = b^2 + c^2 - 2bc\cos A$$

$$\left(4.1\times10^{25}\right)^2 = \left(2.3\times10^{25}\right)^2 + \left(2.9\times10^{25}\right)^2$$
$$-2\left(2.3\times10^{25}\right)\left(2.9\times10^{25}\right)\cos A$$

$$1.7\times10^{51} = 1.4\times10^{51} - 1.3\times10^{51}\cos A$$

$$3.0\times10^{50} = -1.3\times10^{51}\cos A$$

$$\cos A = \frac{3.0\times10^{50}}{-1.3\times10^{51}}$$

$$A = \cos^{-1}\left(-\frac{3.0\times10^{50}}{1.3\times10^{51}}\right)$$

$$A \approx 103.3°$$

$$\frac{\sin 103.3°}{4.1\times10^{25}} = \frac{\sin C}{2.9\times10^{25}}$$

$$4.1\times10^{25}\sin C = 2.9\times10^{25}\sin 103.3°$$

$$\sin C = \frac{2.9\times10^{25}\sin 103.3°}{4.1\times10^{25}}$$

$$C = \sin^{-1}\left(\frac{2.9\times10^{25}\sin 103.3°}{4.1\times10^{25}}\right)$$

$$C \approx 43.5°$$

31. (continued)

$$B = 180° - (43.5° + 103.3°) = 33.2°$$

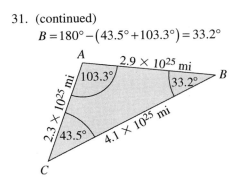

33.

$$a^2 = b^2 + c^2 - 2bc\cos A$$

$$\left(12\sqrt{3}\right)^2 = 12.9^2 + 9.2^2 - 2(12.9)(9.2)\cos A$$

$$432 = 166.41 + 84.64 - 237.36\cos A$$

$$180.95 = -237.36\cos A$$

$$\cos A = \frac{180.95}{-237.36}$$

$$A = \cos^{-1}\left(-\frac{180.95}{237.36}\right)$$

$$A \approx 139.7°$$

$$\frac{\sin 139.7°}{12\sqrt{3}} = \frac{\sin B}{12.9}$$

$$12\sqrt{3}\sin B = 12.9\sin 139.7°$$

$$\sin B = \frac{12.9\sin 139.7°}{12\sqrt{3}}$$

$$B = \sin^{-1}\left(\frac{12.9\sin 139.7°}{12\sqrt{3}}\right)$$

$$B \approx 23.7°$$

$$C = 180° - (23.7° + 139.7°) = 16.6°$$

35.

$$a^2 = b^2 + c^2 - 2bc\cos A$$

$$2bc\cos A = b^2 + c^2 - a^2$$

$$\cos A = \frac{b^2 + c^2 - a^2}{2bc}$$

Adapt the new formula to the given triangle, and solve for angle C first.

$$\cos C = \frac{a^2 + b^2 - c^2}{2ab}$$

$$\cos C = \frac{39^2 + 37^2 - 52^2}{2(39)(37)}$$

$$\cos C = \frac{186}{2886}$$

$$C = \cos^{-1}\left(\frac{31}{481}\right)$$

$$C \approx 86.3°$$

37. $m^2 = 1435^2 + 692^2 - 2(1435)(692)\cos 99°$

$$m^2 \approx 2{,}848{,}774$$

$$m \approx 1688 \text{ mi}$$

39. $d^2 = 1.8^2 + 2.6^2 - 2(1.8)(2.6)\cos 51°$

$d^2 = 3.24 + 6.76 - 9.36\cos 51°$

$d^2 \approx 10 - 9.36\cos 51°$

$d \approx \sqrt{10 - 9.36\cos 51°}$

$d \approx 2.0272$ mi

$d \approx 2.0272$ mi $\cdot 5280$ ft/mi $\approx 10,703.6$ ft

The runway cannot be constructed.

41. $198^2 = 354^2 + 423^2 - 2(354)(423)\cos P$

$39,204 = 125,316 + 178,929 - 299,484\cos P$

$-265,041 = -299,484\cos P$

$\cos P = \dfrac{-265,041}{-299,484}$

$P = \cos^{-1}\left(\dfrac{265,041}{299,484}\right)$

$P \approx 27.7°$

The heading is 27.7° north of west, or a heading of 297.7°.

43. After 5 hours, the distances are $5 \cdot 450 = 2250$ miles, and $5 \cdot 425 = 2125$ miles.

The angle between paths is $270° - 225° = 45°$.

$d^2 = 2250^2 + 2125^2 - 2(2250)(2125)\cos 45°$

$d^2 \approx 2,816,416.4$

$d \approx 1678.2$ mi

45. Call the point at the bottom left corner of the board D. Triangle DAB is a 45-45-90 triangle with legs of length 4 cm, so side AB is $4\sqrt{2}$ cm.

Use Pythagorean Theorem on triangle DBC.

$BC = \sqrt{10^2 + 4^2} = \sqrt{116} = 2\sqrt{29}$

Side AC is 6, so the perimeter is

$P = 6 + 4\sqrt{2} + 2\sqrt{29} \approx 22.4$ cm.

Again we use right triangle DBC.

$\tan C = \dfrac{4}{10}$

$C = \tan^{-1}(0.4)$

$C \approx 21.8°$

We apply the Law of Sines to solve for B.

$\dfrac{\sin B}{6} = \dfrac{\sin 21.8°}{4\sqrt{2}}$

$4\sqrt{2}\sin B = 6\sin 21.8°$

$\sin B = \dfrac{6\sin 21.8°}{4\sqrt{2}}$

$B = \sin^{-1}\left(\dfrac{6\sin 21.8°}{4\sqrt{2}}\right)$

$B \approx 23.2°$

$A = 180° - (23.2° + 21.8°) = 135°$

47. $20^2 = 12^2 + 9^2 - 2(12)(9)\cos C$

$175 = -216\cos C$

$\cos C = \dfrac{175}{-216}$

$C = \cos^{-1}\left(-\dfrac{175}{216}\right)$

$C \approx 144.1°$

$\dfrac{\sin 144.1°}{20} = \dfrac{\sin B}{9}$

$20\sin B = 9\sin 144.1°$

$\sin B = \dfrac{9\sin 144.1°}{20}$

$B = \sin^{-1}\left(\dfrac{9\sin 144.1°}{20}\right)$

$B \approx 15.3°$

$A \approx 180° - (15.3° + 144.1°) = 20.6°$

49. A regular pentagon can be made from five triangles, each with an angle of $\dfrac{360°}{5} = 72°$.

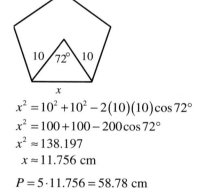

$x^2 = 10^2 + 10^2 - 2(10)(10)\cos 72°$

$x^2 = 100 + 100 - 200\cos 72°$

$x^2 \approx 138.197$

$x \approx 11.756$ cm

$P = 5 \cdot 11.756 = 58.78$ cm

51. Consider each side of the triangle as the hypotenuse of a right triangle. We compute:

$\overline{BC} = \sqrt{12^2 + 5^2} = 13$

$\overline{AC} = \sqrt{3^2 + 4^2} = 5$

$\overline{AB} = \sqrt{9^2 + 1^2} = \sqrt{82}$

$13^2 = 5^2 + \sqrt{82}^2 - 2(5)(\sqrt{82})\cos A$

$62 = -10\sqrt{82}\cos A$

$\cos A = \dfrac{62}{-10\sqrt{82}}$

$A = \cos^{-1}\left(-\dfrac{31}{5\sqrt{82}}\right)$

$A \approx 133.2°$

51. (continued)

$$\frac{\sin 133.2°}{13} = \frac{\sin B}{5}$$

$$13 \sin B = 5 \sin 133.2°$$

$$\sin B = \frac{5 \sin 133.2°}{13}$$

$$B = \sin^{-1}\left(\frac{5 \sin 133.2°}{13}\right)$$

$$B \approx 16.3°$$

$$C = 180° - (16.3° + 133.2°) = 30.5°$$

53. $\sqrt{20^2 + 30^2} = \sqrt{1300} \approx 36.06$

The length of the diagonal is $\sqrt{1300}$ ft.

$$\alpha = \tan^{-1}\left(\frac{20}{30}\right) \approx 33.7°$$

$$A = \frac{1}{2} bc \sin \alpha$$

$$A = \frac{1}{2}(15)\left(\sqrt{1300}\right)\sin 33.7°$$

$$A \approx 150 \text{ ft}^2$$

55. $180° - (42° + 65°) = 73°$

$$A = \frac{c^2 \sin A \sin B}{2 \sin C}$$

$$A = \frac{299^2 \sin 42° \sin 65°}{2 \sin 73°}$$

$$A \approx 28,346.7 \text{ ft}^2$$

a. $\dfrac{28,346.7}{43,560} \approx 0.65$ or 65%

b. $3,000,000(0.65) = \$1,950,000$

57. $s = \dfrac{a+b+c}{2}$

$$s = \frac{1289 + 1063 + 922}{2}$$

$$s = 1637 \text{ km}$$

$$A = \sqrt{s(s-a)(s-b)(s-c)}$$

$$A = \sqrt{1637(1637-1289)(1637-1063)(1637-922)}$$

$$A = \sqrt{1637(348)(574)(715)}$$

$$A \approx 483,529 \text{ km}^2$$

59. The sum of the two smaller sides is 889, which is less than the longer one.
$387 + 502 = 889 < 902$

61. $53.9 = 78 \cos 25° + 37 \cos 117° \approx 53.9$

We have the following equations.

$$a^2 = b^2 + c^2 - 2bc \cos A$$
$$b^2 = a^2 + c^2 - 2ac \cos B$$

Substitute the right side of the first equation in for a^2 in the second equation.

$$b^2 = \left(b^2 + c^2 - 2bc \cos A\right) + c^2 - 2ac \cos B$$

$$b^2 = b^2 + 2c^2 - 2bc \cos A - 2ac \cos B$$

$$0 = 2c^2 - 2bc \cos A - 2ac \cos B$$

$$2c^2 = 2bc \cos A + 2ac \cos B$$

Divide both sides of the equation by $2c$.

$$c = b \cos A + a \cos B$$

63. $-3 \sec \theta + 7\sqrt{3} = 5\sqrt{3}$

$$-3 \sec \theta = -2\sqrt{3}$$

$$\sec \theta = \frac{2\sqrt{3}}{3}$$

$$\cos \theta = \frac{3}{2\sqrt{3}}$$

$$\cos \theta = \frac{\sqrt{3}}{2}$$

$$\theta = \frac{\pi}{6}$$

65.
$$\sin^2 x + \cos^2 x = 1$$

$$\frac{\sin^2 x}{\cos^2 x} + \frac{\cos^2 x}{\cos^2 x} = \frac{1}{\cos^2 x}$$

$$\tan^2 x + 1 = \sec^2 x$$

$$\sin^2 x + \cos^2 x = 1$$

$$\frac{\sin^2 x}{\sin^2 x} + \frac{\cos^2 x}{\sin^2 x} = \frac{1}{\sin^2 x}$$

$$1 + \cot^2 x = \csc^2 x$$

67. $\sin 75° = \sin(45° + 30°)$

$$= \sin 45° \cos 30° + \cos 45° \sin 30°$$

$$= \left(\frac{\sqrt{2}}{2}\right)\left(\frac{1}{2}\right) + \left(\frac{\sqrt{2}}{2}\right)\left(\frac{\sqrt{3}}{2}\right)$$

$$= \frac{\sqrt{2}}{4} + \frac{\sqrt{6}}{4}$$

$$= \frac{\sqrt{6} + \sqrt{2}}{4}$$

Mid-Chapter Check

1. $\dfrac{\sin A}{a} = \dfrac{\sin B}{b}$

   $a\sin B = b\sin A$

   $\sin B = \dfrac{b\sin A}{a}$

3. $a^2 = b^2 + c^2 - 2bc\cos A$

   $a^2 = 250^2 + 207^2 - 2(250)(207)\cos 31°$

   $a^2 = 62,500 + 42,849 - 103,500\cos 31°$

   $a^2 \approx 16,632.18$

   $a \approx 129$ m

   $\dfrac{\sin 31}{129} = \dfrac{\sin B}{250}$

   $129\sin B = 250\sin 31°$

   $\sin B = \dfrac{250\sin 31°}{129}$

   $B = \sin^{-1}\left(\dfrac{250\sin 31°}{129}\right)$

   $B \approx 86.5°$

   $C = 180° - (86.5° + 31°)) = 62.5°$

5. $\dfrac{\sin 44°}{2.1} = \dfrac{\sin C}{2.8}$

   $2.1\sin C = 2.8\sin 44°$

   $\sin C = \dfrac{2.8\sin 44°}{2.1}$

   $C = \sin^{-1}\left(\dfrac{2.8\sin 44°}{2.1}\right)$

   $C \approx 67.9°$

   or $C = 180° - 67.9° = 112.1°$

   Consider $C = 67.9°$.

   $B = 180° - (67.9° + 44°) = 68.1°$

   $\dfrac{\sin 44°}{2.1} = \dfrac{\sin 68.1°}{b}$

   $b\sin 44° = 2.1\sin 68.1°$

   $b = \dfrac{2.1\sin 68.1°}{\sin 44°}$

   $b \approx 2.8$ km

   Consider $C = 112.1°$.

   $B = 180° - (112.1° + 44°) = 23.9°$

   $\dfrac{\sin 44°}{2.1} = \dfrac{\sin 23.9°}{b}$

   $b\sin 44° = 2.1\sin 23.9°$

   $b = \dfrac{2.1\sin 23.9°}{\sin 44°}$

   $b \approx 1.2$ km

7. $\dfrac{75}{\sin 25°} = \dfrac{h}{\sin 20°}$

   $h\sin 25° = 75\sin 20°$

   $h = \dfrac{75\sin 20°}{\sin 25°}$

   $h \approx 60.7$ ft

9. Adding the appropriate radii to get lengths.

   $a = 4 + 12 = 16$ cm

   $b = 9 + 12 = 21$ cm

   $c = 9 + 4 = 13$ cm

   $21^2 = 16^2 + 13^2 - 2(16)(13)\cos\beta$

   $441 = 256 + 169 - 416\cos\beta$

   $16 = -416\cos\beta$

   $\cos\beta = \dfrac{16}{-416}$

   $\beta = \cos^{-1}\left(-\dfrac{1}{26}\right)$

   $\beta \approx 92.2°$

   $\dfrac{\sin 92.2°}{21} = \dfrac{\sin\alpha}{16}$

   $21\sin\alpha = 16\sin 92.2°$

   $\sin\alpha = \dfrac{16\sin 92.2°}{21}$

   $\alpha = \sin^{-1}\left(\dfrac{16\sin 92.2°}{21}\right)$

   $\alpha \approx 49.6°$

   $\gamma = 180° - (49.6° + 92.2°) = 38.2°$

Reinforcing Basic Concepts

Exercise 1:

   $\dfrac{\sin 35°}{11.6} = \dfrac{\sin B}{20}$

   $11.6\sin B = 20\sin 35°$

   $\sin B = \dfrac{20\sin 35°}{11.6}$

   $B = \sin^{-1}\left(\dfrac{20\sin 35°}{11.6}\right)$

   $B \approx 81.5°$

   $C \approx 180° - (81.5° + 35°) = 63.5°$

Angles	Sides
$A = 35°$	$a = 11.6$ cm
$B \approx 81.5°$	$b = 20$ cm
$C \approx 63.5°$	$c = 18$ cm

The measurements are very close.

7.3 Exercises

1.   scalar

3.   directed line

5.   Answers will vary.

7.
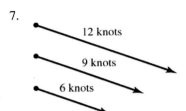

9.
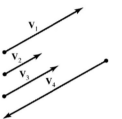

11.
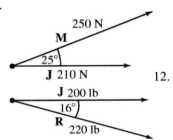

12.

13.
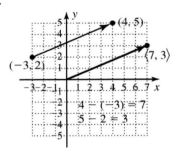

15.
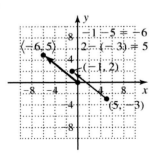

17. Terminal point: $(-2+7, -3+2) = (5, -1)$

$$|\mathbf{v}| = \sqrt{7^2 + 2^2} = \sqrt{53}$$

19. Terminal point: $(2+(-3), 6+(-5)) = (-1, 1)$

$$|\mathbf{v}| = \sqrt{(-3)^2 + (-5)^2} = \sqrt{34}$$

21. a.
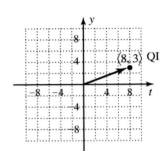

  b. $|\mathbf{v}| = \sqrt{8^2 + 3^2} = \sqrt{73}$

  c. $\theta_r = \tan^{-1}\left|\dfrac{3}{8}\right| = \tan^{-1}\dfrac{3}{8} \approx 20.6°$

23. a.
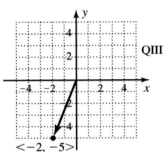

  b. $|\mathbf{v}| = \sqrt{(-2)^2 + (-5)^2} = \sqrt{29}$

  c. $\theta_r = \tan^{-1}\left|\dfrac{-5}{-2}\right| = \tan^{-1}\dfrac{5}{2} \approx 68.2°$

25. $a = 12\cos 25° \approx 10.9$
     $b = 12\sin 25° \approx 5.1$
     $\langle -10.9, 5.1 \rangle$

27. $a = 140.5\cos 41° \approx 106.0$
     $b = 140.5\sin 41° \approx 92.2$
     $\langle 106.0, -92.2 \rangle$

29. $a = 10\cos 15° \approx 9.7$
     $b = 10\sin 15° \approx 2.6$
     $\langle -9.7, -2.6 \rangle$

31. a. $\mathbf{u}+\mathbf{v}=\langle 2+(-3),3+6\rangle=\langle -1,9\rangle$

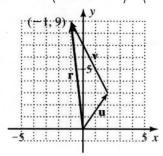

  b. $\mathbf{u}-\mathbf{v}=\langle 2-(-3),3-6\rangle=\langle 5,-3\rangle$

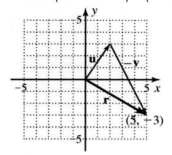

  c. $2\mathbf{u}+1.5\mathbf{v}=\langle 4,6\rangle+\langle -4.5,9\rangle=\langle -0.5,15\rangle$

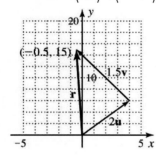

  d. $\mathbf{u}-2\mathbf{v}=\langle 2,3\rangle-\langle -6,12\rangle=\langle 8,-9\rangle$

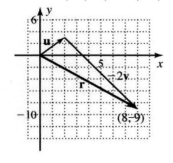

33. a. $\mathbf{u}+\mathbf{v}=\langle 7+1,-2+6\rangle=\langle 8,4\rangle$

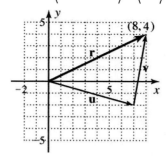

  b. $\mathbf{u}-\mathbf{v}=\langle 7-1,-2-6\rangle=\langle 6,-8\rangle$

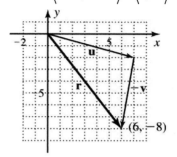

  c. $2\mathbf{u}+1.5\mathbf{v}=\langle 14,-4\rangle+\langle 1.5,9\rangle=\langle 15.5,5\rangle$

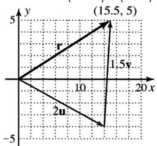

  d. $\mathbf{u}-2\mathbf{v}=\langle 7,-2\rangle-\langle 2,12\rangle=\langle 5,-14\rangle$

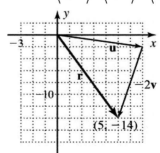

35. a. $\mathbf{u}+\mathbf{v}=\langle-4+1,2+4\rangle=\langle-3,6\rangle$

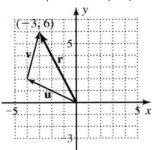

b. $\mathbf{u}-\mathbf{v}=\langle-4-1,2-4\rangle=\langle-5,-2\rangle$

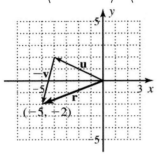

c. $2\mathbf{u}+1.5\mathbf{v}=\langle-8,4\rangle+\langle1.5,6\rangle=\langle-6.5,10\rangle$

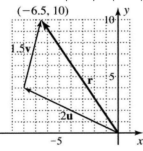

d. $\mathbf{u}-2\mathbf{v}=\langle-4,2\rangle-\langle2,8\rangle=\langle-6,-6\rangle$

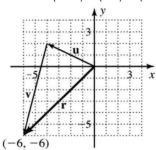

37. True

39. False

41. True

43. $\mathbf{u}+\mathbf{v}=\langle1+7,4+2\rangle=\langle8,6\rangle$

    $\mathbf{u}-\mathbf{v}=\langle1-7,4-2\rangle=\langle-6,2\rangle$

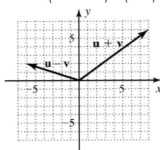

45. $\mathbf{u}+\mathbf{v}=\langle-1+(-8),-3+(-3)\rangle=\langle-9,-6\rangle$

    $\mathbf{u}-\mathbf{v}=\langle-1-(-8),-3-(-3)\rangle=\langle7,0\rangle$

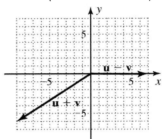

47. $\mathbf{u}+\mathbf{v}=\langle-5+2,-3+(-3)\rangle=\langle-3,-6\rangle$

    $\mathbf{u}-\mathbf{v}=\langle-5-2,-3-(-3)\rangle=\langle-7,0\rangle$

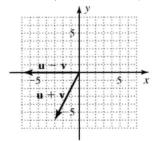

49.

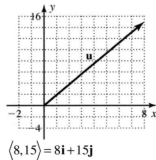

$\langle8,15\rangle=8\mathbf{i}+15\mathbf{j}$

$|\mathbf{u}|=\sqrt{8^2+15^2}=\sqrt{289}=17$

51.

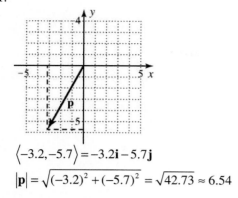

$$\langle -3.2, -5.7 \rangle = -3.2\mathbf{i} - 5.7\mathbf{j}$$
$$|\mathbf{p}| = \sqrt{(-3.2)^2 + (-5.7)^2} = \sqrt{42.73} \approx 6.54$$

53. a.

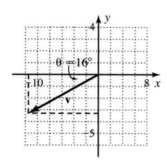

b. $a = 12\cos 16° \approx 11.5$
$b = 12\sin 16° \approx 3.3$
$\mathbf{v} = \langle -11.5, -3.3 \rangle$

c. $\mathbf{v} = -11.5\mathbf{i} - 3.3\mathbf{j}$

55. a.

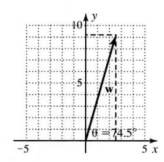

b. $a = 9.5\cos 74.5° \approx 2.5$
$b = 9.5\sin 74.5° \approx 9.2$
$\mathbf{w} = \langle 2.5, 9.2 \rangle$

c. $\mathbf{w} = 2.5\mathbf{i} + 9.2\mathbf{j}$

57. a. $\mathbf{p} = \mathbf{v}_1 + \mathbf{v}_2 = (2-4)\mathbf{i} + (-3+5)\mathbf{j} = -2\mathbf{i} + 2\mathbf{j}$
$$|\mathbf{p}| = \sqrt{(-2)^2 + 2^2} = \sqrt{8} = 2\sqrt{2}$$
$$\theta_r = \tan^{-1}\left|\frac{2}{-2}\right| = \tan^{-1}(1) = 45°$$
In QII, $\theta = 135°$

57. b. $\mathbf{q} = \mathbf{v}_1 - \mathbf{v}_2 = (2-(-4))\mathbf{i} + (-3-5)\mathbf{j} = 6\mathbf{i} - 8\mathbf{j}$
$$|\mathbf{q}| = \sqrt{6^2 + (-8)^2} = 10$$
$$\theta_r = \tan^{-1}\left|\frac{-8}{6}\right| = \tan^{-1}\left(\frac{4}{3}\right) \approx 53.1°$$
In QIV, $\theta = 306.9°$

c. $\mathbf{r} = 2\mathbf{v}_1 + 1.5\mathbf{v}_2 = 4\mathbf{i} - 6\mathbf{j} + -6\mathbf{i} + 7.5\mathbf{j}$
$$= -2\mathbf{i} + 1.5\mathbf{j}$$
$$|\mathbf{r}| = \sqrt{(-2)^2 + (1.5)^2} = \sqrt{6.25} = 2.5$$
$$\theta_r = \tan^{-1}\left|\frac{1.5}{-2}\right| = \tan^{-1}(0.75) \approx 36.9°$$
In QII, $\theta = 143.1°$

d. $\mathbf{s} = \mathbf{v}_1 - 2\mathbf{v}_2 = 2\mathbf{i} - 3\mathbf{j} - (-8\mathbf{i} + 10\mathbf{j}) = 10\mathbf{i} - 13\mathbf{j}$
$$|\mathbf{s}| = \sqrt{10^2 + (-13)^2} \approx 16.4$$
$$\theta_r = \tan^{-1}\left|\frac{-13}{10}\right| = \tan^{-1}(1.3) \approx 52.4°$$
In QIV, $\theta = 307.6°$

59. a. $\mathbf{p} = \mathbf{v}_1 + \mathbf{v}_2 = 5\sqrt{2}\mathbf{i} + 7\mathbf{j} + (-3\sqrt{2}\mathbf{i} - 5\mathbf{j})$
$$= 2\sqrt{2}\mathbf{i} + 2\mathbf{j}$$
$$|\mathbf{p}| = \sqrt{\left(2\sqrt{2}\right)^2 + 2^2} \approx 3.5$$
$$\theta = \tan^{-1}\left|\frac{2}{2\sqrt{2}}\right| = \tan^{-1}\left(\frac{\sqrt{2}}{2}\right) \approx 35.3°$$

b. $\mathbf{q} = \mathbf{v}_1 - \mathbf{v}_2 = 5\sqrt{2}\mathbf{i} + 7\mathbf{j} - (-3\sqrt{2}\mathbf{i} - 5\mathbf{j})$
$$= 8\sqrt{2}\mathbf{i} + 12\mathbf{j}$$
$$|\mathbf{q}| = \sqrt{\left(8\sqrt{2}\right)^2 + 12^2} \approx 16.5$$
$$\theta = \tan^{-1}\left|\frac{12}{8\sqrt{2}}\right| = \tan^{-1}\left(\frac{3\sqrt{2}}{4}\right) \approx 46.7°$$

c. $\mathbf{r} = 2\mathbf{v}_1 + 1.5\mathbf{v}_2$
$$= 10\sqrt{2}\mathbf{i} + 14\mathbf{j} + (-4.5\sqrt{2}\mathbf{i} - 7.5\mathbf{j})$$
$$= 5.5\sqrt{2}\mathbf{i} + 6.5\mathbf{j}$$
$$|\mathbf{r}| = \sqrt{\left(5.5\sqrt{2}\right)^2 + (6.5)^2} \approx 10.1$$
$$\theta = \tan^{-1}\left|\frac{6.5}{5.5\sqrt{2}}\right| = \tan^{-1}\left(\frac{1.3}{1.1\sqrt{2}}\right) \approx 39.9°$$

d. $\mathbf{s} = \mathbf{v}_1 - 2\mathbf{v}_2 = 5\sqrt{2}\mathbf{i} + 7\mathbf{j} - (-6\sqrt{2}\mathbf{i} - 10\mathbf{j})$
$$= 11\sqrt{2}\mathbf{i} + 17\mathbf{j}$$
$$|\mathbf{s}| = \sqrt{\left(11\sqrt{2}\right)^2 + 17^2} \approx 23.0$$
$$\theta = \tan^{-1}\left|\frac{17}{11\sqrt{2}}\right| = \tan^{-1}\left(\frac{17}{11\sqrt{2}}\right) \approx 47.5°$$

61. a. $\mathbf{p} = \mathbf{v}_1 + \mathbf{v}_2 = 12\mathbf{i} + 4\mathbf{j} + (-4\mathbf{i}) = 8\mathbf{i} + 4\mathbf{j}$

$|\mathbf{p}| = \sqrt{8^2 + 4^2} \approx 8.9$

$\theta = \tan^{-1}\left|\dfrac{4}{8}\right| = \tan^{-1}(0.5) \approx 26.6°$

   b. $\mathbf{q} = \mathbf{v}_1 - \mathbf{v}_2 = 12\mathbf{i} + 4\mathbf{j} - (-4\mathbf{i}) = 16\mathbf{i} + 4\mathbf{j}$

$|\mathbf{q}| = \sqrt{16^2 + 4^2} \approx 16.5$

$\theta = \tan^{-1}\left|\dfrac{4}{16}\right| = \tan^{-1}(0.25) \approx 14.0°$

   c. $\mathbf{r} = 2\mathbf{v}_1 + 1.5\mathbf{v}_2 = 24\mathbf{i} + 8\mathbf{j} + (-6\mathbf{i}) = 18\mathbf{i} + 8\mathbf{j}$

$|\mathbf{r}| = \sqrt{18^2 + 8^2} \approx 19.7$

$\theta = \tan^{-1}\left|\dfrac{8}{18}\right| = \tan^{-1}\left(\dfrac{4}{9}\right) \approx 24.0°$

   d. $\mathbf{s} = \mathbf{v}_1 - 2\mathbf{v}_2 = 12\mathbf{i} + 4\mathbf{j} - (-8\mathbf{i}) = 20\mathbf{i} + 4\mathbf{j}$

$|\mathbf{s}| = \sqrt{20^2 + 4^2} \approx 20.4$

$\theta = \tan^{-1}\left|\dfrac{4}{20}\right| = \tan^{-1}(0.2) \approx 11.3°$

63. $|\mathbf{u}| = \sqrt{7^2 + 24^2} = 25$

Unit vector: $\left\langle \dfrac{7}{25}, \dfrac{24}{25} \right\rangle$

$\sqrt{\left(\dfrac{7}{25}\right)^2 + \left(\dfrac{24}{25}\right)^2} = 1$

65. $|\mathbf{p}| = \sqrt{(-20)^2 + 21^2} = 29$

$\mathbf{u} = \left\langle -\dfrac{20}{29}, \dfrac{21}{29} \right\rangle$

$|\mathbf{u}| = \sqrt{\left(-\dfrac{20}{29}\right)^2 + \left(\dfrac{21}{29}\right)^2} = 1$

67. $|\mathbf{v}| = \sqrt{20^2 + (-21)^2} = 29$

$\mathbf{u} = \dfrac{20}{29}\mathbf{i} - \dfrac{21}{29}\mathbf{j}$

$|\mathbf{u}| = \sqrt{\left(\dfrac{20}{29}\right)^2 + \left(-\dfrac{21}{29}\right)^2} = 1$

69. $|\mathbf{v}| = \sqrt{3.5^2 + 12^2} = 12.5$

$\mathbf{u} = \dfrac{3.5}{12.5}\mathbf{i} + \dfrac{12}{12.5}\mathbf{j} = \dfrac{7}{25}\mathbf{i} + \dfrac{24}{25}\mathbf{j}$

$|\mathbf{u}| = \sqrt{\left(\dfrac{7}{25}\right)^2 + \left(\dfrac{24}{25}\right)^2} = 1$

71. $|\mathbf{v}_1| = \sqrt{13^2 + 3^2} = \sqrt{178}$

$\mathbf{u} = \left\langle \dfrac{13}{\sqrt{178}}, \dfrac{3}{\sqrt{178}} \right\rangle$

$|\mathbf{u}| = \sqrt{\left(\dfrac{13}{\sqrt{178}}\right)^2 + \left(\dfrac{3}{\sqrt{178}}\right)^2} = 1$

73. $|\mathbf{v}| = \sqrt{6^2 + 11^2} = \sqrt{157}$

$\mathbf{u} = \dfrac{6}{\sqrt{157}}\mathbf{i} + \dfrac{11}{\sqrt{157}}\mathbf{j}$

$|\mathbf{u}| = \sqrt{\left(\dfrac{6}{\sqrt{157}}\right)^2 + \left(\dfrac{11}{\sqrt{157}}\right)^2} = 1$

75. $|\mathbf{p}| = \sqrt{2^2 + 7^2} = \sqrt{53}$

$\cos 52° = \dfrac{|\mathbf{r}|}{\sqrt{53}}$

$|\mathbf{r}| = \sqrt{53}\cos 52° \approx 4.48$

$|\mathbf{q}| = \sqrt{10^2 + 4^2} = \sqrt{116} = 2\sqrt{29}$

$\mathbf{r} = 4.48\left\langle \dfrac{10}{2\sqrt{29}}, \dfrac{4}{2\sqrt{29}} \right\rangle$

$= 4.48\left\langle \dfrac{5}{\sqrt{29}}, \dfrac{2}{\sqrt{29}} \right\rangle$

$\approx \left\langle 4.16, 1.66 \right\rangle$

77. $|\mathbf{p}| = \sqrt{4^2 + (-6)^2} = \sqrt{52}$

$\cos 36° = \dfrac{|\mathbf{r}|}{\sqrt{52}}$

$|\mathbf{r}| = \sqrt{52}\cos 36° \approx 5.83$

$|\mathbf{q}| = \sqrt{8^2 + (-3)^2} = \sqrt{73}$

$\mathbf{r} = 5.83\left\langle \dfrac{8}{\sqrt{73}}, -\dfrac{3}{\sqrt{73}} \right\rangle$

$\approx \left\langle 5.46, -2.05 \right\rangle$

79. $|\mathbf{v}| = \sqrt{5^2 + 9^2 + 10^2} = \sqrt{206} \approx 14.4$

81. Find the vertical component of $\mathbf{W}_2$.

$a = 700 \sin 32°$

Find the angle that makes the vertical component of $\mathbf{W}_1 = 700 \sin 32°$.

$700 \sin 32° = 900 \sin \theta$

$\sin \theta = \dfrac{700 \sin 32°}{900}$

$\theta = \sin^{-1}\left(\dfrac{700 \sin 32°}{900}\right)$

$\theta \approx 24.3°$

83. Horizontal: $a = 100 \cos 37° \approx 79.9$ ft/sec
    Vertical: $b = 100 \sin 37° \approx 60.2$ ft/sec

85. The plane vector makes a 75° angle with the positive x-axis.
    The wind vector makes a 10° angle with the positive x-axis.
    Find the components of each.
    Plane: $a = 250 \cos 75° \approx 64.7$
    $\qquad b = 250 \sin 75° \approx 241.5$

    Wind: $a = 35 \cos 10° \approx 34.5$
    $\qquad b = 35 \sin 10° \approx 6.1$

    $\langle 64.7 + 34.5,\ 241.5 + 6.1 \rangle = \langle 99.2,\ 247.6 \rangle$

    $\theta = \tan^{-1}\left(\dfrac{247.6}{99.2}\right) \approx 68.2°$

    $\sqrt{99.2^2 + 247.6^2} \approx 266.7$
    The true course and speed of the plane is a heading of 68.2° at 266.7 mph.

87. $x = 85 \cos 15° \approx 82.10$
    $y = 85 \sin 15° \approx 22.00$

    $(82.10 \text{ cm},\ 22.00 \text{ cm})$

89. $1 \cdot \mathbf{u} = 1 \cdot \langle a, b \rangle = \langle 1 \cdot a, 1 \cdot b \rangle = \langle a, b \rangle = \mathbf{u}$

91. $\mathbf{u} - \mathbf{v} = \langle a, b \rangle - \langle c, d \rangle$
    $\qquad = \langle a - c,\ b - d \rangle$
    $\qquad = \langle a + (-c),\ b + (-d) \rangle$
    $\qquad = \langle a, b \rangle + \langle -c, -d \rangle$
    $\qquad = \mathbf{u} + (-\mathbf{v})$

93. $(ck)\mathbf{u} = ck\langle a, b \rangle = \langle cka, ckb \rangle = c\langle ka, kb \rangle = c(k\mathbf{u})$
    $c(k\mathbf{u}) = \langle cka, ckb \rangle = \langle kca, kcb \rangle = k\langle ca, cb \rangle = k(c\mathbf{u})$

95. $\mathbf{u} + (-\mathbf{u}) = \langle a, b \rangle + \langle -a, -b \rangle$
    $\qquad = \langle a - a,\ b - b \rangle$
    $\qquad = \langle 0, 0 \rangle$

97. $(c + k)\mathbf{u} = (c + k)\langle a, b \rangle$
    $\qquad = \langle (c + k)a, (c + k)b \rangle$
    $\qquad = \langle ca + ka,\ cb + kb \rangle$
    $\qquad = \langle ca, cb \rangle + \langle ka, kb \rangle$
    $\qquad = c\langle a, b \rangle + k\langle a, b \rangle$
    $\qquad = c\mathbf{u} + k\mathbf{u}$

99. Determine the components of each vector, then add.
    $\mathbf{p} = \langle 1, 3 \rangle;\ \ \mathbf{r} = \langle 3, 3 \rangle;\ \ \mathbf{s} = \langle 4, -1 \rangle$
    $\mathbf{t} = \langle 2, -4 \rangle;\ \ \mathbf{u} = \langle -4, -3 \rangle;\ \ \mathbf{v} = \langle -6, 2 \rangle$
    $\langle 1, 3 \rangle + \langle 3, 3 \rangle + \langle 4, -1 \rangle$
    $\quad + \langle 2, -4 \rangle + \langle -4, -3 \rangle + \langle -6, 2 \rangle$
    $= \langle 0, 0 \rangle$

    Horizontal: $1 + 3 + 4 + 2 + (-4) + (-6) = 0$

    Vertical: $3 + 3 + (-1) + (-4) + (-3) + 2 = 0$

101. Answers will vary.
     Place the first segment at $0°$.
     It will end at $(45, 0)$.

     Place the second to reach the point $(51, 39.6)$,

     and the third to reach $(80, 20)$.

     The second segment has components $\langle 6, 39.6 \rangle$

     and $\theta = \tan^{-1}\left(\dfrac{39.6}{6}\right) \approx 81.4°$.

     The third segment has components $\langle 29, -19.6 \rangle$

     and $\theta = \tan^{-1}\left(\dfrac{-19.6}{29}\right) \approx -34°$.

103. $2\sec^2\theta = \dfrac{1}{1+\sin\theta} + \dfrac{1}{1-\sin\theta}$

$\qquad = \dfrac{1-\sin\theta}{(1+\sin\theta)(1-\sin\theta)}$

$\qquad\quad + \dfrac{1+\sin\theta}{(1+\sin\theta)(1-\sin\theta)}$

$\qquad = \dfrac{1-\sin\theta+1+\sin\theta}{1-\sin^2\theta}$

$\qquad = \dfrac{2}{\cos^2\theta}$

$\qquad = 2\sec^2\theta$

105. $\sec\theta = \dfrac{13}{12} \Rightarrow x = 12,\ r = 13$

Since $\sin\theta > 0,$ y is positive.
The angle θ is in quadrant I.

$y = \sqrt{13^2-12^2} = \sqrt{25} = 5$

$\sin\theta = \dfrac{5}{13};\ \csc\theta = \dfrac{13}{5};\ \cos\theta = \dfrac{12}{13}$

$\sec\theta = \dfrac{13}{12};\ \tan\theta = \dfrac{5}{12};\ \cot\theta = \dfrac{12}{5}$

107.a. $|A| = 2;\ P = 2\pi;\ B = \dfrac{2\pi}{P} = \dfrac{2\pi}{2\pi} = 1$

Phase shift: $\dfrac{\pi}{4}$ units left

$y = 2\sin\left(x+\dfrac{\pi}{4}\right)$

b. $|A| = 2;\ P = 2\pi;\ B = \dfrac{2\pi}{P} = \dfrac{2\pi}{2\pi} = 1$

Phase shift: $\dfrac{\pi}{4}$ units right

$y = 2\cos\left(x-\dfrac{\pi}{4}\right)$

7.4 Exercises

1. equilibrium, zero

3. orthogonal

5. Answers will vary.

7. $\mathbf{F} = \mathbf{F}_1 + \mathbf{F}_2 = \langle -8+2, -3-5\rangle = \langle -6, -8\rangle$
    $-1\mathbf{F} = \langle 6, 8\rangle$

9. $\mathbf{F} = \mathbf{F}_1 + \mathbf{F}_2 + \mathbf{F}_3$
    $\quad = \langle -2+2+5, -7-7+4\rangle$
    $\quad = \langle 5, -10\rangle$
    $-1\mathbf{F} = \langle -5, 10\rangle$

11. $\mathbf{F} = \mathbf{F}_1 + \mathbf{F}_2$
     $\quad = (5+1)\mathbf{i} + (-2+10)\mathbf{j}$
     $\quad = 6\mathbf{i} + 8\mathbf{j}$
     $-1\mathbf{F} = -6\mathbf{i} - 8\mathbf{j}$

13. $\mathbf{F} = \mathbf{F}_1 + \mathbf{F}_2 + \mathbf{F}_3$
     $\quad = (2.5-0.3)\mathbf{i} + (4.7+6.9-12)\mathbf{j}$
     $\quad = 2.2\mathbf{i} - 0.4\mathbf{j}$
     $-1\mathbf{F} = -2.2\mathbf{i} + 0.4\mathbf{j}$

15. $\mathbf{F}_1 = \langle 10\cos 104°, 10\sin 104°\rangle = \langle -2.42, 9.70\rangle$
     $\mathbf{F}_2 = \langle 6\cos 25°, 6\sin 25°\rangle = \langle 5.44, 2.54\rangle$
     $\mathbf{F}_3 = \langle 9\cos(-20°), 9\sin(-20°)\rangle = \langle 8.46, -3.08\rangle$
     $\mathbf{F} = \langle -2.42+5.44+8.46, 9.70+2.54-3.08\rangle$
     $\quad = \langle 11.48, 9.16\rangle$
     $-1\mathbf{F} = \langle -11.48, -9.16\rangle$

17. $\mathbf{F}_1 + \mathbf{F}_2 = \langle 19+5, 10+17\rangle = \langle 24, 27\rangle$
     $\mathbf{F}_3 = \langle -24, -27\rangle$

19. $\mathbf{F}_1 = \langle 2210\cos 40°, 2210\sin 40°\rangle = \langle 1693.0, 1420.6\rangle$
     $\mathbf{F}_2 = \langle 2500\cos 130°, 2500\sin 130°\rangle$
     $\quad = \langle -1607.0, 1915.1\rangle$
     $\mathbf{F}_1 + \mathbf{F}_2 = \langle 86.0, 3335.7\rangle$
     $\mathbf{F}_3 = \langle -86, -3335.7\rangle$
     $|\mathbf{F}_3| = \sqrt{(-86)^2 + (-3335.7)^2} \approx 3336.8$
     $\theta_r = \tan^{-1}\left|\dfrac{-3335.7}{-86}\right| = \tan^{-1}\left(\dfrac{3335.7}{86}\right) \approx 88.5°$
     In QIII, 268.5°

21. $\mathbf{comp_v u} = 50\cos 42° = 37.16\,\text{kg}$

23. $\mathbf{comp_v u} = 1525\cos 65° = 644.49\,\text{lb}$

25. $\mathbf{comp_v u} = 3010\cos 30° = 2606.74\,\text{kg}$

27. **G** makes an angle of 55° with the incline (**v**).
$\mathbf{comp_v G} = 500\cos 55° \approx 286.79\ \text{lb}$

29. Let β be the angle between **G** and the incline.
Let θ be the angle of incline.
$$325\cos\beta = 225$$
$$\cos\beta = \frac{225}{325}$$
$$\beta = \cos^{-1}\left(\frac{225}{325}\right)$$
$$\beta \approx 46.2°$$
$$\theta = 90 - 46.2 = 43.8°$$

31. $W = |\mathbf{F}|D$
$= (75)(15)$
$= 1125\ \text{N-m}$

33. $R = \dfrac{v^2\sin\theta\cos\theta}{16}$
$= \dfrac{175^2\sin 45°\cos 45°}{16}$
$\approx 957.0\ \text{ft}$

35. The component of force in the direction of movement is $250\cos 30°$ lb.
$W = |\mathbf{F}|D$
$= (250\cos 30°)(300)$
$\approx 64{,}951.9\ \text{ft-lb}$

37. $45{,}000 = |\mathbf{F}|\cos 5° \cdot 100$
$$|\mathbf{F}| = \frac{45{,}000}{100\cos 5°}$$
$$|\mathbf{F}| \approx 451.72\ \text{lb}$$

39. $W = |\mathbf{F}|D$
$= (30\cos 20°)(100)$
$\approx 2819.08\ \text{N-m}$

41. $|\mathbf{F}| = \sqrt{15^2 + 10^2} \approx 18.0$
$\theta_f = \tan^{-1}\dfrac{10}{15} \approx 33.7°$
$\theta_v = \tan^{-1}\dfrac{5}{50} \approx 5.7°$
$33.7° - 5.7° = 28°$
$\mathbf{comp_v F} = |\mathbf{F}|\cos\theta = 18.0\cos 28.0° \approx 15.9$
$|\mathbf{v}| = \sqrt{50^2 + 5^2} \approx 50.2$
$W = 15.9(50.2) \approx 800\ \text{ft-lb}$

43. $|\mathbf{F}| = \sqrt{8^2 + 2^2} \approx 8.2$
$\theta_f = \tan^{-1}\dfrac{2}{8} \approx 14.0°$
$\theta_v = \tan^{-1}\dfrac{-1}{15} \approx -3.8°$
$14.0° - (-3.8)° = 17.8°$
$\mathbf{comp_v F} = |\mathbf{F}|\cos\theta = 8.2\cos 17.8° \approx 7.8$
$|\mathbf{v}| = \sqrt{(-1)^2 + 15^2} \approx 15.0$
$W = 7.8(15) \approx 117\ \text{ft-lb}$

45. $\mathbf{F}\cdot\mathbf{v} = \langle 15,10\rangle\cdot\langle 50,5\rangle$
$= (15)(50) + (10)(5) = 800$
verified

47. $\mathbf{F}\cdot\mathbf{v} = \langle 8,2\rangle\cdot\langle 15,-1\rangle$
$= (8)(15) + (2)(-1) = 118$
verified

49. a. $\mathbf{p}\cdot\mathbf{q} = (5)(3) + (2)(7) = 29$

    b. $|\mathbf{p}| = \sqrt{5^2 + 2^2} = \sqrt{29}$
    $|\mathbf{q}| = \sqrt{3^2 + 7^2} = \sqrt{58}$
    $\theta = \cos^{-1}\dfrac{29}{\sqrt{29}\sqrt{58}} = 45°$

51. a. $\mathbf{p}\cdot\mathbf{q} = (-2)(-6) + (3)(-4) = 0$

    b. $\theta = \cos^{-1}\dfrac{0}{|\mathbf{p}||\mathbf{q}|} = \cos^{-1}0 = 90°$

53. a. $\mathbf{p}\cdot\mathbf{q}=\left(7\sqrt{2}\right)\left(2\sqrt{2}\right)+(-3)(9)=1$

   b. $|\mathbf{p}|=\sqrt{7\sqrt{2}^{\;2}+2\sqrt{2}^{\;2}}=\sqrt{106}$

   $|\mathbf{q}|=\sqrt{(-3)^2+9^2}=\sqrt{90}$

   $\theta=\cos^{-1}\dfrac{1}{\sqrt{106}\sqrt{90}}\approx 89.4°$

55. $\mathbf{u}\cdot\mathbf{v}=(7)(4)+(-2)(14)=0$ Yes

57. $\mathbf{u}\cdot\mathbf{v}=(-6)(-8)+(-3)(15)=3$ No

59. $\mathbf{u}\cdot\mathbf{v}=(-2)(9)+(-6)(-3)=0$ Yes

61. $|\mathbf{v}|=\sqrt{7^2+1^2}=\sqrt{50}$

   $\mathbf{u}\cdot\mathbf{v}=(3)(7)+(5)(1)=26$

   $\mathbf{comp_v u}=\dfrac{26}{\sqrt{50}}\approx 3.68$

63. $|\mathbf{v}|=\sqrt{0^2+(-10)^2}=10$

   $\mathbf{u}\cdot\mathbf{v}=(-7)(0)+(4)(-10)=-40$

   $\mathbf{comp_v u}=\dfrac{-40}{10}=-4$

65. $|\mathbf{v}|=\sqrt{6^2+5\sqrt{3}^{\;2}}\approx\sqrt{111}$

   $\mathbf{u}\cdot\mathbf{v}=\left(7\sqrt{2}\right)(6)+(-3)\left(5\sqrt{3}\right)\approx 42\sqrt{2}-15\sqrt{3}$

   $\mathbf{comp_v u}=\dfrac{42\sqrt{2}-15\sqrt{3}}{\sqrt{111}}\approx 3.17$

67. a. $|\mathbf{v}|=\sqrt{8^2+3^2}=\sqrt{73}$

   $\mathbf{u}\cdot\mathbf{v}=2(8)+6(3)=34$

   $\mathbf{proj_v u}=\dfrac{34}{73}\left\langle 8,3\right\rangle\approx\left\langle 3.73,1.40\right\rangle$

   b. $\mathbf{u}_1=\left\langle 3.73,1.40\right\rangle$

   $\mathbf{u}_2=\mathbf{u}-\mathbf{u}_1$
   $=\left\langle 2-3.73,6-1.40\right\rangle$
   $=\left\langle -1.73,4.60\right\rangle$

69. a. $|\mathbf{v}|=\sqrt{(-6)^2+1^2}=\sqrt{37}$

   $\mathbf{u}\cdot\mathbf{v}=(-2)(-6)+(-8)(1)=4$

   $\mathbf{proj_v u}=\dfrac{4}{37}\left\langle -6,1\right\rangle\approx\left\langle -0.65,0.11\right\rangle$

   b. $\mathbf{u}_1=\left\langle -0.65,0.11\right\rangle$

   $\mathbf{u}_2=\mathbf{u}-\mathbf{u}_1$
   $=\left\langle -2+0.65,-8-0.11\right\rangle$
   $=\left\langle -1.35,-8.11\right\rangle$

71. a. $|\mathbf{v}|=\sqrt{12^2+2^2}=\sqrt{148}$

   $\mathbf{u}\cdot\mathbf{v}=(10)(12)+(5)(2)=130$

   $\mathbf{proj_v u}=\left(\dfrac{130}{148}\right)(12\mathbf{i}+2\mathbf{j})\approx 10.54\mathbf{i}+1.76\mathbf{j}$

   b. $\mathbf{u}_1=10.54\mathbf{i}+1.76\mathbf{j}$

   $\mathbf{u}_2=\mathbf{u}-\mathbf{u}_1$
   $=(10-10.54)\mathbf{i}+(5-1.76)\mathbf{j}$
   $=-0.54\mathbf{i}+3.24\mathbf{j}$

73. a. $x=(250\cos 60°)(3)=375$ ft

   $y=(250\sin 60°)(3)-16(3)^2\approx 505.52$ ft

   The projectile is about 375 ft away,
   and about 505.52 ft high.

   b. $(250\sin 60°)t-16t^2=250$
   $-16t^2+(250\sin 60°)t-250=0$
   Solve using quadratic formula.
   $t\approx 1.27$ sec, 12.26 sec

75. a. $x=(200\cos 45°)(3)\approx 424.26$ ft

   $y=(200\sin 45°)(3)-16(3)^2\approx 280.26$ ft

   The projectile is about 424.26 ft away,
   and about 280.26 ft high.

   b. $(200\sin 45°)t-16t^2=250$
   $-16t^2+(200\sin 45°)t-250=0$
   Solve using quadratic formula.
   $t\approx 2.44$ sec, 6.40 sec

77. $y = (90\sin 65°)(1.2) - 16(1.2)^2 \approx 74.84$ ft

To find another time, set height equal to 74.84.
$$(90\sin 65°)t - 16t^2 = 74.84$$
$$-16t^2 + (90\sin 65°)t - 74.84 = 0$$

Solve using quadratic formula.
$t \approx 1.2$ sec, 3.9 sec
$t = 3.9 - 1.2 = 2.7$ sec
The acrobat will again be at this height 2.7 seconds later.

79. $\mathbf{w} \cdot (\mathbf{u} + \mathbf{v}) = \langle e, f \rangle \cdot \langle a+c, b+d \rangle$
$$= e(a+c) + f(b+d)$$
$$= ea + ec + fb + fd$$
$$= (ea + fb) + (ec + fd)$$
$$= \langle e, f \rangle \cdot \langle a, b \rangle + \langle e, f \rangle \cdot \langle c, d \rangle$$
$$= \mathbf{w} \cdot \mathbf{u} + \mathbf{w} \cdot \mathbf{v}$$

81. $\mathbf{0} \cdot \mathbf{u} = \langle 0, 0 \rangle \cdot \langle a, b \rangle = 0(a) + 0(b) = 0$
$\mathbf{u} \cdot \mathbf{0} = \langle a, b \rangle \cdot \langle 0, 0 \rangle = a(0) + b(0) = 0$

83. $\mathbf{u} \cdot \mathbf{v} = (1)(5) + (5)(2) = 15$
$$|\mathbf{u}| = \sqrt{1^2 + 5^2} = \sqrt{26}$$
$$|\mathbf{v}| = \sqrt{5^2 + 2^2} = \sqrt{29}$$
$$\cos\theta = \frac{15}{\sqrt{26}\sqrt{29}}$$
$$\theta = \cos^{-1}\left(\frac{15}{\sqrt{26}\sqrt{29}}\right)$$
$$\theta \approx 56.9°$$

Slope of $1\mathbf{i} + 5\mathbf{j}$: $\dfrac{\Delta y}{\Delta x} = \dfrac{5}{1} = 5$

Slope of $5\mathbf{i} + 2\mathbf{j}$: $\dfrac{\Delta y}{\Delta x} = \dfrac{2}{5}$

$$\tan\theta = \frac{\frac{2}{5} - 5}{1 + \frac{2}{5} \cdot 5} = \frac{-23/5}{3} = -\frac{23}{15}$$

$$\theta_r = \tan^{-1}\left|-\frac{23}{15}\right| = \tan^{-1}\left(\frac{23}{15}\right) = 56.9°$$

The angle between is 56.9°.
Answers will vary.

85. $\dfrac{\sin 120°}{53} = \dfrac{\sin B}{35}$

$$\sin B = \frac{35\sin 120°}{53}$$

$$B = \sin^{-1}\left(\frac{35\sin 120°}{53}\right) \approx 34.9°$$

$$A = 180° - (34.9° + 120°) = 25.1°$$

$$\frac{\sin 120°}{53} = \frac{\sin 25.1°}{a}$$

$$a = \frac{53\sin 25.1°}{\sin 120°} \approx 25.96 \text{ cm}$$

(If exact values are used, the result is 25.98.)

Angles	Sides
$A \approx 25.1°$	$a \approx 25.98$ cm
$B \approx 34.9°$	$b = 53$ cm
$C = 120°$	$c = 35$ cm

87.

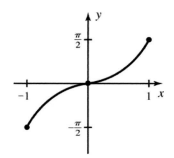

Domain: $[-1, 1]$; Range: $-\dfrac{\pi}{2}, \dfrac{\pi}{2}$

89. $\sin 15° = \sin\left(\dfrac{30°}{2}\right) = \sqrt{\dfrac{1 - \cos 30°}{2}}$

$$= \sqrt{\frac{1 - \frac{\sqrt{3}}{2}}{2}} = \sqrt{\frac{2 - \sqrt{3}}{4}}$$

$$= \frac{1}{2}\sqrt{2 - \sqrt{3}}$$

$\cos 75° = \cos\left(\dfrac{150°}{2}\right) = \sqrt{\dfrac{1 + \cos 150°}{2}}$

$$= \sqrt{\frac{1 + \left(-\frac{\sqrt{3}}{2}\right)}{2}} = \sqrt{\frac{2 - \sqrt{3}}{4}}$$

$$= \frac{1}{2}\sqrt{2 - \sqrt{3}}$$

Identical, since 15° and 75° are complements.

Summary and Concept Review 7.1

1. $A = 180° - (21° + 123°) = 36°$

    $$\frac{\sin 123°}{293} = \frac{\sin 36°}{a}$$
    $$a \sin 123° = 293 \sin 36°$$
    $$a = \frac{293 \sin 36°}{\sin 123°}$$
    $$a \approx 205.35 \text{ cm}$$

    $$\frac{\sin 123°}{293} = \frac{\sin 21°}{b}$$
    $$b \sin 123° = 293 \sin 21°$$
    $$b = \frac{293 \sin 21°}{\sin 123°}$$
    $$b \approx 125.20 \text{ cm}$$

Angles	Sides
$A = 36°$	$a \approx 205.35$ cm
$B = 21°$	$b \approx 125.20$ cm
$C = 123°$	$c = 293$ cm

3. Third angle is $B = 180° - (25° + 110°) = 45°$.

    $$\frac{\sin 45°}{70} = \frac{\sin 25°}{h}$$
    $$h \sin 45° = 70 \sin 25°$$
    $$h = \frac{70 \sin 25°}{\sin 45°}$$
    $$h \approx 41.84 \text{ ft}$$

5. $$\frac{\sin 35°}{67} = \frac{\sin B}{105}$$
    $$67 \sin B = 105 \sin 35°$$
    $$\sin B = \frac{105 \sin 35°}{67}$$
    $$B = \sin^{-1}\left(\frac{105 \sin 35°}{67}\right)$$
    $$B \approx 64.0°$$
    $$180° - 64.0° = 116.0°$$

    Consider $B_1 = 64°$.
    $$C_1 = 180° - (64.0° + 35°)$$
    $$= 81.0°$$
    $$\frac{\sin 35°}{67} = \frac{\sin 81.0°}{c_1}$$
    $$c_1 \sin 35° = 67 \sin 81.0°$$
    $$c_1 = \frac{67 \sin 81.0°}{\sin 35°}$$
    $$c_1 \approx 115.37 \text{ cm}$$

5. (continued)
    Consider $B_2 = 116.0°$.
    $$C_2 = 180° - (116.0° + 35°) = 29.0°$$
    $$\frac{\sin 35°}{67} = \frac{\sin 29°}{c_2}$$
    $$c_2 \sin 35° = 67 \sin 29°$$
    $$c_2 = \frac{67 \sin 29°}{\sin 35°}$$
    $$c_2 \approx 56.63 \text{ cm}$$

Summary and Concept Review 7.2

7. $$9^2 = 12^2 + 15^2 - 360 \cos B$$
    $$81 = 144 + 225 - 360 \cos B$$
    $$-360 \cos B = -288$$
    $$\cos B = \frac{-288}{-360}$$
    $$B = \cos^{-1} 0.8$$
    $$B \approx 36.9°$$

9. Let A, B and C be the angles from largest to smallest.
    $$c^2 = a^2 + b^2 = 2ab \cos C$$
    $$1820^2 = 1250^2 + 720^2 - 2(720)(1250)\cos C$$
    $$1,231,500 = -1,800,000 \cos C$$
    $$\cos C = \frac{1,231,500}{-1,800,000}$$
    $$C = \cos^{-1}\left(-\frac{821}{1200}\right)$$
    $$C \approx 133.2°$$

    $$\frac{\sin B}{1250} = \frac{\sin 133.2°}{1820}$$
    $$1820 \sin B = 1250 \sin 133.2°$$
    $$\sin B = \frac{1250 \sin 133.2°}{1820}$$
    $$B = \sin^{-1}\left(\frac{1250 \sin 133.2°}{1820}\right)$$
    $$B \approx 30.1°$$

    $$A = 180° - (30.1° + 133.2°) = 16.7°$$

Summary and Concept Review 7.3

11.

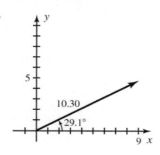

$$\left|\mathbf{v}\right| = \sqrt{9^2 + 5^2} = \sqrt{106} \approx 10.30$$

$$\theta = \tan^{-1}\left|\frac{5}{9}\right| = \tan^{-1}\left(\frac{5}{9}\right) \approx 29.1°$$

13. $a = 18\cos 52° \approx 11.08$
    $b = 18\sin 52° \approx 14.18$

15. $\left|\mathbf{u}\right| = \sqrt{7^2 + 12^2} = \sqrt{193}$

unit vector: $\dfrac{7}{\sqrt{193}}\mathbf{i} + \dfrac{12}{\sqrt{193}}\mathbf{j}$

17. $t = \dfrac{d}{r} = \dfrac{0.5 \text{ mi}}{3 \text{ mph}} = \dfrac{1}{6}$ hr; $\quad \dfrac{1}{6}$ hr $\cdot \dfrac{1 \text{ mi}}{1 \text{ hr}} = \dfrac{1}{6}$ mi

He will end up $\dfrac{1}{6}$ from the finish marker.

Summary and Concept Review 7.4

19. $\mathbf{F} = \mathbf{F}_1 + \mathbf{F}_2$
    $= (-20 + 45)\mathbf{i} + (70 + 53)\mathbf{j}$
    $= 25\mathbf{i} + 123\mathbf{j}$
    $-1\mathbf{F} = -25\mathbf{i} - 123\mathbf{j} = \langle -25, -123 \rangle$

21. $\mathbf{u} \cdot \mathbf{v} = 0$
    $2(-18) + 9d = 0$
    $9d = 36$
    $d = 4$

23. $W = \mathbf{F} \cdot \mathbf{v} = 50(85) + 15(6) = 4340$ ft-lb

25. The component of force in the direction of movement is $75\cos 25°$.
    $W = \left|\mathbf{F}\right|D$
    $= (75\cos 25°)(120)$
    ≈ 8156.77 ft-lb

Mixed Review

1. $A = 180° - (27° + 112°) = 41°$

$$\dfrac{\sin 112°}{19} = \dfrac{\sin 41°}{a}$$
$$a\sin 112° = 19\sin 41°$$
$$a = \dfrac{19\sin 41°}{\sin 112°}$$
$$a \approx 13.44 \text{ in.}$$

$$\dfrac{\sin 112°}{19} = \dfrac{\sin 27°}{b}$$
$$b\sin 112° = 19\sin 27°$$
$$b = \dfrac{19\sin 27°}{\sin 112°}$$
$$b \approx 9.30 \text{ in.}$$

Angles	Sides
$A = 41°$	$a \approx 13.44$ in.
$B = 27°$	$b \approx 9.30$ in.
$C = 112°$	$c = 19$ in.

$$A = \dfrac{19^2 \sin 27° \sin 41°}{2\sin 112°} \approx 58 \text{ in.}^2$$

3. $x = 21\cos 40° \approx 16.09$
   $y = 21\sin 40 \approx 13.50$

5. $180° - (35° + 122°) = 23°$

$$\dfrac{\sin 23°}{120} = \dfrac{\sin 35°}{h}$$
$$h\sin 23° = 120\sin 35°$$
$$h = \dfrac{120\sin 35°}{\sin 23°}$$
$$h \approx 176.15 \text{ ft}$$

7. The plane vector makes a 60° angle with the positive x-axis.
   The wind vector makes a 90° angle with the positive x-axis.
   Find the components of each.
   Plane: $a = 750\cos 60° \approx 375$
   $\qquad\quad b = 750\sin 60° \approx 649.52$
   Wind: $a = 50\cos 90° = 0$
   $\qquad\quad b = 50\sin 90° = 50$
   $\langle 375 + 0,\ 649.52 + 50 \rangle = \langle 375,\ 699.52 \rangle$

$$\theta = \tan^{-1}\left|\dfrac{699.52}{375}\right| \approx 61.8°$$

$$\sqrt{375^2 + 699.52^2} \approx 793.70 \text{ mph}$$

The true course and speed of the plane is a heading of 28.2° at 793.70 mph.

9. $\dfrac{\sin 31^\circ}{36} = \dfrac{\sin B}{24}$

$36\sin B = 24\sin 31^\circ$

$\sin B = \dfrac{24\sin 31^\circ}{36}$

$B = \sin^{-1}\left(\dfrac{24\sin 31^\circ}{36}\right)$

$B \approx 20.1^\circ$

or $B = 180^\circ - 20.1^\circ = 159.9^\circ$
But $159.9^\circ + 31^\circ = 190.9^\circ > 180^\circ$, so this is discarded.
$C = 180^\circ - (20.1^\circ + 31^\circ) = 128.9^\circ$

$\dfrac{\sin 128.9^\circ}{c} = \dfrac{\sin 31^\circ}{36}$

$c\sin 31^\circ = 36\sin 128.9^\circ$

$c = \dfrac{36\sin 128.9^\circ}{\sin 31^\circ}$

$c \approx 54.4$ m

Angles	Sides
$A = 31^\circ$	$a = 36$ m
$B \approx 20.1^\circ$	$b = 24$ m
$C \approx 128.9^\circ$	$c \approx 54.4$ m

11. $\dfrac{\sin 35^\circ}{12} = \dfrac{\sin \theta}{20}$

$12\sin \theta = 20\sin 35^\circ$

$\sin \theta = \dfrac{20\sin 35^\circ}{10} \approx 1.15$

no

$\dfrac{20\sin \alpha}{10} = 1$

$\sin \alpha = \dfrac{1}{2}$

$\alpha = \sin^{-1}\left(\dfrac{1}{2}\right)$

$\alpha = 30^\circ$

The weight barely touches ("tangent") at 30°.

13.   a. $\dfrac{\sin 108.4^\circ}{5142} = \dfrac{\sin 45.5^\circ}{C}$

$C = \dfrac{5142\sin 45.5^\circ}{\sin 108.4^\circ}$

$C \approx 3865$ miles

The distance from Honolulu to Tokyo is 3865 miles.

b. $180^\circ - (108.4^\circ + 45.5^\circ) = 26.1^\circ$

$\dfrac{\sin 108.4^\circ}{5142} = \dfrac{\sin 26.1^\circ}{B}$

$B = \dfrac{5142\sin 26.1^\circ}{\sin 108.4^\circ}$

$B \approx 2384$ miles

The distance from Honolulu to San Francisco is 2384 miles.

15.   Set vertical components equal.
$418\sin 10^\circ = 320\sin \theta$

$\sin \theta = \dfrac{418\sin 10^\circ}{320}$

$\theta = \sin^{-1}\left(\dfrac{418\sin 10^\circ}{320}\right)$

$\theta \approx 13.1^\circ$

17. $\mathbf{u}\cdot\mathbf{v} = (-12)(19) + (-16)(-13) = -20$

$|\mathbf{v}| = \sqrt{19^2 + (-13)^2} = \sqrt{530}$

$\text{comp}_\mathbf{v}\mathbf{u} = \dfrac{-20}{\sqrt{530}} \approx -0.87$

$\mathbf{proj}_\mathbf{v}\mathbf{u} = \dfrac{-20}{530}\langle 19, -13\rangle = -\dfrac{38}{53}\mathbf{i} + \dfrac{26}{53}\mathbf{j}$

19.   Terminal point:
$(5 + (-3),\, -2 + 1) = (2, -1)$

Practice Test

1. $180° - (39° + 68°) = 73°$

$$\frac{\sin 39°}{d} = \frac{\sin 73°}{10}$$

$d \sin 73° = 10 \sin 39°$

$$d = \frac{10 \sin 39°}{\sin 73°}$$

$d \approx 6.58$ mi

The fire is 6.58 miles from the closer tower.

3. Let $a = 15$ in., $b = 6$ in., $B = 20°$.

$$\frac{\sin 20°}{6} = \frac{\sin A}{15}$$

$6 \sin A = 15 \sin 20°$

$$\sin A = \frac{15 \sin 20°}{6}$$

$$A = \sin^{-1}\left(\frac{15 \sin 20°}{6}\right)$$

$A \approx 58.8°$

or $A = 180° - 58.8° = 121.2°$

Consider $A_1 = 58.8°$.

$C_1 = 180° - (58.8° + 20°) = 101.2°$

$$\frac{\sin 101.2°}{c_1} = \frac{\sin 20°}{6}$$

$c_1 \sin 20° = 6 \sin 101.2°$

$$c_1 = \frac{6 \sin 101.2°}{\sin 20°}$$

$c_1 \approx 17.2$ in.

Consider $A_2 = 121.2°$.

$C_2 = 180° - (121.2° + 20°) = 38.8°$

$$\frac{\sin 38.8°}{c_2} = \frac{\sin 20°}{6}$$

$c_2 \sin 20° = 6 \sin 38.8°$

$$c_2 = \frac{6 \sin 38.8°}{\sin 20°}$$

$c_2 \approx 10.99$ in.

Angles	Sides (in.)
$A_1 \approx 58.8°$	$a = 15$
$B = 20°$	$b = 6$
$C_1 \approx 101.2°$	$c_1 \approx 17.21$

Angles	Sides
$A_2 \approx 121.2°$	$a = 15$
$B = 20°$	$b = 6$
$C_2 \approx 38.8°$	$c_2 \approx 11.0$

5. a. $$\frac{\sin 53°}{25} = \frac{\sin \theta}{35}$$

$25 \sin \theta = 35 \sin 53°$

$$\sin \theta = \frac{35 \sin 53°}{25} \approx 1.11$$

No, the target cannot be hit.

b. $$\frac{\sin 53°}{28} = \frac{\sin \theta}{35}$$

$28 \sin \theta = 35 \sin 53°$

$$\sin \theta = \frac{35 \sin 53°}{25} \approx 1$$

Only 1 effective throw can be made.

c. With a range of 35 yd, the target is in range from the bottom left corner of the triangle, and we get an isosceles triangle with angles 53°, 53° and 74°.

$$\frac{\sin 74°}{d} = \frac{\sin 53°}{35}$$

$d \sin 53° = 35 \sin 74°$

$$d = \frac{35 \sin 74°}{\sin 53°}$$

$d \approx 42.13$ yd

$$42.13 \text{ yd} \cdot \frac{1 \sec}{5 \text{ yd}} \approx 8.43 \sec$$

The target is within range for 8.43 sec.

7. $1025^2 = 1020^2 + 977^2 - 2(1020)(977) \cos P$

$-944{,}304 = -1{,}993{,}080 \cos P$

$$\cos P = \frac{-944{,}304}{-1{,}993{,}080}$$

$$P = \cos^{-1}\left(\frac{944{,}304}{1{,}993{,}080}\right)$$

$P \approx 61.7°$

$$\frac{\sin 61.7°}{1025} = \frac{\sin B}{1020}$$

$1025 \sin B = 1020 \sin 61.7°$

$$\sin B = \frac{1020 \sin 61.7°}{1025}$$

$$B = \sin^{-1}\left(\frac{1020 \sin 61.7°}{1025}\right)$$

$B \approx 61.2°$

$M = 180° - (61.2° + 61.7°) = 57.1°$

$$s = \frac{a + b + c}{2}$$

$$s = \frac{1020 + 1025 + 977}{2}$$

$s = 1511$ mi

$A = \sqrt{1511(1511 - 1020)(1511 - 1025)(1511 - 977)}$

$A = \sqrt{1511(491)(486)(534)}$

$A \approx 438{,}795$ mi^2

9. Set vertical components equal.
    $$250\sin 30° = 210\sin\theta$$
    $$\sin\theta = \frac{250\sin 30°}{210}$$
    $$\theta = \sin^{-1}\left(\frac{250\sin 30°}{210}\right)$$
    $$\theta \approx 36.5°$$

11. $\mathbf{F}_1 = \langle 150\cos 42°, 150\sin 42°\rangle$
    $= \langle 111.47, 100.37\rangle$
    $\mathbf{F}_2 = \langle 110\cos 113°, 110\sin 113°\rangle$
    $= \langle -42.98, 101.26\rangle$
    $\mathbf{F}_1 + \mathbf{F}_2 = \langle 68.49, 201.63\rangle$
    $\mathbf{F} = \langle -68.49, -201.63\rangle$
    $|\mathbf{F}| = \sqrt{(-68.49)^2 + (-201.63)^2}$
    ≈ 212.94 N
    $\theta_r = \tan^{-1}\left|\frac{-201.63}{-68.49}\right| = \tan^{-1}\left(\frac{201.63}{68.49}\right) \approx 71.2°$
    In QIII, $\theta = 251.2°$

13. $y = 110\sin 50°(2) - 16(2)^2 \approx 104.53$ ft ft;
    $$-16t^2 + (110\sin 50°)t = 104.53$$
    $$-16t^2 + (110\sin 50°)t - 104.53 = 0$$

    Solve using the quadratic formula.
    $t \approx 1.2$ sec, 3.27 sec
    The ball will reach this same height again after
    3.27 sec.

15. a. $\langle -7-13, -3-(-9)\rangle = \langle -20, 6\rangle$

    b. $\sqrt{(-20)^2 + 6^2} = \sqrt{436} = 2\sqrt{109}$

17. $180° - 35° = 145°$
    $a = 8\cos 145° \approx -6.6$
    $b = 8\sin 145° \approx 4.6$
    $\langle -6.6, 4.6\rangle$

19. a. $\theta_F = \tan^{-1}\left|\frac{7}{-8}\right| = \tan^{-1}\left(\frac{7}{8}\right) \approx 41.2°$
    $\theta_v = \tan^{-1}\left|\frac{9}{2}\right| = \tan^{-1}\left(\frac{9}{2}\right) \approx 77.5°$
    $180° - (\theta_F + \theta_v) \approx 61.3°$

    b. $|\mathbf{F}| = \sqrt{(-8)^2 + 7^2} = \sqrt{113}$
    $|\mathbf{v}| = \sqrt{2^2 + 9^2} = \sqrt{85}$

    The component of force in the direction of
    movement is $\sqrt{113}\cos 61.3°$.
    $$W = |\mathbf{F}|D$$
    $$= \left(\sqrt{113}\cos 61.3°\right)\left(\sqrt{85}\right)$$
    $$\approx 47 \text{ ft-lb}$$

    The work above can be verified by
    computing the dot product of $\mathbf{F}$ and v.
    $$\mathbf{F}\cdot\mathbf{v} = (-8)(2) + (7)(9)$$
    $$= -16 + 63$$
    $$= 47 \text{ ft-lb}$$

Calculator Exploration & Discovery

Exercise 1:
   a. Approximately 50.5 ft
   b. Approximately 50.5 ft
   c. Approximately 224.54 ft
   d. Approximately 3.55 sec

Exercise 3:
   a. Approximately 111.87 ft
   b. Approximately 132.04 ft
   c. Approximately 443.16 ft
   d. Approximately 5.75 sec
   Yes, it will clear the fence.

Strengthening Core Skills

Exercise 1:

Let **u** and **v** be the force vectors for the ropes, and **w** for the weight.

$\mathbf{u} = -|\mathbf{u}|\cos 25°\mathbf{i} + |\mathbf{u}|\sin 25°\mathbf{j}$

$\approx -0.9063|\mathbf{u}|\mathbf{i} + 0.4226|\mathbf{u}|\mathbf{j}$

$\mathbf{v} = |\mathbf{v}|\cos 20°\mathbf{i} + |\mathbf{v}|\sin 20°\mathbf{j}$

$\approx 0.9397|\mathbf{v}|\mathbf{i} + 0.3420|\mathbf{v}|\mathbf{j}$

$\mathbf{w} = -500\mathbf{j}$

The sum of all first components and all second components must be zero.

$-0.9063|\mathbf{u}| + 0.9397|\mathbf{v}| = 0$

$0.4226|\mathbf{u}| + 0.3429|\mathbf{v}| - 500 = 0$

Solving this system, we get

$|\mathbf{u}| = 664.46$ lb, $|\mathbf{v}| = 640.86$ lb.

Exercise 3:

The system remains the same as in the example, except the 180 in the second equation is replaced with 200.

The solution is now

$x = 537.49$ lb,

$y = 547.13$ lb.

Yes, the rope will hold.

Cumulative Review Chapters 1-7

1.   This is a 30-60-90 triangle.

$\beta = 90° - 30° = 60°$

$b = \sqrt{3}a = \sqrt{3}\cdot 20 = 20\sqrt{3}$ m

$c = 2a = 2\cdot 20 = 40$ m

3. $A\cos(Bt + C) - D = 0$

$A\cos(Bt + C) = D$

$\cos(Bt + C) = \dfrac{D}{A}$

$Bt + C = \cos^{-1}\left(\dfrac{D}{A}\right)$

$Bt = \cos^{-1}\left(\dfrac{D}{A}\right) - C$

$t = \dfrac{\cos^{-1}\left(\dfrac{D}{A}\right) - C}{B}$

5.

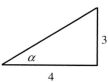

The third side is length 5 (Pythagorean triple), and since cosine is positive, sine is negative.

$\sin\alpha = -\dfrac{3}{5}$; $\csc\alpha = -\dfrac{5}{3}$; $\cos\alpha = \dfrac{4}{5}$

$\sec\alpha = \dfrac{5}{4}$; $\tan\alpha = -\dfrac{3}{4}$; $\cot\alpha = -\dfrac{4}{3}$

7.   a. $\sin(2\alpha) = 2\sin\alpha\cos\alpha$

b. $\sin\left(\dfrac{\alpha}{2}\right) = \pm\sqrt{\dfrac{1 - \cos\alpha}{2}}$

c. $\sin(\alpha + \beta) = \sin\alpha\cos\beta + \cos\alpha\sin\beta$

9.   Using a right triangle, or the Pythagorean Identity, we find that if $\cos 53° \approx 0.6$, then $\sin 53° \approx 0.8$ and if $\cos 72° \approx 0.3$, then $\sin 72° \approx 0.95$.

$\cos 19° = \cos(72° - 53°)$

$= \cos 72°\cos 53° + \sin 72°\sin 53°$

$= (0.3)(0.6) + (0.95)(0.8)$

$= 0.18 + 0.76$

$= 0.94$

$\cos 125° = \cos(72° + 53°)$

$= \cos 72°\cos 53° - \sin 72°\sin 53°$

$= (0.3)(0.6) - (0.95)(0.8)$

$= 0.18 - 0.76$

$= -0.58$

11. The sine regression feature on the calculator provides the equation

$D(t) = 5.704\sin(0.511t - 1.835) + 12.189$.

a. $D(4.5) \approx 14.7$ hr

b.   In the graph, the height is greater than 15 from about $t \approx 4.6$ to $t \approx 8.7$, which corresponds from about April 18 to August 22.

13. $\dfrac{2\cos^2\theta}{\csc^2\theta} + \dfrac{2\sin^2\theta}{\sec^2\theta}$

$= \dfrac{2\cos^2\theta\sec^2\theta + 2\sin^2\theta\csc^2\theta}{\csc^2\theta\sec^2\theta}$

$= \dfrac{4}{\csc^2\theta\sec^2\theta}$

$= 4\sin^2\theta\cos^2\theta$

$= (2\sin\theta\cos\theta)^2$

$= \sin^2(2\theta)$

15. $a^2 = 31^2 + 52^2 - 2(31)(52)\cos 37°$

$a^2 = 961 + 2704 - 3224\cos 37°$

$a^2 \approx 1090.2$

$a \approx 33$ cm

$\dfrac{\sin 37°}{33} = \dfrac{\sin B}{31}$

$33\sin B = 31\sin 37°$

$\sin B = \dfrac{31\sin 37°}{33}$

$B = \sin^{-1}\left(\dfrac{31\sin 37°}{33}\right)$

$B \approx 34.4°$

$C = 180° - (34.4° + 37°) = 108.6°$

17. $90° - 28° = 62°$

The component of force in the direction of movement is $900\cos 62° \approx 422.5$ lb.

19. $\langle -3, 8\rangle, \langle 7, 6\rangle$

$\sqrt{(-3)^2 + 8^2} = \sqrt{73}$

$\sqrt{7^2 + 6^2} = \sqrt{85}$

$\cos\theta = \left\langle \dfrac{-3}{\sqrt{73}}, \dfrac{8}{\sqrt{73}}\right\rangle \cdot \left\langle \dfrac{7}{\sqrt{85}}, \dfrac{6}{\sqrt{85}}\right\rangle$

$\cos\theta = \dfrac{-21}{\sqrt{6205}} + \dfrac{48}{\sqrt{6205}}$

$\cos\theta = \dfrac{27}{\sqrt{6205}}$

$\theta = \cos^{-1}\left(\dfrac{27}{\sqrt{6205}}\right)$

$\theta \approx 70°$

Technology Highlight

Exercise 1:

Graphing Calculator: $3 - 3.464101615i$

Manual: $\left(-2 + \sqrt{-108}\right) + \left(5 - \sqrt{-192}\right)$

$= \left(-2 + 6i\sqrt{3}\right) + \left(5 - 8i\sqrt{3}\right)$

$= 3 - 2i\sqrt{3}$

$\approx 3 - 3.464101615i$

Exercise 3:

Graphing Calculator: $0.2 + 0.6i$

Manual: $\dfrac{2i}{(3+i)}$

$= \dfrac{2i}{3+i} \cdot \dfrac{3-i}{3-i}$

$= \dfrac{6i - 2i^2}{3^2 + 1^2}$

$= \dfrac{2 + 6i}{10}$

$= \dfrac{2}{10} + \dfrac{6}{10}i$

$= 0.2 + 0.6i$

Check: $(0.2 + 0.6i)(3 + i)$

$= 0.6 + 0.2i + 1.8i + 0.6i^2$

$= 0.6 + 0.2i + 1.8i - 0.6$

$= 2i$

8.1 Exercises

1. $3 - 2i$

3. $2;\ 3\sqrt{2}$

5. (b) is correct.

7. a. $\sqrt{-16} = 4i$

 b. $\sqrt{-49} = 7i$

 c. $\sqrt{27} = \sqrt{9 \cdot 3} = 3\sqrt{3}$

 d. $\sqrt{72} = \sqrt{36 \cdot 2} = 6\sqrt{2}$

9. a. $-\sqrt{-18} = -i\sqrt{18}$

 $= -i\sqrt{9 \cdot 2}$

 $= -3i\sqrt{2}$

 b. $-\sqrt{-50} = -i\sqrt{50}$

 $= -i\sqrt{25 \cdot 2}$

 $= -5i\sqrt{2}$

 c. $3\sqrt{-25} = 3i\sqrt{25}$

 $= 3i \cdot 5$

 $= 15i$

 d. $2\sqrt{-9} = 2i\sqrt{9}$

 $= 2i(3)$

 $= 6i$

11. a. $\sqrt{-19} = i\sqrt{19}$

 b. $\sqrt{-31} = i\sqrt{31}$

 c. $\sqrt{\dfrac{-12}{25}} = \dfrac{i\sqrt{12}}{\sqrt{25}} = \dfrac{2\sqrt{3}}{5}i$

 d. $\sqrt{\dfrac{-9}{32}} = \dfrac{i\sqrt{9}}{\sqrt{32}}$

 $= \dfrac{3i}{4\sqrt{2}}$

 $= \dfrac{3\sqrt{2}}{8}i$

13. a. $\dfrac{2 + \sqrt{-4}}{2} = \dfrac{2 + 2i}{2} = 1 + i$

 $a = 1,\ b = 1$

 b. $\dfrac{6 + \sqrt{-27}}{3} = \dfrac{6 + 3i\sqrt{3}}{3} = 2 + i\sqrt{3}$

 $a = 2,\ b = \sqrt{3}$

15. a. $\dfrac{8 + \sqrt{-16}}{2} = \dfrac{8 + 4i}{2} = 4 + 2i$

 $a = 4,\ b = 2$

 b. $\dfrac{10 - \sqrt{-50}}{5} = \dfrac{10 - 5i\sqrt{2}}{5} = 2 - i\sqrt{2}$

 $a = 2,\ b = -\sqrt{2}$

17. a. $5 = 5 + 0i$
$a = 5, b = 0$

b. $3i = 0 + 3i$
$a = 0, b = 3$

19. a. $2\sqrt{-81} = 2(9i) = 18i = 0 + 18i$
$a = 0, b = 18$

b. $\dfrac{\sqrt{-32}}{8} = \dfrac{4\sqrt{2}}{8}i = \dfrac{\sqrt{2}}{2}i = 0 + \dfrac{\sqrt{2}}{2}i$
$a = 0, b = \dfrac{\sqrt{2}}{2}$

21. a. $4 + \sqrt{-50} = 4 + 5i\sqrt{2}$
$a = 4, b = 5\sqrt{2}$

b. $-5 + \sqrt{-27} = -5 + 3i\sqrt{3}$
$a = -5, b = 3\sqrt{3}$

23. a. $\dfrac{14 + \sqrt{-98}}{8} = \dfrac{14 + 7i\sqrt{2}}{8} = \dfrac{7}{4} + \dfrac{7\sqrt{2}}{8}i$
$a = \dfrac{7}{4}, b = \dfrac{7\sqrt{2}}{8}$

b. $\dfrac{5 + \sqrt{-250}}{10} = \dfrac{5 + 5i\sqrt{10}}{10} = \dfrac{1}{2} + \dfrac{\sqrt{10}}{2}i$
$a = \dfrac{1}{2}, b = \dfrac{\sqrt{10}}{2}$

25. a. $(12 - \sqrt{-4}) + (7 + \sqrt{-9})$
$= (12 - 2i) + (7 + 3i)$
$= 12 - 2i + 7 + 3i$
$= (12 + 7) + (-2i + 3i)$
$= 19 + i$

b. $(3 + \sqrt{-25}) + (-1 - \sqrt{-81})$
$= (3 + 5i) + (-1 - 9i)$
$= 3 + 5i - 1 - 9i$
$= (3 - 1) + (5i - 9i)$
$= 2 - 4i$

c. $(11 + \sqrt{-108}) - (2 - \sqrt{-48})$
$= (11 + 6i\sqrt{3}) - (2 - 4i\sqrt{3})$
$= 11 + 6i\sqrt{3} - 2 + 4i\sqrt{3}$
$= (11 - 2) + (6i\sqrt{3} + 4i\sqrt{3})$
$= 9 + 10i\sqrt{3}$

27. a. $(2 + 3i) + (-5 - i)$
$= 2 + 3i - 5 - i$
$= (2 - 5) + (3i - i)$
$= -3 + 2i$

b. $(5 - 2i) + (3 + 2i)$
$= 5 - 2i + 3 + 2i$
$= (5 + 3) + (-2i + 2i)$
$= 8$

c. $(6 - 5i) - (4 + 3i)$
$= 6 - 5i - 4 - 3i$
$= (6 - 4) + (-5i - 3i)$
$= 2 - 8i$

29. a. $(3.7 + 6.1i) - (1 + 5.9i)$
$= 3.7 + 6.1i - 1 - 5.9i$
$= (3.7 - 1) + (6.1i - 5.9i)$
$= 2.7 + 0.2i$

b. $\left(8 + \dfrac{3}{4}i\right) - \left(-7 + \dfrac{2}{3}i\right)$
$= 8 + \dfrac{3}{4}i + 7 - \dfrac{2}{3}i$
$= (8 + 7) + \left(\dfrac{3}{4}i - \dfrac{2}{3}i\right)$
$= 15 + \dfrac{1}{12}i$

c. $\left(-6 - \dfrac{5}{8}i\right) + \left(4 + \dfrac{1}{2}i\right)$
$= -6 - \dfrac{5}{8}i + 4 + \dfrac{1}{2}i$
$= (-6 + 4) + \left(-\dfrac{5}{8}i + \dfrac{1}{2}i\right)$
$= -2 - \dfrac{1}{8}i$

31. a. $5i(-3i) = -15i^2 = 15$

b. $4i(-4i) = -16i^2 = 16$

33. a. $-7i(5 - 3i) = -35i + 21i^2$
$= -21 - 35i$

b. $6i(-3 + 7i) = -18i + 42i^2$
$= -42 - 18i$

35. a. $(-3+2i)(2+3i) = -6 - 9i + 4i + 6i^2$
$= -6 - 9i + 4i - 6$
$= -12 - 5i$

 b. $(3+2i)(1+i) = 3 + 3i + 2i + 2i^2$
$= 3 + 3i + 2i - 2$
$= 1 + 5i$

37. a. Conjugate: $4 - 5i$
$(4+5i)(4-5i) = 4^2 + 5^2 = 41$

 b. Conjugate: $3 + i\sqrt{2}$
$(3-i\sqrt{2})(3+i\sqrt{2}) = 3^2 + (\sqrt{2})^2 = 11$

39. a. Conjugate: $-7i$
$(7i)(-7i) = 7^2 = 49$

 b. Conjugate: $\dfrac{1}{2} + \dfrac{2}{3}i$
$\left(\dfrac{1}{2}-\dfrac{2}{3}i\right)\left(\dfrac{1}{2}+\dfrac{2}{3}i\right) = \left(\dfrac{1}{2}\right)^2 + \left(\dfrac{2}{3}\right)^2$
$= \dfrac{1}{4} + \dfrac{4}{9}$
$= \dfrac{9}{36} + \dfrac{16}{36}$
$= \dfrac{25}{36}$

41. a. $(4-5i)(4+5i) = 4^2 + 5^2 = 41$

 b. $(7-5i)(7+5i) = 7^2 + 5^2 = 74$

43. a. $(3-i\sqrt{2})(3+i\sqrt{2}) = 3^2 + (\sqrt{2})^2 = 11$

 b. $\left(\dfrac{1}{6}+\dfrac{2}{3}i\right)\left(\dfrac{1}{6}-\dfrac{2}{3}i\right) = \left(\dfrac{1}{6}\right)^2 + \left(\dfrac{2}{3}\right)^2$
$= \dfrac{1}{36} + \dfrac{4}{9}$
$= \dfrac{1}{36} + \dfrac{16}{36}$
$= \dfrac{17}{36}$

45. a. $(2+3i)^2 = 2^2 + 2(2)(3i) + (3i)^2$
$= 4 + 12i + 9i^2$
$= 4 + 12i - 9$
$= -5 + 12i$

 b. $(3-4i)^2 = 3^2 + 2(3)(-4i) + (-4i)^2$
$= 9 - 24i + 16i^2$
$= 9 - 24i - 16$
$= -7 - 24i$

47. a. $(-2+5i)^2 = (-2)^2 + 2(-2)(5i) + (5i)^2$
$= 4 - 20i + 25i^2$
$= 4 - 20i - 25$
$= -21 - 20i$

 b. $(3+i\sqrt{2})^2 = 3^2 + 2(3)(i\sqrt{2}) + (i\sqrt{2})^2$
$= 9 + 6i\sqrt{2} + 2i^2$
$= 9 + 6i\sqrt{2} - 2$
$= 7 + 6i\sqrt{2}$

49. $x^2 + 36 = 0;\ x = -6$
$(-6)^2 + 36 = 0$
$36 + 36 = 0$
$72 \neq 0$ no

51. $x^2 + 49 = 0;\ x = -7i$
$(-7i)^2 + 49 = 0$
$49i^2 + 49 = 0$
$-49 + 49 = 0$
$0 = 0$ yes

53. $(x-3)^2 = -9;\ x = 3 - 3i$
$[(3-3i)-3]^2 = -9$
$(3-3i-3)^2 = -9$
$(-3i)^2 = -9$
$9i^2 = -9$
$-9 = -9$ yes

55. $x^2 - 2x + 5 = 0;\ x = 1 - 2i$

$(1-2i)^2 - 2(1-2i) + 5 = 0$

$1 - 4i + 4i^2 - 2 + 4i + 5 = 0$

$1 - 4i - 4 - 2 + 4i + 5 = 0$

$0 = 0$ yes

57. $x^2 - 4x + 9 = 0;\ x = 2 + i\sqrt{5}$

$\left(2+i\sqrt{5}\right)^2 - 4\left(2+i\sqrt{5}\right) + 9 = 0$

$4 + 4i\sqrt{5} + 5i^2 - 8 - 4i\sqrt{5} + 9 = 0$

$4 + 4i\sqrt{5} - 5 - 8 - 4i\sqrt{5} + 9 = 0$

$0 = 0$ yes

59. $x^2 - 2x + 17 = 0;\ x = 1 + 4i,\ 1 - 4i$

$(1+4i)^2 - 2(1+4i) + 17 = 0$

$1 + 8i + 16i^2 - 2 - 8i + 17 = 0$

$1 + 8i - 16 - 2 - 8i + 17 = 0$

$0 = 0$

$1 + 4i$ is a solution.

$(1-4i)^2 - 2(1-4i) + 17 = 0$

$1 - 8i + 16i^2 - 2 + 8i + 17 = 0$

$1 - 8i - 16 - 2 + 8i + 17 = 0$

$0 = 0$

$1 - 4i$ is a solution.

61. a. $i^{48} = \left(i^4\right)^{12} = (1)^{12} = 1$

b. $i^{26} = \left(i^4\right)^6 i^2 = (1)^6(-1) = -1$

c. $i^{39} = \left(i^4\right)^9 i^3 = (1)^9(-i) = -i$

d. $i^{53} = \left(i^4\right)^{13} i^1 = (1)^{13}(i) = i$

63. a. $\dfrac{-2}{\sqrt{-49}} = \dfrac{-2}{7i} \cdot \dfrac{i}{i} = \dfrac{-2i}{7i^2} = \dfrac{2}{7}i$

b. $\dfrac{4}{\sqrt{-25}} = \dfrac{4}{5i} \cdot \dfrac{i}{i} = \dfrac{4i}{5i^2} = -\dfrac{4}{5}i$

65. a. $\dfrac{7}{3+2i} \cdot \dfrac{3-2i}{3-2i} = \dfrac{21-14i}{3^2+2^2}$

$= \dfrac{21-14i}{13}$

$= \dfrac{21}{13} - \dfrac{14}{13}i$

b. $\dfrac{-5}{2-3i} \cdot \dfrac{2+3i}{2+3i} = \dfrac{-10-15i}{2^2+3^2}$

$= \dfrac{-10-15i}{13}$

$= -\dfrac{10}{13} - \dfrac{15}{13}i$

67. a. $\dfrac{3+4i}{4i} \cdot \dfrac{i}{i} = \dfrac{3i+4i^2}{4i^2} = \dfrac{-4+3i}{-4} = 1 - \dfrac{3}{4}i$

b. $\dfrac{2-3i}{3i} \cdot \dfrac{i}{i} = \dfrac{2i-3i^2}{3i^2} = \dfrac{3+2i}{-3} = -1 - \dfrac{2}{3}i$

69. $|a+bi| = \sqrt{a^2+b^2}$

a. $|2+3i| = \sqrt{(2)^2+(3)^2} = \sqrt{13}$

b. $|4-3i| = \sqrt{(4)^2+(-3)^2} = 5$

c. $\left|3+i\sqrt{2}\right| = \sqrt{(3)^2+\left(\sqrt{2}\right)^2} = \sqrt{11}$

71. For $A = 5 + i\sqrt{15}$ and $B = 5 - i\sqrt{15}$,

we must verify that $A + B = 10$ and $AB = 40$.

$A + B = 10$

$\left(5+i\sqrt{15}\right) + \left(5-i\sqrt{15}\right) = 10$

$5 + i\sqrt{15} + 5 - i\sqrt{15} = 10$

$10 = 10$ yes

$AB = 40$

$\left(5+i\sqrt{15}\right)\left(5-i\sqrt{15}\right) = 40$

$5^2 + \left(\sqrt{15}\right)^2 = 40$

$25 + 15 = 40$

$10 = 40$ yes

73. $Z = R + iX_L - iX_C$
    $= 7\Omega + i(6\Omega) - i(11\Omega)$
    $= 7\Omega + 6i\Omega - 11i\Omega$
    $= 7\Omega - 5i\Omega$
    $= 7 - 5i \ \Omega$

75. $V = IZ$
    $= (3 - 2i)(5 + 5i)$
    $= 15 + 15i - 10i - 10i^2$
    $= 15 + 15i - 10i + 10$
    $= 25 + 5i \ V$

77. $Z = \dfrac{Z_1 Z_2}{Z_1 + Z_2}$
    $= \dfrac{(1+2i)(3-2i)}{(1+2i)+(3-2i)}$
    $= \dfrac{3 - 2i + 6i - 4i^2}{1 + 2i + 3 - 2i}$
    $= \dfrac{7 + 4i}{4}$
    $= \dfrac{7}{4} + i \ \Omega$

79. a. $x^2 + 36 = (x + 6i)(x - 6i)$

    b. $m^2 + 3 = \left(m + i\sqrt{3}\right)\left(m - i\sqrt{3}\right)$

    c. $n^2 + 12 = \left(n + 2i\sqrt{3}\right)\left(n - 2i\sqrt{3}\right)$

    d. $4x^2 + 49 = (2x + 7i)(2x - 7i)$

81. $i^{17}(3 - 4i) - 3i^3(1 + 2i)^2$
    $= i(3 - 4i) + 3i(1 + 2i)^2$
    $= i(3 - 4i) + 3i(1 + 4i + 4i^2)$
    $= i(3 - 4i) + 3i(1 + 4i - 4)$
    $= i(3 - 4i) + 3i(-3 + 4i)$
    $= 3i - 4i^2 - 9i + 12i^2$
    $= 3i + 4 - 9i - 12$
    $= -8 - 6i$

83. $\mathbf{u} = \langle -2, 9 \rangle$, $\mathbf{v} = \langle 6, 5 \rangle$
    $|\mathbf{u}| = \sqrt{(-2)^2 + 9^2} = \sqrt{85}$
    $|\mathbf{v}| = \sqrt{6^2 + 5^2} = \sqrt{61}$
    $\cos\theta = \left(\dfrac{\mathbf{u}}{|\mathbf{u}|} \cdot \dfrac{\mathbf{v}}{|\mathbf{v}|} \right)$
    $\cos\theta = \left\langle -\dfrac{2}{\sqrt{85}}, \dfrac{9}{\sqrt{85}} \right\rangle \cdot \left\langle \dfrac{6}{\sqrt{61}}, \dfrac{5}{\sqrt{61}} \right\rangle$
    $\cos\theta = -\dfrac{2}{\sqrt{85}} \cdot \dfrac{6}{\sqrt{61}} + \dfrac{9}{\sqrt{85}} \cdot \dfrac{5}{\sqrt{61}}$
    $\cos\theta = -\dfrac{12}{\sqrt{5185}} + \dfrac{45}{\sqrt{5185}}$
    $\cos\theta = \dfrac{33}{\sqrt{5185}}$
    $\theta = \cos^{-1}\left(\dfrac{33}{\sqrt{5185}} \right)$
    $\theta \approx 62.7°$

85. Begin on the right side of the equation.
    $\dfrac{\cos^2\theta}{1 - \sin\theta} = \dfrac{1 - \sin^2\theta}{1 - \sin\theta}$
    $\qquad\qquad = \dfrac{(1 + \sin\theta)(1 - \sin\theta)}{1 - \sin\theta}$
    $\qquad\qquad = 1 + \sin\theta$

87. $a^2 = b^2 + c^2 - 2ab\cos C$
    $a^2 = 250^2 + 172^2 - 2(250)(172)\cos 32°$
    $a^2 = 62{,}500 + 29{,}584 - 86{,}000\cos 32°$
    $a^2 = 19{,}151.9$
    $a \approx 138.4 \ m$
    $\dfrac{\sin C}{172} = \dfrac{\sin 32°}{138.4}$
    $\sin C = \dfrac{172 \sin 32°}{138.4}$
    $C = \sin^{-1}\left(\dfrac{172\sin 32°}{138.4} \right)$
    $C \approx 41.2°$
    $B = 180° - (41.2° + 32°) = 106.8°$

Angles	Sides
$A = 32°$	$a \approx 138.4 \ m$
$B \approx 106.8°$	$b = 250 \ m$
$C \approx 41.2°$	$c = 172 \ m$

    $P = 138.4 + 250 + 172 = 560.4 \ m$
    $A = \dfrac{1}{2}(250)(172)\sin 32° \approx 11393.3 \ m^2$

Technology Highlight

1. Argument of $z_1 = 2 + 3i$: 56.31°
    Argument of $z_2 = 8 + 2i$: 14.04°

    $56.31° - 14.04° = 42.27°$

    Argument of $\dfrac{z_1}{z_2} = \dfrac{2+3i}{8+2i}$: 42.27°

3. $(87 - 87i)(-187.5 + 62.5i\sqrt{3})$
    $= -16,312.5 + 5437.5i\sqrt{3}$
    $\qquad + 16,312.5i + 5437.5\sqrt{3}$
    $= \left(-16,312.5 + 5437.5\sqrt{3}\right)$
    $\qquad + \left(5437.5\sqrt{3} + 16,312.5\right)i$

    Let $z_1 = 87 - 87i$.
    $|z_1| = \sqrt{87^2 + (-87)^2}$
    $\quad\ = \sqrt{15,138}$
    $\theta_1 = -45°$

    Let $z_2 = -187.5 + 62.5i\sqrt{3}$.
    $|z_2| = \sqrt{(-187.5)^2 + \left(62.5\sqrt{3}\right)^2}$
    $\quad\ = \sqrt{46,875}$
    $\theta_2 = 150°$

    $z_1 z_2 = \sqrt{15,138} \cdot \sqrt{46,875}\,cis\left(150° + (-45°)\right)$
    $\qquad = 10,875\sqrt{6}\,cis\,105°$
    Trigonometric form was more efficient.

8.2 Exercises

1. modulus; argument

3. multiply; add

5. $z = -1 - i\sqrt{3}$
    $|z| = \sqrt{(-1)^2 + \left(-\sqrt{3}\right)^2} = \sqrt{4} = 2$
    $\theta_r = \tan^{-1}\left|\dfrac{-\sqrt{3}}{-1}\right| = \tan^{-1}\sqrt{3} = 60°$
    In QIII, $\theta = 240°$
    $2\left(\cos 240° + i\sin 240°\right)$, z is in QIII

7.
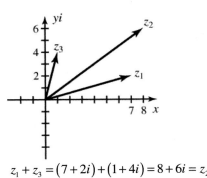

    $z_1 + z_3 = (7 + 2i) + (1 + 4i) = 8 + 6i = z_2$

9.
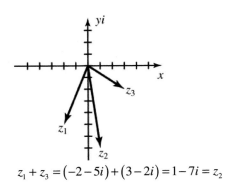

    $z_1 + z_3 = (-2 - 5i) + (3 - 2i) = 1 - 7i = z_2$

11.

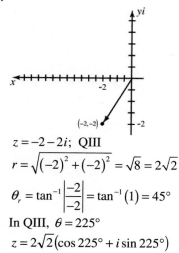

$z = -2 - 2i$; QIII

$r = \sqrt{(-2)^2 + (-2)^2} = \sqrt{8} = 2\sqrt{2}$

$\theta_r = \tan^{-1}\left|\dfrac{-2}{-2}\right| = \tan^{-1}(1) = 45°$

In QIII, $\theta = 225°$

$z = 2\sqrt{2}\left(\cos 225° + i\sin 225°\right)$

13.

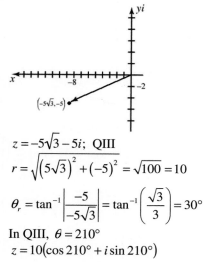

$z = -5\sqrt{3} - 5i$; QIII

$r = \sqrt{\left(5\sqrt{3}\right)^2 + (-5)^2} = \sqrt{100} = 10$

$\theta_r = \tan^{-1}\left|\dfrac{-5}{-5\sqrt{3}}\right| = \tan^{-1}\left(\dfrac{\sqrt{3}}{3}\right) = 30°$

In QIII, $\theta = 210°$

$z = 10\left(\cos 210° + i\sin 210°\right)$

15.

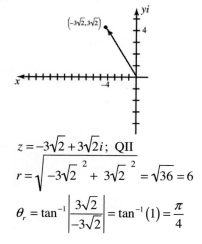

$z = -3\sqrt{2} + 3\sqrt{2}i$; QII

$r = \sqrt{\left(-3\sqrt{2}\right)^2 + \left(3\sqrt{2}\right)^2} = \sqrt{36} = 6$

$\theta_r = \tan^{-1}\left|\dfrac{3\sqrt{2}}{-3\sqrt{2}}\right| = \tan^{-1}(1) = \dfrac{\pi}{4}$

15. (continued)

In QII, $\theta = \dfrac{3\pi}{4}$

$z = 6\left[\cos \dfrac{3\pi}{4} + i\sin \dfrac{3\pi}{4}\right]$

17.

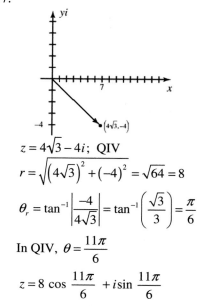

$z = 4\sqrt{3} - 4i$; QIV

$r = \sqrt{\left(4\sqrt{3}\right)^2 + (-4)^2} = \sqrt{64} = 8$

$\theta_r = \tan^{-1}\left|\dfrac{-4}{4\sqrt{3}}\right| = \tan^{-1}\left(\dfrac{\sqrt{3}}{3}\right) = \dfrac{\pi}{6}$

In QIV, $\theta = \dfrac{11\pi}{6}$

$z = 8\left[\cos \dfrac{11\pi}{6} + i\sin \dfrac{11\pi}{6}\right]$

19.

$z = 8 + 6i$; QI

$r = \sqrt{8^2 + 6^2} = 10$

$\theta = \tan^{-1}\left|\dfrac{6}{8}\right| = \tan^{-1}\left(\dfrac{3}{4}\right) \approx 36.9°$

$z = 10\text{cis}\left[\tan^{-1}\left(\dfrac{6}{8}\right)\right] \approx 10\text{cis}36.9°$

21.

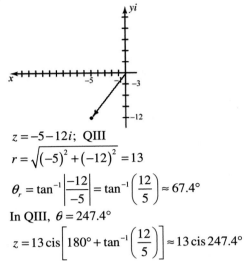

$z = -5 - 12i$; QIII

$r = \sqrt{(-5)^2 + (-12)^2} = 13$

$\theta_r = \tan^{-1}\left|\dfrac{-12}{-5}\right| = \tan^{-1}\left(\dfrac{12}{5}\right) \approx 67.4°$

In QIII, $\theta = 247.4°$

$z = 13\,\text{cis}\left[180° + \tan^{-1}\left(\dfrac{12}{5}\right)\right] \approx 13\,\text{cis}\,247.4°$

23.

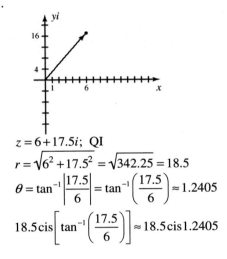

$z = 6 + 17.5i$; QI

$r = \sqrt{6^2 + 17.5^2} = \sqrt{342.25} = 18.5$

$\theta = \tan^{-1}\left|\dfrac{17.5}{6}\right| = \tan^{-1}\left(\dfrac{17.5}{6}\right) \approx 1.2405$

$18.5\,\text{cis}\left[\tan^{-1}\left(\dfrac{17.5}{6}\right)\right] \approx 18.5\,\text{cis}\,1.2405$

25.

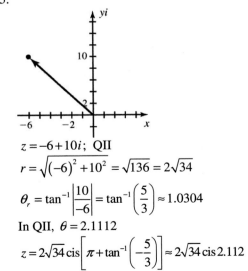

$z = -6 + 10i$; QII

$r = \sqrt{(-6)^2 + 10^2} = \sqrt{136} = 2\sqrt{34}$

$\theta_r = \tan^{-1}\left|\dfrac{10}{-6}\right| = \tan^{-1}\left(\dfrac{5}{3}\right) \approx 1.0304$

In QII, $\theta = 2.1112$

$z = 2\sqrt{34}\,\text{cis}\left[\pi + \tan^{-1}\left(-\dfrac{5}{3}\right)\right] \approx 2\sqrt{34}\,\text{cis}\,2.112$

27. $r = 2, \theta = \dfrac{\pi}{4}$

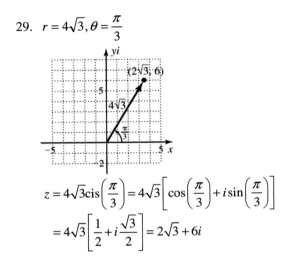

$z = 2\,\text{cis}\left(\dfrac{\pi}{4}\right) = 2\left[\cos\left(\dfrac{\pi}{4}\right) + i\sin\left(\dfrac{\pi}{4}\right)\right]$

$= 2\left[\dfrac{\sqrt{2}}{2} + i\dfrac{\sqrt{2}}{2}\right] = \sqrt{2} + \sqrt{2}i$

29. $r = 4\sqrt{3}, \theta = \dfrac{\pi}{3}$

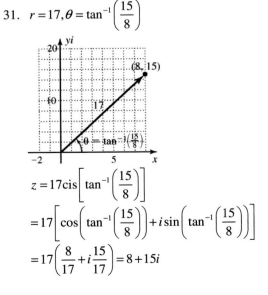

$z = 4\sqrt{3}\,\text{cis}\left(\dfrac{\pi}{3}\right) = 4\sqrt{3}\left[\cos\left(\dfrac{\pi}{3}\right) + i\sin\left(\dfrac{\pi}{3}\right)\right]$

$= 4\sqrt{3}\left[\dfrac{1}{2} + i\dfrac{\sqrt{3}}{2}\right] = 2\sqrt{3} + 6i$

31. $r = 17, \theta = \tan^{-1}\left(\dfrac{15}{8}\right)$

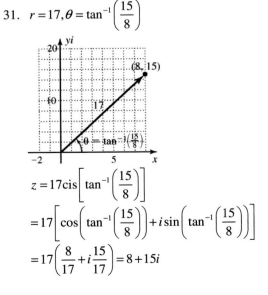

$z = 17\,\text{cis}\left[\tan^{-1}\left(\dfrac{15}{8}\right)\right]$

$= 17\left[\cos\left(\tan^{-1}\left(\dfrac{15}{8}\right)\right) + i\sin\left(\tan^{-1}\left(\dfrac{15}{8}\right)\right)\right]$

$= 17\left(\dfrac{8}{17} + i\dfrac{15}{17}\right) = 8 + 15i$

33. $r = 6, \theta = \pi - \tan^{-1}\left(\dfrac{5}{\sqrt{11}}\right)$

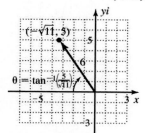

First, pretend that the "$\pi -$" is not there:

$\cos \tan^{-1}\dfrac{5}{\sqrt{11}} = \dfrac{\sqrt{11}}{6}$

$\sin \tan^{-1}\dfrac{5}{\sqrt{11}} = \dfrac{5}{6}$

Now use subtraction identities.

For convenience, let $\theta = \tan^{-1}\dfrac{5}{\sqrt{11}}$.

$\cos(\pi - \theta) = \cos\pi\cos\theta + \sin\pi\sin\theta$

$\qquad = -1\left(\dfrac{\sqrt{11}}{6}\right) + 0 = -\dfrac{\sqrt{11}}{6}$

$\sin(\pi - \theta) = \sin\pi\cos\theta - \cos\pi\sin\theta$

$\qquad = 0 - (-1)\dfrac{5}{6} = \dfrac{5}{6}$

$z = 6\text{cis}\left[\pi - \tan^{-1}\dfrac{5}{\sqrt{11}}\right]$

$\quad = 6\left[\cos(\pi - \theta) + i\sin(\pi - \theta)\right]$

$\quad = 6\left(-\dfrac{\sqrt{11}}{6} + i\dfrac{5}{6}\right) = -\sqrt{11} + 5i$

35. $z_1 = -2 + 2i$

$r_1 = \sqrt{(-2)^2 + 2^2} = \sqrt{8} = 2\sqrt{2}$

$\theta_{1r} = \tan^{-1}\left|\dfrac{2}{-2}\right| = \tan^{-1}(1) = 45°$

In QII, $\theta_1 = 135°$

$z_2 = 3 + 3i$

$r_2 = \sqrt{3^2 + 3^2} = \sqrt{18} = 3\sqrt{2}$

$\theta_2 = \tan^{-1}\left(\dfrac{3}{3}\right) = \tan^{-1}(1) = 45°$

$z_1 z_2 = (-2 + 2i)(3 + 3i)$

$\qquad = -6 - 6i + 6i + 6i^2$

$\qquad = -12 + 0i$

$r_1 r_2 = (2\sqrt{2})(3\sqrt{2}) = 12$

$\theta_1 + \theta_2 = 135° + 45° = 180°$

$12(\cos 180° + i\sin 180°) = -12 + 0i$

37. $z_1 = \sqrt{3} + i$

$r_1 = \sqrt{\left(\sqrt{3}\right)^2 + 1^2} = \sqrt{4} = 2$

$\theta_1 = \tan^{-1}\left(\dfrac{1}{\sqrt{3}}\right) = \tan^{-1}\left(\dfrac{\sqrt{3}}{3}\right) = 30°$

$z_2 = 1 + \sqrt{3}i$

$r_2 = \sqrt{1^2 + \left(\sqrt{3}\right)^2} = \sqrt{4} = 2$

$\theta_2 = \tan^{-1}\left(\dfrac{\sqrt{3}}{1}\right) = \tan^{-1}\left(\sqrt{3}\right) = 60°$

$\dfrac{z_1}{z_2} = \dfrac{\sqrt{3} + i}{1 + \sqrt{3}i} \cdot \dfrac{1 - \sqrt{3}i}{1 - \sqrt{3}i}$

$\qquad = \dfrac{\sqrt{3} - 3i + i - \sqrt{3}i^2}{1^2 + 3^2}$

$\qquad = \dfrac{2\sqrt{3} - 2i}{4} = \dfrac{\sqrt{3}}{2} - \dfrac{1}{2}i$

$\dfrac{r_1}{r_2} = \dfrac{2}{2} = 1$

$\theta_1 - \theta_2 = 30° - 60° = -30°$

$1\left[\cos(-30°) + i\sin(-30°)\right] = \dfrac{\sqrt{3}}{2} - \dfrac{1}{2}i$

39. $z_1 = -4\sqrt{3} + 4i$

$r_1 = \sqrt{\left(-4\sqrt{3}\right)^2 + 4^2} = \sqrt{64} = 8$

$\theta_{1r} = \tan^{-1}\left|\dfrac{4}{-4\sqrt{3}}\right| = \tan^{-1}\left(\dfrac{\sqrt{3}}{3}\right) = \dfrac{\pi}{6}$

In QIV, $\theta_1 = \dfrac{5\pi}{6}$

$z_2 = \dfrac{3\sqrt{3}}{2} + \dfrac{3}{2}i$

$r_2 = \sqrt{\left(\dfrac{3\sqrt{3}}{2}\right)^2 + \left(\dfrac{3}{2}\right)^2} = \sqrt{\dfrac{36}{4}} = \sqrt{9} = 3$

$\theta_2 = \tan^{-1}\left|\dfrac{3/2}{3\sqrt{3}/2}\right| = \tan^{-1}\left(\dfrac{\sqrt{3}}{3}\right) = \dfrac{\pi}{6}$

$z_1 z_2 = (8)(3)\operatorname{cis}\left(\dfrac{5\pi}{6} + \dfrac{\pi}{6}\right)$

$= 24\operatorname{cis}\pi = -24 + 0i$

$\dfrac{z_1}{z_2} = \dfrac{8}{3}\operatorname{cis}\left(\dfrac{5\pi}{6} - \dfrac{\pi}{6}\right) = \dfrac{8}{3}\operatorname{cis}\dfrac{2\pi}{3}$

$= \dfrac{8}{3}\left(-\dfrac{1}{2} + i\dfrac{\sqrt{3}}{2}\right) = -\dfrac{4}{3} + \dfrac{4\sqrt{3}}{3}i$

41. $z_1 = -2\sqrt{3} + 0i$

$r_1 = \sqrt{\left(-2\sqrt{3}\right)^2 + 0^2} = 2\sqrt{3}$

$\theta_{1r} = \tan^{-1}\left|\dfrac{0}{-2\sqrt{3}}\right| = \tan^{-1}(0) = 0; \quad \theta_1 = \pi$

$z_2 = -\dfrac{21}{2} + \dfrac{7\sqrt{3}}{2}i$

$r_2 = \sqrt{\left(-\dfrac{21}{2}\right)^2 + \left(\dfrac{7\sqrt{3}}{2}\right)^2} = \sqrt{\dfrac{588}{4}} = \sqrt{147} = 7\sqrt{3}$

$\theta_{2r} = \tan^{-1}\left|\dfrac{7\sqrt{3}/2}{-21/2}\right| = \tan^{-1}\left(\dfrac{\sqrt{3}}{3}\right) = \dfrac{\pi}{6}; \quad \theta_1 = \dfrac{5\pi}{6}$

$z_1 z_2 = \left(2\sqrt{3}\right)\left(7\sqrt{3}\right)\operatorname{cis}\left(\pi + \dfrac{5\pi}{6}\right) = 42\operatorname{cis}\dfrac{11\pi}{6}$

$= 42\left(\dfrac{\sqrt{3}}{2} - \dfrac{1}{2}i\right) = 21\sqrt{3} - 21i$

$\dfrac{z_1}{z_2} = \dfrac{2\sqrt{3}}{7\sqrt{3}}\operatorname{cis}\left(\pi - \dfrac{5\pi}{6}\right) = \dfrac{2}{7}\operatorname{cis}\dfrac{\pi}{6}$

$= \dfrac{2}{7}\left(\dfrac{\sqrt{3}}{2} + \dfrac{1}{2}i\right) = \dfrac{\sqrt{3}}{7} + \dfrac{1}{7}i$

43. $z_1 z_2 = (9)(1.8)\operatorname{cis}\left(\dfrac{\pi}{15} + \dfrac{2\pi}{3}\right)$

$= 16.2\left[\cos\left(\dfrac{11\pi}{15}\right) + i\sin\left(\dfrac{11\pi}{15}\right)\right]$

$\approx -10.84 + 12.04i$

$\dfrac{z_1}{z_2} = \dfrac{9}{1.8}\operatorname{cis}\left(\dfrac{\pi}{15} - \dfrac{2\pi}{3}\right)$

$= 5\left[\cos\left(-\dfrac{3\pi}{5}\right) + i\sin\left(-\dfrac{3\pi}{5}\right)\right]$

$\approx -1.55 - 4.76i$

45. $z_1 z_2 = 10(4)\operatorname{cis}\left(60° + 30°\right)$

$= 40\left(\cos 90° + i\sin 90°\right)$

$= 40(0 + i) = 0 + 40i$

$\dfrac{z_1}{z_2} = \dfrac{10}{4}\operatorname{cis}\left(60° - 30°\right)$

$= \dfrac{5}{2}\left(\cos 30° + i\sin 30°\right)$

$= \dfrac{5}{2}\left(\dfrac{\sqrt{3}}{2} + \dfrac{1}{2}i\right) = \dfrac{5\sqrt{3}}{4} + \dfrac{5}{4}i$

47. $z_1 z_2 = \left(5\sqrt{2}\right)\left(2\sqrt{2}\right)\operatorname{cis}\left(210° + 30°\right)$

$= 20\left(\cos 240° + i\sin 240°\right)$

$= 20\left(-\dfrac{1}{2} - \dfrac{\sqrt{3}}{2}i\right) = -10 - 10i\sqrt{3}$

$\dfrac{z_1}{z_2} = \dfrac{5\sqrt{2}}{2\sqrt{2}}\operatorname{cis}\left(210° - 30°\right)$

$= \dfrac{5}{2}\left(\cos 180° + i\sin 180°\right)$

$= \dfrac{5}{2}\left(-1 + 0i\right) = -\dfrac{5}{2} + 0i$

49. $r_1 r_2 = 6(1.5) = 9$

$\theta_1 + \theta_2 = 82° + 27° = 109°$

$z_1 z_2 = 6(1.5)\operatorname{cis}\left(82° + 27°\right)$

$= 9\left(\cos 109° + i\sin 109°\right)$

$\approx -2.93 + 8.5i$

$\dfrac{z_1}{z_2} = \dfrac{6}{1.5}\operatorname{cis}\left(82° - 27°\right)$

$= 4\left(\cos 55° + i\sin 55°\right)$

$\approx 2.29 + 3.28i$

51. Distance from u to v:

$$d = \sqrt{(10-2)^2 + \left(\sqrt{3} - \sqrt{3}\right)^2} = 8$$

Distance from v to w:

$$d = \sqrt{(6-10)^2 + \left(5\sqrt{3} - \sqrt{3}\right)^2} = \sqrt{16 + 48} = 8$$

Distance from w to u:

$$d = \sqrt{(2-6)^2 + \left(\sqrt{3} - 5\sqrt{3}\right)^2} = \sqrt{16 + 48} = 8$$

All sides have length 8.

$$u^2 = \left(2 + \sqrt{3}i\right)\left(2 + \sqrt{3}i\right)$$
$$= 4 + 4\sqrt{3}i + 3i^2$$
$$= 1 + 4\sqrt{3}i$$

$$v^2 = \left(10 + \sqrt{3}i\right)\left(10 + \sqrt{3}i\right)$$
$$= 100 + 20\sqrt{3}i + 3i^2$$
$$= 97 + 20\sqrt{3}i$$

$$w^2 = \left(6 + 5\sqrt{3}i\right)\left(6 + 5\sqrt{3}i\right)$$
$$= 36 + 60\sqrt{3}i + 75i^2$$
$$= -39 + 60\sqrt{3}i$$

$$uv = \left(2 + \sqrt{3}i\right)\left(10 + \sqrt{3}i\right)$$
$$= 20 + 12\sqrt{3}i + 3i^2$$
$$= 17 + 12\sqrt{3}i$$

$$uw = \left(2 + \sqrt{3}i\right)\left(6 + 5\sqrt{3}i\right)$$
$$= 12 + 16\sqrt{3}i + 15i^2$$
$$= -3 + 16\sqrt{3}i$$

$$vw = \left(10 + \sqrt{3}i\right)\left(6 + 5\sqrt{3}i\right)$$
$$= 60 + 56\sqrt{3}i + 15i^2$$
$$= 45 + 56\sqrt{3}i$$

$$u^2 + v^2 + w^2$$
$$= \left(1 + 4\sqrt{3}i\right) + \left(97 + 20\sqrt{3}i\right) + \left(-39 + 60\sqrt{3}i\right)$$
$$= 59 + 84\sqrt{3}i$$

$$uv + uw + vw$$
$$= \left(17 + 12\sqrt{3}i\right) + \left(-3 + 16\sqrt{3}i\right) + 45 + 56\sqrt{3}i$$
$$= 59 + 84\sqrt{3}i$$

53. a. $A = 120$ V
$$V(t) = 170\sin\left(f\left(2\pi t\right)\right)$$
$$= 170\sin\left(60(2\pi t)\right)$$
$$= 170\sin\left(120\pi t\right)$$

b. One cycle is $1/60 \approx 0.0167$ sec, so our table should go to 0.008.

t	V	t	V
0	0	0.005	161.7
0.001	62.6	0.006	131.0
0.002	116.4	0.007	81.9
0.003	153.8	0.008	21.3
0.004	169.7		

c. The graph of V is at height 140 at about $t \approx 0.00257$ sec.

55. a. $Z = R + \left(X_L - X_C\right)j$
$$Z = 15 + (12 - 4)j = 15 + 8j; \ \ \text{QI}$$

$$|Z| = \sqrt{R^2 + \left(X_L - X_C\right)^2}$$
$$|Z| = \sqrt{15^2 + (12 - 4)^2} = 17$$
$$\theta = \tan^{-1}\left|\frac{8}{15}\right| = \tan^{-1}\left(\frac{8}{15}\right) \approx 28.1°$$
$$Z = 17\,\text{cis}\,28.1°$$

b. $V_{RLC} = I|Z| = 3(17) = 51$ V

57. a. $Z = R + \left(X_L - X_C\right)j$
$$Z = 7 + (6 - 11)j = 7 - 5j; \ \ \text{QIV}$$

$$|Z| = \sqrt{R^2 + \left(X_L - X_C\right)^2}$$
$$|Z| = \sqrt{7^2 + (6 - 11)^2} = \sqrt{74} \approx 8.60$$
$$\theta_r = \tan^{-1}\left|\frac{-5}{7}\right| = \tan^{-1}\left(\frac{5}{7}\right) \approx 35.5°$$
In QIV, $\theta = 324.5°$
$$Z = 8.6\,\text{cis}\,324.5°$$

b. $V_{RLC} = I|Z| = 1.8(8.60) = 15.48$ V

59. a. $Z = R + (X_L - X_C) j$

   $Z = 12 + (5 - 0) j = 12 + 5j;\ \text{QI}$

   $|Z| = \sqrt{R^2 + (X_L - X_C)^2}$

   $|Z| = \sqrt{12^2 + (5 - 0)^2} = 13$

   $\theta = \tan^{-1}\left|\dfrac{5}{12}\right| = \tan^{-1}\left(\dfrac{5}{12}\right) \approx 22.6°$

   $Z = 13\,\text{cis}\,22.6°$

   b. $V_{RLC} = I\,|Z| = 1.7(13) = 22.1\ \text{V}$

61. Both are in QI.

   $r_I = \sqrt{\left(\sqrt{3}\right)^2 + 1^2} = \sqrt{4} = 2$

   $\theta_I = \tan^{-1}\left|\dfrac{1}{\sqrt{3}}\right| = \tan^{-1}\left(\dfrac{\sqrt{3}}{3}\right) = 30°$

   $I = 2\,\text{cis}\,30°$

   $r_Z = \sqrt{5^2 + 5^2} = \sqrt{50} = 5\sqrt{2}$

   $\theta_Z = \tan^{-1}\left|\dfrac{5}{5}\right| = \tan^{-1}(1) = 45°$

   $Z = 5\sqrt{2}\,\text{cis}\,45°$

   $V = IZ$

   $\quad = 2\left(5\sqrt{2}\right)\text{cis}(30° + 45°)$

   $\quad = 10\sqrt{2}\,\text{cis}\,75°$

63. $r_I = \sqrt{3^2 + (-2)^2} = \sqrt{13}$

   $\theta_{Ir} = \tan^{-1}\left|\dfrac{-2}{3}\right| = \tan^{-1}\left(\dfrac{2}{3}\right) \approx 33.7°\ \theta = 326.3°$

   In QIV, $\theta_I = 326.3°$

   $I = \sqrt{13}\,\text{cis}\,326.3°$

   $r_Z = \sqrt{2^2 + 3.75^2} = 4.25 = \dfrac{17}{4}$

   $\theta_Z = \tan^{-1}\left|\dfrac{3.75}{2}\right| = \tan^{-1}\left(\dfrac{3.75}{2}\right) \approx 61.9°$

   $Z = \dfrac{17}{4}\,\text{cis}\,61.9°$

   $V = IZ$

   $\quad = \sqrt{13}\left(\dfrac{17}{4}\right)\text{cis}(326.3° + 61.9°)$

   $\quad = \dfrac{17\sqrt{13}}{4}\,\text{cis}\,388.2° = \dfrac{17\sqrt{13}}{4}\,\text{cis}\,28.2°$

65. $r_V = \sqrt{2^2 + \left(2\sqrt{3}\right)^2} = \sqrt{16} = 4$

   $\theta_V = \tan^{-1}\left|\dfrac{2\sqrt{3}}{2}\right| = \tan^{-1}\left(\sqrt{3}\right) = 60°$

   $V = 4\,\text{cis}\,60°$

   $r_Z = \sqrt{4^2 + (-4)^2} = \sqrt{32} = 4\sqrt{2}$

   $\theta_{Zr} = \tan^{-1}\left(\dfrac{-4}{4}\right) = \tan^{-1}(1) = 45°$

   In QIV, $\theta_Z = 315°$

   $Z = 4\sqrt{2}\,\text{cis}\,315°$

   $I = \dfrac{V}{Z}$

   $\quad = \dfrac{4}{4\sqrt{2}}\,\text{cis}\left(60° - (-45°)\right)$

   $\quad = \dfrac{\sqrt{2}}{2}\,\text{cis}\,105°$

67. $r_V = \sqrt{3^2 + (-4)^2} = \sqrt{25} = 5$

   $\theta_{Vr} = \tan^{-1}\left|\dfrac{-4}{3}\right| = \tan^{-1}\left(\dfrac{4}{3}\right) = 53.1°$

   In QIV, $\theta_V = 306.9°$

   $V = 5\,\text{cis}\,306.9°$

   $r_Z = \sqrt{4^2 + 7.5^2} = 8.5$

   $\theta_Z = \tan^{-1}\left|\dfrac{7.5}{4}\right| = \tan^{-1}\left(\dfrac{7.5}{4}\right) = 61.9°$

   $Z = 8.5\,\text{cis}\,61.9°$

   $I = \dfrac{V}{Z}$

   $\quad = \dfrac{5}{8.5}\,\text{cis}(306.9° - 61.9°)$

   $\quad = \dfrac{10}{17}\,\text{cis}\,245°$

69. $r_1 = \sqrt{1^2 + 2^2} = \sqrt{5}$

   $\theta_1 = \tan^{-1}\left|\dfrac{2}{1}\right| = \tan^{-1}(2) \approx 63.4°$

   $Z_1 = \sqrt{5}\,\text{cis}\,63.4°$

   $r_2 = \sqrt{3^2 + (-2)^2} = \sqrt{13}$

   $\theta_{2r} = \tan^{-1}\left|\dfrac{-2}{3}\right| = \tan^{-1}\left(\dfrac{2}{3}\right) \approx 33.7°$

69. (continued)

In QIV, $\theta_2 = 326.3°$

$Z_2 = \sqrt{13}\,\text{cis}\,236.3°$

$Z_1 Z_2 = \sqrt{5}\sqrt{13}\,\text{cis}\,(63.4° + 326.3°)$
$= \sqrt{65}\,\text{cis}\,389.7°$
$= \sqrt{65}\,\text{cis}\,29.7°$

$Z_1 + Z_2 = (1 + 2j) + (3 - 2j) = 4$

$Z = \dfrac{Z_1 Z_2}{Z_1 + Z_2} = \dfrac{\sqrt{65}\,\text{cis}\,29.7°}{4}$

71. $\dfrac{r_1}{r_2}\left[\cos(\alpha - \beta) + i\sin(\alpha - \beta)\right]$

$= \dfrac{r_1}{r_2}\left(\cos\alpha\cos\beta + \sin\alpha\sin\beta\right)$

$\qquad + i\dfrac{r_1}{r_2}\left(\sin\alpha\cos\beta + \cos\alpha\sin\beta\right)$

$\dfrac{\cos\alpha + i\sin\alpha}{\cos\beta + i\sin\beta} \cdot \dfrac{\cos\beta - i\sin\beta}{\cos\beta - i\sin\beta}$

$= \dfrac{\cos\alpha\cos\beta - i\cos\alpha\sin\beta + i\cos\beta\sin\alpha - i^2\sin\alpha\sin\beta}{\cos^2\beta - i^2\sin^2\beta}$

$= \dfrac{\cos\alpha\cos\beta + \sin\alpha\sin\beta}{\cos^2\beta + \sin^2\beta} + i\dfrac{\sin\alpha\cos\beta + \cos\alpha\sin\beta}{\cos^2\beta + \sin^2\beta}$

$= \dfrac{\cos\alpha\cos\beta + \sin\alpha\sin\beta}{1} + i\dfrac{\sin\alpha\cos\beta + \cos\alpha\sin\beta}{1}$

Note that $\dfrac{r_1}{r_2}$ times this expression is equal to

$\dfrac{z_1}{z_2}$, and is also equal to the expanded version

of the right side, and we're done.

73. The slope for segment 1 is $\dfrac{\Delta y}{\Delta x} = \dfrac{24}{7}$, so we need

slope $-\dfrac{7}{24}$. We can accomplish this with

$y = -7,\ x = 24,$ or $y = 7,\ x = -24.$

This gives us $24 - 7i$ and $-24 + 7i.$
The magnitude of each is the same as the
magnitude of z_1, so we need to divide each
by 5 to get magnitude one-fifth as great.

$z_2 = \dfrac{24}{5} - \dfrac{7}{5}i,\quad z_3 = -\dfrac{24}{5} + \dfrac{7}{5}i$

75. $350 = 750\sin\left(2x - \dfrac{\pi}{4}\right) - 25$

$375 = 750\sin\left(2x - \dfrac{\pi}{4}\right)$

$\dfrac{1}{2} = \sin\left(2x - \dfrac{\pi}{4}\right)$

$2x - \dfrac{\pi}{4} = \sin^{-1}\left(\dfrac{1}{2}\right)$

$0 \le x < 2\pi \ \Rightarrow\ 0 \le 2x < 4\pi$

$2x - \dfrac{\pi}{4} = \dfrac{\pi}{6},\ \dfrac{5\pi}{6},\ \dfrac{13\pi}{6},\ \dfrac{17\pi}{6}$

$2x = \dfrac{\pi}{6} + \dfrac{\pi}{4},\ \dfrac{5\pi}{6} + \dfrac{\pi}{4},\ \dfrac{13\pi}{6} + \dfrac{\pi}{4},\ \dfrac{17\pi}{6} + \dfrac{\pi}{4}$

$2x = \dfrac{5\pi}{12},\ \dfrac{13\pi}{12},\ \dfrac{29\pi}{12},\ \dfrac{37\pi}{12}$

$x = \dfrac{5\pi}{24},\ \dfrac{13\pi}{24},\ \dfrac{29\pi}{24},\ \dfrac{37\pi}{24}$

77. $\dfrac{1 + \cos\alpha}{1 - \cos\alpha} = \left(\dfrac{1 + \cos\alpha}{1 - \cos\alpha}\right)\dfrac{\sec\alpha}{\sec\alpha}$

$\qquad = \dfrac{\sec\alpha + 1}{\sec\alpha - 1}$

79. The angle at the ship is $180° - (41° + 63°) = 76°.$
Use the Law of Sines.

$\dfrac{\sin 76°}{4} = \dfrac{\sin 41°}{d}$

$d\sin 76° = 4\sin 41°$

$d = \dfrac{4\sin 41°}{\sin 76°}$

$d \approx 2.70 \text{ mi}$

Technology Highlight

Exercise 1:

$r = 1,\ \theta = 0°$

The cube roots are $1, -\dfrac{1}{2} \pm \dfrac{\sqrt{3}}{2}i$

$\left(\text{Note: } \dfrac{\sqrt{3}}{2} \approx 0.8660\right)$

8.3 Exercises

1. $r^5\left[\cos(5\theta)+i\sin(5\theta)\right]$; DeMoivre's

3. complex

5. Answers will vary.
    $z_5 = 2\text{cis}366° = 2\text{cis}6°$
    $z_6 = 2\text{cis}438° = 2\text{cis}78°$
    $z_7 = 2\text{cis}510° = 2\text{cis}150°$
    These are equal to $z_0, z_1,$ and z_2.
    Answers will vary.

7. $r = \sqrt{3^2+3^2} = \sqrt{18} = 3\sqrt{2};\ n = 4$
    $\theta = \tan^{-1}\left|\dfrac{3}{3}\right| = \tan^{-1}(1) = 45°$
    $4\cdot 45° = 180°$
    $(3+3i)^4 = \left(3\sqrt{2}\right)^4\left(\cos180°+i\sin180°\right)$
    $\qquad\qquad = 324(-1+0i)$
    $\qquad\qquad = -324$

9. $r = \sqrt{(-1)^2+\left(\sqrt{3}\right)^2} = \sqrt{4} = 2;\ n = 3$
    $\theta_r = \tan^{-1}\left|\dfrac{\sqrt{3}}{-1}\right| = \tan^{-1}\left(\sqrt{3}\right) = 60°$
    In QII, $\theta = 120°$
    $3\cdot 120° = 360°$
    $\left(-1+\sqrt{3}i\right)^3 = 2^3\left(\cos360°+i\sin360°\right)$
    $\qquad\qquad = 8(1+0i)$
    $\qquad\qquad = 8$

11. $r = \sqrt{\left(\dfrac{1}{2}\right)^2+\left(-\dfrac{\sqrt{3}}{2}\right)^2} = 1;\ n = 5$
    $\theta_r = \tan^{-1}\left|\dfrac{-\sqrt{3}/2}{1/2}\right| = \tan^{-1}\left(\sqrt{3}\right) = 60°$
    In QIV, $\theta = -60°$
    $5\cdot -60° = -300°$, coterminal with $60°$.
    $\left(\dfrac{1}{2}-\dfrac{\sqrt{3}}{2}i\right)^5 = 1^5\left(\cos60°+i\sin60°\right)$
    $\qquad\qquad = 1\left(\dfrac{1}{2}+i\dfrac{\sqrt{3}}{2}\right)$
    $\qquad\qquad = \dfrac{1}{2}+\dfrac{\sqrt{3}}{2}i$

13. $r = \sqrt{\left(\dfrac{\sqrt{2}}{2}\right)^2+\left(-\dfrac{\sqrt{2}}{2}\right)^2} = 1;\ n = 6$
    $\theta_r = \tan^{-1}\left|\dfrac{-\sqrt{2}/2}{\sqrt{2}/2}\right| = \tan^{-1}(1) = 45°$
    In QIV, $\theta = 315°$
    $6\cdot 315° = 1890°$, coterminal with $90°$.
    $\left(\dfrac{\sqrt{2}}{2}-\dfrac{\sqrt{2}}{2}i\right)^6 = 1^6\left(\cos90°+i\sin90°\right)$
    $\qquad\qquad = 1(0+i)$
    $\qquad\qquad = i$

15. $4\text{cis}330° = 4\left(\cos330°+i\sin330°\right)$
    $\qquad\qquad = 4\left(\dfrac{\sqrt{3}}{2}-\dfrac{1}{2}i\right)$
    $\qquad\qquad = 2\sqrt{3}-2i$
    $r = \sqrt{\left(2\sqrt{3}\right)^2+(-2)^2} = \sqrt{16} = 4;\ n = 3$
    $\theta_r = \tan^{-1}\left|\dfrac{-2}{2\sqrt{3}}\right| = \tan^{-1}\left(\dfrac{\sqrt{3}}{3}\right) = 30°$
    In QIV, $\theta = 330°$
    $3\cdot 330° = 990°$, coterminal with $270°$.
    $\left(4\text{cis}330°\right)^3 = 4^3\left(\cos270°+i\sin270°\right)$
    $\qquad\qquad = 64(0-1i)$
    $\qquad\qquad = -64i$

17. $\dfrac{\sqrt{2}}{2}\text{cis}135° = \dfrac{\sqrt{2}}{2}\left(\cos135°+i\sin135°\right)$
    $\qquad\qquad = \dfrac{\sqrt{2}}{2}\left(-\dfrac{\sqrt{2}}{2}+\dfrac{\sqrt{2}}{2}i\right) = -\dfrac{1}{2}+\dfrac{1}{2}i$
    $r = \sqrt{\left(-\dfrac{1}{2}\right)^2+\left(\dfrac{1}{2}\right)^2} = \sqrt{\dfrac{1}{2}} = \dfrac{\sqrt{2}}{2};\ n = 5$
    $\theta_r = \tan^{-1}\left|\dfrac{1/2}{-1/2}\right| = \tan^{-1}(1) = 45°$
    In QII, $\theta = 135°$
    $5\cdot 135° = 675°$, coterminal with $315°$
    $\left(\dfrac{\sqrt{2}}{2}\text{cis}135°\right)^5 = \left(\dfrac{\sqrt{2}}{2}\right)^5\left(\cos315°+i\sin315°\right)$
    $\qquad\qquad = \dfrac{\sqrt{2}}{8}\left(\dfrac{\sqrt{2}}{2}-\dfrac{\sqrt{2}}{2}i\right) = \dfrac{1}{8}-\dfrac{1}{8}i$

19. $r = 2;\ \theta = 90°$

$4 \cdot 90° = 360°$

$3 \cdot 90° = 270°$

$2 \cdot 90° = 180°$

$z^4 = 2^4 \operatorname{cis} 360° = 16$

$z^3 = 2^3 \operatorname{cis} 270° = -8i$

$z^2 = 2^2 \operatorname{cis} 180° = -4$

$z = 2i$

$z^4 + 3z^3 - 6z^2 + 12z - 40$

$= 16 + 3(-8i) - 6(-4) + 12(2i) - 40$

$= 16 - 24i + 24 + 24i - 40 = 0$

21. $r = \sqrt{(-3)^2 + (-3)^2} = \sqrt{18} = 3\sqrt{2}$

$\theta_r = \tan^{-1}\left|\dfrac{-3}{-3}\right| = \tan^{-1}(1) = 45°;\ \theta = 225°$

$4 \cdot 225° = 900°$, coterminal with $180°$

$3 \cdot 225° = 675°$, coterminal with $315°$

$2 \cdot 225° = 450°$, coterminal with $90°$

$z^4 = \left(3\sqrt{2}\right)^4 \operatorname{cis} 180° = -324$

$z^3 = \left(3\sqrt{2}\right)^3 \operatorname{cis} 315° = 54 - 54i$

$z^2 = \left(3\sqrt{2}\right)^2 \operatorname{cis} 90° = 18i$

$z = -3 - 3i$

$z^4 + 6z^3 + 19z^2 + 6z + 18$

$= -324 + 6(54 - 54i) + 19(18i) + 6(-3 - 3i) + 18$

$= -324 + 324 - 324i + 342i - 18 - 18i + 18 = 0$

23. $r = \sqrt{\left(\sqrt{3}\right)^2 + (-1)^2} = 2$

$\theta_r = \tan^{-1}\left|\dfrac{-1}{\sqrt{3}}\right| = \tan^{-1}\left(\dfrac{\sqrt{3}}{3}\right) = 30°;\ \theta = 330°$

$5 \cdot 330° = 1650°$, coterminal with $210°$

$4 \cdot 330° = 1320°$, coterminal with $240°$

$3 \cdot 330° = 990°$, coterminal with $270°$

$2 \cdot 330° = 660°$, coterminal with $300°$

$z^4 = 2^5 \operatorname{cis} 210° = -16\sqrt{3} - 16i$

$z^4 = 2^4 \operatorname{cis} 240° = -8 - 8i\sqrt{3}$

$z^3 = 2^3 \operatorname{cis} 270° = -8i$

$z^2 = 2^2 \operatorname{cis} 300° = 2 - 2i\sqrt{3}$

$z = \sqrt{3} - i$

$z^5 + z^4 - 4z^3 - 4z^2 + 16z + 16$

$= \left(-16\sqrt{3} - 16i\right) + \left(-8 - 8i\sqrt{3}\right) - 4(-8i)$

$\quad -4\left(2 - 2i\sqrt{3}\right) + 16\left(\sqrt{3} - i\right) + 16$

$= -16\sqrt{3} - 16i - 8 - 8i\sqrt{3} + 32i$

$\quad -8 + 8i\sqrt{3} + 16\sqrt{3} - 16i + 16$

25. $r = \sqrt{1^2 + (2)^2} = \sqrt{5}$

$\theta = \tan^{-1}\left|\dfrac{2}{1}\right| = \tan^{-1}(2)$

$z^4 = \sqrt{5}^4 \left[\cos\left(4\tan^{-1}(2)\right) + i\sin\left(4\tan^{-1}(2)\right)\right]$

$\quad = -7 - 24i$

$z^3 = \sqrt{5}^3 \left[\cos\left(3\tan^{-1}(2)\right) + i\sin\left(3\tan^{-1}(2)\right)\right]$

$\quad = -11 - 2i$

$z^2 = \sqrt{5}^2 \left[\cos\left(2\tan^{-1}(2)\right) + i\sin\left(2\tan^{-1}(2)\right)\right]$

$\quad = -3 + 4i$

$z = 1 + 2i$

$z^4 - 4z^3 + 7z^2 - 6z - 10$

$= (-7 - 24i) - 4(-11 - 2i)$

$\quad + 7(-3 + 4i) - 6(1 + 2i) - 10$

$= -7 - 24i + 44 + 8i - 21 + 28i - 6 - 12i - 10 = 0$

27. $r = 1;\ \theta = 0°;\ n = 5$

$\sqrt[5]{1} = 1;\ \dfrac{0° + 360°k}{5} = 72°k$

$z_0 = \operatorname{cis} 0° = 1$

$z_1 = \operatorname{cis} 72° \approx 0.3090 + 0.9511i$

$z_2 = \operatorname{cis} 144° \approx -0.8090 + 0.5878i$

$z_3 = \operatorname{cis} 216° \approx -0.8090 - 0.5878i$

$z_4 = \operatorname{cis} 288° \approx 0.3090 - 0.9511i$

29. $r = 243;\ \theta = 0°;\ n = 5$

$\sqrt[5]{243} = 3;\ \dfrac{0° + 360°k}{5} = 72°k$

$z_0 = 3\operatorname{cis} 0° = 3$

$z_1 = 3\operatorname{cis} 72° \approx 0.9271 + 2.8532i$

$z_2 = 3\operatorname{cis} 144° \approx -2.4271 + 1.7634i$

$z_3 = 3\operatorname{cis} 216° \approx -2.4271 - 1.7634i$

$z_4 = 3\operatorname{cis} 288° \approx 0.9271 - 2.8532i$

31. $r = 27;\ \theta = 270°;\ n = 3$

$\sqrt[3]{27} = 3;\ \dfrac{270° + 360°k}{3} = 90° + 120°k$

$z_0 = 3\operatorname{cis} 90° = 3(0 + i) = 3i$

$z_1 = 3\operatorname{cis} 210° = 3\left(-\dfrac{\sqrt{3}}{2} - \dfrac{1}{2}i\right) = -\dfrac{3\sqrt{3}}{2} - \dfrac{3}{2}i$

$z_2 = 3\operatorname{cis} 330° = 3\left(\dfrac{\sqrt{3}}{2} - \dfrac{1}{2}i\right) = \dfrac{3\sqrt{3}}{2} - \dfrac{3}{2}i$

33. $x^5 - 32 = 0 \Rightarrow x^5 = 32$

$r = 32; \; \theta = 0°; \; n = 5$

$\sqrt[5]{32} = 2; \; \dfrac{0° + 360°k}{5} = 72°k$

$z_0 = 2\operatorname{cis} 0° = 2$

$z_1 = 2\operatorname{cis} 72° \approx 0.6180 + 1.9021i$

$z_2 = 2\operatorname{cis} 144° \approx -1.6180 + 1.1756i$

$z_3 = 2\operatorname{cis} 216° \approx -1.6780 - 1.1756i$

$z_4 = 2\operatorname{cis} 288° \approx 0.6180 - 1.9021i$

35. $x^3 - 27i = 0 \Rightarrow x^3 = 27i$

$r = 27; \; \theta = 90°; \; n = 3$

$\sqrt[3]{27} = 3; \; \dfrac{90° + 360°k}{3} = 30° + 120°k$,

$z_0 = 3\operatorname{cis} 30° = 3\left(\dfrac{\sqrt{3}}{2} + \dfrac{1}{2}i\right) = \dfrac{3\sqrt{3}}{2} + \dfrac{3}{2}i$

$z_1 = 3\operatorname{cis} 150° = 3\left(-\dfrac{\sqrt{3}}{2} + \dfrac{1}{2}i\right) = -\dfrac{3\sqrt{3}}{2} + \dfrac{3}{2}i$

$z_2 = 3\operatorname{cis} 270° = 3(0 - i) = -3i$

37. $x^5 - \sqrt{2} - \sqrt{2}i = 0 \Rightarrow x^5 = \sqrt{2} + \sqrt{2}i$

$r = 2; \; \theta = 45°; \; n = 5$

$\sqrt[5]{2}; \; \dfrac{45° + 360°k}{5} = 9° + 72°k$

$z_0 = \sqrt[5]{2}\operatorname{cis} 9° \approx 1.1346 + 1.1797i$

$z_1 = \sqrt[5]{2}\operatorname{cis} 81° \approx 0.1797 + 1.1346i$

$z_2 = \sqrt[5]{2}\operatorname{cis} 153° \approx -1.0235 + 0.5215i$

$z_3 = \sqrt[5]{2}\operatorname{cis} 225° \approx -0.8123 - 0.8123i$

$z_4 = \sqrt[5]{2}\operatorname{cis} 297° \approx 0.5215 - 1.0235i$

39. $x^3 - 1 = (x - 1)(x^2 + x + 1) = 0$

$x - 1 = 0 \qquad x = 1$

$x^2 + x + 1 = 0$

$x = \dfrac{-1 \pm \sqrt{1^2 - 4(1)(1)}}{2} = -\dfrac{1}{2} \pm \dfrac{\sqrt{3}}{2}i$

These are the same results as in Example 3.

41. $r = \sqrt{(-8)^2 + \left(8\sqrt{3}\right)^2} = \sqrt{256} = 16; \; n = 4$

$\theta_r = \tan^{-1}\left|\dfrac{8\sqrt{3}}{-8}\right| = \tan^{-1}\left(\sqrt{3}\right) = 60°; \; \theta = 120°$

$\sqrt[4]{16} = 2; \; \dfrac{120° + 360°k}{4} = 30° + 90°k$

$z_0 = 2\operatorname{cis} 30° = 2\left(\dfrac{\sqrt{3}}{2} + \dfrac{1}{2}i\right) = \sqrt{3} + i$

$z_1 = 2\operatorname{cis} 120° = 2\left(-\dfrac{1}{2} + \dfrac{\sqrt{3}}{2}i\right) = -1 + \sqrt{3}i$

$z_2 = 2\operatorname{cis} 210° = 2\left(-\dfrac{\sqrt{3}}{2} - \dfrac{1}{2}i\right) = -\sqrt{3} - i$

$z_3 = 2\operatorname{cis} 300° = 2\left(\dfrac{1}{2} - \dfrac{\sqrt{3}}{2}i\right) = 1 - \sqrt{3}i$

43. $r = \sqrt{(-7)^2 + (-7)^2} = \sqrt{98} = 7\sqrt{2}; \; n = 4$

$\theta_r = \tan^{-1}\left|\dfrac{-7}{-7}\right| = \tan^{-1}(1) = 45°; \; \theta = 225°$

$\sqrt[4]{7\sqrt{2}} \approx 1.7738; \; \dfrac{225° + 360°k}{4} = 56.25° + 90°k$

$z_0 = 1.7738\operatorname{cis} 56.25° \approx 0.9855 + 1.4749i$

$z_1 = 1.7738\operatorname{cis} 146.25° \approx -1.4749 + 0.9855i$

$z_2 = 1.7738\operatorname{cis} 236.25° \approx -0.9855 - 1.4749i$

$z_3 = 1.7738\operatorname{cis} 326.25° \approx 1.4749 - 0.9855i$

45. $z^3 - 6z + 4 = 0; \; p = -4, \; q = 4$

$D = \dfrac{4(-6)^3 + 27(4)^2}{108} = \dfrac{-864 + 432}{108} = -4$

$-\dfrac{q}{2} + \sqrt{D} = -\dfrac{4}{2} + \sqrt{-4} = -2 + 2i$

$r = \sqrt{8}; \; \theta = 135°$ (QII)

$\sqrt[3]{r} = \sqrt[3]{\sqrt{8}} = 8^{1/6}; \; \dfrac{135° + 360°k}{3} = 45° + 120°k$

$z_0 = 8^{1/6}\operatorname{cis} 45°$

$z_1 = 8^{1/6}\operatorname{cis} 165°$

$z_2 = 8^{1/6}\operatorname{cis} 285°$

$-\dfrac{q}{2} - \sqrt{D} = -\dfrac{4}{2} - \sqrt{-4} = -2 - 2i$

$r = \sqrt{8}; \; \theta = 225°$ (QIV)

$\sqrt[3]{r} = \sqrt[3]{\sqrt{8}} = 8^{1/6}; \; \dfrac{225° + 360°k}{3} = 75° + 120°k$

$z_0 = 8^{1/6}\operatorname{cis} 75°$

$z_1 = 8^{1/6}\operatorname{cis} 195°$

$z_2 = 8^{1/6}\operatorname{cis} 315°$

47. To use DeMoivre's Theorem, we must multiply 4 by each of the angles given.

$4 \cdot 15° = 60°$

$4 \cdot 105° = 420°$, coterminal with 60°

$4 \cdot 195° = 780°$, coterminal with 60°

$4 \cdot 285° = 1140°$, coterminal with 60°

Raising all four values given to the fourth power results in

$$2^4 \operatorname{cis} 60° = 16\left(\frac{1}{2} + i\frac{\sqrt{3}}{2}\right) = 8 + 8\sqrt{3}i.$$

Verified

49. a. $Z = 3 + 4j; \quad r = 5, \quad \theta = \tan^{-1}\frac{4}{3}$

$$Z^3 = 5^3\left[\cos\left(3\tan^{-1}\frac{4}{3}\right) + j\sin\left(3\tan^{-1}\frac{4}{3}\right)\right]$$

$$= -117 + 44j$$

$$Z^2 = 5^2\left[\cos\left(2\tan^{-1}\frac{4}{3}\right) + j\sin\left(2\tan^{-1}\frac{4}{3}\right)\right]$$

$$= -7 + 24j$$

$$3Z^2 = -21 + 72j$$

b. $$\frac{Z^3}{3Z^2} = \frac{-117 + 44j}{-21 + 72j} \cdot \frac{-21 - 72j}{-21 - 72j}$$

$$= \frac{2457 + 8424j - 924j - 3168j^2}{(-21)^2 + 72^2}$$

$$= \frac{5625 + 7500j}{5625} = 1 + \frac{4}{3}j$$

c. $\dfrac{Z}{3} = \dfrac{3 + 4j}{3} = 1 + \dfrac{4}{3}j$; Verified

51. Answers will vary.

53. a. $z = 1 + 2i; \quad r = \sqrt{1^2 + 2^2} = \sqrt{5}$

$$\theta = \tan^{-1}\left|\frac{2}{1}\right| = \tan^{-1}(2) \approx 63.4°$$

The related right triangle is shown.

53. b. $\sin\theta = \dfrac{2}{\sqrt{5}}, \quad \cos\theta = \dfrac{1}{\sqrt{5}}$

$$\sin(4\theta) = \sin(2(2\theta))$$

$$= 2\sin(2\theta)\cos(2\theta)$$

$$= 2(2\sin\theta\cos\theta)(\cos^2\theta - \sin^2\theta)$$

$$= 2\left[2\left(\frac{2}{\sqrt{5}}\right)\left(\frac{1}{\sqrt{5}}\right)\right]\left[\left(\frac{1}{\sqrt{5}}\right)^2 - \left(\frac{2}{\sqrt{5}}\right)^2\right]$$

$$= \frac{8}{5}\left(-\frac{3}{5}\right)$$

$$= -\frac{24}{25}$$

$$\cos^2(4\theta) = 1 - \sin^2(4\theta)$$

$$\cos^2(4\theta) = 1 - \left(-\frac{24}{25}\right)^2$$

$$\cos^2(4\theta) = 1 - \frac{576}{625}$$

$$\cos^2(4\theta) = \frac{49}{625}$$

$$\cos(4\theta) = -\frac{7}{25}$$

(Note that a quick approximation on the calculator shows us that $\theta = \tan^{-1}(2) \approx 63°$, so $4\theta \approx 252°$, and is in QIII.)

$$z^4 = \sqrt{5}^4\left[\cos(4\theta) + i\sin(4\theta)\right]$$

$$= 25\left(-\frac{7}{25} - \frac{24}{25}i\right)$$

$$= -7 - 24i$$

55. Look at the solutions to Exercise 45, and note that $8^{\frac{1}{4}} = \left(2^3\right)^{\frac{1}{4}} = 2^{\frac{1}{4}} = \sqrt{2}$.

Add the roots from Exercise 45 whose angles add to 360°.

$$8^{\frac{1}{6}}\operatorname{cis} 45° + 8^{\frac{1}{6}}\operatorname{cis} 315°$$

$$= \sqrt{2}\left(\frac{\sqrt{2}}{2} + \frac{\sqrt{2}}{2}i\right) + \sqrt{2}\left(\frac{\sqrt{2}}{2} - \frac{\sqrt{2}}{2}i\right)$$

$$= \frac{2}{2} + \frac{2}{2}i + \frac{2}{2} - \frac{2}{2}i = 2$$

$$8^{\frac{1}{6}}\operatorname{cis} 165° + 8^{\frac{1}{6}}\operatorname{cis} 195°$$

$$\approx (-1.3660 + 0.3660i) + (-1.3660 - 03.660i)$$

$$= -2.7320$$

$$8^{\frac{1}{6}}\operatorname{cis} 285° + 8^{\frac{1}{6}}\operatorname{cis} 75°$$

$$\approx (0.3660 - 1.3660i) + (0.3660 + 1.3660i)$$

$$= 0.7320$$

55. (continued)

Note: Using sum and difference identities, all three solutions can actually be found in exact form. The latter two are $-1-\sqrt{3}$ and $-1+\sqrt{3}$.

57. $I = \dfrac{V}{Z}$

a. $V = 14 - 5i, Z = 3 - 2i$

$$I = \frac{14-5i}{3-2i} \cdot \frac{3+2i}{3+2i}$$

$$= \frac{42+28i-15i-10i^2}{9+6i-6i-4i^2}$$

$$= \frac{52+13i}{13}$$

$$= 4+i$$

b. $ZI = (3-2i)(4+i)$

$$= 12+3i-8i-2i^2$$

$$= 12-5i+2$$

$$= 14-5i$$

$$= V$$

59. $\dfrac{\tan^2 x}{\sec x+1} = \dfrac{\sec^2 x-1}{\sec x+1}$

$$= \frac{(\sec x+1)(\sec x-1)}{\sec x+1}$$

$$= \sec x-1$$

$$= \frac{1}{\cos x} - \frac{\cos x}{\cos x}$$

$$= \frac{1-\cos x}{\cos x}$$

61. $B = 90° - 30° = 60°$

$b = \sqrt{3}a = \sqrt{3} \cdot 2\sqrt{3} = 6$ km

$c = 2a = 2 \cdot 2\sqrt{3} = 4\sqrt{3}$ km

Angles	Sides
$A = 30°$	$a = 2\sqrt{3}$ km
$B = 60°$	$b = 6$ km
$C = 90°$	$c = 4\sqrt{3}$ km

Mid-Chapter Check

1. $(2+3i)+(2-3i) = 2+3i+2-3i$

$$= 4$$

$(2+3i)(2-3i) = 4-6i+6i-9i^2$

$$= 13$$

Both the sum and the product of complex conjugates yield real numbers.

3. $(1+2i)^2 - 2(1+2i)+5 = 0$

$1+4i+4i^2-2-4i+5 = 0$

$1+4i-4-2-4i+5 = 0$

$0 = 0$

5. a. $r = 3\sqrt{2}, \theta = \dfrac{\pi}{4}$

$z = 3\sqrt{2}\,\text{cis}\,\dfrac{\pi}{4}$

$= 3\sqrt{2}\left(\cos\dfrac{\pi}{4} + i\sin\dfrac{\pi}{4}\right)$

$= 3\sqrt{2}\left(\dfrac{\sqrt{2}}{2} + i\dfrac{\sqrt{2}}{2}\right) = 3+3i$

b. $r = 2\sqrt{3}, \theta = \dfrac{11\pi}{6}$

$z = 2\sqrt{3}\,\text{cis}\,\dfrac{11\pi}{6}$

$= 2\sqrt{3}\left(\cos\dfrac{11\pi}{6} + i\sin\dfrac{11\pi}{6}\right)$

$= 2\sqrt{3}\left(\dfrac{\sqrt{3}}{2} - \dfrac{1}{2}i\right) = 3-i\sqrt{3}$

7. $z_1 = -3+3i$

$r_1 = \sqrt{(-3)^2 + 3^2} = \sqrt{18} = 3\sqrt{2}$

$\theta_1 = \tan^{-1}\left|\dfrac{3}{-3}\right| = \tan^{-1}(1) = \dfrac{\pi}{4}$

In QII, $\theta = \dfrac{3\pi}{4}$

$z_2 = 5\sqrt{3}+5i$

$r_2 = \sqrt{(5\sqrt{3})^2 + 5^2} = \sqrt{100} = 10$

$\theta = \tan^{-1}\left|\dfrac{5}{5\sqrt{3}}\right| = \tan^{-1}\left(\dfrac{\sqrt{3}}{3}\right) = \dfrac{\pi}{6}$

$\dfrac{r_1}{r_2} = \dfrac{3\sqrt{2}}{10}$

$\theta_1 - \theta_2 = \dfrac{3\pi}{4} - \dfrac{\pi}{6} = \dfrac{7\pi}{12}$

$\dfrac{z_1}{z_2} = \dfrac{3\sqrt{2}}{10}\,\text{cos}\left(\dfrac{7\pi}{12}\right)$

9. $r = 32;\ \theta = 180°;\ n = 5$

$\sqrt[5]{32} = 2;\ \dfrac{180°+360°k}{5} = 36°+72°k$

$2\,\text{cis}(36°+72°k)$

Reinforcing Basic Concepts

Exercise 1:

i^2 : The product yields a new complex number rotated 180° counterclockwise.

i^3 : The product yields a new complex number rotated 270° counterclockwise.

i^4 : The product yields a new complex number rotated 360° counterclockwise.

Exercise 3:

a. $|z| = \sqrt{\left(\dfrac{\sqrt{2}}{2}\right)^2 + \left(\dfrac{\sqrt{2}}{2}\right)^2} = \sqrt{1} = 1$

$\theta = \tan^{-1}(1) = 45°$

b. $2i\left(\dfrac{\sqrt{2}}{2} + \dfrac{\sqrt{2}}{2}i\right) = i\sqrt{2} + \sqrt{2}i^2$

$= -\sqrt{2} + i\sqrt{2}$

$\left(-\sqrt{2} + i\sqrt{2}\right)\left(\dfrac{\sqrt{2}}{2} + \dfrac{\sqrt{2}}{2}i\right) = -1 - i + i + i^2$

$= -2$

$-2\left(\dfrac{\sqrt{2}}{2} + \dfrac{\sqrt{2}}{2}i\right) = -\sqrt{2} - i\sqrt{2}$

$\left(-\sqrt{2} - i\sqrt{2}\right)\left(\dfrac{\sqrt{2}}{2} + \dfrac{\sqrt{2}}{2}i\right) = -1 - i - i - i^2$

$= -2i$

$-2i\left(\dfrac{\sqrt{2}}{2} + \dfrac{\sqrt{2}}{2}i\right) = -i\sqrt{2} - i^2\sqrt{2}$

$= \sqrt{2} - i\sqrt{2}$

$\left(\sqrt{2} - i\sqrt{2}\right)\left(\dfrac{\sqrt{2}}{2} + \dfrac{\sqrt{2}}{2}i\right) = 1 + i - i - i^2$

$= 2$

$2\left(\dfrac{\sqrt{2}}{2} + \dfrac{\sqrt{2}}{2}i\right) = \sqrt{2} + i\sqrt{2}$

Technology Highlight

Exercise 1:

The greater the step-value, the fewer points used to draw the graph.

Exercise 3:

If n is odd, the rose has n petals. If n is even, the rose has $2n$ petals.

8.4 Exercises

1.   polar

3.   II; IV

5.   To plot the point (r, θ), start at the origin or pole and move $|r|$ units out along the polar axis. Then move counterclockwise an angle measure of θ. You should be r units straight out from the pole in a direction of θ from the positive polar axis. If r is negative, final resting place for the point will be 180° from θ.

7. $\left(4, \dfrac{\pi}{2}\right)$

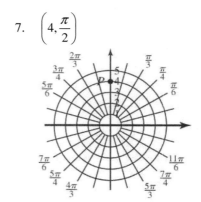

9. $\left(2, \dfrac{5\pi}{4}\right)$

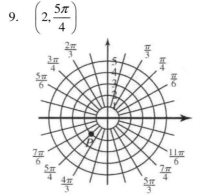

11. $\left(-5, \dfrac{5\pi}{6}\right)$

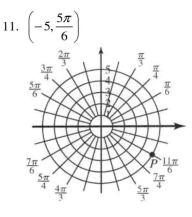

13. $\left(-3, -\dfrac{2\pi}{3}\right)$

15. $P(0,4) \to \left(4, \dfrac{\pi}{2}\right)$

17. $(4, 4)$

$$r = \sqrt{4^2 + 4^2} = \sqrt{16+16} = \sqrt{32} = 4\sqrt{2}$$

$$\theta = \tan^{-1}\left|\dfrac{4}{4}\right| = \tan^{-1}(1) = \dfrac{\pi}{4}$$

$$P(4,4) \to P\left(4\sqrt{2}, \dfrac{\pi}{4}\right)$$

19. $\left(-4, 4\sqrt{3}\right)$

$$r = \sqrt{(-4)^2 + \left(4\sqrt{3}\right)^2} = \sqrt{16+48} = \sqrt{64} = 8$$

$$\theta_r = \tan^{-1}\left|\dfrac{4\sqrt{3}}{-4}\right| = \tan^{-1}\left(\sqrt{3}\right) = \dfrac{\pi}{3}$$

$$\theta = \pi - \dfrac{\pi}{3} = \dfrac{2\pi}{3}$$

$$P\left(-4, 4\sqrt{3}\right) \to P\left(8, \dfrac{2\pi}{3}\right)$$

21. $(-4, 4)$

$$r = \sqrt{(-4)^2 + 4^2} = \sqrt{32} = 4\sqrt{2}$$

$$\theta_r = \tan^{-1}\left|\dfrac{4}{-4}\right| = \tan^{-1}(1) = \dfrac{\pi}{4}$$

$$\theta = \pi - \dfrac{\pi}{4} = \dfrac{3\pi}{4}$$

$$P(-4,\ 4) \to P\left(4\sqrt{2}, \dfrac{3\pi}{4}\right)$$

23. Original Point: $\left(3\sqrt{2}, \dfrac{3\pi}{4}\right)$

$$\left(3\sqrt{2}, \dfrac{3\pi}{4} - 2\pi\right) \to \left(3\sqrt{2}, -\dfrac{5\pi}{4}\right)$$

$$\left(-3\sqrt{2}, \dfrac{3\pi}{4} + \pi\right) \to \left(-3\sqrt{2}, \dfrac{7\pi}{4}\right)$$

$$\left(3\sqrt{2}, \dfrac{3\pi}{4} + 2\pi\right) \to \left(3\sqrt{2}, \dfrac{11\pi}{4}\right)$$

$$\left(-3\sqrt{2}, \dfrac{3\pi}{4} - \pi\right) \to \left(-3\sqrt{2}, -\dfrac{\pi}{4}\right)$$

25. Original Point: $\left(-2, \dfrac{11\pi}{6}\right)$

$$\left(2, \dfrac{11\pi}{6} - \pi\right) \to \left(2, \dfrac{5\pi}{6}\right)$$

$$\left(2, \dfrac{11\pi}{6} - 3\pi\right) \to \left(2, -\dfrac{7\pi}{6}\right)$$

$$\left(2, \dfrac{11\pi}{6} + \pi\right) \to \left(2, \dfrac{17\pi}{6}\right)$$

$$\left(-2, \dfrac{11\pi}{6} - 2\pi\right) \to \left(-2, -\dfrac{\pi}{6}\right)$$

27. C

29. C

31. D

33. B

35. D

37. $(-8,0)$

$r = \sqrt{(-8)^2 + 0^2} = \sqrt{64} = 8$

$\theta_r = 0°, \ \theta = 180°$

$P(-8, 0) \rightarrow P(8, \pi) \ \text{or} \ P(8, 180°)$

39. $(4,4)$

$r = \sqrt{4^2 + 4^2} = \sqrt{32} = 4\sqrt{2}$

$\theta = \tan^{-1}\left|\dfrac{4}{4}\right| = \tan^{-1}(1) = \dfrac{\pi}{4}$

$P(4, 4) \rightarrow P\left(4\sqrt{2}, \dfrac{\pi}{4}\right) \ \text{or P} \ \left(4\sqrt{2}, \ 45°\right)$

41. $\left(5\sqrt{2}, 5\sqrt{2}\right)$

$r = \sqrt{\left(5\sqrt{2}\right)^2 + \left(5\sqrt{2}\right)^2} = \sqrt{100} = 10$

$\theta = \tan^{-1}\left|\dfrac{5\sqrt{2}}{5\sqrt{2}}\right| = \tan^{-1}(1) = \dfrac{\pi}{4}$

$P\left(5\sqrt{2}, \ 5\sqrt{2}\right) \rightarrow P\left(10, \dfrac{\pi}{4}\right) \ \text{or} \ P(10, \ 45°)$

43. $(-5,-12)$

$r = \sqrt{(-5)^2 + (-12)^2} = \sqrt{169} = 13$

$\theta_r = \tan^{-1}\left|\dfrac{-12}{-5}\right| = \tan^{-1}\left(\dfrac{12}{5}\right)$

$\approx 67.4° \approx 1.176 \ \text{radians}$

$\theta = 67.4° + 180° = 247.4° \ \text{or}$

$\theta = 1.176 + \pi = 4.3176 \ \text{radians}$

$P(-5,-12) \rightarrow P(13, \ 247.4°) \ \text{or}$

$P(-5,-12) \rightarrow P(13, \ 4.3176)$

45. $(8, \ 45°)$

$x = 8\cos 45° = 8\left(\dfrac{\sqrt{2}}{2}\right) = 4\sqrt{2}$

$y = 8\sin 45° = 8\left(\dfrac{\sqrt{2}}{2}\right) = 4\sqrt{2}$

$\left(4\sqrt{2}, 4\sqrt{2}\right)$

47. $\left(4, \dfrac{3\pi}{4}\right)$

$x = 4\cos\dfrac{3\pi}{4} = 4\left(\dfrac{-\sqrt{2}}{2}\right) = -2\sqrt{2}$

$y = 4\sin\dfrac{3\pi}{4} = 4\left(\dfrac{\sqrt{2}}{2}\right) = 2\sqrt{2}$

$\left(-2\sqrt{2}, 2\sqrt{2}\right)$

49. $\left(-2, \dfrac{7\pi}{6}\right)$

$x = -2\cos\left(\dfrac{7\pi}{6}\right) = -2\left(\dfrac{-\sqrt{3}}{2}\right) = \sqrt{3}$

$y = -2\sin\left(\dfrac{7\pi}{6}\right) = -2\left(\dfrac{-1}{2}\right) = 1$

$\left(\sqrt{3}, 1\right)$

51. $(-5, -135°)$

$x = -5\cos(-135°) = -5\left(\dfrac{-\sqrt{2}}{2}\right) = \dfrac{5\sqrt{2}}{2}$

$y = -5\sin(-135°) = -5\left(\dfrac{-\sqrt{2}}{2}\right) = \dfrac{5\sqrt{2}}{2}$

$\left(\dfrac{5\sqrt{2}}{2}, \dfrac{5\sqrt{2}}{2}\right)$

53.
$$x^2 = 25 - y^2$$
$$x^2 + y^2 = 25$$
$$(r\cos\theta)^2 + (r\sin\theta)^2 = 25$$
$$r^2\cos^2\theta + r^2\sin^2\theta = 25$$
$$r^2\left(\cos^2\theta + \sin^2\theta\right) = 25$$
$$r^2 = 25$$
$$r = 5$$

55.
$$x = \dfrac{3}{y}$$
$$r\cos\theta = \dfrac{3}{r\sin\theta}$$
$$r^2\cos\theta\sin\theta = 3$$
$$r^2 2\cos\theta\sin\theta = 6$$
$$r^2\sin 2\theta = 6$$

57. $$y = 3x^2 + x$$
$$r\sin\theta = 3(r\cos\theta)^2 + r\cos\theta$$
$$r\sin\theta = 3r^2\cos^2\theta + r\cos\theta$$
$$\frac{r\sin\theta}{r\cos\theta} = \frac{3r^2\cos^2\theta}{r\cos\theta} + \frac{r\cos\theta}{r\cos\theta}$$
$$\tan\theta = 3r\cos\theta + 1$$

We can solve the resulting equation for r.
$$\tan\theta = 3r\cos\theta + 1$$
$$3r\cos\theta = \tan\theta - 1$$
$$r = \frac{\tan\theta - 1}{3\cos\theta}$$

59. $$x^2 - y^2 = x^4 + 2x^2y^2 + y^4$$
$$x^2 - y^2 = (x^2 + y^2)^2$$
$$(r\cos\theta)^2 - (r\sin\theta)^2 = (r^2)^2$$
$$r^2\cos^2\theta - r^2\sin^2\theta = r^4$$
$$\frac{r^2\cos^2\theta}{r^2} - \frac{r^2\sin^2\theta}{r^2} = \frac{r^4}{r^2}$$
$$\cos^2\theta - \sin^2\theta = r^2$$
$$\cos 2\theta = r^2$$

61. $$r = 6\cos\theta$$
$$r^2 = 6r\cos\theta$$
$$x^2 + y^2 = 6x$$

63. $$r = 2\sec\theta$$
$$r\cos\theta = 2$$
$$x = 2$$

65. $$r = \sqrt{r\cos\theta - 1}$$
$$r^2 = r\cos\theta - 1$$
$$x^2 + y^2 = x - 1$$

67. $$r = \frac{1}{1 + \sin\theta}$$
$$r(1 + \sin\theta) = 1$$
$$r + r\sin\theta = 1$$
$$\sqrt{x^2 + y^2} + y = 1$$
$$y - 1 = -\sqrt{x^2 + y^2}$$
$$y^2 - 2y + 1 = x^2 + y^2$$
$$-2y + 1 = x^2$$
$$-2y = x^2 - 1$$
$$y = -\frac{1}{2}x^2 + \frac{1}{2}$$

69. $r = 5$
Circle, Center: $(0,0)$

Cycle	r-value analysis	Location of graph
0 to $\frac{\pi}{2}$	$\lvert r \rvert$ constant at 5	QI $(r=5)$
$\frac{\pi}{2}$ to π	$\lvert r \rvert$ constant at 5	QII $(r=5)$
π to $\frac{3\pi}{2}$	$\lvert r \rvert$ constant at 5	QIII $(r=5)$
$\frac{3\pi}{2}$ to 2π	$\lvert r \rvert$ constant at 5	QIV $(r=5)$

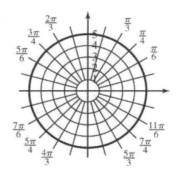

71. $\theta = \frac{\pi}{6}$

Straight line, points of the form $\left(r, \frac{\pi}{6}\right)$,

$\frac{\pi}{6}$ constant, r varies

Cycle	r-value analysis	Location of graph
At $\frac{\pi}{6}$	$\lvert r \rvert$ increases from 0 to ∞	QI $(r>0)$
At $\frac{7\pi}{6}$	$\lvert r \rvert$ increases from 0 to $-\infty$	QI $(r>0)$

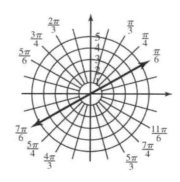

73. $r = 4\cos\theta$

Circle, Center: $(2,0)$

Closed figure limited to QI and QIV

Cycle	r-value analysis	Location of graph
0 to $\dfrac{\pi}{4}$	$\lvert r \rvert$ decreases from 4 to 2	QI $(r > 0)$
$\dfrac{\pi}{4}$ to $\dfrac{\pi}{2}$	$\lvert r \rvert$ decreases from 2 to 0	QII $(r < 0)$
$\dfrac{3\pi}{2}$ to $\dfrac{3\pi}{4}$	$\lvert r \rvert$ increases from 0 to 2	QIII $(r < 0)$
$\dfrac{3\pi}{4}$ to 2π	$\lvert r \rvert$ increases from 2 to 4	QIV $(r > 0)$

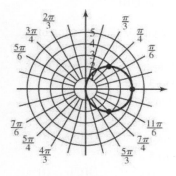

75. $r = 3 + 3\sin\theta$

Cardioid, symmetric about $\theta = \dfrac{\pi}{2}$

Cycle	r-value analysis	Location of graph
0 to $\dfrac{\pi}{2}$	$\lvert r \rvert$ increases from 3 to 6	QI $(r > 0)$
$\dfrac{\pi}{2}$ to π	$\lvert r \rvert$ decreases from 6 to 3	QII $(r > 0)$
π to $\dfrac{3\pi}{2}$	$\lvert r \rvert$ decreases from 3 to 0	QIII $(r > 0)$
$\dfrac{3\pi}{2}$ to 2π	$\lvert r \rvert$ increases from 0 to 3	QIV $(r > 0)$

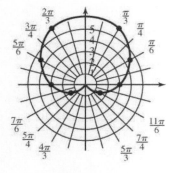

77. $r = 2 - 4\sin\theta$; Limacon, symmetric about $\theta = \dfrac{\pi}{2}$

Cycle	r-value analysis	Location of graph
0 to $\dfrac{\pi}{6}$	$\lvert r \rvert$ decreases from 2 to 0	QI $(r > 0)$
$\dfrac{\pi}{6}$ to $\dfrac{\pi}{2}$	$\lvert r \rvert$ increases from 0 to 2	QIII $(r < 0)$
$\dfrac{\pi}{2}$ to $\dfrac{2\pi}{3}$	$\lvert r \rvert$ decreases from 2 to 0	QIV $(r < 0)$
$\dfrac{2\pi}{3}$ to π	$\lvert r \rvert$ increases from 0 to 2	QII $(r > 0)$
π to $\dfrac{3\pi}{2}$	$\lvert r \rvert$ increases from 2 to 6	QIII $(r > 0)$
$\dfrac{3\pi}{2}$ to 2π	$\lvert r \rvert$ decreases from 6 to 2	QIV $(r > 0)$

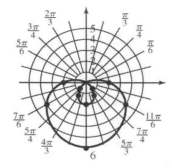

79. $r = 5\cos(2\theta)$

Four-petal rose, symmetric about $\theta = 0$

Cycle	r-value analysis	Location of graph
0 to $\dfrac{\pi}{4}$	$\lvert r \rvert$ decreases from 5 to 0	QI $(r > 0)$
$\dfrac{\pi}{4}$ to $\dfrac{\pi}{2}$	$\lvert r \rvert$ increases from 0 to 5	QIII $(r < 0)$
$\dfrac{\pi}{2}$ to $\dfrac{3\pi}{4}$	$\lvert r \rvert$ decreases from 5 to 0	QIV $(r < 0)$
$\dfrac{3\pi}{4}$ to π	$\lvert r \rvert$ increases from 0 to 5	QII $(r > 0)$
π to $\dfrac{5\pi}{4}$	$\lvert r \rvert$ decreases from 5 to 0	QIII $(r > 0)$

79. (continued)

$\dfrac{5\pi}{4}$ to $\dfrac{3\pi}{2}$ $\lvert r \rvert$ increases from 0 to 5	QI $(r < 0)$
$\dfrac{3\pi}{2}$ to $\dfrac{7\pi}{4}$ $\lvert r \rvert$ decreases from 5 to 0	QII $(r < 0)$
$\dfrac{7\pi}{4}$ to 2π $\lvert r \rvert$ increases from 0 to 5	QIV $(r > 0)$

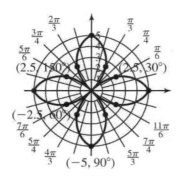

81. $r = 4\sin(2\theta)$

Four-petal rose, symmetric about $\theta = \dfrac{\pi}{2}$

Cycle	r-value analysis	Location of graph
0 to $\dfrac{\pi}{4}$	$\lvert r \rvert$ increases from 0 to 4	QI $(r > 0)$
$\dfrac{\pi}{4}$ to $\dfrac{\pi}{2}$	$\lvert r \rvert$ decreases from 4 to 0	QIII $(r > 0)$
$\dfrac{\pi}{2}$ to $\dfrac{3\pi}{4}$	$\lvert r \rvert$ increases from 0 to 4	QIV $(r < 0)$
$\dfrac{3\pi}{4}$ to π	$\lvert r \rvert$ decreases from 4 to 0	QII $(r < 0)$
π to $\dfrac{5\pi}{4}$	$\lvert r \rvert$ increases from 0 to 4	QIII $(r < 0)$
$\dfrac{5\pi}{4}$ to $\dfrac{3\pi}{2}$	$\lvert r \rvert$ decreases from 4 to 0	QI $(r < 0)$
$\dfrac{3\pi}{2}$ to $\dfrac{7\pi}{4}$	$\lvert r \rvert$ increases from 0 to 4	QII $(r > 0)$
$\dfrac{7\pi}{4}$ to 2π	$\lvert r \rvert$ decreases from 4 to 0	QIV $(r > 0)$

81. (continued)

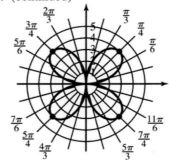

83. $r^2 = 9\sin(2\theta)$

Lemniscate, symmetric about $\theta = \dfrac{\pi}{4}$

Closed image in QI & QIII

Cycle	r-value analysis	Location of graph
0 to $\dfrac{\pi}{4}$	$\lvert r \rvert$ increases from 0 to 3	QI $(r > 0)$
$\dfrac{\pi}{4}$ to $\dfrac{\pi}{2}$	$\lvert r \rvert$ decreases from 3 to 0	QI $(r > 0)$
π to $\dfrac{5\pi}{4}$	$\lvert r \rvert$ increases from 0 to 3	QIII $(r > 0)$
$\dfrac{5\pi}{4}$ to $\dfrac{3\pi}{2}$	$\lvert r \rvert$ decreases from 3 to 0	QIII $(r > 0)$

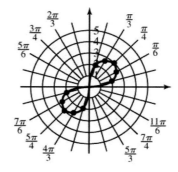

85. $r = 4\sin\left(\dfrac{\theta}{2}\right)$

Symmetric about $\theta = \dfrac{\pi}{2}$ and $\theta = 0$

Cycle	r-value analysis	Location of graph
0 to $\dfrac{\pi}{2}$	$\lvert r\rvert$ increases from 0 to $2\sqrt{2}$	QI $(r > 0)$
$\dfrac{\pi}{2}$ to π	$\lvert r\rvert$ increases from 4 to $2\sqrt{2}$	QII $(r > 0)$
π to $\dfrac{3\pi}{2}$	$\lvert r\rvert$ decreases from 4 to $2\sqrt{2}$	QIII $(r > 0)$
$\dfrac{3\pi}{2}$ to 2π	$\lvert r\rvert$ decreases from $2\sqrt{2}$ to 0	QIV $(r > 0)$
2π to $\dfrac{5\pi}{2}$	$\lvert r\rvert$ increases from 0 to $2\sqrt{2}$	QIII $(r < 0)$
$\dfrac{5\pi}{2}$ to 3π	$\lvert r\rvert$ increases from $2\sqrt{2}$ to 4	QIV $(r < 0)$
3π to $\dfrac{7\pi}{2}$	$\lvert r\rvert$ decreases from 4 to $2\sqrt{2}$	QI $(r < 0)$
$\dfrac{7\pi}{2}$ to 4π	$\lvert r\rvert$ decreases from $2\sqrt{2}$ to 0	QII $(r < 0)$

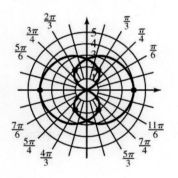

87. $r = 4\sqrt{1 - \sin^2\theta}$, a hippopede

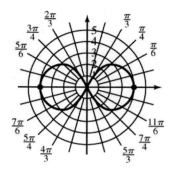

89. $r = 2\cos\theta\cot\theta$, a cissoid

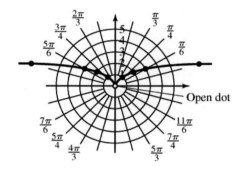

Open dot

91. $r = 8\sin\theta\cos^2\theta$, a bifoliate

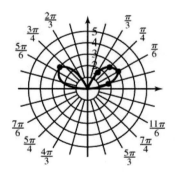

93. $M = \left(\dfrac{r \cos \alpha + R \cos \beta}{2}, \dfrac{r \sin \alpha + R \sin \beta}{2} \right)$

$M = \left(\dfrac{8 \cos 30° + 6 \cos 45°}{2}, \dfrac{8 \sin 30° + 6 \sin 45°}{2} \right)$

$= \left(\dfrac{8 \left(\dfrac{\sqrt{3}}{2} \right) + 6 \left(\dfrac{\sqrt{2}}{2} \right)}{2}, \dfrac{8 \left(\dfrac{1}{2} \right) + 6 \left(\dfrac{\sqrt{2}}{2} \right)}{2} \right)$

$= \left(\dfrac{4\sqrt{3} + 3\sqrt{2}}{2}, \dfrac{4 + 3\sqrt{2}}{2} \right)$

$x = 6 \cos 45° = 6 \left(\dfrac{\sqrt{2}}{2} \right) = 3\sqrt{2}$

$y = 6 \sin 45° = 6 \left(\dfrac{\sqrt{2}}{2} \right) = 3\sqrt{2}$

$(6, 45°) \rightarrow \left(3\sqrt{2}, 3\sqrt{2} \right)$

$x = 8 \cos 30° = 8 \left(\dfrac{\sqrt{3}}{2} \right) = 4\sqrt{3}$

$y = 8 \sin 30° = 8 \left(\dfrac{1}{2} \right) = 4$

$(8, 30°) \rightarrow \left(4\sqrt{3}, 4 \right)$

$M = \left(\dfrac{x_1 + x_2}{2} \right), \left(\dfrac{y_1 + y_2}{2} \right)$

$= \left(\dfrac{3\sqrt{2} + 4\sqrt{3}}{2}, \dfrac{3\sqrt{2} + 4}{2} \right)$

Yes, the results match.

95. $r = 4 + 4 \cos \theta$

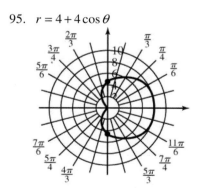

97. $r = 4 \cos(5\theta)$

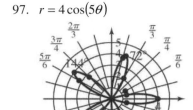
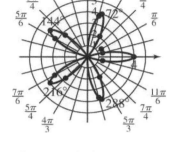

99. $r^2 = 16 \cos(2\theta)$

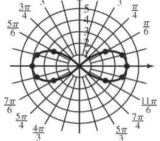

101. $r = 4 \sin \theta$

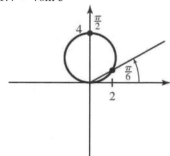

103. a; This is a circle through $(6, 0°)$ symmetric about the polar axis.

105. g; This is a circle through $\left(6, \dfrac{\pi}{2} \right)$ symmetric about $\theta = \dfrac{\pi}{2}$.

107. f; This is a limacon symmetric about $\theta = \dfrac{\pi}{2}$ with an inner loop. Thus $a < b$.

109.b; This is a cardoid symmetric about $\theta = \dfrac{\pi}{2}$

through $\left(6, \dfrac{3\pi}{2}\right)$.

111. $(7200, 45°)$ and $(0, 90°)$

$a = 7200$

$r^2 = 7200^2 \sin(2\theta)$

113.5 blades; $r = 15$ mm

$r = 15\cos(5\theta)$ or $r = 15\sin(5\theta)$

115. $r = a\theta; r = \dfrac{1}{2}\theta$

π, π, π , Answers will vary.

117.Consider $r = a\sqrt{\cos(2\theta)}$ and $r = -a\sqrt{\cos(2\theta)}$.

Both satisfy $r^2 = a^2\cos(2\theta)$. Thus, (r, θ) and $(-r, \theta)$ will both be on the curve. The same is true with $r = a\sqrt{\sin(2\theta)}$ and $r = -a\sqrt{\sin(2\theta)}$.

119. $r = 6$

$A = \pi\, r^2 = \pi(6)^2 = 36\pi$ units^2

The area of the circumscribed circle is 36π units^2.

Area $= (0.25)36\pi = 9\pi$ units^2

The area within the boundaries of the rose is 9π units^2.

121.Begin on right side of equation.

$\dfrac{1+\sin x}{\cos x} = \dfrac{(1+\sin x)(1-\sin x)}{\cos x(1-\sin x)}$

$= \dfrac{1-\sin^2 x}{\cos x(1-\sin x)}$

$= \dfrac{\cos^2 x}{\cos x(1-\sin x)}$

$= \dfrac{\cos x}{1-\sin x}$

123. $z_1 = 15+1i$, $z_2 = 13+9i$

$|z_1| = \sqrt{15^2+1^2} = \sqrt{226}$

$|z_2| = \sqrt{13^2+9^2} = \sqrt{250}$

$|z_1| = \sqrt{226} < \sqrt{250} = |z_2|$

125.Let l_1 be the length of the lower slide.

$\sin 25° = \dfrac{20}{l_1}$

$l_1 = \dfrac{20}{\sin 25°}$

$l_1 \approx 47.3$ m

Let x_1 be the base of the lower slide.

$x_1 = \sqrt{47.3^2 - 20^2} \approx 42.9$ m

Let x_2 be the base of the upper slide.

$105 - 42.9 - 36 = 26.1$ m

Let l_2 be the length of the upper slide.

$l_2 \approx \sqrt{(26.1)^2 + 18^2} \approx 31.7$ m

$L \approx 47.3 + 36 + 31.7$

≈ 115.0 m

The entire length of the slide is about 115.0 m.

Technology Highlights

1. verified

8.5 Exercises

1. parameter

3. direction

5. Answers will vary.

7. $x = t+2;\ t \in [-3,3]$

$y = t^2 - 1$

a. A parabola with vertex at $(2, -1)$.

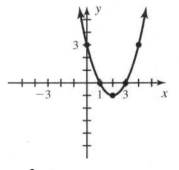

b. $x - 2 = t$

$y = (x-2)^2 - 1$

$y = x^2 - 4x + 4 - 1$

$y = x^2 - 4x + 3$

9. $x = (2-t)^2$; $t \in [0, 5]$

$y = (t-3)^2$

a. A parabola

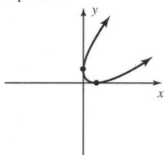

b. $\pm\sqrt{x} = 2-t$

$t = 2 \pm \sqrt{x}$

$y = \left(2 \pm \sqrt{x} - 3\right)^2$

$y = \left(\pm\sqrt{x} - 1\right)^2$

$y = x \pm 2\sqrt{x} + 1$

11. $x = \dfrac{5}{t}$; $t \neq 0$; $t \in [-3.5, 3.5]$

$y = t^2$

a. Power function with $p = -2$

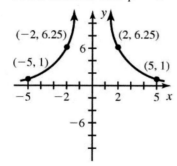

b. $x = \dfrac{5}{t}$

$xt = 5$

$t = \dfrac{5}{x}$

$y = \left(\dfrac{5}{x}\right)^2$

$y = \dfrac{25}{x^2}$, $x \neq 0$

13. $x = 4\cos t$, $t \in [0, 2\pi)$

$y = 3\sin t$

a. Ellipse

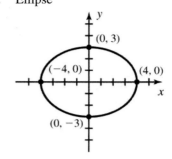

b. $x^2 = (4\cos t)^2$ $\quad y^2 = (3\sin t)^2$

$x^2 = 16\cos^2 t$ $\quad y^2 = 9\sin^2 t$

$\dfrac{x^2}{16} = \cos^2 t$ $\quad \dfrac{y^2}{9} = \sin^2 t$

$\dfrac{x^2}{16} + \dfrac{y^2}{9} = \cos^2 t + \sin^2 t$

$\dfrac{x^2}{16} + \dfrac{y^2}{9} = 1$

15. $x = 4\sin(2t)$; $t \in [0, 2\pi)$

$y = 6\cos t$

a. Lissajous figure

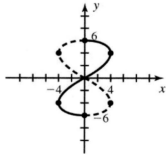

b. $\qquad x = 4\sin 2t$

$\dfrac{x}{4} = \sin 2t$

$\sin^{-1}\left(\dfrac{x}{4}\right) = 2t$

$\dfrac{1}{2}\sin^{-1}\left(\dfrac{x}{4}\right) = t$

$y = 6\cos t$

$y = 6\cos\left[\dfrac{1}{2}\sin^{-1}\left(\dfrac{x}{4}\right)\right]$

17. $x = \dfrac{-3}{\tan t}, \; t \in (0, \pi)$

    $y = 5\sin(2t)$

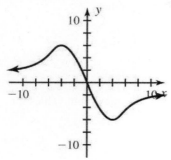

19. $y = 3x - 2$

    i) $x = t$

    $y = 3t - 2$

    ii) $x = \dfrac{1}{3}t$

    $y = 3\left(\dfrac{1}{3}t\right) - 2$

    $y = t - 2$

    iii) $x = \cos t$

    $y = 3\cos t - 2$

21. $y = (x+3)^2 + 1$

    i) $x = t$

    $y = (t+3)^2 + 1$

    ii) $x = t - 3$

    $y = \left[(t-3)+3\right]^2 + 1$

    $y = t^2 + 1$

    iii) $x = \tan t - 3$

    $x + 3 = \tan t$

    $y = \tan^2 t + 1$

    $y = \sec^2 t$

    $t \notin \left(k + \dfrac{1}{2}\right)\pi, \; k \in \mathbb{Z}$

    $t \notin \dfrac{(2k+1)\pi}{2}, \; k \in \mathbb{Z}$

23. $y = \tan^2(x-2) + 1$

    i) $x = t$

    $y = \tan^2(t-2) + 1$

    $t \notin \pi k + \dfrac{\pi}{2} + 2, \; k \in \mathbb{Z}$

    ii) $t = x - 2$

    $x = t + 2$

    $y = \tan^2(t + 2 - 2) + 1$

    $y = \tan^2 t + 1$

    $y = \sec^2 t$

    $t \notin \left(k + \dfrac{1}{2}\right)\pi, \; k \in \mathbb{Z}$

    iii) $x = \tan^{-1} t + 2$

    $y = \tan^2\left(\tan^{-1} t + 2 - 2\right) + 1$

    $y = \tan^2\left(\tan^{-1} t\right) + 1$

    $y = t^2 + 1; \; t \in \mathbb{R}$

25. $y = 4(x-3)^2 + 1$

    i) $x = t$

    $y = 4(t-3)^2 + 1$

    ii) $x = t + 3$

    $y = 4t^2 + 1$

    iii) $x = \dfrac{1}{2}\tan t + 3$

    $y = \sec^2 t$

    These can be verified using a graphing calculator.

27. $x = 8\cos t + 2\cos(4t)$

    $y = 8\sin t - 2\sin(4t)$

    a. Hypocycloid (5-cusp)

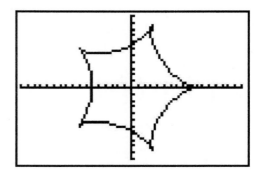

27. b. *x*-intercepts:
$t = 0, x = 10, y = 0$
$t = \pi, \ x = -6, y = 0$

y-intercepts:
$t \approx 1.757, x = 0, y \approx 6.5$
$t \approx 4.527, x = 0, y \approx -6.5$

Min *x*-value: -8.1
Max *x*-value: 10
Min *y*-value: -9.5
Max *y*-value: 9.5

29. $x = \dfrac{2}{\tan t}$

$y = 8 \sin t \cos t$

a. Serpentine curve

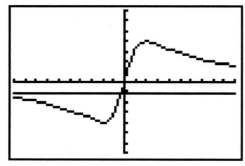

b. *x*-intercept: none
y-intercept: none

Min *x*-value: none
Max *x*-value: none
Min *y*-value: -4
Max *y*-value: 4

31. $x = 2(\cos t + t \sin t)$

$y = 2(\sin t - t \cos t)$

a. Involute of a circle

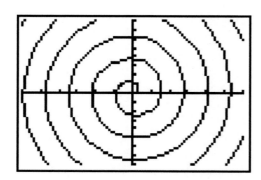

31. b. *x*-intercepts:
$t = 0, x = 2, y = 0$
$t \approx 4.493, x = -9.2, y = 0$
Infinitely many others.

y-intercepts:
$t \approx 2.79, x = 0, y = 5.9$
$t \approx 6.12, x = 0, \ y = -12.4$
Infinitely many others.

No minimum or maximum values for
x or *y* .

33. $x = 3t - \sin t$

$y = 3 - \cos t$

a. Curtate cycloid

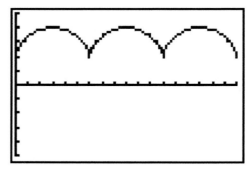

b. *x*-intercept:
none
y-intercept:
$t = 0, \ x = 0, \ y = 2$

Min *x*-value: none
Max *x*-value: none
Min *y*-value: 2
Max *y*-value: 4

35. $x = 2[3 \cos t - \cos(3t)]$

$y = 2[3 \sin t - \sin(3t)]$

a. Nephroid

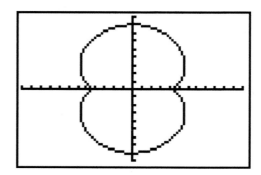

35. b.   *x*-intercepts:

$t = 0, x = 4, y = 0$

$t = \pi, x = -4, y = 0$

y-intercepts:

$t = \dfrac{\pi}{2}, x = 0, y = 8; \ t = \dfrac{3\pi}{2}, x = 0, y = -8$

Min *x*-value: ≈ -5.657
Max *x*-value: ≈ 5.657
Min *y*-value: -8
Max *y*-value: 8

37. $x = 6\sin(2t); \quad y = 8\cos(t)$

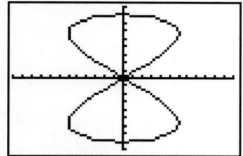

Box to frame curve: width 12, length 16. Over interval $[0, 2\pi]$ graph crosses itself 2 times.

39. $x = 5\sin(7t); \quad y = 7\cos(4t)$

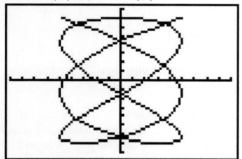

Box to frame curve: width 10, length 14. Over interval $[0, 2\pi]$ graph crosses itself 9 times.

41. $x = 10\sin(1.5t); \quad y = 10\cos(2.5t)$

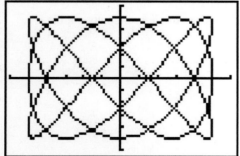

Box to frame curve: width 20, length 20. Over interval $[0, 4\pi]$ graph crosses itself 23 times.

43. $x = \dfrac{a}{\tan t}$

$y = b\sin t \cos t$

The maximum value as graph swells is at

$(x, y) = \left(a, \dfrac{b}{2} \right)$.

The minimum value as graph dips to the valley

is at $(x, y) = \left(-a, \dfrac{-b}{2} \right)$.

45. $x(t) = 2kt$

$y(t) = \dfrac{2k}{1+t^2}$

a.   The curve is approaching $y = 2$ as t

approaches $\dfrac{3\pi}{2}$, but $\cot\left(\dfrac{3\pi}{2} \right)$ is

undefined, and the trig form seems to

indicate a "hole" at $t = \dfrac{3\pi}{2}, x = 0, y = 2$.

The algebraic form does not have this problem and shows a maximum defined at $t = 0, x = 0, y = 2$.

b.   As $|t| \to \infty, y(t) \to 0$

c.   The maximum value occurs at $(0, 2k)$.

47. $x = 75t \cos 36$

$y = 75t \sin 36 - 16t^2$

a.   At $t = 1.24$
$x = 75.239$
$y = 30.062$
Yes, the football goes through hoop.

b.   At $t = 2.7552$
$x = 167.1779$
$y = 0$
Yes, the ball hits the target.

c. $168 - 167.18 = 0.82$ ft

49. $x = 80t \cos 29°$

$y = 80t \sin 29° - 16t^2$

Consider $t = 2.14$ sec.
$x = 80(2.14)\cos 29°$
$x \approx 149.73$ ft
$y = 80(2.144)\sin 29° - 16(2.144)^2$
$y = 9.5769 < 10$ ft
No, the kick is short.

51. $\begin{cases} x = 6\cos t \\ y = 2\sin t \end{cases}$

t	x	y
2	-2.50	1.82
2.09	-2.98	1.74
2.225	-3.65	1.59
3	-5.94	0.28

Left and downward

53. $\begin{cases} x - 5y + z = 3 \\ 5x + y - 7z = -9 \\ 2x + 3y - 4z = -6 \end{cases}$

$7R_1 + R_2$

$\begin{cases} 7x - 35y + 7z = 21 \\ 5x + y - 7z = -9 \end{cases}$
$\overline{\hspace{0.5cm} 12x - 34y = 12}$
(Equation 4)

$4R_1 + R_3$

$\begin{cases} 4x - 20y + 4z = 12 \\ 2x + 3y - 4z = -6 \end{cases}$
$\overline{\hspace{0.5cm} 6x - 17y \hspace{0.8cm} = 6}$
(Equation 5)

$-2R_5 + R_4$

$-12x + 34y = -12$
$\underline{12x - 34y = 12}$
$\hspace{2cm} 0 = 0$

Dependent equations

$12x - 34y = 12$
$-34y = -12x + 12$
$\dfrac{-34y}{-34} = \dfrac{-12x}{-34} + \dfrac{12}{-34}$
$y = \dfrac{6}{17}x - \dfrac{6}{17}$

$x - 5\left(\dfrac{6}{17}x - \dfrac{6}{17}\right) + z = 3$
$x - \dfrac{30x}{17} + \dfrac{30}{17} + z = 3$
$\dfrac{-13x}{17} + z = \dfrac{21}{17}$
$z = \dfrac{13}{17}x + \dfrac{21}{17}$

$\left(x, \dfrac{6}{17}x - \dfrac{6}{17}, \dfrac{13}{17}x + \dfrac{21}{17}\right)$
$\left(t, \dfrac{6}{17}t - \dfrac{6}{17}, \dfrac{13}{17}t + \dfrac{21}{17}\right)$

55. $\begin{cases} x + y - 5z = -4 \\ 2y - 3z = -1 \\ x - 3y + z = -3 \end{cases}$

$-R_1 + R_3$

$\begin{cases} -x - y + 5z = 4 \\ x - 3y + z = -3 \end{cases}$
$\overline{\hspace{0.5cm} -4y + 6z = 1}$
(Equation 4)

$2R_2 + R_4$

$\begin{cases} 4y - 6z = -2 \\ -4y + 6z = 1 \end{cases}$
$\overline{\hspace{1cm} 0 \neq -1}$

Inconsistent, no solutions

57.

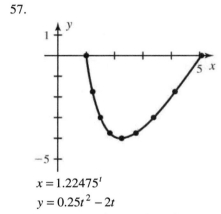

$x = 1.22475^t$
$y = 0.25t^2 - 2t$

The parametric equations fit the data very well.

59. Answers will vary.
Graphing both functions on the same screen, we note that although the paths intersect at approximately $(5.3, 3.7)$ and $(4.1, 1.5)$, the first particle arrives at these locations for $T = 5.00$ and $T = 4.90$, respectively, while the second particle arrives at $T = 2.17$ and $T = 3.40$.
No, the particles would not collide.

61. The ship vector makes a $135°$ angle with the positive x-axis.
The current vector makes a $60°$ angle with the positive x-axis.
Find the components of each.

Ship: $a = 12\cos 135° \approx -8.5$
$\quad\quad b = 12\sin 135° \approx 8.5$

Current: $a = 3\cos 60° = 1.5$
$\quad\quad\quad b = 3\sin 60° \approx 2.6$

$\langle -8.5 + 1.5,\, 8.5 + 2.6 \rangle = \langle -7,\, 11.1 \rangle$

$\theta = \tan^{-1}\left|\dfrac{11.1}{-7}\right| = \tan^{-1}\left(\dfrac{11.1}{7}\right) \approx 57.8°$

$270° + 57.8° = 327.8°$

$\sqrt{(-7)^2 + 11.1^2} \approx 13.1 \text{ mph}$

The true course and speed of the ship is a heading of $327.8°$ at 13.1 mph.

63. $\cos 105° = \cos(45° + 60°)$
$= \cos 45° \cos 60° - \sin 45° \sin 60°$
$= \dfrac{\sqrt{2}}{2} \cdot \dfrac{1}{2} - \dfrac{\sqrt{2}}{2} \cdot \dfrac{\sqrt{3}}{2}$
$= \dfrac{\sqrt{2}}{4} - \dfrac{\sqrt{6}}{4}$
$= \dfrac{\sqrt{2} - \sqrt{6}}{4}$

QIII: $2x \approx 3.9170 + \dfrac{\pi}{6}$
$\quad\quad\quad 2x \approx 4.4409$
$\quad\quad\quad\quad x \approx 2.2203$
$2.2203 + \pi \approx 5.3619$

QIV: $2x = 5.5078 + \dfrac{\pi}{6}$
$\quad\quad\quad 2x \approx 6.0314$
$\quad\quad\quad\quad x \approx 3.0157$
$3.0157 + \pi \approx 6.1573$

65. $\dfrac{\sin 50°}{52} = \dfrac{\sin B}{75}$
$52\sin B = 75\sin 50°$
$\sin B = \dfrac{75\sin 50°}{52}$
$\sin B \approx 1.1049$
Since the sine ratio is greater than 1, no triangle is possible.

Summary and Concept Review 8.1

1. $\sqrt{-72} = i\sqrt{72}$
$\quad\quad = i\sqrt{36 \cdot 2}$
$\quad\quad = 6i\sqrt{2}$

3. $\dfrac{-10 + \sqrt{-50}}{5} = \dfrac{-10 + i\sqrt{25 \cdot 2}}{5}$
$\quad\quad\quad\quad\quad = \dfrac{-10 + 5i\sqrt{2}}{5}$
$\quad\quad\quad\quad\quad = -2 + i\sqrt{2}$

5. $i^{57} = \left(i^4\right)^{14} i = i$

7. $\dfrac{5i}{1 - 2i} \cdot \dfrac{1 + 2i}{1 + 2i} = \dfrac{5i + 10i^2}{1^2 + 2^2}$
$\quad\quad\quad\quad\quad\quad = \dfrac{-10 + 5i}{5}$
$\quad\quad\quad\quad\quad\quad = -2 + i$

9. $(2 + 3i)(2 - 3i) = 2^2 + 3^2 = 13$

11. $x^2 - 9 = -34;\ x = 5i$
$\quad\quad (5i)^2 - 9 = -34$
$\quad\quad\quad 25i^2 - 9 = -34$
$\quad\quad\quad -25 - 9 = -34$
$\quad\quad\quad\quad -34 = -34 \text{ yes}$

$\quad\quad (-5i)^2 - 9 = -34$
$\quad\quad\quad 25i^2 - 9 = -34$
$\quad\quad\quad -25 - 9 = -34$
$\quad\quad\quad\quad -34 = -34 \text{ yes}$

Summary and Concept Review 8.2

13. $r = \sqrt{(-1)^2 + (-\sqrt{3})^2} = \sqrt{4} = 2$

$\theta_r = \tan^{-1}\left|\dfrac{-\sqrt{3}}{-1}\right| = \tan^{-1}(\sqrt{3}) = 60°$

In QIII, $\theta = 240°$

$z = 2(\cos 240° + i\sin 240°)$

15. $z = 5(\cos 30° + i\sin 30°)$

$= 5\left(\dfrac{\sqrt{3}}{2} + \dfrac{1}{2}i\right)$

$= \dfrac{5\sqrt{3}}{2} + \dfrac{5}{2}i$

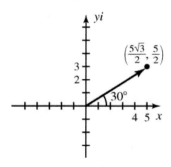

17. $I = \dfrac{V}{Z}$

$= \dfrac{4\sqrt{3} - 4j}{1 - \sqrt{3}j} \cdot \dfrac{1 + \sqrt{3}j}{1 + \sqrt{3}j}$

$= \dfrac{4\sqrt{3} + 12j - 4j - 4\sqrt{3}j^2}{1^2 - 3^2}$

$= \dfrac{8\sqrt{3} + 8j}{4}$

$= 2\sqrt{3} + 2j$

Summary and Concept Review 8.3

19. $r = \sqrt{(-1)^2 + (\sqrt{3})^2} = \sqrt{4} = 2; \; n = 5$

$\theta_r = \tan^{-1}\left|\dfrac{\sqrt{3}}{-1}\right| = \tan^{-1}(\sqrt{3}) = 60°$

In QII, $\theta = 120°$

$5 \cdot 120° = 600°$, coterminal with $240°$.

$(-1 + \sqrt{3}i)^5 = 2^5(\cos 240° + i\sin 240°)$

$= 32\left(-\dfrac{1}{2} - \dfrac{\sqrt{3}}{2}i\right)$

$= -16 - 16i\sqrt{3}$

21. $r = 125; \; \theta = 90°$

$\sqrt[3]{125} = 5; \; \dfrac{90°}{3} + \dfrac{360°k}{3} = 30° + 120°k$

$z_0 = 2.3348\,\text{cis}\,15° \approx 2.2553 + 0.6043i$

$z_1 = 2.3348\,\text{cis}\,135° \approx -1.6510 + 1.6510i$

$z_2 = 2.3348\,\text{cis}\,255° \approx -0.6043 - 2.2553i$

$z_0 = 5\,\text{cis}\,30° = 5\left(\dfrac{\sqrt{3}}{2} + \dfrac{1}{2}i\right) = \dfrac{5\sqrt{3}}{2} + \dfrac{5}{2}i$

$z_1 = 5\,\text{cis}\,150° = 5\left(-\dfrac{\sqrt{3}}{2} + \dfrac{1}{2}i\right) = -\dfrac{5\sqrt{3}}{2} + \dfrac{5}{2}i$

$z_1 = 5\,\text{cis}\,270° = 5(0 - i) = -5i$

23. $r = \sqrt{2^2 + 2^2} = \sqrt{8} = 2\sqrt{2}; \; n = 4$

$\theta = \tan^{-1}\left|\dfrac{2}{2}\right| = \tan^{-1}(1) = 45°$

The other roots will have the same value for r and will be spaced $90°$ apart.

$45° + 90° = 135°$

$2\sqrt{2}\,\text{cis}\,135° = 2\sqrt{2}(\cos 135° + i\sin 135°)$

$= 2\sqrt{2}\left(-\dfrac{\sqrt{2}}{2} + \dfrac{\sqrt{2}}{2}i\right)$

$= -2 + 2i$

The remaining two must be conjugates of the two we have roots we already know.

$2 - 2i$ and $-2 - 2i$

25. $\dfrac{5\sqrt{3}}{2} + \dfrac{5}{2}i;\ r = \sqrt{\left(\dfrac{5\sqrt{3}}{2}\right)^2 + \left(\dfrac{5}{2}\right)^2} = 5$

$\theta = \tan^{-1}\left|\dfrac{\dfrac{5}{2}}{\dfrac{5\sqrt{3}}{2}}\right| = \tan^{-1}\left(\dfrac{\sqrt{3}}{3}\right) = 30°$

$\left(\dfrac{5\sqrt{3}}{2} + \dfrac{5}{2}i\right)^3 = 5^3\,\text{cis}\,(3\cdot 30°)$

$= 5^3\,\text{cis}\,90°$

$= 125i$

$-\dfrac{5\sqrt{3}}{2} + \dfrac{5}{2}i;\ r = \sqrt{\left(-\dfrac{5\sqrt{3}}{2}\right)^2 + \left(\dfrac{5}{2}\right)^2} = 5$

$\theta_r = \tan^{-1}\left|\dfrac{\dfrac{5}{2}}{-\dfrac{5\sqrt{3}}{2}}\right| = \tan^{-1}\left(\dfrac{\sqrt{3}}{3}\right) = 30°$

In QII, $\theta = 150°$

$\left(-\dfrac{5\sqrt{3}}{2} + \dfrac{5}{2}i\right)^3 = 5^3\,\text{cis}\,(3\cdot 150°)$

$= 5^3\,\text{cis}\,450°$

$= 125i$

$(-5i)^3 = -125i^3 = 125i$

Summary and Concept Review 8.4

27. $r = 4 + 4\cos\theta$

Cardioid, Symmetric about $\theta = 0$

Cycle	r-value analysis	Location of graph
0 to $\dfrac{\pi}{2}$	$\|r\|$ decreases from 8 to 4	QI $(r > 0)$
$\dfrac{\pi}{2}$ to π	$\|r\|$ decreases from 4 to 0	QII $(r > 0)$
π to $\dfrac{3\pi}{2}$	$\|r\|$ increases from 0 to 4	QIII $(r > 0)$
$\dfrac{3\pi}{2}$ to 2π	$\|r\|$ increases from 4 to 8	QIV $(r > 0)$

27. (continued)

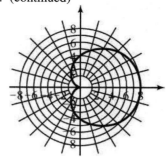

29. $r = 8\sin(2\theta)$

Four-petal rose,

Symmetric about $\theta = \dfrac{\pi}{2}$ and $\theta = 0$

Cycle	r-value analysis	Location of graph
0 to $\dfrac{\pi}{4}$	$\|r\|$ increases from 0 to 8	QI $(r > 0)$
$\dfrac{\pi}{4}$ to $\dfrac{\pi}{2}$	$\|r\|$ decreases from 8 to 0	QI $(r > 0)$
$\dfrac{\pi}{2}$ to $\dfrac{3\pi}{4}$	$\|r\|$ increases from 0 to 8	QIV $(r < 0)$
$\dfrac{3\pi}{4}$ to π	$\|r\|$ decreases from 8 to 0	QIV $(r < 0)$
π to $\dfrac{5\pi}{4}$	$\|r\|$ increases from 0 to 8	QIII $(r > 0)$
$\dfrac{5\pi}{4}$ to $\dfrac{3\pi}{2}$	$\|r\|$ decreases from 8 to 0	QIII $(r > 0)$
$\dfrac{3\pi}{2}$ to $\dfrac{7\pi}{4}$	$\|r\|$ increases from 0 to 8	QII $(r < 0)$
$\dfrac{7\pi}{4}$ to 2π	$\|r\|$ decreases from 8 to 0	QII $(r < 0)$

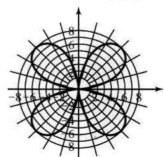

Summary and Concept Review 8.5

Mixed Review

31. $x = (2-t)^2$; $t \in [0,5]$

$y = (t-3)^2$

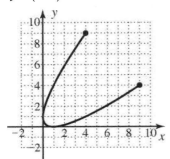

$$x = (2-t)^2$$
$$\pm\sqrt{x} = 2-t$$
$$\pm\sqrt{x} - 2 = -t$$
$$2 \pm \sqrt{x} = t$$

$$y = \left(2 \pm \sqrt{x} - 3\right)^2$$
$$y = \left(-1 \pm \sqrt{x}\right)^2$$

33. Answers will vary.
An example is included here.

$$x - 5 = t$$
$$x = t + 5$$

$$y = 2(t+5-5)^2 - 1$$
$$y = 2t^2 - 1$$

1. a. $\sqrt{-18} + \sqrt{-50} = i\sqrt{9 \cdot 2} + i\sqrt{25 \cdot 2}$
$$= 3i\sqrt{2} + 5i\sqrt{2}$$
$$= 8i\sqrt{2}$$

b. $(1-2i)^2 = 1^2 - 2(1)(2i) + (2i)^2$
$$= 1 - 4i + 4i^2$$
$$= -3 - 4i$$

c. $\dfrac{3i}{1+i} = \dfrac{3i}{1+i} \cdot \dfrac{1-i}{1-i}$
$$= \dfrac{3i - 3i^2}{1^2 + 1^2}$$
$$= \dfrac{3 + 3i}{2}$$
$$= \dfrac{3}{2} + \dfrac{3}{2}i$$

d. $(2 + i\sqrt{3})(2 - i\sqrt{3}) = 2^2 + \left(\sqrt{3}\right)^2$
$$= 4 + 3$$
$$= 7$$

3. a. $z = 4 - 5i$
$$z^2 - 8z + 41 = 0$$
$$(4-5i)^2 - 8(4-5i) + 41 = 0$$
$$16 - 40i + 25i^2 - 32 + 40i + 41 = 0$$
$$16 - 40i - 25 - 32 + 40i + 41 = 0$$
$$0 = 0 \text{ yes}$$

$$z = 4 + 5i$$
$$z^2 - 8z + 41 = 0$$
$$(4+5i)^2 - 8(4+5i) + 41 = 0$$
$$16 + 40i + 25i^2 - 32 - 40i + 41 = 0$$
$$16 + 40i - 25 - 32 - 40i + 41 = 0$$
$$0 = 0 \text{ yes}$$

b. $z^2 - 6iz + 7 = 0$
$a = 1, b = -6i, c = 7$

$$z = \frac{-(-6i) \pm \sqrt{(-6i)^2 - 4(1)(7)}}{2(1)}$$

$$z = \frac{6i \pm \sqrt{36i^2 - 28}}{2}$$

$$z = \frac{6i \pm \sqrt{-64}}{2}$$

$$z = \frac{6i \pm 8i}{2}$$

$$z = \frac{14i}{2} = 7i \text{ or } z = \frac{-2i}{2} = -i$$

5. $r = \sqrt{\left(2\sqrt{3}\right)^2 + \left(-2\right)^2} = 4$

$\theta_r = \tan^{-1}\left|\dfrac{-2}{2\sqrt{3}}\right| = \tan^{-1}\left(\dfrac{\sqrt{3}}{3}\right) = 30°$

In QIV, $\theta = 330°$

$6 \cdot 330° = 1980°$, coterminal with $180°$.

$\left(2\sqrt{3} - 2i\right)^6 = 4^6 \operatorname{cis} 180°$

$\qquad = 4096\left(\cos 180° + i\sin 180°\right)$

$\qquad = 4096\left(-1 + 0i\right) = -4096$

7. $Z = R + j\left(X_L - X_C\right)$

$Z = 12 + j\left(15.2 - 9.4\right)$

$\quad = 12 + 5.8j$

$|Z| = \sqrt{12^2 + 5.8^2} \approx 13.33$

$\theta = \tan^{-1}\left|\dfrac{5.8}{12}\right| = \tan^{-1}\left(\dfrac{5.8}{12}\right) \approx 25.8°$

$Z = 13.33\left(\cos 25.8° + i\sin 25.8°\right)$

$V_{RLC} \approx 6.5\left(13.33\right) \approx 86.6 \text{ V}$

9.

a. $\left(3.5, \dfrac{2\pi}{3}\right)$

$x = 3.5\cos\left(\dfrac{2\pi}{3}\right) = \dfrac{7}{2}\left(-\dfrac{1}{2}\right) = -\dfrac{7}{4}$

$y = 3.5\sin\left(\dfrac{2\pi}{3}\right) = \dfrac{7}{2}\left(\dfrac{\sqrt{3}}{2}\right) = \dfrac{7\sqrt{3}}{4}$

$\left(-\dfrac{7}{4}, \dfrac{7\sqrt{3}}{4}\right)$

b. $\left(-4, \dfrac{5\pi}{4}\right)$

$x = -4\cos\left(\dfrac{5\pi}{4}\right) = -4\left(-\dfrac{\sqrt{2}}{2}\right) = 2\sqrt{2}$

$y = -4\sin\left(\dfrac{5\pi}{4}\right) = -4\left(-\dfrac{\sqrt{2}}{2}\right) = 2\sqrt{2}$

$\left(2\sqrt{2}, 2\sqrt{2}\right)$

11. $r = 5$; number of leaves is 7

$y = 5\sin\left(7\theta\right)$

13. $x = 3\cos t \qquad y = -4\sin t$

$\dfrac{x}{3} = \cos t \qquad \dfrac{y}{-4} = \sin t$

$\dfrac{x^2}{9} = \cos^2 t \qquad \dfrac{y^2}{16} = \sin^2 t$

$\dfrac{x^2}{9} + \dfrac{y^2}{16} = \sin^2 t + \cos^2 t$

$\dfrac{x^2}{9} + \dfrac{y^2}{16} = 1$

15. $r = \sqrt{\left(-\dfrac{5\sqrt{2}}{2}\right)^2 + \left(-\dfrac{5\sqrt{2}}{2}\right)^2} = 5$

$\theta_r = \tan^{-1}\left|\dfrac{-\dfrac{5\sqrt{2}}{2}}{-\dfrac{5\sqrt{2}}{2}}\right| = \tan^{-1}\left(1\right) = 45°$

In QII, $\theta = 225°$

$4 \cdot 225° = 900°$, coterminal with $180°$

$3 \cdot 225° = 675°$, coterminal with $315°$

$2 \cdot 225° = 450°$, coterminal with $90°$

$z^4 = \left(5\right)^4 \operatorname{cis} 180° = -625$

$z^3 = \left(5\right)^3 \operatorname{cis} 315° = \dfrac{125\sqrt{2}}{2} - \dfrac{125\sqrt{2}}{2}i$

$z^2 = \left(5\right)^2 \operatorname{cis} 90° = 25i$

$z = -\dfrac{5\sqrt{2}}{2} - \dfrac{5\sqrt{2}}{2}i$

$\dfrac{1}{25}z^4 + z^2 + 25 - 25i$

$= \dfrac{1}{25}\left(-625\right) + 25i + 25 - 25i$

$= -25 + 25i + 25 - 25i = 0$

17. $x = 3\cos t \qquad y = 3\sin t$

$\dfrac{x}{3} = \cos t \qquad \dfrac{y}{3} = \sin t$

$\dfrac{x^2}{9} = \cos^2 t \qquad \dfrac{y^2}{9} = \sin^2 t$

$\dfrac{x^2}{9} + \dfrac{y^2}{9} = \sin^2 t + \cos^2 t$

$\dfrac{x^2}{9} + \dfrac{y^2}{9} = 1$

19. $r = 1;\ \theta = 0°;\ n = 6$

$$\sqrt[8]{1} = 1;\ \frac{0° + 360°k}{8} = 45°k$$

$z_0 = \text{cis}\, 0° = 1$

$z_1 = \text{cis}\, 45° = \frac{\sqrt{2}}{2} + \frac{\sqrt{2}}{2}i$

$z_2 = \text{cis}\, 90° = i$

$z_3 = \text{cis}\, 135° = -\frac{\sqrt{2}}{2} + \frac{\sqrt{2}}{2}i$

$z_4 = \text{cis}\, 180° = -1$

$z_5 = \text{cis}\, 225° = -\frac{\sqrt{2}}{2} - \frac{\sqrt{2}}{2}i$

$z_6 = \text{cis}\, 270° = -i$

$z_7 = \text{cis}\, 315° = \frac{\sqrt{2}}{2} - \frac{\sqrt{2}}{2}i$

$z_8 = \text{cis}\, 360° = 1$

Practice Test

1.
$$\frac{-8 + \sqrt{-20}}{6} = \frac{-8 + i\sqrt{4 \cdot 5}}{6}$$
$$= \frac{-8 + 2i\sqrt{5}}{6}$$
$$= -\frac{4}{3} + \frac{\sqrt{5}}{3}i$$

3. a.
$$\left(\frac{1}{2} + \frac{\sqrt{3}}{2}i\right) + \left(\frac{1}{2} - \frac{\sqrt{3}}{2}i\right)$$
$$= \frac{1}{2} + \frac{\sqrt{3}}{2}i + \frac{1}{2} - \frac{\sqrt{3}}{2}i$$
$$= 1$$

b.
$$\left(\frac{1}{2} + \frac{\sqrt{3}}{2}i\right) - \left(\frac{1}{2} - \frac{\sqrt{3}}{2}i\right)$$
$$= \frac{1}{2} + \frac{\sqrt{3}}{2}i - \frac{1}{2} + \frac{\sqrt{3}}{2}i$$
$$= i\sqrt{3}$$

c.
$$\left(\frac{1}{2} + \frac{\sqrt{3}}{2}i\right)\left(\frac{1}{2} - \frac{\sqrt{3}}{2}i\right)$$
$$= \left(\frac{1}{2}\right)^2 + \left(\frac{\sqrt{3}}{2}\right)^2$$
$$= \frac{1}{4} + \frac{3}{4}$$
$$= 1$$

5. $(3i + 5)(5 - 3i) = 15i - 9i^2 + 25 - 15i$
$$= 15i + 9 + 25 - 15i$$
$$= 34$$

7. $\dfrac{z_1}{z_2} = \dfrac{6\sqrt{5}}{3\sqrt{5}}\,\text{cis}\,\dfrac{\pi}{8} - \dfrac{\pi}{12} = 2\,\text{cis}\,\dfrac{\pi}{24}$

9. $Z = R + j(X_L - X_C)$
$Z = 18 + j(6.1 - 1.4)$
$\quad = 18 + 4.7j$
$|Z| = \sqrt{18^2 + 4.7^2} \approx 18.6$
$\theta = \tan^{-1}\left|\dfrac{4.7}{18}\right| = \tan^{-1}\left(\dfrac{4.7}{18}\right) \approx 14.6°$
$Z = 18.6(\cos 14.6° + i\sin 14.6°)$
$V_{RLC} \approx 2.5(18.6) \approx 46.5 \text{ V}$

11. $r = \sqrt{2^2 + \left(2\sqrt{3}\right)^2} = \sqrt{16} = 4$

$\theta = \tan^{-1}\left|\dfrac{2\sqrt{3}}{2}\right| = \tan^{-1}\left(\sqrt{3}\right) = 60°$

$5 \cdot 60° = 300°$
$4 \cdot 60° = 240°$
$3 \cdot 60° = 180°$
$2 \cdot 60° = 120°$

$z^4 = 4^5\,\text{cis}\,300° = 512 - 512i\sqrt{3}$
$z^4 = 4^4\,\text{cis}\,240° = -128 - 128i\sqrt{3}$
$z^3 = 4^3\,\text{cis}\,180° = -64$
$z^2 = 4^2\,\text{cis}\,120° = -8 + 8i\sqrt{3}$
$z = 2 + 2i\sqrt{3}$

$z^5 + 3z^3 + 64z^2 + 192$
$= \left(512 - 512i\sqrt{3}\right) + 3(-64) + 64\left(-8 + 8i\sqrt{3}\right) + 192$
$= 512 - 512i\sqrt{3} - 192 - 512 + 512i\sqrt{3} + 192 = 0$

13. $u = z^2;\ u^2 - 6u + 58 = 0$

$u = \dfrac{-(-6) \pm \sqrt{(-6)^2 - 4(1)(58)}}{2}$

$\quad = \dfrac{6 \pm \sqrt{36 - 232}}{2}$

$\quad = \dfrac{6 \pm \sqrt{-196}}{2}$

$\quad = \dfrac{6 \pm 14i}{2}$

$\quad = 3 \pm 7i$

$z^2 = 3 \pm 7i$, so we need to find the square roots of $3 + 7i,\ 3 - 7i$.

13. (continued)

For each, $r = \sqrt{3^2 + 7^2} = \sqrt{58}$.

Consider $3 + 7i$.

$$\theta = \tan^{-1}\left|\frac{7}{3}\right| = \tan^{-1}\left(\frac{7}{3}\right) \approx 66.8°$$

$$\sqrt{\sqrt{58}} = \sqrt[4]{58};$$

$$\frac{66.8° + 360°k}{2} = 33.4° + 180°k$$

$$z_0 \approx \sqrt[4]{58}\,\text{cis}\,33.4° \approx 2.3039 + 1.5191i$$

$$z_1 = \sqrt[4]{58}\,\text{cis}\,213.4° \approx -2.3039 - 1.5191i$$

Consider $3 - 7i$.

$$\theta_r = \tan^{-1}\left|\frac{-7}{3}\right| = \tan^{-1}\left(\frac{7}{3}\right) \approx 66.8°$$

In QIV, $\theta = 293.2°$

$$\sqrt{\sqrt{58}} = \sqrt[4]{58};$$

$$\frac{293.2° + 360°k}{2} = 146.6° + 180°k$$

$$z_0 \approx \sqrt[4]{58}\,\text{cis}\,146.6° \approx -2.3039 + 1.5191i$$

$$z_1 = \sqrt[4]{58}\,\text{cis}\,326.6° \approx 2.3039 - 1.5191i$$

15. $r = 4 + 8\cos\theta$
    Limacon

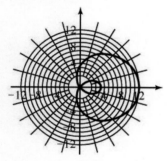

17. $x = 4\sin t$
    $y = 5\cos t$
    Vertical ellipse

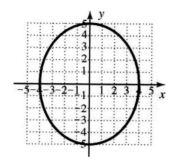

$$x = 4\sin t \qquad y = 5\cos t$$

$$\frac{x}{4} = \sin t \qquad \frac{y}{5} = \cos t$$

$$\frac{x^2}{16} = \sin^2 t \qquad \frac{y^2}{25} = \cos^2 t$$

$$\frac{x^2}{16} + \frac{y^2}{25} = \sin^2 t + \cos^2 t$$

$$\frac{x^2}{16} + \frac{y^2}{25} = 1$$

19. $x = 4T - 4\sin T$
    $y = 4 - 4\cos T$

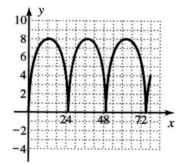

Maximum y-value: 8
Minimum y-value: 0
Period: 8π

Calculator Exploration and Discovery

Exercise 1:

$$\begin{cases} 2x - y - z = -1 \\ -3x + 2y + z = 4 \\ 3x - 3y = -9 \end{cases}$$

R1+R2

$$\begin{cases} 2x - y - z = -1 \\ -3x + 2y + z = 4 \end{cases}$$

$$-x + y\ \ \ \ = 3 \qquad \text{Equation 4}$$

3R4+R3

$$\begin{cases} -3x + 3y = 9 \\ 3x - 3y = -9 \end{cases}$$

$$0 = 0$$

(Dependent equations)

$$3x - 3y = -9$$
$$-3y = -3x - 9$$
$$y = x + 3$$

$$2x - y - z = -1$$
$$2x - (x+3) - z = -1$$
$$2x - x - 3 - z = -1$$
$$x - 3 - z = -1$$
$$-z = -x + 2$$
$$z = x - 2$$

$$(x, x+3, x-2)$$
$$(t, t+3, t-2)$$

Strengthening Core Skills

Exercise 1:

$$z_1 = \operatorname{cis} \alpha$$
$$z_2 = \operatorname{cis} \beta$$

$$\frac{z_1}{z_2} = \frac{\operatorname{cis} \alpha}{\operatorname{cis} \beta}$$

$$= \frac{\cos \alpha + i \sin \alpha}{\cos \beta + i \sin \beta}$$

$$\frac{z_1}{z_2} = \frac{\operatorname{cis} \alpha}{\operatorname{cis} \beta}$$

$$= \operatorname{cis}(\alpha - \beta)$$

$$= \cos(\alpha - \beta) + i \sin(\alpha - \beta)$$

$$= \frac{\cos \alpha + i \sin \alpha}{\cos \beta + i \sin \beta} \cdot \frac{\cos \beta - i \sin \beta}{\cos \beta - i \sin \beta}$$

$$= \frac{\cos \alpha \cos \beta - i \cos \alpha \sin \beta + i \sin \alpha \cos \beta - i^2 \sin \alpha \sin \beta}{\cos^2 \beta + \sin^2 \beta}$$

$$= \frac{(\cos \alpha \cos \beta + \sin \alpha \sin \beta) + (\sin \alpha \cos \beta - \cos \alpha \sin \beta)i}{1}$$

$$= (\cos \alpha \cos \beta + \sin \alpha \sin \beta) + (\sin \alpha \cos \beta - \cos \alpha \sin \beta)i$$

By direct comparison, we see that

$$\cos(\alpha - \beta) = \cos \alpha \cos \beta + \sin \alpha \sin \beta \text{ ; and}$$

$$\sin(\alpha - \beta) = \sin \alpha \cos \beta - \cos \alpha \sin \beta.$$

Exercise 3:

$$z_1 = -3 + i\sqrt{3}; \quad r_1 = \sqrt{(-3)^2 + \left(\sqrt{3}\right)^2} = \sqrt{12} = 2\sqrt{3}$$

$$\theta_{1r} = \tan^{-1}\left|\frac{\sqrt{3}}{-3}\right| = \tan^{-1}\left(\frac{\sqrt{3}}{3}\right) = \frac{\pi}{6}$$

In QII, $\theta_1 = \dfrac{5\pi}{6}$

$$z_1 = 2\sqrt{3}e^{\frac{5\pi}{6}i}$$

$$z_2 = \sqrt{3} + i; \quad r_2 = \sqrt{\left(\sqrt{3}\right)^2 + 1^2} = \sqrt{4} = 2$$

$$\theta_2 = \tan^{-1}\left|\frac{1}{\sqrt{3}}\right| = \tan^{-1}\left(\frac{\sqrt{3}}{3}\right) = \frac{\pi}{6}$$

$$z_2 = 2e^{\frac{\pi}{6}i}$$

$$\frac{z_1}{z_2} = \frac{2\sqrt{3}e^{\frac{5\pi}{6}i}}{2e^{\frac{\pi}{6}i}} = 2e^{\frac{2\pi}{3}i}$$

$$= \sqrt{3}\left(\cos\frac{2\pi}{3} + i\sin\frac{2\pi}{3}\right)$$

$$= \sqrt{3}\left(-\frac{1}{2} + \frac{\sqrt{3}}{2}i\right)$$

$$= -\frac{\sqrt{3}}{2} + \frac{3}{2}i$$

Exercise 5:

$$z = 3\operatorname{cis}\left(\frac{137\pi}{180}\right) = 3e^{\frac{137\pi}{180}i}$$

$$z^4 = \left(3e^{\frac{137\pi}{180}i}\right)^4 = 3^4 e^{\frac{137\pi}{45}i} = 81e^{\frac{137\pi}{45}i}$$

$$= 81\left[\cos\left(\frac{137\pi}{45}\right) + i\sin\left(\frac{137\pi}{45}\right)\right]$$

$$\approx 81(-0.9903 - 0.1392i)$$

$$\approx -80.21 - 11.27i$$

Cumulative Review Chapters 1-8

1. $\quad -6\tan x = 2\sqrt{3}$

$$\tan x = \frac{2\sqrt{3}}{-6}$$

$$\tan x = -\frac{\sqrt{3}}{3}$$

$$x = \tan^{-1}\left(-\frac{\sqrt{3}}{3}\right)$$

$$x = \frac{5\pi}{6} \text{ or } x = \frac{11\pi}{6}$$

$$x = \frac{5\pi}{6} + \pi k, \ k \in \mathbb{Z}$$

3. $\quad 25\sin\left(\dfrac{\pi}{3}x - \dfrac{\pi}{6}\right) + 3 = 15.5$

$$25\sin\left(\frac{\pi}{3}x - \frac{\pi}{6}\right) = 12.5$$

$$\sin\left(\frac{\pi}{3}x - \frac{\pi}{6}\right) = \frac{12.5}{25}$$

$$\sin\left(\frac{\pi}{3}x - \frac{\pi}{6}\right) = \frac{1}{2}$$

$$\frac{\pi}{3}x - \frac{\pi}{6} = \sin^{-1}\left(\frac{1}{2}\right)$$

$$\frac{\pi}{3}x - \frac{\pi}{6} = \frac{\pi}{6} + 2\pi k$$

$$\frac{\pi}{3}x = \frac{\pi}{3} + 2\pi k$$

$$x = 1 + 6k, \ k \in \mathbb{Z}$$

$$\frac{\pi}{3}x - \frac{\pi}{6} = \frac{5\pi}{6} + 2\pi k$$

$$\frac{\pi}{3}x = \pi + 2\pi k$$

$$x = 3 + 6k, \ k \in \mathbb{Z}$$

5. $180° - 72° = 108°$
    $180° - (40° + 108°) = 32°$

    Let d be the distance from the point 2000 m from the base to the peak of the mountain.
    $$\frac{\sin 32°}{2000} = \frac{\sin 108°}{d}$$
    $$d \sin 32° = 2000 \sin 108°$$
    $$d = \frac{2000 \sin 108°}{\sin 32°}$$
    $$d \approx 3589 \text{ m}$$

    Let h be the height of the mountain.
    $$\sin 40° \approx \frac{h}{3589}$$
    $$h \approx 3589 \sin 40°$$
    $$h \approx 2307 \text{ m}$$

7. $\cos t = \dfrac{12}{13}$

    Since t is in QIV, y is negative.
    $$y = -\sqrt{13^2 - 12^2} = -5; \quad \sin t = -\frac{5}{13}$$

    $$\sin(2t) = 2\sin t \cos t$$
    $$= 2\left(-\frac{5}{13}\right)\left(\frac{12}{13}\right)$$
    $$= -\frac{120}{169}$$

    $$\cos(2t) = 2\cos^2 t - 1$$
    $$= 2\left(\frac{12}{13}\right)^2 - 1$$
    $$= \frac{119}{169}$$

9. $r = 4\cos(2\theta)$
    Four-petal rose

    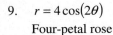

11. $\cos\theta = \dfrac{u \cdot v}{\|u\| \cdot \|v\|}$
    $$= \frac{-4(3) + 5(7)}{\sqrt{(-4)^2 + 5^2}\,\sqrt{3^2 + 7^2}}$$
    $$= \frac{23}{\sqrt{41 \cdot 58}}$$
    $$= \frac{23}{\sqrt{2378}}$$

    $$\theta = \cos^{-1}\left(\frac{23}{\sqrt{2378}}\right) \approx 61.9°$$

13. $\sin 37° = \dfrac{h}{10}$
    $$h = 10\sin 37°$$
    $$h \approx 6.0181 \text{ m}$$

    $$A = \frac{1}{2}(25)(6.0181) \approx 75.2 \text{ m}^2$$

15. $\sec\theta - \cot\theta = \dfrac{\cos\theta}{1 + \sin\theta}$
    $$\frac{1}{\cos\theta} - \frac{\cos\theta}{\sin\theta} = \frac{\cos\theta}{1 + \sin\theta}$$

    Determine those values of θ for which the denominators are 0.

$\cos\theta = 0$	$\sin\theta = 0$	$1 + \sin\theta = 0$
$\theta = \dfrac{\pi}{2}, \dfrac{3\pi}{2}$	$\theta = 0, \pi$	$\sin\theta = -1$ $\theta = \pi$

    The relation is not defined at $\theta = 0, \dfrac{\pi}{2}, \pi, \dfrac{3\pi}{2}$.

17. $\alpha = 32°$
    coterminal angle: $360° + 32° = 392°$

    $\beta = 0.7169$
    coterminal angle: $2\pi + 0.7169 \approx 7.0001$

19. $\theta = 125° \cdot \dfrac{\pi}{180°} = \dfrac{25\pi}{36}$

    $$A = \frac{1}{2}(6)^2\left(\frac{25\pi}{36}\right) = 39.3 \text{ ft}^2$$

21. $\tan 52° = \dfrac{h}{100}$
    $$h = 100\tan 52°$$
    $$h \approx 128 \text{ yd}$$

23. $\cos(2\theta) = \cos^2\theta - \sin^2\theta$

$\cos(2\theta) = \cos^2\theta - (1 - \cos^2\theta)$

$\cos(2\theta) = \cos^2\theta - 1 + \cos^2\theta$

$\cos(2\theta) = 2\cos^2\theta - 1$

$\cos(2\theta) = \cos^2\theta - \sin^2\theta$

$\cos(2\theta) = 1 - \sin^2\theta - \sin^2\theta$

$\cos(2\theta) = 1 - 2\sin^2\theta$

25. $\sin\left(\dfrac{\pi}{8}\right)\cos\left(\dfrac{\pi}{12}\right) - \cos\left(\dfrac{\pi}{8}\right)\sin\left(\dfrac{\pi}{12}\right)$

$= \sin\left(\dfrac{\pi}{8} - \dfrac{\pi}{12}\right)$

$= \sin\left(\dfrac{3\pi}{24} - \dfrac{2\pi}{24}\right)$

$= \sin\left(\dfrac{\pi}{24}\right)$

27. $\dfrac{\sin 32°}{10} = \dfrac{\sin B}{20}$

$10\sin B = 20\sin 32°$

$\sin B = \dfrac{20\sin 32°}{10}$

$\sin B \approx 1.0598$

Since the sine ratio is greater than 1, no triangle is possible.

No, the hyena will not be detected.

29. $z = 1 - \sqrt{3}i$

$r = \sqrt{1^2 + \left(-\sqrt{3}\right)^2} = 2;\ n = 4$

$\theta = \tan^{-1}\left|\dfrac{-\sqrt{3}}{1}\right| = \tan^{-1}\left(\sqrt{3}\right) = 60°$

In QIV, $\theta = 300°$

$4 \cdot 300° = 1200°,$ coterminal with $120°$

$z^4 = 2^4\operatorname{cis}120°$

$= 16\left(\cos 120° + \sin 120°\right)$

$= 16\left(-\dfrac{1}{2} + \dfrac{\sqrt{3}}{2}i\right)$

$= -8 + 8i\sqrt{3}$

A Exercises

1. b^x; b; b; x

3. a; 1

5. False; for $|b| < 1$ and $x_2 > x_1$, $b^{x_2} < b^{x_1}$, so the function is decreasing.

7. $P(t) = 2500 \cdot 4^t$

$P(2) = 2500 \cdot 4^2 = 40{,}000$

$P\left(\dfrac{1}{2}\right) = 2500 \cdot 4^{1/2} = 5000$

$P\left(\dfrac{3}{2}\right) = 2500 \cdot 4^{3/2} = 20{,}000$

$P\left(\sqrt{3}\right) = 2500 \cdot 4^{\sqrt{3}} \approx 27{,}589.162$

9. $f(x) = 0.5 \cdot 10^x$

$f(3) = 0.5 \cdot 10^3 = 500$

$f\left(\dfrac{1}{2}\right) = 0.5 \cdot 10^{1/2} \approx 1.581$

$f\left(\dfrac{2}{3}\right) = 0.5 \cdot 10^{2/3} \approx 2.321$

$f\left(\sqrt{7}\right) = 0.5 \cdot 10^{\sqrt{7}} \approx 221.168$

11. $V(n) = 10{,}000\left(\dfrac{2}{3}\right)^n$

$V(0) = 10{,}000\left(\dfrac{2}{3}\right)^0 = 10{,}000$

$V(4) = 10{,}000\left(\dfrac{2}{3}\right)^4 \approx 1975.309$

$V(4.7) = 10{,}000\left(\dfrac{2}{3}\right)^{4.7} \approx 1487.206$

$V(5) = 10{,}000\left(\dfrac{2}{3}\right)^5 \approx 1316.872$

13. $y = 3^x$

y-intercept: $(0, 1)$

At $x = 2$, $y = 9$. $(2, 9)$

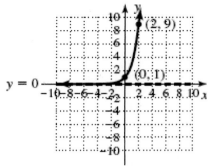

increasing

15. $y = \left(\dfrac{1}{3}\right)^x$

y-intercept: $(0, 1)$

At $x = -2$, $y = 9$. $(-2, 9)$

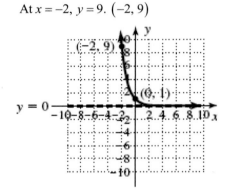

decreasing

17. $y = 3^x + 2$

Translate the graph of $y = 3^x$ up 2 units.

Asymptote: $y = 2$

y-intercept: $(0, 3)$

At $x = 1$, $y = 5$. $(1, 5)$

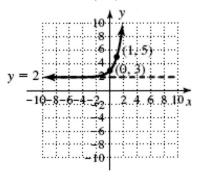

19. $y = 3^{x+3}$

Translate the graph of $y = 3^x$ left 3 units.

Asymptote: $y = 0$

At $x = -3$, $y = 1$. $(-3, 1)$

At $x = -1$, $y = 9$. $(-1, 9)$

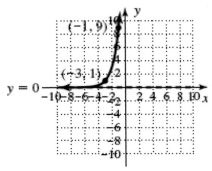

21. $y = 2^{-x}$

Reflect the graph of $y = 2^x$ in the y-axis.

Asymptote: $y = 0$

y-intercept: $(0, 1)$

At $x = -3$, $y = 8$. $(-3, 8)$

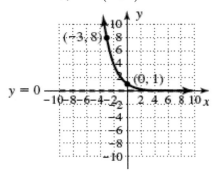

23. $y = 2^{-x} + 3$

Reflect the graph of $y = 2^x$ in the y-axis and translate up 3 units.

Asymptote: $y = 3$

y-intercept: $(0, 4)$

At $x = -2$, $y = 7$. $(-2, 7)$

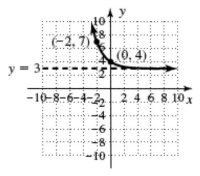

25. $y = 2^{x+1} - 3$

Translate the graph of $y = 2^x$ left 1 unit and down 3 units.

Asymptote: $y = -3$

At $x = -1$, $y = -2$. $(-1, -2)$

At $x = 2$, $y = 5$. $(2, 5)$

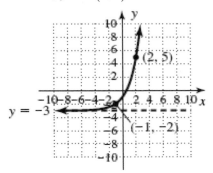

27. $y = \left(\dfrac{1}{3}\right)^x + 1$

Translate the graph of $y = \left(\dfrac{1}{3}\right)^x$ up 1 unit.

Asymptote: $y = 1$

y-intercept: $(0, 2)$

At $x = -2$, $y = 10$. $(-2, 10)$

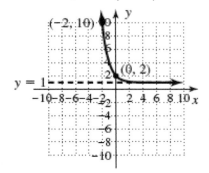

29. $y = \left(\dfrac{1}{3}\right)^{x-2}$

Translate the graph of $y = \left(\dfrac{1}{3}\right)^x$ right 2 units.

Asymptote: $y = 0$

y-intercept: $(0, 9)$

At $x = 2$, $y = 1$. $(2, 1)$

29. (continued)

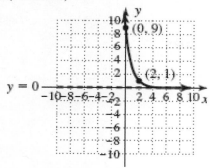

31. $f(x) = \left(\dfrac{1}{3}\right)^x - 2$

Translate the graph of $y = \left(\dfrac{1}{3}\right)^x$ down 2 units.

Asymptote: $y = -2$

y-intercept: $(0, -1)$

At $x = -2$, $y = 7$. $(-2, 7)$

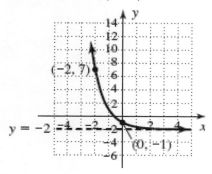

33. $y = 5^{-x}$

Reflect the graph of $y = 5^x$ in the y-axis.
Asymptote: $y = 0$

y-intercept: $(0, 1)$

At $x = -1$, $y = 5$. $(-1, 5)$

The equation corresponds to graph e.

35. $y = 3^{-x+1} = 3^{-(x-1)}$

Reflect the graph of $y = 3^x$ in the y-axis and
translate right 1 unit.
Asymptote: $y = 0$

y-intercept: $(0, 3)$

At $x = 1$, $y = 1$. $(1, 1)$

The equation corresponds to graph a.

37. $y = 2^{x+1} - 2$

Translate the graph of $y = 2^x$ left 1 unit and
down 2 units.
Asymptote: $y = -2$

At $x = -1$, $y = -1$. $(-1, -1)$

At $x = 1$, $y = 2$. $(1, 2)$

The equation corresponds to graph b.

39. $e^1 \approx 2.718282$

41. $e^2 \approx 7.389056$

43. $e^{1.5} \approx 4.481689$

45. $e^{\sqrt{2}} \approx 4.113250$

47. $f(x) = e^{x+3} - 2$

Translate the graph of $f(x) = e^x$ left 3 units
and down 2 units.
Asymptote: $y = -2$

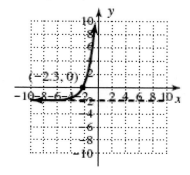

49. $r(t) = -e^t + 2$

Reflect the graph of $r(t) = e^t$ in the x-axis and
translate up 2 units.
Asymptote: $y = 2$

y-intercept: $(0, 1)$

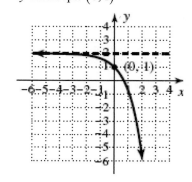

51. $p(x) = e^{-x+2} - 1$

Reflect the graph of $p(x) = e^x$ in the y-axis
and translate left 2 units and down 1 unit.
Asymptote: $y = -1$

At $x = 2$, $y = 0$. $(2, 0)$

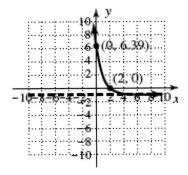

53. $10^x = 1000$

$10^x = 10^3$

$x = 3$

55. $25^x = 125$

$5^{2x} = 5^3$

$2x = 3$

$x = \dfrac{3}{2}$

57. $8^{x+2} = 32$

$(2^3)^{x+2} = 2^5$

$2^{3x+6} = 2^5$

$3x + 6 = 5$

$3x = -1$

$x = -\dfrac{1}{3}$

59. $32^x = 16^{x+1}$

$(2^5)^x = (2^4)^{x+1}$

$2^{5x} = 2^{4x+4}$

$5x = 4x + 4$

$x = 4$

61. $\left(\dfrac{1}{5}\right)^x = 125$

$(5^{-1})^x = 5^3$

$5^{-x} = 5^3$

$-x = 3$

$x = -3$

63. $\left(\dfrac{1}{3}\right)^{2x} = 9^{x-6}$

$(3^{-1})^{2x} = (3^2)^{x-6}$

$3^{-2x} = 3^{2x-12}$

$-2x = 2x - 12$

$-4x = -12$

$x = 3$

65. $\left(\dfrac{1}{9}\right)^{x-5} = 3^{3x}$

$(3^{-2})^{x-5} = 3^{3x}$

$3^{-2x+10} = 3^{3x}$

$-2x + 10 = 3x$

$10 = 5x$

$2 = x$

67. $25^{3x} = 125^{x-2}$

$(5^2)^{3x} = (5^3)^{x-2}$

$5^{6x} = 5^{3x-6}$

$6x = 3x - 6$

$3x = -6$

$x = -2$

69. $\dfrac{e^4}{e^{2-x}} = e^3 e$

$e^{4-(2-x)} = e^{3+1}$

$e^{2+x} = e^4$

$2 + x = 4$

$x = 2$

71. $(e^{2x-4})^3 = \dfrac{e^{x+5}}{e^2}$

$e^{6x-12} = e^{x+5-2}$

$e^{6x-12} = e^{x+3}$

$6x - 12 = x + 3$

$5x = 15$

$x = 3$

73. $P(t) = 1000 \cdot 3^t$

a.   12 hr $= \dfrac{1}{2}$ day

$P\left(\dfrac{1}{2}\right) = 1000 \cdot 3^{1/2} \approx 1732$

$P(1) = 1000 \cdot 3^1 = 3000$

$P\left(\dfrac{3}{2}\right) = 1000 \cdot 3^{3/2} \approx 5196$

$P(2) = 1000 \cdot 3^2 = 9000$

73. b. Yes, the outputs show that the population is tripling every 24 hours.

c. As $t \to \infty, P \to \infty$.

d.

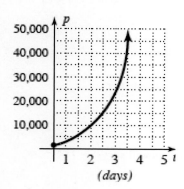

75. $T(x) = T_R + (T_0 - T_R)e^{kx}$

$T_R = -10°, T_0 = 73°, k \approx -0.031, x = 15$

$T(15) = -10 + (73 - (-10))e^{-0.031(15)}$

$= -10 + (83)e^{-0.465}$

≈ 42

No, the drinks will not be cold enough after just 15 minutes.

$35 = -10 + (73 - (-10))e^{-0.031x}$

Using the TABLE feature of a graphing calculator, we see that $T(20) \approx 35$, so they will have to wait about 5 minutes.

77. $V(t) = V_0 \left(\dfrac{4}{5}\right)^t$

a. $V(1) = 125,000 \left(\dfrac{4}{5}\right)^1 = 100,000$

The earthmover will be worth $100,000.

b. $64,000 = 125,000 \cdot \left(\dfrac{4}{5}\right)^t$

$\dfrac{64}{125} = \left(\dfrac{4}{5}\right)^t$

$\left(\dfrac{4}{5}\right)^3 = \left(\dfrac{4}{5}\right)^t$

$3 = t$

In 3 years, it will depreciate to $64,000.

79. $V(t) = V_0 \left(\dfrac{5}{6}\right)^t$

a. $V(5) = 216,000 \cdot \left(\dfrac{5}{6}\right)^5 \approx \$86,806$

The x-ray machine will be worth approximately $86,806.

b. $125,000 = 216,000 \cdot \left(\dfrac{5}{6}\right)^t$

$\dfrac{125}{216} = \left(\dfrac{5}{6}\right)^t$

$\left(\dfrac{5}{6}\right)^3 = \left(\dfrac{5}{6}\right)^t$

$3 = t$

In 3 years, it will depreciate to $125,000.

81. $R(t) = R_0 \cdot 2^t$

a. $R(4) = 2.5 \cdot 2^4 = 40$

A revenue of $40 million is being generated.

b. $320 = 2.5 \cdot 2^t$

$128 = 2^t$

$2^7 = 2^t$

$7 = t$

It will be 7 years before the business will be generating revenue of $320 million.

83. $T(x) = 0.85^x$

$T(7) = 0.85^7 \approx 0.32$

The transparency is 32%.

85. $T(x) = 0.85^x$

$T(11) = 0.85^{11} \approx 0.17$

The transparency is 17%.

87. $P(t) = P_0 (1.05)^t$

$P(10) = 20,000(1.05)^{10} \approx \$32,578$

89. $Q(t) = Q_0 \left(\dfrac{1}{2}\right)^{t/h}$

a. $Q(24) = 64 \cdot \left(\dfrac{1}{2}\right)^{24/8}$

$= 64 \cdot \left(\dfrac{1}{2}\right)^3$

$= 8$

8 grams remain after 24 minutes.

89. b.
$$1 = 64\left(\frac{1}{2}\right)^{t/8}$$
$$\frac{1}{64} = \left(\frac{1}{2}\right)^{t/8}$$
$$\left(\frac{1}{2}\right)^6 = \left(\frac{1}{2}\right)^{t/8}$$
$$6 = \frac{t}{8}$$
$$48 = t$$
After 48 minutes, only 1 gram remains.

91.
$$10^{2x} = 25$$
$$10^{2x} = 5^2$$
$$\left(10^x\right)^2 = 5^2$$
$$10^x = 5$$
$$\left(10^x\right)^{-1} = \left(5\right)^{-1}$$
$$10^{-x} = 5^{-1} = \frac{1}{5}$$

93.
$$3^{0.5x} = 5$$
$$\left(3^{0.5x}\right)^2 = 5^2$$
$$3^x = 5^2$$
$$3 \cdot 3^x = 3 \cdot 5^2$$
$$3^{x+1} = 75$$

95. $f(x) = \left(\frac{1}{2}\right)^x$

$$f(20) = \left(\frac{1}{2}\right)^{20} \approx 9.5 \times 10^{-7}$$
Answers will vary.

97. $\left(1 + \frac{1}{x}\right)^x$

a. $\dfrac{f(x+0.01) - f(x)}{x + 0.01 - x}$

$$= \frac{\left(1 + \dfrac{1}{x+0.01}\right)^{x+0.01} - \left(1 + \dfrac{1}{x}\right)^x}{0.01}$$

We use the TABLE feature.
At $x = 1$, 0.3842
At $x = 4$, 0.0564
At $x = 10$, 0.0114
At $x = 20$, 0.0031
The rate of growth seems to be approaching 0.

97. b.   Using the TABLE feature, we see that at $e = 2.718281828...$, $x = 16,608$.

c.   Yes, the secant lines are becoming virtually horizontal. $(y = e)$

B Exercises

1. $\log_b x$; b; b; greater

3. $(1,0)$; 0

5. 5; Answers will vary.

7. $3 = \log_2 8$
$$2^3 = 8$$

9. $-1 = \log_7 \frac{1}{7}$
$$7^{-1} = \frac{1}{7}$$

11. $0 = \log_9 1$
$$9^0 = 1$$

13. $\frac{1}{3} = \log_8 2$
$$8^{1/3} = 2$$

15. $1 = \log_2 2$
$$2^1 = 2$$

17. $\log_7 49 = 2$
$$7^2 = 49$$

19. $\log_{10} 100 = 2$
$$10^2 = 100$$

21. $\log_e (54.598) \approx 4$
$$e^4 \approx 54.598$$

23. $4^3 = 64$
$$\log_4 64 = 3$$

25. $3^{-2} = \frac{1}{9}$
$$\log_3 \frac{1}{9} = -2$$

27. $e^0 = 1$
$0 = \log_e 1$

29. $\left(\dfrac{1}{3}\right)^{-3} = 27$
$\log_{\frac{1}{3}} 27 = -3$

31. $10^3 = 1000$
$\log 1000 = 3$

33. $10^{-2} = \dfrac{1}{100}$
$\log \dfrac{1}{100} = -2$

35. $4^{\frac{3}{2}} = 8$
$\log_4 8 = \dfrac{3}{2}$

37. $4^{\frac{-3}{2}} = \dfrac{1}{8}$
$\log_4 \dfrac{1}{8} = \dfrac{-3}{2}$

39. $\log_4 4 = 1$, since $4^1 = 4$.

41. $\log_{11} 121 = 2$, since $11^2 = 121$.

43. $\log_e e = 1$, since $e^1 = e$.

45. $\log_4 2 = \dfrac{1}{2}$, since $4^{\frac{1}{2}} = 2$.

47. $\log_7 \dfrac{1}{49} = -2$, since $7^{-2} = \dfrac{1}{49}$.

49. $\log_e \dfrac{1}{e^2} = -2$, since $e^{-2} = \dfrac{1}{e^2}$.

51. $\log 50 \approx 1.6990$

53. $\ln 1.6 \approx 0.4700$

55. $\ln 225 \approx 5.4161$

57. $\log \sqrt{37} \approx 0.7841$

59. $f(x) = \log_2 x + 3$
Translate graph of $f(x) = \log_2 x$ up 3 units.
Asymptote: $x = 0$
At $x = 1$, $y = 3$. $(1, 3)$

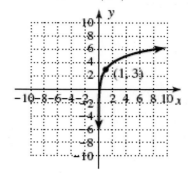

61. $h(x) = \log_2 (x - 2) + 3$
Translate graph of $h(x) = \log_2 x$ right 2 units
and up 3 units.
Asymptote: $x = 2$
At $x = 3$, $y = 3$. $(3, 3)$

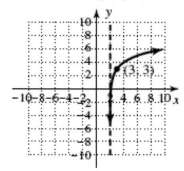

63. $q(x) = \ln(x + 1)$
Translate graph of $q(x) = \ln x$ left 1 unit.
Asymptote: $x = -1$
At $x = 0$, $y = 0$. $(0, 0)$

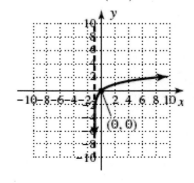

65. $Y_1 = -\ln(x+1)$

   Reflect graph of $Y_1 = \ln x$ in the x–axis,

   and translate left 1 unit.

   Asymptote: $x = -1$

   At $x = 0$, $y = 0$. $(0, 0)$

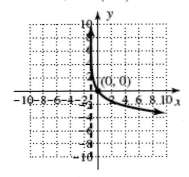

67. $y = \log_b(x+2)$

   Translate the graph of $y = \log_b x$ left 2 units.

   Asymptote: $x = -2$

   At $x = -1$, $y = 0$. $(-1, 0)$

   The equation corresponds to graph II.

69. $y = 1 - \log_b x$

   Reflect the graph of $y = \log_b x$ in the x-axis,

   translate up 1 unit.

   Asymptote: $x = 0$

   At $x = 1$, $y = 1$. $(1, 1)$

   The equation corresponds to graph VI.

71. $y = \log_b x + 2$

   Translate the graph of $y = \log_b x$ up 2 units.

   Asymptote: $x = 0$

   At $x = 1$, $y = 2$. $(1, 2)$

   The equation corresponds to graph V.

73. $y = \log_6\left(\dfrac{x+1}{x-3}\right)$

   $\dfrac{x+1}{x-3} > 0$, $x \neq 3$

   critical values: -1 and 3

   pos   neg   pos
   ───────○──────○──────→
          -1   3

   $x \in (-\infty, -1) \cup (3, \infty)$

75. $y = \log_5 \sqrt{2x-3}$

   $2x - 3 > 0$

   $2x > 3$

   $x > \dfrac{3}{2}$

   $x \in \left(\dfrac{3}{2}, \infty\right)$

77. $y = \log(9 - x^2)$

   $9 - x^2 > 0$

   $(3+x)(3-x) > 0$

   critical values: 3 and -3

   neg   pos   neg
   ───────○──────○──────→
          -3   3

   $x \in (-3, 3)$

79. $f(x) = -\log_{10} x$

   $f(7.94 \times 10^{-5}) = -\log_{10}(7.94 \times 10^{-5})$

   ≈ 4.1

   This is an acid solution.

81. $M(I) = \log\left(\dfrac{I}{I_0}\right)$

   a. $I = 50,000 I_0$

   $M(50,000 I_0) = \log\left(\dfrac{50,000 I_0}{I_0}\right)$

   $= \log 50,000$

   ≈ 4.7

   b. $I = 75,000 I_0$

   $M(75,000 I_0) = \log\left(\dfrac{75,000 I_0}{I_0}\right)$

   $= \log 75,000$

   ≈ 4.9

83. $M(I) = \log\left(\dfrac{I}{I_0}\right)$

   1989: $\log\left(\dfrac{I}{I_0}\right) = 6.2$

   $\dfrac{I}{I_0} = 10^{6.2}$

   $I = 10^{6.2} I_0$

83. (continued)

2006: $\log\left(\dfrac{I}{I_0}\right) = 6.7$

$\dfrac{I}{I_0} = 10^{6.7}$

$I = 10^{6.7} I_0$

$\dfrac{10^{6.7} I_0}{10^{6.2} I_0} = \dfrac{10^{6.7}}{10^{6.2}} = 10^{6.7-6.2} = 10^{0.5} \approx 3.2$

The 2006 quake on the northwest side was about 3.2 times as intense as the 1989 quake on the southeast side.

85. $M(I) = 6 - 2.5 \cdot \log\left(\dfrac{I}{I_0}\right)$

a. $M(27I_0) = 6 - 2.5 \cdot \log\left(\dfrac{27I_0}{I_0}\right)$

$= 6 - 2.5 \cdot \log(27)$

≈ 2.4

b. $M(85I_0) = 6 - 2.5 \cdot \log\left(\dfrac{85I_0}{I_0}\right)$

$= 6 - 2.5 \cdot \log(85)$

≈ 1.2

87. $D(I) = 10 \cdot \log\left(\dfrac{I}{I_0}\right)$

a. $D(10^{-14}) = 10 \cdot \log\left(\dfrac{10^{-14}}{10^{-16}}\right)$

$= 10 \cdot \log(10^2)$

$= 10 \cdot 2$

$= 20$ dB

b. $D(10^{-4}) = 10 \cdot \log\left(\dfrac{10^{-4}}{10^{-16}}\right)$

$= 10 \cdot \log(10^{12})$

$= 10 \cdot 12$

$= 120$ dB

89. $D(I) = 10 \cdot \log\left(\dfrac{I}{I_0}\right)$

Hair Dryer:

$10 \cdot \log\left(\dfrac{I}{I_0}\right) = 75$

$\log\left(\dfrac{I}{I_0}\right) = 7.5$

$\dfrac{I}{I_0} = 10^{7.5}$

$I = 10^{7.5} I_0$

Air Compressor:

$10 \cdot \log\left(\dfrac{I}{I_0}\right) = 110$

$\log\left(\dfrac{I}{I_0}\right) = 11.0$

$\dfrac{I}{I_0} = 10^{11.0}$

$I = 10^{11.0} I_0$

$\dfrac{10^{11.0} I_0}{10^{7.5} I_0} = \dfrac{10^{11.0}}{10^{7.5}} = 10^{11.0-7.5} = 10^{3.5} \approx 3162$

The sound of the air compressor is about 3162 times as intense as the hair dryer.

91. $H = (30T + 8000) \cdot \ln\left(\dfrac{P_0}{P}\right)$

$T = -10,\ P = 34,\ P_0 = 76$

$H = \left[30(-10) + 8000\right] \cdot \ln\left(\dfrac{76}{34}\right)$

$= (-300 + 8000) \cdot \ln\left(\dfrac{76}{34}\right)$

$= (7700) \cdot \ln\left(\dfrac{76}{34}\right)$

≈ 6194 m

The height of Mt. McKinley is approximately 6194 meters.

93. $H = (30T + 8000) \cdot \ln\left(\dfrac{P_0}{P}\right)$

  a. $T = 8$, $P = 39.3$, $P_0 = 76$

  $H = \left[30(8) + 8000\right] \cdot \ln\left(\dfrac{76}{39.3}\right)$

  $= (240 + 8000) \cdot \ln\left(\dfrac{76}{39.3}\right)$

  $= (8240) \cdot \ln\left(\dfrac{76}{39.3}\right)$

  ≈ 5434 m

  The Semo La pass is approximately 5434 meters high.

  b. $T = 12$, $P = 47.1$, $P_0 = 76$

  $H = \left[30(12) + 8000\right] \cdot \ln\left(\dfrac{76}{47.1}\right)$

  $= (360 + 8000) \cdot \ln\left(\dfrac{76}{47.1}\right)$

  $= (8360) \cdot \ln\left(\dfrac{76}{47.1}\right)$

  ≈ 4000 m

  The marker gave a height of 4000 meters.

95. $N(A) = 1500 + 315 \ln A$

  a. $N(10) = 1500 + 315 \ln(10) \approx 2225$ items

  b. $N(50) = 1500 + 315 \ln(50) \approx 2732$ items

  c. Using the TABLE feature, we estimate a budget of $117,000 is needed.

  d. $\dfrac{N(39.4) - N(39.3)}{39.4 - 39.3}$

  $= \dfrac{\left[1500 + 315\ln(39.4)\right] - \left[1500 + 315\ln(39.3)\right]}{0.1}$

  $= \dfrac{315\left[\ln(39.4) - \ln(39.3)\right]}{0.1} = \dfrac{315\ln\left(\dfrac{39.4}{39.3}\right)}{0.1}$

  $\approx \dfrac{0.8}{0.1} = \dfrac{8}{1}$ Verified.

97. $C(x) = 42\ln x - 270$

  a. $C(2500) = 42\ln 2500 - 270$
  ≈ 58.6 cfm

  b. $42\ln x - 270 = 40$
  $42\ln x = 310$
  $\ln x = \dfrac{310}{42}$
  $x = e^{310/42} \approx 1605$ ft^2

99. $P(x) = 95 - 14 \cdot \log_2 x$

  a.   1 day: $P(1) = 95 - 14 \cdot \log_2(1)$
  $= 95 - 14 \cdot 0$
  $= 95 - 0 = 95\%$

  b.   4 days: $P(4) = 95 - 14 \cdot \log_2(4)$
  $= 95 - 14 \cdot 2$
  $= 95 - 28 = 67\%$

  c.   16 days: $P(16) = 95 - 14 \cdot \log_2(16)$
  $= 95 - 14 \cdot 4$
  $= 95 - 56 = 39\%$

101. $f(x) = -\log_{10} x$

  $f(5.1 \times 10^{-5}) = -\log_{10}(5.1 \times 10^{-5})$
  ≈ -4.3

  Black coffee is considered an acid.

103.a.   Threshold of audibility
  0 dB

  b.   Lawn Mower
  90 dB

  c.   Whisper
  15 dB

  d.   Loud rock concert
  120 dB

  e.   Lively party
  100 dB

  f.   Jet engine
  140 dB

  Many sources give the threshold of pain as 120dB. Answers will vary.

105.a. $\log_{64} \dfrac{1}{16} = x$

  Convert to exponential form.

  $64^x = \dfrac{1}{16}$

  $\left(4^3\right)^x = 4^{-2}$

  $4^{3x} = 4^{-2}$

  $3x = -2$

  $x = -\dfrac{2}{3}$

105.b. $\log_{4/9}\left(\dfrac{27}{8}\right) = x$

Convert to exponential form.

$$\frac{4^x}{9} = \frac{27}{8}$$

$$\left(\frac{2}{3}\right)^{2x} = \left(\frac{2}{3}\right)^{-3}$$

$$2x = -3$$

$$x = -\frac{3}{2}$$

c. $\log_{0.25} 32 = x$

Convert to exponential form.

$$0.25^x = 32$$

$$\left(\frac{1}{4}\right)^x = 32$$

$$\left(2^{-2}\right)^x = 2^5$$

$$2^{-2x} = 2^5$$

$$-2x = 5$$

$$x = -\frac{5}{2}$$

Mid-Chapter Check

1.   a. $27^{\frac{2}{3}} = 9$

$$\frac{2}{3} = \log_{27} 9$$

    b. $81^{\frac{5}{4}} = 243$

$$\frac{5}{4} = \log_{81} 243$$

3.   a. $4^{2x} = 32^{x-1}$

$$\left(2^2\right)^{2x} = \left(2^5\right)^{x-1}$$

$$2^{4x} = 2^{5x-5}$$

$$4x = 5x - 5$$

$$5 = x$$

    b. $\left(\dfrac{1}{3}\right)^{4b} = 9^{2b-5}$

$$\left(3^{-1}\right)^{4b} = \left(3^2\right)^{2b-5}$$

$$3^{-4b} = 3^{4b-10}$$

$$-4b = 4b - 10$$

$$-8b = -10$$

$$b = \frac{5}{4}$$

5. $V(t) = V_0\left(\dfrac{9}{8}\right)^t$

    a. $V(3) = 50{,}000\left(\dfrac{9}{8}\right)^3 \approx \$71{,}191.41$

    b.   Using the TABLE feature, we estimate the value will double in 6 years.

7.   a. $T(x) = T_R + (T_0 - T_R)e^{kx}$

$T_R = 75^\circ,\ T_0 = 200^\circ,\ k = -0.28,\ x = 3$

$$T(3) = 75 + (200 - 75)e^{-0.28(3)}$$

$$= 75 + (125)e^{-0.84}$$

$$\approx 129^\circ$$

    b. $105 = 75 + (200 - 75)e^{-0.28x}$

Using the TABLE feature of a graphing calculator, we see that $T(5) \approx 105$, so the gnocci has cooled to 105° after 5 min.

9.   a. $\dfrac{2}{3} = \log_{27} 9$

$$27^{\frac{2}{3}} = 9$$

$$\left(3^3\right)^{\frac{2}{3}} = 9$$

$$3^2 = 9$$

    b. $1.4 \approx \ln 4.0552$

$e^{1.4} \approx 4.0552$;   Verified

Reinforcing Basic Concepts

Exercise 1:

$$14 - 11.8 = 2.2$$

$$10^{2.2} \approx 158$$

About 158 times

Exercise 3:

$$7.5 - 3.4 = 4.1$$

$$10^{4.1} \approx 12{,}589$$

About 12,589 times

Exercise 5:

$$9.1 - 4.5 = 4.6$$

$$10^{4.6} \approx 39{,}811$$

About 39,811 times

C Exercises

1. e

3. extraneous

5. $\ln(4x+3)+\ln 2 = 3.2$
    $\ln 2(4x+3) = 3.2$
    $\ln(8x+6) = 3.2$
    $8x+6 = e^{3.2}$
    $8x = e^{3.2}-6$
    $x = \dfrac{e^{3.2}-6}{8}$
    $x \approx 2.316566275$

7. $\ln x = 3.4$
    $e^{\ln x} = e^{3.4}$
    $x = e^{3.4}$
    $x \approx 29.964$

9. $\log x = \dfrac{1}{4}$
    $10^{\log x} = 10^{\frac{1}{4}}$
    $x = 10^{\frac{1}{4}}$
    $x \approx 1.778$

11. $e^x = 9.025$
    $\ln e^x = \ln 9.025$
    $x = \ln 9.025$
    $x \approx 2.200$

13. $10^x = 18.197$
    $\log 10^x = \log 18.197$
    $x = \log 18.197$
    $x \approx 1.260$

15. $4e^{x-2}+5 = 70$
    $4e^{x-2} = 65$
    $e^{x-2} = 16.25$
    $\ln e^{x-2} = \ln 16.25$
    $x-2 = \ln 16.25$
    $x = 2 + \ln 16.25$
    $x \approx 4.7881$

17. $10^{x+5} - 228 = -150$
    $10^{x+5} = 78$
    $\log 10^{x+5} = \log 78$
    $x+5 = \log 78$
    $x = -5 + \log 78$
    $x \approx -3.1079$

19. $-150 = 290.8 - 190e^{-0.75x}$
    $-440.8 = -190e^{-0.75x}$
    $\dfrac{-440.8}{-190} = e^{-0.75x}$
    $\dfrac{58}{25} = e^{-0.75x}$
    $\ln\left(\dfrac{58}{25}\right) = \ln e^{-0.75x}$
    $\ln\left(\dfrac{58}{25}\right) = -0.75x$
    $\dfrac{\ln\left(\dfrac{58}{25}\right)}{-0.75} = x$
    $-1.1221 \approx x$

21. $3\ln(x+4)-5 = 3$
    $3\ln(x+4) = 8$
    $\ln(x+4) = \dfrac{8}{3}$
    $x+4 = e^{\frac{8}{3}}$
    $x = e^{\frac{8}{3}}-4$
    $x \approx 10.3919$

23. $-1.5 = 2\log(5-x)-4$
    $2.5 = 2\log(5-x)$
    $1.25 = \log(5-x)$
    $10^{1.25} = 10^{\log(5-x)}$
    $10^{1.25} = 5-x$
    $x = 5-10^{1.25}$
    $x \approx -12.7828$

25. $\dfrac{1}{2}\ln(2x+5)+3 = 3.2$
    $\dfrac{1}{2}\ln(2x+5) = 0.2$
    $\ln(2x+5) = 0.4$
    $e^{\ln(2x+5)} = e^{0.4}$
    $2x+5 = e^{0.4}$
    $2x = e^{0.4}-5$
    $x = \dfrac{e^{0.4}-5}{2}$
    $x \approx -1.7541$

27. $\ln(2x)+\ln(x-7) = \ln(2x(x-7))$
    $= \ln(2x^2-14x)$

29. $\log(x+1) + \log(x-1) = \log((x+1)(x-1))$
$$= \log(x^2 - 1)$$

31. $\log_3 28 - \log_3 7 = \log_3\left(\dfrac{28}{7}\right)$
$$= \log_3(4)$$

33. $\log x - \log(x+1) = \log\left(\dfrac{x}{x+1}\right)$

35. $\ln(x-5) - \ln x = \ln\left(\dfrac{x-5}{x}\right)$

37. $\ln(x^2 - 4) - \ln(x+2) = \ln\left(\dfrac{x^2 - 4}{x+2}\right)$
$$= \ln\left[\dfrac{(x+2)(x-2)}{x+2}\right]$$
$$= \ln(x-2)$$

39. $\log_2 7 + \log_2 6 = \log_2(7 \cdot 6)$
$$= \log_2 42$$

41. $\log_5(x^2 - 2x) + \log_5 x^{-1} = \log_5\left[x^{-1}(x^2 - 2x)\right]$
$$= \log_5(x-2)$$

43. $\log 8^{x+2} = (x+2)\log 8$

45. $\ln 5^{2x-1} = (2x-1)\ln 5$

47. $\log\sqrt{22} = \log 22^{\frac{1}{2}} = \dfrac{1}{2}\log 22$

49. $\log_5 81 = \log_5 3^4 = 4\log_5 3$

51. $\log(a^3 b) = \log a^3 + \log b$
$$= 3\log a + \log b$$

53. $\ln\left(x\sqrt[4]{y}\right) = \ln x + \ln y^{\frac{1}{4}}$
$$= \ln x + \dfrac{1}{4}\ln y$$

55. $\ln\left(\dfrac{x^2}{y}\right) = \ln x^2 - \ln y$
$$= 2\ln x - \ln y$$

57. $\log\left(\sqrt{\dfrac{x-2}{x}}\right) = \log\left(\dfrac{x-2}{x}\right)^{\frac{1}{2}}$
$$= \dfrac{1}{2}\log\left(\dfrac{x-2}{x}\right)$$
$$= \dfrac{1}{2}\left[\log(x-2) - \log x\right]$$

59. $\ln\left(\dfrac{7x\sqrt{3-4x}}{2(x-1)^3}\right)$
$$= \ln\left(7x\sqrt{3-4x}\right) - \ln\left(2(x-1)^3\right)$$
$$= \ln 7x + \ln\sqrt{3-4x} - \left(\ln 2 + \ln(x-1)^3\right)$$
$$= \ln 7x + \ln(3-4x)^{\frac{1}{2}} - \ln 2 - \ln(x-1)^3$$
$$= \ln 7 + \ln x + \dfrac{1}{2}\ln(3-4x) - \ln 2 - 3\ln(x-1)$$

61. $\log_7 60 = \dfrac{\log 60}{\log 7} = \dfrac{\ln 60}{\ln 7} \approx 2.104076884$

63. $\log_5 152 = \dfrac{\log 152}{\log 5} = \dfrac{\ln 152}{\ln 5} \approx 3.121512475$

65 $\log_3 1.73205 = \dfrac{\log 1.73205}{\log 3} = \dfrac{\ln 1.73205}{\ln 3}$
$$\approx 0.499999576$$

67. $\log_{0.5} 0.125 = \dfrac{\log 0.125}{\log 0.5} = \dfrac{\ln 0.125}{\ln 0.5} = 3$

69. $f(x) = \log_3 x = \dfrac{\log x}{\log 3}$
$$f(5) = \dfrac{\log 5}{\log 3} \approx 1.4650$$
$$f(15) = \dfrac{\log 15}{\log 3} \approx 2.4650$$
$$f(45) = \dfrac{\log 45}{\log 3} \approx 3.4650$$

outputs increase by 1; $f(3^3 \cdot 5) \approx 4.4650$

71. $h(x) = \log_9 x = \dfrac{\log x}{\log 9}$

$h(2) = \dfrac{\log 2}{\log 9} \approx 0.3155$

$h(4) = \dfrac{\log 4}{\log 9} \approx 0.6309$

$h(8) = \dfrac{\log 8}{\log 9} \approx 0.9464$

outputs are multiples of 0.3155;
$h(2^4) = 4(0.3155) \approx 1.2619$

73. $\log 4 + \log(x-7) = 2$

$\log[4(x-7)] = 2$

$\log(4x - 28) = 2$

$4x - 28 = 10^2$

$4x - 28 = 100$

$4x = 128$

$x = 7$

Check:

$\log 4 + \log(32 - 7) = 2$

$\log 4 + \log 25 = 2$

$\log(4 \cdot 25) = 2$

$\log 100 = 2$

$\log 10^2 = 2$

$2 = 2$

75. $\log(2x - 5) - \log 78 = -1$

$\log\left(\dfrac{2x-5}{78}\right) = -1$

$\dfrac{2x-5}{78} = 10^{-1}$

$\dfrac{2x-5}{78} = \dfrac{1}{10}$

$2x - 5 = 7.8$

$2x = 12.8$

$x = 6.4$

Check:

$\log[2(6.4) - 5] - \log 78 = -1$

$\log(12.8 - 5) - \log 78 = -1$

$\log 7.8 - \log 78 = -1$

$\log\left(\dfrac{7.8}{78}\right) = -1$

$\log(0.1) = -1$

$\log 10^{-1} = -1$

$-1 = -1$

77. $\log(x - 15) - 2 = -\log x$

$\log(x - 15) + \log x = 2$

$\log[x(x - 15)] = 2$

$\log(x^2 - 15x) = 2$

$x^2 - 15x = 10^2$

$x^2 - 15x = 100$

$x^2 - 15x - 100 = 0$

$(x + 5)(x - 20) = 0$

$x + 5 = 0$ or $x - 20 = 0$

$x = -5$ $x = 20$

Check $x = -5$:

$\log(-5 - 15) - 2 = -\log(-5)$

The solution $x = -5$ is outside the domain and is discarded.

Check $x = 20$:

$\log(20 - 15) - 2 = -\log 20$

$\log 5 - 2 = -\log 20$

$-1.3010 = -1.3010$

The solution is $x = 20$.

79. $\log(2x + 1) = 1 - \log x$

$\log(2x + 1) + \log x = 1$

$\log[x(2x + 1)] = 1$

$\log(2x^2 + x) = 1$

$2x^2 + x = 10^1$

$2x^2 + x = 10$

$2x^2 + x - 10 = 0$

$(2x + 5)(x - 2) = 0$

$2x + 5 = 0$ or $x - 2 = 0$

$2x = -5$ $x = 2$

$x = -\dfrac{5}{2}$

Check $x = -\dfrac{5}{2}$:

$\log\left[2\left(-\dfrac{5}{2}\right) + 1\right] = 1 - \log\left(-\dfrac{5}{2}\right)$

The solution $x = -\dfrac{5}{2}$ is outside the domain and is discarded.

Check $x = 2$:

$\log[2(2) + 1] = 1 - \log 2$

$\log 5 = 1 - \log 2$

$0.6990 = 0.6990$

The solution is $x = 2$.

81. $\log(5x+2) = \log 2$

$$5x+2 = 2$$
$$5x = 0$$
$$x = 0$$

83. $\log_4(x+2) - \log_4 3 = \log_4(x-1)$

$$\log_4\left(\frac{x+2}{3}\right) = \log_4(x-1)$$
$$\frac{x+2}{3} = x-1$$
$$x+2 = 3x-3$$
$$5 = 2x$$
$$\frac{5}{2} = x$$

85. $\ln(8x-4) = \ln 2 + \ln x$

$$\ln(8x-4) = \ln(2x)$$
$$8x-4 = 2x$$
$$6x = 4$$
$$x = \frac{2}{3}$$

87. $\log(2x-1) + \log 5 = 1$

$$\log(10x-5) = 1$$
$$10x-5 = 10^1$$
$$10x = 15$$
$$x = \frac{3}{2}$$

89. $\log_2 9 + \log_2(x+3) = 3$

$$\log_2(9x+27) = 3$$
$$9x+27 = 2^3$$
$$9x+27 = 8$$
$$9x = -19$$
$$x = -\frac{19}{9}$$

91. $\ln(x+7) + \ln 9 = 2$

$$\ln(9x+63) = 2$$
$$9x+63 = e^2$$
$$9x = e^2 - 63$$
$$x = \frac{e^2 - 63}{9}$$

93. $\log(x+8) + \log x = \log(x+18)$

$$\log(x^2+8x) = \log(x+18)$$
$$x^2+8x = x+18$$
$$x^2+7x-18 = 0$$
$$(x+9)(x-2) = 0$$
$$x+9 = 0 \quad \text{or} \quad x-2 = 0$$
$$x = -9 \qquad\qquad x = 2$$

-9 is extraneous.
The solution is $x = 2$.

95. $\quad\ln(2x+1) = 3 + \ln 6$

$$\ln(2x+1) - \ln 6 = 3$$
$$\ln\left(\frac{2x+1}{6}\right) = 3$$
$$\frac{2x+1}{6} = e^3$$
$$2x+1 = 6e^3$$
$$2x = 6e^3 - 1$$
$$x = 3e^3 - \frac{1}{2} \approx 59.75661077$$

97. $\log(-x-1) = \log(5x) - \log x$

$$\log(-x-1) = \log 5$$
$$-x-1 = 5$$
$$-x = 6$$
$$x = -6$$

-6 is extraneous.
There is no solution.

99. $\quad\ln(2t+7) = \ln(3) - \ln(t+1)$

$$\ln(2t+7) = \ln\left(\frac{3}{t+1}\right)$$
$$2t+7 = \frac{3}{t+1}$$
$$(2t+7)(t+1) = 3$$
$$2t^2+9t+7 = 3$$
$$2t^2+9t+4 = 0$$
$$(t+4)(2t+1) = 0$$
$$t+4 = 0 \quad \text{or} \quad 2t+1 = 0$$
$$t = -4 \qquad\qquad 2t = -1$$
$$t = -\frac{1}{2}$$

-4 is extraneous.

The solution is $t = -\frac{1}{2}$.

101. $\log(x-1) - \log x = \log(x-3)$

$$\log\left(\frac{x-1}{x}\right) = \log(x-3)$$

$$\frac{x-1}{x} = x-3$$

$$x-1 = x^2 - 3x$$

$$0 = x^2 - 4x + 1$$

$a = 1,\ b = -4,\ c = 1$

$$x = \frac{-(-4) \pm \sqrt{(-4)^2 - 4(1)(1)}}{2(1)}$$

$$x = \frac{4 \pm \sqrt{16-4}}{2}$$

$$x = \frac{4 \pm \sqrt{12}}{2}$$

$$x = \frac{4 \pm 2\sqrt{3}}{2}$$

$$x = 2 \pm \sqrt{3}$$

$x = 2 - \sqrt{3}$ is extraneous.

The solution is $x = 2 + \sqrt{3}$.

103.

$$7^{x+2} = 231$$

$$\ln 7^{x+2} = \ln 231$$

$$(x+2)\ln 7 = \ln 231$$

$$x+2 = \frac{\ln 231}{\ln 7}$$

$$x = \frac{\ln 231}{\ln 7} - 2$$

$$x \approx 0.7968$$

105.

$$5^{3x-2} = 128,965$$

$$\ln 5^{3x-2} = \ln 128,965$$

$$(3x-2)\ln 5 = \ln 128,965$$

$$3x - 2 = \frac{\ln 128,695}{\ln 5}$$

$$3x = \frac{\ln 128,695}{\ln 5} + 2$$

$$x = \frac{\ln 128,965}{3\ln 5} + \frac{2}{3}$$

$$x \approx 3.1038$$

107.

$$2^{x+1} = 3^x$$

$$\ln 2^{x+1} = \ln 3^x$$

$$(x+1)\ln 2 = x\ln 3$$

$$x\ln 2 + \ln 2 = x\ln 3$$

$$x\ln 2 - x\ln 3 = -\ln 2$$

$$x(\ln 2 - \ln 3) = -\ln 2$$

$$x = \frac{-\ln 2}{\ln 2 - \ln 3}$$

$$x = \frac{\ln 2}{\ln 3 - \ln 2}$$

$$x \approx 1.7095$$

109.

$$5^{2x+1} = 9^{x+1}$$

$$\ln 5^{2x+1} = \ln 9^{x+1}$$

$$(2x+1)\ln 5 = (x+1)\ln 9$$

$$2x\ln 5 + \ln 5 = x\ln 9 + \ln 9$$

$$2x\ln 5 - x\ln 9 = \ln 9 - \ln 5$$

$$x(2\ln 5 - \ln 9) = \ln 9 - \ln 5$$

$$x = \frac{\ln 9 - \ln 5}{2\ln 5 - \ln 9}$$

$$x \approx 0.5753$$

111. $\dfrac{250}{1+4e^{-0.06x}} = 200$

$$\frac{250}{200} = 1 + 4e^{-0.06x}$$

$$\frac{5}{4} - 1 = 4e^{-0.06x}$$

$$\frac{1}{4} = 4e^{-0.06x}$$

$$\frac{1}{16} = e^{-0.06x}$$

$$\ln\left(\frac{1}{16}\right) = \ln e^{-0.06x}$$

$$-\ln 16 = -0.06x$$

$$\frac{\ln 16}{0.06} = x$$

$$46.2 \approx x$$

113. $P = \dfrac{C}{1+ae^{-kt}}$

$1+ae^{-kt} = \dfrac{C}{P}$

$ae^{-kt} = \dfrac{C}{P}-1$

$e^{-kt} = \dfrac{\frac{C}{P}-1}{a}$

$\ln e^{-kt} = \ln\left(\dfrac{\frac{C}{P}-1}{a}\right)$

$-kt = \ln\left(\dfrac{\frac{C}{P}-1}{a}\right)$

$\ln\left(\dfrac{\frac{C}{P}-1}{a}\right)$

$t = \dfrac{\ln\left(\dfrac{\frac{C}{P}-1}{a}\right)}{-k}$

$C = 450,\ a = 8,\ P = 400,\ k = 0.075$

$t = \dfrac{\ln\left(\dfrac{\frac{450}{400}-1}{8}\right)}{-0.075} = \dfrac{\ln\left(\frac{1}{64}\right)}{-0.075} = \dfrac{\ln 64}{0.075} \approx 55.45$

115. $P(t) = \dfrac{750}{1+24e^{-0.075t}}$

a. $P(0) = \dfrac{750}{1+24e^{-0.075(0)}}$

$= \dfrac{750}{1+24}$

$= \dfrac{750}{25}$

$= 30$

The farmer initially put 30 fish in the lake.

115.b. $300 = \dfrac{750}{1+24e^{-0.075t}}$

$1+24e^{-0.075t} = \dfrac{750}{300}$

$24e^{-0.075t} = \dfrac{5}{2}-1$

$24e^{-0.075t} = \dfrac{3}{2}$

$e^{-0.075t} = \dfrac{1}{16}$

$\ln e^{-0.075t} = \ln\left(\dfrac{1}{16}\right)$

$-0.075t = -\ln 16$

$t = \dfrac{\ln 16}{0.075}$

$t \approx 37$

It will be about 37 months.

117. $H = (30T + 8000)\ln\left(\dfrac{P_0}{P}\right);\ P_0 = 76$ cmHg

a. $H = 18,250$ m; $T = -75°C$

$18,250 = \left[30(-75)+8000\right]\ln\left(\dfrac{76}{P}\right)$

$18,250 = (-2250+8000)\ln\left(\dfrac{76}{P}\right)$

$18,250 = 5750\ln\left(\dfrac{76}{P}\right)$

$\dfrac{18,250}{5750} = \ln\left(\dfrac{76}{P}\right)$

$e^{\frac{73}{23}} = \dfrac{76}{P}$

$P = \dfrac{76}{e^{\frac{73}{23}}}$

$P \approx 3.2$ cmHg

119. $T = T_R + (T_0 - T_R)e^{kh}$

$32 = -20 + \left[75-(-20)\right]e^{-0.012h}$

$32 = -20 + 95e^{-0.012h}$

$52 = 95e^{-0.012h}$

$\dfrac{52}{95} = e^{-0.012h}$

$\ln\left(\dfrac{52}{95}\right) = \ln e^{-0.012h}$

$\ln\left(\dfrac{52}{95}\right) = -0.012h$

$\dfrac{\ln\left(\dfrac{52}{95}\right)}{-0.012} = h$

$50.2 \approx h$

They will have to wait about 50.2 minutes.

121. $T = k \ln\left(\dfrac{V_n}{V_f}\right)$

$3 = 5\ln\left(\dfrac{28,500}{V_f}\right)$

$\dfrac{3}{5} = \ln\left(\dfrac{28,500}{V_f}\right)$

$e^{0.6} = \dfrac{28,500}{V_f}$

$V_f = \dfrac{28,500}{e^{0.6}}$

$V_f = \$15,641$

123. $T(p) = \dfrac{-\ln p}{k}$

a. $k = 0.072; \ p = 1 - 0.35 = 0.65$

$T(0.65) = \dfrac{-\ln 0.65}{0.072} \approx 6 \text{ hr}$

b. $\dfrac{-\ln p}{0.072} = 24$

$-\ln p = 24(0.072)$

$-\ln p = 1.728$

$\ln p = -1.728$

$p = e^{-1.728}$

$p \approx 0.178 = 17.8\%$

125. $V_s = V_e \ln\left(\dfrac{M_s}{M_s - M_f}\right)$

$V_s = 6 \text{ km/sec}, \ V_e = 8 \text{ km/sec}, \ M_s = 100 \text{ tons}$

$6 = 8\ln\left(\dfrac{100}{100 - M_f}\right)$

$\dfrac{6}{8} = \ln\left(\dfrac{100}{100 - M_f}\right)$

$e^{0.75} = \dfrac{100}{100 - M_f}$

$100 - M_f = \dfrac{100}{e^{0.75}}$

$-M_f = \dfrac{100}{e^{0.75}} - 100$

$M_f = 100 - \dfrac{100}{e^{0.75}}$

$M_f \approx 52.76 \text{ tons}$

133. (continued)

If $u = 2$, then $e^x = 2$.

127. $P(t) = 5.9 + 12.6\ln t$

a. $P(5) = 5.9 + 12.6\ln 5$

$\approx 26 \text{ planes}$

b. $5.9 + 12.6\ln t = 34$

$12.6\ln t = 28.1$

$\ln t = \dfrac{28.1}{12.6}$

$t = e^{\frac{28.1}{12.6}}$

$t \approx 9 \text{ days}$

129. a. $\log_3 20 = \log_3 (4 \cdot 5)$

$= \log_3 4 + \log_3 5$

$= 1.2619 + 1.4649$

$= 2.7268$

b. $\log_3 \dfrac{4}{5} = \log_3 4 - \log_3 5$

$= 1.2619 - 1.4649$

$= -0.203$

c. $\log_3 25 = \log_3 5^2$

$= 2\log_3 5$

$= 2(1.4649)$

$= 2.9298$

131. a.   d

b.   e

c.   b

d.   f

e.   a

f.   c

133. $3e^{2x} - 4e^x - 7 = -3$

Let $u = e^x$.

$3u^2 - 4u - 7 = -3$

$3u^2 - 4u - 4 = 0$

$(3u + 2)(u - 2) = 0$

$3u + 2 = 0 \quad \text{or} \quad u - 2 = 0$

$3u = -2 \qquad\qquad u = 2$

$u = -\dfrac{2}{3}$

If $u = -\dfrac{2}{3}$, then $e^x = -\dfrac{2}{3}$.

This is not possible.

$e^x = 2$

$\ln e^x = \ln 2$

$x = \ln 2$

$x \approx 0.69314718$

135.a. $f(x) = y = 2^{x+1}$
Interchange x and y.
$x = 2^{y+1}$
Solve for y.
$$x = 2^{y+1}$$
$$\ln x = \ln 2^{y+1}$$
$$\ln x = (y+1)\ln 2$$
$$\frac{\ln x}{\ln 2} = y+1$$
$$\frac{\ln x}{\ln 2} - 1 = y$$
$$f^{-1}(x) = \frac{\ln x}{\ln 2} - 1$$

b. $f(x) = y = 2\ln(x-3)$
Interchange x and y.
$$x = 2\ln(y-3)$$
$$\frac{x}{2} = \ln(y-3)$$
$$e^{\frac{x}{2}} = e^{\ln(y-3)}$$
$$e^{\frac{x}{2}} = y-3$$
$$e^{\frac{x}{2}} + 3 = y$$
$$f^{-1}(x) = e^{\frac{x}{2}} + 3$$

137.a. $y = 2^x$
$\ln y = x\ln 2$
$e^{\ln y} = e^{x\ln 2}$
$y = e^{x\ln 2}$

b. $y = b^x$
$\ln y = \ln b^x$
$\ln y = x\ln b$
$e^{\ln y} = e^{x\ln b}$
$y = e^{xr}$ where $r = \ln b$

139. Answers will vary.

D Exercises

1.   compound

3. $Q_0 e^{-rt}$

5.   Answers will vary.

7. $I = prt$
$I = \$229.50$; $r = 6.25\% = 0.0625$;
$t = \dfrac{9}{12} = 0.75$
$229.50 = p(0.0625)(0.75)$
$229.50 = 0.046875p$
$\dfrac{229.50}{0.046875} = p$
$\$4896 = p$

9. $I = prt$
$I = \$297.50 - \$260 = \$37.50$;
$p = \$260$; $t = \dfrac{3}{52}$
$37.50 = 260r\left(\dfrac{3}{52}\right)$
$37.50 = 15r$
$\dfrac{37.50}{15} = r$
$2.5 = r$
$r = 250\%$

11. $A = p(1+rt)$
$A = \$2500$; $r = 6.25\% = 0.0625$; $t = \dfrac{31}{12}$
$2500 = p\left[1 + 0.0625\left(\dfrac{31}{12}\right)\right]$
$2500 = \dfrac{223}{192}p$
$2500 \cdot \dfrac{192}{223} = p$
$\$2152.47 \approx p$

13. $A = p(1+rt)$

$A = \$149,925;\ p = \$120,000;$

$r = 4.75\% = 0.0475$

$149,925 = 120,000(1+0.0475t)$

$\dfrac{149,925}{120,000} = 1+0.0475t$

$1.249375 = 1+0.0475t$

$0.249375 = 0.0475t$

$\dfrac{0.249375}{0.0475} = t$

$5.25 \text{ yr} = t$

15. $I = prt$

$I = \$240 - \$200 = \$40;\ p = \$200;$

$t = \dfrac{13}{52} = 0.25$

$40 = 200r(0.25)$

$0.2 = 0.25r$

$\dfrac{0.2}{0.25} = r$

$0.8 = r$

$r = 80\%$

17. $A = p(1+r)^t$

$A = \$48,428;\ p = \$38,000;$

$r = 6.25\% = 0.0625$

$48,428 = 38,000(1+0.0625)^t$

$\dfrac{48,428}{38,000} = (1.0625)^t$

$\ln\left(\dfrac{48,428}{38,000}\right) = \ln(1.0625)^t$

$\ln\left(\dfrac{48,428}{38,000}\right) = t\ln(1.0625)$

$\dfrac{\ln\left(\dfrac{48,428}{38,000}\right)}{\ln(1.0625)} = t$

$4 \text{ yr} \approx t$

19. $A = p(1+r)^t$

$A = 3\cdot\$1525 = \$4575;\ p = \$1525;$

$r = 7.1\% = 0.071$

$4575 = 1525(1+0.071)^t$

$\dfrac{4575}{1525} = (1.071)^t$

$\ln(3) = \ln(1.071)^t$

$\ln(3) = t\ln(1.071)$

$\dfrac{\ln(3)}{\ln(1.071)} = t$

$16 \text{ yr} \approx t$

21. $P = \dfrac{A}{(1+r)^t}$

$A = \$10,000;\ r = 5.75\% = 0.0575;\ t = 5$

$P = \dfrac{10,000}{(1+0.0575)^5}$

$= \dfrac{10,000}{(1.0575)^5}$

$\approx \$7561.33$

23. $A = p\left(1+\dfrac{r}{n}\right)^{nt}$

$A = \$129,500;\ p = \$90,000;$

$r = 7.125\% = 0.07125;\ n = 52$

$129,500 = 90,000\left(1+\dfrac{0.07125}{52}\right)^{52t}$

$\dfrac{129,500}{90,000} = \left(1+\dfrac{0.07125}{52}\right)^{52t}$

$\ln\left(\dfrac{259}{180}\right) = \ln\left(1+\dfrac{0.07125}{52}\right)^{52t}$

$\ln\left(\dfrac{259}{180}\right) = 52t\ln\left(1+\dfrac{0.07125}{52}\right)$

$\dfrac{\ln\left(\dfrac{259}{180}\right)}{52\ln\left(1+\dfrac{0.07125}{52}\right)} = t$

$5 \text{ yr} \approx t$

25. $A = p\left(1+\dfrac{r}{n}\right)^{nt}$

$A = \$10,000;\ p = \$5000;$

$r = 9.25\% = 0.0925;\ n = 365$

$10,000 = 5000\left(1+\dfrac{0.0925}{365}\right)^{365t}$

$\dfrac{10,000}{5000} = \left(1+\dfrac{0.0925}{365}\right)^{365t}$

$\ln(2) = \ln\left(1+\dfrac{0.0925}{365}\right)^{365t}$

$\ln(2) = 365t\ln\left(1+\dfrac{0.0925}{365}\right)$

$\dfrac{\ln(2)}{365\ln\left(1+\dfrac{0.0925}{365}\right)} = t$

$7.5 \text{ yr} \approx t$

27. $A = p\left(1+\dfrac{r}{n}\right)^{nt}$

$p = \$10;\ r = 10\% = 0.10;\ n = 10;\ t = 10$

$A = 10\left(1+\dfrac{0.10}{10}\right)^{10(10)}$

$A = 10(1+0.01)^{100}$

$A = 10(1.01)^{100}$

$A \approx \$27.05$

No, the investment will not triple in value.

29. $A = p\left(1+\dfrac{r}{n}\right)^{nt}$

a. $p = \$175{,}000;\ r = 8.75\% = 0.0875;$
     $n = 2;\ t = 4$

$A = 175{,}000\left(1+\dfrac{0.875}{2}\right)^{2(4)}$

$A = 175{,}000(1+0.04375)^{8}$

$A = 175{,}000(1.04375)^{8}$

$A \approx \$246{,}496.05$

No, there will not be sufficient funds.

b. $A = \$250{,}000;\ p = \$175{,}000;\ n = 2;\ t = 4$

$250{,}000 = 175{,}000\left(1+\dfrac{r}{2}\right)^{2(4)}$

$\dfrac{250{,}000}{175{,}000} = \left(1+\dfrac{r}{2}\right)^{8}$

$\sqrt[8]{\dfrac{10}{7}} = \sqrt[8]{\left(1+\dfrac{r}{2}\right)^{8}}$

$\sqrt[8]{\dfrac{10}{7}} = 1+\dfrac{r}{2}$

$\sqrt[8]{\dfrac{10}{7}} - 1 = \dfrac{r}{2}$

$2\left(\sqrt[8]{\dfrac{10}{7}} - 1\right) = r$

$0.0912 \approx r$

A minimum interest rate of 9.12% will allow the dairy to meet its goal.

31. $A = pe^{rt}$

$A = \$2500;\ p = \$1750;\ r = 4.5\% = 0.045$

$2500 = 1750e^{0.045t}$

$\dfrac{2500}{1750} = e^{0.045t}$

$\dfrac{10}{7} = e^{0.045t}$

$\ln\left(\dfrac{10}{7}\right) = \ln e^{0.045t}$

$\ln\left(\dfrac{10}{7}\right) = 0.045t$

$\dfrac{\ln\left(\dfrac{10}{7}\right)}{0.045} = t$

$7.9\ \text{yr} \approx t$

33. $A = pe^{rt}$

$A = \$10{,}000;\ p = \$5000;\ r = 9.25\% = 0.0925$

$10{,}000 = 5000e^{0.0925t}$

$\dfrac{10{,}000}{5000} = e^{0.0925t}$

$2 = e^{0.0925t}$

$\ln(2) = \ln e^{0.0925t}$

$\ln(2) = 0.0925t$

$\dfrac{\ln(2)}{0.0925} = t$

$7.5\ \text{yr} \approx t$

35. $A = pe^{rt}$

a. $p = 12{,}500\ \text{euros};\ r = 8.6\% = 0.086;\ t = 5$

$A = 12{,}500e^{0.086(5)}$

$A = 12{,}500e^{0.43}$

$A \approx 19{,}215.72\ \text{euros}$

No, he will not meet his investment goal.

b. $A = 20{,}000\ \text{euros};\ p = 12{,}500\ \text{euros};\ t = 5$

$20{,}000 = 12{,}500e^{r(5)}$

$\dfrac{20{,}000}{12{,}500} = e^{5r}$

$1.6 = e^{5r}$

$\ln 1.6 = \ln e^{5r}$

$\ln 1.6 = 5r$

$\dfrac{\ln 1.6}{5} = r$

$0.094 \approx r$

$r \approx 9.4\%$

A minimum interest rate of 9.4% will enable him to meet this goal.

37. $A = pe^{rt}$

   a. $p = 12{,}000$ euros; $r = 5.5\% = 0.055$; $t = 7$

   $A = 12{,}000e^{0.055(7)}$

   $A = 12{,}000e^{0.385}$

   $A \approx 17{,}635.37$ euros

   No, they will not have enough to make repairs.

   b. $A = 20{,}000$ euros; $r = 5.5\% = 0.055$; $t = 5$

   $20{,}000 = pe^{0.055(7)}$

   $20{,}000 = pe^{0.385}$

   $\dfrac{20{,}000}{e^{0.385}} = p$

   $13{,}609 \text{ euros} \approx p$

   They need to deposit a minimum of 13,609 euros.

39. $T = \dfrac{1}{r} \cdot \ln\left(\dfrac{A}{P}\right)$

   $T = 8$; $r = 5\% = 0.05$; $P = \$200{,}000$

   $8 = \dfrac{1}{0.05} \cdot \ln\left(\dfrac{A}{200{,}000}\right)$

   $0.4 = \ln\left(\dfrac{A}{200{,}000}\right)$

   By definition, $y = \ln x$ if and only if $x = e^{y}$.

   $\dfrac{A}{200{,}000} = e^{0.4}$

   $A = 200{,}000e^{0.4}$

   $\approx \$298{,}364.94$

   No, they will not have enough for the new facility.

   $T = 8$; $r = 5\% = 0.05$; $A = \$350{,}000$

   $8 = \dfrac{1}{0.05} \cdot \ln\left(\dfrac{350{,}000}{P}\right)$

   $0.4 = \ln\left(\dfrac{350{,}000}{P}\right)$

   By definition, $y = \ln x$ if and only if $x = e^{y}$.

   $e^{0.4} = \dfrac{350{,}000}{P}$

   $P = \dfrac{350{,}000}{e^{0.4}}$

   $P \approx \$234{,}612.02$

   $\$234{,}612.02$ should be invested.

41. $A = \dfrac{P\left[(1+R)^{nt} - 1\right]}{R}$

   $A = \$10{,}000$; $P = \$90$; $R = \dfrac{r}{n} = \dfrac{0.0775}{12}$

   $10{,}000 = \dfrac{90\left[\left(1 + \dfrac{0.0775}{12}\right)^{12t} - 1\right]}{\dfrac{0.0775}{12}}$

   $\dfrac{775}{12} = 90\left[\left(1 + \dfrac{0.0775}{12}\right)^{12t} - 1\right]$

   $\dfrac{155}{216} = \left(1 + \dfrac{0.0775}{12}\right)^{12t} - 1$

   $\dfrac{371}{216} = \left(1 + \dfrac{0.0775}{12}\right)^{12t}$

   $\ln\left(\dfrac{371}{216}\right) = \ln\left(1 + \dfrac{0.0775}{12}\right)^{12t}$

   $\ln\left(\dfrac{371}{216}\right) = 12t\ln\left(1 + \dfrac{0.0775}{12}\right)$

   $\dfrac{\ln\left(\dfrac{371}{216}\right)}{12\ln\left(1 + \dfrac{0.0775}{12}\right)} = t$

   $7 \text{ yr} \approx t$

43. $A = \dfrac{P\left[(1+R)^{nt} - 1\right]}{R}$

   $A = \$30{,}000$; $P = \$50$; $R = \dfrac{r}{n} = \dfrac{0.062}{12}$

   $30{,}000 = \dfrac{50\left[\left(1 + \dfrac{0.062}{12}\right)^{12t} - 1\right]}{\dfrac{0.062}{12}}$

   $155 = 50\left[\left(1 + \dfrac{0.062}{12}\right)^{12t} - 1\right]$

   $3.1 = \left(1 + \dfrac{0.062}{12}\right)^{12t} - 1$

   $4.1 = \left(1 + \dfrac{0.062}{12}\right)^{12t}$

   $\ln 4.1 = \ln\left(1 + \dfrac{0.062}{12}\right)^{12t}$

   $\ln 4.1 = 12t\ln\left(1 + \dfrac{0.062}{12}\right)$

   $\dfrac{\ln(4.1)}{12\ln\left(1 + \dfrac{0.062}{12}\right)} = t$

   $23 \text{ yr} \approx t$

45. $A = \dfrac{P\left[(1+R)^{nt}-1\right]}{R}$

    a. $P = \$250;\ R = \dfrac{r}{n} = \dfrac{0.085}{12};\ t = 5$

$$A = \dfrac{250\left[\left(1+\dfrac{0.085}{12}\right)^{12(5)}-1\right]}{\dfrac{0.085}{12}}$$

       $A \approx \$18,610.61$

       No, this monthly amount is not sufficient.

    b. $A = \$22,500;\ R = \dfrac{r}{n} = \dfrac{0.085}{12};\ t = 5$

$$22,500 = \dfrac{P\left[\left(1+\dfrac{0.085}{12}\right)^{12(5)}-1\right]}{\dfrac{0.085}{12}}$$

$$159.375 = P\left[\left(1+\dfrac{0.085}{12}\right)^{60}-1\right]$$

$$\dfrac{159.375}{\left[\left(1+\dfrac{0.085}{12}\right)^{60}-1\right]} = P$$

       $\$302.25 \approx P$

47. $A = p + prt$

    a. $A = p + prt$

       $A - p = prt$

       $\dfrac{A-p}{pr} = t$

    b. $A = p + prt$

       $A = p(1+rt)$

       $\dfrac{A}{1+rt} = p$

49. $A = P\left(1+\dfrac{r}{n}\right)^{nt}$

    a. $A = P\left(1+\dfrac{r}{n}\right)^{nt}$

       $\dfrac{A}{P} = \left(1+\dfrac{r}{n}\right)^{nt}$

       $\sqrt[nt]{\dfrac{A}{P}} = \sqrt[nt]{\left(1+\dfrac{r}{n}\right)^{nt}}$

       $\sqrt[nt]{\dfrac{A}{P}} = 1+\dfrac{r}{n}$

       $\sqrt[nt]{\dfrac{A}{P}} - 1 = \dfrac{r}{n}$

       $n\left(\sqrt[nt]{\dfrac{A}{P}} - 1\right) = r$

49. b. $A = P\left(1+\dfrac{r}{n}\right)^{nt}$

       $\dfrac{A}{P} = \left(1+\dfrac{r}{n}\right)^{nt}$

       $\ln\left(\dfrac{A}{P}\right) = \ln\left(1+\dfrac{r}{n}\right)^{nt}$

       $\ln\left(\dfrac{A}{P}\right) = nt \ln\left(1+\dfrac{r}{n}\right)$

       $\dfrac{\ln\left(\dfrac{A}{P}\right)}{n \ln\left(1+\dfrac{r}{n}\right)} = t$

51. $Q(t) = Q_0 e^{rt}$

    a. $Q(t) = Q_0 e^{rt}$

       $\dfrac{Q(t)}{e^{rt}} = Q_0$

    b. $Q(t) = Q_0 e^{rt}$

       $\dfrac{Q(t)}{Q_0} = e^{rt}$

       $\ln\left(\dfrac{Q(t)}{Q_0}\right) = \ln e^{rt}$

       $\ln\left(\dfrac{Q(t)}{Q_0}\right) = rt$

       $\dfrac{\ln\left(\dfrac{Q(t)}{Q_0}\right)}{r} = t$

53. $P = \dfrac{AR}{1-(1+R)^{-nt}}$

       $A = \$125,000;\ R = \dfrac{r}{n} = \dfrac{0.055}{12};\ t = 30$

$$P = \dfrac{125,000\left(\dfrac{0.055}{12}\right)}{1-\left[1+\left(\dfrac{0.055}{12}\right)\right]^{-12(30)}}$$

       $P \approx \$709.74$

55. $Q(t) = Q_0 e^{rt}$

   a. $2000 = 1000 e^{r(12)}$

       $2 = e^{12r}$

       $\ln 2 = \ln e^{12r}$

       $\ln 2 = 12r$

       $\dfrac{\ln 2}{12} = r$

       $0.0578 \approx r$

       $r \approx 5.78\%$

      The growth rate is 5.78%.

   b. $200{,}000 = 1000 e^{(0.0578)t}$

       $200 = e^{0.0578t}$

       $\ln 200 = \ln e^{0.0578t}$

       $\ln 200 = 0.0578t$

       $\dfrac{\ln 200}{0.0578} = t$

       $91.67 \approx t$

      It takes 91.67 hours to produce 200,000 bacteria.

57. $r = \dfrac{\ln 2}{t}$

   $r = \dfrac{\ln 2}{8}$

   $r \approx 0.087$

   $Q_0 e^{-rt} = Q(t)$

   $Q_0 e^{-0.087(3)} = 0.5$

   $Q_0 = \dfrac{0.5}{e^{-0.261}}$

   $Q_0 \approx 0.65$ grams

59. $r = \dfrac{\ln 2}{t}$

   $r = \dfrac{\ln 2}{432}$

   $Q_0 e^{-rt} = Q(t)$

   $10 e^{\left(-\frac{\ln 2}{432}\right)t} = 2.7$

   $e^{-\frac{\ln 2}{432}t} = 0.27$

   $\ln e^{-\frac{\ln 2}{432}t} = \ln 0.27$

   $-\dfrac{\ln 2}{432}t = \ln 0.27$

   $t = \dfrac{\ln 0.27}{\left(-\dfrac{\ln 2}{432}\right)}$

   $t \approx 816$

It will take 816 years for 10 grams to decay to 2.7 grams.

61. $T = -8267 \ln p$

   $17{,}255 = -8267 \ln p$

   $\dfrac{17{,}255}{-8267} = \ln p$

   $-\dfrac{2465}{1181} = \ln p$

   $e^{-\frac{2465}{1181}} = e^{\ln p}$

   $e^{-\frac{2465}{1181}} = p$

   $0.124 \approx p$

About 12.4% of the original amount remained.

63. $A = p e^{rt}$

   $p = \$10{,}000;\ r = 6.2\% = 0.062;$

   $t = 2010 - 1890 = 120$

   $A = 10{,}000 e^{0.062(120)}$

   $A = 10{,}000 e^{7.44}$

   $A \approx \$17{,}027{,}502.21$

   Answers will vary.

65. Refer to solution for Exercise 30.

Summary and Concept Review

1. $y = 2^x + 3$

   Translate the graph of $y = 2^x$ up 3 units.

   Asymptote: $y = 3$

   y-intercept: $(0, 4)$

3. $y = -e^{x+1} - 2$

Reflect the graph of $y = e^x$ in the x-axis and translate left 1 unit and down 2 units.
Asymptote: $y = -2$

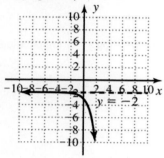

5. $4^x = \dfrac{1}{16}$

$4^x = 4^{-2}$

$x = -2$

7. $20{,}000 = 142{,}000(0.85)^t$

$\dfrac{20{,}000}{142{,}000} = 0.85^t$

$\ln\left(\dfrac{10}{71}\right) = \ln 0.85^t$

$\ln\left(\dfrac{10}{71}\right) = t \ln 0.85$

$\dfrac{\ln\left(\dfrac{10}{71}\right)}{\ln 0.85} = t$

$12.1 \text{ yr} \approx t$

9. $\log_5 \dfrac{1}{125} = -3$

$5^{-3} = \dfrac{1}{125}$

11. $5^2 = 25$

$\log_5 25 = 2$

13. $3^4 = 81$

$\log_3 81 = 4$

15. $\ln\left(\dfrac{1}{e}\right) = -1$, since $e^{-1} = \dfrac{1}{e}$.

17. $f(x) = \log_2 x$

Asymptote: $x = 0$

At $x = 1$, $y = 0$. $(1, 0)$

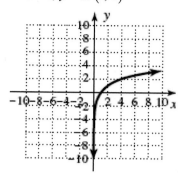

19. $f(x) = 2 + \ln(x - 1)$

Translate graph of $f(x) = \ln x$ right 1 unit and up 2 units. Asymptote: $x = 1$

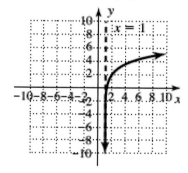

21. $f(x) = \ln(x^2 - 6x)$

$x^2 - 6x > 0$

$x(x - 6) > 0$

Zeros: $x = 0$, $x = 6$

$x = -1$: $(-1)(-1-6) = (-1)(-7) = 7 \to$ pos

$x = 1$: $(1)(1-6) = (1)(-5) = -5 \to$ neg

$x = 7$: $(7)(7-6) = (7)(1) = 7 \to$ pos

Domain: $x \in (-\infty, 0) \cup (0, 6)$

23. a. $\ln x = 32$

$x = e^{32}$

b. $\log x = 2.38$

$x = 10^{2.38}$

c. $e^x = 9.8$

$\ln e^x = \ln 9.8$

$x = \ln 9.8$

d. $10^x = \sqrt{7}$

$\log 10^x = \log \sqrt{7}$

$x = \log \sqrt{7}$

25. a. $\ln 7 + \ln 6 = \ln(7 \cdot 6)$

$= \ln 42$

b. $\log_9 2 + \log_9 15 = \log_9(2 \cdot 15)$

$= \log_9 30$

c. $\ln(x+3) - \ln(x-1) = \ln\left(\dfrac{x+3}{x-1}\right)$

d. $\log x + \log(x+1) = \log\left[x(x+1)\right]$

$= \log(x^2 + x)$

27. a. $\ln\left(x\sqrt[4]{y}\right) = \ln x + \ln \sqrt[4]{y}$

$= \ln x + \ln y^{\frac{1}{4}}$

$= \ln x + \dfrac{1}{4}\ln y$

b. $\ln\left(\sqrt[3]{pq}\right) = \ln \sqrt[3]{p} + \ln q$

$= \ln p^{\frac{1}{3}} + \ln q$

$= \dfrac{1}{3}\ln p + \ln q$

c. $\log\left(\dfrac{\sqrt[3]{x^5 \cdot y^4}}{\sqrt{x^5 y^3}}\right)$

$= \log\left(\sqrt[3]{x^5 y^4}\right) - \log \sqrt{x^5 y^3}$

$= \log x^{\frac{5}{3}}y^{\frac{4}{3}} - \log x^{\frac{5}{2}}y^{\frac{3}{2}}$

$= \log x^{\frac{5}{3}} + \log y^{\frac{4}{3}} - \log x^{\frac{5}{2}} - \log y^{\frac{3}{2}}$

$= \dfrac{5}{3}\log x + \dfrac{4}{3}\log y - \dfrac{5}{2}\log x - \dfrac{3}{2}\log y$

27. d. $\log\left(\dfrac{4\sqrt[3]{p^5 q^4}}{\sqrt{p^3 q^2}}\right)$

$= \log 4\sqrt[3]{p^5 q^4} - \log \sqrt{p^3 q^2}$

$= \log 4p^{\frac{5}{3}}q^{\frac{4}{3}} - \log p^{\frac{3}{2}}q$

$= \log 4 + \log p^{\frac{5}{3}} + \log q^{\frac{4}{3}} - \left(\log p^{\frac{3}{2}} + \log q\right)$

$= \log 4 + \dfrac{5}{3}\log p + \dfrac{4}{3}\log q - \dfrac{3}{2}\log p - \log q$

29. $2^x = 7$

$\ln 2^x = \ln 7$

$x \ln 2 = \ln 7$

$x = \dfrac{\ln 7}{\ln 2}$

31. $e^{x-2} = 3^x$

$\ln e^{x-2} = \ln 3^x$

$x - 2 = x \ln 3$

$x - x \ln 3 = 2$

$x(1 - \ln 3) = 2$

$x = \dfrac{2}{1 - \ln 3}$

33. $\log x + \log(x-3) = 1$

$\log\left[x(x-3)\right] = 1$

$x(x-3) = 10^1$

$x^2 - 3x = 10$

$x^2 - 3x - 10 = 0$

$(x+2)(x-5) = 0$

$x + 2 = 0 \quad \text{or} \quad x - 5 = 0$

$x = -2 \qquad\qquad x = 5$

Check $x = -2$:

$\log(-2) + \log(-2-3) = 1$

The solution $x = -2$ is outside the domain and is discarded.

Check $x = 5$:

$\log(5) + \log(5-3) = 1$

$\log 5 + \log 2 = 1$

$1 = 1$

The solution is $x = 5$.

35. $R(h) = \dfrac{\ln 2}{h}$

   a. $R(3.9) = \dfrac{\ln 2}{3.9} \approx 0.1777$
The rate of decay is 17.77%.

   b. $0.0289 = \dfrac{\ln 2}{h}$

           $h = \dfrac{\ln 2}{0.0289}$
           $h \approx 23.98$
The half-life is 23.98 days.

37. $I = prt$
     $I = \$627.75 - \$600 = \$27.75;$
     $p = \$600; \; t = \dfrac{3}{12} = 0.25$
     $27.75 = 600r(0.25)$
     $27.75 = 150r$
     $\dfrac{27.75}{150} = r$
     $0.185 \approx r$
         $r \approx 18.5\%$

39. $A = \dfrac{P\left[(1+R)^{nt} - 1\right]}{R}$

   a. $P = \$260; \; R = \dfrac{r}{n} = \dfrac{0.075}{12} = 0.00625; \; t = 4$

       $A = \dfrac{260\left[(1+0.00625)^{12(4)} - 1\right]}{0.00625}$

       $A = \dfrac{260\left[(1.00625)^{48} - 1\right]}{0.00625}$
       $A \approx \$14{,}501.72$
No, this monthly amount is not sufficient.

   b. $A = \$15{,}000; \; R = \dfrac{r}{n} = 0.00625; \; t = 4$

         $15{,}000 = \dfrac{P\left[(1+0.00625)^{12(4)} - 1\right]}{0.00625}$

         $93.75 = P\left[(1.00625)^{48} - 1\right]$

         $\dfrac{93.75}{\left[(1.00625)^{48} - 1\right]} = P$

          $\$268.93 \approx P$
He must deposit a minimum of $268.93 each month.

Mixed Review

1. a. $\log_2 30 = \dfrac{\log 30}{\log 2} = \dfrac{\ln 30}{\ln 2} \approx 4.9069$

   b. $\log_{0.25} 8 = \dfrac{\log 8}{\log 0.25} = \dfrac{\ln 8}{\ln 0.25} = -1.5$

   c. $\log_8 2 = \dfrac{1}{3}$ since $8^{\frac{1}{3}} = 2.$

3. a. $\log_{10} 20^2 = 2\log_{10} 20$

   b. $\log 10^{0.05x} = 0.05x \log 10 = 0.05x$

   c. $\ln 2^{x-3} = (x-3)\ln 2$

5. $y = 5 \cdot 2^{-x}$
Reflect the graph of $y = 2^x$ in the y-axis and stretch vertically by a factor of 5.
Asymptote: $y = 0;$ y-intercept: $(0, 5)$

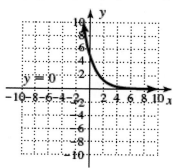

7. $y = \log_2(-x) - 4$
Reflect the graph of $y = \log_2 x$ in the y-axis and translate down 4 units.
Asymptote: $x = 0$
At $x = -2, \; y = -3. \; (-2, -3)$
At $x = -8, \; y = -1. \; (-8, -1)$

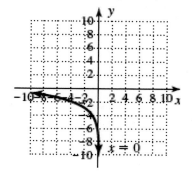

9. a. $\log_5 625 = 4$
$$5^4 = 625$$

b. $\ln 0.15x = 0.45$
$$e^{0.45} = 0.15x$$

c. $\log(0.1 \times 10^8) = 7$
$$10^7 = 0.1 \times 10^8$$

11. a. $\log(2x^2 - 3x - 2)$
$$2x^2 - 3x - 2 > 0$$
$$(2x+1)(x-2) > 0$$

Zeros: $x = -\dfrac{1}{2},\ x = 2$

$x = -1:\ \log\left[2(-1)^2 - 3(-1) - 2\right]$
$$= \log(2 + 3 - 2)$$
$$= \log 3 \rightarrow \text{yes}$$

$x = 0:\ \log\left[2(0)^2 - 3(0) - 2\right]$
$$= \log(-2) \rightarrow \text{no}$$

$x = 3:\ \log\left[2(3)^2 - 3(3) - 2\right]$
$$= \log(18 - 9 - 2)$$
$$= \log 7 \rightarrow \text{yes}$$

Domain: $x \in \left(-\infty, -\dfrac{1}{2}\right) \cup (2, \infty)$

b. $\ln\left|x^3 - 8\right|$
$$x^3 - 8 \neq 0$$
$$x \neq 2$$
Domain: $x \in (-\infty, 2) \cup (2, \infty)$

13. $10^{x-4} = 200$
$$\log 10^{x-4} = \log 200$$
$$(x-4)\log 10 = \log(100 \cdot 2)$$
$$x - 4 = \log 10^2 + \log 2$$
$$x - 4 = 2 + \log 2$$
$$x = 6 + \log 2$$

15. $\log_2(2x - 5) + \log_2(x - 2) = 4$
$$\log_2(2x - 5)(x - 2) = 4$$
$$(2x - 5)(x - 2) = 2^4$$
$$2x^2 - 9x + 10 = 16$$
$$2x^2 - 9x - 6 = 0$$
$a = 2;\ b = -9;\ c = -6$

$$x = \frac{-b \pm \sqrt{b^2 - 4ac}}{2a}$$

$$x = \frac{-(-9) \pm \sqrt{(-9)^2 - 4(2)(-6)}}{2(2)}$$

$$x = \frac{9 \pm \sqrt{81 + 48}}{4} = \frac{9 \pm \sqrt{129}}{4}$$

The solution is $x = \dfrac{9}{4} + \dfrac{\sqrt{129}}{4}$.

17. $M(I) = \log\left(\dfrac{I}{I_0}\right)$

$$6.5 = \log\left(\frac{I}{2 \times 10^{11}}\right)$$

$$\frac{I}{2 \times 10^{11}} = 10^{6.5}$$
$$I = 10^{6.5}(2 \times 10^{11})$$
$$I \approx 6.3 \times 10^{17}$$

19. $r(n) = 2(0.8)^n$

n	$r(n) = 2(0.8)^n$
1	1.6 m
2	1.28 m
3	1.02 m
4	0.82 m
5	0.66 m
6	0.52 m

Practice Test

1. $\log_3 81 = 4$
    $3^4 = 81$

3. $\log_b\left(\dfrac{\sqrt{x^5}\,y^3}{z}\right)$

    $= \log_b\left(\sqrt{x^5}\,y^3\right) - \log_b z$

    $= \log_b \sqrt{x^5} + \log_b y^3 - \log_b z$

    $= \log_b x^{\frac{5}{2}} + \log_b y^3 - \log_b z$

    $= \dfrac{5}{2}\log_b x + 3\log_b y - \log_b z$

5. $5^{x-7} = 125$
    $5^{x-7} = 5^3$
    $x - 7 = 3$
    $x = 10$

7. $\log_a 45 = \log_a 9 \cdot 5$
    $\qquad = \log_a 9 + \log_a 5$
    $\qquad = \log_a 3^2 + \log_a 5$
    $\qquad = 2\log_a 3 + \log_a 5$
    $\qquad = 2(0.48) + 1.72$
    $\qquad = 0.96 + 1.72$
    $\qquad = 2.68$

9. $g(x) = -2^{x-1} + 3$

    Reflect the graph of $g(x) = 2^x$ in the y-axis
    and translate right 1 unit and up 3 units.
    Asymptote: $y = 3$
    At $x = 1$, $y = 2$. $(1, 2)$

    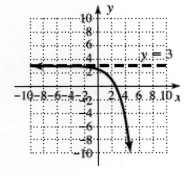

11. a. $\log_3 100 = \dfrac{\log 100}{\log 3} = \dfrac{2}{\log 3} \approx 4.19$

    b. $\log_6 0.235 = \dfrac{\log 0.235}{\log 6} = \dfrac{\ln 0.235}{\ln 6} = -0.81$

13. $3^{x-1} = 89$
    $\ln 3^{x-1} = \ln 89$
    $(x-1) = \ln 89$
    $x - 1 = \dfrac{\ln 89}{\ln 3}$
    $x = 1 + \dfrac{\ln 89}{\ln 3}$

15. $3000 = 8000(0.82)^t$
    $\dfrac{3000}{8000} = 0.82^t$
    $\ln\left(\dfrac{3}{8}\right) = \ln 0.82^t$
    $\ln\left(\dfrac{3}{8}\right) = t \ln 0.82$
    $\dfrac{\ln\left(\dfrac{3}{8}\right)}{\ln 0.82} = t$
    $5 \text{ yr} \approx t$

17. $Q(t) = -2600 + 1900\ln(t)$
    $-2600 + 1900\ln(t) = 3000$
    $1900\ln(t) = 5600$
    $\ln(t) = \dfrac{5600}{1900}$
    $\ln(t) = \dfrac{56}{19}$
    $t = e^{\frac{56}{19}}$
    $t \approx 19.1 \text{ months}$

19. $A = \dfrac{P\left[(1+R)^{nt} - 1\right]}{R}$

    a. $P = \$50$; $R = \dfrac{r}{n} = \dfrac{0.0825}{12} = 0.006875$;
        $t = 5$

        $A = \dfrac{50\left[(1+0.006875)^{12(5)} - 1\right]}{0.006875}$

        $A = \dfrac{50\left[(1.006875)^{60} - 1\right]}{0.006875}$

        $A \approx \$3697.88$
        No, this amount is not sufficient.

19. b. $A = \$4000;\ R = \dfrac{r}{n} = 0.006875;\ t = 5$

$$4000 = \frac{P\left[\left(1 + 0.006875\right)^{12(5)} - 1\right]}{0.006875}$$

$$27.5 = P\left[\left(1.006875\right)^{60} - 1\right]$$

$$\frac{27.5}{\left[\left(1.006875\right)^{60} - 1\right]} = P$$

$$\$54.09 \approx P$$

He must save a minimum of $54.09 monthly.

Calculator Exploration and Discovery

Exercise 1:

$$P(t) = \frac{c}{1 + ae^{-bt}} = \frac{2500}{1 + 25e^{-0.5t}}$$
$$a = 25,\ b = 0.5,\ c = 2500$$

Exercise 3:

$$P(0) = \frac{3000}{1 + 15e^{-0.5(0)}}$$
$$= \frac{3000}{1 + 15e^{0}}$$
$$= \frac{3000}{1 + 15(1)}$$
$$= \frac{3000}{16}$$
$$\approx 187.5$$

(b) gives the larger initial population.

Exercise 5:

The population increases more quickly as b increases, so it would surpass 200 more quickly if $b = 0.6$.

Exercise 7:

Use a graphing calculator to verify answers.

Strengthening Core Skills

Exercise 1:

Answers will vary.

Exercise 3:

Answers will vary.

Notes

Notes